MEDICAL AND DENTAL
SPACE PLANNING

MEDICAL AND DENTAL
SPACE PLANNING

A Comprehensive Guide to Design, Equipment, and Clinical Procedures

THIRD EDITION

Jain Malkin

JOHN WILEY & SONS, INC.

Cover Credits

Gowned Waiting Lounge:
Scripps Polster Breast Center
Design: Jain Malkin Inc.
Photographer: Glenn Cormier, InSite

Dental Operatory:
Design: Lawrence Man Architects
Photographer: Lucy Chen

Screened Background Rendering:
Courtesy Janice Thayer-Johnson, Signature Environments

Library of Congress Cataloging-in-Publication Data:

Malkin, Jain.
   Medical and dental space planning : a comprehensive guide to design, equipment, and clinical procedures / Jain Malkin.—3rd ed.
      p. cm.
   Includes index.
   ISBN 0-471-38574-3 (cloth : alk. paper)
    1. Medical offices—Design and construction. 2. Dental offices—Design and construction. I. Title.

R728 .M235 2002
725'.23—dc21

2001045585

Printed in the United States of America.
10 9 8 7 6 5 4 3 2 1

To **Stuart,**
for his good cheer, enduring patience,
and encouragement throughout the two years
of researching and writing this book,
a task that seemed as if it would never end

And in memory of my **Mother,**
whose energy and drive, love for the written word,
and intellectual curiosity have shaped my life

Contents

Preface

In 1970, I decided to specialize in healthcare design. I spent many weeks at the library researching the literature on medical and dental space planning, color and its effect on patients, and the psychological aspects of illness—how do patients and visitors react to hospitals? Why do people fear a visit to the doctor or dentist? What role does lighting play in patient rooms?

Much to my surprise, very little had been written on these topics. I found nothing in architecture or design publications, but did come across an occasional article in obscure publications sometimes dating from the 1940s. There were a few articles in the *American Journal of Occupational Therapy* on the effect of the environment on the patient, and there were numerous articles on color preferences of various ethnic groups or cultural taboos with respect to color. A handful of articles on limited aspects of office space planning were scattered in medical or dental practice management magazines and Department of Health, Education, and Welfare publications. Here was a field with few resources and vast potential.

Most medical and dental offices in 1970 were either colorless and clinical or drab and dreary. There was no middle ground. Clinical offices had high levels of illumination, easy-to-clean shiny surfaces, and a lot of medical or dental instruments in view—clean and clinical. At the other end of the spectrum were offices with brown shag carpeting, residential pendant lights, nubby, earth-tone upholstery fabric that wouldn't show soil, and poorly styled wood furniture that appeared to have been rescued from a Salvation Army truck. Dusty pothos plants in macrame hangers complete the picture of these dingy and unhygienic environments.

I concluded that I would have to do my own empirical research to gather enough data on which to base my design work. I spent the better part of a year visiting hospitals, interviewing staff and patients, and observing how patients were handled. I wanted to see the facility through the patients' eyes. I also visited many physicians and dentists and asked about their practices—what kinds of instruments they used; what size treatment room would be optimal; what kinds of changes would make their offices more efficient; and what critical adjacencies existed between rooms or treatment areas.

I documented my visits with photographs of confusing signage, waiting rooms furnished with Goodwill rejects, dismal lighting, corridors jammed with medical equipment, and procedure rooms that resembled Dr. Jekyll's laboratory. At the end of my research, I had accumulated over 2000 photos and reams of notes, which I analyzed, and, from this, I formulated my design philosophy. My dual majors, Psychology and Environmental Design, provided a theoretical background with which to interpret the data. This database, combined with my current 30 years of experience designing hundreds of medical and dental offices, has resulted in this book.

A person with no prior experience in healthcare design can study this book and become familiar not only with current economic and practice management issues, but also with medical and dental procedures, equipment associated with each medical or dental specialty, room sizes, traffic flow, construction methods, codes, interior finishes, and more. I have attempted to synthesize my research and experience so that others will not have to follow such a laborious course of study in order to become proficient in a field that requires such highly specialized knowledge.

Today, probably more than a thousand architects and designers across the country list healthcare as one of their specialties. In its infancy when I started out, the field has now reached maturity. No longer concerned with discovering the basic rules and principles, healthcare design specialists can devote themselves to refining what has been learned and to innovation.

The first edition of this book was published in 1982 and featured exclusively my own work. However, the second edition (1990) and the new third edition, in order to give a broader perspective, include examples of work by other practitioners, who are credited under each photo. I thank each of these architects, designers, and photographers for sharing their work.

The third edition updates the book on digital technology—electronic medical records, digital imaging, digital diagnostic instruments, and networked communications—and how these impact the design of medical and dental offices. The milieu in which physicians and dentists practice—the impact of managed care, the Internet, the baby boomer generation, the age wave, the large number of uninsured Americans—is presented as a backdrop for understanding the pressures on the healthcare system and, also, implications for facility design.

Expanded chapters include new medical specialties: reproductive enhancement (in vitro fertilization), pain management, breast care centers, LASIK eye surgery, and medical oncology. Nowhere have changes in technology been more apparent than in dentistry and diagnostic imaging. These and most other chapters have been totally rewritten. Nearly 100 new or revised space plans, totally revised space programs for all specialties, and 90 percent new photos of facilities and equipment have been added to all chapters, and the text has been rewritten to include new developments in medical and dental treatment and to familiarize readers with state-of-the-art medical and dental equipment. Fabrics and interior finishes representative of recent technological advances are introduced as well as ergonomically appropriate furniture. The lighting chapter has been revised to acquaint readers with new types of lamps and fixtures and innovative solutions to enhance both aesthetics and function.

A major change since the last edition of this book is the rigor of regulatory agency review of office-based surgery practices, far more stringent mandatory regulation (certification, licensing, and accreditation) of ambulatory surgical centers, and interest by group practices and large managed-care organizations in seeking voluntary accreditation from one or more national agencies as well as Medicare certification. Ambulatory-care enterprises such as a breast care center, urgent care, women's center, or radiation therapy that may physically be located in a medical office building but are covered under the hospital's license, will most likely be subject to a JCAHO survey and accreditation. This book will help clarify the roles of these various agencies, explain which aspects of the regulations apply to the built environment, and answer many questions that often arise when trying to understand compliance. I've also tried to clarify OSHA issues that affect design, which required wading through several inches of "interpretive letters" to find those kernels that impacted safety of personnel and were within the province of design professionals as opposed to policies and procedures followed by staff to protect themselves.

I offer special thanks to my colleagues, architect Bill Yeaple, Ph.D., for his invaluable assistance in research and in acquiring updated photos of equipment; and architects Osia Orailoglu; Joost Bende, AIA; and Chris Shinall for their assistance in updating space plans; and to my executive assistant, Mary Anne Jones, for her extraordinary help and perseverance in preparing the manuscript. I would also like to thank the AIA Academy of Architecture for Health for providing me with an advance draft of the new *Guidelines for Design and Construction of Hospital and Health Care Facilities,* chapter on ambulatory care.

On a final note, although the book attempts to familiarize readers with basic code information, codes vary geographically and the architect or designer must check local and state codes, as well as the evolution of the Americans with Disabilities Act (ADA) legislation.

Acknowledgments

The author wishes to acknowledge Bill Rostenberg, FAIA, of the SmithGroup for his advice, expertise, and critique of the diagnostic imaging portion of this chapter. I am most grateful for his generosity of time and spirit. I am also appreciative of the expertise of Scott Jenkins whose 30 years of experience planning diagnostic imaging equipment sites and providing technical assistance has been most helpful in pointing out what designers often overlook.

The author thanks Lee Palmer, a biotechnology engineer with over 30 years' experience in the dental field as a space planner and equipment selection consultant, for his generosity of spirt and invaluable expertise in reviewing this chapter. Thanks also to architect T. Michael Hadley for sharing his innovative work and to Dr. Larry Emmott, a passionate technology buff who writes a column for *Dental Products Report*.

Introduction: Changing Perspectives

HEALTHCARE FINANCE

Dramatic changes have occurred in the delivery of healthcare since the first edition of this book when undiscounted fee-for-service reigned. The seminal event that kicked off a series of radical changes in the traditional fee structure began in 1984, with the federal government's prospective pricing program whereby Medicare and Medicaid reimbursements were made on a fixed, flat-fee basis, rather than as a percentage of an individual physician's fee. Based upon a current list of 500 diagnosis-related groups (DRGs) of procedures, the physician/provider receives a flat fee, regardless of actual cost. Each DRG has a "weight" established for it based primarily on Medicare billing and cost data. Each weight reflects the relative cost, across all hospitals, of treating cases classified in that DRG. Since Medicare and Medicaid comprise approximately 33 percent of the national healthcare budget, hospitals and physicians have been forced to take a hard look at ways to reduce costs. Following the lead of the federal government, some states also have initiated prospective pricing programs, and insurance companies have followed suit, issuing guidelines and directives, and making physicians feel that third-party payers, rather than they, are managing their patients' care.

During the 1990s, the demands of investors increasingly influenced the delivery of healthcare services as a growing number of hospitals, home healthcare services, skilled nursing facilities, and HMOs (health maintenance organizations) became for-profit entities, publicly traded on Wall Street. Investor ownership profoundly influenced the "product" of healthcare by intensifying competition, creating a focus on cost containment, reducing the autonomy of physicians, and, ultimately, reducing healthcare services to a commodity. But by 1997, healthcare stocks were performing poorly because cost containment and competition had reduced profit margins and Medicare and Medicaid had made serious budget cuts. Then came the scandals leading to the collapse of two of the most celebrated companies — Columbia/HCA and Oxford Health Plans.

Just when healthcare finance seemed as if it couldn't get any worse, it did. The Balanced Budget Act of 1997 required that Medicare expenditures be cut by $115 billion over a period of five years, placing enormous pressure on hospitals to reduce costs.

On the insurance front, the biggest change over the past five years has been the growth of HMO enrollment from 50.6 million Americans in 1995 to 80.9 million in 2000; however, this trend is slowing.[1] A more detailed discussion of HMOs and market penetration can be found in Chapter 6, and an excellent financial summary of the American healthcare system in the 1990s is available in *The New England Journal of Medicine*.[2] According to this article, in 1997, only about one-third of HMOs recorded a profit, since they faced considerable competition from each other and from physician-owned health plans and those sponsored by hospitals. Additionally, consumer dissatisfaction with restrictions on care and a rash of bad press has led to a proliferation of managed care alternatives, and in Washington, patients' rights legislation looks as if it may pass in the 2001 Congress.

Although some states have remained relatively unaffected by managed care and physicians in those states are doing well with discounted fee-for-service reimbursement, physicians in states like California, Rhode Island, Delaware, Hawaii, and Pennsylvania — those with the

---

[1]Russell C. Coile, Jr., *Futurescan 2001*, Health Administration Press, Society for Healthcare Strategy and Market Development, Chicago, 2001, p. 15.

[2]Robert Kuttner, 1999. "Health Policy Report: The American Healthcare System — Wall Street and Healthcare," *New England Journal of Medicine* 340(8): 664–668.

highest managed-care penetration[3]—have seen serious erosion of their income. This has led physicians into entrepreneurial niche enterprises, such as ambulatory surgery ventures, oncology care, cardiac care, and free-standing radiology centers, in competition with hospitals.

Today, medical insurance is complicated and has become a battleground wherein healthcare providers, consumers, employers, and insurance companies are each trying to retain control of their respective interests. Whether healthcare will ever be "reformed" to include the uninsured and to fulfill the original promise of managed care—to provide closely integrated services, eliminating waste, and enhancing clinical outcomes–remains unclear. The ever-shifting sands of healthcare politics reveal, however, a certain sensitivity to public opinion. Recent announcements by Blue Cross and other large payers promise to allow physicians to make the final decision on treatments for their patients. And some have further proposed to reward physicians with bonuses for receiving high patient satisfaction scores as opposed to rewarding them for restricting access and containing costs. As managed care loses popularity, a "consumer choice" model is emerging in which hospitals are competing on new facilities and amenities. (Never underestimate the power of the American consumer.)

REGULATORY ISSUES AFFECTING PHYSICIANS

A number of recent regulatory issues will significantly affect physicians.

Ambulatory Payment Classifications (APCs)

Medicare's prospective payment system has hit ambulatory care. Similar to DRGs, the APC classifications fall into three categories: surgical, medical, and ancillary. Therapies such as physical therapy, speech, occupational therapy and also laboratory work are excluded and are paid on a fee schedule, as mammography screening and durable medical equipment will be. Imposed by HCFA (Healthcare Financing Administration) in August 2000, APCs will affect ambulatory surgery, which has become a battleground between physicians and hospitals. Seventy percent of all surgery is done in an outpatient setting.[4] The less complex (and more lucrative) cases are siphoned off by physicians to be performed in an ambulatory surgical center, while the hospital is left with complex cases and declining reimbursement.

HIPAA

The Health Insurance Portability and Accountability Act of 1996 will continue to result in many changes and costs for both physicians and dentists.[5] HIPAA is a mandate from the federal government to automate health-related financial and clinical data to protect patient privacy. In coming years, this will result in significant cost for software, compliant hardware, employee training, personnel security policies, considerable documentation, and monitoring of compliance. The use of a single HIPAA-defined administrative standard for electronic transactions, such as claims processing and verification of eligibility, is one of the goals. Although HIPAA refers only to electronic data, one wonders how, or if, this will also affect paper records storage, commonly accessible even to janitorial staff, in open rooms and/or unlocked chart file cabinets.

FORCES SHAPING HEALTHCARE

Institute of Medicine (IOM) Report

One of the hottest issues in healthcare in 2001 was the IOM report, *To Err Is Human: Building a Safer Health*

---

[3]IHS® Health Group: 2000 Managed Care Profile Map.

[4]*Russ Coile's Health Trends*, Aspen Publishers, Inc., Frederick, Maryland, 2000, 12(9): 2.

[5]*Russ Coile's Health Trends*, Aspen Publishers, Inc., Frederick, Maryland, 2000, 12(4): 3.

Home telemedicine monitoring, Aviva™ central station. (*Photo courtesy: American TeleCare, Eden Prairie, MN.*)

Home telemedicine monitoring, Aviva™ patient station. (*Photo courtesy: American TeleCare, Eden Prairie, MN.*)

System, which was followed by *Crossing the Quality Chasm.* The IOM is a private, nonprofit institution that provides health policy advice under a congressional charter granted to the National Academy of Sciences. These two reports have placed medical errors on every provider's radar screen based upon the assertion that medical errors are probably the eighth leading cause of death in the United States—more than motor vehicle accidents, breast cancer, or AIDS.[6] Healthcare represents more than half of the *preventable* accidents. Medical informatics and the avoidance of handwritten physicians' orders will solve some of these problems, as will electronic medical records, making the chart instantly available at any location, providing access to information about patients' allergies, notifying the clinical team about negative drug interactions, and flagging dosages that

exceed standards. Clinical pathways for treatment of various illnesses are expected to weed out practices with poor clinical outcomes.

Telemedicine

According to Kirby Vosburgh, Associate Director of CIMIT (Center for the Integration of Medicine and Innovative Technology in Boston), healthcare will be moving into the home, changing "house calls to mouse calls."[7] Internet-enabled medicine will allow patients and providers to communicate in cyberspace (see Figures 1 and 2), listening to a patient's heart or lungs, and monitoring blood pressure

---

[6]The National Academy of Sciences "NEWS," March, 2001 *(www.news@nas.edu).*

[7]Lecture by Kirby Vosburgh, Ph.D., "The Electronic Outpatient/Home Environment—from House Calls to Mouse Calls," (Vancouver, British Columbia, October, 2000, "Beyond 2000: An International Conference on Architecture for Health."

via computer. Telemedicine is especially useful for clinical consultations with physicians who are located in rural areas. This is expected to reduce the number of office visits and to help manage chronic illnesses, such as hypertension, and the number of acute complications that result from poor management of these conditions. Payment for "televisits" is expected within five years, and 50 percent of physicians will treat patients on-line, according to a survey by the American Medical Association.

Medical Informatics

The use of information systems in running a medical practice and managing patient care makes a vast store of clinical data instantly available to physicians. An aggregate database of millions of clinical encounters can be accessed with powerful software programs that will even run on a palm-top PC. Currently, patients with identical conditions may receive radically different treatments from different providers, whereas the use of a prognosis "calculator" enables physicians to quantify the advantages and disadvantages of various clinical strategies, to review research findings, and to calculate drug dosages while the patient is still in the exam room (Figures 3-29a and b). Another aspect of medical informatics is the computer-based provider order entry (CPOE), which is expected to greatly reduce errors due to illegibility.

The Experience Economy

A new approach to marketing underscores the value of creating an experience that engages customers in a personal way.[8] Staged experiences create memorable and lasting impressions that can bond customers—in this case, patients—to a specific provider. As an example, Starbucks has effectively demonstrated that a basic commodity like a cup of coffee can be presented in an environment that elevates the experience in such a way that customers will pay considerably more for the product than they would at the corner diner. Similarly, experiences can be *designed* and *scripted* in the healthcare setting to help differentiate a provider from competitors and to ensure a level of customer service that exceeds expectations (including Starbucks cafes that are now being installed in some hospital lobbies). Baby Boomers, as a consumer group, have been characterized as being finicky and discriminating, and willing to spend the time to evaluate a variety of goods and services before making a commitment. In the new economy, Baby Boomers will fuel the demand for memorable experiences and will often be willing to pay more for these services.

The New Consumer

Much has been written about the new consumer: a more well-educated comparison shopper, empowered by the Internet, with the analytical ability to review research and form an opinion about treatment options. This group has grown from 25 percent of the population 20 years ago to 45 percent today. By 2005, they will constitute 52 percent of the population.[9]

Universal Beliefs
According to a study by Yankelovich Research, the new consumer has three universal beliefs:[10]

- Doctors can be wrong.

- People know their own bodies best; self-reliance is wise.

- Quality is important, and consumers want the best for less; value is being redefined.

Patients are realizing, largely due to their personal experiences with managed care—but also influenced by the

---

[8]B. Joseph Pine II and James Gilmore, *The Experience Economy,* Harvard Business School Press, Boston, 2000.

[9]Institute for the Future Executive Summary: The New Healthcare Consumer (Menlo Park, CA: 1998): 1.

[10]A report delivered at Healthcare Forum Summit, 1998.

media—that cost containment pressures and the complexities of the healthcare system leave them vulnerable to being ignored, being denied treatment, or being exposed to medical error unless they aggressively take responsibility for educating themselves and "managing" their own healthcare. These *empowered consumers* are a new factor, identified in a Price Waterhouse Coopers forecast of the healthcare industry (with projections to the year 2010) as the most important force behind change.[11] It, and other similar forecasts characterize Baby Boomers as "adversarial, fickle, and impatient" and point out that providers are "not prepared to serve the highly differentiated expectations of these strong-willed and knowledgeable individuals."[12]

Baby Boomers Empowered by the Internet

A major change agent has been the explosion of Internet sites, giving patients access to self-care information, journal articles, and chat rooms associated with specific diseases 24 hours a day, seven days a week. Consumers with the motivation and education to do this type of research and the ability to understand what they are reading have been arriving at their doctors' offices prepared to discuss potential diagnoses and treatment options. Some physicians have not been prepared for, nor have they welcomed, this sort of collegiality and "partnership" with patients, and they have responded in a variety of ways that express how uncomfortable they are when their authority is being challenged. But if the research published in the past few years is any indication, this trend will accelerate, not diminish. From the physician's perspective, valuable examination time can be squandered by having to sort through a stack of studies that may or may not be relevant to the patient's condition. Nevertheless, the new consumer's desire to "take charge" and to play a proactive role seems to be a force that physicians will have to contend with.

Responding to the Pace of Change

Healthcare providers will need to develop strategies to meet consumer demands.[13] These include the following:

- More choices—of health plans, open provider networks, treatment options to help maintain market share.

- More control—the new consumers are more active and participatory in their healthcare and are interested in self-care.

- Superior customer service, being consumer-friendly.

- Branding—a way of differentiating services with direct-to-consumer marketing, offering an ombudsman, and perhaps offering complementary and alternative therapies

- Access to information—the new consumers devour information and become frustrated when access is limited.

Barriers to Consumer-Focused Healthcare

The transformation of the healthcare system to meet the demands of the new consumer may be slowed by third-party payers as mediators between the physician/patient interaction; the difficulty of measuring and comparing the quality and price of health services; and the gap in information and authority between consumers and providers/physicians who have attended medical school and are more knowledgeable.[14]

The Baby Boomer Bulge

The majority of Baby Boomers will not reach age 65 until 2010. As that population ages, it is expected to challenge and change society's view of aging as it has changed other societal structures. The increase in the numbers of persons who have attended college will impact the healthcare system sometime after 2005 as income

---

[11]"SMG Market Letter," (Chicago, IL: SMG Marketing Group Inc., 2000), 14(1): 1.
[12]Ibid:1.

[13]*Institute for the Future Executive Summary: The New Healthcare Consumer* (Menlo Park, CA: 1998): 1.
[14]Ibid:1–2.

inequality declines slightly. (Research has shown that health status increases proportionately with educational level.) The current 74 percent Caucasian population will decrease to 64 percent by 2010, with Asians comprising 5 percent, African-Americans 12 percent and, in certain western states, Latinos approximately 15 percent of the population, according to forecasts.[15]

Tiered access to healthcare will be reflected by the top tier, comprised of empowered patients with discretionary income, education, and the ability to use technology like the Internet; the next tier, who have access to health insurance but have little or no choice of health plans (this includes those who are temporarily employed and early retirees who have less or no discretionary income); and the third tier, comprised of the uninsured and those on Medicaid, who have no access to technology and no ability to participate in decisions about their health or treatment options.[16]

Disconnect Between Values and Economic Reality

The sense of mission and the core values that attract many to a career in healthcare has been jeopardized by the notion that economic performance is more important than properly caring for patients. The "business of medicine" is creating a corrosive environment for doctors, nurses, and patients.

According to noted ethicist Emily Friedman, every healthcare decision is both a business decision and a values decision. The last decade of the twentieth century has been a tug-of-war between those two polar forces. Some have pondered whether, 10 or 15 years from now, when we look back on the decade of the 1990s, policy-makers will feel any shame about having turned physicians into hamsters who are running faster and faster on a wheel to only stay in place, measuring their production

by time and motion studies, thereby reducing a valued patient/physician relationship to a commodity.

As we enter the twenty-first century, physicians are being faced with seismic changes in a system that has served them well for a hundred years: the shift to electronic medical records, telemedicine, and medical informatics in all its forms; digital imaging; and the erosion of authority by virtue of vast medical data banks now available to consumers, not in a medical library, but in their own homes. These are tremendous cultural changes for midcareer physicians. Recent medical school graduates, on the other hand, will be far more comfortable in this new environment.

ABOUT THIS BOOK

A Reader's Guide

For medical practices, it is essential that you read Chapter 3 first, as it is the foundation for all the specialty practices that follow. Chapters on sports medicine, physical therapy, diagnostic imaging, and ambulatory surgical centers are relatively self-contained. The dental chapter can be read independently of the medical chapters, although there are cross-references to other chapters on lighting, construction methods, furniture, interior finishes, and color.

A Word of Advice to Providers

Physicians and dentists should not lease office space prior to having a space planner prepare a program (list of rooms, sizes, and critical adjacencies) and a summary of total square footage required. This would be analogous to shopping for a suit of clothes without knowing what size one wears. In fact, if you are considering two or three alternative spaces, the fee invested in a program and schematic space plan will pay huge rewards in demonstrating which space most appropriately lends itself to your practice's needs. In fact, a smaller space with specific dimensions or a specific configuration may accom-

---

[15]*Institute for the Future Executive Summary: The New Battlegrounds* (Menlo Park, CA: 1998): 2.

[16]Ibid: 3.

modate you better than a larger one. Signing a ten-year-lease on an inefficient, awkward space can hamper your practice and be costly in more ways than one.

The Heterogeneous Nature of the Clinical Office

This book addresses a wide variety of clinical offices, from solo practitioners of primary care with a single employee in the front office to large group practices with dozens of physicians, medical assistants, and support staff. The latter category includes multispecialty group practices, specialists who may be accessed by referral only, and hospital-based clinics. But, according to a leader in the redesign of clinical practice, "despite the heterogeneity of the clinical office as a place of work, almost all its forms share in common one property: historical stability of design in the face of enormous changes in both the environment and agenda of healthcare."[17] Hopefully, the information and resources introduced in this book will stimulate innovation and encourage providers to consider new possibilities, in addition to explaining the basic principles of medical space planning.

Meeting the Challenges Ahead

As physicians regroup to meet the challenges ahead, competent medical space planners will be needed, and they will be expected to be familiar with new technology, the types of medical procedures being performed, and the latest techniques and equipment. To that end, this book will be an invaluable guide.

---

[17]Charles Kilo, M.D., MPH, *Idealized Design of Clinical Office Practices*, Conference Proceedings, Symposium on Healthcare Design, San Francisco, 1998, 458.

CHAPTER I
Psychology: Implications for Healthcare Design

OVERVIEW

A visit to the physician or dentist traumatizes many people. The basis for the fear, even more than lack of familiarity with procedures and a feeling of helplessness, may stem from the perception of invasion of one's personal space.

Touch and proximity can be comforting elements in other cultures, whereas Americans maintain larger territorial boundaries. For example, an American may maintain an imaginary barrier 24 inches in front of him or her as a safe conversational distance for strangers, while a person from the Middle East may reduce that safe boundary to 12 inches.

During a medical or dental examination, a person is most vulnerable, both emotionally and physically. One's territorial limits are invaded by strangers who poke, probe, and prod. And when the examination demands that the patient be naked, clad only in a gown, even the barrier of clothing ceases to protect. Is it any wonder that a visit to the dentist or physician can intimidate even the most stouthearted among us? How, then, can practitioners break through this barrier to examine and treat patients without arousing fear and anxiety?

First, the patient must perceive the positive aspects of the care he or she is receiving through an understanding of the procedures and how they will enhance his or her enjoyment of life. The relief of pain and the prevention of disease are joys in themselves. Second, the diagnostic and therapeutic milieu must *promote health* rather than aggravate illness and cause anxiety. The environment must be clean, cheerful, and nonthreatening, with contemporary furnishings, pleasing colors, interesting textures, and compatible works of art. The staff should be neatly groomed, well trained, friendly, and interested in the patients' well-being.

PATIENT SATISFACTION

Patient satisfaction is the new buzzword. It's the difference between providing what a patient *needs* and what a patient *wants.* It is important not only to satisfy clinical needs, but also to meet psychological expectations, which includes comfort and compassionate care. It is interesting to note that the two preceding sentences appeared in the last edition of this book written 12 years ago and they are still current. The fact that patient satisfaction is still regarded as a "new" trend demonstrates that it is still a work in progress and has not achieved enough critical mass to settle in as one of the basic components of patient care. Yet far more research has been done in the past five years to more closely define patient and customer satisfaction. The Picker Institute (www.picker.org) and the Center for Health Design (www.healthdesign.org) jointly sponsored research that culminated in a document published December 1997, *Consumer Perceptions of the Healthcare Environment: An Investigation to Determine What Matters,* a copy of which can be obtained from either organization. An effective video is also available. The Center for Health Design has also worked closely with JCAHO (Joint Commission on Accreditation of Healthcare Organizations) to develop standards to assess the built environment relative to what matters most to patients in order to reduce anxiety and provide a more patient-centered environment.

Principal components of patient satisfaction are a warm and caring staff, comfortable surroundings, and the ability of patients and visitors to easily find their way around the medical center without getting lost. Convenience and ease of access are critically important as is privacy. Why privacy has only *this past year* hit the radar screens of regulatory agencies that create standards and inspect healthcare facilities is not entirely clear as it has *always* been important to patients. Of course, the federal HIPAA (Health Insurance Portability and Accountability Act of 1996) legislation kicked it into high gear. It's a fact that change occurs at glacial speed in the healthcare industry, which is both good and bad. It's good when evaluating clinical procedures or pharmaceutical agents that may threaten a patient's life, but it's bad when something as simple as providing privacy for someone who is registering for surgery requires, literally, an act of Congress.

CONSUMER PERCEPTIONS OF THE HEALTHCARE ENVIRONMENT

In the aforementioned research sponsored by the Picker Institute and the Center for Health Design, the following issues were raised by consumers with respect to expectations in the ambulatory-care setting.* According to this report, in ambulatory care consumers want a physical environment that:

Facilitates Connection to Staff. Patients want to be noticed upon arrival and not be overlooked when they are called for their appointment.

Is Conducive to Well-Being. Patients want creature comforts to keep them from becoming bored or anxious and

---

Consumer Perceptions of the Healthcare Environment: An Investigation to Determine What Matters, Lafayette, California, Center for Health Design and Picker Institute, Boston, 1998, pp. 10–13.

consideration regarding room temperature, color, lighting, and avoidance of environmental stressors such as noise.

Is Convenient and Accessible. Patients want to get in and out of the clinic as fast as possible. Ease of wayfinding was highly valued.

Is Confidential and Private. Patients want confidentiality and privacy especially in the waiting room and during the clinical encounter. Patients do not want to overhear confidential information about other patients, nor do they want to be overheard.

Is Caring for the Family. Patients want play areas for their children and accommodation for family who accompany them into exam rooms or for diagnostic treatments.

Is Considerate of People's Impairments. Patients want seating and signage that accommodates the elderly and those with various impairments. They also requested consideration of those who arrive at the clinic feeling quite ill who would like a quiet place where they may be able to lie down.

Is Close to Nature. Patients highly value views of gardens, sky, natural light, as well as contact with nature in terms of aquariums, indoor plants, and water elements.

THE NEW CONSUMERISM

The rise of consumerism and the Internet have radically changed patient/physician relationships. There was a time when people never dared to question a physician's diagnosis or recommendations for treatment. Physicians and other healthcare professionals were placed on a pedestal, and even malpractice suits were infrequent. Sociologists attribute this loss of innocence to the Vietnam War, the Watergate scandal, the dumping of toxic waste, and other events that have caused some to question whether those in authority actually have our well-being in mind. Added to this are the efforts of people like Ralph Nader, who educated consumers to examine critically the safety of products and practices commonly in use. The result is a new group of consumers who focus on wellness, who put responsibility for health in their own hands, who play an active role in keeping themselves fit, and who shop for healthcare services with a critical eye. The powerful explosion of self-care Web sites on the Internet, coupled with unprecedented access to health data and medical research from one's home "24/7" has dramatically changed the patient/physician interface.

Shopping for healthcare services began in the 1980s. Prior to this, people visited the family doctor with whom they had grown up, or they selected a practitioner in the neighborhood. However, with the mobility that characterizes our society, people move frequently, and long-term relationships with healthcare providers are often not possible. Managed care has also impacted the "sacred" physician/patient relationship: physicians may be denied access to the care they think is best for an individual patient and patients may be forced to change physicians when they change employment or when health maintenance organization (HMO) physician panels change. Interest in holistic medicine and the proliferation of public information regarding the prevention of disease have also fueled the consumer-driven market.

One would expect a consumer-driven market to spawn competition among healthcare providers who, in the context of this book, are physicians and dentists, not hospitals. Dentists have historically been savvy about marketing and sensitive to consumer issues and there was a time when physicians had more impetus to attend to such concerns. Today, however, reimbursement for medical care has been impacted so dramatically by managed care and HCFA (Health Care Financing Administration) that just keeping the door open and the lights on can be a challenge. And, to be sure, there are large groups of patients who do not have the luxury of "shopping" for healthcare services: they may be uninsured and happy to receive any care at all. That's the reality. Despite this, the issues raised in this chapter are important and should be considered when remodeling or planning new offices.

FIRST IMPRESSIONS COUNT

Once the patient walks into the office, the waiting room should establish immediate rapport and put the patient at ease. First impressions are very important. Out-of-date furniture, worn upholstery, and grimy spots on walls may give the patient a message that the doctor does not care about patient comfort, or that he or she is reluctant to replace things when they wear out. No doubt, it's more a matter of heavy workloads and the fact that physicians rarely walk through their own waiting rooms. But perception is reality. It may *subliminally* suggest that the doctor is outdated on medical matters as well, which can lead to a lack of confidence and breed anxiety in the patient.

Subliminal Cues. There is no substitute for live green plants in a waiting room. Plastic plants suggest that live plants probably could not survive the environment, and the patient may fare no better. Healthy, lustrous greenery, on the other hand, promotes feelings of well-being.

A poorly illuminated waiting room not only makes it difficult to read, but subliminally suggests to patients that the staff is trying to hide something—perhaps poor housekeeping. It is surprising how often one finds badly soiled carpet and upholstery. Professional cleaning of these items should be routinely scheduled. Burned-out light bulbs are the ultimate insult, indicating a consummate inattention to detail.

A closed, sliding glass window with a buzzer for service tells patients that they are not really welcome—that they are intruding on the staff's privacy. The receptionist should always be in view of patients and accessible to them.

WAITING: A FRUSTRATING INCONVENIENCE

Waiting, unhappily, is one of the frustrations that often accompanies a visit to the doctor. Patients who are in pain or who are alarmed about an undiagnosed illness will accept waiting, realizing that doctors cannot always schedule appointments accurately. Well patients, however, such as those in a screening facility, have a different attitude and are not willing to accept discomfort or inconvenience without registering complaints.

Few wait with pleasure. In fact, waiting tends to concentrate one's attention on the details of the surroundings, making the presence or lack of good interior design more noticeable. Burned-out light bulbs, waxy and dusty plastic plants, and the crooked magazine rack become exaggerated irritants.

Many people visit a physician or dentist during their work day. Excessive waiting leads to anxiety and hostility, with worries about time away from the office and being late for meetings. An emergency at the hospital or the delivery of a baby are situations that people will forgive. They understand medical emergencies. But physicians who make a continual practice of overbooking are, perhaps without realizing it, offending their patients.

Research About Waiting

A study designed to investigate the effect of waiting time in the ambulatory setting revealed the following*:

- Time spent in the waiting room itself was not as important as total time spent waiting to receive care.

- Patients who were occupied while in the waiting room were less likely to be dissatisfied.

- A long wait in the treatment room engendered dissatisfaction with the clinicians.

- A short time in the waiting room raising expectations for a quick visit, followed by a lengthy wait in the treatment room, resulted in feelings of anger and resentment.

---

*K. H. Dansky, 1997. "Patient Satisfaction with Ambulatory Healthcare Services: Waiting Time and Filling Time." *Hospital & Health Services Administration* 42(2):165–177.

- Unoccupied time while waiting was perceived as longer, suggesting that strategies to fill time (watching a video, working a jigsaw puzzle, studying an aquarium, searching the Internet) are worthwhile.

- Informing patients how long they will have to wait increased patient satisfaction.

Seating Arrangements

Americans, in particular, do not like to be in close proximity to strangers. Middle Eastern and Latin cultures, by contrast, encourage closeness and touching. In the Arab world, olfaction, as expressed by breathing in the face of a friend, is considered a necessary part of social grace. To deny a friend of the smell of one's breath is a cause of shame. Middle Easterners and Latinos will huddle together much more closely than will Americans in a crowd.

Thus, seating arrangements in a waiting room designed for Americans should not force strangers to sit together—this only intensifies the stress of visiting the physician or dentist. Yet, in deference to the ethnic diversity that characterizes the American population, flexibility should be built in to allow waiting in family groups as well as offer seating that minimizes interaction with strangers, since both options may alleviate stress for the widest number of individuals. Individual chairs should be provided and arranged so that strangers do not have to face one another with a distance of less than 8 feet between them. Chairs should be placed against walls or in configurations that offer a degree of security, so that seated persons do not feel they are in jeopardy of being approached from behind. Careful planning in this regard will assure patient comfort.

Cultural Differences

If the medical office or clinic serves an ethnic population, it is important to research how that group uses space.

Some cultural groups, for example, tend to bring many relatives when one family member has to visit the doctor. Perhaps this is due to the need for emotional support provided by the presence of the family. People who do not speak English well or those from rural areas might easily become intimidated by modern technology. Books by Robert Summer and Edward T. Hall are excellent resources on the cultural use of space.

PERCEIVED STATUS DIFFERENCE

One of the reasons patients feel intimidated may be due to the perceived status difference between the physician or technician and themselves. The patient sits in a powerless position while being acted upon by others. Feelings of helplessness are accelerated when physicians do not establish rapport and make eye contact with patients. This can be facilitated by the layout of the examination room and the way it is furnished.

Body Language Indicates Stress

A number of research studies have explored the subject of physician/patient rapport and the importance of maintaining it during the clinical encounter. The patient's body language may indicate when the patient is uncomfortable with the physician, dentist, or technician. Averted eyes—looking away from the doctor—is one sign. Body positioned away from the doctor is another. Stereotyped behavior (tapping toes, shaking a leg, or rocking) is another. At these signs, the doctor must reestablish contact with the patient to break the "distance" barrier. Touching the patient's hand or arm and asking if he or she is okay is both friendly and reassuring. Interestingly, several studies have demonstrated that if the physician asks the patient's opinion about the cause of the illness, rapport increases considerably and it also provides some fairly accurate clues to the source of the problem that the physician might otherwise not discover.

Preserving Patients' Dignity

Another example of patient discomfort may occur when a radiologist or tech speaks from a remote control room to a gowned patient splayed on the X-ray table. Every effort should be made to treat the patient as an equal, to explain each step of a medical or dental procedure, to make the patient a partner in his or her treatment, and to allow the patient as much dignity as possible during what can best be described as humiliating medical examinations such as gastrointestinal X-ray studies or sigmoidoscopies. An individual's most private bodily functions are scrutinized by strangers, causing great psychological stress.

SEEING THE DOCTOR AS A PERSON

The consultation room (and occasionally, but rarely, the waiting room) may contain the doctor's personal memorabilia. Such items help the patient to see the doctor as a person with a family, hobbies, and interests outside of medicine. This reassures the patient, establishes rapport, and reduces the intimidation factor. In other than a solo practice (one physician), however, personal items should be kept out of the waiting room.

Style of Furnishings Should Not Be Trendy

There is considerable opportunity for the doctor to express his or her personality and style preferences in furniture and interior design. Indeed, for obstetricians, gynecologists, plastic surgeons, and pediatricians, the sky is the limit. But most physicians, surgeons in particular, must carefully select furniture that will convey a solid, conservative image. Patients need to feel that their surgeon is not impulsive—that he or she is a serious person not subject to frivolities and trendy decor. This is true for oral surgeons as well. General dentists who practice solo have more leeway in expressing personal interests (such as sailing or mountain climbing) with office decor than those who practice in a group.

Even if patients are not consciously aware of the message they are getting from the office interior design, they are subconsciously reading it. The body language of the office environment tells patients things that might subconsciously undermine their confidence in the physician or dentist. Confidence can be reinforced through attention to patients' comfort.

Although patients sometimes abuse nice furnishings by putting their feet on chairs or placing gum on the upholstery, unfortunately, that's the price that must be paid to make patients feel comfortable. The replacement factor should be built into the office overhead. The fact is, most patients do not abuse the pleasant surroundings provided for them, so why make the many suffer for the transgressions of the few? The psychological benefits of an office designed to serve patients far outweighs any drawbacks.

CHAPTER 2
General Parameters of Medical Space Planning

BUILDING SHELL DESIGN

Efficient medical offices begin with an intelligently designed building shell. All too often, medical office buildings (MOBs) are planned by designers or architects who are unfamiliar with the special requirements of medical tenants; thus, the structure of the building does not lend itself to an efficient layout of suites. Structural column locations, stair placement, elevators, electrical room, mechanical shafts, public restrooms (if provided), and window modules either impede of facilitate layout of individual suites.

Other factors that influence the design of an MOB are the shape and size of the site, the specific requirements of a particular tenant or client, a beautiful view, or the architect's desire to impose a unique design on the project. All of these factors have to be weighed and balanced along with applicable codes, zoning restrictions, and the client's budget. A building that is completely functional and efficient, but totally insensitive to aesthetics may not rent as quickly as the owners may wish. But an MOB designed primarily for aesthetic merit, with only secondary concern for internal planning efficiency, will also be difficult to lease.

Floor Area Efficiency

To begin with, an MOB should contain at least 12,000 square feet of rentable space per floor in order to accommodate suites of varying sizes and configurations as well as to increase the efficiency of stairs and elevators. Larger buildings often have 20,000 square feet per floor. The elevator, mechanical equipment room, electrical room, and public restrooms can be placed in the core with rental space wrapped around the perimeter (Figures 2-1 and 2-2) or the

services may be located at the ends of a double-loaded public corridor (Figure 2-4). Figure 2-1 gives 80 percent rentable space and Figure 2-3 gives 89 percent rentable space, but it must be noted that Figure 2-1 includes restrooms. Medical buildings usually are designed to an 85 percent efficiency, but architectural features such as an atrium or a large lobby can reduce the efficiency to 80 percent.

The core factor is 12 percent in Figure 2-2, reflecting the gain in efficiency due to the large floor plate. The building shell in Figure 2-2 is designed to accommodate large users on the 60-foot-bay-depth side. If the building is leased to smaller tenants, public corridors penetrating the 60-foot depth may have to be added, thereby reducing somewhat the potential rentable area.

Special attention must be paid to locating stairwells when one tenant intends to lease an entire floor or half a floor. In such case, the public exit stairwell may fall within an individual suite—a nonpublic space. One way to handle this is to provide a third stair in the center of the building so that, even if one tenant takes half a floor, two stairs remain accessible for tenants on the other half of the floor (Figure 2-4).

Figure 2-2 shows a layout with one stair set in, to allow a 52-foot bay depth between it and the end of the building, so that a large suite can run across the end of the building either at the 52-foot depth or at a 32-foot depth utilizing a 20-foot "allowable" dead-end corridor, extending from the stairwell. One must remember, however, when locating a suite across the end of a building: If the occupancy load is high enough, two exits may be required, with a separation equal to one-half the distance of the diagonal of the suite. In a large suite, this would be achieved by extending another corridor perpendicular to the public corridor for the secondary exit.

In spite of these issues, especially with a floor plate as large as that shown in Figure 2-2, setting in the stair on one

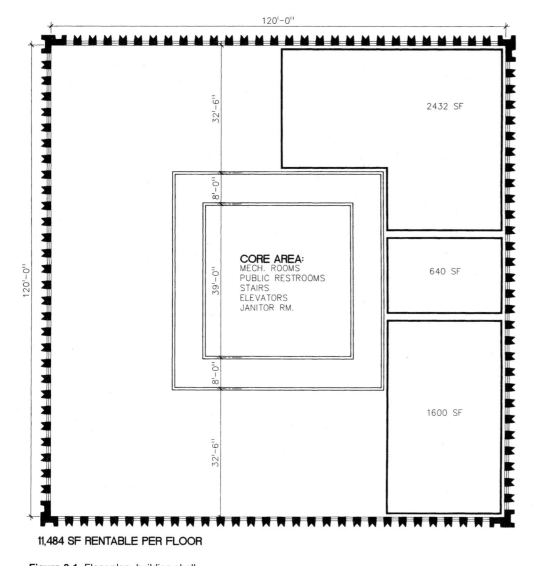

120'-0"

32'-6"

2432 SF

8'-0"

120'-0"

39'-0"

CORE AREA:
MECH. ROOMS
PUBLIC RESTROOMS
STAIRS
ELEVATORS
JANITOR RM.

640 SF

8'-0"

1600 SF

32'-6"

11,484 SF RENTABLE PER FLOOR

Figure 2-1. Floor plan, building shell.

end provides great flexibility with respect to the size of suites that may be accommodated. It should be noted that the stairwells themselves must be located with a separation (generally measured to the center of each door) of one-half the diagonal of the floor.

Structural Support

The structural support system for the building should allow as much flexibility as possible for the layout of tenant spaces. For a multistory building, a moment-resistant steel frame offers considerably more flexibility in space planning and window placement than does a building supported with "K" braces, for example. Of course, moment-resistant steel is a considerably more expensive option. Regardless of the type of system used, it is imperative that the structural engineer work very closely with the medical space planner, so that structural elements can be accommodated within the planning grid.

Perimeter columns, ideally, would be flush with the inside face of the exterior wall (Figure 2-2) so that they do not protrude into the room or, at the least, are flush with the exterior face of the building so that protrusion into the room is minimized. On the interior, columns for a 32-foot bay depth would fall as shown in Figure 2-3 on the inside face of the public corridor wall, spanning 32 feet 6 inches center to center, creating a column free space in between.

For a 44-foot bay depth, the intermediate column should occur either 17 or 18 feet on-center, measured from the column on the exterior wall, and depending upon whether it is flush with the exterior face or extends totally from the inside of the exterior wall (Figures 2-4 and 2-5). Here, there will be a 12-foot-deep row of rooms across the exterior wall. There would then be a 4-foot-wide corridor, and the column should fall on the far side of the corridor, extending into the center row of rooms (Figure 2-5, lower diagram). Obviously, one would not want that intermediate column to fall within the corridor space.

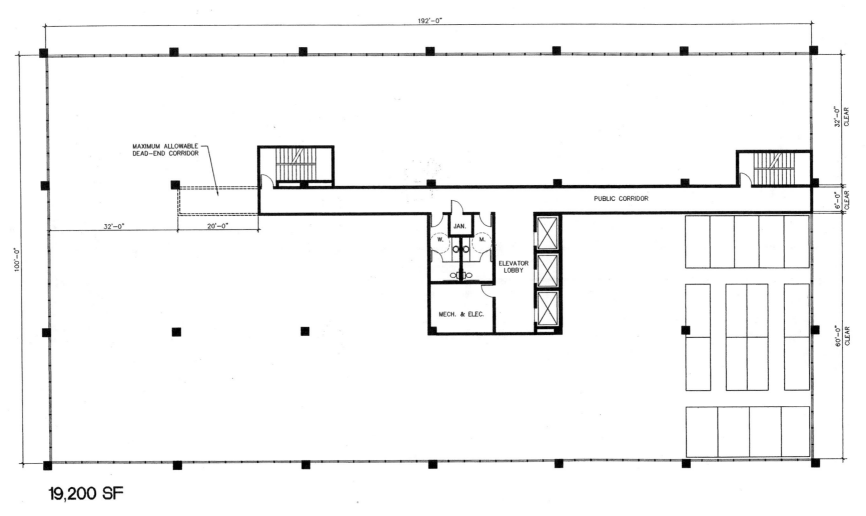

MAXIMUM ALLOWABLE
DEAD-END CORRIDOR

192'-0"

32'-0" CLEAR

6'-0" CLEAR

100'-0"

60'-0" CLEAR

32'-0"

20'-0"

PUBLIC CORRIDOR

JAN.

W.

M.

ELEVATOR
LOBBY

MECH. & ELEC.

19,200 SF

Figure 2-2. Floor plan, building shell. (*Design: Jain Malkin Inc.*)

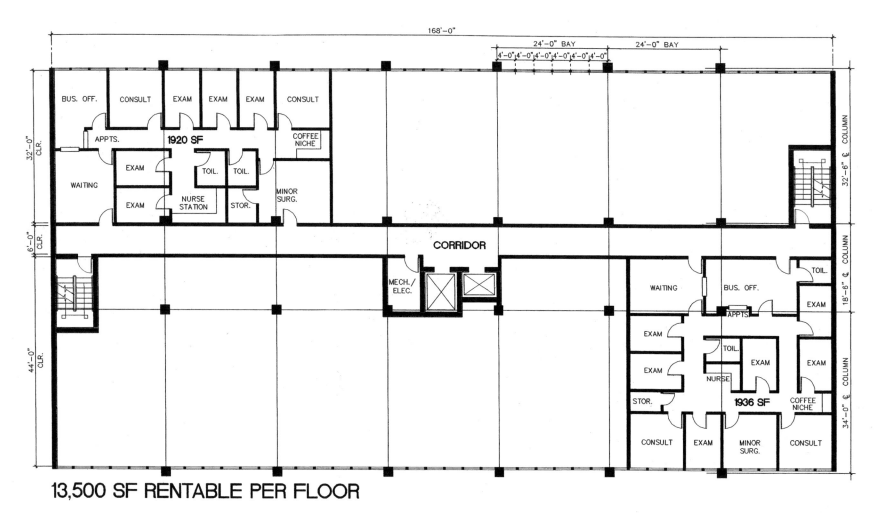

168'-0"

24'-0" BAY **24'-0" BAY**

4'-0" 4'-0" 4'-0" 4'-0" 4'-0" 4'-0"

32'-0" CLR.

BUS. OFF. | CONSULT | EXAM | EXAM | EXAM | CONSULT

APPTS. | **1920 SF** | COFFEE NICHE

EXAM | TOIL. | TOIL.

WAITING

EXAM | NURSE STATION | STOR. | MINOR SURG.

6'-0" CLR.

CORRIDOR

32'-6" ℄ COLUMN

44'-0" CLR.

MECH./ ELEC.

18'-6" ℄ COLUMN

WAITING | BUS. OFF. | TOIL.

APPTS | EXAM

EXAM

EXAM | TOIL. | EXAM | EXAM

NURSE

STOR. | **1936 SF** | COFFEE NICHE

CONSULT | EXAM | MINOR SURG. | CONSULT

34'-0" ℄ COLUMN

13,500 SF RENTABLE PER FLOOR

Figure 2-3. Floor plan, building shell. (*Design: Jain Malkin Inc.*)

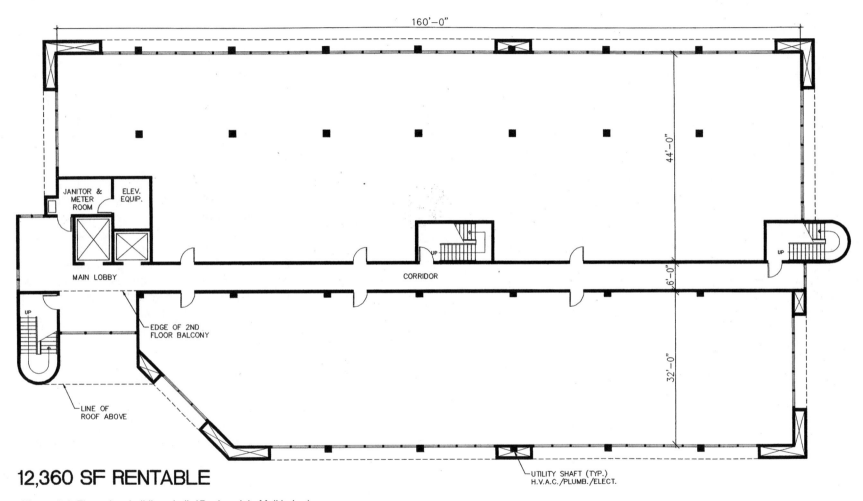

160'-0"

44'-0"

6'-0"

32'-0"

JANITOR &
METER
ROOM

ELEV.
EQUIP.

MAIN LOBBY

CORRIDOR

UP

UP

UP

EDGE OF 2ND
FLOOR BALCONY

LINE OF
ROOF ABOVE

UTILITY SHAFT (TYP.)
H.V.A.C./PLUMB./ELECT.

12,360 SF RENTABLE

Figure 2-4. Floor plan, building shell. (*Design: Jain Malkin Inc.*)

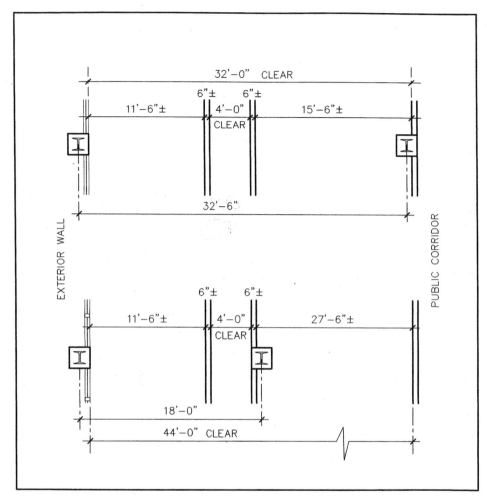

Figure 2-5. Placement of columns. (*Design: Jain Malkin Inc.*)

Another option for locating the intermediate column in a 44-foot-bay depth is illustrated in Figure 2-3. It occurs in the wall of the business office or waiting room, making it 34 feet on center, measured from the column on the exterior wall.

It is difficult to give absolute dimensions for locating columns, because there are so many variables. The "box-in" size of the columns, whether one uses 4-foot-wide or 5-foot-wide interior corridors, and the fact that high-rise buildings have larger columns, affect the spacing between them.

Locations of structural columns should not adversely affect the flexibility of the space, if the building is engineered properly. Most rooms are small; thus, the density of partitions is high. Long spans are not necessary. A tradeoff inevitably arises here. Reducing the span between columns makes it possible to use lighter-weight beams, thereby reducing the cost of the building. However, more columns, closer together, reduce space planning flexibility. The occurrence of perimeter columns at intervals, creating 20-foot-wide or 24-foot-wide bays, and interior columns spaced as shown in Figure 2-4, often works well. Where the spaces on both sides of the corridor are a 32-foot depth, all columns may be contained in the perimeter walls, with none occurring within tenant spaces.

PLANNING MODULE

A considerable amount of standardization exists in the sizes of rooms in a medical suite. For the most part, suites can be laid out on either a 4-foot or a 4-foot 6-inch planning grid. Having said that, however, one must acknowledge the odd-sized treatment rooms, toilets, and specialty rooms such as radiology.

The author prefers a 4-foot planning module. Based on this, there are four common bay depths that accommodate efficiently suites of certain sizes. To begin with, a *28-foot bay depth* works well for small suites anywhere from 500 to 1500 square feet. It can even accommodate an 1800-square-foot suite as shown in Figure 2-6. These

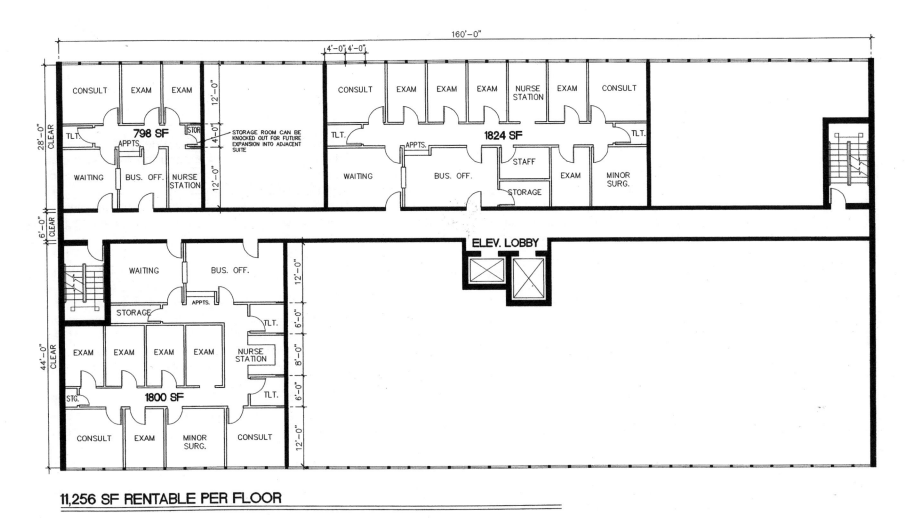

Figure 2-6. Floor plan, building shell. (*Design: Jain Malkin Inc.*)

suites are extremely easy to plan because they involve two 12-foot-deep rows of rooms separated by a 4-foot-wide corridor.

A *32-foot bay depth* is the most common and ac-commodates suites anywhere from 1200 to 3000 square feet. This is similar to the 28-foot bay depth in that it is also a double-loaded corridor, except that the row of rooms closest to the public corridor is 16 feet deep. This is where the waiting room and business office would generally be located. A 3000-square-foot suite, at a 32-foot bay depth, would be 92 feet long and would involve long walking distances. Therefore, a 3000-square-foot suite would be accommodated better in a 44-foot bay depth where a center core, or island, may be used.

A *44-foot bay depth* works well for suites between 1800 and 4000 square feet. Figures 2-3 and 2-6 illustrate how a central core may be used. With suites less than 1800 square feet, a 44-foot-bay depth does not allow enough windows. It creates a narrow, deep suite.

Suite Bay Depths

28 feet	• suites	500 to 1,500 square feet
32 feet	• suites	1,200 to 3,000 square feet
44 feet	• suites	1,800 to 4,000 square feet
60 feet	• suites	4,000 to 10,000 square feet

For purposes of illustration, an identical suite is created in a 28-foot bay depth and a 44-foot bay depth in Figure 2-6, and in a 32-foot bay depth in Figure 2-3. Consultation rooms are 12×12 feet, and exam rooms are usually 8×12 feet in size. Minor surgery rooms are generally 12×12 feet. Thus, a fairly predictable layout of rooms can be expected.

If suites are laid out with a storage room at the end of a corridor, as shown in the 798-square-foot suite in Figure 2-6 and in the suites in Figure 2-3, a tenant can expand into an adjoining suite by eliminating the storage room and continuing the corridor, with no other remodeling necessary in the existing suite.

Suites over 4000 square feet work well in a 60-foot bay depth. Starting at the public corridor wall and moving toward the exterior wall, this allows for a 16-foot-deep row of rooms, a 4-foot-wide corridor, two 12-foot-deep rows of rooms back to back, another 4-foot corridor, and a 12-foot-deep row of rooms parallel to the exterior wall. One may have a number of transverse corridors running perpendicular to the two aforementioned ones, as illustrated in the block diagram in Figure 2-2. This bay depth works for suites anywhere from 4000 to 10,000 square feet. It is not impossible to design a suite less than 4000 square feet in a 60-foot bay depth; however, unless it is a corner suite with windows on two sides as shown in Figure 2-2, it becomes a narrow, deep suite with few windows.

Suites over 10,000 square feet, depending on the size of the building, may become a full-floor tenant. In this case, if they were a tenant in the building shown in Figure 2-3, the suite would have a bay depth of 82 feet. In the building shown in Figure 2-4, the tenant could take one-half of the floor (to the right of the center stair) and achieve a large square space. The third stair, centrally located, would provide the two required exits for the tenants on the other half of the floor.

One cannot state unequivocally, for example, that a 4000-square-foot suite would be more efficient in a 44-foot bay depth than in a 60-foot bay depth. The type of medical specialty, penetrations of stairs and elevators, and the spacing between columns may, in an individual building, make one bay depth preferable to another. If both are available in the building, it would be wise to provide alternate layouts to see which works best. The reader is referred to the radiology suite in Figure 5-5 for an example of a 7400-square-foot suite that runs in an "L" shape along the 44-foot bay depth and continues across the end of the building.

If one designs a medical building so that suites on one side of the public corridor have a depth of 32 feet, and the other, a depth of 44 feet (Figures 2-3 and 2-4), one would have considerable flexibility to place tenants where the suites can be laid out most efficiently. If feasibility studies prepared prior to the design of the building shell show that there is a considerable need for large suites, then one side of the building might be designed at a 60-foot bay depth. Sometimes a suite can be laid out equally well in two different bay depths, and the only differ-ence may be that one requires more circulation area than another.

The average medical suite for a solo practitioner would be 1200 square feet. Few suites are smaller than that. The bulk of suites the designer will encounter fall in the range of 1200 to 2500 square feet. There may be large orthopedic or internal medicine suites ranging from 3500 to 8000 square feet. Since the terms of financing often specify that the building must be 50 percent pre-leased before construction begins, it is often possible to know who the large tenants with special needs will be, and the building can be shaped with those requirements in mind.

An MOB constructed purely on speculation with little preleasing would be difficult to plan without a profile or feasibility study of physicians in the area, their space needs were they to lease space, and their respective spe-cialties.

Alternate Planning Module

In recent years, there has been a trend toward larger exam rooms as well as wider internal corridors. This is difficult to accomplish with a planning module of 4 feet, since three windows 4 feet wide would lead to a room 12 feet wide, whereas 9 or 10 feet would be the goal for the width of a "large" exam room. Some prefer an exam room 9 feet wide×12 feet long, yet others prefer more of a square room 10×10 feet or 9×10 feet in size (Figure 3-40). A wider exam room allows the door to open to shield the patient and still preserve the handicapped access setback on the pull side of the door (Figure 3-38). Internal corridors would be 5 feet, rather than 4 feet clear.

Although at first it seems an odd number, a planning module of 3 feet will work well, provided the shell archi-tecture and facade also comply (Figure 2-7). Windows, and columns, have to tie to the 3-foot grid. This provides exam rooms that are 9 feet wide, center to center, or 8 feet 6 inches clear, and consultation rooms that are 12 feet wide on center, as they would be when using a plan-ning module of 4 feet.

The 3-foot planning module provides bay depths of 33, 45, and 60 feet. A 33-foot bay depth would have, starting at the exterior wall, a row of 12-foot-deep rooms, a corri-dor of 5 feet, and a 16-foot-wide row of rooms near the building's public corridor. The only compromise occurs at the end of the building where, if one has continuous win-dows wrapping the building with mullions on a 3-foot grid, a corridor of 5 feet, rather than 6 feet, puts a partition in the center of a lite of glass. This irregularity occurs only on the ends of the building.

Considering a 45-foot bay depth, starting at the exteri-or wall, one would have a 10-foot-wide row of rooms, 5-foot-wide corridor, another 5-foot-wide corridor, and a 15-foot-deep row of rooms along the public corridor.

Window Placement

Window placement is a significant issue in a medical office building. With so many small rooms, it is important that windows fall in the right place and that structural columns occur on the coordinates of the planning module so that they can be buried in the walls. Windows with mul-lions at 4 feet on center function well when a 4-foot plan-ning grid is utilized. This permits exam rooms to be 8 feet wide (7 feet 6 inches clear) and consultation rooms to be 12 feet wide (11 feet 6 inches clear) along the window wall. The 4-foot window module can be reduced to a 2-foot module to permit even greater flexibility, but this amounts to an increased construction cost. When win-dows are irregularly sized, or something other than the 4-foot module, partitions have to jog in order to meet a mul-lion.

It is important that windows start at 42 inches off the floor so that cabinets can be put under them, and patient privacy in an exam room is not violated. Even in a waiting room or lobby, windows should not start at the floor because it limits the area of seating. The glazing color should be gray, not bronze, because the latter tends to make skin look jaundiced.

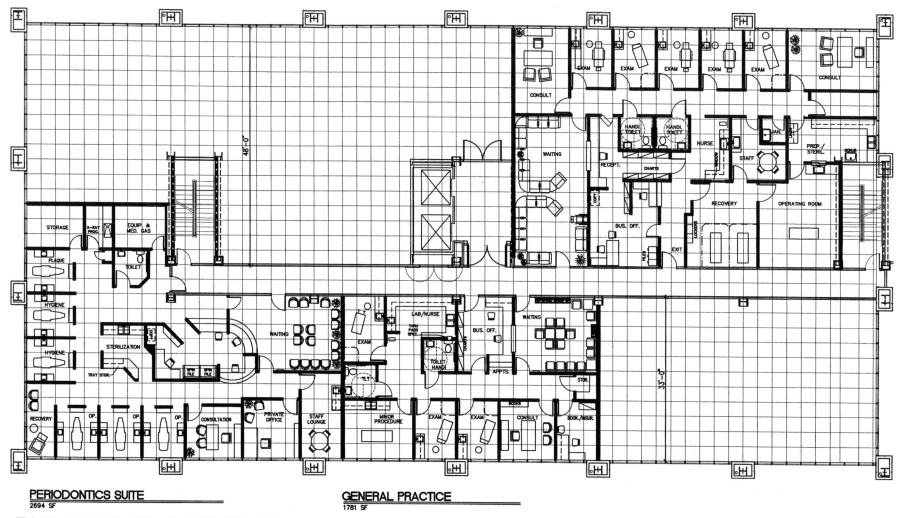

PLASTIC SURGERY
3302 SF

PERIODONTICS SUITE
2694 SF

GENERAL PRACTICE
1781 SF

BUILDING FLOOR PLAN ON 3 FEET PLANNING GRID
15,720 SF

Figure 2-7. Floor plan, building shell, using a 3-foot planning module. (*Design: Jain Malkin Inc.*)

Ceiling Heights

An 8-foot or 8-foot 6-inch ceiling height is suitable for individual suites with the exception of a few individual rooms such as radiology, outpatient surgery, or physical therapy, which require a 9- or 10-foot-high ceiling. A standard suspended acoustic ceiling works well, but ideally, for acoustical reasons, should be laid out individually in each room with interior partitions extending above the finished ceiling 6 to 9 inches.

AMENITIES

When a dentist or physician evaluates one building against another, various factors are considered in addition to lease terms and a possible equity position. Amenities such as a health club, a conference center, dedicated parking for physicians, and a coffee shop or deli may make one building more attractive than another. A building's image is important, but less so than for corporate users, who will generally seek out the most upscale building their budgets will allow.

Physicians try to tailor the image to their patient profile. Plastic surgeons and other specialists who perform largely elective procedures may be more interested in a high-profile building. However, a primary care physician with a broad spectrum of patients may choose a more modest building that will not make low-income patients feel uncomfortable. This physician would be more interested in other attributes of the building such as freeway access, convenient parking for patients, and proximity to the hospital.

BUILDING SHELL CONFIGURATIONS

The building shell configurations illustrated in this chapter are straightforward and highly functional. Other considerations sometimes prevail. The site may be best suited to a square building, a cruciform building, or perhaps one in a T shape. If located on a prominent corner, the part of the building that faces the corner might be sculpted or articulated in such a way as to make it more dramatic.

Sometimes, in an attempt to make an architectural statement, the exterior of the building will have a stair-step configuration. This can greatly reduce the efficiency of the suites unless careful consideration is given to the length of each staggered section to make sure that a row of rooms will fit within it. Niches in the exterior wall can be even more of a problem, resulting in very irregular room shapes. Buildings that are oval or have a circular configuration are next to impossible to utilize for medical office buildings.

BUILDING STANDARDS

It is important to define building standards for tenant improvements in order to establish an acceptable level of quality for construction items. These building standards would normally be prepared by the medical space planner for review by the owner and tenant improvement contractor. The items included are construction details for each type of partition, sound attenuation, suite entry hardware, door closers, interior doors, casework style and details, plumbing fixtures, ceiling system, light fixtures, electrical hardware, interior finishes, design of reception window, and so forth.

These items are generally accepted by all tenants in the building. Some may wish to upgrade light fixtures, add wallcoverings, or upgrade the carpet, but the basic construction items will be consistent throughout the building. This assures the owner, who has to maintain the building, that replacement parts will be on hand, and, if a tenant moves out, the owner won't be left with a suite having French Provincial residential hardware, for example.

TENANT IMPROVEMENT ALLOWANCES

Owners or developers offer tenants a *tenant improvement allowance,* expressed as a per-square-foot amount, to build their suites. These amounts vary from building to building and also reflect geographical differences in construction costs. At the lower end of the spectrum, tenants cannot build even a simple suite without adding $25 to $30 per foot, from their own pockets, to the allowance. At the upper end of the spectrum, tenants may be able to build a "plain vanilla" suite (one with minimum casework, building standard lighting, and painted walls) at the tenant improvement allowance, without adding money to it.

Generally speaking, tenants don't expect to be able to build a medical or dental suite within the tenant improvement allowance. Suites such as family practice, pediatrics, and dermatology, however, would be less expensive to build than an ophthalmology suite, for example, which has a great deal of electrical work.

At the upper end in terms of construction cost would be radiology suites, oral surgery, ambulatory surgical centers, and many dental suites. All of these contain a great deal of plumbing, electrical, and special construction details that make them extremely expensive to construct. For this reason, physicians and dentists are highly desirable tenants. They invest so much in tenant improvements that they move infrequently. Commercial office tenants often move every few years, whereas it is not unusual for a physician to occupy a space for 10 to 15 years.

An alternate method of dealing with tenant improvements is to present tenants with a *work letter* stipulating exactly how many of each item (i.e., lineal feet of casework, number of electrical outlets, number of doors, lineal feet of partitions) they will receive per. 1000 square feet of rentable space. These quantities are tied to the per-square-foot allowance. In theory, if the tenant did not exceed those quantities of each item, per 1000 square feet, the suite would be built with no out-of-pocket expenses.

POLITICS

When designing tenant suites, one becomes aware of a fundamental issue: conflicting goals of various parties regarding tenant privileges and limitations. Of particular concern are ownership of the building (whether the tenants may participate in ownership), tenant improvement

allowances offered by the owners, whether tenants may have their own radiology equipment, and whether tenants will be permitted to engage their own contractors.

In essence, owners generally want to give as little as possible but lease the building quickly and at high rents, and tenants want to move into custom suites, designed according to their every whim, without having to foot any out-of-pocket expenses. The tug-of-war usually continues until the tenant actually takes occupancy of the suite, and then, little by little, the issues seem to resolve themselves. However, the space planner is often caught in the middle.

If retained by the owner of the building to do space planning for the tenants, the designer's obligation is to protect the rights of the owner; when employed by an individual tenant, the designer is charged with negotiating with the building owner to secure the greatest number of goods for the tenant. When one is the space planner for the building and also engaged to provide custom interior design services for a tenant, one must wear two hats and represent both parties well.

LEASING CONSIDERATIONS

Leasing a medical building requires a great deal of strategy. It is helpful if the leasing agent is experienced in dealing with physicians. Targeting one or two key physician groups is the best way to kick off the leasing effort. Physicians are often reluctant to be the first to lease space in a new building. It takes a couple of leaders who are not afraid to risk being first in order to interest other physicians. The strategy involves determining who those key physicians are and going after them. Their interest in the project signals the seal of approval to others in the medical community.

Strategy also comes into play when determining optimum locations for various suites within the building. Some of this is a factor of the building shell itself, as suites of a certain size might be better accommodated in one location than another. Apart from that consideration, however, high-volume suites are best located, if not on the ground floor, then at least near the elevator, to limit foot traffic down the corridor.

Radiology, due to the weight of the equipment, would usually be found on the ground floor and, for ease of access, so would the clinical lab. Specialties such as general practice or internal medicine, which use radiology and lab services a great deal, would wisely be located adjacent to those suites. Low-volume specialties such as plastic surgery, neurology, or cardiac surgery might be located on upper floors, perhaps in a corner suite.

For corner suites, one would not locate a 1500-square-foot tenant in a choice corner. These suites should be saved to use as an inducement to woo a prime tenant. Remember, however, when a suite is located across the end of a building, if the suite is of sufficient size to require two exits, there will have to be a separation between them. This is sometimes difficult to achieve at the end of a building.

Another issue to think about when laying out suites on a floor and taking into account the tenant's preference for location is that it is important to not leave any "holes" or unleasable size spaces between suites. In order to avoid this, tenants cannot always be located exactly where they would wish to be. This is where the space planner's skill as a mediator comes into play.

The first tenants to express interest in a new medical building are often radiology, clinical lab, and pharmacy, but they are often the last actually to confirm a lease since they depend on the other tenants for their livelihood. If the building is only 50 percent leased upon completion and these tenants have to move in, they will suffer. Furthermore, they will want to know, in advance of signing a lease, who the major tenants are, so that they can project whether the composition of the building will generate enough revenue for them. A fully equipped radiology suite represents an investment of several million dollars in equipment and construction costs. Such equipment is not easily relocated. Understandably, such tenants want very specific information on the other tenants in the building before committing to a lease.

HOSPITAL-BASED MOBs

Medical office buildings that are adjacent to and affiliated with hospitals have very special needs that will be touched on only briefly in this discussion. The major consideration lies in the interface with the hospital. Will the hospital actually be occupying space in the MOB? If so, and if inpatients have access to these facilities, the MOB will be subject to more stringent standards and codes, thereby greatly increasing construction costs.

If the MOB is to be physically connected to the hospital, great thought must be given to the configuration of each floor with regard to stairwells, elevators, and point of entry to the hospital, so that future expansion is not hampered, and circulation between the hospital and the MOB is efficient. One disadvantage to physicians in a hospital-affiliated MOB is that sometimes the hospital imposes limitations upon individual tenants whose services or practices are likely to compete with hospital departments. This is particularly true of diagnostic imaging, clinical lab, physical therapy, and pharmacy services.

Hospitals benefit by having on-campus MOBs to provide a core group of admitting physicians who are loyal to the hospital. This also increases utilization of the hospital's ancillary services.

CHAPTER 3
Practice of Medicine: Primary Care

The field of medicine is continually expanding as new knowledge and concepts are put into practice. But at the base level of the health care delivery system, we begin with the primary fields of medicine: general practice, pediatrics, family practice, and internal medicine. Physicians in these areas are responsible for the total healthcare needs of their patients. They are termed "primary" medical specialties because they are normally the entry-level physician one would consult about a medical problem.

If the problem requires a specialist, the family practitioner or internist will then refer the patient to a specialist —perhaps a urologist, neurologist, orthopedist, or allergist. There are certain obvious exceptions to this primary-care referral system. People frequently consult allergists, plastic surgeons, dermatologists, obstetricians and gynecologists, or orthopedists on their own if they feel certain they have a problem that falls into that specialist's domain.

While a primary physician may refer patients to a specialist to consult on a special problem, he or she will be in contact with the specialist and will retain overall responsibility for the patient's care. This provides for continuity of care—one physician who records a continuing health history for a patient and who oversees and coordinates total healthcare over a period of years. This is particularly important for patients with long-term disabilities such as diabetes, heart disease, or hypertension. In managed-care systems, the primary-care referral physician is often called the "gatekeeper," since access to specialty care is controlled by this individual.

A general practitioner (G.P.) is a doctor who, having completed medical school and an internship, began his or her medical practice. A G.P. gains a broad general knowledge through experience that enables him or her to treat most medical disorders encountered by his or her patients. Doctors in family practice have had at least three years' training and service in all major areas of medicine such as surgery, obstetrics and gynecology, pediatrics, internal medicine, geriatrics, and psychiatry. The practice of family medicine is based on four principles of care: continuity, comprehensiveness, family orientation, and commitment to the person.* For the purpose of space planning, the needs of general practice and family practice physicians are identical.

FAMILY PRACTICE

The individual rooms that comprise this suite, with modifications, form the specialized suites to be discussed in future chapters. Together, these rooms constitute the basic medical suite.

Therefore, the philosophy behind the design of these individual rooms (waiting room, business office, exam room, consultation room, nurse station) will be discussed in depth in this chapter.

---

*I. R.. McWhinney, *An Introduction to Family Medicine,* Oxford University Press, New York, 1981.

Functions of a Medical Suite

1. Administrative
   a. Waiting and reception
   b. Business (appointments, bookkeeping, insurance, clerical)
   c. Medical records

2. Patient care
   a. Examination
   b. Treatment/minor surgery
   c. Consultation

3. Support services
   a. Nurse station/laboratory
   b. X-ray, darkroom
   c. Storage
   d. Staff lounge

Figure 3-1 shows the relationship of rooms. The patient enters the waiting room, checks in with the receptionist (usually an opening or window with a transaction counter between the business office and waiting room), and takes a seat in the waiting room. Since most medical offices require advance appointments (as opposed to walk-ins),

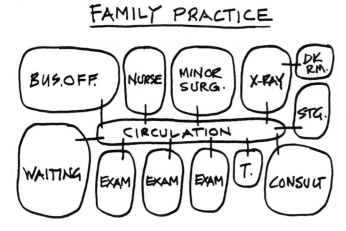

Figure 3-1. Schematic diagram of a family practice suite.

the nurse will have pulled the patient's medical record prior to the patient entering the office.

Later, a nurse or medical assistant calls the patient to the examination area. Usually, the nurse or assistant will then weigh the patient, request a urine sample (if required), record blood pressure, and take a short history. This is done either at the nurse station or in the exam room. The nurse may also record the patient's temperature.

In the exam room, the nurse or aide prepares the patient for the examination and arranges the instruments the physician will need. The doctor enters the room, washes his or her hands, chats with the patient about symptoms, makes notes in the patient's chart, and proceeds to examine the patient, often with a nurse or assistant in attendance. After the examination, the patient is asked to dress and may be instructed to meet the physician in the consultation room, where a diagnosis and recommended treatment are discussed. As it slows down the physician to have to return repeatedly to a consultation room with each patient, more commonly, the doctor diagnoses and prescribes right in the exam room. The patient leaves the office, passing an appointment desk or window where future appointments may be booked and where payment for services may be made or arranged.

Obvious deviations to the above may occur when, for example, a patient breaks a limb. In this case, the patient may be sent to an X-ray room first, and then proceed to a minor surgery room to have a cast applied without ever entering an exam room.

Flow

The efficiency of the medical practice will be largely influenced by the flow of patients, staff, and—to a lesser degree—supplies through the suite. The layout of rooms must be based on a thorough understanding of how staff interface with patients and, most important, separation of incoming and outgoing traffic. This is rarely possible in a small office for one or two practitioners but is increasingly important as the size of the office grows.

In Figure 3-2, for example, exam rooms and consultation rooms are arranged in four clusters, enabling four physicians to practice simultaneously. It assumes a fifth physician will, at any time, have a day off. Patients, after checking in with the receptionist, proceed to one of four nurse stations to be weighed. If a urine specimen is required, toilets between each two nurse stations have specimen pass-throughs. For those arriving for lab work only, or for those who know they need lab work after having visited the physician and who are now on their way out of the suite, the lab is conveniently located near the waiting room. The exit/check-out path of travel is more or less separate from the ingress, and patients can exit from both sides of the suite without passing through the waiting room. Circulation for staff is direct, enabling them to quickly access all parts of the suite without having to navigate a maze. Medical records and the business office are centrally located.

Electronic Communication Systems

Flow can be enhanced and managed by custom light-signaling communication systems that consist of a panel of colored signal lights mounted on the wall of exam and procedure rooms, nurse stations, and the reception area. By glancing at a panel or pressing a button, physicians and staff can silently be notified of messages and emergencies, let others in the office know where they are located, and tell nurses and technicians where they are needed. The sequence memory program advances automatically, telling the doctor which patient is next. Monitor panels at nurse stations indicate at a glance the status of exam rooms, while another panel at the reception desk notifies clinical staff when patients have arrived and which provider they're scheduled to see. Expeditor Systems of Alpharetta, Georgia, is a leading vendor of these systems.

An add-on to the Expeditor communication system, called Practice Profiler®, provides room utilization analysis and documentation of the entire patient encounter. It measures the time a patient spends waiting in the exam room before the doctor arrives, the amount of time the doctor spends with the patient, and a monthly report on physician and staff productivity is e-mailed to subscribers. This type of data can help physicians become more efficient in the eternal quest to see more patients each day without sacrificing quality.

Physician Extenders

In recent years, physicians—especially those in group practices—have increasingly added physician extenders (PEs) to their patient care management teams. Also referred to as "mid-level providers," these generic terms usually refer to physician assistants (PAs), medical assistants (MAs), and advanced practice nurses (APNs). According to the American Association of Colleges of Nursing, APNs are advanced registered nurses, typically with master's degrees, who fall into four categories:

1. *Nurse practitioners,* who provide primary-care diagnosis and treatment, immunizations, physical exams, and management of common chronic problems

2. *Certified nurse midwives,* who provide prenatal, postpartum, and gynecological care to healthy women, and deliver babies in a variety of settings

3. *Clinical nurse specialists,* who are trained in a range of specialized areas such as oncology, cardiac care, and pediatrics

4. *Certified registered nurse anesthetists,* who, according to the American Association of Colleges of Nursing, administer more than 65 percent of all anesthetics given to patients

At least 45 states allow advanced practice nurses to prescribe medications, and 16 states allow APNs to practice independently without physician supervision.

Clearly, the use of physician extenders dovetails with the economics of managed care. Studies by the Medical Group Management Association (MGMA) and the American Medical Association (AMA) Center for Health Policy Research indicate that PEs can increase a physi-

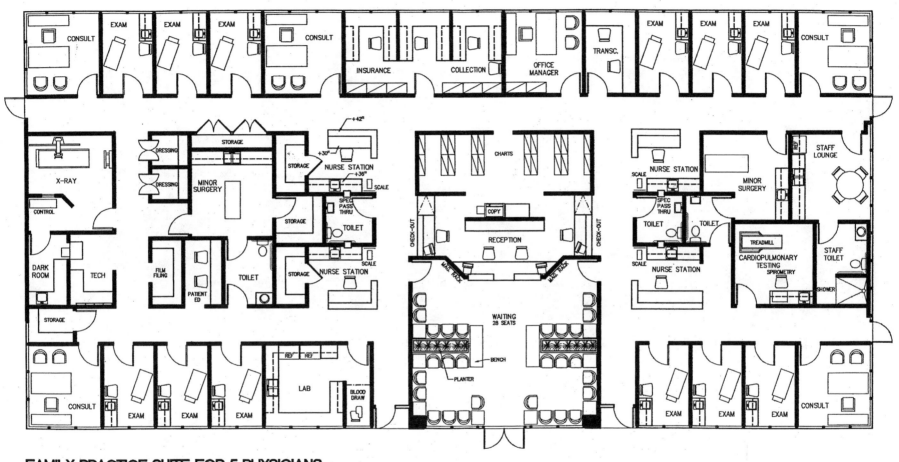

FAMILY PRACTICE SUITE FOR 5 PHYSICIANS

7270 SQUARE FEET

Figure 3-2. Space plan for family practice, 7270 square feet. (*Design: Jain Malkin Inc.*)

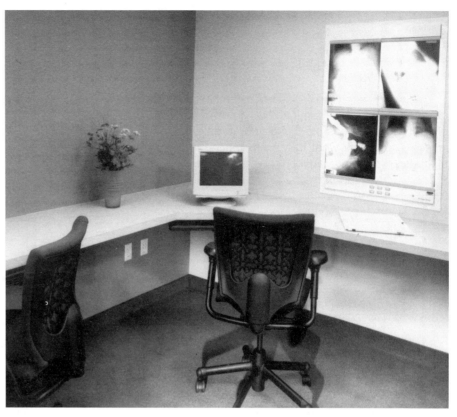

Figure 3-3. Primary care, community clinic, physician extenders' office. (*Architecture: Moon Mayoras Architects, San Diego, CA; Interior design: Jain Malkin Inc.; Photographer: Steve McClelland.*)

Figure 3-4. Primary care, community clinic, physician extenders' office (opposite side of room). (*Architecture: Moon Mayoras Architects, San Diego, CA; Interior design: Jain Malkin Inc.;*)

cian's productivity and income and that patients are generally pleased with the quality of care delivered. Under Medicare regulations, services provided by a PA in most physicians' offices are reimbursed the same as if provided by a physician.

If the medical practice includes physician extenders, they will require shared or private offices, based on the tasks they perform and their roles in the practice (Figures 3-3 and 3-4). Thus, a four-physician office with two PAs and one NP is a seven-provider office for the purpose of determining the number of exam and treatment rooms.

Office of the Future

Two forces—managed care and digital technology—are exerting pressure on physicians to rethink the *process* of how they practice medicine. These pressures are particularly painful for mid-career and older physicians who may not be as comfortable with digital technology as young physicians and for whom the severe decline in reimbursement and the loss of control in determining the course of treatment for a specific patient are barriers to the way they are accustomed to practicing medicine.

Change is indeed difficult and access to healthcare is a vital, as well as emotional, issue. What health plans and third-party payers will cover and what the physician believes is best for the patient are often at odds, creating great tension. It's not that younger physicians find this situation less frustrating, but their expectations may be lower since they were familiar with the new environment in which healthcare is practiced prior to entering medical school. They knew what they were getting into and one might even say that anyone going into medicine now must have the heart of a missionary as one can no longer expect it will lead to a life of wealth and privilege.

As healthcare becomes more of a commodity, "processing" more patients in less time is a strategy for dealing with low reimbursement and the ever-growing demand for care. However, most physicians don't want to run in and out of exam rooms, spending mere minutes with each patient, never really getting to know them or to develop a trusting relationship. This sets the stage for looking at a new way of practicing medicine that uses physician extenders for more routine examinations as well as digital technology to free up more time for the physician to spend with the patients who require complex diagnostic assessments.

The re-engineering of clinic and physicians' office environments to optimize provider utilization and enhance patient satisfaction has been the goal of a consortium of medical equipment manufacturers founded by Welch Allyn and Midmark Corporation, leaders, respectively, in the areas of diagnostic instrumentation and examination/procedure tables and modular cabinetry

Goals of the Office of the Future Project

1. Enhance provider productivity through product integration, efficient layout, equipment access, and usage.

2. Eliminate redundancy among various manufacturers' equipment, sharing technology platforms wherever possible.

3. Create an overall environment that promotes patient satisfaction with the clinical experience.

4. Take a leadership role in device compatibility related to telemedicine, medical information systems, and other communication technologies.

5. Incorporate new tools and technologies previously available and affordable only in higher-cost settings.

6. Maximize cost effectiveness of initial acquisition of ongoing operating/support expenses.

Flexibility and Interconnectivity

Modularity and flexibility are built into the Office of the Future, allowing it to be customized to each provider's requirements. Several levels of interconnectivity provide for the sharing of images, patient records, admissions and accounting information among different sites. The Version 4.5 (Figure 3-5) primary-care procedure room is the most recent edition, resulting from research and

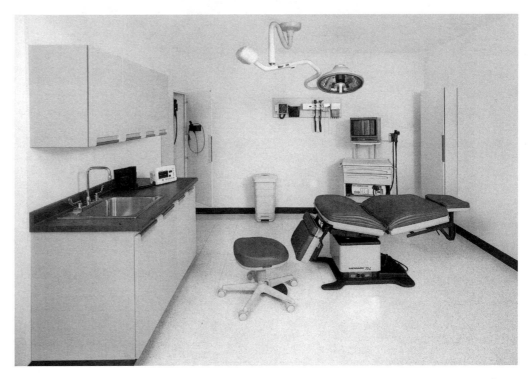

Figure 3-5. Office of the Future, Version 4.5, primary-care procedure room. (*Photo courtesy: Welch Allyn®, Skaneates Falls, NY.*)

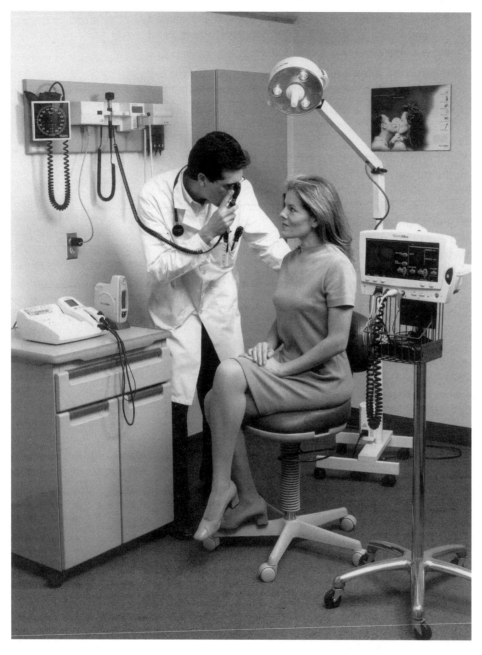

Figure 3-6. Primary-care procedure room displaying digital instrumentation that can download results to an electronic medical record. (*Photo courtesy: Welch Allyn®, Skaneates Falls, NY.*)

collaboration among manufacturers. It features automated patient identification, computerized medical records, and direct data input from medical devices, and it combines personal computer (PC) and video monitors to eliminate redundancy. Integration of multiprocedure video platforms (such as sigmoidoscopy and colposcopy) and telemedicine-ready diagnostic equipment are also featured, although a colposcope is not included in this photo.

Multipurpose Procedure Room

This procedure room has a digital vital signs monitor attached to a blood pressure cuff on the countertop. The telemedicine mobile cart (rear wall) has a video monitor that, when connected to a cable in the wall, can transmit an image to a "remote" physician. A PC/CPU (central processing unit) fits inside the cart. The vital signs monitor replaces the traditional diagnostic instrument panel on the wall at the rear of this room except that it lacks an otoscope (for examining ears) and an ophthalmoscope (for examining eyes), which (unless one uses the telemedicine cart) are available as battery-powered manual instruments. On the right in this photo is the Midmark *Dressing Nook* and, on the left, is a Midmark cabinet for storage of endoscopy scopes. Thus, this room can be used for many procedures. What is unique, and new, is the interconnectivity of these diagnostic devices and the fact that they all produce digital output that can record directly to an electronic medical record and also be transmitted, along with video images of procedures, to remote locations for consultation by a specialist. In fact, a physician at a remote location can even watch the procedure in real time and help "direct" the fiberoptic scope or comment during the procedure.

Manual Versus Digital Instrumentation

The dramatic contrast between the use of traditional manual diagnostic instruments and the digital revolution is illustrated in Figure 3-6. [The furniture and exam table in this photo have been placed, not according to principles of medical space planning, but for the sake of illustrating the point.] The Welch Allyn/Midmark diagnostic instrument panel mounted on the wall relies on the practitioner's sens-

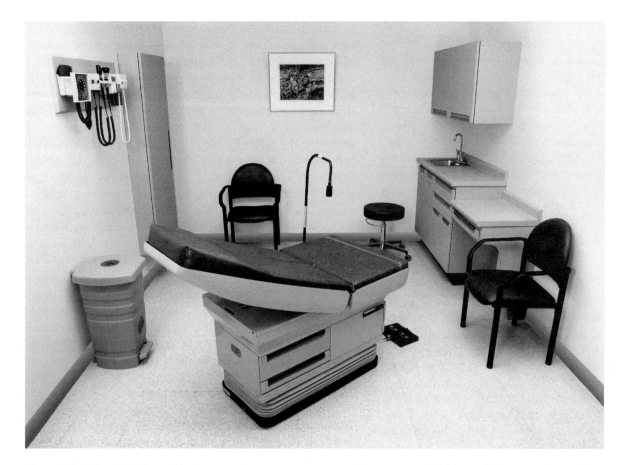

Figure 3-8. Exam room Dressing Nook. (*Photo courtesy: Midmark Corporation, Versailles, OH.*)

Figure 3-7. Office of the Future, Version 4.5, primary-care exam room. (*Photo courtesy: Welch Allyn®, Skaneates Falls, NY.*)

es—hand to eye and eye to brain—versus automated vital signs capture (the instrument on the mobile cart) that requires no clinical expertise and could be performed by an aide. If one rolls the telemedicine cart into the room, one has an otoscope and ophthalmoscope inside the drawer that are connected to the video monitor which can capture images from these devices for saving to a PC or electronically transmit them to a telemedicine physician.

On the cabinet in Figure 3-6 are the Sure Sight™ vision screener (item on right) and the AudioPath™ hearing screening device, which also does tympanometry. Both devices produce digital output that can be connected to an electronic medical record.

The Office of the Future, Version 4.5, primary-care exam room (Figure 3-7) features similar interconnectivity of diagnostic devices as does the procedure room. One of the productivity features is the Midmark Dressing Nook (Figure 3-8), which allows a provider to take a patient history or chart while talking to the patient who is undressing or dressing.

Examination Room

It is clear the "future" has arrived. One can see how the practice of medicine will be transformed by digital technology. But, psychologically, are physicians ready and willing to abrogate their responsibilities and sensory contact with patients to a machine, to artificial intelligence? Physicians who have been in practice for many years would likely pride themselves on being able to tell a great deal by looking at a patient's skin tone, or examining their tongues, or picking up some elusive quality during the process of monitoring vital signs. After all, medicine is a science *and* an art. And with interest in integrative medicine (integration of allopathic or Western medicine and complementary therapies) steadily growing, it won't be easy to forge a marriage between digital technology and energy medicine. Buck Rogers meets Andrew Weil.

Placebo Effect

In integrative medicine, rapport between the physician and patient is key to a successful outcome. According to Herbert Benson, M.D., author of *Timeless Healing: The Power and Biology of Belief,* the placebo effect (belief that causes self-healing) is greatly enhanced when the patient *believes* that the physician is capable of healing him; when the physician *believes* in the efficacy of the treatment; and when, together, there is a belief in the relationship—rapport has been established.

In the end, digital technology need not preclude developing a warm and caring relationship with patients. By automating the more routine aspects of a patient visit, the physician may have more time to spend as diagnostician and teacher.

Institute for Healthcare Improvement[*]

This nonprofit, Boston-based research and education organization, established in 1991, focuses on accelerating the pace of improvement in healthcare systems. It

---

*All IHI information was provided by permission of Donald Berwick, M.D., M.P.P., President and CEO, Institute for Healthcare Improvement.

is based on broad collaboration, rather than competition, between people and organizations that are committed to major reform. Initiatives that might be of interest to readers of this book are those relating to subsystems of office practice such as workflow and patient flow, patient satisfaction, physical office design, and the elimination of delays and waiting in all aspects of patient care delivery. The organization's mission statement for the Idealized Design of Clinical Office Practices™ project (initiated in January 1999) states that it will "design, test, and deploy new models of office-based practices...capable of fundamentally improved performance levels, better clinical outcomes, higher satisfaction, lower costs, and improved efficiency in a more rewarding work setting." Forty-two prototype sites from 23 organizations are participating in this study. Readers are encouraged to consult the IHI Web site (www.ihi.org) for more information about the innovative work undertaken by this organization. A brief outline of the philosophical principles underpinning the IHI vision for idealized office-based care follows.

Principles for Office-Based Practices

We believe that the following Principles serve as a foundation upon which clinical offices will be designed; they represent the fundamental underpinnings of office-based care. The ideal clinical office will create systems to assure that these Principles are achieved.

1. Paramount focus on the clinician-patient relationship

2. Individualized access to care and information at all times

3. Knowledge-based care is the standard

4. Individuals control their own care to the extent that each individual desires

5. Minimal waiting for all involved in the processes of care

6. Seamless transfer and communication of information and coordination of care

7. Financial performance sufficient to ensure unhindered viability

8. Patient and practice management will be based on real-time data, including measures of process, satisfaction, finance, outcomes, and epidemiology

9. Continual improvement and waste reduction in all processes and services

10. Individual health linked to broader community health

11. A model work environment

Few can disagree with IHI's premise:

> The clinical office lies at the heart of health care. For most patients most of the time, it is the portal of entry, the communications hub, the primary locus of care, and, in these days of integrated care, the coordinating center. For most doctors, too, it is home base; they speak of *the* hospital, but *my* office.

Nor can one fail to observe that, despite seismic pressures on physicians and the healthcare system in general, the clinical office practice has changed little in decades.

> The average clinical office practice of today bears remarkable similarity in form, process, design, and activity to the offices of a decade, two decades, even a half-century ago. In the typical office setting, patients still phone in for appointments, register upon arrival, wait in waiting rooms, disrobe in examination rooms, listen in consulting rooms, and wave good-bye to the receptionist in a sequence of actions that would look nearly identical if we could compare, say, 1950 to 1998. A few differences would be noticeable, of course—the desktop computer instead of the typewriter, the otoscope now fiberoptic, the furniture modular, the increased ability to provide certain treatments such as antibiotics and chemotherapeutics, and the credit card taken and checked automatically. But, the core sequence, the systems that support the work and, more importantly, the assumptions about

what work is to be done, would all be almost identical—1950 equals 1998.*

The Institute for Healthcare Improvement and projects like the Office of the Future, although they approach radical change from completely different avenues, will likely impact the future design of medical offices and clinics. The opportunity for redesign is vast.

Waiting Room

The waiting room is the patient's introduction to a physician or dentist. One forms a first impression of the practitioner by the image projected in the waiting room. This is where psychology plays a significant role. Outdated furniture with torn and faded upholstery may simply be the result of a doctor's busy schedule or his or her reluctance to focus on it as an important aspect of patient care. But, whatever the actual reason, such a neglected waiting room conveys to a patient that this is a doctor who may be as outdated in his or her medical expertise and technology as the waiting room indicates. The neglect of the waiting room generalizes to other areas, and patients may feel that this is a physician or dentist who might be neglectful in their care—one who manages to slide along with minimum standards. Designing the waiting room as a comfortable, cheerful space with appealing colors, soft lighting, and attractive furnishings is paramount (Color Plate 1, Figure 3-9). Note, in this photo, that privacy has cleverly been provided at the reception desk by setting it back from the waiting room yet openings in the wall in front of it afford visibility of waiting patients. A tabletop fountain (Color Plate 2, Figure 3-10) is a stress-relieving amenity at the entry to the suite. These items are discussed in greater detail in Chapter 12.

---

*Lecture handout by Charles Kilo, M.D., M.P.H., *Idealized Design of Clinical Office Practices*, Symposium on Healthcare Design, San Francisco, November 1998.

Table 3-1.
Table 3-1.
Analysis of Program.
Family Practice

No. of Physicians:	1		2		3	
Consultation		12×12=144	2@	12×12=288	3@	12×12=432
Exam Rooms	3@	8×12=288	6@	8×12=576	9@	8×12=864
Waiting Room		12×14=168		14×18=252		18×20=360
Business Office		12×14=168		16×18=288[a]		18×30=540[a]
Nurse Station		8×10=80	2@	8×8=128	3@	8×8=192
Toilets	2@	7×8=112	2@	7×8=112	3@	7×8=168
Storage		6×6=36		6×8=48		8×10=80
Cast Room	Use Minor Surgery		Use Minor Surgery		Use Minor Surgery	
Staff Lounge		8×10=80		10×12=120		10×12=120
Minor Surgery		12×12=144		12×12=144		12×12=144
X-ray Area[b]		—		12×25=300		12×25=300
Laboratory (if any)	Combined with nurse station		10×10=100		16×16=256[c]	
Subtotal		1220 ft²		2356 ft²		3456 ft²
20% Circulation		244	470		690	
Total		1464 ft²		2826 ft²		4146 ft²

[a]Includes insurance clerk, bookkeeper, and office manager.
[b]Includes darkroom, control, film filing, and dressing area.
[c]Includes lab, waiting, and blood draw.

Security
Depending on the demographics and location of the medical practice, the door between the waiting room and the medical office may have a lock that can be released by the receptionist. Irate patients or those who may be mentally unstable can pose a threat to staff.

Function and Comfort
In addition to the psychological aspects of the waiting room design, it must, above all, be functional. Unless the office is located in a warm climate, the waiting room should include a secure space for hanging coats and stashing boots and umbrellas (Figure 3-11). A patient must be able to enter the room and proceed directly to the receptionist's window without tripping over people or furniture. After checking in, the patient should be able to select a magazine from a conveniently located rack, and find a seat. When called, the seated patient should be able to move quickly into the examination area without disturbing other patients.

Should the patient be disabled, traffic aisles must be wide enough to accommodate a wheelchair, and there should be an open space in the room where the person in a wheelchair can comfortably remain, without clogging the traffic flow. Persons who are disabled do not like to feel they are a burden to the nonhandicapped population. They prefer to be independent, and they must be considered in the planning stages of a project so their needs and rights to access can be humanely and sympathetically handled.* Architects and space planners are familiar with the Americans with Disabilities Act (ADA), which must be adhered to in any medical or dental office, or public building, for that matter.

Size of Waiting Room
The size of the waiting room can be determined after interviewing the physician and staff (see the Appendix for a client interview form). The composition of the doctor's patient population and his or her work habits will indicate parameters the designer must follow. Common sense dictates that a physician who sees people without advance appointments will need a much larger waiting room than one who follows an appointment schedule.

Low-volume practices such as surgical specialties or psychiatry require smaller waiting rooms than do high-volume specialties such as general practice, orthopedics, pediatrics, internal medicine, and obstetrics and gynecology (OB-GYN). In addition, practices that accommodate a large number of emergencies need a larger waiting room. Accident cases will frequently be brought through the staff entrance to avoid exposing what might be a gory sight to those in the waiting room. The larger the patient volume, the larger the waiting room needs to be.

*Readers are referred to two excellent books on this subject: *Beautiful Universal Design* by Cynthia Leibrock and James Evan Terry (John Wiley, 1999) and *Design Details for Health* by Cynthia Leibrock (John Wiley, 2000).

Figure 3-11. Built-in brochure rack and closet in clinic waiting area. (*Architecture: OSM; Photo courtesy: Jain Malkin Inc.*)

A convenient formula for determining the number of seats is as follows:

$$2P \times D - E = S$$

where

P = Average number of patients per hour (per physician)
D = Number of doctors
E = Number of exam rooms
S = Seating
L = Late factor

The waiting room must accommodate at least one hour's patients. If a physician sees an average of four patients per hour, and has three examining rooms, and it is assumed that each patient is accompanied by one friend or relative, a solo practitioner would require five seats in the waiting room:

$$2(4) \times 1 - 3 = 5$$

Because this is a one-physician practice, it would be wise to assume that the doctor will run half an hour late, so the waiting room must accommodate 1.5 hours' patients. This expansion factor can be expressed as:

$$\frac{2P \times D = L}{2} \qquad \frac{2(4) \times 1 = 4}{2}$$

Thus, the waiting room should accommodate $S + L,$ or *nine persons,* plus an area for children, if space permits. The late factor can generally be reduced as the number of physicians is increased. Using the above formulas for a two-physician family practice, including a late factor, 18 seats would be required:

$$2(4) \times 2 - 6 \quad = 10$$
$$\frac{2(4) \times 2}{2} \qquad = \frac{8}{18}$$

A quick rule of thumb is 2.5 seats per exam room which, in this case, also yields 18 seats.

It is important to understand that these formulas are only a guide. The specifics of each practice and space limitations of the suite will often dictate waiting room capacity. The formula, and good common sense, may tell you that ideally 45 seats should be provided, but the physical limitations of the space and the physicians' intent to squeeze in as many exam rooms as possible may limit seating capacity to 25.

In medical space planning, as in life, rarely does the ideal prevail. The designer has to skillfully juggle the client's requests, the client's budget, building codes, structural limitations of the given space, and the principles of medical space planning. Tradeoffs and compromises are the reality from which suites are built.

Once the number of waiting room seats has been estimated, the size of the room can be determined, allowing 18 to 20 square feet per person. The author has found 18 square feet per person a workable guide for the average medical office. Nevertheless, the amount of space required for a comfortable waiting room will vary according to the room's configuration and the location of the entry foyer and the reception window.

Accommodating Children

An area may be provided for children. A table and chairs or a toy box is welcomed by parents. Special furniture can be fabricated (see Pediatrics), which will keep children occupied, quiet, and out of danger of being stepped on. Interactive toys (Figures 3-12, 12-16, 12-17, and 12-18) available from People Friendly Places, Inc. (Northbrook, Illinois), keep young children engaged. Keep in mind that a children's corner must be located away from door swings or other hazards on which children might injure themselves. The children's area must be in sight of the receptionist, who is charged with keeping order.

Amenities

A large aquarium (Figures 3-13, 3-93, and 4-50) is a nice addition to a waiting room. It is restful and enjoyed by adults and children alike. Other amenities include a desk or countertop with a computer and Internet access.

As medical offices become more digital, it will be necessary to provide carrels in the waiting room where patients can update their electronic medical records. Although not yet widespread, it is currently possible for a patient medical record to be encoded on a "smart card" that can be downloaded at a provider's office. As providers address HIPAA, they will be making substantial investments in information technology that may require accommodation in the way patients are registered, processed, and followed during their care. Futurists predict that the home will increasingly become the site for healthcare: Patients will self-monitor their vital signs, which will simultaneously be transmitted to a provider's office, and telemedicine-type consults will enable the physician and patient to see each other and speak in real time (see the two figures in the Introduction). A prescription can be sent via the Internet directly to a pharmacy; however, appropriate security measures mandated by HIPAA will have to be in place.

A considerable amount of educational literature is dispensed in some offices. Wall-mounted brochure racks prevent a cluttered appearance (Figures 3-11, 12-3).

Patient Privacy

Some physicians prefer maximum communication between front office staff and patients and favor a waiting room separated from the business office by only a low partition. Although this may comfort the patient psychologically by removing what may be perceived as a barrier, it often results in a loss of privacy for staff, who frequently have to discuss delicate matters with a patient. The patient might suffer embarrassment, knowing that the adjacent waiting patients may overhear the conversation.

For this reason, many offices use a 4- to 6-foot-wide window with a plastic laminate shelf, starting at 42 inches off the floor (Figure 3-14). It should be noted that the ADA (Americans with Disabilities Act) requires accommoda-

Figure 3-12. Interactive play toy engages toddlers. (*Photo courtesy: People Friendly Places, Inc., Northbrook, IL*)

Figure 3-13. Aquarium adds interest to waiting room. (*Design: Jain Malkin Inc.; Photographer: John Christian.*)

tion for wheelchair users at 34-inch countertop height; however, a section of 30-inch-high counter is even friendlier (Color Plate 3, Figure 3-15). This means either the entire reception transaction counter be no higher than 34 inches or a portion of it be at that height. A sliding glass window may be added for additional staff privacy, but it does convey a negative image of closing out the patients. If glass is used, it should always be clear, not obscure, so that patients have visual contact with staff.

There is a tradeoff here in that lowering the countertop to 30 or 34 inches exposes all the clutter (and there is usually a lot) on the desktop as well as the unsightly backs of computers. If a section of the reception counter has a 42-inch-high transaction shelf, it makes it easy for patients to sign in or to write a check without bending. On the staff side, it provides space for storage of frequently used

Figure 3-14. Reception window, internal medicine suite. (*Design: Jain Malkin Inc.; Photographer: Jain Malkin.*)

forms in a slotted rack (Figure 3-16) and also conceals staplers, tape dispenser, telephone, and other items as well as keeps confidential paperwork away from prying eyes.

A decorative vertical panel or frosted glass (Figures 3-17 and 3-18) can be added to a 30-inch-high work surface to conceal the back of the monitor. As flat-panel monitors become more commonplace, accommodating the bulky cathode ray tube (CRT) will cease to be an issue (Figure 7-8).

To deal effectively with issues of patient privacy when designing the waiting room, do not place chairs too close to the reception window; position the receptionist's tele-

Figure 3-16. Built-in cubby-hole slots for office forms at reception desk eliminate the clutter of tiered letter trays. (*Interior design: Jain Malkin Inc.; Photographer: Steve McClelland.*)

Figure 3-17. Street-level registration desk, primary-care community clinic. (*Architecture: Moon Mayoras Architects, San Diego, CA; Interior design: Jain Malkin Inc.; Photographer: Steve McClelland.*)

Figure 3-18. Patient check-out features privacy screens between patients, frosted glass panels to conceal backs of computers, and exquisite lighting treatment (see Figure 4-17 for space plan). Memorial Breast Care Center at Anaheim Memorial Hospital, Anaheim, CA. (*Architecture and interior design: Taylor & Associates Architects, Newport Beach, CA; Photographer: Farshid Assasi.*)

phone to the side of the window opening to help mask conversations; and provide an area, in the front office, where staff and patients may discuss a sensitive topic without it being overheard (Figure 3-18, Color Plate 3, Figure 3-19, and Figure 3-22).

Toilet Rooms

There is disagreement as to the practicality of providing a toilet room in the waiting area. It saves staff the trouble of frequently directing patients to the bathroom of the examination area, but it has the disadvantage of patients emptying their bladders before the nurse can request a urine specimen. In pediatric offices, however, a toilet in the reception area is desirable to enable mothers to change a baby's diaper (see Figures 3-84 and 3-85). Ceramic tile floors and wainscot are the most practical long-term finishes for bathrooms. For little additional cost, an interesting tile pattern can be created as in Figure 3-20. Note that dark grout is optimal on the floor to conceal stains. Dark tile provides excellent contrast with white sink and toilet for low-vision individuals. The wall-hung sink in this photo meets the ADA requirements and conceals the unsightly P-trap drain.

Reception

Since the receptionist often books appointments and maintains the day's schedule, she must see the patient on arrival and just before leaving. She must also have a good view of the waiting room from her chair so that she can see who is waiting (Color Plate 3, Figure 3-19). Few practitioners use manual appointment books now as computers are preferable. Despite working on a computer, adequate "clear" countertop work space is required, in addition to a place for the phone and to write messages; a place for a printer, fax machine, and countertop copier (for copying insurance eligibility cards) nearby; and, if possible, an L-shaped return facing the corridor appointment "good-bye" window so that, while remaining

seated, she can swivel around, greet an exiting patient, book an appointment, or accept payment for services (Figure 3-21).

In an office with two or three front office staff, the appointments/cashier workstation and reception window may be separated (Color Plate 3, Figure 3-19) to provide greater privacy for the exiting patient.

Figure 3-20. Clinic bathroom is both functional and attractive. Montefiore Medical Center in the Bronx. (*Architecture and interior design: Guenther Petrarca, New York, NY; Photographer: ©Christopher Lovi.*)

GENERAL PRACTICE

1664 SF

Figure 3-21. Space plan for general (family) practice, 1664 square feet. (Design: Jain Malkin Inc.)

Front office personnel may occasionally help in the back office, assisting the doctor in the examining room at times, weighing patients, or recording histories, but usually their duties will be confined to the business office.

It is desirable to design the business office in such a way that staff can easily cover one another's station. An efficient layout can sometimes mean that one fewer person is required, considerably reducing the overhead.

Patient Education

Patient education is an important part of healthcare that many physicians try to accommodate in their suite design. It is generally located at the front of the suite, and may even be an alcove off the waiting room. For reasons of privacy, however, it is advisable to create a room, perhaps 8×10 feet, and build carrels or partitions between patients. A 30-inch-high countertop would have a small television monitor, and a videocassette recorder (VCR) would be housed in an open compartment underneath (Figure 4-135). Shallow cabinets provide storage space for videotapes. Tapes cover all sorts of topics: presurgical instructions, information about various diseases or injuries, ways to lower health risks, and they may even allow a patient to view his or her own surgery. The use of videotapes allows the doctor to communicate a great deal of information, in a professional manner, without having to explain each concept or procedure personally.

Business Office

Frequently referred to as the *front office* in medical jargon (versus the *back office* or examination area), this is the heart of the medical office. Appointments are scheduled here; patients are billed; medical records are stored here; patients are greeted from this room; and routine insurance and bookkeeping duties are performed here.

In a small practice, two people may perform all these tasks. In a large practice, several persons may occupy the business office. A convenient rule of thumb is one secretary for each two doctors in a low-volume practice and one secretary per physician in a high-volume practice. If a physician is seeing four to six patients per hour, the secretary may be spending more time with patients than the doctor does, since the secretary's work would involve arranging and rescheduling patient appointments on the telephone whenever the doctor is delayed or has to rearrange his or her daily schedule, filing medical charts, sending reports to referring physicians, billing patients, collecting money, filing insurance claims, answering the phone, and ordering supplies. In larger practices, there is more division of labor—one individual does billing and collections, another accounts payable, another insurance, a medical records clerk, a transcriptionist, and so forth, as well as an office manager or administrator.

A convenience in the business office is a gate door with a plastic laminate shelf or a 30-inch-high section of countertop that has a piano hinge to enable staff to lift it to exit the room. Either of these options permits communication with patients as they are exiting the office and suffices for brief greetings or a routine discussion about a bill without the patient having to enter the bookkeeper's or the business office.

Depending on the width of the corridor (the standard corridor width is 48 inches clear; however, in high-volume suites, 60-inch width is preferable), the gate door might be located in a recess or alcove so that a patient who stops to chat will not be blocking corridor traffic (Figure 4-56). However, for longer conversations and more privacy, the patient would enter through that door and proceed to the bookkeeper's office. A guest chair should be provided in the bookkeeper's office for this purpose.

Workroom and Storage Needs
Unless one has worked in a medical business office, or at least spent several days observing the flow of paper and communication, it is difficult to plan adequately sized work spaces, storage areas, and accommodation of equipment. Furthermore, upper cabinets are often too high for the average 5-foot-4-inch woman to reach; the cabinets—if 12-inch overall depth—may be too shallow to house reams of paper, boxes of envelopes, and computer forms, and they are often poorly utilized. It is not uncommon for front office staff to say they have no storage space only to find the upper cabinets only 25 percent full. A series of full-height cabinets at least 15 inches deep with adjustable shelves is far more practical. Alternatively, one could provide a workroom as in Figure 4-160 off of the business office, and out of public view, with simple open shelves, a countertop for postage meter, printers, fax machine, and space for a floor model copier, if needed. It is always desirable to place copiers in a room that is well ventilated and has no occupants. Copiers, especially large floor models, are a health hazard in terms of air quality. Sometimes the rear wall of the appointments/check-out counter accommodates the workroom function (Figure 3-22). Note the vertical slots on the left-hand side for patient charts.

Another option is to create a workroom (Figures 3-23 and 4-19) at the entry to the business office as this pro-

Figure 3-22. Friendly sit-down height check-out/appointment desk at Montefiore Medical Center in the Bronx (family practice clinic). The rear wall provides space for fax machine, copier, and supplies. (*Architecture and interior design: Guenther Petrarca, New York, NY; Photographer: Lynn Massimo.*)

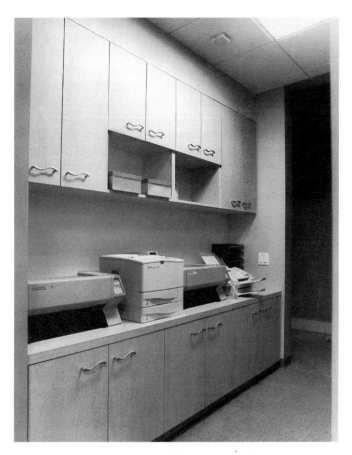

Figure 3-23. Business office workroom accommodates several printers with paper feed slots in cabinet below, fax machine, and floor model copier (out of view) on opposite wall. Business office staff access it from one end and clinic staff from the other. Scripps Breast Care Center, La Jolla, CA. (*Interior architecture and design: Jain Malkin Inc.; Photographer: Glenn Cormier.*)

vides easy access to others in the clinic for faxing, copying, and printing without having to disturb those working in the front office. Do not underestimate the number of machines and equipment that may have to be accommodated, including a large shredder and/or storage container for confidential material (anything with patients' names, test results, reports) that will be picked up by a contract vendor for shredding. HIPAA regulations regarding confidential handling of patient data will increase the need for paper shredding.

Clearly, the issue is not just having enough storage, but having it where it's needed, so that one does not have to keep getting up to get forms that are frequently used; one does not tear one's stockings due to inadequate knee space; the countertop is neither too shallow nor too deep; adequate clear desk space is available despite a computer, telephone, typewriter, calculator, pencil sharpener, stapler, reference books, and possibly a credit card machine. Cubbies for forms are quite useful (Figure 3-16) in keeping the desk clear of clutter.

Casework and Countertops
It has been standard in the design of medical offices to build in all workstations in the business office, insurance, transcription, and similar areas. Lining the perimeter of the room with 24- to 30-inch-deep plastic-laminate-clad countertops takes full advantage of every inch of space in a way that freestanding desks or workstations rarely do, especially in small rooms or irregularly shaped spaces.

Having said that, it is easy to mindlessly draw countertops, turning the 90 degree corner, and continuing, placing a task chair every 5 feet, giving the client false confidence that an efficient work space has been carefully developed for each of these persons, without truly taking into consideration the tasks each performs and the way in which they interface with patients and coworkers. Staff move into the space and are shocked to learn that their equipment barely—or possibly doesn't—fit. The paper feed on their large printer requires a 15-inch grommeted slot in the countertop, there is no space for the hospital printer, and the space between the countertop and the 42-inch-high transaction shelf where two manuals are kept for ready access is half an inch too short. A 5-foot-long countertop space at 24-inch depth does not place the computer screen at an ergonomic viewing distance, the keyboard does not fit on the countertop, and, without a keyboard tray, there is not enough clear work space to handle papers or write notes.

Ergonomic Considerations

Work surfaces designed for computer monitors should allow the screen to be positioned at least 18 inches from the front of the keyboard tray. Getting it elevated to a comfortable viewing height can be a problem. The modular work station in Figure 3-24 takes advantage of the corner depth. Despite ergonomic research on optimal distances and conditions, considerable individual variation and preferences exist. WorkRite Ergonomic Accessories, Inc., Novato, California, offers numerous products that enable workers to meet individual needs. One of the most useful products is a metal insert that spans a standard right-angled countertop, creating a diagonal "bridge" and thereby adding considerable space in front of the CRT. Another useful item is the multiple-adjustment arm that lifts the CRT off the desk, getting it to whatever height the worker desires and also freeing up desk space. The patented PowerLift™ feature quickly shifts the CRT from sit-down to stand-up height. The vendor's Web site (www.backbenimble.com) helps buyers select appropriate ergonomic accessories by "walking" them through all the tasks they perform until the total order is configured.

Improving Ergonomics

A solution to concealing the back of the monitor, at the same time resulting in more usable desktop area, is provided by NOVA® Office Furniture, Inc. This unit allows the user's head to be oriented slightly downward instead of tilted back, which is more common and often results in neck strain (Figure 3-25). It is sold as a component that can be built into freestanding desks or custom millwork. NOVA has done considerable research to design a product that reduces eyestrain and musculoskeletal complaints (Figures 3-26 and 3-27), but it requires meticulous location of overhead lighting to avoid glare on the glass. It seems to work best in reception/admitting functions where the desktop CRT can become a barrier between staff and patient. The downside is that when a new employee occupies the workstation, if this "option" is not embraced, retrofitting the desk can be costly. NOVA works well in large nurse stations where numerous monitors can take up desktop space and nurses are merely accessing information, rather than doing word processing. Another solution for lowering the height of monitors is shown in Figure 10-90.

Figure 3-24. Modular workstation puts computer screen at proper viewing distance and provides lowered shelf for keyboard. (*Photo courtesy: Steelcase Inc., Grand Rapids, MI.*)

Figure 3-25. Desk features recessed computer with dark glass, antiglare cover. (*Photo courtesy: Nova Solutions, Inc., Effingham, IL. Covered by various U.S. patents.*)

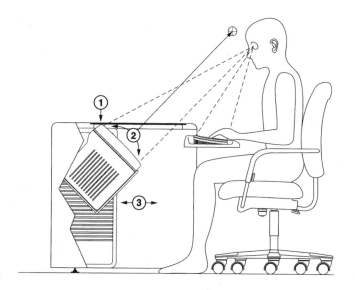

CREATING THE CORRECT DOWNWARD GAZE ANGLE™ WORKSTATION

*Remove Monitor Base.

1. Screen should point slightly above the user's face (bottom edge of monitor is nearer to the eye than top edge).

2. Install monitor as high as possible without raising glass.

3. Preferred position: top edge of monitor is at back edge of glass.

Figure 3-26. Illustration of the NOVA workstation. (*Photo courtesy: Nova Solutions, Inc., Effingham, IL. Covered by various U.S. patents.*)

It is necessary to spend considerable time interviewing the office manager and key staff to understand how they work and perhaps offer advice on a more efficient layout than they have considered. Realize that they may be reluctant to admit that they cannot understand the space plan or be able to visualize the adjacencies inherent in the plan, nor may they be able to interpret the casework elevations and locations of electrical outlets, phones, or computer connections. Thus, it is necessary to demonstrate with a tape measure, foam core, or other tools critical distances, heights, and spaces.

Computer Systems

Today, all medical and dental offices are computerized. Some offices use computers only for word processing and for billing. Others use computers to link their offices

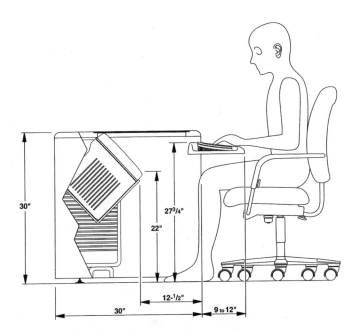

Figure 3-27. Illustration of the NOVA® workstation with critical dimensions. (*Photo courtesy: Nova Solutions, Inc., Effingham, IL. Covered by various U.S. patents.*)

proper ergonomic viewing distance, they must not be so deep that it creates back strain if the employee needs to reach over it to transact business with patients. Keyboard trays and ergonomic task chairs with multiple adjustments reduce workers' compensation claims and absenteeism and increase productivity.

The number of peripheral items connected to the computer can consume considerable space. If the office has a dedicated computer that is networked with the hospital, this will generally be located in the front office. Other computers will be proprietary to the medical practice and generally networked to each other. Printers must be carefully placed close to those who use them most to prevent employees from having to continually walk over to the printer to retrieve something.

It is important to be aware of the effects of glare from overhead lighting and from windows when laying out workstations using CRTs. Glare causes reflections on the screen that lead to eyestrain and stress.

Bookkeeping

Some practices use an outside bookkeeping service. The daily charges for service and payments received are recorded and forwarded to the bookkeeping service, which, in turn, handles billing and collections. Monthly reports are sent to the physician. In this case, space for billing and collections can be minimized as in Figures 3-35 and 4-159. Occasionally, a large practice will have its own billing office off site in less expensive accommodations.

In many offices, the bookkeeper is in a separate room adjacent to, but not part of, the business/reception area. The insurance secretary may also have a separate office to provide working conditions with fewer interruptions. The business office of a busy practice is an extremely hectic place. Phones ring continually; people are rushing around. It is not a good place for people who need concentration. If space permits, it is always better to protect the bookkeeper and insurance secretary by giving them private offices. Sometimes modular workstations are used to provide privacy when private offices are not feasible. These

with the hospital and with support services such as a laboratory or radiology group. This enables a doctor to preadmit a patient to the hospital, book radiology procedures, or schedule surgery, and receive an immediate reply.

Practitioners with a totally computerized office will have sophisticated software that handles appointment scheduling, patient accounting, patient histories, patient and insurance billing, revenue projections, collection letters, referring physician reports, patient medication data reports, statements, and insurance claims tracking. With an integrated software system, patient data can be tabulated to produce a variety of reports that allow the practitioner to analyze the practice. These may include cross-referencing of diagnoses and procedures and demographic analysis of marketing efforts.

Although countertops that accommodate computers need to be deep enough to keep a large monitor at the often have paper management accessories and hinged flipper-door storage to make use of vertical surfaces.

Insurance

Most medical treatment is paid by third-party payers—insurance companies. Under managed care, many individuals are enrolled in HMOs whereby a monthly prepaid fee entitles one to receive healthcare, often with a co-pay at each visit. Much has been written about the complexity and mountains of paperwork associated with billing (and collecting from) insurance companies, which is complicated by the lack of uniformity among them in terms of billing forms and procedures. This amounts to a great deal of paperwork, and a medical office of any size usually has at least one full-time employee doing nothing but insurance forms. He or she requires a desk with an L- or U-shaped return, a computer, one or two printers, and access to medical records and to the copy machine. Numerous file cabinets are needed, as well as open-shelf storage, for the multitude of business forms and manuals. A guest chair should be provided for a patient. As government control increases, more and more procedures are covered by third-party payers, and the personnel required to process these forms has steadily increased. It should be noted that it is now possible to process claims electronically (paperless) with many of the large insurance companies, which speeds the process.

Medical Transcription

Medium-volume to large-volume practices often have a part-time or full-time medical transcriptionist who works from dictation tapes and transcribes the physicians' notes. This task is best accommodated in a separate room since an environment with little distraction is optimal. Only a countertop work surface is required. It should be 30 inches high with a fully adjustable keyboard tray. A small room is adequate, provided it has a window and natural light.

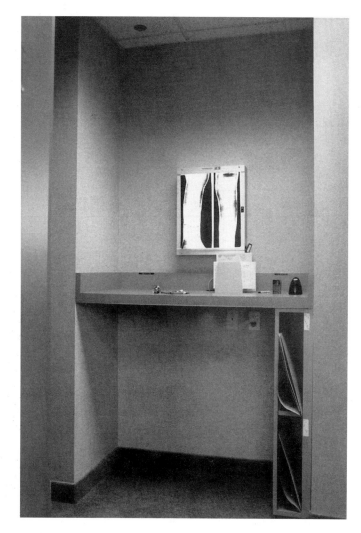

Figure 3-28. Dictation niche. (*Design: Jain Malkin Inc.; Photographer: John Christian.*)

Some physicians send their tapes out of the office for transcription; others may have a dictation line to a word processing unit on the telephone. The notes would be recorded and the typed manuscript would be delivered to the physician's office. Voice recognition software is another option that appeals to some physicians.

Figure 3-29a. Exam room physician/patient interface using computer with patient management and clinical best practices databases integrated with an electronic medical record. (*Photo courtesy: Physician Micro Systems, Inc., Seattle, WA.*)

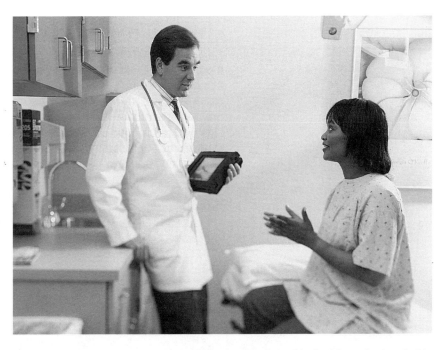

Figure 3-29b. Examination room physician/patient interface with physician using handheld computer with patient management and clinical best practices databases, activated by a light pen. (*Photo courtesy: Cerner Corporation, Kansas City, MO.*)

Dictation

Occasionally, a physician will request a dictation niche (Figures 3-28 and 4-3) in the corridor central to the exam rooms to be used after examining each patient, rather than saving it for the end of the day. This is also a good place to locate a wall-mounted telephone so that the doctor can take a quick call without returning to the consultation room. An X-ray view box and an open storage compartment for X-ray films would be essential features for many, but not for all, physicians (Figure 3-28). Some physicians prefer to dictate in the exam room while the patient is still present, and it seems likely this will be the preferred site with electronic medical records and the previously described interconnectivity of diagnostic instrumentation and total patient management systems (Figures 3-29a and 3-29b).

Office Manager

Large offices frequently have an office manager or a business manager who hires personnel, orders supplies and drugs, and assists the physicians in secretarial or business matters in the capacity of executive assistant. The office manager should have a private office. It need not be large—10×12 feet is adequate—and it should be located so that it faces the business office. In fact, the walls facing the business office may have glass, starting 48 inches off the floor, so that the manager can oversee the staff at all times (Figure 3-52).

Medical Records

An important function of the business office is the storage of medical records. In order to protect the physician from legal complications, as well as to provide continuity of care for patients, accurate records must be maintained where they are easy to retrieve. Primary physicians keep more extensive and more detailed records than urologists or radiologists, for example, who see patients on a referral basis.

The preferred method of record storage is the lateral file cabinet (Figure 3-30). This may be a cabinet without doors (Figure 3-31), or with retractable doors that store in the top of each shelf opening. The shelves may be stationary, or they may pull out for easier access. When filing is done laterally, the file folder tab must be on the side so that it sticks out of the file cabinet.

Color-coded file jackets are the most efficient system for medical offices (Figure 3-32). The standard file jacket

Figure 3-30. Lateral file cabinet. (*Photo courtesy: Tab Products, Vernon Hills, IL.*)

Figure 3-31. Open-shelf filing cabinet. (*Photo courtesy: Tab Products, Vernon Hills, IL.*)

accepts 8×11-inch papers, but radiology files require jumbo file jackets, which are 14×17 inches. The patient's name may be encoded alphabetically, by color, and/or number. Thus, a misfiled folder immediately becomes obvious, as the colors do not conform to the surrounding jackets.

Additionally, one can encode by color special features such as the sex of the patient, certain unusual medical disorders, or the date the patient initially sought consultation. This facilitates pruning files for inactive charts or selecting case studies of patients with various medical disorders for follow-up. Various companies manufacture these specialized file jackets with the color-coding system. Ames Color File (Sommerville, Massachusetts) publishes a particularly good brochure explaining the details and refinements available with this system of medical record storage.

Group practices frequently utilize a large room for medical records with a mechanical retrieval system. This eliminates the need for aisles in front of all shelves, since the files move to the operator, and the access aisle is in front of the operator. This equipment can be purchased with manual controls or it may be motorized (Figure 3-33).

It is not necessary to buy factory-fabricated file cabinets. They may be custom built on the job, particularly if the space allotted to medical chart storage does not accommodate standard file cabinet widths. These job-built file storage units would consist of open shelves with a clear height of 12 inches. However, steel file cabinets have the advantage of being able to be moved to another office, they provide greater fire resistance, and they can be locked for security.

Prefabricated file units without retractable doors are less expensive and offer open-shelf easy access to charts (Figure 3-31). Small- to medium-sized offices may use space-saving files that are two cabinets deep with the front one sliding on a track (Figure 3-34).

It is important for the designer to project the physician's future needs for medical chart storage in the new office. The designer must ascertain, from the client interview, the number of new patients added to the practice each week or month. That number would be projected for three

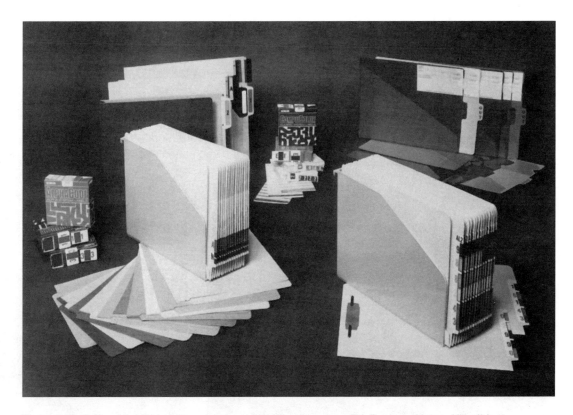

Figure 3-32. Color-coded file jackets and accessories. (*Photo courtesy: Tab Products, Vernon Hills, IL.*)

to five years (the length of most medical leases) and added to the existing number of medical charts. The thickness of charts must also be factored into the equation. Physicians who see many patients with chronic conditions may have many charts 2 inches thick, whereas a surgeon's charts may be estimated at four per inch. Charts should be pruned each year to eliminate patients who have not been seen in three years. These "aged" charts can be placed in storage at a local warehouse that offers a quick retrieval system for physicians.

Medical records should be located so that they are convenient to the receptionists, nurses, and bookkeeper. Charts are usually pulled in the morning for patients to be seen that day. The only other time staff would need access to charts would be primarily for phone calls or pre-

Figure 3-33. Medical records room utilizing high density motorized filing system. (*Interior design: Jain Malkin Inc.; Photographer: Steve McClelland.*)

Figure 3-34. Sliding file system. SIDE-TRAC®. (*Photo courtesy: Tab Products, Vernon Hills, IL.*)

scription refills. Medical records would normally be located in the business office, but could be placed elsewhere in the suite. The bookkeeper needs convenient access to medical records for billing patients and filing insurance claims. Occasionally, for patients who are involved in litigation, attorneys and legal assistants will come to the office to copy charts.

Electronic Medical Records

Although contemplated as "the future" a number of years ago, the electronic medical record (EMR) has been slow to win the hearts and minds of physicians. According to Rosemarie Nelson, Welch Allyn's Office of the Future Director, as of this writing (the year 2001), fewer than 3 to

5 percent of physicians have electronic medical records. It may be 10 years down the road before physicians' offices are totally electronic with completely integrated systems of medical records, billing, scheduling, as well as digital diagnostic instruments, analyzers, weight scales, and tools for recording vital signs that are networked and record data in real time on the patient's electronic medical record. In theory, the physician would type input on a handheld or laptop computer (Figures 3-29a and 3-29b), which transmits it directly to the patient's chart. When the patient exits the room, all data will have been recorded on the chart. By use of a "smart card" (a small card that can be carried in the wallet with a computer chip that has the patient's medical record), the patient would not have to continually repeat his or her medical history each time a provider is consulted or a visit to the emergency room is made.

A company called MediVation (medivation.com) develops, for medical practices, a home page, and then creates private pages, with full security, for each patient. The patient can receive personal messages that are password protected.

Technology currently exists that will enable the patient to download a medical-social family history form, fill it out, but not have to submit it over the Internet. When it is downloaded from the physician's office, it prints with a bar code. When the patient brings it into the physician's office, it is scanned with a bar code scanner that downloads the information to the patient's medical record.

Private Entrance

A medical office, regardless of size, must have two entrances—one for patients and a private one for the doctor, so that he or she can enter the office without meeting patients in the waiting room (Figure 3-35). In large suites, usually over 3000 square feet, local building codes may require two exits (separated by a distance equal to one-half the length of the maximum overall diagonal dimension of the area served, measured in a straight line between exits). Occasionally, to save space, the staff entrance is through a room such as the staff lounge, the business office, or a special procedures room, although the latter option is less desirable (Figures 4-52, 4-107, and 4-133).

Examination Room

Good traffic flow is imperative for the efficiency of a medical office. Several factors influence the location of the exam rooms:

1. Nurses are responsible for controlling traffic to and from the exam rooms, so the nurse station and exam rooms should be clustered together. This enables nurses to prepare the patients in each room quickly, while traveling back and forth to the nurse station to clean instruments or obtain items needed for the examination (Figures 3-2 and 3-35).

2. Exam rooms must be close to the consultation room to save the physician unnecessary steps, but it is preferable that patients not pass the consultation room when making their way to the exam room, although this is sometimes unavoidable.

3. The exam room corridor(s) should be arranged so that patients must pass the business office when exiting the suite (Figures 3-53 and 3-104). This provides control so that future appointments may be booked, medications explained, and payment for services discussed. A convenient feature is a full-height, 12-inch-deep recessed storage cabinet for drug samples located in the corridor near the check-out area to enable the provider to dispense a product as the patient exits (Figures 4-113 and 4-120).

The exam room is the background for diagnosis. As such, it should be designed very functionally, with an understanding of the equipment that needs to be provided and the psychological needs of the patient (refer to

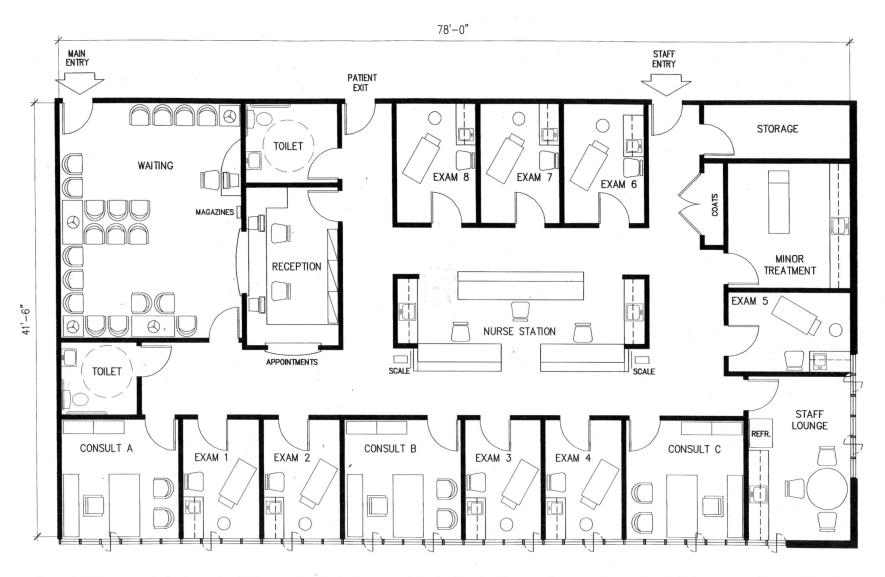

Figure 3-35. Space plan for family practice, 3300 square feet. Centralized nurse station enables physicians to write orders at transaction shelf. The business office and billing functions are off site. (*Design: Jain Malkin Inc.*)

Chapter 1). If the amenities of the room can help the patient relax (wallcovering, flooring, color, and artwork), it makes the examination easier.

It is desirable that patients' vital signs (blood pressure, pulse, etc.) be at normal levels prior to an examination. Anxiety, resulting from fear of a clinical and unfamiliar environment, elevates patients' vital signs and may give false readings. This is often referred to as "white coat syndrome." Numerous journal articles have noted how often this condition leads to elevated blood pressure and results in healthy individuals being treated for hypertension.

Physician/Patient Interface

A number of journal articles have been written about the physician/patient interface with respect to increasing patient satisfaction and patient compliance (adherence to treatment and drug regimens). In general, these studies have demonstrated that specific interview techniques can be employed by the practitioner to achieve these goals, but there is another aspect related to the rapport established between doctor and patient. Even a brief encounter of several minutes face to face with the physician can enhance patient satisfaction if the patient feels he or she has the full attention of the physician and if rapport has been established. This leads one to wonder if the exam room layout and furnishings could be reconsidered from this perspective, placing the patient and physician eye to eye to achieve greatest rapport (Figures 3-36 and 3-37). An excellent annotated bibliography on doctor-patient communication is available from the American Academy on Physician and Patient in New York City.

A future challenge will be to integrate a computer screen or laptop computer into the exam room, enabling both the physician and the patient to look at it together. It will be possible with a Microsoft Windows® platform to view, on one screen, an X-ray, a lab report, charting notes from a previous visit, and even a video image of an endoscopy procedure. Assuming flat-panel monitors will eventually become the norm, integrating them into a

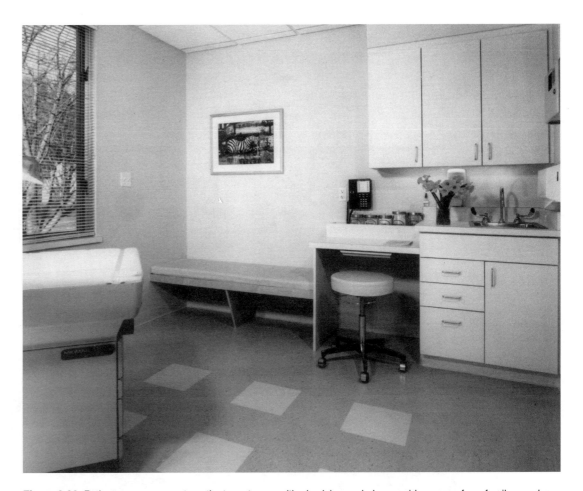

Figure 3-36. Patient exam room puts patient eye to eye with physician and also provides space for a family member or siblings. Family Practice Clinic at Frisbie Memorial Hospital, Rochester, NH. (*Architecture and interior design: TRO/The Ritchie Organization, Newton, MA; Photographer: Edward Jacoby.*)

"compact" setting will be less difficult than working with bulky CRTs.

Layout
Looking at the room in Figure 3-38, the physician, upon entering the room, can easily walk to the sink to wash his or her hands, pivot around to face the patient on the exam table, reach for instruments on the countertop with the left hand, and examine the patient with the right. This room

Figure 3-37. Combined examination and consultation room, known as a "Mayo room," enhances patient/physician rapport by eliminating the traditional desk as a barrier. Built-in X-ray view box facilitates discussion of films. A newer version of this room would accommodate access to digital diagnostic images and electronic medical records. Mayo Clinic, Scottsdale, AZ. (*Architecture and interior design: Hammel Green and Abrahamson, Inc., Minneapolis, MN; Photographer: Mark Boisclair.*)

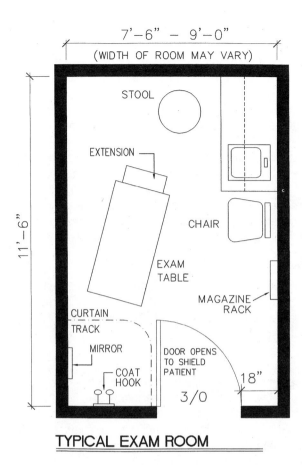

TYPICAL EXAM ROOM

7'-6" – 9'-0"
(WIDTH OF ROOM MAY VARY)

11'-6"

STOOL

EXTENSION

CHAIR

EXAM TABLE

MAGAZINE RACK

CURTAIN TRACK

MIRROR

COAT HOOK

DOOR OPENS TO SHIELD PATIENT

18"

3/0

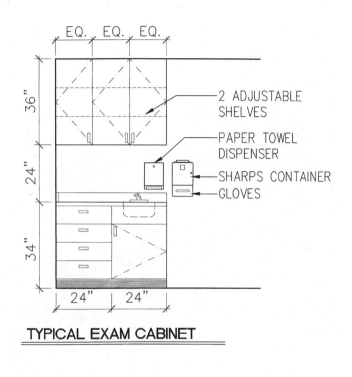

TYPICAL EXAM CABINET

EQ. EQ. EQ.

36"

24"

34"

2 ADJUSTABLE SHELVES

PAPER TOWEL DISPENSER

SHARPS CONTAINER

GLOVES

24"   24"

Figure 3-38. Standard examination room layout. (*Design: Jain Malkin Inc.*)

layout puts the physician on the patient's right side, which is standard, even for most left-handed practitioners. Physicians are trained to examine from the right side as this makes it easier to palpate certain organs. It should be noted that an attempt to place plumbing back to back (mirror image) will result in left- and right-handed exam rooms. This is foolish economy. Every exam room should be identical in layout to be efficient so that the practitioner has the same degree of comfort and orientation in each room. One could almost draw a vertical line through this room dividing it into two zones—the right side for the physician or provider and the left for the patient. In a "right-handed room," the entry door will be on the right side and the exam table on the left, as one would face the room upon entering.

Despite this rationale, one may find practitioners with other preferences such as in Figure 3-39 where the sink cabinet faces the wall with the door (this layout wouldn't work were there windows on this wall), although the physician still addresses the patient from the right side. The patient is exposed as the foot or stirrup end of the exam table faces the door, but a cubicle drape can be

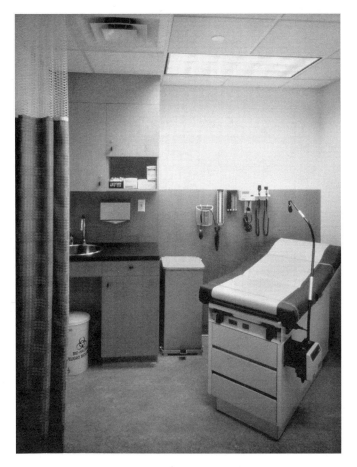

Figure 3-39. Examination room. Montefiore Medical Center in the Bronx. (*Architecture and interior design: Guenther Petrarca, New York, NY; Photographer: ©Christopher Lovi.*)

pulled across the width of the room. The wooden wall panel behind the wall-mounted examination instruments is an attractive feature of the room.

Size

The first functional consideration is size: 8×12 feet is the ideal size for exam rooms (gives a clear dimension of 7 feet 6 inches×11 feet 6 inches inside the room) as it comfortably allows for a full-size exam table, a built-in sink cabinet with storage above, dressing area, small writing desk (usually wall mounted), a stool on casters for the doctor, a guest chair for the patient, a treatment stand (if required), and perhaps a small piece of portable medical equipment.

If the room is used for purposes other than routine examinations, such as stress testing, the room would contain an electrocardiogram (ECG) unit and a treadmill, as well as an exam table, and it should be 9×12 feet or 10×12 feet in size. If a dressing area is not required, the length of the room can be shortened to 10 feet.

The reader may wish to refer to Chapter 2 for a discussion of alternate sizes of exam rooms with respect to planning grids. Practitioners may prefer a wider exam room (9×12 feet) as in Figure 3-40 or even a square room 10×10 feet as in Figure 3-40 although, if these occur on exterior walls and the planning grid is 4 feet, the wall will have to jog 2 feet one way or the other (creating an awkward unusable space in front of the window) to terminate at a mullion.

Dressing Area

If space permits, it is desirable to provide a dressing area for patients. This need be no more than a 3-×3-foot, surface-mounted drapery cubicle track at the ceiling (with radius corner), with a built-in bench or a chair, clothes hooks, hangers, a mirror, and perhaps a shelf for disposable gowns. It provides patients with privacy in undressing.

The alternative is that patients must disrobe in the open exam room, with the fear that the nurse or doctor may walk in on them while they are naked or while they are squeezing into a girdle or pantyhose. Older people, and those with orthopedic girdles or braces, tend to be more sensitive about this than younger people.

There is also the possibility of creating a private dressing alcove with a 30-inch-wide door or panel hinged to the wall. It is perpendicular to the wall when in use and folds flat against the wall when not in use. The chair can be used either inside the dressing area when the hinged panel is extended or outside when the panel is folded flat against the wall. Called the Dressing Nook, such a product is currently manufactured by Midmark Corporation

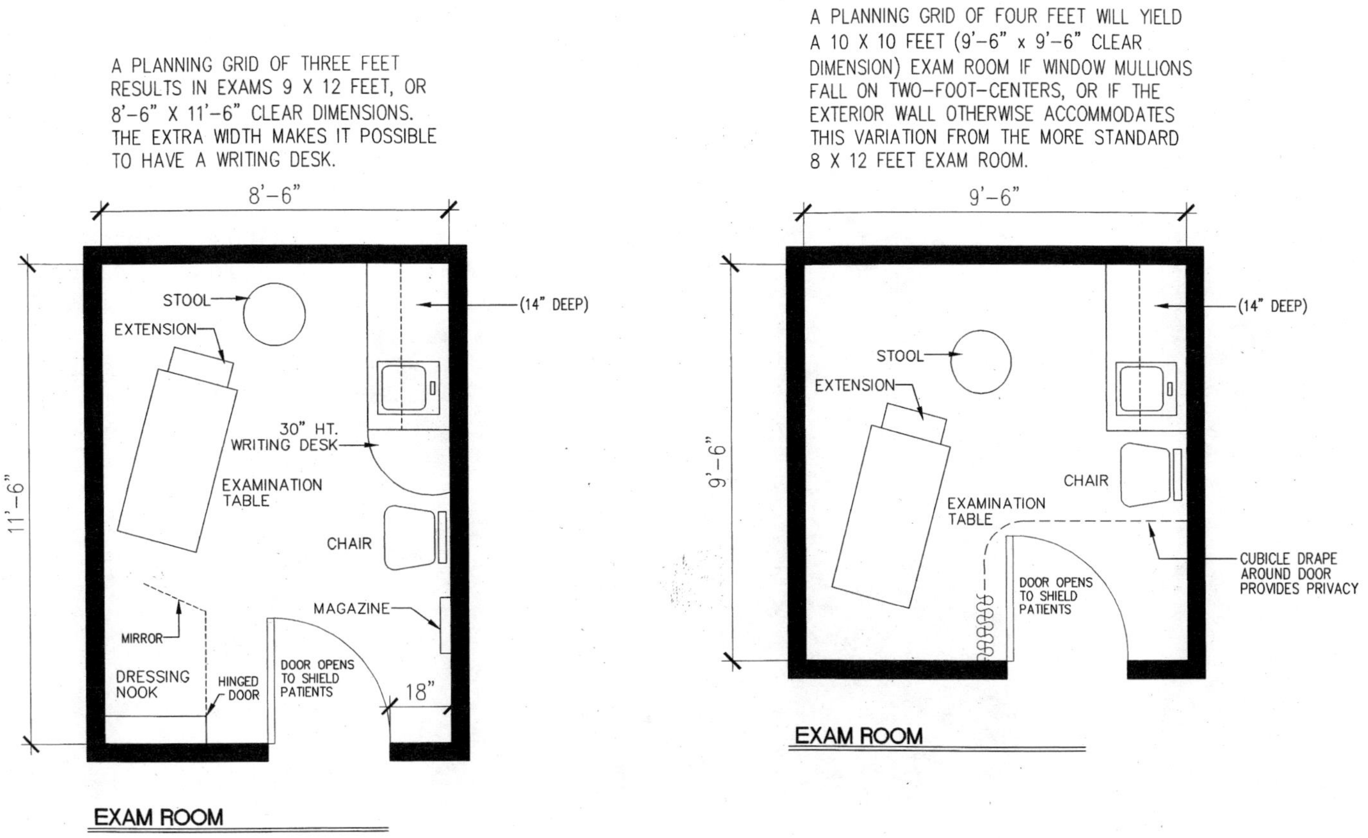
A PLANNING GRID OF THREE FEET RESULTS IN EXAMS 9 X 12 FEET, OR 8'-6" X 11'-6" CLEAR DIMENSIONS. THE EXTRA WIDTH MAKES IT POSSIBLE TO HAVE A WRITING DESK.
8'-6"
11'-6"
STOOL
EXTENSION
(14" DEEP)
30" HT. WRITING DESK
EXAMINATION TABLE
CHAIR
MAGAZINE
MIRROR
DRESSING NOOK
HINGED DOOR
DOOR OPENS TO SHIELD PATIENTS
18"
EXAM ROOM
A PLANNING GRID OF FOUR FEET WILL YIELD A 10 X 10 FEET (9'-6" x 9'-6" CLEAR DIMENSION) EXAM ROOM IF WINDOW MULLIONS FALL ON TWO-FOOT-CENTERS, OR IF THE EXTERIOR WALL OTHERWISE ACCOMMODATES THIS VARIATION FROM THE MORE STANDARD 8 X 12 FEET EXAM ROOM.
9'-6"
9'-6"
STOOL
EXTENSION
(14" DEEP)
CHAIR
EXAMINATION TABLE
CUBICLE DRAPE AROUND DOOR PROVIDES PRIVACY
DOOR OPENS TO SHIELD PATIENTS
EXAM ROOM

Figure 3-40. Alternative layouts and sizes for examination rooms. (*Design: Jain Malkin Inc.*)

(Figure 3-8). As an alternate, one may place a cubicle drape around the door as in Figure 3-40.

With certain medical specialties, for example, ear, nose, and throat (ENT) or orthopedics, patients rarely undress, or if they do so, they primarily undress just to the waist, so private dressing cubicles would not be a priority in these practices.

It should be noted that cubicle drape fabric is specially fabricated for this purpose. It is 72 inches wide, has two "good" sides in terms of pattern and appearance, and can be washed at a temperature of 160 degrees Fahrenheit. Manufacturers include Maharam, Carnegie, DesignTex, and Momentum.

Position of Exam Table

The second functional consideration is the position of the examining table. The foot or stirrup end of the table should be angled away from the door (Figure 3-41) as well as the wall, so that the doctor has access to all sides of the patient, and the patient is out of view of passersby in the corridor when the door is opened. Related to the position of the exam table is the placement of the wall-mounted diagnostic instrument panel (Figures 3-6, 3-39, 3-41, and 3-42).

The door to an exam room should be hinged so that it opens away from the wall (does not stack against the wall). While this might seem awkward in most rooms, it is desirable in a medical exam room because it shields the

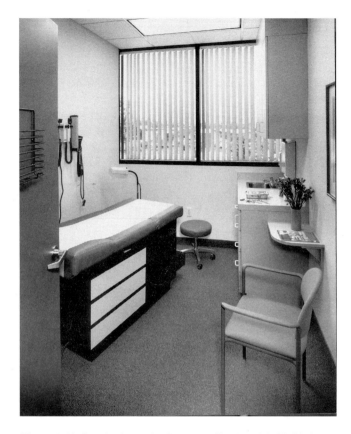

Figure 3-41. Standard examination room. (*Design: Jain Malkin Inc.; Photographer: Robinson/Ward.*)

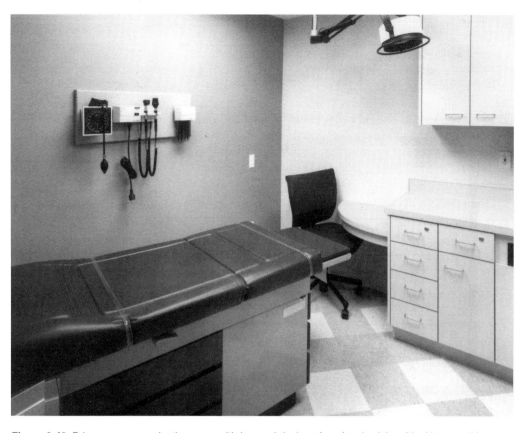

Figure 3-42. Primary-care examination room with lowered desk surface for physician. (*Architecture: Moon Mayoras Architects, San Diego, CA; Interior design: Jain Malkin Inc.; Photographer: Steve McClelland.*)

patient from corridor traffic, should the door be opened accidentally, and gives the patient more privacy when dressing, since one has to walk around the open door to enter the room. It should be noted that the ADA requires 18 inches of clear space on the pull side of the door, making it awkward to open the door to shield the patient in a 7-foot-6-inch-wide room as it puts the door almost in the center of the room (Figure 3-38).

Cabinets
The sink cabinet may be located either on the foot wall opposite the door or on the long wall, to the right, as one

enters the room. Either location is functional in a room in which pelvic or proctologic examinations are done.

The sink cabinet need have only a small sink (a 12-×12-inch stainless steel bar sink works well), as instruments will be washed at the nurse station or lab. In addition, the sink should have a single-lever faucet. The sink cabinet should be a minimum of 48 inches long, 24 inches deep, and 34 inches high. If space permits, it might have a built-in compartment for trash with a hinged "trash slot" cut into the face of the cabinet door (Figure 3-42). Each exam room needs a container for general waste as well as biohazardous waste.

An upper cabinet may be provided (48 inches long, 14 inches deep, 36 inches high), over the base cabinet, for storage of disposable gowns, sheets, and other paper products (Figure 3-38). Shallow drawers in the base cabinet store instruments, syringes, surgical gloves, dressings, tongue depressors, and the like. Paper towel and liquid soap dispensers should be mounted on the wall near the sink, as well as sharps containers and a rack for holding boxes of gloves (Figure 3-43). These items are often provided by the paper or supply vendors who service the units but, if the designer does not oversee the installation, they may be placed with no regard for the aesthetics of the room.

Obstetricians and gynecologists often like to warm their specula prior to examinations. For this purpose, an electrical outlet may be provided in the drawer in which the specula are stored. The more expensive pelvic examination tables have a built-in warmer.

A small wall-hung writing shelf may be provided in an exam room to enable the physician to complete most examinations in the exam room without returning to the consultation room. The prefabricated unit in Figure 3-44 can be customized to house a laptop computer. It has storage for a chart, a place for prescription pads, and a tackable surface, and it is self-closing. If the sink cabinet is located on the long wall or the foot wall, the countertop can be extended, and lowered, from 34 inches to 30 inches, to serve as a writing desk (Figures 3-36 and 3-42). A rolling stool that stores under the "desk," when not in use, should be provided for the physician.

The patient may sit on the exam table (Figure 3-42) or on a guest chair while the physician is taking a patient history or writing a diagnosis. Over time, the use of laptop computers or fully loaded PC tablets (Figures 3-29a and 3-29b) will become more common and may influence the character of the physician/patient interface.

The cabinetry should be clad with plastic laminate, rather than painted. The additional cost when fabricating cabinets is minimal, and well worth it, when one considers the abuse of the painted surfaces plus the inconvenience, and cost, of repainting.

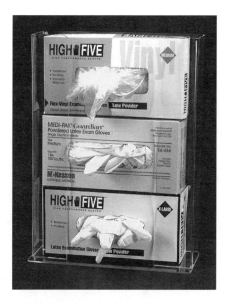

Figure 3-43. Plexiglas glove box holder. (*Photo courtesy: Custom Comfort, Inc., Orlando, FL.*)

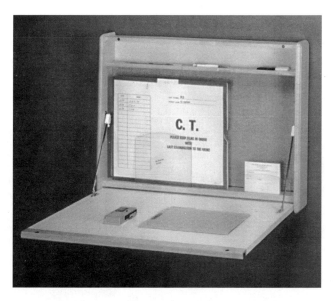

Figure 3-44. Wall-mounted fold-down physician's writing desk. (*Photo courtesy: Peter Pepper Products, Inc., Compton, CA.*)

Windows

There is controversy over the benefit of windows in exam rooms. There is no need for natural light in an exam room for most specialties (it is recommended for dermatology exam rooms, however), so the inclusion of windows would be either a matter of the physician's preference or a given of the building's architecture. However, natural light makes the room more pleasant, especially if the patient is kept waiting. If present, the glass should start at a height sufficient (generally 42 inches) to afford the patient a measure of privacy.

Gray glass is superior to bronze since the latter casts an unhealthy tint on a patient's skin. Horizontal slat wooden blinds or vertical blinds are particularly well suited to windows in exam rooms, as the slats can be tilted to provide privacy without cutting off the light or view entirely.

Too many windows in a medical building can make it difficult to lay out the rooms efficiently unless one wishes to have partitions that terminate in the middle of a window, instead of at a wall or a mullion. This is particularly common when the architect who designed the building was not familiar with medical space planning, and a window module was designed that was not compatible with the size of the rooms in a medical office—basically a 4-foot module.

Electrical Requirements

Three grounded duplex electrical outlets should be provided in an examination room—one above the cabinet countertop, one at the foot of the table, and one near the head of the table. Except for the outlet over the countertop, which would run horizontally at a height of 42 inches, the other outlets may be a standard 15-inch height. Some physicians use a wall-mounted diagnostic instrument panel that would be positioned on the long wall, at approximately 60-inch height, near the head of the exam table (Figures 3-39, 3-41, and 3-42). It requires an electrical outlet that may be placed low on the wall, or high, depending on how much electrical cord one wants visible. Rooms used for ophthalmic or ENT examinations have special electrical requirements, to be discussed in Chapter 4.

Certain exam rooms, such as pediatric or orthopedic exam rooms, often require only two electrical outlets, one over the countertop and the other near the foot of the exam table. Outlets in a pediatric exam room must be carefully guarded and located where a child cannot reach them.

Some examinations, such as OB-GYN exams, require an additional light source, which is usually a high-intensity quartz halogen lamp on a mobile floor stand. Some practitioners like a ceiling-mounted high-intensity lamp at the foot of the exam table. This requires support in the ceiling for mounting it (Figure 3-42). A halogen light may also be bracketed to the end of the exam table (Figure 3-39).

It may be necessary to shield a specialized exam room (one used for electrocardiograph machinery, for example) against electrical interference from surrounding medical offices or equipment, although this is increasingly rare with current equipment.

Exam Table

The standard exam table is 27 inches wide×54 inches long plus stirrups and pull-out footrest (Figures 3-39 and 3-42) if it is to be used for pelvic or urologic examinations. If not used for these purposes, the table will have a pull-out foot board that extends the length of the table to about 6 feet. There are specialized tables for cystoscopic (urological) examinations (Figure 4-158).

The examining room, as described above, will be suitable for most physicians, but some medical specialties require modifications, and these are discussed in future chapters. Most notably, orthopedic surgeons use an 80-inch-long exam table, which is sometimes placed against a wall. Pediatricians also often place their exam tables against the wall.

The combination consultation room and examination room popularized some years ago by the Mayo Clinic (Figure 3-37) is an alternative that has a place in some practices. The Mayo brothers were pioneers in exploring options for the design of exam rooms to enhance productivity. Whatever the design of the exam room, the formula for a productive and efficient office is in the relationship between exam rooms, consultation rooms, nurse stations, and support areas.

Treatment/Minor Surgery

Each family practice or general practice suite will have a minor surgery or procedure room (Figure 3-45). It is sometimes called a *treatment room.* It is a large exam room (usually 12×12 feet) that serves a variety of purposes. It may be used as a cast room, in which case a plaster trap should be provided in the sink, and cabinets should contain a bin for plaster and for the remains of casts that have been removed (see Chapter 4, Orthopedic Surgery).

It may be used as an ECG room, as an operating room for minor surgical procedures using local anesthetics, and as an emergency exam room for accident cases. In treating emergencies, the physician may need one or more aides in the room plus certain medical equipment not usually stored in other exam rooms. Add to that the relatives who accompany the patient and frequently wish to remain in the treatment room, and the need for an oversized, multipurpose exam room becomes clear.

A minor surgery room should have a 10- to 12-foot length of upper and lower cabinets—one full wall of built-ins. Usually, this room will have a ceiling-mounted surgical light over the treatment table, in addition to standard fluorescent lighting (Figure 3-45). Proper illumination is mandatory for this room.

If the suite is so situated within the layout of the medical building as to make possible a direct entrance to the minor surgery room, it is desirable. Accident cases or those with contagious diseases do not have to walk through the waiting room if they can enter the minor surgery room directly. This would be an unmarked door in the public corridor of the medical building provided with a buzzer, or the door might simply state *Emergency Entrance—Ring Bell for Service.*

The receptionist taking the emergency call would ask the patient to go to the door marked *Emergency Entrance* and ring the bell.

Consultation Room

This room functions as a private office for the most part, but some physicians do consult with patients here. Routine consultation can be handled in a well-designed exam room, saving the physician the trouble of continually returning to his or her private office with each patient.

Certain physicians (e.g., internists, oncologists) spend a good deal of time interviewing the patient on the initial visit. In such cases, physicians may feel that the consultation room provides a more conducive atmosphere for establishing the relationship or for discussing serious illnesses. Surgeons also tend to use their private offices for consultation with patients, but this remains a matter of individual preference for each physician.

The consultation room is also used by the physician for reading, returning phone calls, dictating notes, or just relaxing. The minimum size for this room is 10×12 feet, but 12×12 feet is better. The room must accommodate a desk with computer, credenza, bookshelves for the doc-

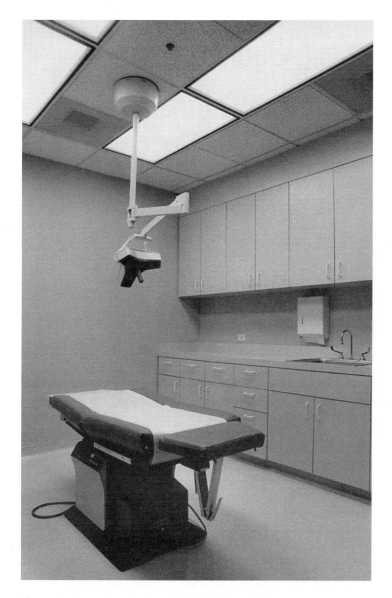

Figure 3-45. Minor surgery room. (*Design: Jain Malkin Inc.; Photographer: John Christian.*)

Figure 3-46. Diplomas, attractively framed. (*Design: Jain Malkin Inc.; Photographer: Michael Denny.*)

Figure 3-47. Shared physician office. Montefiore Medical Center in the Bronx. (*Architecture and interior design: Guenther Petrarca, New York, NY; Photographer: Lynn Massimo.*)

tor's library, two guest chairs, a coat closet (optional), and perhaps a private bathroom.

The room should be furnished like a living room or study with cut pile carpet, textured wallcoverings, comfortable furniture, and artwork. If the doctor has a hobby that lends itself to expression in room decor, this is the one room in the suite that can be highly personalized. Family photos, armed forces honors, and personal memorabilia humanize the doctor's image and provide a clue to him or her as a person, apart from the medical practice.

The physician's diplomas and credentials should be nicely framed and displayed in the consultation room. If grouped artistically (Figure 3-46), they can complement the room's decor.

A consultation room should have natural light if possible. In addition, table lamps or indirect lighting may add to the room's homelike ambience. It is desirable to locate the consultation room at the rear of the suite to give the physician more privacy and to ensure that patients do not pass it on their way to the examining room. Still, some assertive patients find their way to the consultation room uninvited and unannounced.

It may be possible to locate an outdoor exit in the private office. The physician may thus enter or leave without being seen by patients. If such a door is not possible, then a private rear entrance to the suite, as previously discussed, is mandatory.

In certain suites, such as pediatrics, the consultation room is used so minimally that several physicians may share one. Their combined medical library would be stored here, and each doctor would have a small desk and telephone (see Figure 3-47).

At the other extreme, a physician will occasionally request a consultation room with a sofa large enough to sleep on, a table with reading lamp, a refrigerator, and bathroom with shower, in addition to the usual components of a private office. Such an office may serve a cardiac surgeon who, due to many emergency surgeries, may have to spend the night at the office (if it is near the hospital) or just catch up on sleep during the day between surgeries.

Figure 3-48. Nurse station. (*Design: Jain Malkin Inc.; Photographer: John Christian.*)

Figure 3-49. Nurse station, pediatric community clinic. (*Interior design: Jain Malkin Inc.; Photographer: Steve McClelland.*)

Nurse Station and Laboratory

The nurse station is an area where the doctor's nurses or assistants perform a variety of tasks such as weighing patients, sterilizing instruments, dispensing drug samples, giving injections, taking a patient's temperature, performing routine lab tests, communicating with patients by telephone, or handling office paperwork (Figures 3-48 and 3-49).

The nurse station may be only a 6-foot length of countertop (with cabinets below and above) recessed in a niche in the corridor (Figure 3-52), or it may be an 8-×12-foot room or area adjacent to the exam rooms (Figure 3-2). The size of the nurse station depends on the num-

Figure 3-50. Pneumatic blood draw chair. (*Photo courtesy: Custom Comfort, Inc., Orlando, FL.*)

ber of nurses or aides who will use it, the type of medical practice, and the functions to be performed by those individuals. The nurse station in Figure 3-35 offers physicians maximum access to nurses and numerous stand-up-height writing shelves.

The number of physician extenders can be estimated on the basis of each doctor requiring one or two assistants, depending on whether the practice is a high-volume specialty. This person, depending on training, may assist the physician in the exam room or may actually perform certain examinations. Obstetricians and gynecologists have been using nurse practitioners in this expanded role for routine pelvic and gynecologic examinations. Since OB-GYN is a very high-volume specialty, the use of nurse practitioners saves the physician time on routine examinations and permits him or her to concentrate on patients with more demanding medical problems.

Therefore, the nurse station in an OB-GYN suite must be large enough to accommodate the nurse practitioners and other aides who need a knee space for sitting down and writing notes, one or two scales (all OB-GYN patients are weighed each visit), with a writing shelf nearby. Sometimes scales are recessed into the floor, if practical, in terms of cost and construction parameters. This recess in the concrete slab can be carpeted with the adjacent floor carpet. An area of approximately 24 inches should be allowed for each scale. This is not the size of the recess but the floor space necessary to accommodate a standard medical scale with balance rod.

There is an advantage to locating the nurse station near the front of the suite in a small office (under 1500 square feet). The nurse has easy access to patients as he or she leads them from the waiting room to the exam room, and the nurse can cover for business office staff when they are momentarily away from their desks. In larger suites, each doctor may have a nurse or medical assistant working from a nurse station convenient to his or her pod of exam rooms (see Figures 3-2 and 3-52).

In some medical offices, the nurse station is combined with the laboratory. In otolaryngology (ENT), for example, this is true since few lab tests are performed in the office.

The nurse station/lab would be used for preparing throat cultures and for cleanup of instruments in the sink or for sterilizing instruments. With the widespread use of disposable syringes, gowns, sheets, and even many examination instruments, relatively few items have to be washed or sterilized.

In an OB-GYN practice, the laboratory would usually be a separate room because a good deal of lab work is generated in the suite. Each patient supplies a urine sample for analysis, which is performed in the lab, and each patient having a pelvic exam and Pap smear will have a tissue culture that will have to be prepared for sending to a cytology lab.

A number of other routine tests would be performed within the lab, plus many gynecologists do D&Cs (dilation and curettage), terminations of pregnancy, and other types of minor surgery procedures in a well-equipped minor surgery room in the office. These procedures can be messy and require an adequate area for cleanup and a good-sized nurse station, plus lab support facilities.

A lab should have a double-compartment sink, a knee space area for a microscope, and a full-size refrigerator, if necessary (otherwise an undercounter one). It may also have a blood drawing station with a specialized blood draw chair (Figures 3-50 and 5-79) as standard tablet-arm chairs are not functional for this purpose. It is advisable to shield the patient whose blood is being drawn from the sight of other patients, who often become faint upon observing the procedure. The countertop will have a centrifuge for spinning down blood before sending it out to a lab and may have (if more lab work is done within the suite) a countertop analyzer. Refer to Chapter 5 for photos of clinical analyzers.

It is desirable to have at least one toilet room adjacent to the lab so that a specimen pass-through door in the wall can give the lab technician access to urine specimens without leaving the lab (see Figure 3-21). The reader is referred to Chapter 5 for more detailed specifications of a small laboratory and to the Appendix for a diagram of a specimen pass-through.

The nurse station of an orthopedic surgery suite would be of minimal size since there are no lab tests performed, and no blood is drawn. The supplies needed for examinations or for making or removing casts would be stored in the respective rooms, and very little would have to be carried into a room for a procedure. In fact, orthopedic offices have tech workstations rather than nurse stations.

By contrast, a family practice or G.P. suite would have a large nurse station. Since such a wide variety of medical procedures are performed and there is such a wide range of patients, it would be impractical to store in each exam room all the supplies one might need. Therefore, the nurse prepares the exam room with any special supplies, injections, dressings, and instruments that she anticipates will be required. A good many of these items will be stored in the nurse station, and each nurse station might have its own autoclave for sterilization of instruments. In addition, the nurse might give allergy or other injections at the nurse station; blood might be drawn for tests to be done in the suite's own lab or sent out for processing; patients are weighed at each visit; and many other routine tasks are carried out here.

A nurse station should always have a sink and often has an undercounter refrigerator and a knee-space work area with telephone (Figures 3-47 and 3-48). Most nurse stations have a scale space, with a nearby shelf, for recording the weight in the patient's chart. The reader is referred to Chapter 4 for nurse station requirements for each medical specialty.

Legislation Affecting In-House Labs
Regarding the laboratory, the physician decides whether to do lab tests within the office or send the work out. Some do not even like to draw blood in their office, preferring to send the patient to a lab, if one is conveniently located in the medical building.

Stark Legislation
In the past, physicians may have had a financial interest in a lab to which they referred their patients, but with the federal Stark legislation enacted a number of years ago, this is rare. Only under the "safe harbor" provision, and

under certain conditions, for example, in rural areas where an independent lab may not be available, may physicians own a lab. Otherwise, financial interest in a lab, or other ancillary services, is viewed as a potential conflict of interest.

It is estimated that today fewer than 10 percent of medical practices do lab work in house as CLIA (Clinical Laboratory Improvement Act), federal legislation enacted in 1988, imposes a level of compliance that results in high overhead and—with the decrease in reimbursement—it becomes a drain, rather than an economic incentive. Also, under managed care, a patient's insurance may dictate what lab must be used.

CLIA Compliance
Lab tests physicians may commonly do in their offices—and are allowed to do without CLIA compliance (although they still need to register with CLIA)—are what are referred to as "waived tests," something equivalent to the kinds of self-tests one could purchase at a pharmacy. These include dipstick urine tests for pregnancy or diabetes.

Physicians who elect to do what are called "nonwaived" tests in the office would come under CLIA regulations. The most commonly performed tests include blood counts, glucose tolerance tests, kidney and liver function tests, and cholesterol testing or a full lipid panel. This work would require benchtop hematology and chemistry analyzers. See Chapter 5 for photos of automated analyzers and more detailed information about laboratories.

Drug Testing
Large family practice suites and clinical laboratories may wish to do testing for drugs as part of employment-required physical exams. A toilet room designed for this purpose is discussed in Chapter 5.

OSHA Issues
The Occupational Safety and Health Administration (OSHA) of the U.S. Department of Labor protects workers from occupational hazards and risks. It publishes guidelines, standards, and regulations governing a multitude of settings, products, and situations, most of which have to

Figure 3-51. Opti-Klens I eyewash faucet diverter. (*Photo courtesy: Desert Assembly, Inc., Henderson, NV.*)

do with processes and procedures, none of which come under the purview of the architect or designer. OSHA also evaluates products such as sharps disposal containers to determine if they meet OSHA standards. Periodically, worksites, including medical and dental offices, may be visited by OSHA inspectors. Designers should be aware of the following issues:

1. Personal-use or edible items cannot be stored in the same refrigerator as blood or tissue samples. However, according to OSHA, refrigerators containing medications or other substances stored for medical procedures (e.g., challenge solutions for glucose tolerance tests) are not subject to the restriction.

2. An eyewash diverter valve device mounted to a faucet is required in any workplace where the eyes of the employee may be exposed to injurious materials. In OSHA interpretations letters, it is not clear where, in a medical or dental office, they might be required. However, a large primary-care office might have one; urgent-care clinics (for walk-in patients) and ophthalmologists often have one for patients. The device must meet American National Standards Institute (ANSI) Z358.1-1990, as does the Opti-Klens® unit in Figure 3-51.

3. In offices where staff are exposed to bloodborne pathogens, staff should remove their lab coats prior to leaving the suite. The idea is to not carry home organisms on one's clothing. Although not required by OSHA in physicians' or dentists' offices, depending on the specialty, the practitioner may wish to provide a locker room and change area for staff. Disposable items with bodily fluids must be red-bagged and labeled "biohazardous waste" and collected by a service. A biohazardous storage room, usually near the staff entrance to the suite, will house the waste until it is picked up. It can also be stored in a soiled utility room. [Note: Some suite plans in this book lack this room as it was not a requirement when these suites were designed.]

4. Occupational exposure to bloodborne pathogens including hepatitis B and C viruses as well as human immunodeficiency virus (HIV) poses great risk to healthcare workers. Needle-stick injuries are a serious hazard and OSHA has researched every aspect of this problem and published numerous standards and documents relating to how injuries occur and how they can be reduced. Standards for selecting the safest sharps disposal container and suggestions for training staff are covered in the Occupational Exposure to Bloodborne Pathogens Standard.

Placement of Sharps Disposal Containers

It is of interest to note that one of the three factors most often related to sharps injuries is inappropriate placement of the sharps container. It should be visible and placed at an arm's reach and below eye level at the point of use. According to OSHA, the fixture should be below the eye level of 95 percent of adult female workers, which results in an optimal installation range of 56 to 52 inches at a standing workstation and 42 to 38 inches for a seated workstation.

A word of warning: When a physician's office staff conveys to the designer OSHA standards and regulations that must be met, it is advisable to check it out by calling OSHA. In the author's experience, much of the time, either no regulation exists or, if it does, its effect on the built environment has been misunderstood. The problem is that individual OSHA inspectors may cite a facility for a perceived infraction that cannot be found in a literal reading of the OSHA text. In addition, each state has its own OSHA interpretations. Physicians' office staffs are right to treat employee safety issues seriously and to want to address them to the letter of the law since the liability and risks are substantial for noncompliance. However, much of the compliance deals with staff training, keeping procedure manuals updated, and making certain the staff actively follow the procedures they have outlined to protect patients and employees. In that regard, an excellent resource for OSHA compliance training, consulting, and compliance products is HPTC in Plymouth, Michigan (www.hptcinc.com).

Other Support Services

X-Ray Room

This discussion will focus on the one-room X-ray unit that can be found in a family practice or internal medicine suite (Figure 3-52). Rather simple radiographic examinations are performed here—films of extremities, chests, gallbladders, appendixes, and so forth. More complicated procedures will be performed in a radiologist's office. A large internal medicine practice might have a suite of radiographic rooms within its facility with a full-time radiologist on staff. But usually a patient who requires GI (gastrointestinal) studies, thyroid scans, computed tomography (CT) scans, radiation oncology therapy, or other specialized or complicated diagnostic imaging procedures will be referred to a local hospital on an outpatient basis or to a nearby radiology clinic.

A 10×14-foot room is adequate (not taking into account the dressing area and darkroom) for most X-ray machines used in a family practice or internal medicine office, although a slightly larger room would be more comfortable. Usually, a 9-foot ceiling height is required. There should be a place inside or outside the room for a patient to dress (ideally a 3-×4-foot alcove with a drapery or door for privacy), a control area for the technician, and a place to process the film. Although the equipment breaks down into components, it is advisable to provide a minimum 3-foot-wide door in this room for ease in moving the equipment. Although new imaging equipment is digital and filmless, many physicians have existing equipment that is not and it is unlikely most will trade it in as long as it's still serviceable. *Therefore, the discussion about filmless imaging will be confined to Chapter 5.*

The radiography room does not need a sink or prep area unless GI studies are performed or contrast media are used, in which case a bathroom must be located close to the radiographic room (Figure 5-5).

Two or more walls of an X-ray room will have to be shielded with lead to protect office occupants as well as passersby from radiation scatter. It is necessary to obtain a radiation physicist's report, which takes into account the type of equipment and the location of the room within the suite and within the medical office building, in order to know which walls must be shielded, the thickness of the lead, and the height of the lead panels. Frequently, the door to the room must also be lead-lined. Such a door is very heavy and must have a heavy-duty door closer. The control partition, if located within the room, must also be lead-lined. It is possible to buy prefabricated, lead-lined control partitions with glass viewing panels from X-ray supply houses.

If the control area is located outside the X-ray room, there must be a lead-lined glass window to enable the operator to observe the patient at all times (Figure 4-122). The control area need not be large—3 feet square is generally adequate.

There are considerable variations in size of radiology equipment, power requirements, and other specifications from one manufacturer to another. Therefore, it is advisable to obtain planning guides for each piece of equipment before proceeding.

A valuable reference in designing radiology rooms is the catalog of radiology accessories marketed by each manufacturer. These catalogs are available online through the Internet and, in addition, some are available as printed catalogs as well. General Electric has a particularly good one, in which many items are pictured with dimensions and pertinent data. This will familiarize the designer with the numerous accessory items (cassette pass boxes, film illuminators, film dryers, automatic processors) that must be accommodated in a radiology room or suite.

A lead-lined cassette pass box should be located in the wall between the darkroom and the radiography room. The pass box is used for passing exposed and unexposed film back and forth between the rooms.

The manufacturer's literature will specify utility requirements and critical distances between equipment. Additional support is usually needed in the ceiling to support the tube stand. The X-ray unit, if new, will often be supplied by a local distributor who will assist the designer in locating the equipment in the room. Or, if the physician is relocating existing equipment to a new office, it will usually be moved and reinstalled by a skilled technician who can offer assistance as to the equipment's requirements.

Darkroom

In the future, most radiographic equipment will be digital but, currently, most general practice and internal medicine clinics—if they do radiography—will have a darkroom. It should be set up with a "wet" and a "dry" side (Figure 10-78). A 6-×8-foot room is the minimum size, although, if designed to meet the ADA, and in view of the fact that a darkroom door always opens inward, the room would have to be larger. The room should have two full-width countertops either parallel to each other or at right angles. The wet side contains the sink, automatic processor, and replenisher tanks, while the dry side is used for loading cassettes. A light-proof metal film storage bin should be located under the dry side of the counter. Ideally, the cassette pass box would be positioned in the wall close to the film storage bin.

Sometimes a rack for storage of cassettes is provided. A floor drain must be located near the processor. One outlet should be provided over the counter on both the wet and the dry sides. An outlet is needed for the film storage bin as well. The processor requires only cold water if it is a recent model with an internal temperature control.

Local codes normally require a vacuum breaker on piping to darkroom tanks to prevent the chemical waste from backing up into the water supply. Also, acid-resistant pipe is recommended, since chemical waste is highly corrosive.

The room must have an exhaust fan, and some codes require that the door have a light-proof louver ventilation panel. The darkroom door must be 36 inches wide and have a light seal. It should open inward, so that if someone tries to enter while film is exposed, the technician inside the room can put a foot against the door to prevent it from opening. Some darkrooms have a red warning light that is activated when developing is in progress.

The darkroom must have two sources of light. A 75-watt incandescent fixture, surface-mounted to the ceiling, will suffice for general illumination, but a safelight must be provided for working with exposed film. The safelight may be plugged into an outlet at 60 to 72 inches off the floor,

and it can work by a pull chain or be wired into a wall switch. If the latter, the switch should be located away from the incandescent light switch so that the technician does not confuse them and hit the wrong one while the film is exposed. Any recessed light fixtures and the exhaust fan must have a light-sealed housing.

Counters and cabinets in a darkroom may be at a 36-inch or 42-inch height, according to personal preference. If designed to meet the ADA, the countertop must not exceed the 34-inch height. There is no need for closed storage in the darkroom. All shelves should be open shelves.

A small viewing area is required outside the procedure room, near the darkroom (Figure 4-124). This may consist of nothing more than a double-panel view box illuminator, either surface mounted to the wall or recessed (Figure 4-133). The X-ray technologist checks the films for resolution and clarity before handing them to the physician for diagnosis. If the film is not good, the patient is still at hand, with little time lost in having to take the film again. In a larger X-ray suite of rooms, the viewing area will be larger, with several banks of film illuminators and a place for two or more persons to sit down.

The film will be developed by an automatic film processor which may be a small tabletop unit such as dentists, otolaryngologists, or plastic surgeons use, or a floor model that sits outside the darkroom in the tech work area (Figures 3-52 and 4-124) with a feed tray that fits through the wall into the darkroom (see Figure 5-25). The exposed film is fed into the processor from the darkroom and "daylights" (drops out after processing) into the tech work area. See Chapter 5 for more detail. The suite in Figure 4-127 is set up for digital radiography but still accommodates storage of old film files.

Storage

Medical offices should have a storage room at least 6 feet square with two or more walls of adjustable shelves for storage of office supplies, sterile supplies, pharmaceutical items, housekeeping supplies, and cartons of toilet paper, hand towels, and facial tissue. If the office does not use a janitorial service, the vacuum cleaner and mop and pail would be stored here.

Staff Lounge

Any suite with more than two employees should have a staff lounge. The room need not be larger than 10×12 feet with a built-in sink cabinet 6 to 8 feet in length, an undercounter refrigerator, microwave oven, garbage disposal, a small table and chairs, and possibly lockers for personal effects. Do not underestimate the countertop area required considering coffee maker, appliances, dish drying rack, and space for the box of dougnuts. Remember that a refrigerator with an ice maker will require a water line. A larger staff lounge might include a sofa where an employee can lie down as well as a full-size refrigerator. This is a private room where the staff may take coffee breaks or eat their lunch. A staff lounge is an amenity that pleases employees and makes their jobs a little more pleasant. Furthermore, one does not want staff eating food in the nurse station, in the lab, or at the reception desk.

INTERNAL MEDICINE

The practice of internal medicine is broad. It encompasses subspecialties such as pulmonary disease, nephrology, oncology, hematology, gastroenterology, endocrinology, and cardiovascular disease—the major emphases. Before planning an internal medicine suite, it is important to analyze the physicians' respective specialties and practice schedules. Internists often function as general-practice primary-care physicians for adults, providing a full spectrum of care (generally excluding gynecological examinations), or they may practice only their subspecialty such as cardiology, pulmonology, or endocrinology. The combinations of subspecialties in a group practice will obviously influence the program of rooms. Table 3-2 provides a general idea of a typical complement of rooms and Figure 3-52 shows the relationship of rooms.

With such a broad range of areas of expertise, it is common for internists to practice in groups rather than as solo practitioners. A designer must also understand the structure of a physician's workday. Physicians tend to visit their hospitalized patients in the morning, before

Table 3-2.
Analysis of Program.
Internal Medicine

No. of Physicians:		2		3		4
Consultation	2@	12×12=288	3@	12×12=432	4@	12×12=576
Exam Rooms	6@	8×12=576	8@	8×12=768	10@	8×12=960
Waiting Room		14×18=252		20×20=400		20×24=480
Business Office		16×20=320		20×20=400		24×26=624
Office Manager		10×12=120		10×12=120		10×12=120
Nurse Stations	2@	8×8=128	3@	8×8=192	3@	8×8=192
Toilets	2@	7×8=112	3@	7×8=168	4@	7×8=224
Storage		6×8=48		6×8=48		8×10=80
Flex Sig. Room[a]		12×18=216		12×18=216		12×18=216
Staff Lounge		10×12=120		12×12=144		12×14=168
Laboratory[b]		10×12=120		10×12=120		10×14=140
ECG/Treadmill		10×12=120		10×12=120		10×12=120
Pulmonary Function Testing		—		(Optional)		14×16=224
Radiology[c]		—		12×25=300		12×25=300
Subtotal		2420 ft²		3428 ft²		4424 ft²
20% Circulation		484		685		884
Total		2904 ft²		4113 ft²		5308 ft²

[a]Includes workroom and toilet (flexible sigmoidoscopy room); used for various types of special procedures.
[b]Includes lab, sub-waiting, and blood draw. Optional: Patients may be sent out for blood draw.
[c]Includes darkroom, control, film filing, radiology room, and viewing area.

office hours. Office hours typically begin at 9 A.M. and continue to 12 noon. Medical offices are usually closed from noon to 2 P.M. and open again from 2 to 5 P.M. Surgeons try to do the bulk of their surgery in the morning and reserve the afternoon for office visits by patients.

In a five-person practice, for example, physicians' schedules will usually be arranged so that no more than three are in the office at any one time (Figure 3-53). This negates the need for each of the five to have the use of exam rooms all at the same time. By efficiently coordinating their schedules, the group can function well in less space, without sacrificing income or service to patients. One doctor may have a day off, while a second may be seeing patients at a satellite office, and a third may be seeing patients at the hospital, leaving the other two in our hypothetical group of five in

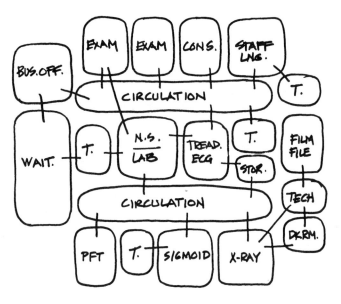

INTERNAL MEDICINE

Figure 3-52. Schematic diagram of an internal medicine suite.

the primary office. At a busier point in the day, schedules may be arranged so that three or four of the internists are in the primary office seeing patients.

Internal medicine is a medium-volume practice. It is based on diagnosis, which requires long history-taking interviews by the physician and sometimes a complicated battery of tests. The internist, being primarily a diagnostician, spends a good deal of time with a patient. However, follow-up visits may be considerably shorter, so overall, a well-organized, efficient practice can process a fairly high number of patients each day.

Some internists prefer to do the initial interview in the consultation room, whereas others find it more efficient to do it in the exam room. If the consultation room is used, it should be large—12×12 feet—with comfortable seating.

There is a lot of lab work associated with internal medicine, and one must determine which tests are to be done within the suite and which are to be sent out. If a sub-

stantial number of tests are to be done within the suite, a 12-×12-foot minimum size lab should be set up. The reader is referred to Chapter 5, Small Laboratory, for further details. Remember, however, the previous comments about CLIA regulations and how few physicians currently do lab work in their offices.

An internist needs *three* exam rooms or *five* for each two physicians, provided there is a procedure room that can also be used. Ten exam rooms should suffice for a group of five physicians, allowing that at least one person is absent at any time and a second person may be absent for certain periods of the day.

A small X-ray room should be provided for chest films. Gallbladder and gastrointestinal studies are referred to a radiologist or, as appropriate, are performed in an endoscopy suite, discussed later in this chapter. Refer to Family Practice for details of the X-ray suite.

A large storage room may be needed for storing specialized, seldom used equipment and for storing X-ray films.

Electrocardiograph (ECG) Room

A standard exam room (8×12 feet) can be used for ECG studies. Some physicians dedicate a special room to this function, while others feel that dedicated rooms result in a loss of flexibility. Since the equipment is portable, it can be moved from room to room as needed (Figure 3-54). A monitoring unit on a mobile cart is brought to the patient and electrodes attached to wires on the machine are placed on the patient's chest, leg, and wrist. The patient lies on a physical therapy–type table (or exam table) for this procedure. The instrument records the changes in electrical potential occurring during the heartbeat by imaging the vibrations and producing a printout—the electrocardiogram—which is then interpreted by the internist. This test is often performed by a nurse or aide.

This type of ECG (where the patient lies supine) is called *static*. By contrast, a *dynamic* ECG involves an active patient whose heartbeat is monitored while he or she is walking on a motorized treadmill that is hardwired to the ECG machine and monitor, which control the ele-

103'-6"

70'-0"

PUBLIC ENTRY

STAFF ENTRY

LAB ENTRY

WAITING

TRANS.

STORAGE

CONSULT

EXAM

EXAM

CONSULT

TLT.

MINOR TREATMENT

NURSE

EXAM

RECEPT.

APPTS.

CRASH CART

LINEN

ECHO EXAM & HOLTER

TREADMILL

EXAM

ECG

EXAM

BUS. MGR.

CHART FILES (SPACE-SAVER TYPE)

ECG TECH

P.T. TABLE

DK. RM.

NURSE

COPIER

VIEWING & SORT.

PROC.

BOOK.

FILES

TLT.

DRES'G.

CONTROL

X-RAY

STAFF ENTRY

INSUR.

SIGMOID

FILM FILING

DRES'G.

SCALE

SUPPLY

PREP.

X-RAY WAITING

EXAM

LAB WTG.

DRYING CAB

STORAGE

FOUNTAIN

EXAM

EXAM

EXAM

BLOOD DRAW

RECOVERY COT

STOR.

SPEC. PASS THRU

COATS

NURSE

SCALE

EXAM

REF.

LAB

STAFF

TLT.

CONSULT

EXAM

EXAM

CONSULT

TLT.

CONSULT

INTERNAL MEDICINE

7245SF

Figure 3-53. Space plan for internal medicine, 7245 square feet. (*Design: Jain Malkin Inc.*)

vation and speed of the treadmill (Figure 3-55). One can program the remote control for the desired protocol. The treadmill is not easy to move around, so if dynamic ECGs are done, it is better to locate the equipment in one room and leave it there. Space for a "crash" cart with defibrillator and portable oxygen is required wherever stress testing is done (Figure 3-56). In addition, a treadmill room also requires an exam table where the patient can lie down during the recovery phase. Working to maximum exertion can cause dizziness or nausea. In positioning the treadmill, there needs to be a wall in front of the patient for a "perceived exertion" chart, and the exam table must be near the treadmill in case the patient feels light-headed or unstable. The physician and tech need ready access to the right side of the patient to quickly replace an electrode that might have fallen off if the patient starts to perspire profusely. A cardiologist is always present during a treadmill test although he or she may not remain in the room for the entire test period.

An ECG room without a treadmill can be the size of a standard exam room (8×12 feet) with space for a 2-×6-foot table for the patient to lie on, the portable monitoring equipment, and the standard exam room sink cabinet. The ECG machine stores enough paper for numerous tests and additional paper can be stored on the mobile cart and in a central storage room. The cart also stores the silver chloride disposable electrodes. Patients remove only their shirts or blouse for a static ECG procedure.

Echocardiography

Echocardiography is a noninvasive procedure that images the heart with ultrasound technology. The unit is portable and sits on a cart with a VCR and image printer (Figure 3-57). Sometimes the test is done while the

Figure 3-54. Portable electrocardiogram machine Eclipse 850. (*Photo courtesy: ©1999 Spacelabs Burdick, Inc., Deerfield, WI. Reproduced with permission.*)

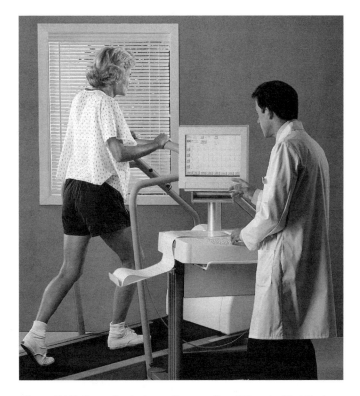

Figure 3-55. Dynamic electrocardiogram. Quest Exercise Test System. (*Photo courtesy: ©1999 Spacelabs Burdick, Inc., Deerfield, WI. Reproduced with permission.*)

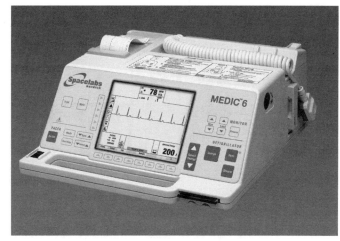

Figure 3-56. Cardiac defibrillator. (*Photo courtesy: ©1999 Spacelabs Burdick, Inc., Deerfield, WI. Reproduced with permission.*)

patient is on a treadmill (Figure 3-58). This can be performed in any standard examination room, but it requires absolute quiet. The patient lies on a flat table with the technician working from the patient's right side (Figure 3-61). Room lights should be dimmable.

The sonographer listens to sounds as they're coming toward and away from the probe; thus, extraneous noise makes it difficult to isolate the sounds although some sonographers wear headphones. "2-D Echo plus Doppler" means two-dimensional imaging (appears on a CRT) plus sound. It is important to eliminate glare on the CRT screen. Additionally, there is a need for storage of echo tapes, which are VHS cassettes. In the future, these will most likely be stored in a compressed digital format.

Holter Monitoring

Holter monitoring is a noninvasive procedure for recording cardiac activity on a 24-hour basis. Electrodes applied to the patient's chest are connected via lead wires to a Holter recording unit worn on the patient's belt. The data are recorded on microcassettes or standard-sized audiocassettes, depending on the individual unit. In addition, the patient keeps a written diary of activities and events that is later correlated with the data on the tape. The patient returns to the office with the cassette, and the Holter tech then plays it on a Holter analyzer located at the workstation (Figure 3-59). A digital Holter recording device with built-in fax and modem allows Holter reports

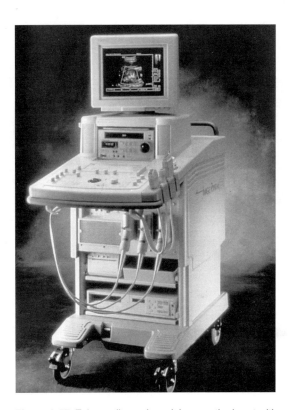

Figure 3-57. Echocardiography unit images the heart with ultrasound technology. SONOS Ultrasound Unit. (*Photo courtesy: Agilent Technologies, Inc., Andover, MA.*)

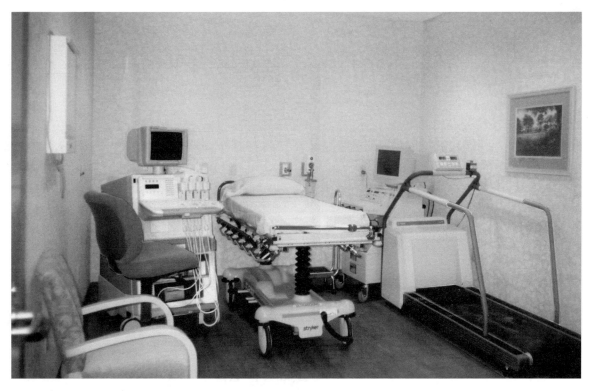

Figure 3-58. Echocardiography examination room accommodates both static and dynamic (treadmill) imaging. (*Interior design: Jain Malkin Inc.; Photographer: Jain Malkin.*)

Figure 3-59. Holter analyzer. (*Photo courtesy: ©1999 Spacelabs Burdick, Inc., Deerfield, WI. Reproduced with permission.*)

to be sent by e-mail through the Internet to consulting physicians. Compatibility with Windows software provides composite screen formats for comparison and analysis of multiple cardiac data.

The patient can be fitted for the monitoring equipment in any standard exam room. A physical therapy–type table is adequate, and the room should have some cabinetry for storing supplies. The recorded cassettes can be stored in a storage room or at the tech's workstation. Note the relationship of test rooms in Figure 3-52 in the central core of the suite with a workstation for the tech who does echo, ECG, and Holter. The X-ray facility is also in the core with a sub-waiting area.

Vascular Lab

Diagnostic studies of the blood vessels are performed in a vascular lab to detect blood clots, calcium buildup, fatty deposits, and so forth. A vascular lab might be set up with two rooms, one for carotid artery studies of the neck and one for studies of the extremities. A third room would be an office for the sonographers (Figure 3-60).

A three-room suite as described above might handle approximately 14 to 20 cases per day. The time required with each patient varies, but the norm is a 20- to 30-minute patient history-taking and 40- to 60-minute test period, followed by a 15-minute period of calculation and

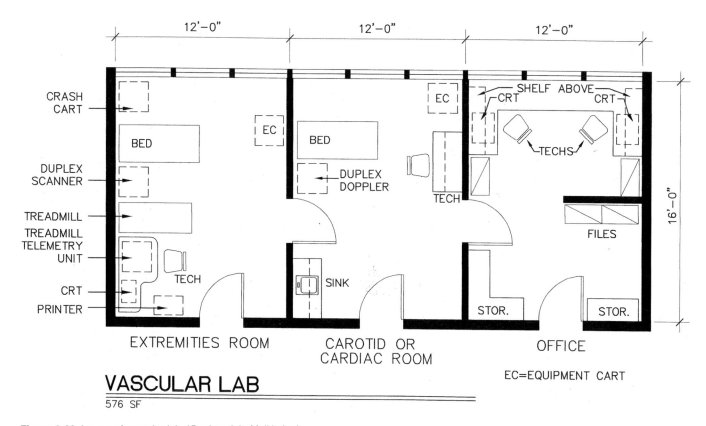

Figure 3-60. Layout of vascular lab. (*Design: Jain Malkin Inc.*)

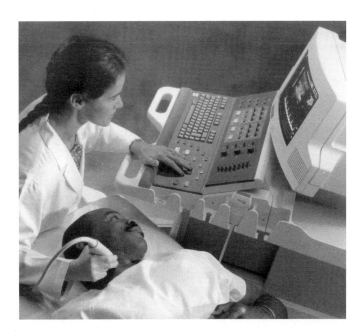

Figure 3-61. Duplex Doppler ultrasonic imaging system. (*Photo courtesy: ATL Ultrasound, Bothell, WA.*)

recording of data. Patients are usually gowned for tests, but procedures are noninvasive.

The carotid room uses a duplex Doppler ultrasonic imaging system (Figure 3-61). As a point of information, power Doppler detects flow, duplex Doppler gives direction of flow. A photo of the blood vessel can be produced, which can be placed in the patient's chart. The room also needs a desk for the sonographer and a sink cabinet, with storage above, for supplies and linen. A nice amenity to relax patients is a back-lit film transparency overhead of a view of nature (Figure 3-62).

The extremities room uses a Stryker gurney cart that is mobile and allows for flexible positioning of the patient. There would be a treadmill alongside the tech's desk, with the treadmill telemetry unit on the desk. The duplex Doppler imaging scanner would be on one side of the bed. A resuscitation cart should be nearby. Other equipment can be stored on a mobile cart. The room

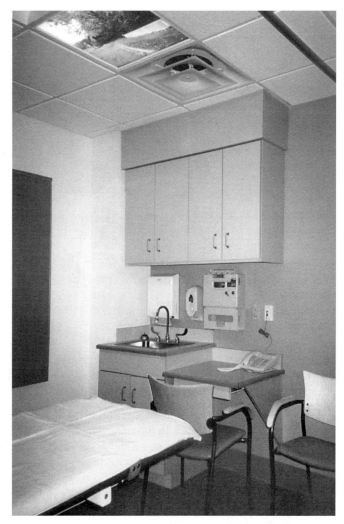

Figure 3-62. Examination room for Doppler ultrasonic imaging features a back-lit film transparency of a view of nature overhead. (*Interior design: Jain Malkin Inc.; Photographer: Jain Malkin.*)

needs to be large enough to accommodate all this equipment (Figure 3-59). The same consideration with respect to dimming of room lights, quiet, and control of glare, hold true in a vascular lab, as they do for echocardiography.

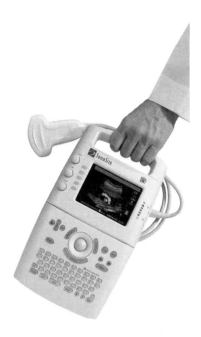

Figure 3-63. Handheld SonoSite 180 portable ultrasound system. (*Photo courtesy: SonoSite, Inc., Bothell, WA.*)

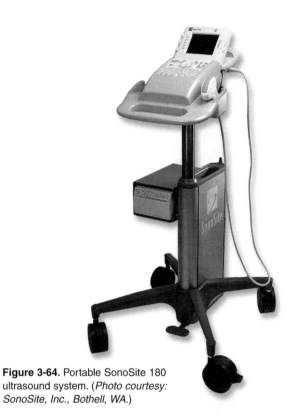

Figure 3-64. Portable SonoSite 180 ultrasound system. (*Photo courtesy: SonoSite, Inc., Bothell, WA.*)

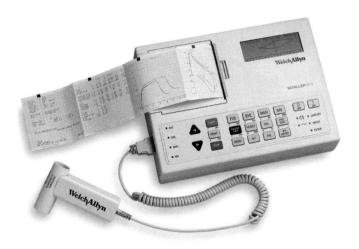

Figure 3-65. Spirometer (the disposable flow sensor eliminates the need to sterilize between patients). (*Photo courtesy: Welch Allyn®, Skaneates Falls, NY.*)

A portable ultrasound unit (Figures 3-63 and 3-64) that can be used in a vascular lab, in the operating room (OR), or in a physician's office for basic examinations is gaining in popularity. It shows the velocity of blood flow but at present is not duplex Doppler. This unit can be used for OB-GYN and other specialties such as cardiology. Exam presets exist within the system. For example, if one plugs in a transvaginal probe, one will automatically access the exams appropriate for that transducer. Therefore, this instrument can be used in a variety of settings.

Pulmonary Function Testing

People with impaired lung functions are diagnosed in the pulmonary function lab. Pulmonary dysfunction may be acute or chronic. A patient recovering from pneumonia,

for example, may need assessment and nebulizer treatment for a finite period but a patient with lung cancer or emphysema may need long-term evaluation and treatment for the remainder of his or her life. The composition of a pulmonary specialist's practice (age of patients, volume of patients, proximity to a hospital's outpatient respiratory therapy unit) will determine the extent, if any, to which inhalation therapy is done within the office.

The spirometer, an instrument for measuring *lung capacity* (Figure 3-65), is the basic tool for pulmonary function studies. It, along with an analysis of blood gases and other clinical tests, helps the physician to evaluate the extent and nature of lung damage. A bronchodilator medication is often administered when spirometer studies are performed.

Pulmonary function studies are noninvasive and can be performed quickly and inexpensively with computer calculations and comparisons to predicted normal values. These studies allow the physician to monitor the course of disease and to measure the effects of therapeutic intervention.

Those seeking treatment may complain of shortness of breath, chronic cough, allergic manifestations, or dizziness, or they may suffer from exposure to noxious dusts and fumes. Spirometry is generally included in annual routine health examinations, and it is required by law as part of the mandated screening program for people who are occupationally exposed to hazardous fumes. Pulmonary function testing (also called PFT) provides a quantitative estimation of lung impairment.

In this specialty, as in many others, declining reimbursement in recent years has led physicians to make fewer investments in equipment and the additional space that may be required to accommodate it. Patients requiring more complicated tests would likely be referred to a hospital's outpatient pulmonary medicine.

Most pulmonologists will have, in their offices, spirometry, ECG, and a method of measuring stress on the heart and lungs via a bike or treadmill hooked up to a sophisticated instrument that can measure and integrate several modalities.

In recent years, spirometers have become miniaturized (Figure 3-66). With pneumotachometers, spirometers also measure the flow of expired air from the lungs. Diagnostic instruments may be combined in a microprocessor-based complete pulmonary function system (Figure 3-67) that measures lung volume, residual volume, and diffusion (how gases pass into the blood). The metabolic analyzer (also called a metabolic "cart") measures oxygen consumption and carbon dioxide production. Used with an exercise bike or a treadmill (Figure 3-68), it measures, through expired gases, the cardiopulmonary stress response to a graduated workload. It is also used in sports medicine facilities to train athletes and in rehab settings. It should be noted that arterial blood gases can be measured before, during, and after exercise testing.

Although many pulmonologists would not have this equipment in their offices, one would find a body *plethysmograph* or "body box" (Figure 3-69) in a large clinic set-

Figure 3-66. Spirometer. (*Photo courtesy: Medical Graphics Corporation, St. Paul, MN.*)

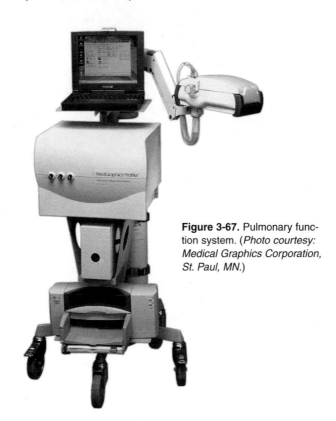

Figure 3-67. Pulmonary function system. (*Photo courtesy: Medical Graphics Corporation, St. Paul, MN.*)

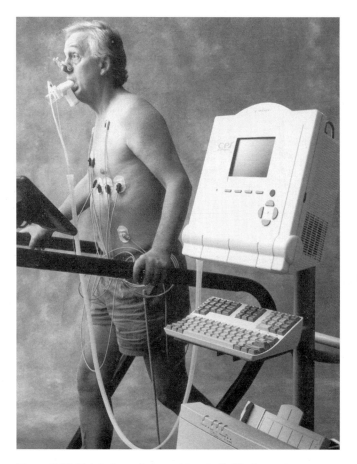

Figure 3-68. Metabolic analyzer and treadmill. (*Photo courtesy: Medical Graphics Corporation, St. Paul, MN.*)

Figure 3-69. Plethysmograph for pulmonary function studies. (*Photo courtesy: Medical Graphics Corporation, St. Paul, MN*)

ting. Along with complete pulmonary function capabilities, it measures thoracic lung volumes, airway resistance, and specific airway conductance. The technician sits outside to observe and coach the patient who is seated inside the pressure-type "body box." The unit is approximately 30×42 inches in size.

Once the patient has been screened, the treatment phase would be called *inhalation* or *respiratory therapy.* The treatment generally consists of breathing mechanically pressurized air with medication. Currently, most patients' treatment can be managed by the use of nebu-

lizers (inhalers) in the home, greatly reducing the use of the Bird intermittent positive-pressure breathing (IPPB) apparatus, which may require an outpatient visit, but can be rented for home use. Nebulizers are devices for aerosolizing metered doses of medications such as antibiotics and bronchodilators to the lungs to thin mucous secretions. The Bird IPPB machine would not be found in a physician's office but may be available in a large clinic or hospital; therefore, accommodation for this device will not be discussed here. The treatment might also consist of chest physiotherapy, in which a patient lies

80'-0"

32'-0"

EXAM TABLE

BIKE

TREADMILL

NURSE STATION

METABOLIC CART   ECG

REF.

PFT

SPIROMETER

REF.

STAFF LOUNGE

TOILET

TOILET

EXAM

EXAM

CONSULT

EXAM

CONSULT

DRESSING CUBICLES

EXAM

EXAM

EXAM

BOOK./INSUR.

DISPLAY

RECEPTION

BUS. OFF.

CHARTS

COPY

PATIENT EDUCATION

WAITING

INTERNAL MEDICINE

2640 SF

Figure 3-70. Space plan for internal medicine, 2640 square feet. (*Design: Jain Malkin Inc.*)

on an angled bed and gravity flow drains different lobes of the lung. The therapist, after administering bronchodilator medication, cups the patient's back, and the patient coughs up the mucous.

Layout of Rooms

There is no generally accepted standard layout for a pulmonary function lab because it depends largely on the specific pieces of equipment the practitioner has and whether cardiovascular screening will be included. In the last instance, it is called a *cardiopulmonary lab.* Figure 3-70 shows a layout in which PFT and cardiopulmonary screening are performed.

Typically, in such a combined setting, one might have an ergometer exercise bicycle, a treadmill, telemetry, a physical therapy–type table, ECG, spirometer, a crash cart with defibrillator and oxygen, and a desk for the tech. One may also find a computerized metabolic testing unit (Figure 3-67) used primarily with an exercise bike, occasionally with a treadmill, previously discussed.

The majority of pulmonologists do only diagnostic testing in their offices and then refer the patient to a hospital outpatient facility for inhalation therapy, if the use of in-home nebulizers is not adequate. But this is rare; most treatment can be provided in the home.

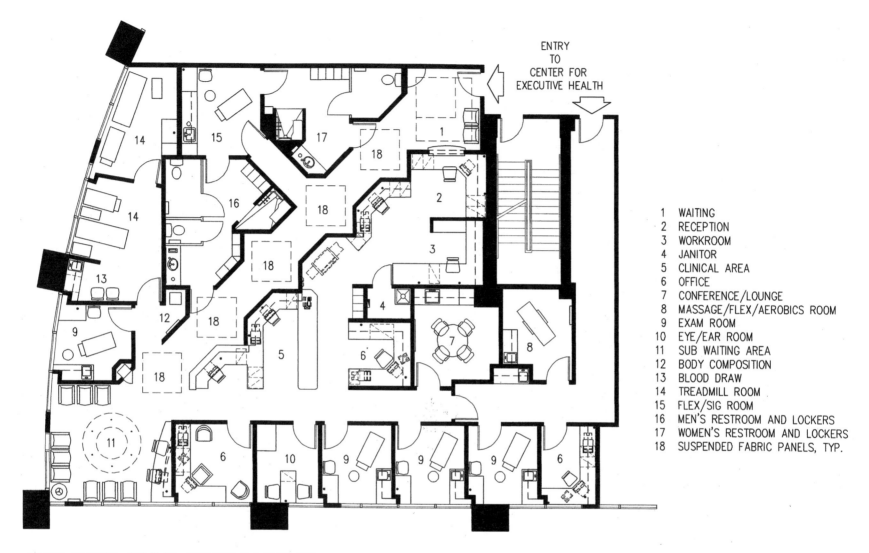

ENTRY TO CENTER FOR EXECUTIVE HEALTH

1 WAITING
2 RECEPTION
3 WORKROOM
4 JANITOR
5 CLINICAL AREA
6 OFFICE
7 CONFERENCE/LOUNGE
8 MASSAGE/FLEX/AEROBICS ROOM
9 EXAM ROOM
10 EYE/EAR ROOM
11 SUB WAITING AREA
12 BODY COMPOSITION
13 BLOOD DRAW
14 TREADMILL ROOM
15 FLEX/SIG ROOM
16 MEN'S RESTROOM AND LOCKERS
17 WOMEN'S RESTROOM AND LOCKERS
18 SUSPENDED FABRIC PANELS, TYP.

CENTER FOR EXECUTIVE HEALTH

3484 SF

Figure 3-71. Space plan for health assessment/screening clinic located at Scripps Memorial Hospital, La Jolla, CA. (*Interior architecture and design: Jain Malkin Inc.*)

Accommodating the equipment shown in Figure 3-69 requires considerable space as each patient needs privacy. If no partitions, screens, or curtains exist in the room, then it can only be used for one patient at a time, despite the inventory of equipment and diagnostic instrumentation.

Executive Health Centers. Sometimes a cardiopulmonary lab is part of an executive health screening facility (Figure 3-71) and, if so, a high-profile "corporate" image may be appropriate. Windows are a desirable feature in this room. A wood-look sheet vinyl floor is less institutional than vinyl composition tile and easy to maintain, but carpet is also functional.

Tech Work Areas

In general, technicians are able to operate multiple types of diagnostic instruments since equipment is so automated it requires little training. Pulmonary function studies, and certainly respiratory therapy, require a trained respiratory therapist or nurse or an aide with PFT training. The volume of patients would determine staffing for ECG, Holter, echocardiography, and pulmonary testing. Techs often have workstations or desks in the room with the equipment so they can monitor the patient while doing desk work. Their work areas need to have space for supplies used in the procedures, a place to store microcassettes or tapes of patients' test results, and file cabinets for computer printouts of test results. In the future, compressed digital storage will become more common.

Physicians' Consults

Physicians are always present or nearby when stress testing is done. Therefore, consultation rooms for the cardiologists and pulmonologists associated with the testing should be adjacent to the test area.

Sigmoidoscopy

Both a general internal medicine physician who does not have a subspecialty in gastroenterology and a family practice physician would likely use a multipurpose procedure room for the occasional need to look at an unprepped colon. The patient would be given a Fleet enema prior to the procedure to empty the lower portion of the colon and this would enable the physician to check for anal fissures, bleeding or a tear in the sphincter. Patients would be referred to a colon and rectal surgeon if any repair was indicated.

Internists with a subspecialty in gastroenterology (whether in a subspecialty practice or part of a general internal medicine practice) would most likely have a dedicated room for what is called "flex sig" examinations of the lower colon with a flexible sigmoidoscope, a tube with fiber-optic light, an eyepiece at one end, and a tiny camera at the other. The patient is asked to adhere to a liquid diet the day before the procedure, then "prepare" the colon with a Fleet enema for the procedure, usually scheduled the next morning. The patient is not sedated and the procedure causes only mild and momentary discomfort. Therefore, no prep or recovery rooms are required; however, a workroom (6×8 feet) opening onto the procedure room is ideal (Figure 3-52) to provide suitable accommodation for washing and drying the scopes, which are very expensive and delicate and must be handled with care. A toilet room should open onto the flex sig room (Figure 3-52).

Layout of Procedure Room
A procedure room 10×12 feet in size is adequate. If space is tight, although it's not ideal, the washing and drying of scopes can be handled in the procedure room (as in Figure 3-72), where flex sig is part of a multiphasic executive health screening clinic. In this instance, the scopes are soaked in trays containing glutaraldehyde (a powerful disinfectant) placed on the countertop. Glutaraldehyde has a strong odor that must be exhausted from the room (note air grille running horizontally in the sink backsplash) to the exterior of the building. With adequate ventilation,

Figure 3-72. Flexible sigmoidoscopy examination room located at Center for Executive Health. (*Interior architecture and design: Jain Malkin Inc.; Photographer: Steve McClelland.*)

there is no detectable chemical odor. The tall cabinet at left contains drying racks for the scopes. Details are covered in the Endoscopy section.

The examination table used for a sigmoid procedure is usually larger than a standard exam table and is often motorized to adjust the height and position of the patient. In laying out the exam table and casework in this room, it is important to note that the patient lies on his or her left side with knees bent with the physician, obviously, working from behind the patient. A nurse usually stands at the

patient's head to help relax the patient and provide reassurance.

Internal Medicine—Summary

A large internal medicine suite (5000 to 7000 square feet) will have a sigmoidoscopy room, an ECG room with treadmill, and a lab with its own waiting area, blood draw, and toilet with specimen pass-through. Certain types of X-rays may be done in the office and, if so, an X-ray room with adjoining darkroom and film viewing area will be included in the suite. The business office in a suite of this size will be composed of separate rooms for transcription, business manager, insurance, medical records, bookkeeper, and receptionist. A sizable staff lounge should also be included. The reader is referred to Chapter 6 for guidance in designing suites of this size.

Endoscopy

The development of fiber optics has made possible the examination of the colon, the lungs (bronchoscopy), and the upper gastrointestinal tract with an endoscope. This noninvasive instrument has revolutionized surgery, by reducing problems from invasive surgery and helping doctors detect, and in some cases treat, diseases at an early stage. These 4- to 5-foot-long flexible "tubes" have powerful fiber-optic lights and allow viewing through an eyepiece (fiberscope) or, most often, on a separate video monitor (videoscope). Light is transmitted down the tube to enable the internist to examine the colon, for example, in search of tumors or polyps. The procedure is viewed, in real time, on a video monitor placed on a cart or a ceiling-mounted arm, visible to both patient and physician during the procedure (Figure 3-73). At any point, the physician can print a photo to give to the patient or save an image to a computer for later use and comparison.

Endoscopies would generally not be performed in a physician's office unless it were a large clinic with a specialized suite designed to meet all life safety requirements. A medical office building may have an endoscopy center set up as an independent business

Figure 3-73. Proximal video camera system with standard eyepiece coupler for use with flexible fiberoptic endoscopes. (*Photo courtesy: Welch Allyn®, Skaneates Falls, NY.*)

for the convenience of gastroenterologists in the building. It would most likely be owned by gastroenterologists and, if the center is properly designed and accredited, any qualified physician could have privileges there. Sometimes endoscopies are performed in ambulatory surgery centers in special rooms dedicated to this purpose.

Endoscopy on the Rise

In recent years, colon cancer has been given considerable exposure in the news media, greatly increasing the volume of procedures both for flex sig (examining the lower 6 inches of the colon) and for colonoscopy (examining the upper and lower colon with the scope penetrating as far as 6 feet). In 2000, the ongoing debate about the efficacy of colonoscopy (an expensive procedure and one that insurance companies and HMOs would rather not pay for) in terms of saving lives tilted in favor of the procedure for individuals over 45 years of age. In fact, because many precancerous polyps occur in the upper colon where they cannot be seen in a flex sig procedure, many now view that procedure with skepticism as it may give a false sense of security. Despite this, because it is an inexpensive screening tool, flex sigs are often performed as part of a comprehensive physical examination for adults.

As further evidence of this trend, in 2000, CEO David Lawrence announced that Kaiser Permanente Health Plan would offer colonoscopy to all members over a certain age, even though the enormous cost to provide this examination would impose short-range economic hardship and the benefits would not be realized unless the member (patient) stayed with Kaiser for many years. Kaiser's mission is to form lifelong partnerships with its members and, therefore, it is in Kaiser's best interest to keep members healthy. The economic benefits of early detection and treatment are well known and often offset the cost of early screening.

For all of these reasons, including the aging population demographic, the volume of endoscopy procedures will increase as will the need to design efficient suites.

Components of an Endoscopy Suite

An endoscopy suite would include:

- Procedure room

- Dressing area with lockers for male/female (M/F) staff

- Dressing area with lockers for patients

- Bathrooms (patients and staff)

- Workroom between procedure rooms

- Prep and recovery room

- Physicians' dictation/charting

- Reception/administration/waiting

- Linen storage

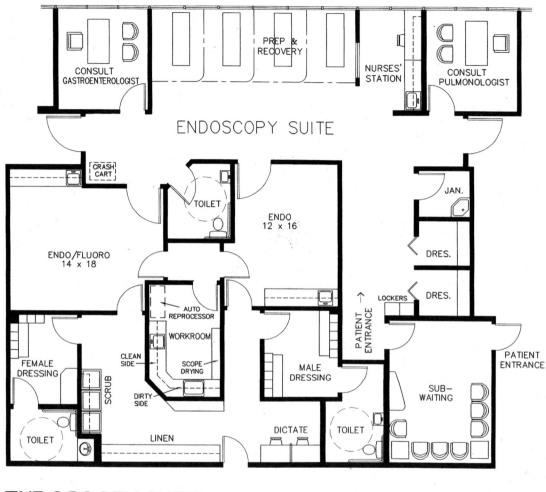

ENDOSCOPY SUITE

ENDOSCOPY SUITE
2737 SF

Figure 3-74. Layout of endoscopy suite, 2737 square feet. (*Design: Jain Malkin Inc.*)

The same procedure room can be used by pulmonologists to do bronchoscopies and by gastroenterologists to examine the upper GI tract (esophagus, duodenum, and stomach) and the lower GI tract (colon). As a point of information, endoscopy procedure rooms are not considered sterile. However, there is a benefit to having dedicated rooms when a high volume of physicians use the facility and a high volume of cases exists. Many hospitals, in fact, separate rooms by function in order to do more procedures simultaneously and to facilitate scheduling with physicians.

In a large group practice or a multispecialty ambulatory clinic, one might find a layout of rooms similar to that shown in Figure 3-74. The number of procedure rooms is related to the projected volume of cases. Procedure rooms must be large enough to accommodate a Stryker cart or gurney, the endoscopy cart with video monitor, considerable storage for clean linen and supplies, and a resuscitation cart (Figure 3-75). Hampers for soiled linen and a clock with second hand are also required. The floor should be sheet vinyl with a self-coved base. The door to the room must be wide enough to accommodate gurney traffic. Rooms need central oxygen and suction, ideally coming from the ceiling. There are typically two monitors on the endo cart, one is video for the procedure and the other for patient information. The patient is given conscious sedation through a vein in his or her arm or hand.

The patient may intermittently wake up and watch the procedure, then doze off, but there is no memory of pain or discomfort afterward.

Procedure Room Lighting. Room lighting is darkened during this procedure. Indirect perimeter lighting, which could be dimmed, combined with standard 2×4 fluorescents overhead, when more light is required, would be ideal.

Fluoroscopic Examinations. Fluoroscopy may be used in a large procedure room with a C-arm X-ray to explore bile

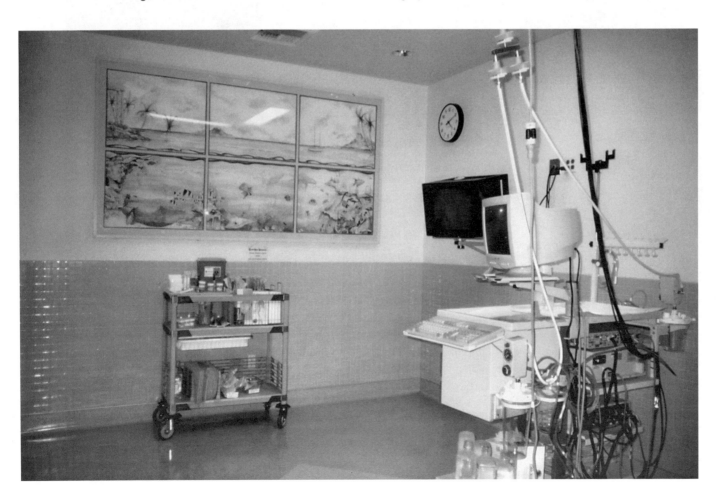

Figure 3-75. Endoscopy procedure room. (*Photographer: Jain Malkin.*)

Internal Medicine **83**

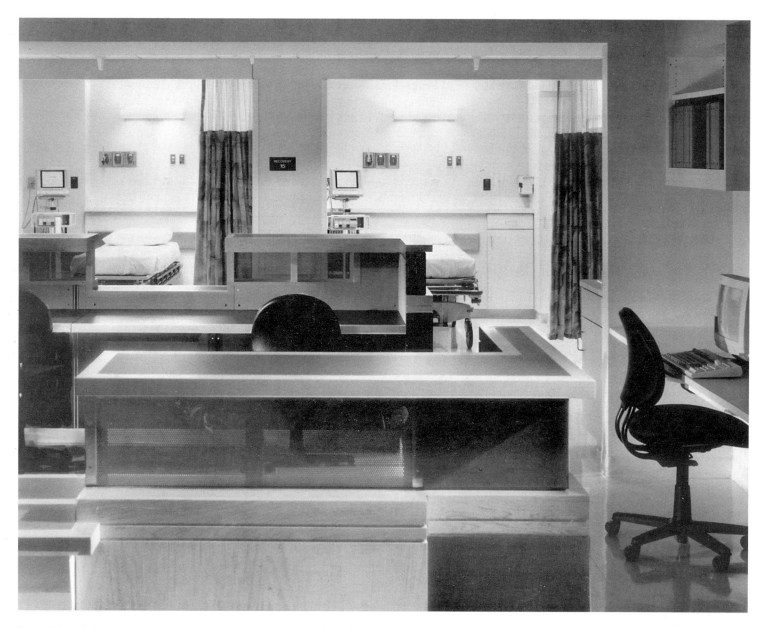

Figure 3-76. Endoscopy recovery area provides maximum privacy for patients and gives nurses maximum visibility. Saint Francis Hospital, Hartford, CT. (*Interior architecture and design: TRO/The Ritchie Organization, Newton, MA; Photographer: Hedrich Blessing.*)

ducts and the pancreas during an upper GI exam. These organs are accessed through the duodenum with tools that feed through the scope tube into those small ducts where the camera on the end of the scope won't fit. Contrast media are injected into the organ. This is called ERCP (endoscopic retrograde colangio-pancreatography).

Flow

Patients are typically prepped and recovered in the same area. Figure 3-76 shows an attractively designed hospital-based prep/recovery area with private rooms, while Figure 3-77 shows a prep/recovery area in a medical office building endoscopy center. Patients often remove their clothes and change into a gown with the cubicle curtain closed, and their clothes are stored in a basket under the gurney, which follows the patient into the procedure room which negating the need for dressing rooms. The gurney is usually used as the procedure table since it can be adjusted in height and saves time in not having to transfer the patient to another table. The nurse sets up a monitor in the prep area for blood pressure and pulse oximetry and this monitor follows the patient into the procedure room. A monitor that attaches to the gurney is best so that two people (one for the gurney and one for the monitor stand) do not have to transport the patient into the procedure room and back again.

The patient is continually monitored during the procedure and given oxygen, as needed. The recovery period is generally 30 minutes during which time patients are monitored and observed by a nurse. Physicians will often dictate between patients or after several are seen in a morning. These procedures are usually performed in the morning for the convenience of patients who are required to fast and not drink water.

Workroom for Cleaning Scopes

This is one of the most important rooms in the suite. All equipment is cleaned and readied for use in this room. Supplies are stored here, as are the cleaned scopes, which are typically hung in a long cabinet with glass doors (Figure 3-78). Scopes are very expensive and are handled with great care.

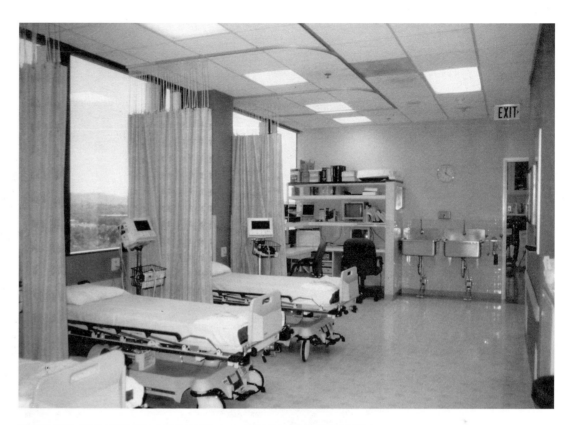

Figure 3-77. Endoscopy prep and recovery area. (*Photographer: Jain Malkin.*)

Some technicians prefer a separate sink for cleaning scopes used In upper GI and bronchoscopy procedures. In any case, a workroom requires at least two sinks set into countertops at right angles to each other or parallel. The sinks need to be deep and should be *lower* than the standard 34-inch-high countertop. For most people, a 30-inch height is fine. As the scopes are long and require quite a bit of handling to properly clean, the lowered sink is more comfortable.

The nurse or tech spends a few minutes precleaning and leak-testing the scope after each procedure, then manually reprocessing or putting the scope in an AER (automated endoscope reprocessor). The nurse also preps each patient. Therefore, it is unlikely the same

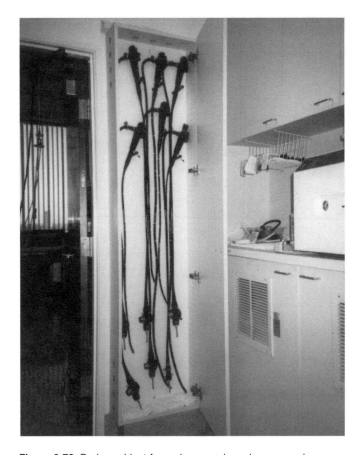

Figure 3-78. Drying cabinet for endoscopes in endoscopy workroom. (*Photographer: Jain Malkin.*)

person can also keep an eye on recovering patients while reprocessing scopes. Somewhere in the suite, if not in the workroom, there need to be deep cabinets for storing disposables, room for the scope transport cases (these look like hard-shell briefcases), and shelves for large binders for storing the forceps used in biopsies. Each forceps is specific to each size scope, and these are often color-coded by the staff into binders for easy retrieval.

The workroom is a busy area, packed with instruments, sterilization equipment, bottles of solutions, racks, and more. It can easily become cluttered, and therefore the room size should not be underestimated (Figure 3-79). A room 8×14 feet is the minimum functional size.

Infection Control Issues. Endoscopic procedure rooms are clean, but not sterile. GI scopes are cleaned with liquid chemical germicide (LCG) using a very specific procedure, which can be facilitated or impeded by the layout of the room, the height of the sink, and the locations of air and suction. Scopes used for bronchoscopies are usually cleaned by sterile technique. With tuberculosis on the rise, strict infection-control procedures must be followed. Proper reprocessing of endoscopes cannot and should not be underestimated as it enhances and contributes to patient safety. Attention to reprocessing equipment, procedures, and facility design can have enormous economic benefits or drawbacks.

Cleaning Process—Overview. Scopes must be reprocessed with a protocol developed by the scope manufacturer, LCG manufacturer, AER manufacturer, appropriate professional organizations such as SGNA (Society of Gastroenterology Nurses and Associates, Inc.) and AORN (Association of periOperative Registered Nurses), and all appropriate regulatory bodies. Scopes are always precleaned by drawing water and detergent into them, soaking, washing, scrubbing, and inserting a cleaning brush through the channels as part of the process. They are leak-tested in the sink. At this point, they can be high-level disinfected by manually soaking in trays containing glutaraldehyde or in an automated endoscope reprocessor. In the manual process, scopes are rinsed off after soaking, then taken to the "clean side" to blow out with compressed air, and hung in a cabinet to dry.

Liquid chemical germicides recently introduced into the market have reduced soak times in the AER to as low as 5 minutes (from previous lows of 20 minutes). Ten air exchanges per hour or a filter device to limit vapor exposure are usually recommended when using glutaraldehyde and other LCGs. Although neutralization is seldom required, the LCG can usually be neutralized in a 5-gallon carboy and then dumped down the drain (a

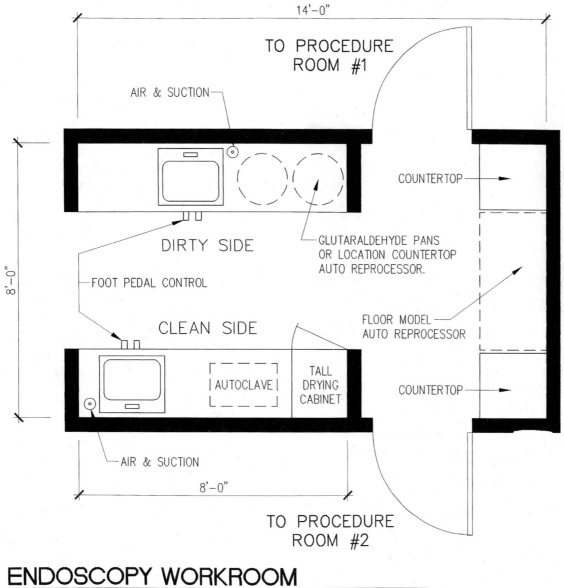

14'-0"

TO PROCEDURE
ROOM #1

AIR & SUCTION

8'-0"

COUNTERTOP

DIRTY SIDE

GLUTARALDEHYDE PANS
OR LOCATION COUNTERTOP
AUTO REPROCESSOR.

FOOT PEDAL CONTROL

CLEAN SIDE

FLOOR MODEL
AUTO REPROCESSOR

AUTOCLAVE

TALL
DRYING
CABINET

COUNTERTOP

AIR & SUCTION

8'-0"

TO PROCEDURE
ROOM #2

ENDOSCOPY WORKROOM

Figure 3-79. Layout of endoscopy workroom. (*Design: Jain Malkin Inc.*)

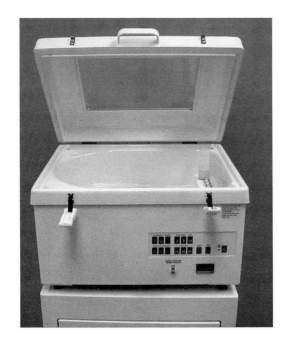

Figure 3-80. Countertop model endoscopy automatic reprocessor unit. (*Photo courtesy: Medivators Inc., Eagan, MN.*)

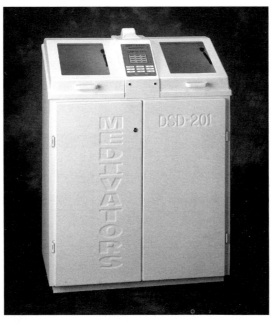

Figure 3-81. Floor model endoscope automatic reprocessor unit. (*Photo courtesy: Medivators Inc., Eagan, MN*)

Biopsy forceps and endotherapy devices introduced down the scope channels are of the one-time disposable or reusable type. The reprocessing protocol involves immersion in detergent, ultrasonic cleaning, rinsing, lubrication, followed by steam sterilization in an autoclave.

Glutaraldehyde Ventilation Strategies. Glutaraldehyde is used for cold sterilization and high-level disinfection of medical instruments. Although not proven to be a carcinogenic agent, it is an irritant that can be absorbed by inhalation, by ingestion, and through the skin. It has a strong odor and requires specific ventilation measures, including*:

- 10 air exchanges per hour

- A room large enough to ensure adequate dilution of vapors

- Exhaust vents located at the source of the vapor discharge (Figure 3-71—note exhaust grille at rear of sink)

- Additional exhaust vents at floor level (glutaraldehyde vapors are heavier than air and this pulls the vapors down away from the breathing zone)

- Fresh air supply at ceiling across (opposite) from exhaust vents

- Consideration of outside air intakes, windows, or other openings to prevent re-entry of discharged vapor or exposure to other occupancies—this air must not be recirculated

- Employing scope cleaning procedures and taking air samples to monitor vapor levels at completion of construction

Layout of Workroom. The room should have a dirty side and a clean side, with the dirty side being larger.

*The above recommendations are from *The Safe and Effective Handling of Glutaraldehyde Solutions,* SGNA Monograph Series, ©1996 Society of Gastroenterology Nurses and Associates, Inc., Chicago.

floor drain facilitates the process). AERs include detergent, disinfectant, filtered water, air, and alcohol treatment cycles. They are designed to minimize chemical vapors and exposure and ensure a uniformly reprocessed instrument. Each AER usually requires a ½-inch water line with an accessible shutoff valve capable of providing 2 to 4 gallons of flow per minute, potable cold or hot water, a floor drain, and typically 120 volts ac (alternating current) with a 20-ampere line (fused and dedicated circuit). Suction and air connections are not required. The machines have internal air compressors that inject air through the endoscope channels. The countertop model in Figure 3-80 is designed for facilities that process more than 100 procedures per month, whereas the dual-basin floor model in Figure 3-81 is intended for higher volume.

Dirty Side. The deep, large sink at 30-inch height would have a countertop space on the right and left. The dirty scope would be laid down on the left, held in the sink to be manually washed with brushes, then placed in the automatic disinfector reprocessor or soaked in trays to the right of the sink. Suction should be placed on the right side of the sink. The autoclave can be placed on the clean or dirty side. After the scopes are disinfected, they are rinsed off, then carried to the clean side to blow out with air and hung to dry. Even with the automatic reprocessor, scopes need to be hung in a drying cabinet. Locate a rack for gloves near the sink.

Clean Side. The sink should be on the right side with most of the countertop on the left. The sink here should also be lowered. Alcohol is used in the final stage of reprocessing. It is induced into the channels of the scope by syringe to dry any remaining water. Then the channels must be purged by air. Compressed air is needed on the right side of the sink. (The air compressor fits under the sink.) Bacteria grow quickly in damp, dark places. Therefore, air is used to blow dry all of the channels, and scopes must be hung in a tall cabinet so that they can be fully extended whether manual or automatic reprocessing (Figure 3-77). Locate a rack for gloves near the sink. A 6-inch-deep shelf over the sink is very useful on both the dirty and clean sides.

Miscellaneous Considerations. City water needs to be filtered; it's too contaminated. With the automatic reprocessor machines, leave space for an external pre-filtration system. Foot-pedal control for water at both sinks is ideal, but it must be a high-quality unit that has good temperature control and provides adequate flow.

Storage. Provide adequate storage in the workroom for boxes of gloves, masks, and disposable gowns, which provide a better barrier than linen. Storage for many gallon bottles of solutions must be accommodated.

Regulatory Agencies. Endoscopy facilities are state licensed, they require Medicare certification, and it is anticipated that they will soon have to be accredited by JCAHO or AAAHC (see Chapter 15) in order to get managed care contracts.

Recovery Room
The recovery room is standard in all respects, with oxygen and suction at each bed and privacy curtains separating each patient. Recovery time is normally half an hour, and recovering patients should be in view of nursing staff (Figures 3-73 and 3-75).

Interior Design

The interior design of an internal medicine suite should be tailored to the functional needs of the patient population. If the internist is a cardiologist or a pulmonologist, for example, those patients may, for the most part, be elderly. Therefore, a conservative color palette and furnishings might be appropriate. An oncologist, on the other hand, would have a broad age range of patients and a more upbeat design might be in order. A more important consideration is the socioeconomic level of the patients served to tune the design to their expectations and comfort. Color Plate 4, Figure 3-82, is a cardiac surgeon's waiting room. Patients visit the office preoperatively and postoperatively, on two or three afternoons a week. The remainder of the time, the office is a home away from home for the surgeon —a place to relax, sleep, prepare slides for lectures, and meet with colleagues to discuss cases.

PEDIATRICS

A pediatrician treats children from birth through adolescence (age 18). The office visits are frequent and of relatively short duration in the exam room, but frequently involve a protracted period of time in the waiting room. This is a high-volume specialty, and the practice is almost always composed of two or more physicians. It is rare to find more than three pediatricians working in the same office, although a busy practice may staff a second or third office.

Waiting Room

Waiting rooms must be larger than for other specialties, as parents often bring all their children and sometimes a grandparent, when one child has to visit the doctor. Pediatric offices often have a *sick-baby,* or contagious, waiting room and a *well-baby* waiting room (Figure 3-83). The reason for this is to limit contagion. Since physicians do not make house calls, children with infectious diseases are brought into the office, where well children who are waiting for a routine checkup or an injection are vulnerable to contracting them.

If space is limited, a sick-baby waiting room can be devised by direct entry into an exam room (Figure 3-84).

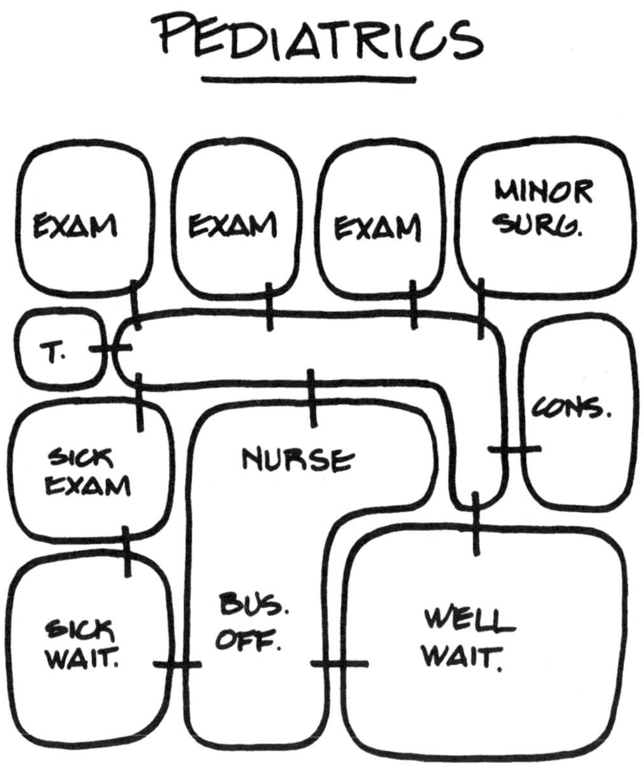

PEDIATRICS

Figure 3-83. Schematic diagram of pediatrics suite.

Table 3-3.
Analysis of Program.
Pediatrics

No. of Physicians:		2		3
Business Office		12×16=192		14×18=252
Exam Rooms[a]	6@	8×10=480	9@	8×10=720
Adolescent Exam		8×12=96		8×12=96
Minor Surgery		—		12×12=144
Toilets	2@	7×8=112	2@	7×8=112
Consultation Room	2@	10×12=240	3@	10×12=360
Nurse Station		10×12=120		12×12=144
Staff Lounge		10×12=120		10×12=120
Waiting Room/Sick Baby 1		2×14=168		12×14=168
Well Baby		18×20=360		22×26=572
Storage		6×8=48		6×8=48
Subtotal		1936 ft^2		2736 ft^2
20% Circulation		387		547
Total		2323 ft^2		3283 ft^2

[a]Designer may wish to make one exam room 10x12 feet for use as a minor surgery room, as well as provide a staff lounge, if space permits.

One exam room would have a door to the outside or building corridor, as the case may be, and would have a buzzer or bell to summon the nurse for entry. The nurse would tell the mother, over the phone, to come to that door and buzz. The door would be marked *Contagious Entrance.* The sick-baby exam should be near a toilet, and the room must have a sink.

If the suite is large enough to have a contagious waiting room, one exam room in close proximity to the waiting room should be designed as a sick-baby exam room, with a sink cabinet and a toilet nearby. The other exam rooms should be clustered around the nurse station (Figure 3-85).

In this specialty, it is a good idea to have a toilet accessible from the waiting room so that parents may change diapers in advance of entering the exam room, and the

PEDIATRICS

2992 SF

Figure 3-84. Space plan for pediatrics, 2992 square feet. (*Design: Jain Malkin Inc.*)

60'-0"

40'-0"

CONSULT

BABY CHANGING STATION

HANDI. TLT.

EXAM

SCALE

SIBLINGS EXAM

SCALE

EXAM

EXAM

MINOR SURGERY

EXAM

EXAM

CONSULT

STORAGE

REF

SHOTS

NURSE

CHARTS

STAFF LOUNGE

REF

HANDI. TLT.

BABY CHANGING STATION

INFANT SHELF

PLAY PIT

WELL-BABY WAITING

SICK BABY WAITING

COPY

CHARTS

RECEPTION

BOOK.

BUILT-IN SEATING

PEDIATRICS
2400 SF

Figure 3-85. Space plan for pediatrics, 2400 square feet. (*Design: Jain Malkin Inc.*)

Figure 3-86. Fold-down baby changing station. (*Photo courtesy: Koala Corporation, Denver, CO.*)

Figure 3-87. Toddler seat. (*Photo courtesy: Koala Corporation, Denver, CO.*)

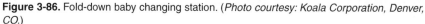

staff is not continually interrupted in order to direct children to the bathroom (Figures 3-83 and 3-84). The bathroom should have a sink countertop large enough to change diapers on, a shelf for disposable diapers, talcum and paper towels, and a large trash receptacle. An amenity is a wall-mounted, drop-down baby changing station (Figure 3-86). A wall-mounted seat keeps toddlers secure while a parent uses the restroom (Figure 3-87). A compactor for dirty diapers, purchased at a baby store, would be useful.

Doctors disagree on the practicality of having a child's-height drinking fountain in the waiting room. If the room is not well supervised, it can lead to mayhem.

The waiting room should contain some tables or flat areas built into the seating where parents can put down an infant in a carrier without occupying an adult's seat (Figure 3-88). A pediatric waiting room may be as large as space and budget permit. Each patient is accompanied by one to three people. Children can get pretty rowdy playing in a pediatrician's waiting room, so an effort

Figure 3-88. Pediatric waiting room. Note magnetized tic-tac-toe board at rear of playpit. (*Design: Jain Malkin Inc.; Photographer: John Waggaman.*)

Figure 3-89. Children's playpit. (*Design: Jain Malkin Inc.; Photographer: Michael Denny.*)

should be made to occupy them with something unique. A carpeted playpit (Figure 3-89) or seating unit (Figure 3-88) can be designed.

Built of plywood, then padded and upholstered with carpet, these custom-built units appeal to children's need for physical movement. Their pent-up energy can be released while "driving" a fire truck (Figure 3-90) or riding "Nessie" (Figure 3-91). In fact, a waiting room that is designed imaginatively can be so appealing to children that it results in tantrums when it is time to leave. Custom play furniture

must be designed to eliminate sharp corners and edges against which a toddler may fall and become injured.

The waiting room should also contain bins for toys and racks for magazines, at a height accessible to children. Pediatricians disagree in their choice of toys for this room. More conservative physicians tend to feel that toys spread infection (drooling on toys, fingers in mouth, etc.) and will limit the type of amusements they condone. Younger pediatricians seem to be more relaxed and icon-oclastic (many refuse to wear white coats, which may

Figure 3-90. Play fire engine. (*Photo courtesy: People Friendly Places, Inc., Northbrook, IL.*)

Figure 3-91. Sea monster. (*Photo courtesy: People Friendly Places, Inc., Northbrook, IL.*)

Figure 3-92. Clown puzzle wallgraphic. (*Design: Jain Malkin Inc.; Photographer: Michael Denny.*)

frighten children) and feel that germs are everywhere and inevitable. If a child is not exposed to germs in the office, he or she will surely be exposed to infection from playmates.

In a pediatric waiting room, one may break the rule about providing individual chairs. One may take liberties in furnishings here, since it is a homogeneous population —mostly parents from the same neighborhood, approximately the same age, and sharing a common interest—

their children. Thus, parents do not seem to mind sitting next to each other in continuous (common seat and back) seating. Figures 3-84, 3-87, and 3-92 show this type of seating, which saves space and accommodates a maximum number of people in a small waiting room. Whatever the type of seating provided, one may wish to provide a few standard-height chairs, with arms, for pregnant women, who often find it difficult to get out of low, lounge-type seating.

Figure 3-93. Pediatric waiting room, community clinic, features saltwater aquarium with built-in bench, recessed niche for TV, and upholstered corral for toddlers. (*Interior design: Jain Malkin Inc.; Photographer: Steve McClelland.*)

Other design ideas for the waiting area include a large built-in saltwater aquarium and an upholstered "corral" to keep toddlers safely in view (Figure 3-93). A clever wall-mounted unit by People Friendly Places, Inc., keeps toddlers engaged (Figure 3-12), while a puppet theater appeals to older kids (Figure 3-94). Colorful wall murals based on children's art would be appropriate for a young patient population (Figure 3-95). A colorful design using geometric patterns would appeal to a larger age range (Color Plate 5, Figure 3-96). A unique des-

tination treatment, with celestial theme, cues wayfinding (Color Plate 6, Figure 3-97). There is no end to the fanciful design ideas that can be implemented in a pediatric office. In the Victor Yacktman outpatient pediatric facility, Color Plate 6, Figures 3-97 and 3-98, public areas feature photos of physicians wearing funny hats and making funny faces. The reader is referred to Chapter 12 for additional information on furnishings and interior finish specifications. Note Figures 12-16, 12-17, and 12-18.

Figure 3-94. Puppet theater in waiting room keeps children occupied. (*Design: Jain Malkin Inc.; Photographer: Jain Malkin.*)

Figure 3-95. Children's art makes wonderful wallgraphics. (*Design: Jain Malkin Inc.; Photographer: John Waggaman.*)

Examination Rooms

Number of Exam Rooms. Each pediatrician should have a minimum of three exam rooms, but four is better. It is important to plan for growth. A pediatric practice grows rapidly, and before long, a two-physician practice with five or six exam rooms will be able to use eight. Thus, the designer should guide the client at the outset to lease a large enough space. Since examinations are short, the physician can quickly move on to the next patient while the mother is dressing the child and the nurse cleaning up the last exam room.

It is a good idea to make one exam room large enough to accommodate an infant exam table and a child's table, since it is more efficient to examine two siblings in the same room (Figure 3-84).

Adolescent Patients. Most pediatric practices (particularly true with older physicians who have been in practice a number of years) must accommodate a number of adolescent patients. A standard-sized adult exam room (8×12 feet) should be provided, with a standard-sized pelvic exam table and decor suitable to a teenager. Care must be taken in the interior design of the office not to gear it too much to infants and toddlers, as it may offend the older patients who are quite sensitive about being considered children. Rooms designed to accommodate older children should have a floor scale. Since children may be shy or modest about being weighed at the nurse station, it is best to have a scale in the exam room (Color Plate 6, Figure 3-97). The family-centered exam room in Figure 3-97 is part of a large outpatient pediatric clinic associated with a hospital.

Location of Sinks. Some physicians consider it unnecessary to have a sink in every exam room if a sink is available nearby in the corridor. However, it is more efficient to have a sink in each exam room, since children may vomit or urinate during an examination and having a sink in the room saves time, by eliminating the need to leave the room in order to clean it up or wash hands. Today, with extreme concern about infection control, a sink in the exam room seems mandatory.

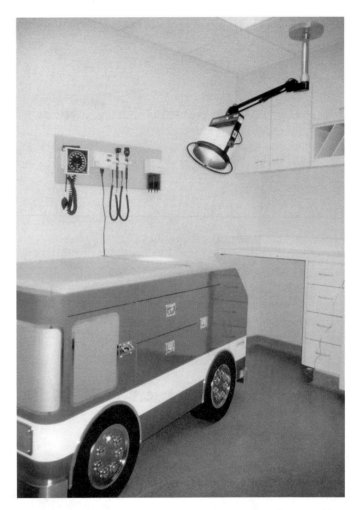

Figure 3-100. Pediatric exam room. Child climbs stairs at foot end of fire truck to reach the tabletop. Exam table by Good Time Medical, Chicago, IL. (*Interior design: Jain Malkin Inc.; Photographer: Jain Malkin.*)

Size of Rooms. Pediatric exam rooms may be quite small, particularly an infant room. They need not have a door that opens to shield the patient. In fact, frequently exam rooms are so small that a pocket door is the most practical solution. An infant room may be no more than 6×8 feet (see Figure 3-83). For a standard (noninfant) pedo exam room, 8×10 feet is a good size. A guest chair for the parent should be included and, if space permits, a small writing desk for the doctor (Color Plate 5, Figure 3-99). The rooms in these space plans may seem small, but pediatricians often prefer to make the exam rooms minimum size in order to squeeze in an "extra" exam room.

Exam Tables. Pediatric exam tables are available as manufactured items (Figures 3-100 and 3-101), but may be custom-built with storage underneath (Figure 3-102). The table must also have a paper roll holder inside the cabinet with a slot in the table top so that a continuous roll of paper can be pulled over the vinyl-covered exam table pad and quickly changed between patients.

The size is 2×4 feet for an infant table (this increases to 6 feet if a lowered portion for a baby scale is included) or 2×6 feet for a child's table. The table is always placed against a wall to minimize the hazard of a child falling off. It should be positioned so that the doctor can examine from the right side of the patient, unless the doctor is left-handed and examines with the left hand. If a lowered area for a baby scale is not incorporated into the table, a portion of the sink cabinet countertop should be lowered for this purpose. It is better, however, to reserve this lowered portion of the sink cabinet for a doctor's writing desk. The infant exam table in Figure 3-103 has a digital scale and digital infantometer to measure infant length (with optional electrical or battery operation).

Figure 3-102. Infant exam room with custom-built exam table with lowered section to accommodate infant scale. (*Design: Jain Malkin Inc.; Photographer: Michael Denny.*)

Figure 3-103. Infant exam table with built-in digital scale and measuring device. (*Photo courtesy: Hausmann Industries, Inc., Northvale, NJ.*)

Figure 3-101. Pediatric exam table with built-in measuring device and space for infant scale. (*Photo courtesy: Good Time Medical, Chicago, IL.*)

PEDIATRICS (PLAN DONE PRIOR TO ADA)

4500 SF

Figure 3-104. Space plan for pediatrics, 4500 square feet. (*Design: Jain Malkin Inc.*)

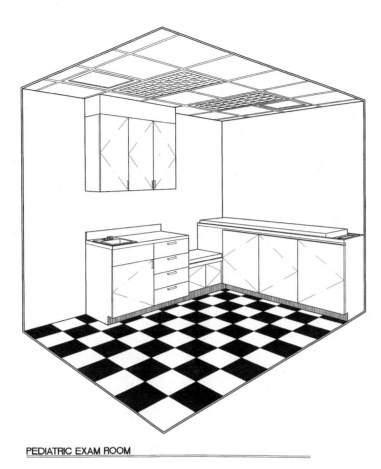

PEDIATRIC EXAM ROOM

Figure 3-105. Pediatric examination table, with wrap-around bench for parent, and sink cabinet. (*Design: Jain Malkin Inc.*)

It is possible to design an exam table that wraps around the corner to incorporate a bench for the parent, a scale space, and a sink cabinet (see Figures 3-104, 3-105, and 3-106). It should be noted that any storage that is accessible to children in an exam room should be locked. Otherwise, they will empty the cabinets regularly or catch their fingers in the doors or drawers.

Some method by which one may measure an infant's length may be incorporated into the exam table (Figure 3-100). The length of the table on one side can be routed

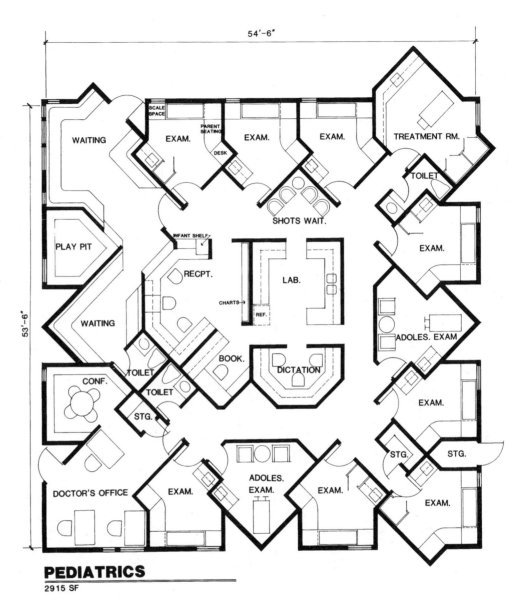

PEDIATRICS
2915 SF

Figure 3-106. Space plan for pediatrics, 2915 square feet. (*Design: Jain Malkin Inc.*)

Figure 3-107. Nurse station, pediatric community clinic. Note infant exam table with scale and measuring device. Blood draw chair fits in niche. (*Interior design: Jain Malkin Inc.; Photographer: Steve McClelland.*)

with a slot for a yardstick, and a sliding wooden arm may be pushed up to the baby's feet to hold the child steady and, at the same time, indicate on the tape the child's length. A table that weighs and measures infants is sometimes located in the nurse station (Figure 3-107).

Interior Design. Exam rooms should be gaily decorated with one or two walls of colorful patterned wallcovering or a wallcovering border placed at a height where children can note it, perhaps a patterned tile floor and ceiling tiles (Color Plate X, Figure 3-98), and artwork of interest to children. Pediatric exam rooms should never be carpeted. Sheet vinyl or vinyl composition tile are recommended. Wallcovering even catches the attention of infants and serves to distract them, thus making the doctor's examination that much easier. One of the papered walls should be the long wall behind the exam table so that babies can see it while lying down. Art images that are pictorial with a lot of detail (items to identify, count, or name the color) can be used by nurses to gauge the developmental status of a young child.

Nurse Station

Pediatric suites require large nurse stations because the nurses administer many injections. After an injection, a patient must be observed for 15 to 20 minutes in order to note any negative reaction to the drug. A few chairs or a bench must be provided either in the corridor adjacent to the nurse station or perhaps within the nurse station (Figure 3-105). The nurse can attend to other business, but still keep a watchful eye on the patient. A full-size refrigerator must be accommodated in the nurse station. Pediatricians who administer allergy shots should have a nurse station located near the front of the suite, so that patients coming just for injections can enter and leave without adding to the congestion in the examination area of the suite. The nurse station should have a knee space area with telephone, space for a microscope, and a double sink.

Business Office

The business office is as described under Family Practice, although sometimes the nurse station can be combined with the business office (Figure 3-84). This is efficient in a small office, as the staff can cover for one another during critical periods of the day.

The pediatric business office should have a reception window facing both the sick and the well waiting rooms (see Figure 3-84). The appointment/cashier counter needs to have a wide shelf or a secure niche in the wall where a parent may put an infant in a carrier while he or she is writing a check or chatting with the staff (Figures 3-83 and 3-84).

The reception window should be designed in such a manner as to appear "friendly" and nonclinical. That shown in Color Plate 7, Figure 3-108, incorporates French windows, ivory painted trim, and a fanciful carpet inset—all very residential in character. The reception window in Figure 3-109 and the adjacent wallgraphic are bright and playful, executed in primary colors.

A busy practice, with perhaps three physicians seeing patients simultaneously, benefits greatly from a separation of incoming and outgoing traffic. Figure 3-103 is designed for patients to enter through one door and leave through another, without exiting through the waiting room. This greatly enhances productivity and reduces crowding and stress. Note that both the reception and the cashier counters are very wide, to accommodate a number of transactions simultaneously. The electrical plan and reflected ceiling plan for this suite (Figure 3-103) can be found in Chapter 13.

Consultation Room

Pediatricians spend little time in a consultation room and seldom see patients there. Therefore, it is not uncommon for two physicians to share a private office (see Figure 3-105). Basically, it is used for housing medical reference books and for returning phone calls. Pediatricians dispense a lot of literature and pamphlets on child care, so

Figure 3-109. Fabric canopy makes a reception desk festive. (*Design: Jain Malkin Inc.; Photographer: Jain Malkin.*)

a wall rack should be provided for the organized storage of these materials, either at the nurse station or in the corridor adjacent to exam rooms.

Corridor

One corridor should be selected for a 20-foot refraction lane. An eye chart would be tacked to a door or placed on the wall at the end of the corridor for a brief eye test. A circle inset into the carpet can mark where the child's heels should be placed to assure a distance of 20 feet. An alternative to this is an automated refractor that sits on a 2-×4-foot table with the patient on one side and the aide or tech on the other or a handheld automated refractor which is even quicker (Figure 4-80). Corridors should be cheerful and may have cartoon characters or colorful graphics (Figure 3-95 and Color Plate 5, Figure 3-96).

Hearing Test Room

Some pediatricians like to do a preliminary hearing test to screen patients who need to be referred to an ENT spe-cialist. Sometimes this can be set up in a dual-purpose room. The hearing test can be performed in a multipurpose consulting room or in a small 8-×8-foot room dedicated to that purpose. One needs a table 24×48 inches on which to place the equipment (Figure 4-143), a chair for the patient, and one for the technician. Walls of the room must have sound insulation and, inside the room, walls may be covered with carpet to provide further sound attenuation. The room should be located at the rear of the suite away from the hectic front office (see Figure 3-104).

Storage

The office needs a small storage room, 6 × 8 feet, for drug samples, disposable supplies, office forms and stationery, and handout pamphlets.

Interior Design

The suite should be colorful and imaginatively designed to reduce the children's anxiety and make them forget any negative associations they may have had about visiting the doctor. All rooms except exam rooms may be carpeted.

CHAPTER 4
Medicine: Specialized Suites

The American Board of Medical Specialties recognizes, as of this writing, 25 medical specialties and about a dozen and a half subspecialties. The specialties are Allergy and Immunology, Anesthesiology, Colon and Rectal Surgery, Dermatology, Family Practice, Internal Medicine, Neurological Surgery, Nuclear Medicine, Obstetrics and Gynecology, Ophthalmol-ogy, Orthopedic Surgery, Otolaryngology, Pathology, Pedi-atrics, Physical Medicine and Rehabilitation, Plastic Surgery, Preventive Medicine, Psychiatry, Neurology, Radiology, General Surgery, Thoracic Surgery, Urology, Emergency Medicine, and Medical Genetics.

Subspecialties under Internal Medicine are Cardiovascular Disease, Endocrinology, Diabetes and Metabolism, Gastro-enterology, Hematology, Infectious Disease, Medical Oncol-ogy, Nephrology, Pulmonary Disease, Rheumatology, Adolescent Medicine, Clinical Cardiac Electrophysiology, Critical Care Medicine, Clinical and Laboratory Immunology, Geriatric Medicine, and Sports Medicine. Subspecialties under Pediatrics are Pediatric Cardiology, Pediatric Gastro-enterology, Pediatric Endocrinology, Pediatric Hematology-Oncology, Neonatal-Perinatal Medicine, Nephrology, Pediatric Critical Care Medicine, Pediatric Emergency Medicine, Pediatric Infectious Diseases, Pediatric Rheumatology, Sports Medicine, Medical Toxicology, Adolescent Medicine, and Clinical Laboratory Immunology. There are a few other sub-specialties under Psychiatry and Neurology, such as Child and Adolescent Psychiatry and Child Neurology.

Although Family Practice, Pediatrics, and Internal Medicine are primary medical practices, they are also listed as specialties by the American Board of Medical Specialties, since physicians in these specialties must take and pass specialty boards that certify their competence in their respective fields. These three "specialties," then, are primary-practice physicians, whereas many of the other specialties listed above tend to be referral specialties—patients are referred by their primary-care physicians.

This chapter will discuss the requirements of the medical specialties the designer or architect is most likely to encounter in a medical office building. It is assumed that the reader will have read Chapter 3, which is the foundation for Chapter 4.

As a general comment, the same economic pressures and regulatory issues that have affected primary-care physicians have impacted specialty care. When the second edition of this book was published in 1990, physicians wanted to do as many tests as possible in their offices to capture the additional revenue. Today, in many parts of the United States, reimbursement is so low that the more procedures one does, the more one loses. Medicare is the largest payer in the United States, and what it will or will not cover and the amount it pays influences other payers as well as the types of procedures physicians are willing to do in their offices. If it's not reimbursed, the patient may be referred to the local hospital for the procedure.

In writing the new edition of this book, the author sent sections of the text to several physicians in each specialty asking them to review it for accuracy. It was surprising to note the following commonalities in their responses:

- More space for administration for increased paperwork associated with managed care.

- No great interest in upgrading to digital diagnostic instrumentation due to cost and retraining unless forced to buy new equipment.

- When electronic medical records become prevalent, it may be practical to provide an area in the waiting room for patients to update their charts or medical histories (Figure 4-137).

- A computer at all staff workstations and centrally located at nurse stations. This makes it easy to retrieve lab results.

- Anticipated increase in regulation (codes, accreditation, and licensing) of office-based surgery, specifically affecting dermatologists, plastic surgeons, otolaryngologists, and oral surgeons.

- Increased emphasis on patient privacy as a response to HIPAA (see the Introduction), JCAHO, and other regulatory or accreditation agencies.

SURGICAL SPECIALTIES

To avoid redundancy, certain issues common to all surgical specialties with respect to minor surgery rooms and office-based outpatient surgery suites will be discussed here, rather than under each specialty heading. However, the Plastic Surgery section has the most complete discussion of office-based surgery suites in terms of layout and design issues.

Physicians with specialties in OB-GYN, otolaryngology (ENT), ophthalmology, dermatology, plastic surgery, general surgery, urology, and, occasionally, orthopedic surgery, will have a minor surgery or special procedures room where they may use local anesthetics, which requires no special accommodation.

Conscious Sedation/Minor Procedures

The next step up is conscious sedation, which involves intravenous (IV) sedatives like Valium®, often combined with an agent that acts like an amnesiac so that the memory of pain is erased. When conscious sedation is administered, monitoring equipment and a resuscitation cart are required. Urologists often use this type of sedation when performing cystoscopies, but many physicians are reluctant to assume the liability and risks of using conscious sedation in their offices unless they do many procedures that require it and have properly trained staff to monitor patients. As an option, a surgeon may contract with an anesthesia service to assist in a procedure. An anesthesiologist or nurse anesthetist with a portable anesthesia machine will come to the surgeon's office as scheduled.

Office-Based Surgery

Plastic surgeons are the most likely physicians to have an office-based surgery center within their suite, followed by dermatologists and, occasionally, otolaryngologists. As statutes and codes vary widely from state to state, the following comments reflect national trends driven by Medicare for facility certification or AAAHC accreditation. See also Chapters 7 and 15 for more in-depth discussion of regulations and codes.

As a prelude, it should be noted that physicians setting up office-based surgery suites have historically had considerable flexibility in the layout of these facilities, generally trying to fit two pounds of program into a one-pound container. Operating room sizes, space around each recovery bed, and ancillary rooms (clean and soiled utilities, scrub area, staff and patient dressing areas) have been left largely to the discretion of the physician, sometimes resulting in "funky" layouts. It is common to find a "prep room" in which clean and soiled are accommodated side by side, rather than in separate rooms. Minimum-width corridors and clearances may also have been compromised. Unless physicians seek Medicare certification in order to be able to bill a fee for the use of the facility (in addition to the surgeon's fees), they often can avert close scrutiny on these issues. However, numerous states and national accreditation agencies are currently raising the bar on office-based surgical facilities to ensure greater patient safety and standardization. This will result in larger surgery suites and greater cost.

In fact, surgery performed in office-based settings is gaining the attention of state legislators and regulators throughout the nation. A recent article in *AORN Journal* (April 2001) forecasts that 20 percent of surgical procedures in 2001 will be performed in physicians' offices. The article details the ongoing measures in various states to assure patient safety.

Even JCAHO (Joint Commission on Accreditation of Healthcare Organizations) has stepped up to the plate with its Office-Based Surgery (OBS) Standards, approved 2001, intended for physicians and dentists performing operative and invasive procedures in an office setting. To be eligible for accreditation under the OBS standards, a provider must meet all of the following criteria:

- The practice comprises three or fewer licensed independent practitioners performing surgical procedures.

- The organization or practice must be physician owned or operated such as a professional services corporation, private physician practice, or small group practice.

- Invasive surgical services are provided to patients and local anesthesia, minimal sedation, conscious sedation, or general anesthesia are administered. Practices providing procedures such as excisions of skin lesions, moles, and warts or draining of abscesses limited to the skin and subcutaneous tissue typically do not fall under OBS standards.

- OBS practices that render four or more patients incapable of self-preservation at the same time are required to meet the provisions of the Life Safety Code, NFPA 101, of the National Fire Protection Association (NFPA).

Office-based surgery suites often fall into a "gray area" in terms of codes. For example, the Uniform Building Code (UBC) classifies them as a "B" or office occupancy if fewer than five individuals are incapable of self-preservation, which limits the enterprise to two ORs and three recovery beds or one OR and four recovery beds. (NFPA 101 limits it to four persons or fewer.) The local department of public health will, in many jurisdictions, send an inspector to review life safety issues and this individual may demand accommodations that go beyond what is stipulated in the local building code and in NFPA 101 Life Safety Code.

An example might be that the surgery portion of the suite be separate from the physician's office practice with a dedicated entry and reception office. This seems unwarranted in a one-physician practice in which the doctor can only be in one place or the other. However, from the standpoint of patient safety, in theory, nothing would preclude the physician from allowing an "outside" physician to see patients while he is performing surgery and the front office staff might be distracted when called upon to assist in an emergency to evacuate a patient.

Nevertheless, this results in the need for additional staff and additional space, which might exceed the physician's budget.

Physicians will want to be accredited by one of a number of possible agencies that vary, in terms of physical design considerations, from flexible to rigorous. See Plastic Surgery for more detail.

To reflect the range of options the architect or designer may encounter, the suite plans in this book demonstrate both types of office-based surgery suites—those that meet physicians' functional needs but may be somewhat idiosyncratic in layout, as well as those meeting more rigorous standards, which is where things are headed.

OBSTETRICS AND GYNECOLOGY

This is a high-volume practice, so patient flow must be carefully analyzed. Obstetrical patients usually make monthly visits, which entail weighing and a brief examination. Gynecology patients require a more lengthy pelvic examination. This type of practice requires a large staff as each physician needs one or two nurses; often, two

OB/GYN

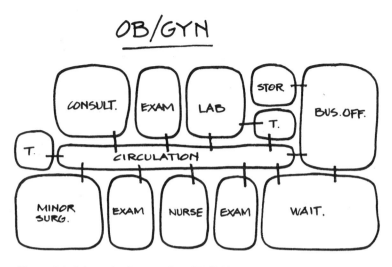

Figure 4-1. Schematic diagram of an OB-GYN suite.

Table 4-1.
Analysis of Program.
Obstetrics and Gynecology

No. of Physicians:	1	2
		(Plus Nurse Practitioner)
Exam Rooms	2@ 8 ×12 × 192	7@ 8 ×12 ×672
Exam/Ultrasound	10 ×10 × 100	10 ×10 ×100
Consultation Room	12 ×12 ∇ 144	2@ 12 ×12 ×288
Nurse Station	8 ×10 × 80[a]	2@ 8 ×12 ×192
Laboratory	—	12 ×16 ×192
Toilets	2@ 7 × 8 × 112	4@ 7 × 8 × 224
Minor Surgery	12 ×12 × 144	12 ×14 ×168
Staff Lounge	10 ×12 × 120	12 ×14 ×168
Storage	6 × 8 × 48	10 ×12 ×120
Nurse Practitioner	—	10 ×10 ×100
Business Office/Bookkeeping	12 ×16 × 192	12 ×30 × 360[b]
Medical Records	—	10 ×14 ×140
Waiting Room	12 ×20 × 240	14 ×30 ×420
Subtotal	1372 ft²	3144 ft²
20% Circulation	274	629
Total	1646 ft²	3773 ft²

[a]Combined with lab.

[b]Includes reception, bookkeeping, and insurance.

physicians share three nurses or aides in addition to the front office staff. It is customary for a female nurse to be present during pelvic examinations, necessitating more staff per doctor than required with many other medical specialties. Figure 4-1 shows the relationship of rooms.

Nurse Practitioner

A trend in this field is the use of nurse practitioners and midwives to perform routine patient examinations. A registered nurse (R.N.) with additional training in OB-GYN can be certified to work in this capacity (refer to Chapter 3 for more detail). This frees physicians from routine pelvic examinations and Pap smears on healthy patients, allowing them to concentrate on diagnosis of disease. Offices using nurse practitioners will need larger nurse stations or perhaps a small private office for them (Figure 4-2).

Patient Flow

There probably would not be more than three doctors working in an office at one time even if it were a four- or five-person practice, since one or two doctors may be delivering babies, making hospital rounds, or taking the day off. There should be three to four exam rooms per physician. The patient flow is from waiting room to weighing area, to toilet (urine specimen), to exam room. A good space plan will channel patients to each area by the most direct route with no backtracking or unnecessary steps. If possible, the nurse station/sterilization/lab areas should be located toward the front of the suite (centralized) so that the staff can cover for each other, and duplication of personnel is avoided.

Waiting Room

The waiting room of an OB-GYN suite should be large and comfortable. Unexpected deliveries frequently make the doctor late and necessitate a long wait for patients.

Figure 4-2. Space plan for OB-GYN, 4488 square feet. The plan was designed for two physicians with a nurse practitioner and a part-time physician who does not have a consultation room. (*Design: Jain Malkin Inc.*)

OB-GYN

4488 SF

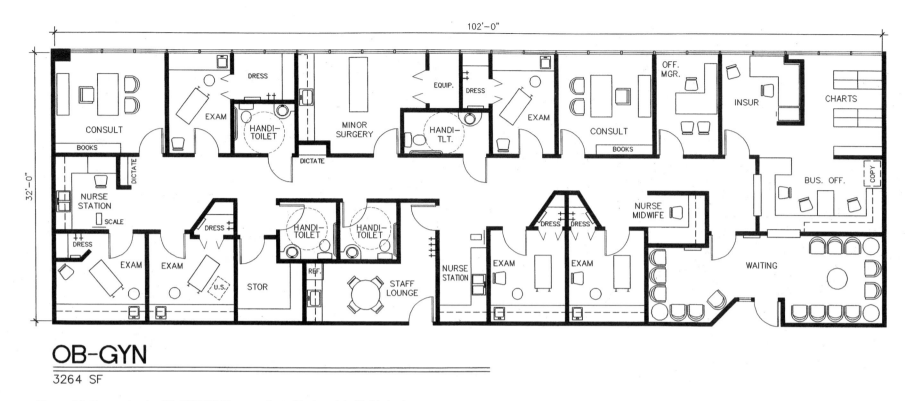

OB-GYN

3264 SF

Figure 4-3. Space plan for OB-GYN, 3264 square feet. (*Design: Jain Malkin Inc.*)

The patient is apt to be more forgiving if her wait is in a well-designed room with good lighting, current magazines, comfortable seating, and interesting artwork on the walls. A play area for children would be a practical addition to the waiting room, since many patients are young mothers, who are apt to bring their children with them.

Exam Rooms

Exam rooms may have attractive wallcovering, carpet, and a dressing area where patients may disrobe in privacy and hang underwear out of sight. Upon dressing, they may check makeup and hair in a mirror before leaving the exam room. This dressing area may be a 3-×3-foot corner of a room with a ceiling-mounted cubicle drape and a

chair or built-in bench. Or, it can be a hinged space-saver panel that opens perpendicular to the wall. Note that in Figure 4-3 the dressing area is spacious and offers total privacy. Remember that the door to the exam room must open to shield the patient.

The position of the sink cabinet is particularly important in an OB-GYN exam room. The physician should be able to examine the patient with the right hand and reach for instruments from the cabinet with the left hand (Figure 4-4). The exam table used here is a pelvic table with stirrups. Such tables often have a built-in speculum warmer. Alternatively, one drawer of the sink cabinet may have an electrical outlet at the rear for warming instruments. Three electrical outlets are required: One must be located near the foot of the table for the examination lamp used for pelvic exams; one should be located above the sink countertop; and the third would be located on the long wall, near the head of the table.

It should be noted that some OB-GYN physicians prefer a wider examination room with a cabinet that runs along the wall at the foot of the exam table (Figure 4-5). This cabinet is at a 30-inch height so that the physician, when seated, can comfortably reach instruments and equipment. Note that, in this instance, patient education is handled in the exam room, with a TV monitor built into the cabinet. Monitors are wired to VCR units in the business office. The nurse selects the proper tape for the patient's viewing; thus, time spent waiting in an exam room can be productive. Figure 4-6 shows the cabinets opened. These exam rooms are carpeted, except for a 3-foot-wide strip running in front of the built-in cabinet, which has wood parquet.

It is pleasant to have windows in an OB-GYN exam room. The wait is frequently very long and being able to look outside makes the wait a little more bearable. Polyvinyl chloride (PVC) vertical blinds serve exam rooms well since they permit light and view to enter the room while protecting the occupant's privacy. Narrow-slat horizontal metal blinds are also functional, but collect dust.

Many physicians write a prescription in the exam room, but others ask the patient to dress and come to the consultation room. In any case, it is a good idea to provide a writing desk in the exam room so that the physician can make notations on the patient's chart and write a prescription, which may be done either manually or digitally.

Minor Surgery/Special Procedures

OB-GYN suites will have a minor surgery room where a variety of procedures will be performed (Figure 4-7). See also Figure 3-5, although it is not specifically set up for OB-GYN, the accompanying text addresses it. The plan in Figure 4-8 shows an ideal procedure room as it has an equipment storage room, a workroom for prep, cleanup, and sterilization, and natural light. The sink should be a large one with foot pedal control that can be used as a scrub sink. Special procedure rooms such as this always

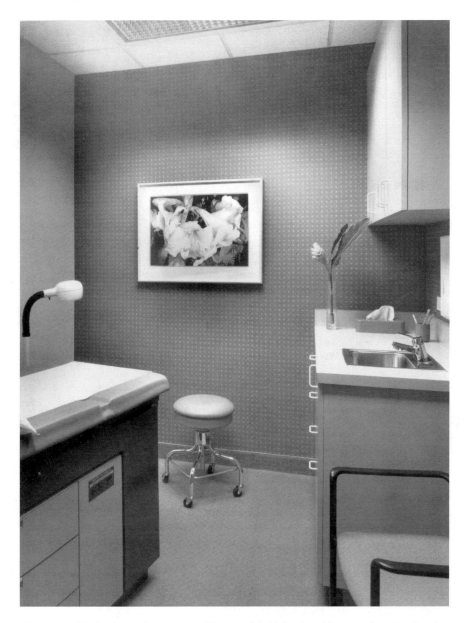

Figure 4-4. OB-GYN examination room. (*Design: Jain Malkin Inc.; Photographer: Kim Brun.*)

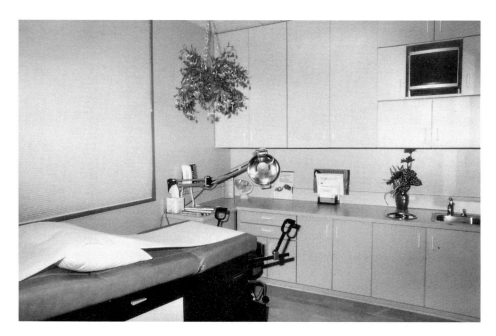

Figure 4-5. OB-GYN examination room with cabinet at foot of exam table. (*Casework design: Ashvin Contractor, San Jose, CA; Interior Design: Jain Malkin Inc.; Photographer: Jain Malkin.*)

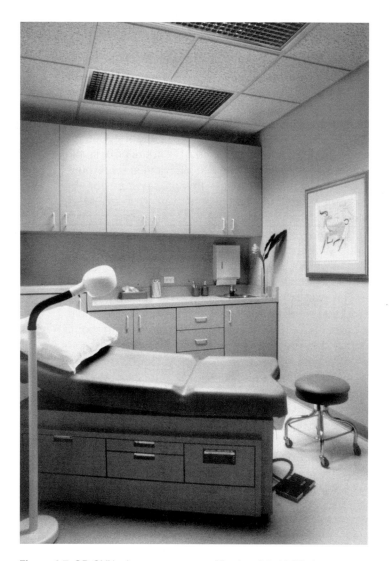

Figure 4-7. OB-GYN minor surgery room. (*Design: Jain Malkin Inc.; Photographer: Kim Brun.*)

Figure 4-6. OB-GYN exam room, interior of casework. (*Casework design: Ashvin Contractor, San Jose, CA; Interior Design: Jain Malkin Inc.; Photographer: Jain Malkin.*)

have a sink in them; however, it should be noted that operating rooms such as may be found in plastic surgery or dermatology suites would not have a sink as regulatory agencies would view this as a breach of infection control. Sinks and drains are considered a potential source of pathogens.

Types of Procedures

The kinds of procedures that may be performed in this room include (if the gynecologist has a subspecialty in urology) cystoscopies; hysteroscopies (looking inside the uterus with a fiber-optic scope); D&Cs; colposcopies (examination of the cervix with magnification); and LEEP (loop electrosurgical excision procedure), which is the newest procedure to replace core biopsies. The colposcope (Figure 4-9) and all other equipment is portable. Sedation is not required, which negates the need for a recovery area. Suction (may be central or portable) is required in this room, but other medical gases are not. The room may have a video monitor (as explained in Chapter 3, Office of the Future) associated with the colposcope or other fiber-optic scopes, in which case glare on the screen from windows or light fixtures may be a problem. The video monitor enables the patient to view the procedure and, with a printer, an image can be captured as a still photo for future reference. With a telemedicine connection, video images can be viewed at remote locations. Lighting in this room should be able to be dimmed if video monitors are used.

Room Size

The size of the room may vary from 12×14 feet to 14×16 feet, depending on the number of assistants who must be in the room and the amount of medical equipment. Usually, an adjustable-height standard procedure table as in Figure 3-5 would be used.

Ultrasound

A common piece of equipment in an OB-GYN office is an ultrasound machine, which is used to observe the developing fetus and also to image growths such as fibroids and cysts. It requires a trained sonographer. The room should

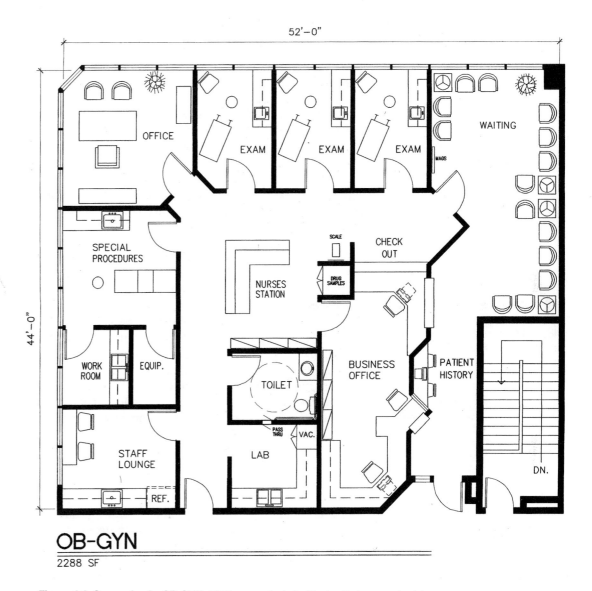

OB-GYN

2288 SF

Figure 4-8. Space plan for OB-GYN, 2288 square feet. An ideal suite for one physician. (*Design: Jain Malkin Inc.*)

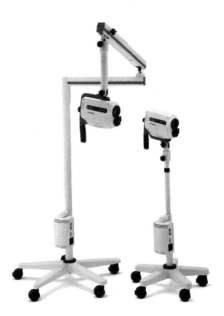

Figure 4-9. Colposcope. (*Photo courtesy: Welch Allyn®, Skaneates Falls, NY.*)

be located close to a bathroom, as women are usually asked to drink a large quantity of water prior to the procedure and, immediately after, will need to void. Although this equipment is portable, it is large (Color Plate 7, Figure 4-10) and awkward to move from room to room. It is usually placed in a large (10×12 feet) exam room that can also be used for standard examinations. A small ultrasound unit (Figure 3-63) is becoming increasingly popular and can be tucked into a corner of a small exam room. Two guest chairs should be provided for family members who want to "experience" the heartbeat of the fetus. An ultrasound room should have lighting that can be dimmed.

Patient Education

Many printed educational pamphlets are distributed, so suitable storage racks should be provided in the waiting room or in the corridor near the nurse station (Figure 4-11). A provision should be made for patient education. It might be a niche off a corridor, which would have a built-in countertop with privacy partitions, a TV monitor, and a compartment under the countertop for a VCR as in Figure 4-15. Patients would wear headphones. In lieu of this, one might provide a patient education room, preferably located near the front of the suite.

Disposal of Infectious Waste

A large amount of trash is generated in this practice. A disposable gown, sheet, and exam table paper must be discarded after each patient, as well as paper hand towels and other disposable items. Each exam room should have a large trash receptacle, which may be built into the cabinet or freestanding.

It should be noted that many cities, as well as OSHA, have regulations for dealing with infectious waste. These used to apply only to hospitals, but with the presence of HIV and other "super" viruses, medical offices are also required to separate their trash (refer to Chapter 3, OSHA Issues). Provision has to be made in the examination

Figure 4-11. Reading nook, women's clinic. (*Design: Jain Malkin Inc.; Photographer: Kim Brun.*)

room for two receptacles. Paper from the exam table, paper towels, and wrappings from disposables could go into one container, and items coming into contact with patients' body fluids would be disposed of in a "red-bagged" infectious waste receptacle. (These bags must be labeled to indicate they contain infectious waste.)

Specimen Toilets

Since each patient must empty her bladder before an examination, an OB-GYN suite needs a minimum of two toilet rooms. If it is possible to locate the toilet rooms near the nurse station or lab (Figure 4-12), a specimen pass-through (see the Appendix) in the wall can eliminate the need for the patient to carry the urine specimen to the nurse station. Toilet rooms need a hook for hanging a handbag and coat, a shelf for sanitary napkins and tampons, and a receptacle for sanitary napkin disposal. It would be a nice touch to wallpaper the bathrooms.

Laboratory

The laboratory should be at least 10×12 feet and must include a sit-down space for a microscope and a countertop space for centrifuge and an autoclave. Space should be allotted for an undercounter refrigerator. If the physicians elect to do a good deal of lab work in the suite, include a blood draw area and adequate countertop space for an automated clinical analyzer. The reader is referred to Chapter 3 for a discussion of CLIA regulations and an explanation of why physicians do little lab work in their suites these days.

Interior Design

Physicians in this specialty often like a well-appointed consultation room. Furnishings may be more elegant and refined than one might find in a consultation room of a general practice physician, for example. The room may be designed along the lines of a residential library or den, with a wood parquet floor and Oriental rug, bookshelves, fabric wallcovering, elegant upholstery fabrics, and an unusual desk. Window treatment, likewise, may be more like one would find in a residence rather than in a medical office.

The waiting room, as well as the rest of the suite, ought to be designed to appeal to women. This may take the form of sunny colors and a garden theme with floral upholstery fabrics, or it may be elegant and sophisticated (Color Plate 8, Figure 4-13), perhaps a warm gray background punctuated by polished chrome and Plexiglas fur-

Figure 4-12. Space plan for OB-GYN, 1600 square feet. (*Design: Jain Malkin Inc.*)

niture, dramatic lighting, accented by violet and chartreuse in the upholstery.

If a physician's leanings are traditional, the style could be formal with wood moldings, Chippendale chairs with petit point upholstery, fabric wallcoverings, and Oriental rugs on a wood floor. Or, the traditional style might be less formal—country French. The options are many. This specialty allows the designer a great amount of freedom; obstetricians and gynecologists usually like to present a well-decorated office to their patients. Whatever the design style, chairs should not be so soft or so low that it is difficult for pregnant women to disengage themselves.

In summary, the patients here—due to the nature of the specialty—are generally happy, and this upbeat mood should be enhanced by the interior design. All rooms except the laboratory, minor surgery, and toilets may be carpeted. If the practice includes a number of women who are incontinent, exam rooms with hard-surface floors (e.g., wood-look sheet vinyl) may be more practical.

WOMEN'S HEALTH CENTERS

Women's health centers arose in the mid-1980s in response to various social and economic changes. Taking responsibility for one's own health, consumer education, questioning traditional medical practices, and a more assertive population of women who work outside the home were all contributing factors. When market analysts revealed the following, the magnitude of the women's market became evident:

- Women are the decision makers on family healthcare.

- Women are the major users of medical and health services and, as women outnumber men in the population at large, they will continue to exert a major influence on the marketing of healthcare services.

- Women were often dissatisfied with the patronizing manner of some healthcare professionals.

Motivated by a desire to meet the demands of this "new" consumer, healthcare providers have been courting women with marketing incentives that differ considerably from the traditional doctor-knows-best approach of former years. Promises of no waiting, evening and Saturday office hours, convenient parking, child care, and health education seminars are attractive incentives.

These are not the only things that draw women to these facilities. The attitude of the staff is often dramatically different in a market-driven practice than in the traditional healthcare setting. There is an expressed respect for women and an opportunity for them to participate in their own healthcare. There are no secrets. Patients are not kept waiting. Prices are quoted in advance. Lab test results—even normal ones—are related to the patient. During patient/physician consultations, the patient is clothed and seated at the same level as the physician. There is a special emphasis on making the patient feel like a welcome guest.

Common to many women's centers is an all-female professional staff that may include family practitioners, internists, psychiatrists and psychologists, nurse practitioners, nutritionists, obstetrician/gynecologists, and social workers. These professionals focus their attention on gender differences in each area of specialization and thereby offer patients a measure of understanding that is sometimes lacking in healthcare provided by professionals outside the women's center network. This is a major issue for women who are looking for continuity of care, instead of maintaining a relationship with five or six practitioners in different offices.

Psychological and Mental Health Issues: Refocusing the Primary-Care Agenda

The women's primary-care agenda shifted in the 1990s as sex and gender-specific aspects of primary care became a focus of academic medicine. Research and policy-making organizations staged conferences to define pressing issues in women's health, and a fairly clear picture emerged. The real needs of many women were underserved. Victims of rape, incest, domestic violence, poverty, drug abuse, and various mental disorders often had no access to appropriate care and still don't in 2002. Many of these issues must be approached from a community health perspective, taking into account cultural or ethnic factors.

As the decade of the 1980s progressed, the changing roles of women added additional psychological stresses, resulting from balancing child care, work outside the home, spousal relationships or divorce, and care of aging parents. This was often referred to as the "superwoman syndrome." These issues continued unabated into the

1990s with even more pressure to be successful, provide well for one's children, and participate in the booming economy. Men and women in the 1990s worked even longer hours; consumer spending soared, as did the number of self-help books promising a plan for balancing one's life. A new term, the "sandwich generation," gave recognition to the pressures of child care on one side and parent care on the other, as the U.S. population continues to push toward having the largest number of centenarians in the history of the world. It is a well-established fact that, whether for one's own parents or one's in-laws, it is the female—sister or wife—to whom elder care usually falls.

Summarizing the lesser-known gender-specific issues arising from the research of the last half of the 1990s reveals the following:

- Women's unique requirements for health and well-being have been largely ignored by the healthcare system.

- Gender-specific care is far more than that which deals with the female reproductive system. Being female is not the same as not being male. The distinction between sex and gender is crucial. Sex refers to chromosomal structure, while gender is what society and culture make of those biological characteristics*.

- There is a vast unmet need for mental health screening, assessment, and treatment in the primary-care setting as an integral part of core services.

- A full-service women's center removes some of the social barriers and stigma associated with accessing mental healthcare.

- Women access mental health services through their primary-care provider. Many women with mental health problems never see a mental health professional.

- Safety and confidentiality are huge issues in mental health treatment for women.

---

*S. R. Kunkel and R. C. Atchley, 1996. *American Journal of Preventive Medicine* 12(5):295.

- Women access mental health services through a women's center because their problems are taken seriously.

- In the traditional primary-care setting, women's mental health issues are often misdiagnosed as physical diseases by physicians whose biomedical training does not enable them to identify the psychosocial genesis of the symptoms.

Translating Women's Primary-Care Needs to the Built Environment

The overarching need to create a safe haven, a psychologically supportive care environment that makes women feel secure and comfortable can best be achieved by a women's center, a place where women do not encounter men in the waiting room. Interior design should be based on research aimed at reducing stress. Research exists in five principal areas to inform design decisions:

- *Connection to Nature:* Even a three-minute view of nature in the form of a garden or water element (or even a realistic photograph of nature) has been shown to have immediate physiological benefits in terms of stress reduction. These features can be incorporated into waiting areas and treatment settings. Natural light in as many rooms as possible is desirable.

- *Pleasant Diversions:* Music, aromatherapy, an aquarium, engaging pieces of art or sculpture all address the multisensory nature of human beings. Moments of joy and delight distract patients from pain and help them cope with the burden of illness.

- *Social Support:* Although this is not a design issue, compassionate caregivers, social worker/case managers, and peer support groups enhance well-being and foster coping skills.

- *Elimination of Environmental Stressors:* Noise, lack of privacy, overheard conversations, poor air quality, and glare from inappropriate lighting design create stress for patients and caregivers alike. These are features of the built environment that can be controlled by competent design professionals.

- *Options and Choice:* Whether it is the selection of alternate styles of seating in the waiting room, options for things to do while waiting, passive or active participation in one's healthcare, or access to a resource library, providing options greatly reduces stress.

Customer Service Focus

Some of the newly opened centers are affiliated with a hospital, but other clinics are operated by physicians or entrepreneurial for-profit corporations. The for-profits tend to operate their facilities with an eye on the bottom line—that healthcare can be packaged and delivered as a product and earn a profit at the same time. Viewing healthcare as a business, rather than as a community service, makes the for-profits particularly sensitive to marketing trends and customer satisfaction. This is good news for designers. A client who is aware of marketing opportunities understands that the design of the facility will attract patients and, in turn, will lead to many patient referrals.

Women find these facilities comfortable and nonclinical, with carpeted floors, wallcoverings, and residential-style lighting and furniture. Clients who are attentive to these issues may actually reduce their marketing costs due to increased referrals by satisfied patients.

Design and Planning Issues

To design a women's health center properly, one has to understand the range of services offered—and this varies from facility to facility. These may include gynecology, mammography, osteoporosis screening, primary care, internal medicine, diet and exercise programs, nutrition counseling, weight loss clinics, counseling on family or social problems, and prenatal care. Great emphasis is placed on prevention and patient education. Seminars and

lectures by healthcare experts occur regularly. Other features may include a library or reading area for information on healthcare topics.

Those who plan women's health centers should consider the following:

- Secure parking, close to the building entrance.

- Understandable wayfinding: entrances clearly marked, no maze-like internal corridors.

- Privacy issues addressed in all settings:
  Reception check-in
  Those waiting should not overhear telephone or other conversations with or about other patients.
  Exam room integrity: Patient should not be able to overhear conversations in adjacent exam rooms.
  Secure dressing areas.

- Include children's play spaces in waiting rooms. Arrange seating in waiting rooms in privacy groupings, broken up by low planter walls so that patients are not forced to stare at each other.

- Include in waiting rooms a self-serve coffee/tea bar, areas to plug in computers, a fax machine, a free phone for local calls. A TV should not dominate the room—it causes stress for those who are forced to watch offensive programming. If long waits are inevitable, provide a pager to allow patients to sit outdoors in a garden or browse in nearby shops as appropriate. Provide a variety of current magazines addressing diverse interests.

- Small vases with a fresh flower in exam rooms, colored gowns, a magazine rack, a mirror for checking one's hair or makeup before exiting, and a proper place to store one's clothes indicate an attention to detail that reinforces confidence in the clinical care (Figure 4-4).

- A kitchen for nutritional counseling and food prep demonstrations is included in some women's centers.

- Color and design should appeal to women, but not be overly frilly. Too often, facilities try to appear "feminine" by using inexpensive French Provincial furniture, velvet cushions, or artwork framed with ruffles and lace. This may appeal to some women, but the majority may prefer a more sophisticated treatment (Color Plate 8, Figure 4-14).

- The reception window should be wide and open so that the patient does not feel closed out and isolated.

- Patient education carrels should be located in view of one of the receptionists, but should afford privacy for the patient (Figure 4-15).

- A large multipurpose meeting room is needed for lectures and seminars. It should be furnished with tablet-arm chairs and a number of small tables that can be pushed together for meetings (Figure 4-15).

- Exam rooms need dressing cubicles for patient privacy and for hanging clothing. Medical equipment and instruments should be stored out of sight so that the room appears nonthreatening to the patient. Exam rooms (except those used for minor surgery) should be carpeted. It should be noted that recent developments in commercial carpet fibers and backings as well as antimicrobial and stain-resistant properties make carpet a viable option for exam rooms.

- The physician's consultation room or private office should have—in addition to a desk—some lounge chairs or a small sofa and coffee table to provide an informal, friendly, residential setting.

- A library, if space allows, can be located in a separate room or in a nook off the entry, but within view of the receptionist or cashier. For brochures, which are meant to be handed out, a rack in the reception area or corridor would be sufficient (Figure 4-11).

- The scale at the nurse station should be placed to afford privacy for those self-conscious about their weight. Ample storage areas for drug samples and other items must be provided in the nurse station, as well.

- One room will be a breast exam room, which means that the patient will usually lie down on a divan or high

WOMEN'S HEALTH CENTER

3450 SF

Figure 4-15. Space plan for women's health center, 3450 square feet. (*Design: Jain Malkin Inc.*)

bed and watch a video describing how to do a breast self-exam. There also needs to be a chair for a nurse or aide.

- Light fixtures should not shine into patients' eyes; therefore, alternatives such as wall sconces, wall washers, indirect perimeter lighting, or low voltage downlighting should be used (Color Plate 9, Figure 4-16). Limit the use of lay-in 2×4 fluorescent lighting in examination or treatment rooms.

- If the facility is to be staffed primarily by women, the height of such items as X-ray view boxes, countertops, and cabinets must be considered. The average height of a woman is 5 feet, 4 inches.

- Patients appreciate a specimen pass-through between the restroom and lab so that the patient does not have to carry the specimen into the corridor.

- Cabinets in the minor surgery room can house large pieces of equipment, such as the suction machine, the colposcope, and the emergency crash cart, which tend to be anxiety-provoking items (Figure 4-7). More casework is needed here compared with a standard exam room. Also, the floor should be sheet vinyl or other easily cleaned material.

- For acoustical privacy, exam rooms should have solid-core doors, Fiberglas® insulation batting in the walls, and walls that continue above the finished ceiling.

A Women's Center for the Millennium

Much has been written about the effects of the Internet on culture and the economy. Instant wealth for many individuals—especially those under the age of 25—has been a unique occurrence as has instant access to information. One thing is certain: two forces—the Internet and the Baby Boomer generation—will create seismic change in our institutions, in the way we define aging, and in what we expect from our healthcare system.

A women's center for the first decade of the new millennium will address the full continuum of women's health and, with the huge number of Baby Boomer women in their mid-50s, the focus on postmenopausal issues may exceed the prior emphasis on birthing. The significant increase in persons living to the age of 100 and the overall Baby Boomer emphasis on healthy lifestyles requires educational programs relating to aging.

Marketing to women and making sure that they have a pleasant experience is especially important for women's centers associated with a hospital as it's usually the woman who decides where her family will access care. In fact, various market research sources indicate that women make between 80 and 84 percent of healthcare decisions in the United States. Women communicate differently than men and approach illness from different points of view, yet these subtle differences are often ignored. Understanding women's unique requirements for health and well-being will increase market share and establish loyalty.

BREAST CENTERS

Historically, mammography screening has been available to women in diagnostic imaging (radiology) centers and, occasionally, in the offices of large OB-GYN practices. In recent years, however, more comprehensive breast care services have been provided in specialized facilities that offer women more psychosocial support and a full range of services, should they be diagnosed as symptomatic. Even when mammography is part of a diagnostic imaging suite, the goal is usually to separate it from the other imaging modalities, creating a separate entrance and identity (Figures 5-4 and 5-5).

Depending on the anticipated volume of procedures and the potential as a feeder to oncology services, the breast center may be totally independent of diagnostic imaging, having its own ultrasound, mammography, and stereotactic rooms, as well as film filing and reading areas. The proliferation of well-designed, high-profile breast centers in recent years is a reflection of the increased awareness of the benefits of early detection as well as a response to reaching out to women who make most of the healthcare decisions for their families.

The scale and range of breast care centers is demonstrated by the small facility in Figure 4-18 and the somewhat larger one in Figure 4-17, both associated with a community hospital but located in an MOB; Figure 6-6, associated with a large primary-care clinic; Figure 4-19, also under a hospital's license but located in a medical office building with direct access to an ambulatory surgical center; and the largest of these facilities (Figure 4-38) is part of a cancer center, which includes chemotherapy infusion, also associated with a large community hospital, but located in a campus MOB. Interior photos of all of these facilities are included in the book and will be cross-referenced later in this discussion. Some have been placed in the Oncology section, others here in the Breast Centers section, and a few appear in Chapters 6 and 13. All of these facilities have outstanding design features in addition to being highly functional in terms of space planning and critical adjacencies.

Psychological Context

The possibility of breast cancer strikes such a chord of fear and terror in many women that the anticipation of having a mammogram is filled with dread. This, despite the fact that more women die of heart disease every year than breast cancer. Understanding this context of fear of the unknown, and perhaps the subconscious fear of the possibility of losing a breast if a lesion or tumor is discovered, causes some women to arrive at the facility in an anxious state of mind. Therefore, a design that is calming and soothing will be appreciated. Research shows that connecting people to nature with a view of a garden, or a water element like a large fountain, and natural light has immediate physiological benefits in terms of reducing stress. Even a simulated view of nature as in

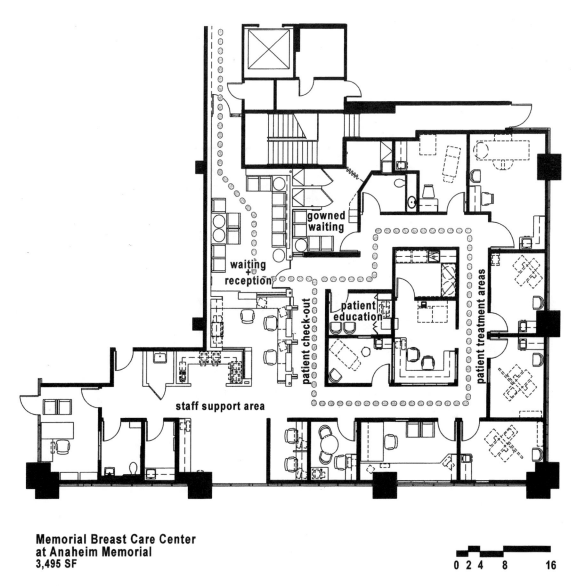

**Memorial Breast Care Center
at Anaheim Memorial**
3,495 SF

0 2 4   8   16

Figure 4-17. Space plan, 3495 square feet. Memorial Breast Care Center at Anaheim Memorial Hospital, Anaheim, CA. (*Architecture and interior design: Taylor & Associates Architects, Newport Beach, CA.*)

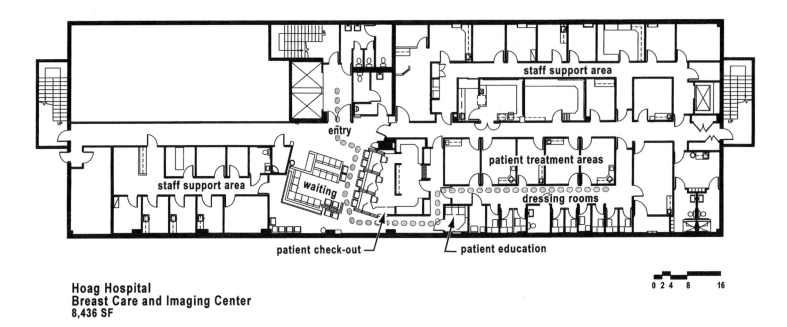

Hoag Hospital
Breast Care and Imaging Center
8,436 SF

0 2 4 8 16

Figure 4-18. Space plan, 8436 square feet. Hoag Hospital Breast Care and Imaging Center. (*Architecture and interior design: Taylor & Associates Architects, Newport Beach, CA.*)

Color Plates 9, 25, and 28, Figures 4-20, 5-70, and 7-15, respectively, is effective. Providing options and choice also reduces stress. Patients who visit the Scripps Breast Care Center (Figures 4-19 and 4-21 and Color Plates 10, 11, Figures 4-22, 4-23, and 4-24) have a choice of five options to fill their time while waiting for the procedure. After gowning, they may sip tea from a china tea service and read magazines; watch a video on breast self-exam; visit the resource library to select a book or video (using wireless headphones) or go on line to research women's health topics; tour the corridors to see the many works of art and contemporary crafts; or visit the positive appearance center to select a gift. Pleasant diversions, according to research, also reduce stress. These include aquariums (Figure 4-50), fountains, soothing music, interactive works of art, or anything that distracts one from worry and fear.

Psychological Support

One of the advantages of screening at a breast center, as opposed to having a mammogram at a diagnostic imaging facility, is the psychosocial support that is often available to women who prove to be symptomatic. In the typical scenario, a woman who learns she has a suspicious growth has to wait an agonizing week or two to book an appointment with a primary-care physician who will likely refer the patient for further diagnostic studies. That interval of time can be torturous, whereas, in a breast center, psychosocial support is immediately available through counselors and nurses. Further diagnostic tests can be conducted at the same site with care coordinated by a concerned and familiar team of individuals. A connection to the breast center can be maintained even after surgery and other types of therapy, by virtue of counseling and educational programs as well as support groups.

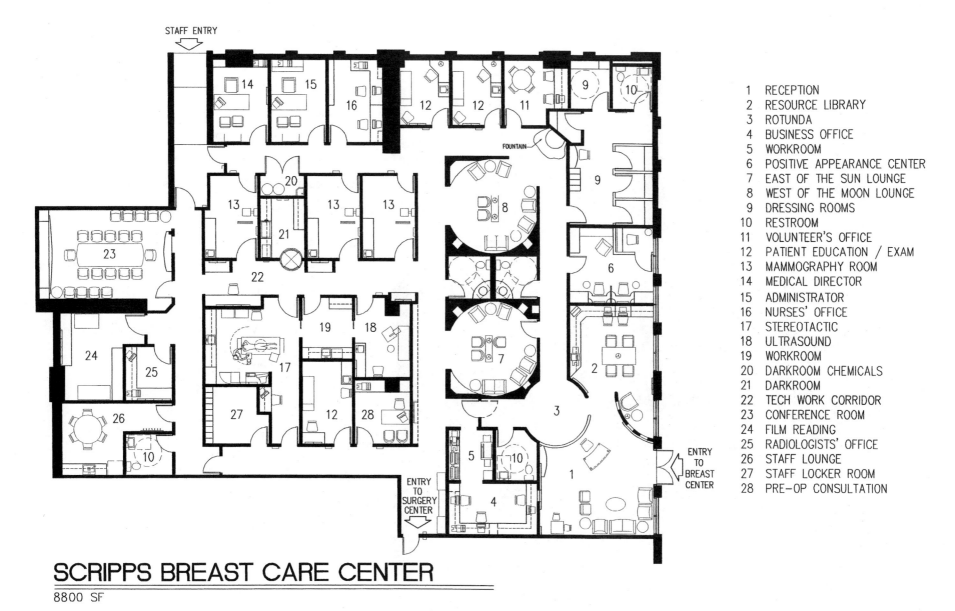

STAFF ENTRY

14 15 16 12 12 11 9 10 FOUNTAIN

20 13 13 13 9

21 8

22 23 6

24 19 18 7

25 17 2

26 27 12 28 3

10 5 10 1

ENTRY TO SURGERY CENTER 4 ENTRY TO BREAST CENTER

1   RECEPTION
2   RESOURCE LIBRARY
3   ROTUNDA
4   BUSINESS OFFICE
5   WORKROOM
6   POSITIVE APPEARANCE CENTER
7   EAST OF THE SUN LOUNGE
8   WEST OF THE MOON LOUNGE
9   DRESSING ROOMS
10 RESTROOM
11 VOLUNTEER'S OFFICE
12 PATIENT EDUCATION / EXAM
13 MAMMOGRAPHY ROOM
14 MEDICAL DIRECTOR
15 ADMINISTRATOR
16 NURSES' OFFICE
17 STEREOTACTIC
18 ULTRASOUND
19 WORKROOM
20 DARKROOM CHEMICALS
21 DARKROOM
22 TECH WORK CORRIDOR
23 CONFERENCE ROOM
24 FILM READING
25 RADIOLOGISTS' OFFICE
26 STAFF LOUNGE
27 STAFF LOCKER ROOM
28 PRE-OP CONSULTATION

SCRIPPS BREAST CARE CENTER

8800 SF

Figure 4-19. Space plan, 8800 square feet. Scripps Breast Care Center, La Jolla, CA. (*Architecture and interior Design: Jain Malkin Inc.*)

Figure 4-21. Ethel Rosenthal Resource Library. Scripps Breast Care Center, La Jolla, CA. (*Interior architecture and Design: Jain Malkin Inc.; Photographer: Glenn Cormier.*)

Scope of Services

Screening and Diagnosis

- Screening and diagnostic mammography
- Clinical breast examination
- Ultrasound and ultrasound-guided biopsy
- Stereotactic-guided core biopsy
- Stereotactic-guided mammotomy biopsy
- Needle localization biopsy

Education and Outreach

- Education in breast self-examination and breast health
- Positive appearance center with wigs, scarves, hats, and prostheses
- Resource library with Internet access and guidance

Wellness Programs

- Healthy lifestyle programs
- Nutrition counseling
- Complementary therapy resources

Professional and Support Services

- Peer survivor program ("buddy" matching)
- Support groups
- Genetic risk assessment and counseling
- Patient and family education
- Multidisciplinary pretreatment planning conferences
- Second-opinion consultation services
- Lymphedema/rehab services

Space Planning Considerations

The space planner may wish to consider these space-planning features:

- Lay out procedure rooms with separate entries for tech and patient: techs enter rooms from a tech work corridor that includes workstations, view box, and access to darkroom (Figures 4-18 and 4-19).

- Locate closet for darkroom chemicals close to rear entry of suite so that deliveries can be made without having to walk through suite with hand cart; pipe chemicals through wall to darkroom (Figure 4-19).

- Instead of a conventional reception window, consider using a concierge desk, staffed by a volunteer, in the main lobby to greet and check in patients (Color Plate 10, Figure 4-22).

- If possible, provide a connection to a surgery center. This provides the greatest privacy and convenience for women who have had a needle localization and now have to proceed to surgery for biopsy (Figure 4-19).

- Separate "screening" mammography patients from "symptomatic" in gowned waiting (Figure 4-19 and Color Plate 11, Figure 4-24).

- Provide a separate and identifiable entry when part of a larger clinic setting (Figures 4-38 and 6-6).

- Provide acoustically and visually isolated (from patients) staff area with lounge, conference room, restrooms, film reading, film filing, and offices for radiologists and medical director (Figures 4-18, 4-19, 4-38, and 6-6).

- Provide a resource library near the lobby (Figures 4-19, 4-21, and 6-6).

Interior Design Amenities

- Provide wall sconces and other indirect lighting in all procedure rooms as well as exam/patient education rooms (Figure 13-3).

- Consider a painting for the floor under the stereotactic table (protected by piece of Lexan®), where patient is lying on stomach, looking down.

- Furnish the lobby or waiting room like a living room with a variety of seating, interesting ceilings, lighting, and artwork (Color Plates 11 and 26, Figures 4-24 and 6-8, respectively).

- Even a small waiting room can become an extraordinary work of art by virtue of geometry, ceiling design, lighting, and use of color (Color Plate 40, Figure 13-8). Consider a separate lounge for the men who often accompany patients.

- An intimate, serene inner sanctum was created in a challenging below-grade space with low ceiling and no windows, by building banquette seating around the perimeter, complemented by exquisite detailing, careful attention to lighting, and a few surprises such as the opening in the ceiling (Color Plate 12, Figure 4-25).

- Provide elegant, private dressing rooms (Figure 4-26).

- A considerable amount of literature is dispensed, which requires racks to keep it sorted and neat (Figures 3-11, 4-11, 4-91, and 12-3).

- Include pleasant diversions to reduce stress such as a large aquarium (Figure 4-50) and trompe l'oeil (French for "fool the eye")–style murals (Color Plates 9 and 18, Figures 4-20 and 4-101, respectively).

- In oncology consultation rooms, consider building into a table, an audio cassette recorder to enable a patient to record the physician's comments to replay later at home. In the anxiety of the moment, it's easy to forget what was said.

Figure 4-26. Dressing room. Hoag Hospital Breast Care and Imaging Center. (*Architecture and interior design: Taylor & Associates Architects, Newport Beach, CA; Photographer: Farshid Assassi.*)

- Gowned waiting can be designed as a living room with an inset area rug and an opening on one or two sides to provide a view of something interesting. The suite plan in Figure 4-19 provides two 18-foot-diameter gowned waiting rooms, one for screening mammography patients and the other for symptomatic patients. Derived from a popular Norwegian fairy tale, the West of the Moon lounge (Color Plate 11, Figure 4-24) opens, on one side, to a view of three large oil paintings commissioned by an artist to represent the three phases of a woman's life: the young maiden, the nurturing mother, and the wise elder. They combine symbolism such as a butterfly for metamorphosis, a lotus flower representing higher consciousness, and they also incorporate the sun and the moon, the two themes of the gowned waiting lounges. Another opening in the room exposes a view of a carved granite fountain that looks like a large boulder.

- Consider a "theme" to anchor the design. As an example, the aforementioned gowned waiting areas are developed around the sun and the moon. The lounge for symptomatic patients, named East of the Sun, celebrates the summer solstice, which research indicates has, for centuries, been regarded as the peak of women's energy and healing. It is much celebrated in Northern Europe. The ceiling (which is round) has a cut in it similar to a sundial marker pointing northwest, exactly where the sun would be on June 21. It, as well as a marker in the inset carpet design, points to a recessed niche with a custom sculpture of a sundial and text explaining the concept. The other lounge, West of the Moon, is dedicated to the Triple Goddess of the Moon legend that can be found in many cultures, tying the phases of the moon (waxing, full, waning) to the three phases of a woman's life. In this lounge, a recessed niche with a custom sculpture represents this concept. The three large paintings and the concepts for the two lounges are mutually reinforcing. In addition, the 12-foot-diameter entry rotunda (Color Plate 11, Figure 4-23) introduces Hygeia and Panacea, daughters of Aesclepius, the god of healing in 4th century

B.C. Greece, representing, respectively, *prevention and treatment.* They welcome women to the Scripps Breast Care Center.

- Locate the positive appearance center near the front of the suite as this is a retail space.

- Historically, facilities designed specifically for women have often had period-style furniture and somewhat frilly decor. Determined to demonstrate a more modern approach, the architect for the Anaheim Memorial Breast Center combined soft pastel colors with contemporary architectural forms such as cantilevered glass panels and strong ceiling elements that intersect each other and connect one space to the next (Figure 3-18 and Color Plate 40, Figure 13-8). Note the elegant sandblasted pattern on the glass. The Scripps Breast Care Center also departs from expectations about appropriate colors for a breast center. The geranium red accent used throughout (the most auspicious color in feng shui) is a counterpoint to the warm gray walls and carpet. The stereotactic room in Color Plate 13, Figure 4-27, is a welcome change from the cold, clinical VCT floor environments one typically encounters. The wood-grain sheet vinyl and maple casework, combined with two complementary colors (violet and yellow), create a soothing ambience. The lavender border has metallic silver spirals known as the "Archimedes spiral," which Carl Jung identifies as one of the earliest forms associated with healing in many cultures.

Correlation of Suite Plans and Photos

Because all of the facilities featured have high-profile design that should be correlated to the respective space plans, following is a list of locations of interior photos.

Suite plan Figure 4-17: Figure 3-18 and Color Plate 40, Figure 13-8

Suite plan Figure 4-18: Color Plate 12, Figures 4-25 and 4-26.

Suite plan Figure 4-19: Figures 3-23, 4-20, 4-21, Color Plates 10, 11, and 13, Figures 4-22, 4-23, 4-24, and 4-27, and Figures 4-28, 4-30, and 5-20.

Suite plan Figure 6-6: Color Plate 26, Figure 6-8

Explanation of Treatment Modalities

Mammography

An X-ray is taken of the breast, which is compressed between two horizontal plates. The control screen that protects the tech is usually integrated into the equipment (Figures 4-28 and 4-29). The room often has a sink cabinet and may have a desk for the tech. There are no restrictions about finishes in this room with carpet and wallcovering having become standard. Some mammography rooms are quite elaborate in their interior design features, incorporating crown moulding and commissioned works of art.

Stereotactic

In this room, the patient lies on her stomach on a special table with an opening through which the breast protrudes. To accommodate staff, the table is high. The breast is compressed on a panel while two stereotactic X-rays (taken from two different angles) are taken. The precise location of the suspicious lesion is analyzed by a computer based on the X-rays. Following this, a device that will direct a probe and needle into the breast is positioned by the computer at the proper angle. The target area is deadened with a local anesthetic. The needle has a notched opening on the tip that cuts a small amount of breast tissue while a vacuum pulls the tissue into the probe. A machine equipped with a new device called the Mammotome™, manufactured by Biopsys Medical Inc. in Irvine, California, enables the physician to obtain several tissue samples within a full circle with only one needle insertion, as opposed to several when doing core-needle biopsy. The stereotactic room can also used for needle localizations prior to surgical biopsies. Typically, the nee-

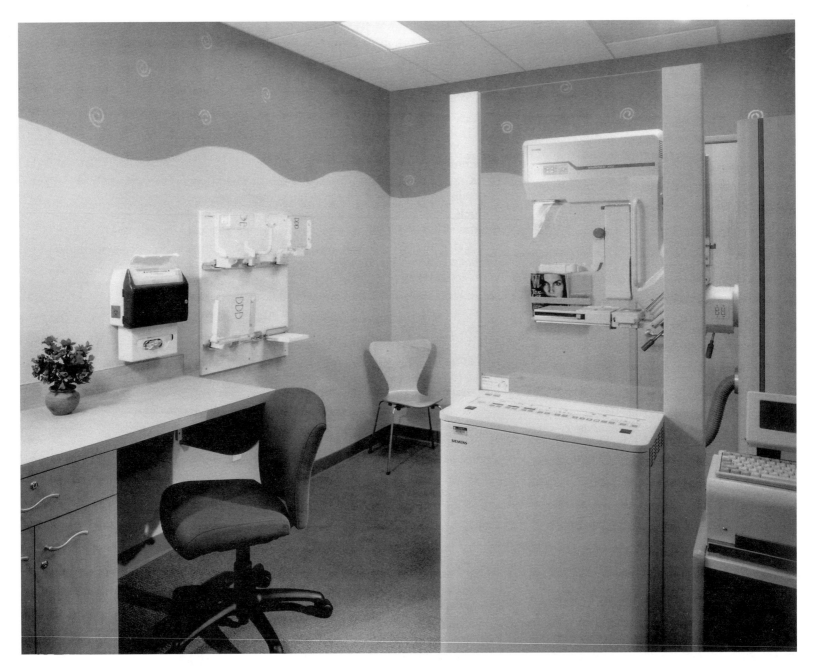

Figure 4-28. Mammography room. Scripps Breast Care Center, La Jolla, CA. (*Interior architecture and Design: Jain Malkin Inc.; Photographer: Glenn Cormier.*)

dle is placed and a paper cup is put over it to protect it while the patient dresses and drives to an ambulatory surgical center for the biopsy. This is inconvenient and most likely adds to the patient's anxiety. If direct access to a surgery center is possible, as in Figure 4-19, it is optimal.

Ultrasound

Used as an adjunct to mammography and physical examination, ultrasound helps physicians decide if a biopsy is necessary for suspicious breast lesions by providing more information about whether the "area" is a cyst or a solid mass. The ATL High Definition™ Digital Ultrasound, according to the manufacturer, may reduce the number of surgical breast biopsies by 40 percent, is less costly than surgery, and does not cause internal scarring. The aforementioned Mammotome device is also compatible with ultrasound equipment, allowing the physician to position the probe in the exact spot where tissue acquisition is desired. Refer to the Obstetrics and Gynecology and Women's Health Center sections for discussion of lighting and layout of ultrasound rooms. Also see Figures 4-10 and 4-30.

Tech Areas

Ideally, patients will not see other patients' X-rays mounted on view box illuminators, nor will they overhear staff conversations to ensure patient confidentiality. The tech corridor in Figure 4-19 provides entry into all procedure rooms as well as access to the darkroom. Placed conveniently outside each procedure room are stand-up-height viewing areas to enable techs to check films. Remember that the techs in a breast center are all women, which means casework, countertops (with vertical slots underneath for sorting X-rays), and mounting heights for stand-up view boxes must be appropriate for the average 5-foot-4-inch-high woman.

The radiologist will most likely use film alternators in the reading room (Figure 5-22). Radiologists will some-

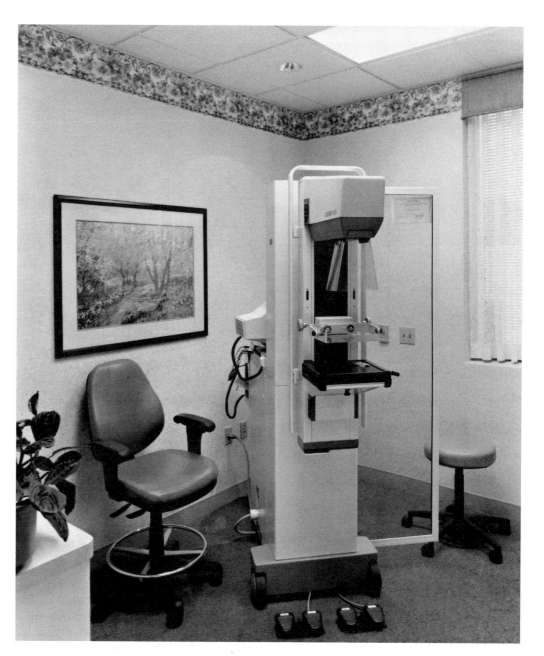

Figure 4-29. Mammography room. Saint Jude Breast Center. (*Architecture and interior design: Haynes and Oakley Architects, Sierra Madre, CA; Photographer: John Connell Photography.*)

Donor Opportunities

Breast care centers are valued highly by hospital foundations because they are highly visible and attractive to donors. If the facility has a high-profile design that distinguishes it, it is astonishing the amounts of money that can be raised to name individual rooms, the lobby, the positive appearance center, and the facility itself. A high-profile center may cost $100 per square foot in 2001 to construct (tenant improvement cost), but can attract $5 to $10 million in underwriting, depending on the geographic location, the foundation's outreach and skill, the prestige of the physicians associated with it, and the unique design properties of the facility.

REPRODUCTIVE ENHANCEMENT (ASSISTED REPRODUCTIVE TECHNOLOGIES)

Overview

Who would not be smitten by the emotional context that surrounds this ultra-high-technology specialty? The hopes and dreams of so many to have a family are linked to a successful outcome and the fact that it all happens within the walls of this facility—life is created here. Couples, singles, both heterosexual and homosexual, and occasionally individuals who travel from remote parts of the world find their way to the portals of the most celebrated and clinically successful specialists in reproductive enhancement. This is a relatively new field that has been much in the news in recent years with articles celebrating the astonishing technological accomplishments, which are, at times, flanked by controversy surrounding multiple births, surrogates who later decide to keep the baby themselves, frozen eggs that have been stolen and sold without the donors' knowledge, and eggs that have been carelessly handled and transplanted into the wrong person. Registries have sprung up on the Internet offering, at exorbitant prices, "designer" eggs and sperm of individuals who exemplify an aesthetic ideal, have very high SAT scores, or are gifted musicians, athletes, or high achiev-

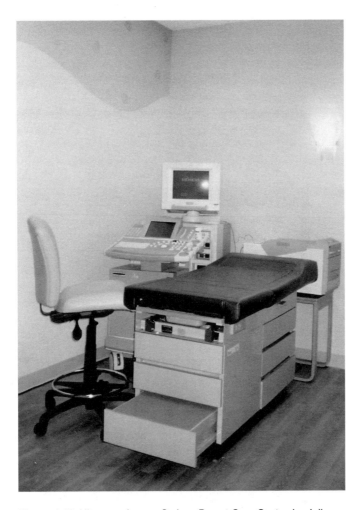

Figure 4-30. Ultrasound room. Scripps Breast Care Center, La Jolla, CA. (*Interior architecture and Design: Jain Malkin Inc.; Photographer: Glenn Cormier.*)

times request cubicle drapes or some other means of partitioning to control distractions. The film viewing area should be in the quietest part of the suite and will be adjacent to the radiologist's office. A large conference room is common to these facilities as there are numerous staff conferences regarding treatment planning and case presentations.

ers at Ivy League schools. Despite this backlash, the need to pass on one's genes and to procreate is among the most primal of nature's urges and, as this specialty matures, the Brave New World queasiness will no doubt subside. These procedures are a touchstone for moral, ethical, and spiritual conflict as society attempts to grapple with what a mere 15 years ago would have been considered science fiction.

Access to Information

The Internet is a tremendous source of information on infertility treatments with a surprising number of Web sites by assisted reproductive technologies that read more like medical textbooks. This means that patients may arrive at the physician's office with a highly sophisticated understanding of all of the techniques, success rates of each, and sheaf of journal articles.

Psychological Considerations

One could say that everything associated with these procedures creates stress. In the words of Elizabeth Barrett Browning, "…let me count the ways," starting with what brings individuals to seek this sort of help—years of yearning and trying to conceive. Couples deal with guilt, blame, worry, and hope, living by ovulation cycles, and the optimum day to "do it," and what started out as pleasurable sex has become fraught with anxiety, akin to a project or a job. The pressure is tremendous. And women, at some point, feel that biological clock running out of time.

Once one enters reproductive therapy, there are no guarantees or magic bullets. One enters the world of critical timetables, cycles, and many steps in a process that are dependent on each other. Failure at any stage may mean aborting the process and starting over. Consider the highs and lows of waiting for news about results of blood tests, sperm motility, viability of the eggs, and whether fertilization has taken place. Add to this the hormonal changes resulting from fertility drugs that can cause strong emotions and unpredictable outbursts. Trying to conceive is a stressful process and infertility

treatment an ongoing enterprise. With all the magic associated with a successful outcome, the day-to-day reality of the ordeal can be physiologically and psychologically grueling. To help individuals and couples manage these emotions, counseling sessions teach coping skills, stress management, and relaxation techniques. The financial impact of infertility treatment is substantial. Individuals who have tried unsuccessfully for several years to conceive may have mortgaged their homes, borrowed from friends and family, sold their automobile, to be able to continue with the treatment. This compounds the emotional stress.

Designing for Comfort

Designing to meet patients' psychological needs in this specialty leads one to think of comfort in every conceivable manner. One would avoid sharp angles, geometric forms that create visual tension, high levels of illumination, hard, shiny, surfaces, materials that are cold to the touch, and seating that is lined up like soldiers against the wall. Granted that design and color are always, to a certain degree, subjective, and what constitutes comfort may be open to interpretation. Nevertheless, one should strive to create a serene environment, with a variety of seating, including some oversized chairs that metaphorically form a cocoon around a person. Employ a soothing color palette leaning toward warm, rather than cool, colors. Wood can be used on the face of the reception desk and elsewhere to add warmth (Figure 13-4). Walls and ceilings may have curved forms, and lighting should be varied, avoiding entirely 2×4-foot lay-in fluorescent luminaires (Color Plate 13, Figure 4-31, and Figure 13-7). High levels of illumination and glare can create tension.

Artwork used in the waiting room must be selected carefully. One must avoid anything that might hit a nerve such as photos of parents and children, although there are places in the office where this can be quite successful as relevant art, but not in the waiting room. Art that is whimsical can be quite successful. In Color Plate 13, Figure 4-31, an artist was commissioned to create a series of five gouache and pastel pieces reminiscent of Cirque du Soleil characters. These are placed along one wall; on the opposite wall are actual Cirque du Soleil sculptures and other whimsical works of art. Be mindful that art images should not represent what appears to be overweight female forms because women undergoing hormone therapy for infertility experience water retention, they feel bloated, and their ovaries may actually triple in size.

Procedures and Terminology

A few years ago, this field was often referred to as IVF, or in vitro fertilization, but, as the field has become more technologically advanced and an expanded number of services are offered, assisted reproductive technologies (ART) is the preferred term.

Assisted reproductive technologies include the following:

- Infertility diagnosis prescreening

- Artificial insemination—large numbers of washed motile sperm are placed into the female reproductive tract, often the uterus

- Intrauterine insemination (IUI)—sperm are placed directly into the uterus

- Hormonal therapy to induce ovulation

- Reproductive laser surgery to treat endometriosis and other uterine or tubal problems that can affect fertility

- Ovulation induction with artificial insemination

- Gamete intrafallopian transfer (GIFT)—eggs and sperm are injected directly into the woman's fallopian tubes via laparoscopy

- Zygote intrafallopian transfer (ZIFT)—a zygote (newly fertilized egg) is inserted directly into the woman's fallopian tubes

- Intracytoplasmic sperm injection (ICSI)—using micromanipulation technology, a single sperm is injected into the center of the cytoplasm of the egg to achieve fertilization

- Testicular epididymal sperm aspiration (TESA)—sperm are retrieved using an open testicular biopsy technique

- In vitro fertilization (IVF)—eggs are retrieved from the ovary and fertilized by the man's sperm in the lab; several days later, a number of fertilized embryos are transferred into the uterus; the remaining embryos can be cryopreserved for use in subsequent cycles

- Assisted hatching—micromanipulation of the embryo to increase implantation success

- Egg donation—women whose ovaries have been removed, or do not function normally, can receive donated eggs from another woman; these eggs are fertilized by the husband's sperm in the lab and later implanted into the uterus

- Gestational surrogacy—transferring the embryo into another woman who carries the pregnancy to term

- Traditional surrogacy—artificially inseminating a woman who carries a baby to term; the baby will then be raised by its genetic father and his partner

- Embryo cryopreservation—freezing and storage of embryos in liquid nitrogen

- Hysteroscopy with tubal cannulization—visual examiniation of the interior of the uterus to check for abnormalities

- Laparoscopy—procedures using a fiber-optic scope passed into the abdomen through a tiny incision below the navel

- Psychological services

Regulatory Issues

Although IVF is not specifically defined in the codes, the facility can be viewed as having three basic components that *are* well defined in various codes and can be relied on to guide decisions. These are the examination/medical office component, which, in most codes, is a business occupancy (assuming this is not a hospital-based facility); the clinical laboratory; and the operating room suite. One should consult the state's business and professions code, if such exists, as well as the state's department of health services. There are nationally recognized accreditation agencies such as AAAHC and AAAASF (refer to the Plastic Surgery section and Chapter 7 for detailed discussion of these agencies) that will accredit these facilities, and there is JCAHO, but practitioners may also wish to consider state accreditation agencies for ambulatory care. As an example, in California, it's the Institute for Medical Quality, a subsidiary of the California Medical Association. This agency is approved by the Medical Board of California to verify compliance with assembly bill AB-595, also known as the Spiers Bill. Similar bills may have been enacted in other states, but in California, as of 1996, any medical practice from solo to small group to multiservice ambulatory centers that administers general anesthesia must be either licensed by the Department of Health Services, obtain Medicare certification, or be accredited.

Clearly, licensing and Medicare certification are quite rigorous in terms of facility design, whereas many accreditation agencies focus more on policies and procedures such as infection control measures, patients' rights, hospital transfer agreements, quality management/quality improvement, calibration logs of equipment, documentation of periodic safety drills, testing of back-up power, pharmaceutical control logs, and review of medical charts. Achieving Medicare certification will most likely mean that the surgery center portion of the suite—even if it's just one procedure room with ancillary spaces—will be isolated from the medical office, having its own entry, business office, and waiting area. This is what is demanded for office-based surgery facilities. However, it is clearly a gray area for IVF suites because the nature of what is done in the procedure room is "procedures" rather than surgery.

General Anesthesia Is the Trigger

If general anesthesia is used, the facility will have to be licensed or accredited. The *AIA Guidelines for Design* *and Construction of Hospital and Healthcare Facilities* should be used as a guide, along with NFPA 101 Life Safety Code. Many physicians do not use general anesthesia for these procedures and, instead, use monitored anesthesia care (IV sedation with oxygen), which causes a twilight sleep and does not involve intubation. An anesthesiologist would participate during these procedures and resuscitation equipment should be available in the procedure room.

Clinical Lab Regulatory Issues

Certification. Certification is both mandatory and voluntary for the clinical lab component of the suite, which involves blood draw, the andrology lab, and the IVF/embryology lab. Currently, three states—California, New York, and Florida—require clinics to be licensed as a tissue bank if human tissue is collected, processed, stored, or distributed for purposes of transplantation in either the andrology or the embryology lab. States also issue licenses for clinical laboratories and one would have to be certified by CLIA (Clinical Laboratory Improvement Act), a federal program regulated by the Health Care Financing Administration (HCFA). The reader is referred to a discussion of CLIA in Chapters 3 and 5.

On July 21, 1999, the Department of Health and Human Services released to state officials and health authorities a model certification program developed by the Centers for Disease Control and Prevention (CDC) encouraging the adoption of this program by individual states. It contained a set of quality standards that states could use for inspecting and certifying laboratories used in fertility clinics that provide assisted reproductive technology. However, certification of these laboratories by states is voluntary.

Accreditation. For physicians to become members of the Society of Assisted Reproductive Technology (SART), the andrology and embryology laboratories must pass a national laboratory accreditation inspection program for reproductive laboratories developed by the College of American Pathologists (CAP) and the American Society for Reproductive Medicine (ASRM). Using a checklist, the CAP/ASRM Reproductive Laboratory Accreditation Program examines all aspects of quality assurance in the laboratory, including methodology, reagents, control media, equipment, specimen handling, procedure manuals, reports and proficiency testing, qualifications of personnel, safety, and the overall management policies that distinguish a quality laboratory. Upon successful completion of the inspection process, the laboratory will be awarded CAP accreditation. In some states, CAP accreditation satisfies the state's regulatory agency.

Reimbursement. Since most third-party payers do not reimburse for assisted reproductive technologies, achieving Medicare certification to be able to bill a facility fee becomes a moot point.

Process and Patient Flow

The initial visit starts with a comprehensive physical and gynecological exam, a review of family and social history, and a review of male-related infertility issues. This initial interview and examination may take 45 to 50 minutes. Because the reasons for infertility problems are so diverse, the number of procedures to address these problems are similarly diverse. To give some idea of what is involved, consider two of the most frequent procedures, egg retrieval and egg transfer. In addition to taking hormones, the woman will take a medication at home and within a specified period of time—generally 35 hours—must come to the office for the egg retrieval. This is an ultrasound-guided needle aspiration procedure that is typically done under conscious sedation. Patients are understandably very nervous prior to this procedure. Afterward, the patient is transferred on a gurney to the recovery room where she remains for approximately an hour. Eggs and embryos are kept inside an incubator while in the embryology lab except when they are removed to be inseminated, changed to a new culture medium, or prepared for transfer to the uterus. The

IVF lab acts as a temporary womb to support fragile gametes (eggs and sperm) and nurtures newly formed embryos until they are transferred to the uterus; therefore, the environment has to be very carefully controlled.

Sperm Collection
The collection room, sometimes referred to euphemistically as the donor room, is where sperm are collected. This room should be furnished like a comfortable lounge, with a TV and VCR. The pressure on a man to perform is enormous. A man may ejaculate through masturbation or with the help of a partner in the room. Although there are many steps involved, a simple explanation is that sperm are first separated from the seminal fluid through repeated washing and spinning in a centrifuge, later to be subjected to *capacitation* (alterations to the surface of the sperm head accomplished by incubating it in a specially prepared culture to increase its ability to penetrate the egg).

Micromanipulation
During the process of micromanipulation, which uses a specialized inverted microscope, sperm are introduced into the egg by the embryologist. About 16 to 20 hours after insemination, the embryologist transfers each egg to a new growth medium to enhance its development and encourage cell division if fertilization has occurred.

Embryo Transfer
Finally, an ultrasound-guided embryo transfer to the uterus is performed. It's important that the woman be as relaxed as possible during embryo transfer as many stress-related hormones such as adrenalin can cause the uterus to contract. The nurse coordinator or counselor often sits at the bedside to coach the patient in relaxation techniques, often using guided imagery. Following the procedure, the patient is usually asked to lie on her back or side for one to two hours in the recovery area. This is a delicate procedure and it's important that no bleeding occurs and that the embryos are not damaged.

Schedule of Visits

Patients make frequent visits, which often involve blood draw and ultrasound examinations. Patients are often asked to drink a great deal of water prior to an ultrasound examination; therefore, a bathroom should open off the examination room (Figure 4-32) or immediately adjacent. The initial interview usually takes place in the physician's office or consultation room, followed by a discussion with the financial counselor. There are quite a number of sequential visits that need to be scheduled. Often, a close bond forms between the patient and the nurse coordinator who, over time, offers reassurance, support, and guidance.

Clinic Components

The program in Table 4-2 is based on an embryology lab equipped to process 300 to 600 retrievals per year. The space plans in Figures 4-32, 4-33, and 4-34 represent, respectively, a one-physician practice, a three-physician practice, and a four-physician practice. It should be noted that IVF procedure rooms are clean rooms, but not sterile. A number of procedures can be done in a smaller "minor" procedure room. These rooms should not have sinks as they compromise infection control.

Critical Adjacencies

Embryology/IVF Laboratory. Ideally, as exemplified by Figures 4-32, 4-33, and 4-34, the IVF lab is contiguous with the procedure rooms. If the distance to the place of egg retrieval or embryo transfer (the procedure room) exceeds 100 feet, then the use of an infant isolette or other method of maintaining temperature and pH for the eggs and embryos must be employed. Intercom communication is recommended if direct communication is not possible. The laboratory should be in a low-traffic, secured area with access limited to the embryologist and techs who work in the lab. Security is of utmost importance to maintain the sterile conditions of the space as well as to protect the specimens.

Table 4-2. Analysis of Program. Advanced Reproductive Technologies

Business/Administration			
Waiting Room		$20 \times 20 =$	400
Reception		—	180
Business Office[a]		—	550
Conference Room		—	300
Staff Lounge		$12 \times 12 =$	144
Staff Toilets	2@	$7 \times 8 =$	112
Storage		$8 \times 10 =$	80
Office Manager		$10 \times 12 =$	120
Financial Counselor		$10 \times 12 =$	120
Donor Program Coordinator		$8 \times 10 =$	80
Lab Director		$10 \times 12 =$	120
OR Nurse		$8 \times 10 =$	80
IVF Coordinator		$8 \times 10 =$	80
Psychologist		$10 \times 12 =$	120
Resource Library/Patient Education		$10 \times 12 =$	120
Clinical Areas			
Exam Rooms	6@	$10 \times 10 =$	600
Nurse Stations	2@	$8 \times 12 =$	192
Blood Draw		$6 \times 8 =$	48
Collection Room		$10 \times 10 =$	100
Toilets	3@	$7 \times 8 =$	168
Consultation Rooms	3@	$12 \times 12 =$	432
Andrology Lab		$10 \times 12 =$	120
Embryology Lab		—	720
Micromanipulation Area			
Cryopreservation Prep and Storage			
Male/Female Gowning/Lockers			
Storage (Med Gases and Supplies)			
Procedures/Operating Suite			
OR		$20 \times 20 =$	400
Procedure Room		$14 \times 16 =$	224
Scrub		—	24
Clean Utility		$8 \times 10 =$	80
Soiled Utility		$8 \times 10 =$	80
Central Supply		$10 \times 10 =$	100
Recovery Areas	2@	$8 \times 10 =$	160
Janitor Closet		$4 \times 6 =$	24
Miscellaneous[b]		—	80
Subtotal			6158 ft^2
20% Circulation			1232
Total			7390 ft^2

[a]Includes medical records, billing, and workroom (mail/copy).
[b]Biohazardous storage, medical gas storage, vacuum, and generator.
Note: This program supports three physicians.

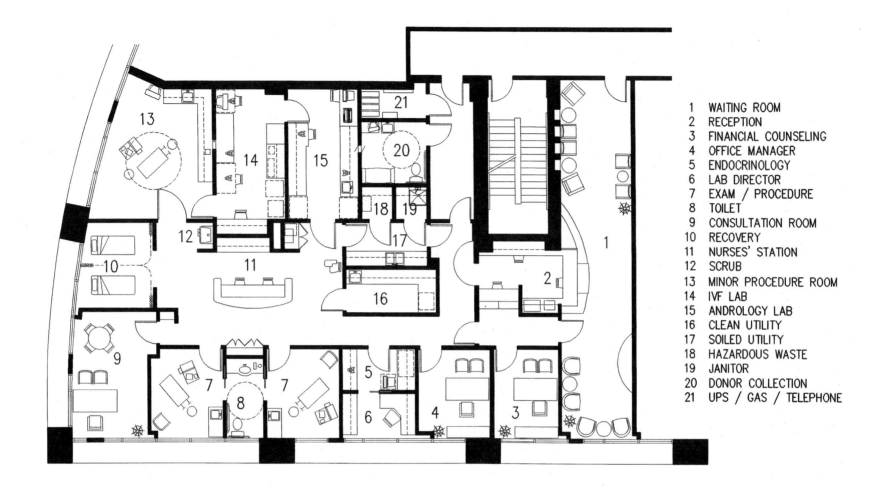

1 WAITING ROOM
2 RECEPTION
3 FINANCIAL COUNSELING
4 OFFICE MANAGER
5 ENDOCRINOLOGY
6 LAB DIRECTOR
7 EXAM / PROCEDURE
8 TOILET
9 CONSULTATION ROOM
10 RECOVERY
11 NURSES' STATION
12 SCRUB
13 MINOR PROCEDURE ROOM
14 IVF LAB
15 ANDROLOGY LAB
16 CLEAN UTILITY
17 SOILED UTILITY
18 HAZARDOUS WASTE
19 JANITOR
20 DONOR COLLECTION
21 UPS / GAS / TELEPHONE

SMOTRICH CENTER FOR REPRODUCTIVE ENHANCEMENT

3414 SF

Figure 4-32. Space plan, 3414 square feet. Smotrich Center for Reproductive Enhancement, La Jolla, CA. (*Design: Jain Malkin Inc.*)

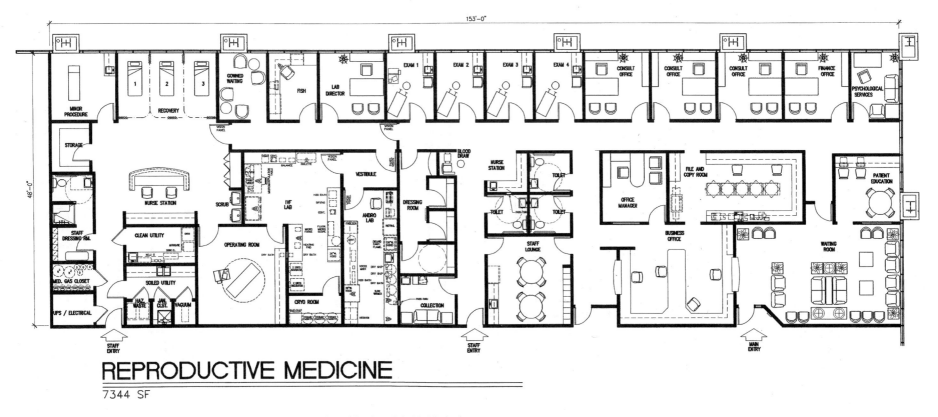

153'—0"

48'—0"

REPRODUCTIVE MEDICINE

7344 SF

Figure 4-33. Space plan for reproductive medicine, 7344 square feet. (*Design: Jain Malkin Inc.*)

Andrology Lab. This is not a clean room (although sterile technique is used) and it need not be adjacent to the IVF lab. Semen analysis is done here as well as sperm capacitation and cryopreservation.

Media Prep Room. Various culture media are prepared in this room. It can be within the IVF lab or adjacent to it.

Collection Room. This is best located in a quiet area of the suite and should be reasonably close to the andrology lab where semen is analyzed and sperm undergo the capacitation process. In fact, in some facilities (Figures 4-32 and 4-33) the collection room is adjacent to the andrology lab and there is a pass-through between the two rooms. However, it has an interlock that prevents someone in the lab from looking into the collection room.

Laboratory Equipment

Most of the equipment in the andrology and embryology laboratories is highly specialized for use in ART labs. The pieces of equipment are too numerous to be able to include photos in this chapter. Instead, following are the names of respected vendors for the larger pieces of equipment. Each has a Web site featuring equipment options and specifications.

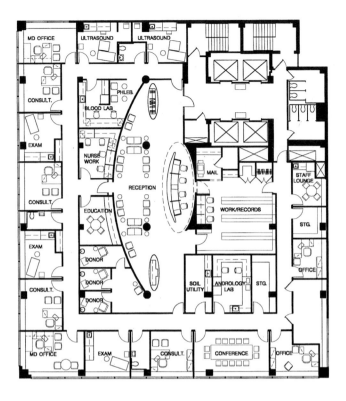

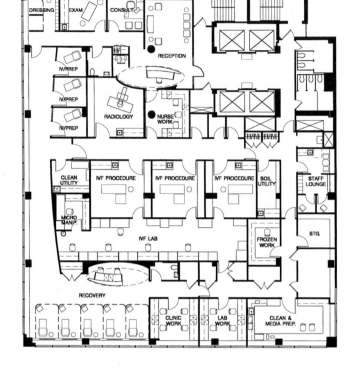

Figure 4-34. Space plan, 18,000 square feet. In vitro fertilization clinic. (*Planning and interior design: Perkins & Will, New York, NY.*)

THE CENTER FOR HUMAN REPRODUCTION
18,000 S.F.

Heraeus (incubators)

Forma Scientific, Inc. (incubators, cryopreservation dry shippers, laminar-flow bench workstations)

MVE (liquid nitrogen freezers)

Nikon (inverted microscope) (Note: a video camera may be used with this.)

Eppendorf (micromanipulator, centrifuges)

Mid-Atlantic Diagnostics: K-System (air suspension workbench with stereo microscope built into a vertical laminar flow cabinet)

Barnstead/Thermolyne (test tube mixers, rotators, and shakers)

Thermo Forma (microcentrifuges)

Diagnostics Products Corporation (Immulite endocrine analyzer)

A list of the principal pieces of equipment follows. It should be noted that there are consultants specific to the IVF field who specify equipment and do the laboratory layout, although the embryologist will have considerable input and may, in fact, take entire responsibility for the design and equipment selection (Figure 4-35). The relationship of each piece of equipment to another affects the electrical plan, requiring careful coordination.

General Lab Equipment. Includes refrigerators and freezers; cryogenic storage tanks; specialized microscopes; air suspension tables; centrifuges; test tube mixers, shakers, and rotators.

Andrology Lab. Includes laminar-flow hood; refrigerator; centrifuges, both large and small; phase microscope with fluorescence; warming oven; water-jacketed CO_2 incubator; dry shipper tanks (Figure 4-35).

Embryology Lab. Includes laminar-flow hood; stereo microscopes; stage warmers; centrifuges, large and small; computers and printer; incubators (tabletop model, water-jacketed CO_2, and high-effieciency particulate air [HEPA]–filtered CO_2); water purification system; waterline pressure pump and tank; dry heat ovens.

Embryology Micromanipulation Area. Includes air suspension table (to minimize vibration); inverted microscope; video camera, monitor, and recorder; stage warmer. The video camera and monitor enable the embryologist to perform the procedure at magnification on the monitor, rather than looking through the microscope. It also shows (if the OR has a large monitor) the embryo being loaded into the syringe just prior to the transfer procedure.

Cryopreservation Area. Includes laminar-flow hood, planar cell freezer, heat sealer, stereo dissecting microscope, liquid nitrogen tanks.

Microscopes need to be at sit-down workstations and must be at a comfortable height for the embryologist. This can differ depending on whether that individual is short or tall, which can sometimes be accommodated by adjusting the chair height. The selection of a task chair for this position is also very important as individual comfort and ergonomic features matter.

Note that there should *not* be overhead cabinets above the balance table in the micromanipulation area, the computerized semen analyzer, the cryopreservation counters, or the autoclave area. Areas under the cryopreservation countertop should be open to accommodate liquid nitrogen storage tanks on wheels. CO_2 lines should be centrally piped to the workbenches where it is needed. The endocrine analyzer can, if space is limited, be located outside the lab.

Lab Storage. If an adequate water purification system is not centrally installed, there will be a need to store quantities of ultra-pure water, which is delivered in large bottles. There are also many chemicals that need to be stored to support the lab functions.

Utility Requirements

HVAC/Air Quality Standards. Air quality is an important factor when trying to maintain process integrity. Testing reliability, results, and personal protection can be affected by airborne contamination. Air quality in laboratories is defined by Federal Standard 209E with classifications of Class 1, 10, 100, 1000, and so on. This Class number is the maximum allowable number of particles 0.5 micron and larger per cubic foot of air; the lower the number, the cleaner the air. International Standard ISO14644-1 classifications are rated as ISO Class 1, ISO Class 2, and so forth. According to both standards, Class 1 is the cleanest, ultra-pure air. ISO Class 2 correlates most closely to Federal Standard Class 100. The standard for an embryology lab is Class 100 air quality. The labs will have several laminar-flow hoods for carrying out certain procedures. The room should have a four-stage HEPA filtration system that purifies the air of the entire lab. The labs must have individual temperature, humidity, and velocity controls and there must be access to overhead ducts for periodic cleaning and changing of air filters. Air intake must not be near any source of contaminiation, and air from the hoods may need to be ducted directly to the outdoors, due to the chemicals used.

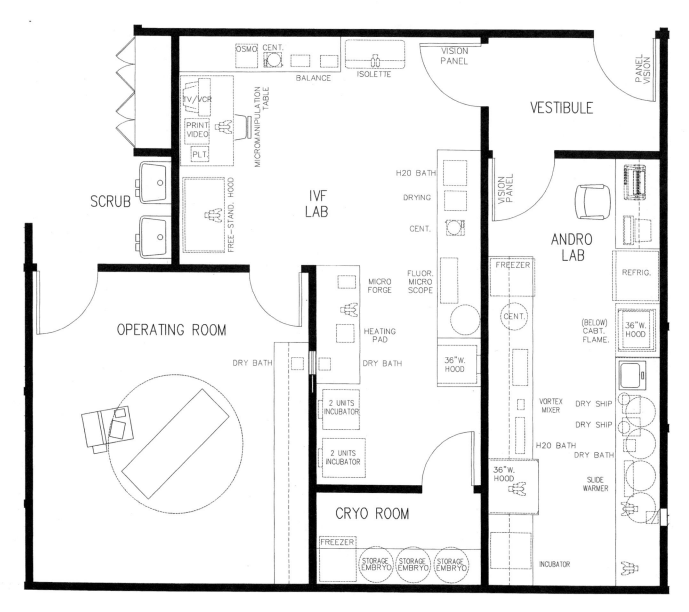

Figure 4-35. Layout, embryology and andrology labs. (*Planning: Jain Malkin Inc.*)

Lighting. Lighting in each section of the lab should be individually dimmable. It must be an incandescent source as fluorescents generate a frequency that may affect cellular development of the embryos. Procedures in exam rooms are generally done in full light, but being able to dim the lights during ultrasound is advisable. This could also be accomplished by being able to turn off the overhead lights and have just a wall sconce remain (Color Plate 14, Figure 4-36). In large procedure rooms, a ceiling-mounted surgical light is required. Here, as well, being able to dim the lights is important during ultrasound-guided procedures. There will be a large video monitor placed so that the patient can see when the embryologist loads the syringe for the embryo transfer. Room lighting needs to be placed to avoid glare on monitors.

Electrical. Of utmost importance in the labs is an uninterrupted power source for incubators, alarm systems, and monitors. Various types of back-up power systems are available. In addition, surge protection is needed for all electrical and electronic equipment.

Security and Alarm Systems. Laboratory security sometimes involves video cameras. Depending on the number of people who have access to the lab, a fingerprint identification system or magnetic card reader may be required. Alarm systems monitor incubators, gas and liquid nitrogen tanks, and cryotank monitors, relaying a message when equipment malfunctions. Successful results in this specialty demand precise temperature control and environmental conditions. Forma Scientific makes a monitor/alarm system that can interface with up to 24 pieces of equipment. It also makes the Sensaphone® telephone dialing system that interfaces with the alarm system to automatically dial several sequential telephone numbers of laboratory staff if something is amiss at the lab.

Medical Gases. There are a large number of medical gas cylinders within this suite. Even if general anesthesia is not used, there will be a need for centrally piped oxygen in the procedure rooms and the recovery room. The IVF culture area and micromanipulation area require vacuum and CO_2. The cryopreservation area requires liquid nitrogen (LN_2) and vacuum, and the media prep and andrology areas require CO_2 and vacuum.

Plumbing. Sinks must be precisely located in the laboratory areas. In addition, certain pieces of equipment may need to be connected to water and drain. As in any lab, noncorrosive piping must be used and sinks should be stainless steel. Eyewash diverters on sinks must meet OSHA requirements.

Interior Design Considerations
Embryology Laboratory. Purity of materials is of utmost importance. Off-gasing of volatile organic compounds (VOCs) from synthetic materials and contact cements used in plastic laminate casework should be reduced to the minimum possible. At completion of construction, high-velocity air filtration and fans should be used to exhaust as much of the construction dust and off-gasing of materials as possible prior to commissioning the lab. Usually, for two weeks prior to using human specimens, mouse or hamster eggs may be used to test conditions. Walls and floors should have no seams or crevices to reduce the possibility of contamination and make cleaning easier. Sheet flooring such as linoleum (made with natural materials) can be self-coved at the base to eliminate crevices. In terms of color, labs should be fairly neutral but white creates too much glare. A beige floor and walls work well. Embryologists often prefer to work on dark-colored (charcoal) countertops because it makes it easier to see dust. The doors to laboratories must have a sign saying *Authorized Staff Only.*

Procedure Room. Physicians often prefer a medium to dark floor in these rooms to eliminate glare. Note that the door will require a sign *Proper Surgical Attire Required.*

Accommodation of Celebrities

Well-established ART practices often attract celebrities, foreign dignitaries, and even heads of state who will be ushered into the office through a private entry, bypassing the waiting room. Occasionally, to accommodate these individuals, the office is closed so that no one but staff is present during the visit.

Relevant Art

A collection of fertility dolls from various cultures is interesting and relevant. Although not recommended for the waiting room, in a corridor, a large photo wall can be attractively created with photos of parents and their babies. Physicians in this specialty receive hundreds of photos from grateful patients. These range from poorly composed snapshots taken with disposable cameras to professionally posed photos with twins or triplets wearing matching outfits with a seasonal theme such as Easter bunnies or valentines. They are fetchingly adorable. Most photos will be color, which will make the overall effect quite busy. A solution is to take all of them to a professional photo lab and have an internegative made to convert them to crisp black-and-white prints, in exactly the desired sizes to fit the designer's selection of frames. Additionally, magazine and newspaper articles featuring the physician(s) can be attractively matted and professionally framed. The physician's diplomas should be prominently displayed in his or her consultation room (private office). Frames need not match and are more interesting if they complement each other, but don't match. This is not the time to go to Aaron Brothers to buy a picture frame. Patients need to have confidence in the fertility specialist since they are investing a great deal of time, emotion, and money in this endeavor.

ONCOLOGY

Oncologists treat cancer. Patients are referred by their primary-care physician or a specialist such as a urologist, gynecologist, gastroenterologist, or dermatologist, to name a few. Once a tumor or lesion has been identified, surgery is usually the first form of treatment, often followed by chemotherapy and/or radiation therapy. This discussion will focus on medical oncology, not radiation therapy. [The author's other book, *Hospital Interior Architecture,* also published by John Wiley, has an extensive chapter on radiation oncology facilities; however, several photos of linear accelerator installations are included in Chapter 5.]

The oncologist manages the patient's cancer treatments, conferring from time to time with the primary-care physician or specialist who referred the patient. Many medical oncologists prefer to do chemotherapy infusion in their offices rather than refer the patient to the hospital. This offers convenience for patients and a feeling of security that they are being treated under the watchful eye of their oncologist. The initial visit will typically be lengthy—perhaps an hour—and will occur in the oncologist's consultation room (private office). A view box illuminator or monitor for reading digital X-rays is required. These practices may include one or two physicians, or they may consist of a large group of 10 or 12 oncologists who are the prominent group providing major cancer care at the hospital on the MOB campus. Surgeons may become well known for certain types of surgical techniques, attracting patients from considerable distances. As an example, the suite plan in Figure 4-37 was designed for a gynecological oncologist.

The large cancer center in Figure 4-38 represents an unusually good functional layout of rooms, maintains appropriate critical adjacencies, and also has aesthetic flair with numerous curves, ceiling treatments, and design details.

Patient Flow

A course of chemo infusion may require visits once or twice a month for six months for certain regimens, or three days per week once a month, or two visits per month. The average infusion time is four hours, which means that patients get to know each other and provide encouragement and support to each other. Patients often arrive with a close friend or family member for company, necessitating a guest chair.

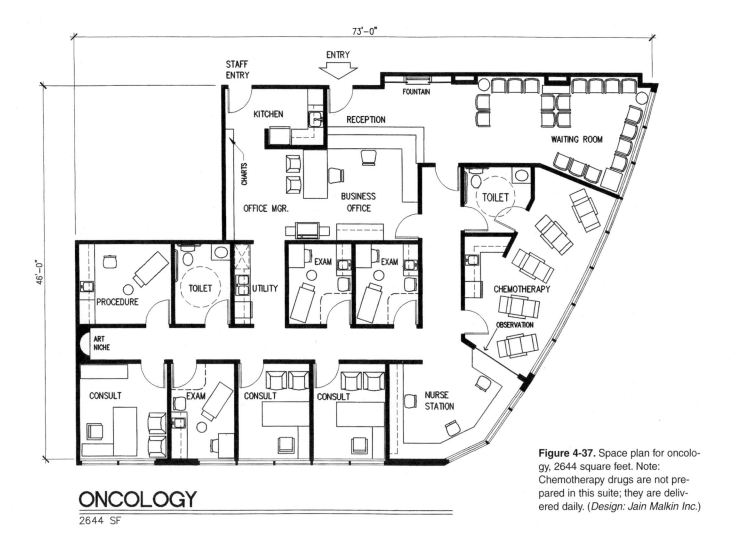

73'–0"

STAFF
ENTRY

ENTRY

FOUNTAIN

KITCHEN

RECEPTION

WAITING ROOM

CHARTS

OFFICE MGR.

BUSINESS
OFFICE

TOILET

46'–0"

PROCEDURE

TOILET

UTILITY

EXAM

EXAM

CHEMOTHERAPY

OBSERVATION

ART
NICHE

CONSULT

EXAM

CONSULT

CONSULT

NURSE
STATION

ONCOLOGY

2644 SF

Figure 4-37. Space plan for oncology, 2644 square feet. Note: Chemotherapy drugs are not prepared in this suite; they are delivered daily. (*Design: Jain Malkin Inc.*)

Patients first go to an exam room 75 percent of the time to see a doctor or nurse practitioner to reassess their situation and find out how they've been doing. Next, blood is drawn to verify that the white count is high enough to receive the next dose of chemo. Some practitioners draw blood in the exam room, while others use a blood draw chair in the lab. Still others do it in the recliner chair of the infusion bay as the IV is put in so that blood can be drawn for the CBC (complete blood count) so that the patient doesn't have to be stuck twice with a needle. A countertop CBC analyzer located in the lab provides results in 90 seconds.

Although in most facilities it is assumed that patients will be tethered to a recliner chair and not walk around during infusion, if the patient is feeling well, there is no reason why he or she cannot work a puzzle at a table or sit in a living room setting socializing with friends.

Many patients who visit oncologists do not receive chemotherapy. These patients may be on medications

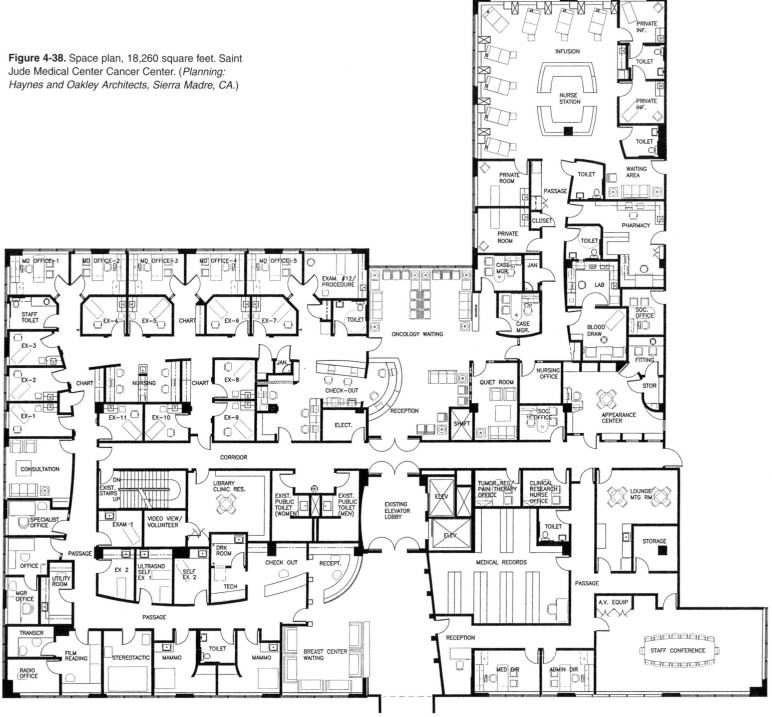

Figure 4-38. Space plan, 18,260 square feet. Saint Jude Medical Center Cancer Center. (*Planning: Haynes and Oakley Architects, Sierra Madre, CA.*)

that need to be monitored from time to time. For example, a patient with a slow-growth prostate cancer who is on medication to reduce the growth of the tumor will require frequent PSA (prostate-specific antigen) tests to monitor progress. In this practice, there are many return visits and a great deal of rapport and camaraderie often develops between the patients and staff over the years.

Space-Planning Considerations

Nurse Station
The nurse station should be at the front of the suite, convenient to exam rooms. Registered nurses, nurse practitioners, and/or medical assistants may work out of this room. The room will require a scale and may have a Pyxis™ Omnicell™ unit for dispensing and charging medications (Figure 4-39), a desk-height workstation with telephone and computer, ample storage for supplies, and a handwash sink. A full-height refrigerator is needed if a refrigerated medication dispensing unit like Pyxis or Omnicell is not used.

Laboratory
This is the most complex room in the suite and is often poorly designed, from a functional standpoint, because of the designer's lack of understanding of the numerous pieces of equipment that must be accommodated or, as is often the case, the space available falls far short of what is required for this room. This can result in printers tucked under countertops (Figures 4-40 and 4-41), computer keyboards placed in awkward locations (Figure 4-42), and pieces of equipment that should be placed side by side (Figures 4-43 and 4-44) tethered to each other by cords running along a wall.

Typically, the R.N. who mixes the chemicals also administers them to the patient. Because chemo drugs are highly toxic, this room is kept locked so that janitorial staff do not have access to it. Some oncologists have installed machines like Pyxis that keep an inventory of drugs, help to prevent error in dispensing medication, and provide

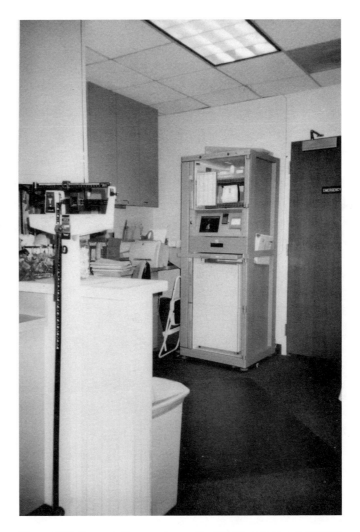

Figure 4-39. Nurse station, oncology suite. (*Photographer: Jain Malkin.*)

greater assurance that patients will be charged for all the meds. The Pyxis or Omnicell system automatically interacts with the billing system and charges the patient's account, as drugs are dispensed, and then also automatically reorders. There could be three or four drugs dispensed in one chemo preparation. Other meds like flu vaccines would be kept refrigerated at the nurse station.

Figure 4-40. Nurse station and lab, oncology suite. (*Photographer: Jain Malkin.*)

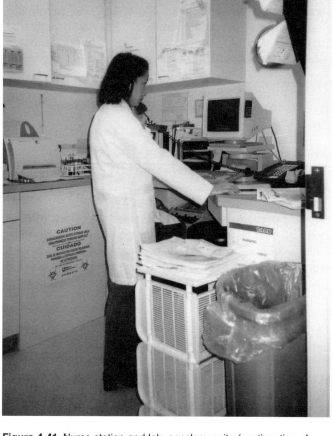

Figure 4-41. Nurse station and lab, oncology suite (continuation of Figure 4-40). (*Photographer: Jain Malkin.*)

Integration of Equipment. The large piece of equipment in Figure 4-42 is a blood count analyzer. This unit is close to the sink because it has a drain line that empties into the sink. It is an example of how, when adding new pieces of technology, in an effort to save money the physician may not want to make a hole in the cabinet to enable the drain line to connect to the plumbing under the sink. Over time, with a number of machines added, the room

becomes cluttered with jury-rigged connections. The lab in Figures 4-40, 4-41, 4-43, and 4-44 has several printers that would ideally be stacked in a vertical column with adjustable shelves, as indicated in the space plan layout shown in Figure 4-45. The blood count analyzer has a printer, as does the Pyxis, and there is a printer connected to the medical management software that prints labels, and another printer directly connected to a refer-

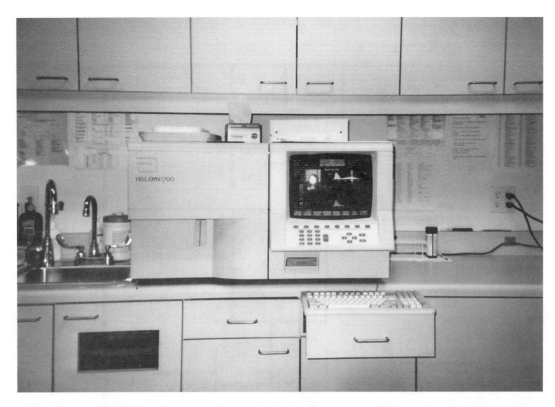

Figure 4-42. Laboratory, oncology suite. Note clinical analyzer on countertop. (*Photographer: Jain Malkin.*)

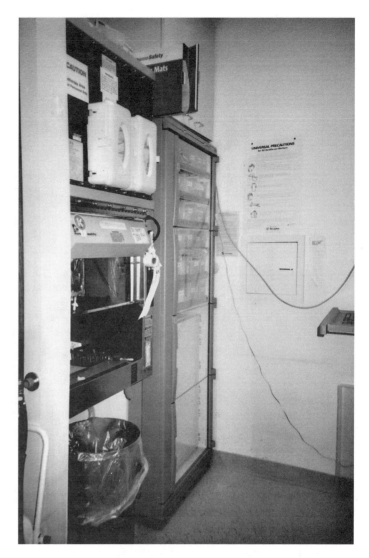

Figure 4-43. Laboratory, used for chemotherapy drug preparation (opposite side of room depicted in Figure 4-42). Note biological safety cabinet and, to the right, refrigerated medication inventory and dispensing unit. (*Photographer: Jain Malkin.*)

ence lab. A room 10×16 feet would be ideal. There also needs to be a kneespace workstation with telephone and computer monitor. If an automated medication dispensing unit is not used, a refrigerator for chemicals will be required. There will also be a centrifuge on the countertop as blood specimens that are sent out need to be spun down first. Generally, only blood counts are done in the office; all other lab work is sent out.

Biological Safety Cabinet. Chemotherapy infusion chemicals are mixed in a biological safety cabinet (Figures 4-43 and 4-46), which is a unit that protects the nurse or tech. It has laminar flow and a HEPA filter and generally need not be vented to the outside. The nurse must wear gloves, mask, gown, and safety goggles for

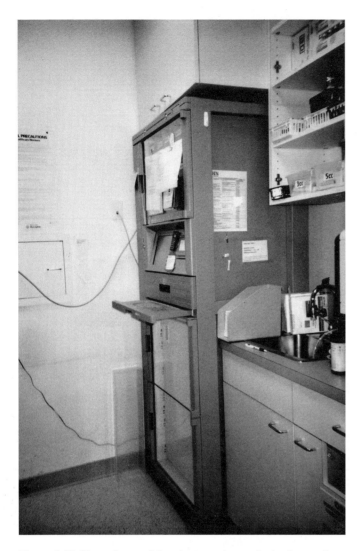

Figure 4-44. Chemotherapy laboratory, oncology suite (wall opposite that depicted in Figure 4-43). Note that the tall cabinet is a refrigerated medication inventory and dispensing unit. (*Photographer: Jain Malkin.*)

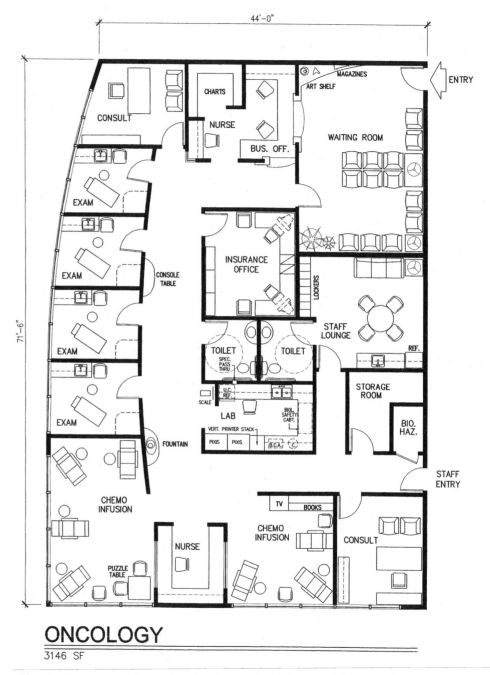

ONCOLOGY
3146 SF

Figure 4-45. Space plan for oncology, 3146 square feet. (*Design: Jain Malkin Inc.*)

mixing of chemicals, but only the gown and fresh gloves are worn when the chemicals are administered to the patient. The cabinet by Forma Scientific is called Class II Type A or AB, which refers to ventilated cabinets with open fronts that use inward airflow for personnel protection, have HEPA-filtered laminar airflow for product protection, and have HEPA-filtered exhausted air for environmental protection per NSF (National Science Foundation) Standard 49. Biological safety cabinets are the primary containment devices used in laboratories to prevent the escape of aerosols. As an optional feature, the cabinet can be vented to exhaust to the outdoors. Local codes must always be consulted in these matters.

Utility Requirements. The benchtop model includes a built-in drain valve, a service valve, and one plugged penetration. The unit incorporates two separate circuit breakers and two line cords, one for the blower/motor and interior lights and one for the electrical outlet.

Patient Visibility

A nurse station is always adjacent to the chemo infusion area so that patients are constantly observed. In addition, nurses are continually circulating through the infusion area to change bags of chemicals on the IV stands as they are emptied. If the lab is contiguous with the infusion area, there is often a window through which one could observe patients. The lab should be as close to the infusion area as possible so that nurses always maintain contact with patients and chemicals do not need to be carried throughout the suite.

OSHA

OSHA has many requirements for biohazardous waste and protection of workers, more fully discussed in Chapter 3. Among these are an eyewash device at the sink in the lab. The closet for biohazardous waste needs to be locked and should ideally be located near the service or staff entrance to the suite for easy collection by a contracted vendor.

OSHA's Office of Occupational Medicine, in a report titled "Exposure to Hazardous Drugs," describes antineo-

Figure 4-46. Biological safety cabinet used for preparation of chemotherapy drugs. (*Photographer: Jain Malkin.*)

Figure 4-47. Chemotherapy infusion lounge. (*Photographer: Jain Malkin.*)

Universal precautions must be followed for this laundry. However, cytotoxic drugs (chemicals that are directly toxic to cells, preventing their reproduction or growth) are not necessarily rendered harmless by laundering, according to OSHA, and should be prewashed to remove as much of the drugs as possible before coming into contact with other laundry. Proper storage of contaminated linen should be provided so that housekeeping personnel do not risk exposure.

Off-Site Preparation of Chemotherapy Drugs

Some oncologists do not prepare chemotherapy drugs in their offices. They are prepared off site at the hospital pharmacy or delivered by a pharmaceutical supply vendor. In this case, there may not be a lab or the lab will be quite minimal as in Figure 4-37 where, in addition, patients are sent to the lab in the building for their blood tests.

Chemotherapy Infusion

Although spaces designed for this function are often nothing more than a large room with a group of recliner chairs, often placed too closely together, gregarious individuals welcome the closeness and conviviality such a setting often fosters (Figure 4-47). According to research, providing options and choices reduces stress. The environment in Figure 4-48 offers more space for each chair; includes individual sloped magazine racks, CD players, and VCRs; has views of nature and access to natural light (if the patient were to turn and look out the window); maintains good visual contact with the nurse station; and displays variety in lighting. The chair has speakers built into the back at shoulder level and "therapeutic" music. The space plan for this infusion unit is presented in Figure 4-38.

Other Planning Considerations

Personal Space. Provide a place for personal belongings such as briefcases, books, or handbags so that they are not on the floor where the nurse might trip on them. The casework in Figure 4-49 between every two chairs provides a measure of privacy, a place to attach the bracket

plastic drugs (cytochemotherapeutic agents) as agents capable of inhibiting tumor growth by disrupting cell division and killing actively growing cells. The potential hazards for oncology nurses who prepare the chemicals are substantial unless very strict protocols are followed. The exposure occurs by inhalation of the aerosolized drug (thought to be the primary exposure route), percutaneous (through the skin) absorption, and accidental ingestion. All surfaces of the room should be easy to clean, with few crevices or seams. A high-quality sheet vinyl with self-coved base is ideal. An additional issue is the laundering of linen or uniforms that have been contaminated with chemotherapeutic drugs or infectious agents.

for a personal TV, and the end of the cabinet lifts up for access to commonly used supplies needed by nurses.

Nonclinical Appearance. A wood-look sheet vinyl floor adds warmth to the room. There are no restrictions against plants or carpet if a living room option is provided with a puzzle table and lounge chairs. Locating the infusion area on an upper floor (if there is an option) sometimes conveys the feeling of being in a treehouse as in Figure 4-49. Research shows that connecting patients to nature by way of views, water elements, or even simulated views of nature greatly reduces stress.

Patient Safety. Allowing adequate space around each chair is necessary to assure patient safety. In a "code" situation, staff must have ready access to all sides of the patient, especially the head.

Visibility. Patients typically want to know that they can be seen by the nurse and they often find it diverting to watch the activity at the nurse station. There is always the trade-off (especially when a beautiful view is available outside the windows) of turning the chairs so that they face the view, which means that they generally no longer face the nurse station.

Waste Receptacles. It is hard to imagine how much waste is generated in an infusion setting unless one observes the activity for several hours. Infusions are packed in thick plastic pouches hanging on IV stands. The idea is to enable the nurse to discard the empty bag without having to walk very far to do it. The same is true for sharps containers, yet one wouldn't want to see them exposed next to the patient. The shorter the distance one has to walk to dispose of sharps or chemo bags the less opportunity there is for exposure or needle sticks. It takes a very thoughtful designer to address these functional issues so that these items are built in and unobtrusive. In addition, there are numerous large waste carts on casters that are unattractive to look at and rarely are they well accommodated by the designer.

Figure 4-48. Chemotherapy infusion provides options for privacy and many amenities for patients. Saint Jude Medical Center Cancer Center. (*Architecture and interior design: Haynes and Oakley Architects, Sierra Madre, CA; Photographer: Barbara White Architectural Photography.*)|

interactive work of art, a library of videotapes, and a table with a jigsaw puzzle are welcome diversions. Think about a humor corner with decor and resources all focused on laughter and mirth. The 7000-square-foot medical oncology center in Figure 6-5 features a large saltwater aquarium in the main lobby, adjacent to a resource library (Figure 4-50).

Interior Design

There are no special restrictions in terms of interior design for this specialty with the exception of what common sense would dictate for the lab and nurse station. Chemo infusion can be carpeted, have textured vinyl wallcoverings, and use wall sconce lighting. Preferably, ambient light will not come from fixtures located directly over patient chairs. (Some feel carpet should not be used because drops of chemotherapy agents that spill must be cleaned up and they are hard to inactivate without using a bleach-and-water solution. Options would be a wood-look sheet vinyl or a solution-dyed carpet that *can* be cleaned with bleach.) Glare must be considered from the standpoint of a patient reclining in a chair. Even downlights with a polished Alzak® (looks like polished chrome) interior and compact fluorescent lamps can create a tremendous hot spot directly in the eyes of a seated patient. Lighting that can be adjusted by the patient, or increased when the nurse needs it, would be optimal.

The oncologist's practice is composed of equal numbers of men and women; therefore, the design style, colors, and vocabulary of details should reflect the community the practice serves. Recliner chairs in the infusion room need not be covered with uncomfortable—and cold to the touch—vinyl upholstery fabric but must be wiped clean of blood, IV solutions, and chemotherapy spills. Woven Crypton® provides the same benefits, yet has the ambience of a fine-woven fabric with no limitation on beautiful colors and patterns.

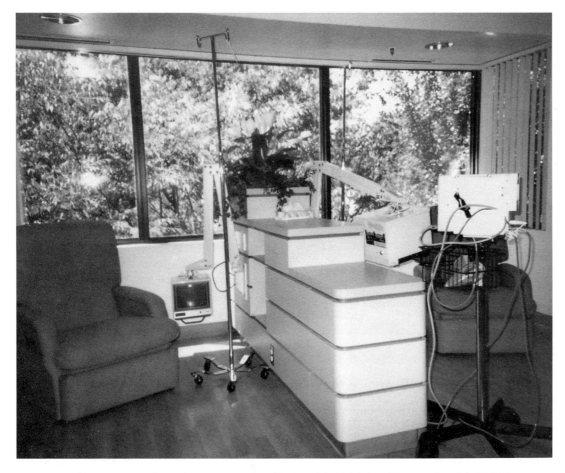

Figure 4-49. Chemotherapy infusion in a treetop setting. (*Design: Jain Malkin Inc.; Photographer: Jain Malkin.*)

Hand Washing. Locate sinks in several locations to make it convenient for nurses and doctors to wash their hands. This is essential for infection control.

Other Amenities. A restroom must be nearby, along with a place for self-serve beverages. Family and friends must be accommodated as most patients seem to arrive with another individual for emotional support. Pleasant diversions such as a saltwater aquarium, an

Figure 4-50. Reception/waiting area. Hope Cancer Care Center, Morton Grove, IL. (*Architecture and interior design: Mekus Studios, Chicago, IL; Photographer: Jon Miller® Hedrich Blessing.*)

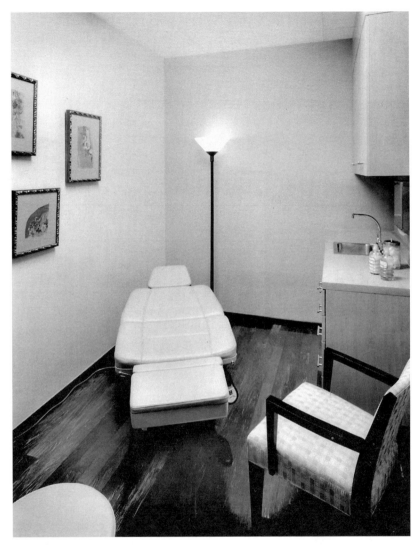

Figure 4-51. Examination room, vascular surgery. (Interior architecture and *Design: Jain Malkin Inc.; Photographer: Steve McClelland.*)

GENERAL SURGERY

This is a low-volume practice in large part dependent on referrals from primary-care physicians. The suite can be small, because most of a surgeon's work is done in a hospital. Patients are examined and interviewed preoperatively and postoperatively in the office, and sutures may be removed or dressings changed.

A surgeon's office (solo practitioner) will usually contain two or three standard- sized exam rooms (Figure 4-51), a large consultation room (12×12 or 12×14 feet), a small business office, a waiting room, and a restroom. (If one exam room is larger—10×12 feet—it can be used for minor surgery.) A small nurse station, a niche in the corridor, will suffice for the sterilization of instruments and storage of dressings and supplies (Figure 4-52). An undercounter refrigerator should be built into the cabinet. Figure 4-53 diagrams the relationship of rooms.

The waiting room need not accommodate more than eight chairs, since patients are well scheduled and usually do not have to wait a long time. The waiting room in Color Plate 14, Figure 4-54, was designed for a prominent vascular surgeon and reflects his love of contemporary art and architecture. It's a serene retreat for patients who have an abundant choice of current magazines and dozens of art books while they sip tea or freshly brewed coffee. Surgeons usually perform surgery in the morning and see patients in the office during the afternoon. The consultation room is larger than for many medical specialties because it may be used for consulting with patients. A double-panel X-ray view box should be located near the desk.

In a two-surgeon office, it is likely that schedules will be arranged so that one sees patients in the office while the other does surgery. In a three-surgeon practice, perhaps two would see patients at the same time, sharing four or five exam rooms and a minor surgery room (Figures 4-55 and 4-56).

In a one-physician practice, two employees can usually run the business office—answering the phone, book-

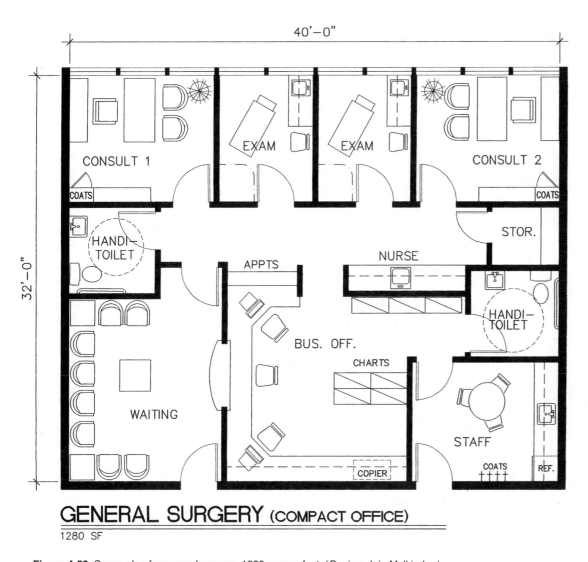

GENERAL SURGERY (COMPACT OFFICE)

1280 SF

Figure 4-52. Space plan for general surgery, 1280 square feet. (*Design: Jain Malkin Inc.*)

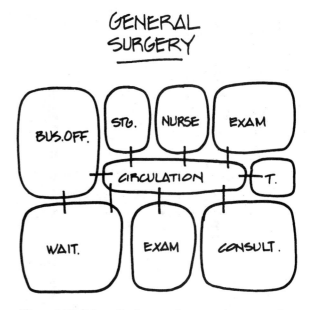

GENERAL SURGERY

Figure 4-53. Schematic diagram of a general surgery suite.

ing appointments, handling insurance, and billing patients. A three- or four-physician practice will have an expanded business office with more staff performing the tasks of reception, bookkeeping, insurance, and surgery scheduling (Figure 4-55).

All rooms of this suite may be carpeted. The decor should be cheerful with warm colors but, above all, it must convey a solid, conservative image due to the nature of the specialty. A patient wants to think of a surgeon as a serious person not subject to frivolities and trendy decor.

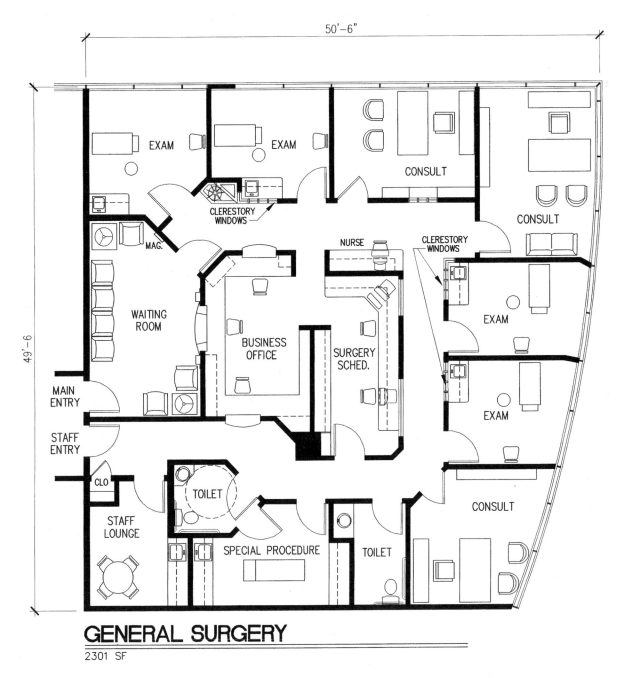

50'–6"

49'–6

EXAM

EXAM

CONSULT

CONSULT

CLERESTORY WINDOWS

MAG.

NURSE

CLERESTORY WINDOWS

WAITING ROOM

BUSINESS OFFICE

SURGERY SCHED.

EXAM

MAIN ENTRY

STAFF ENTRY

EXAM

CLO

TOILET

CONSULT

STAFF LOUNGE

SPECIAL PROCEDURE

TOILET

GENERAL SURGERY

2301 SF

Figure 4-55. Space plan for general surgery, 2301 square feet. (*Design: Jain Malkin Inc.*)

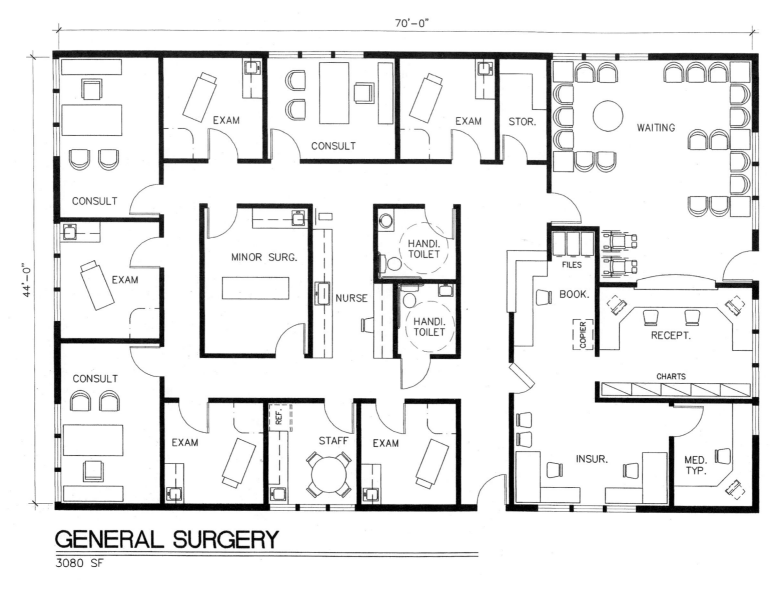

GENERAL SURGERY

3080 SF

Figure 4-56. Space plan for general surgery, 3080 square feet. (*Design: Jain Malkin Inc.*)

Table 4-3.
Analysis of Program.
Otolaryngology

No. of Physicians:	1		2	
Exam Rooms	3@	10 × 10 = 300	5@	10 × 10 = 500
Consultation Rooms		12 × 14 = 168	2@	12 × 14 = 336
Business Office		12 × 18 = 216		12 × 18 = 216
Nurse Station/Lab		8 × 10 = 80		8 × 12 = 96
Waiting Room		14 × 16 = 224		14 × 20 = 280
Audio Room with Dispensing		8 × 18 = 144		8 × 18 = 144
Toilets	2@	7 × 8 = 112	2@	7 × 8 = 112
Minor Surgery		12 × 12 = 144		—
Outpatient Surgery				
Operating Room		—		14 × 16 = 224
Scrub		—		4 × 5 = 20
Nurse Station		—		6 × 8 = 48
Soiled Utility		—		8 × 8 = 64
Cleaned Utility		—		8 × 8 = 64
Med Gas Storage		—		3 × 4 = 12
Janitor Closet		—		3 × 4 = 12
Equipment (air and suction)		—		4 × 4 = 16
Recovery (2 beds)		—		10 × 14 = 140
Storage		8 × 8 = 64		8 × 8 = 64
X-Ray (Optional)		—		9 × 12 = 108
Darkroom (Optional)		—		6 × 6 = 36
Staff Lounge		10 × 10 = 100		10 × 12 = 120
Subtotal		1552 ft²		2612 ft²
20% Circulation		310		522
Total		1862 ft²		3134 ft²

Note: The one-physician suite outlined above would serve an otolaryngologist who does not do office-based surgery; the two-physician suite is designed for practitioners who do.

OTOLARYNGOLOGY

An otolaryngologist treats diseases of the ears, nose, and throat and tumors of the head and neck. The surgical specialty is more commonly known as ENT (ear, nose, and throat), and its practitioners sometimes practice facial plastic surgery as well.

For maximum efficiency, a solo practitioner needs three examination rooms, a waiting room that seats 10 or 11 persons, an audio test room and hearing aid dispensing area, a minor surgery room (or if facial plastic surgery is practiced, an outpatient surgery suite and recovery room), occasionally an X-ray room and darkroom, a business office, a consultation room, and a nurse station/lab (Figures 4-57 and 4-58). A two-physician suite may not be much larger, but would have an additional consultation room and two or three additional exam rooms. Figure 4-59 shows the relationship of rooms.

In-house X-ray is declining due to OSHA and other regulatory issues, the cost of a technician, and liability in reading films. In addition, the most complex problems are now diagnosed by CT scan or magnetic resonance imaging (MRI), which have become the standard of care.

The consultation room is large (12×14 feet) since patients are often brought into this room to discuss fees for surgery or to discuss the feasibility of a surgical procedure. The X-ray room can be as small as 8×12 feet, depending on the physician's equipment, since films are limited to the head and neck. The reader is referred to Chapter 3 for space-planning details of an X-ray room, control area, darkroom, and lead shielding. The darkroom can be small, since the physician will probably have a tabletop model automatic film processor similar to the kind used by dentists. The designer must obtain the specs on utility requirements from the manufacturer of the unit.

Exam Rooms

Examination rooms should be 10×10 feet ideally with the sink cabinet located on the long wall. A motorized examination chair (see Figure 4-60) is located in the center of

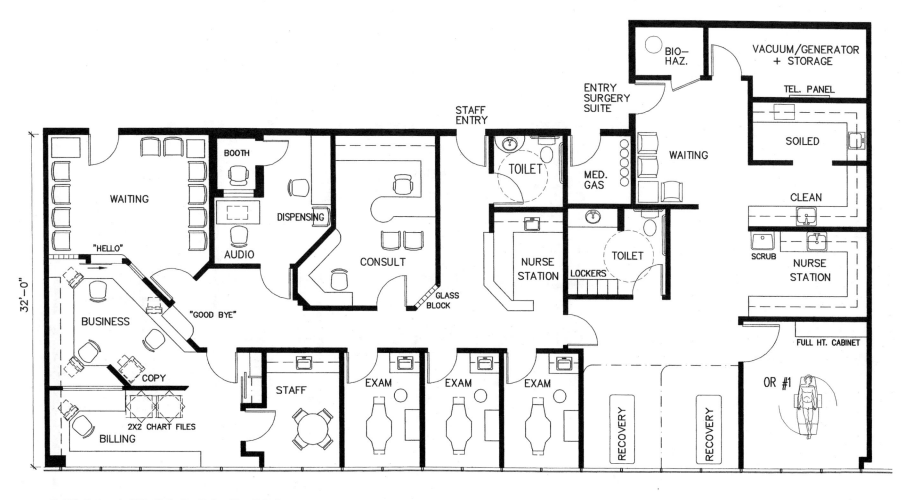

OTOLARYNGOLOGY (WITH SURGERY SUITE)

2883 SF

Figure 4-57. Space plan for otolaryngology (with surgery suite), 2883 square feet. (*Design: Jain Malkin Inc.*)

Figure 4-58. Space plan for otolaryngology, 2698 square feet. (*Design: Jain Malkin Inc.*)

59'-6"

28'-0"

OFF. MGR.

S.M.P. UNIT | MEMBOX
DESK
EXAM

S.M.P. UNIT | MEMBOX
DESK
EXAM

S.M.P. UNIT | MEMBOX
DESK
EXAM

TOILET

STOR.

CONSULT

TOILET

FAN PROJECTION
AUDIO BOOTH

AUDIO

WAITING

BUS. OFF.

CHARTS

COPY

INSUR.

REF.

STAFF LOUNGE

NURSE STA.

PROC

DKRM.

VIEW BOXES

CONTROL CONSOLE

X-RAY

JAN.

WORK ROOM

VIEW BOXES

RECOVERY

MINOR SURG.

63'-0"

29'-6"

OTOLARYNGOLOGY
2698 SF

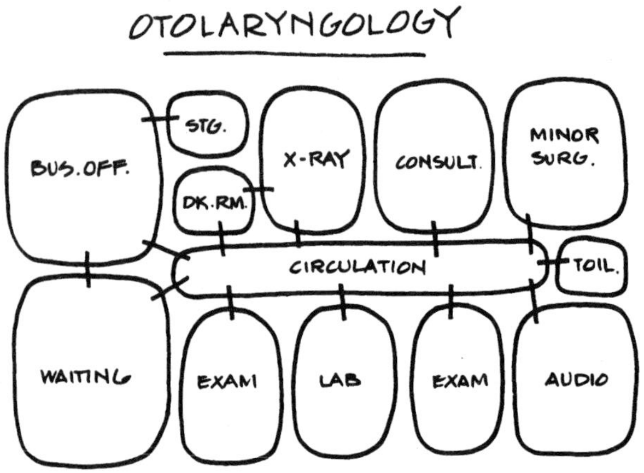

OTOLARYNGOLOGY

BUS.OFF.

STG.

DK.RM.

X-RAY

CONSULT.

MINOR SURG.

CIRCULATION

TOIL.

WAITING

EXAM

LAB

EXAM

AUDIO

Figure 4-59. Schematic diagram of an otolaryngology suite.

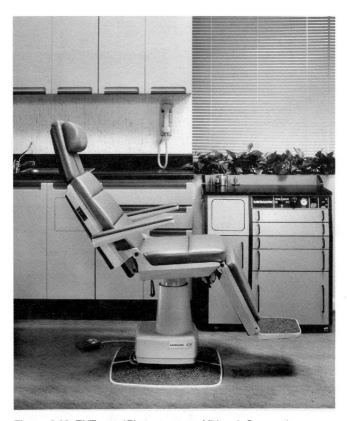

Figure 4-60. ENT cart. (*Photo courtesy: Midmark Corporation, Versailles, OH.*)

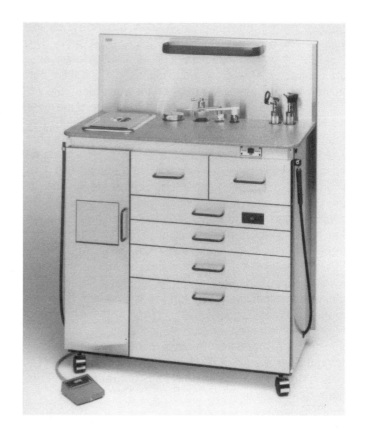

Figure 4-61. ENT cabinet for otolaryngology exam room. Deluxe MaxiCabinet. (*Photo courtesy: Global Surgical Corporation, St. Louis, MO.*)

the room with the patient facing the door. The chair swivels 360 degrees. The physician works off of a cart along the wall, to the right of the patient. Most of the time, the physician is seated on a stool with casters. Each exam room needs an X-ray view box recessed into the wall.

The unit from which the physician works is usually a specialized manufactured instrument cabinet on casters (Figures 4-60 and 4-61) containing a suction unit and pump, compressed air, a cautery, an electrical panel for instruments, racks for solution bottles, and a shelf and drawers for medications, cotton jars, irrigation syringes, and atomizers. The unit also has a pull-out writing shelf.

Approximately 23 inches wide×18 inches deep×46 inches high at the rear panel, it requires a grounded duplex outlet. Some units have Corian® tops and plastic laminate faces. [These are often referred to as Storz/SMR carts by physicians, but the SMR division of Storz Instrument was acquired by Global Surgical Corp. in 1994.]

Sometimes the medical examination cabinet is purchased without suction and air features, in which case the designer needs to provide a vacuum system within the suite. Many physicians prefer central suction. A small room, 4 feet 6 inches×5 feet, should be provided close to the examination rooms to eliminate long-distance piping.

Vacuum pumps and air compressors are noisy, so the walls of this room should be well insulated. Usually, two separate 20-ampere circuits will be required. A local vacuum contractor or a competent plumbing contractor can provide the designer with specs on the equipment and will install the plastic piping. The piping would be done after the HVAC (heating, ventilating, and air conditioning) has been completed, but before the partitions are closed up.

One exam room may be slightly larger to accommodate digital fiber-optic diagnostic equipment (Figure 4-62). This involves a Sony monitor, an image capture device (miniature camera on tip of fiberoptic scope), and a printer. Both physician and patient can watch the procedure on video and the patient can leave with a photo. With a different probe, one can examine the ear, nose, throat, and larynx.

A nice feature in exam rooms and the recovery room is a wall-mounted cosmetic mirror—perhaps a small plastic laminate cabinet with two hinged doors, which, when opened, reveal a good-quality mirror and two rows of makeup lights on either side. A light over the mirror will only create a shadow on the face. In designing the mirror, being able to visualize the head from both sides, or profiles, is desirable. A dressing area is not required in ENT exam rooms.

Office-Based Surgery

If the physician does only ENT and no facial plastic surgery, a minor surgery room (refer to Chapter 3) would be used for special procedures and for emergency care. As the practice matures, some otolaryngologists tend toward more cosmetic and reconstructive facial plastic surgery because it is more lucrative and, perhaps, more interesting than routine ENT procedures. Procedures such as nose reconstruction, facelifts, eye tucks, and face peels as well as routine tonsillectomies and sinus surgery may be performed in the office in a well-equipped outpatient surgery room with ancillary recovery room and scrub and prep areas (Figure 4-57). Regulations have tightened on office-based surgery, requiring far more space than practitioners previously allocated.

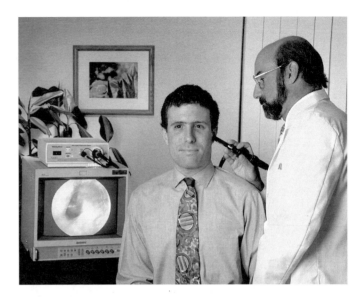

Figure 4-62. Diagnostic ENT VideoScope enables the patient or family member to visualize the medical problem and also facilitates telemedicine consultations. (*Photo courtesy: AMD Telemedicine, Lowell, MA.*)

The surgery room should contain one wall of built-in cabinets, and the sink should have a plaster trap and foot-lever control for hot, warm, and cold water. Scrub and prep can be done in the surgery room if the room is large enough and if patient volume is low. An electrical outlet is required in the floor for the motorized table. Other electrical outlets and connections for suction, compressed air, and instruments should be located by the physician, since this room allows for a variety of options with respect to work habits. The reader is referred to Plastic Surgery section for a detailed discussion of an office-based surgery suite, requirements for third-party payers, and accreditation issues.

Audio Testing

A basic part of an otolaryngologist's practice involves diagnosing and treating patients with a hearing loss. An audiometric test booth is used for testing hearing. It is a soundproofed booth approximately 30×40 inches (or

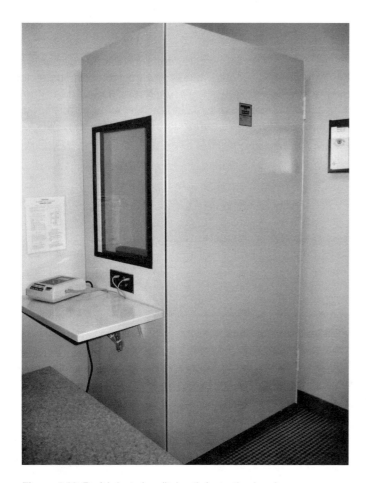

Figure 4-63. Prefabricated audio booth for testing hearing. (*Photographer: Jain Malkin.*)

Figure 4-64. Audio booth with cartoon design. (*Design: Jain Malkin Inc.; Photographer: Jain Malkin.*)

may be larger) with a door at one end. The patient sits inside and listens to sounds of different frequencies through headphones. The technician or audiologist sits outside the booth, at a counter facing the patient, and looks into the booth through a window so that the patient is always in view (Figure 4-63). This countertop contains the audio equipment from which sounds are transmitted to the patient in the booth. The patient's responses are digitally recorded, and a graph of hearing loss is produced for the physician to evaluate.

The audio booth is available as a prefabricated unit (Figure 4-64) that breaks down into components (the large ones) and is assembled in the room by an installation technician. Smaller units are preassembled. The booth has a roof-integrated ventilation system, lighting, and a prewired medical jack panel to connect it to the testing equipment. The audio testing room must be located in a quiet part of the suite, away from the heavy traffic of the waiting room and business office. If the prefab booth is to be handicapped accessible, it will require a large room and a small ramp to get over the 4-inch-high "ledge."

A custom audio booth can be built on the job, but rigorous construction specifications must be adhered to in order to achieve a sound transmission class of 55 to 60 decibels. Double-stud walls with several layers of sound board, insulation batting, and a solid-core door with an acoustic seal on all sides would be required.

Hearing Aid Dispensing

The audiologist will make a mold of the ear and fit and adjust the hearing aid when it arrives. From time to time, patients will return to have their hearing aids fine tuned. This can take place in the same room as the audio testing if a desk is provided for the audiologist and if there is suitable storage. An L- or U-shaped desk works best. The computerized equipment that tunes the hearing aid sits on the desk and the patient sits to the side of the desk facing the audiologist (Figure 4-65).

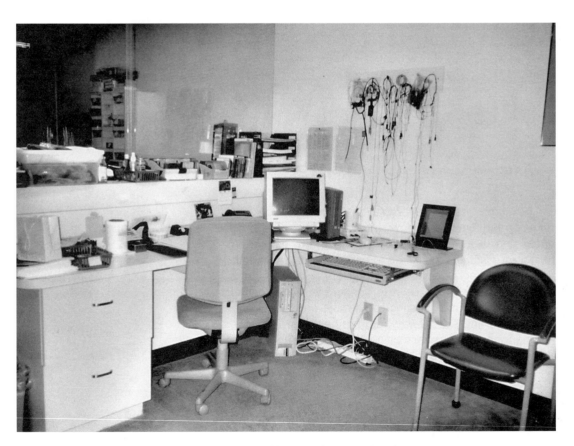

Figure 4-65. Audiologist's desk for fitting hearing aids. (*Photographer: Jain Malkin.*)

Interior Design

There are no special requirements for interior design in this suite. If the practice tends toward facial plastic surgery, the office design should reinforce the image of the surgeon as a successful, skilled professional with refined aesthetic taste. The reader is referred to the Plastic Surgery section in this chapter for additional discussion of this topic.

OPHTHALMOLOGY

This specialty is characterized by a variety of options in suite design. Therefore, the individual practitioner must make the basic decisions on preferred work habits before the designer can begin.

The constant demand for specialized eye care means that the ophthalmologist may attain a capacity patient load within the first two years of practice. Thus, it is important to project at the outset what the ophthalmologist's space needs will be in two or three years. Often, young ophthalmologists setting up their first offices will try to be too economical. They set up an undersized office based on their patient projection (usually underestimated) at that moment. Then, for the remainder of their lease (usually five years), they are handicapped by a small, poorly laid out office, which greatly inhibits the growth of their practice.

Patient Volume

Many ophthalmologists schedule three patients per hour for regular eye examinations, although the testing portion of the examination and updating the patient's medical history is done by a tech or medical assistant prior to the physician entering the room. Added to that are unscheduled patients—emergency and trauma—and postoperative patients, and it is not unusual for an ophthalmologist to see four or five patients an hour. Individual practice habits may differ, with some doctors spending more time informally chatting with patients than those who choose to work in a more restricted, tightly scheduled manner. The more relaxed ophthalmologist may see only two patients per hour, particularly if he or she does all the testing with little assistance from aides, but this is rare, especially with declining reimbursement and the pressures of managed care.

Required Rooms

A solo practitioner needs at least two refraction rooms, plus a third multipurpose or surgery/treatment room (Figure 4-66). While a patient whose examination has been concluded is gathering up possessions and receiving medications and instructions from the tech or aide, the doctor has already stepped into the next refraction room and has begun to examine the patient with no loss of time. The surgery room can be used for removing a foreign body from the eye or for other emergency visits, or the doctor may see an unscheduled patient in this room while he or she is between patients without interrupting scheduled patients in the refraction rooms. The surgery room can also be used for photography or for visual fields testing or othoptic evaluations. Some ophthalmologists do not require a large multipurpose treatment room as they do all their procedures in the exam room, including removal of cysts, suturing lacerations, and so on. However, an ophthalmologist who does cosmetic procedures on eyelids and forehead can perform these in the office in a surgery room. These are typically done using local anesthetic.

An ophthalmologist does not need a nurse station or lab as such, but it is advisable to provide a work space in a niche off the corridor (Figure 4-67) for an assistant or tech. This is where phone calls can be received or made to reschedule patients, prescriptions authorized, and medications dispensed. Ophthalmologists dispense a number of eyedrops and medications, which may be stored in a rack in each examining room or at the assistant's work area.

Table 4-4.
Analysis of Program.
Ophthalmology

No. of Physicians:	1	2	4
Refracting Rooms	3@ 10 × 12 = 360[a]	4 total = 700[b]	8@ 10 × 12 = 960
Surgery	11 × 12 = 132	2@ 12 × 12 = 288	12 × 22 = 264
Consultation	10 × 12 = 120	2@ 10 × 12 = 240	4@ 10 × 12 = 480
Fields Room	8 × 8 = 64	—	8 × 8 = 64
Data Collection	—	10 × 10 = 100	10 × 14 = 140
Waiting Room	12 × 18 = 216	16 × 28 = 448	22 × 26 = 572
Drops	6 × 10 = 60	8 × 12 = 96	Use Waiting Room
Toilets	2@ 7 × 8 = 112	2@ 7 × 8 = 112	2@ 7 × 8 = 112
Business Office	12 × 14 = 168	12 × 16 = 192	12 × 20 = 240
Storage	4 × 6 = 24	6 × 8 = 48	6 × 8 = 48
Optician, Lab, and Contact Lens	10 × 24 = 240	(Nondispensing Physician)	18 × 30 = 540
Staff Lounge	—	8 × 10 = 80	12 × 12 = 144
Subtotal	1496 ft²	2304 ft²	3564 ft²
20% Circulation	299	461	713
Total	1795 ft²	2765 ft²	4277 ft²

[a]Using mirrors.
[b]Twenty-four-foot refracting rooms (two "interlocking" together occupy approximately 10×35 ft).

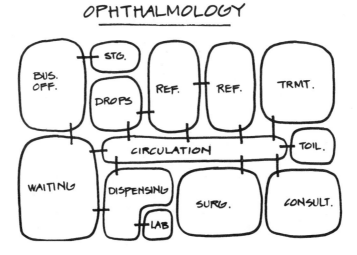

Figure 4-66. Schematic diagram of an ophthalmology suite.

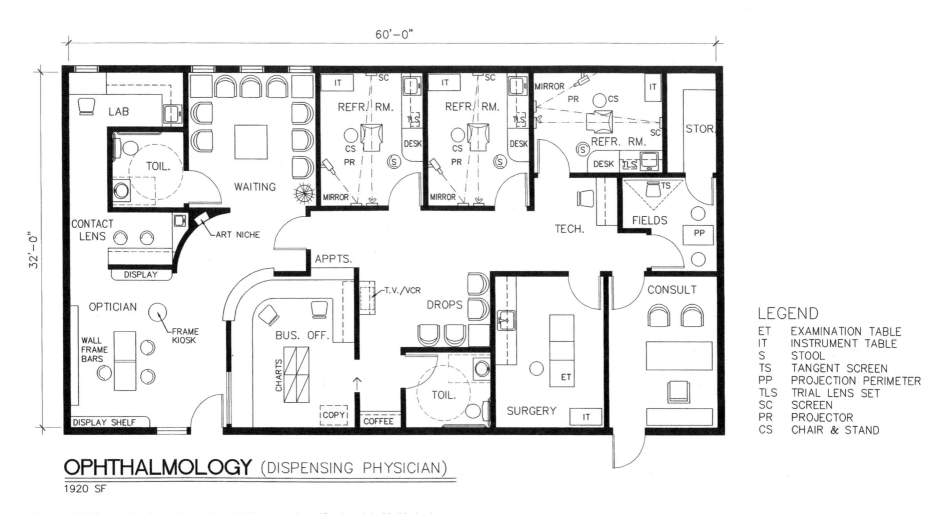

Figure 4-67. Space plan for ophthalmology, 1920 square feet. (*Design: Jain Malkin Inc.*)

Optical Dispensing

It is not uncommon for ophthalmologists to practice as solo practitioners with the help of an assistant or technician. An optician may also be part of the practice, in which case an area approximately 10×24 feet is needed, divided into a lab, a contact lens area, and a fitting area (Figures 4-67 and 4-68). The lab has walls lined with cabinets and work counters and requires shadow-free lighting.

The contact lens area requires a small fitting table 2×4 feet with a mirrored top. The patient sits on one side and the optician on the other. The room may also have a storage cabinet and a small sink. The fitting area has a long table divided into a number of fitting stations, each with a mirror, and it may have panels of eyeglass frames (*frame bars*) located on either side of the patient. The optician sits on a stool behind the table and works from drawers and cabinets to the side and behind. Attractive wall frame

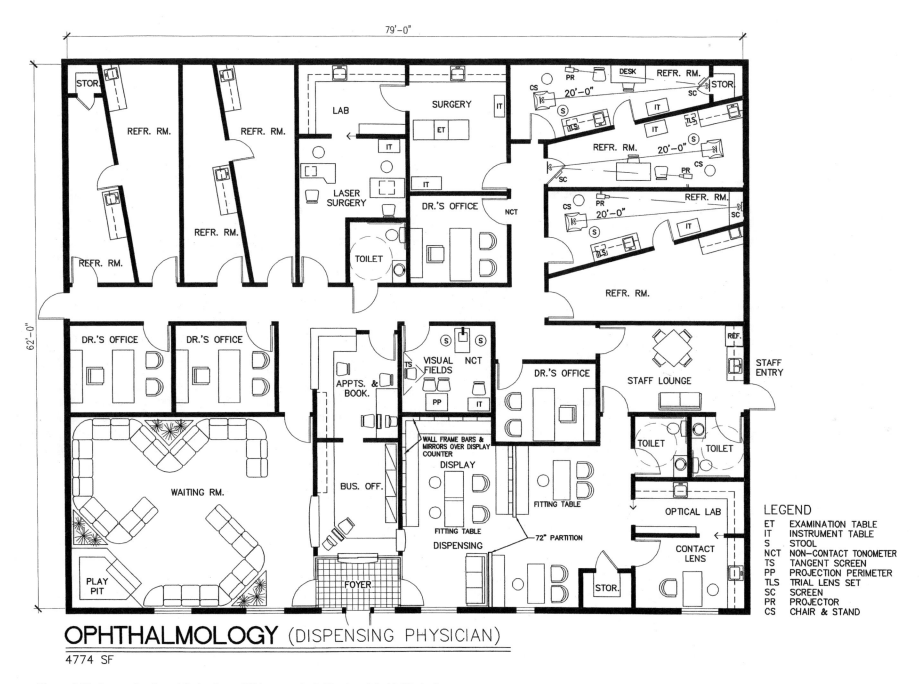

Figure 4-68. Space plan for ophthalmology, 4774 square feet. (*Design: Jain Malkin Inc.*)

bars can be purchased ready made, or they may be designed and custom fabricated to hold the many eyeglass frames to be displayed.

Ophthalmologists who offer the services of an optician are called *dispensing physicians*. As a marketing strategy, it is advisable to give as much visibility as possible to the dispensing area so that waiting patients are tempted to walk over and look at the frames.

Multipurpose Exam Room

Ophthalmologists used to arrange their offices so that different tests were performed in different rooms. Some ophthalmologists may still practice that way. However, it is far more efficient for the patient to remain in one room. Each time the patient has to gather his belongings and move to another room, then again get comfortable, valuable time (and money) is lost. For most ophthalmology practices, a complete examination and treatment can be done in the same room with the patient in the same chair.

Refraction Room

The most important room is the refraction room, a multipurpose examination room with equipment and instruments grouped around the patient and the doctor sitting either in front of the patient or just to one side. Right-handed physicians may prefer to examine from the patient's right side although, if the physician wants to write notes while facing the patient, the preference may be to locate the cabinet (with writing desk) to the left of the patient as in Figure 4-67. The dimensions of this room are crucial, and both the ophthalmologist's work habits and instruments will dictate the critical distances that must be observed.

Refraction rooms have two basic sizes. Since a standard eye chart is designed for a distance of 20 feet from chart to patient's eye, the traditional refraction room is approximately 24 feet long (20 feet for the refraction lane plus 4 feet for the examining chair and space to walk around it) as in Figure 4-68. However, with the aid of projectors and mirrors, the room length may be reduced to 12 to 14 feet. A 9- or 10-foot-wide×12-foot-long room would be suitable. Today it is rare to find refraction rooms longer than 12 feet.

To compensate for a room length of less than 24 feet, two mirrors are placed on the wall in front of the patient, and a screen is placed on the wall behind the patient (Figures 4-67 and 4-69). A projector (Figure 4-70), usually wall mounted, projects the text characters onto one of the front mirrors, which, in turn, projects it back to the screen behind the patient. The second mirror, in front of the patient, reflects the image from the rear screen. The refracting lane, in this case, is the distance measured between the second mirror and the screen plus the distance between the mirror and the patient. The letters of the eye chart can be adjusted in size by the projector so that correct visual acuities can always be maintained.

There are several types of procedures performed in the refracting room, but the primary task is to determine the refractive power of the eye. To do this, the tech or physician selects various lenses from a partitioned rack (Figure 4-71), a *trial lens box* (approximate size 12½×20½×2½ inches), and places them in a holder through which the patient looks. The patient is asked to read the test letters to determine which lens is best. Sometimes a *refractor*, an instrument containing lenses, is used.

The interior of the eye, the fundus, is examined by an *ophthalmoscope*, a handheld light source, while the conjunctiva, lens, iris, and cornea (the front portions of the eye) are examined with a *slit lamp*, an illuminated microscope (Figure 4-72), which may be mounted on an arm of the instrument stand (Figure 4-73) or may be on a mobile instrument table. A *keratometer* (Figure 4-74) measures the curvature of the cornea. The Radiusgauge™ in Figure 4-75 measures the curvature and thickness of contact lenses.

A direct ophthalmoscope (Figure 4-76) is used to view and illuminate the retina, head of the optic nerve, retinal arteries, and vitreous humor even through an undilated pupil. The focus in the eyepiece is equal to the image on the video monitor.

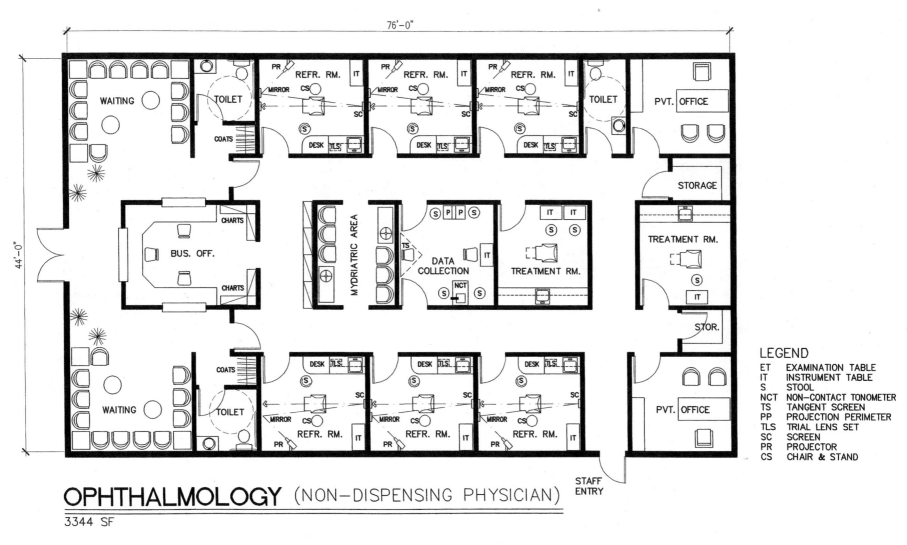

76'-0"

44'-0"

WAITING

TOILET

COATS

PR REFR. RM. IT
MIRROR CS
S
SC
DESK TLS

PR REFR. RM. IT
MIRROR CS
S
SC
DESK TLS

PR REFR. RM. IT
MIRROR CS
S
SC
DESK TLS

TOILET

PVT. OFFICE

STORAGE

CHARTS

BUS. OFF.

CHARTS

MYDRIATRIC AREA

TS

S P P S

DATA COLLECTION
IT
S NCT S

IT IT
S S

TREATMENT RM.

TREATMENT RM.
S
IT

STOR.

WAITING

TOILET

COATS

DESK TLS
S
SC
MIRROR CS
PR REFR. RM. IT

DESK TLS
S
SC
MIRROR CS
PR REFR. RM. IT

DESK TLS
S
SC
MIRROR CS
PR REFR. RM. IT

PVT. OFFICE

STAFF ENTRY

LEGEND

ET   EXAMINATION TABLE
IT   INSTRUMENT TABLE
S   STOOL
NCT NON–CONTACT TONOMETER
TS   TANGENT SCREEN
PP   PROJECTION PERIMETER
TLS TRIAL LENS SET
SC   SCREEN
PR   PROJECTOR
CS   CHAIR & STAND

OPHTHALMOLOGY (NON–DISPENSING PHYSICIAN)
3344 SF

Figure 4-69. Space plan for ophthalmology, 3344 square feet. (*Design: Jain Malkin Inc.*)

Figure 4-70. Ophthalmology automated chart projector (can be wall mounted). (*Photo courtesy: Leica Microsystems Inc., Bannockburn, IL.*)

Figure 4-71. Trial lens box. (*Photo courtesy: Marco Ophthalmic, Jacksonville, FL.*)

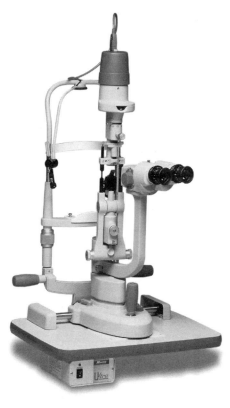

Figure 4-72. Slit lamp. (*Photo courtesy: Marco Ophthalmic, Jacksonville, FL.*)

Examining chairs are available in tilt or nontilt models. If the physician prefers to write notes at a desk that enables him or her to face the patient, the room would be set up with the chair positioned so that the instrument stand console is to the patient's right, although this means that a right-handed physician is always reaching for instruments with the left hand as well as reaching across the patient. An alternative is a mobile trial lens cart with a pull-out writing shelf. Located to the patient's right, with the instrument stand on the patient's left (the physician's right as he or she faces the patient), it allows the physician to face the patient while writing notes and use the right hand both to select trial lenses and to manipulate the slit lamp and other instruments. The chair should be positioned in the room so that the physician can walk behind it (allow 3 to 4 feet behind it) even when the chair is in the reclined position. The chair and attached instrument stand console together are approximately 4 feet wide (Figure 4-73). A clear space of 24 to 30 inches to the right side of the patient and 5 to 6 feet to the left is desirable (measured from the center of the chair). As with any medical equipment, the designer must verify dimensions and critical spatial relationships before designing the room. This chapter lists general dimensions, but each manufacturer's literature must be consulted for specifics.

The physician may work off of the instrument stand as well as the sink cabinet located to the left of the patient. The instrument stand console may be specially wired so

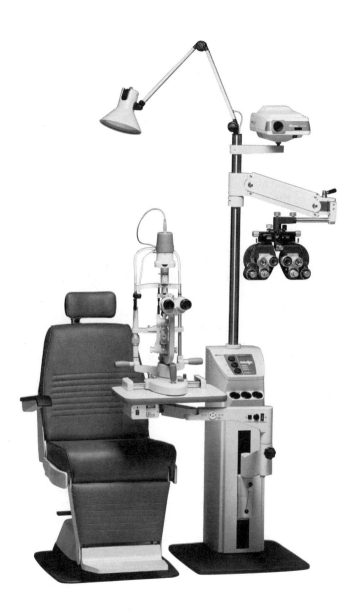

Figure 4-74. Keratometer. (*Photo courtesy: Marco Ophthalmic, Jacksonville, FL.*)

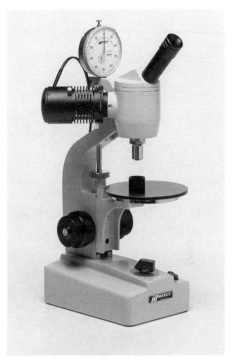

Figure 4-75. Radiusgauge™ used to measure hard or gas-permeable contact lenses. (*Photo courtesy: Marco Ophthalmic, Jacksonville, FL.*)

Figure 4-73. Chair and instrument stand. Note chart projector mounted on post and slit lamp on table. (*Photo courtesy: Marco Ophthalmic, Jacksonville, FL.*)

Figure 4-76. Direct video ophthalmoscope enables the patient or family member to see what the physician is seeing and also facilitates telemedicine consultations. (*Photo courtesy: AMD Telemedicine, Lowell, MA.*)

Figure 4-77. Refraction room (*Design: Jeffrey B. Morris, M.D.; Photographer: Robinson/Ward.*)

checked with reference to controlling room lights from the instrument stand. Low-voltage wiring is usually required.) Indirect lighting works best in an ophthalmology exam room. For example, fluorescent lamps around the perimeter of the room with uplighting source shielded by the fixture eliminate the brightness of overhead lights when patients' eyes are dilated.

Other electrical requirements for the room include an outlet for a *fixation light* mounted on the wall at approximately a 72-inch height directly behind the patient; an outlet for the *projector,* usually at a 60-inch height on the wall to the left of the patient or behind the patient (the designer must specify wood blocking in the wall to support the weight of the projector); a duplex outlet above the countertop for miscellaneous instruments and recharger modules for the cordless hand instruments; and a floor outlet (15-ampere circuit) for the instrument stand console.

One duplex outlet should be located at a 12-inch height on the wall to the left of the examining chair, and all outlets should be grounded. The electrical requirements of refraction rooms are highly specialized. A thorough review of the practitioner's habits and specific instrumentation is necessary before planning the electrical layout.

The trial lens case may be placed on a countertop (Figure 4-71), or it may fit in a drawer or be built into a mobile cart designed for that purpose. If it is to fit in a drawer, the designer must determine if the rack should be tilted for easier visibility, in which case the drawer must be deeper.

A more contemporary style of refraction chair and instrumentation is shown in Figure 4-78. Capable of performing all refraction procedures by remote control (offering greater flexibility to the operator), it offers direct wireless data transfer and speeds the examination process. Moreover, it works well for disabled patients who can remain in the wheelchair and pull up under the shelf. The phoropter (eyepiece unit) slides up and down the pole to adjust height. The trial lens case fits into the top drawer of the pedestal. The room requires the standard projector, mirrors, and screen. An interesting feature is that the patient's current prescription for lenses can be loaded into the computer to be used as a comparison with the

that the physician can control the room lights, fixation light, projection chart, and other instruments from it. Or, the sink cabinet may be extended to include a knee space and an electrical panel for remote control of the room's overhead lights, projector, fixation light, and nurse call buzzer. (Switches and controls may be located on the face of the cabinet or in the knee-space opening so that they are within easy reach of the ophthalmologist during the examination.) Thus, the ophthalmologist, from a seated position alongside the patient, may control illumination and instrumentation from either the instrument stand or the wall cabinet, or both (Figure 4-77).

Room lights should have a three-way switch so that they can be controlled from the wall and the console, and they should have a dimmer control. (Local codes must be current exam and the new prescription can be downloaded to an electronic medical record, enabling both uploading and downloading of data.

All refracting rooms should be exactly alike in layout, arrangement of instruments, and quality of equipment. If one room has a better slit lamp than another, the rooms will not get equal usage. Patients will be shifted around so the doctor can use favored equipment, defeating the basic efficiency of the suite.

The distance the doctor must walk between refraction rooms should be minimal. To this end, some ophthalmologists request connecting doors between two refraction rooms (Figure 4-68). Although it saves steps, it creates an acoustic problem. And since many persons with poor eyesight happen to be elderly, they may also suffer from a hearing loss, which means the doctor may have to shout to be understood — all the more reason to provide good sound insulation around these rooms and walls that continue beyond the finished ceiling.

Mydriatic Area

Prior to an eye examination, the patient may receive eyedrops to dilate the pupil. The patient is often asked to wait in a secondary waiting area adjacent to the refraction room called a *drop* or *mydriatic room* for 15 to 20 minutes before being admitted to the refraction room for the examination.

Automated Refraction

An *automated refractor* (Figure 4-79) is an electronic tabletop instrument (also available as a handheld unit as in Figure 4-80) for objectively measuring the patient's visual acuity. It is commonly used by a technician, thereby reducing the number of physician-performed refractions and streamlining those that are necessary. One of the advantages of this unit, in addition to the time it saves over the conventional method of refraction, is that it does not rely on the patient's sub-

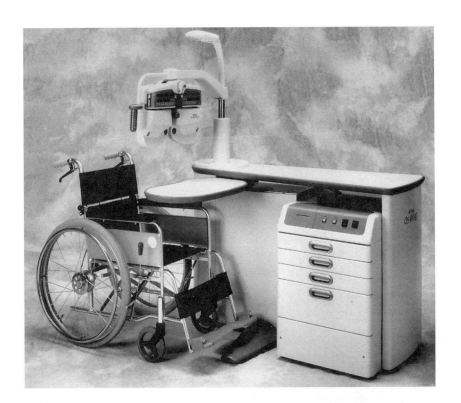

Figure 4-78. Auto Optester remote control refraction instrument with Os-Wing ophthalmic console system. (*Photo courtesy: Nikon Instruments Inc., Melville, NY.*)

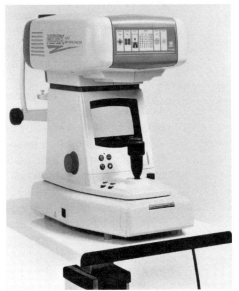

Figure 4-79. Automated refractor. (*Photo courtesy: Marco Ophthalmic, Jacksonville, FL.*)

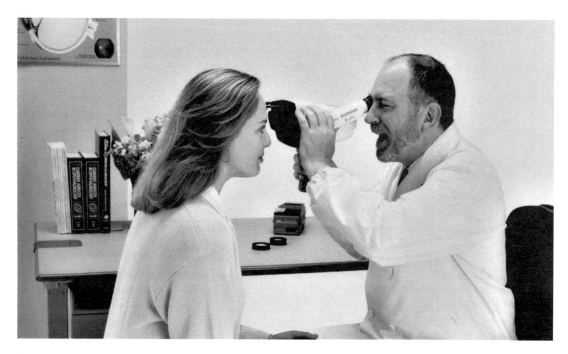

Figure 4-80. Handheld Retinomax K-Plus2 Auto refractometer. (*Photo courtesy: Nikon Instruments Inc., Melville, NY.*)

jective comparison: *Is this clearer than that?* The patient looks into the viewing window of the unit and adjusts a knob until the image is in focus. The machine automatically gives a digital readout of the patient's visual acuity. It can also compare the patient's current prescription with the new one.

When used as a general screening device, this machine would be located in the *data collection room* along with the other instruments used by aides (Figure 4-69).

After a patient has been refracted by this instrument, he or she moves to an examination room where the ophthalmologist would review the findings and study the patient's medical history.

In spite of the advantages afforded by an automated refractor, many ophthalmologists prefer the traditional method of refraction done in the examination room. It is generally performed by a technician or aide who also takes the patient history in advance of the ophthalmologist's entering the room. The ophthalmologist then exam-

ines the eye with a slit lamp and may use the Non-Contact™ Tonometer (Figure 4-81) to check for glaucoma or perform other procedures, as required, to diagnose the patient's problem.

Visual Fields

The charting of visual fields used to be done with a *tangent screen,* which is a piece of black felt with meridians marked off (Figure 4-82), but is now commonly done with automated digital equipment. As tangent screens are still in use, the concept will be explained. Tangent screens may be rigid or roll-up, the former being preferred because they permit greater accuracy. They are available in four sizes, ranging from 1 to 2 meters, the smaller screen giving the smallest amount of information. A 1.5-meter screen is commonly used, and if it is placed in a dedicated room, the room need be only 8×8 feet. A 1-meter screen needs a room only 6×6 feet in size.

The tangent screen may be in the data collection room, in a refracting room, or in a visual fields room, depending on the practitioner's preference and the composition of the practice. A glaucoma specialist may have one in each refracting room. Others may have only one screen in the data collection room.

The patient sits at a specified distance from the screen (which resembles a target), and pins are placed in the felt to chart the limits of the patient's visual field. If the screen is placed in the refraction room, it is convenient to locate it on the wall behind the patient. Thus, the physician can spin the patient's chair around to face it. The chair must be 1.5 meters (60 inches) away from the screen (with a 1.5-meter screen).

However, the tangent screen is a basic screening device and not terribly accurate, since one has no control over movement of the patient's head. Perimetry is a more advanced method of doing peripheral and central fields. An *automated projection perimeter* is a computerized piece of equipment that sits on a 24×30-inch instrument table (Figure 4-83). The patient's visual field is charted automatically and accurately since the patient's head is firmly held.

The instrument fits in a room as small as 6×6 feet. It may be placed in a visual fields room or in a data collection room, but the room's illumination must be controlled by a dimmer, since the procedure is done in a dark room. Not all ophthalmologists will have this piece of equipment.

Procedure/Surgery Room

A number of procedures can be done in a large (12×14 feet) room similar to special procedure rooms in primary-care offices. A full wall of casework should be provided, with an undercounter refrigerator and a sink with foot-pedal control. An autoclave for sterilizing instruments will sit on the countertop. A ceiling-mounted surgical light is required along with a sheet vinyl floor.

Lasers

Laser surgery makes possible the correction of many vision problems on an outpatient basis in the ophthalmologist's office. Lasers are used to treat diabetic retinopathy, macular degeneration, retinal tears, glaucoma, and retinal vein occlusion and to open the clouded posterior capsule that sometimes forms following cataract surgery.

Laser light is within the normal visible spectrum, but it is coherent light of a single wavelength—all the energy works together and in one direction. This allows it to be focused precisely on a certain point.

Choosing a wavelength color that the eye tissue being treated can absorb, controlling the power and time of exposure, and varying the size of the laser beam allow the physician to use the laser to seal tears, make tiny openings, evaporate small amounts of tissue, and stop bleeding.

Ophthalmologists use several types of lasers. The color associated with each type enables it to target specific tissues without damaging others. Yttrium aluminum garnet (YAG) lasers use infrared rays in the near-visible spectrum to treat problems in the front of the eye. The YAG is called a *photo disruption laser,* and it uses rapid, tiny bursts of energy to make tiny openings in the eye. Other lasers are

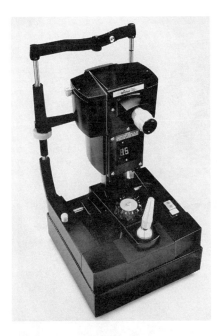

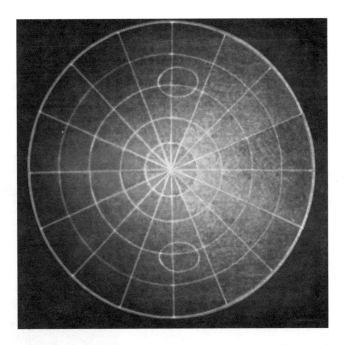

Figure 4-81. Non-Contact™ II Tonometer. (*Photo courtesy: Reichert Ophthalmic Instruments, Buffalo, NY.*)

Figure 4-82. Tangent screen. (*Photo courtesy: Richmond Products.*)

Figure 4-83. Projection perimeter. (*Photo courtesy: Marco Ophthalmic, Jacksonville, FL.*)

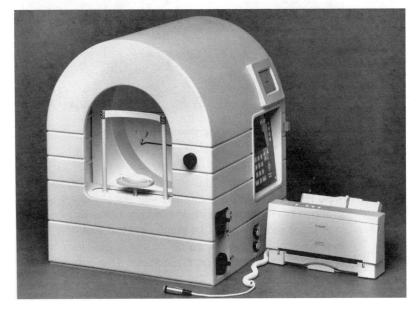

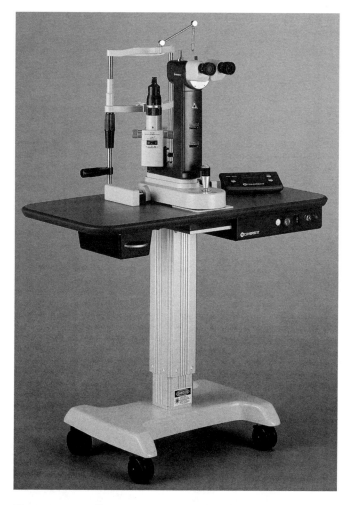

Figure 4-84. Aura™ Nd:YAG ophthalmic laser. (*Photo courtesy: Coherent Medical Group, Santa Clara, CA.*)

called *photocoagulation lasers* that use heat (light) to spot-weld tears and leaks in the retinal vessels of the eye and to produce openings in the iris in the front of the eye.

A laser room may be as small as 8×8 feet or 10×10 feet. Ophthalmic lasers come out of a slit-lamp microscope, which sits on a portable stand. The ophthalmologist sits on one side of the table and the patient on the other, resting the chin in a support to immobilize the head

(Figure 4-84). A sink cabinet 6 to 8 feet long is a general requirement for any special procedure room, and room lights must be able to be dimmed during the procedure.

As lasers are expensive, some physicians have them in their office, while others may do laser procedures in an outpatient eye clinic at a nearby hospital. The advantages of laser surgery are many: The eye is not opened surgically; there is no needle or stitches; and the risk of infection is minimal.

It should be noted that laser use requires the observance of safety precautions. The American National Standards Institute (ANSI) publishes standards for the safe use of laser systems. Specific safety devices and warning labels must be used. The eyes are most susceptible to laser injury.

Rooms in which lasers are in use must have a warning sign posted on the door that reads *DANGER—Laser Radiation—Avoid Eye or Skin Exposure to Direct or Scattered Radiation.* When using infrared wavelengths such as the YAG, the word "invisible" must be included in the warning sign.

It is important to have nonspecular (nonreflecting) and fire-resistant material in or near the beam path. Doors may require safety latches or interlocks to prevent unexpected entry into laser-controlled areas. If the door to the room has a window, it must have a window shade that can be rolled down during laser use. Everyone in the room must wear goggles to protect his or her eyes. (Goggles are specific to each type of laser that is used.)

Whereas older argon and some YAG lasers require a direct water connection, newer ones do not. The reader is referred to Chapter 7 for additional discussion of lasers. The Nd:YAG laser pictured in Figure 4-84 is cooled by air convection and does not require water, while the multiwavelength laser, used by retinal specialists, has an internal water-cooling system.

Fluorescein Angiography

Not all ophthalmologists do fluorescein angiograms in their offices. Some refer their patients to a retinal subspecialist or to an outpatient eye clinic associated with a nearby hospital. Fluorescein dye is injected into the patient's arm. The resulting photographs of the retina show if there is leakage of fluids, edema, or poor circulation. This procedure can be done in a minor treatment or special procedure room, and it is performed by a technologist, not the physician.

No special accommodation is required in the room, as the patient sits on a standard chair on one side of an instrument table, with the tech on the other side. A small darkroom should be nearby. A workroom for the tech is optional and depends on what other rooms are close at hand. A retinal specialist would have a dedicated room for angiograms, with an adjacent office for the photographer, and a mydriatic or drop room nearby. The entire procedure, including waiting time for dilation of the pupil, can take as long as 45 minutes.

Office-Based Surgery

It is a matter of personal preference whether an ophthalmologist chooses to do surgery (nonlaser) within the office. Some may elect, for a variety of reasons, to use an ambulatory surgical center located in the medical office building or one located in a nearby hospital. The advantages of performing surgery in one's office are convenience for the patient, convenience in scheduling procedures, and revenue generated for the medical practice. Disadvantages include the initial cost to create a surgery facility that meets state licensing and/or Medicare certification criteria, the cost of equipping it, additional coverage, and the risks assumed, however slight, when performing surgery outside the hospital or ambulatory surgical center settings.

Since eye surgery is generally not elective in nature, a physician would want to be certain the office-based surgery facility meets requirements for reimbursement by third-party payers. In fact, the majority of patients needing surgery are over 65 years of age, and Medicare reimbursement would be essential to an ophthalmologist's practice.

Removal of cataracts is one of the most common types of ophthalmic surgery. It is generally performed using a local anesthetic (eyedrops) and is sometimes accompanied by conscious sedation, administered by a nurse anesthetist or an anesthesiologist. This type of surgery is performed in a sterile room, which means it's generally done in an ambulatory surgical center. An incision is made; the clouded lens (cataract) is removed; and an intraocular lens (artificial lens) is inserted. The surgical portion of the procedure takes 15 to 30 minutes. The patient recovers in a recliner chair for about 15 minutes before being released to go home.

Some ophthalmologists do all of their surgery in an ambulatory surgical center. Others do only those surgeries requiring general anesthesia in an ambulatory surgical center, and procedures done with a local anesthetic such as cataract surgery and radial keratotomy are done in the office. Some use a room no larger than a standard minor treatment or special procedure room, with an adjacent nurse station, small recovery area, and clean utility room. When general anesthesia is used, state fire marshal and Medicare certification requirements become strict. Many Life Safety Code regulations must be met. The reader is referred to Chapter 7 for a more complete discussion of this issue.

The designer should note that ophthalmic surgery is done while looking through a microscope. Therefore, vibration can be a problem. If the office is in a medical building near a railroad track or close to a major freeway, there could be some undesirable vibration, depending on the height of the building, the location of the suite within the building, and the type of structural system that supports the building.

Laser Eye Surgery

Photorefractive Keratectomy
Photorefractive keratectomy (PRK) is a procedure to correct mild nearsightedness. In PRK, the surgeon scrapes away the outer surface of the cornea and then reshapes the underlying tissues with a cool ultraviolet beam. Only

"eyedrop" anesthesia is required. As this procedure may result in scar tissue and can correct only mild nearsightedness, it is losing ground to the highly touted LASIK procedure.

LASIK

LASIK—an acronym for laser in situ keratomileusis—has been made possible by the excimer laser (Figure 4-85), which reshapes the cornea to correct nearsightedness, farsightedness, and astigmatism. Using an instrument called a microkeratome, the surgeon folds back a thin protective flap of corneal tissue. The excimer laser then removes a predetermined amount of tissue from the inner cornea to correct the refractive error. The corneal flap is replaced in its original position where it bonds without sutures.

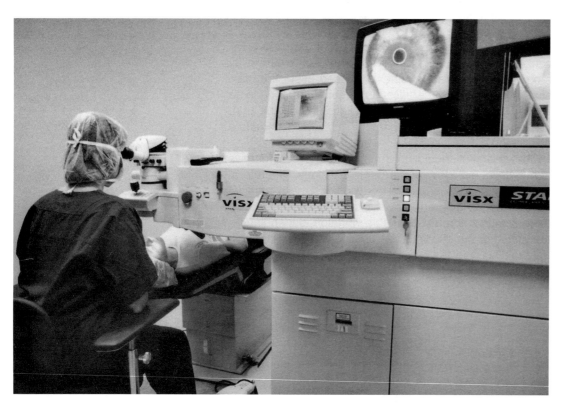

Figure 4-85. LASIK surgery equipment. (*Photo courtesy: Jain Malkin Inc.; Photographer: Don Kohlbauer.*)

So popular is this procedure that a number of ophthalmologists do nothing but LASIK in specialized facilities designed for this purpose (Figure 4-86). Taking only 15 minutes for the entire procedure, it is hugely profitable and carries little risk in competent hands. As this is an elective procedure, insurance companies do not cover it. LASIK surgeons often use multimedia marketing (TV, print ads, telemarketing, and Web sites) to drive up patient volume and may even resort to customer-pleasing gimmicks such as limousine service. Although some LASIK specialists may abhor this level of commercialism, others unabashedly buy time on local TV stations to create advertorials that depict the surgeon and satisfied patients. Because there is great competition among practitioners, marketing services are a standard part of the practice. A waiting room that can double as a seminar room in the evening works well. An adjacent storage room for folding chairs, a credenza for refreshments, and a large screen TV are needed (Figures 4-86 and 4-87).

Layout of Rooms

A facility will generally have one procedure room approximately 12×15 feet, which may be connected to a small lab (for sterilizing instruments), two standard pre-op refraction rooms, a small topographic room, a small slit-lamp room to be used by the surgeon postsurgically to check the patient prior to discharge, and a small recovery room in which the patient spends a few moments in a recliner chair while receiving discharge instructions. The patient does not change clothes or gown; however, lockers for handbags, briefcase, and coats are useful. The "topo" room has a tabletop autorefractor and a diagnostic instrument that measures the curvature of the cornea to produce a topographical map of the surface. Both instruments fit on a 2-×4-foot table with a stool for the tech on one side and a chair for the patient on the other.

LASIK Room

HVAC Considerations. Although this is not a sterile room, sterile technique is followed. Eyedrop anesthetic is used. Control of humidity and temperature is essential for

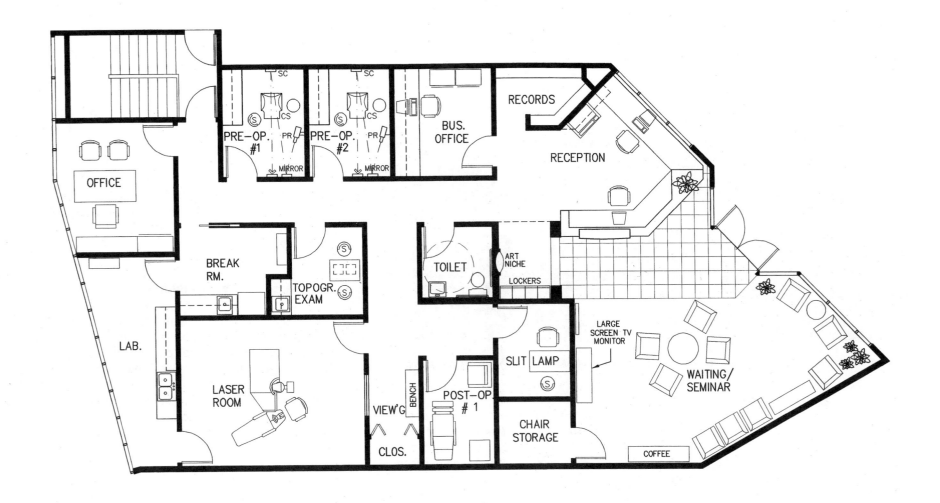

LASER EYE SURGERY

2400 SF

Figure 4-86. Space plan for laser eye surgery, 2400 square feet. (*Design: William Smith Associates, San Diego, CA.*)

Figure 4-87. Waiting room, LASIK surgery center. (*Interior Design: Jain Malkin Inc.; Photographer: Don Kohlbauer.*)

installed to filter the fluorine out of the air. A built-in detection system monitors gas leaks.

Observation Window. An observation window (with a blind controlled from the procedure room) that enables a family member to watch is a popular feature (Figure 4-86).

Lighting. There are no special lighting requirements. However, there is an advantage to being able to dim the lights when using some accessory devices on the machine.

Finishes. Reflectance of walls and floors is not a problem as the laser beam is narrowly focused on the eye. A large window (glass), whether exterior or interior, depending on placement in relation to the machine, can create annoying glare.

Other Considerations

An ophthalmologist may accumulate 11 to 12 lineal feet of medical charts in a year, so the file area should accommodate about 48 lineal feet per doctor. Inactive charts can be stored in file transfer boxes in the storage room or off site.

The consultation room functions as a private office, a place to relax between patients, to read mail, or to make phone calls. It is rarely used for consulting with patients; thus, it can be small.

Interior Design

The interior design of this suite should be cheerful, and lighting is of critical importance. The waiting room should have good reading light, as many of the patients are elderly, which means they need a high intensity of light to be able to read with comfort. Those with cataracts, however, will find glare very uncomfortable. A high level of indirect light, supplemented by table lamps, would meet the needs of most individuals.

proper functioning of the equipment and mixing of gases. Relative humidity of 35 to 65 and temperature of 60 to 80 degrees Fahrenheit is the desired range according to VIS-X, the leading manufacturer of the Excimer laser. A dehumidifier may be required. The surgeon needs to be able to adjust the room humidity and temperature to keep the machine calibrated.

The room should have positive pressure to keep the air clean and, ideally, a HEPA filter. The HVAC must be separate from the rest of the facility to achieve this level of control and should be activated by controls within the procedure room. In case of a gas leak, the room air must be evacuated in two minutes.

Ideally, the exhaust would be vented to the outdoors but, if this is not possible, a room scrubber system can be

Figure 4-90. Reception desk, LASIK surgery center. (*Interior Design: Jain Malkin Inc.; Photographer: Don Kohlbauer.*)

Figure 4-91. Built-in brochure rack. (*Design: OSM Architects; Photographer: Jain Malkin.*)

In refraction rooms, the designer must be extremely careful to select wallcoverings that have absolutely no visual rhythm or figure-ground reversal. People who visit an ophthalmologist have a variety of vision problems, some of which include distortions. A person who sees a triple image or one whose vision is blurred might experience considerable discomfort in looking at a busy wallpaper or a geometric design. As the lens ages, it thickens and yellows. To know how colors might be perceived by the elderly, one can look through a pair of yellow lenses.

The waiting room in Color Plate 15, Figure 4-88, would be quite appropriate for an ophthalmologist's office if patients are predominantly elderly. Note the design of the reception window in Color Plate 16, Figure 4-89, using modular furniture systems and the open, welcoming reception desk in Figure 4-90. Many educational brochures are dispensed in this specialty, necessitating brochure racks (Figure 4-91).

PLASTIC SURGERY

Plastic surgery suites vary considerably, depending on the focus of the practice (cosmetic or reconstructive) and whether there is an intention to provide skin care or spa services (a recent trend). Skin care/spa services may include microdermabrasion skin resurfacing, chemical peels, permanent hair removal by a diode laser, facials, body and cellulite treatments, as well as makeup tattooing of eyeliner or brows. These procedures are explained in greater detail, and room requirements discussed, in the Dermatology section of this chapter and at the end of this section.

Another factor that will influence space planning is whether the plastic surgeon uses an advertising practice model. Some practitioners allocate a significant budget for advertising, publicity, or media consultants, and many offer educational seminars. As an example, a plastic surgeon in a building that contains a sizable breast care center may wish to conduct seminars on breast reconstruction for mastectomy candidates or may wish to conduct a seminar on skin resurfacing techniques. In these practices, the waiting room may have to double as a meeting room for slide presentations. If the design of the office makes a great first impression, it will be more valuable to entice prospective patients into the office than to conduct a seminar off site at a hotel. Plastic surgery is highly competitive since most procedures are elective and not reimbursed by insurance. Plastic surgeons have great earning power as they have been relatively unaffected by the vagaries of managed care and they realize that making an investment in outstanding interior design can enhance their image.

A plastic surgeon with a cosmetically oriented practice needs to "market" his or her skills and successes. Dentists specializing in cosmetic or aesthetic dentistry are in somewhat the same situation in terms of being interviewed by prospective patients and having to "sell the case." Often, people self-refer, based on a successful outcome of a friend or relative, but the quest for an idealized self-image and the desire to restore one's youthful appearance cause many women (83 percent of plastic surgery patients are women) to interview a number of plastic surgeons.

As it is time consuming for the busy surgeon to do these initial evaluations, factors that increase the likelihood of that patient returning to have the procedure are worthwhile. This means that the appearance and function of the office are important. The prospective patient has to make a number of stops during that initial evaluation and the office should seem orderly and well organized. The patient may be greeted by the patient care coordinator who will discuss the type of procedure the patient has in mind and who may take the patient into a private office and allow her to peruse a book of "before and after" photos of patients who have had that procedure. The next stop might be the physician's consultation room where the physician will interview the patient, perhaps sketch some possibilities, and show slides of patients who started out with a similar problem that has now been resolved. After the surgeon determines which procedures are necessary to accomplish the goal, the patient would move to the financial counseling office, or patient care coordinator, to discuss fees and payment plans and to answer any "process" questions. Ideally, the financial counseling office and consultation room would be near the front of the suite so that these patients do not have to mix with those who have already been scheduled for procedures and may be there for the pre-op workup or post-op visits.

Plastic surgeons often do surgery in their offices in a properly equipped office-based surgery center, described more completely later in this section. Those who don't, will do their cases in an ambulatory surgery center, which may be available in the medical office building; or a freestanding surgery center where they have privileges; or a hospital, which is probably the least desirable alternative for plastic surgery unless it is so extensive that the patient has to stay overnight and receive an intensive level of monitoring. It should be mentioned that there are, in some cities, 72-hour-stay recovery-care centers which allow more complicated cases to be safely handled in an ambulatory surgical setting.

There are a number of reasons for performing plastic surgery on an outpatient basis in the surgeon's office. Principally, the patient is more comfortable in a physician's office because it is a less clinical environment than a hospital, and it affords more privacy. Patients undergoing cosmetic procedures are often very concerned about bumping into friends and neighbors. It is not uncommon for people to visit a plastic surgeon in another city in order to safeguard their "secret."

There are other advantages to surgery outside the hospital setting. The surgeon has more control over scheduling when procedures are done in the office, and the patient avoids the generally frightening experience of being admitted to a hospital. It usually lowers the cost for the patient and permits the physician to charge a fee for the use of the operating room, rather than lose that fee to the hospital.

In some plastic surgery practices, approximately 95 percent of the surgery caseload can be performed in a properly equipped operating suite within the office. *Liposuction* has become one of the most commonly performed procedures for removing unwanted fat from the stomach, buttocks, thighs, or other areas. Briefly, in this procedure, an incision is made in the skin, a *cannula* (tube) is inserted, and the fat is suctioned out. Other procedures commonly performed by plastic surgeons include facelifts, breast augmentation (or reduction), rhinoplasty (reshaping the nose), hair transplants, hand surgery, skin grafts for burn survivors and repair of cleft palate (both usually done in a hospital setting), breast reconstruction associated with cancer surgery, and other disfiguring malformations of the face and head. The top three cosmetic procedures in the United States are liposuction, breast augmentation, and eyelid lifts.

Circulation Patterns and Patient Flow

If a plastic surgeon is going to do office-based surgery, the optimum flow would be that shown in Figures 4-92,

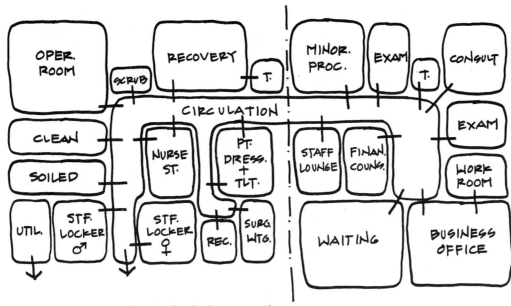

Figure 4-92. Schematic diagram of a plastic surgery suite.

Table 4-5.
Analysis of Program.
Plastic Surgery

No. of Physicians:		1			2	
		(Without Surgery Suite)			(With Surgery Suite)	
Consultation Rooms[a]		12 × 16 = 192		2@	12 × 16 = 384	
Exam Rooms	2@	8 × 12 = 192		4@	8 × 12 = 384	
Minor Treatment		10 × 12 = 120			10 × 12 = 120	
Nurse Station		8 × 10 = 80			8 × 10 = 80	
Operating Suite[b]		—			—	1600
Primary Waiting Room		16 × 16 = 256			16 × 18 = 288	
Surgery and Post-Op Waiting		10 × 10 = 100			10 × 12 = 120	
Business Office		16 x 20 = 320			16 x 24 = 384	
Financial Counseling		10 × 12 = 120			10 × 12 = 120	
Toilets	2@	7 × 8 = 112		3@	7 × 8 = 168	
Storage	2@	6 × 8 = 96		2@	6 × 8 = 96	
Shampoo/Makeup		—			12 × 12 = 144	
Spa Services/Skin Care		20 × 30 = 600			—	
Staff Lounge		12 × 12 = 144			12 × 12 = 144	
Subtotal		2332 ft²			4032 ft²	
20% Circulation		466			806	
Total		2799 ft²			4838 ft²	

[a]Used both as private office and for consultation with new patients.
[b]Includes (2) ORs, nurse station, scrub, clean and soiled utility rooms, recovery, equipment storage (vacuum, med gases, air, generator), patient toilet/lockers, and male/female staff dressing. 1600 square feet is a minimum.

Note: The above is merely an approximation, since plastic surgery suites can vary considerably in size and number of rooms, depending on the physician's scope of procedures and practice philosophy.

4-93, and 4-94, in which surgical patients are separated from the pre-op and post-op examination areas of the suite. There are separate waiting rooms, but there is no duplication of staff required since the receptionist can monitor both rooms, although, ideally, in terms of Medicare, even the reception/business office for the surgery suite should be separate. To comply with Medicare certification, there should be complete separation of the surgery suite from the office practice during hours of operation of the surgery center and it must be a separate business entity maintaining separate records. The door to the surgery suite (from the medical office) should be able to be secured by means of a keypad to prevent unauthorized entry. Few plastic surgeons, however, seek Medicare certification; AAAHC accreditation is more common.

The flow through the suite for elective cases would begin with the initial consultation and, if the patient decides to proceed, would then include one or two pre-op visits, the actual surgery, plus multiple post-op visits. Trauma cases or emergencies would generally be seen at the hospital initially with follow-up visits in the office.

The practice documents results with "before" and "after" photos of patients. Photographs are an important part of the plastic surgery practice. These photos can be taken in the examination room (where a pull-down panel of blue fabric is mounted to the wall as a background) or in a small windowless 6-×8-foot room designed for that purpose (Figure 4-95).

With most procedures, the patient is operated on in the morning, spends one or two hours in the recovery room, and goes home that afternoon. The doctor's afternoons would be spent visiting hospitalized patients, conducting consultations in the office with prospective patients, and seeing postoperative patients to change dressings or remove sutures. If the doctor doesn't have a surgery facility in house, the schedule may be arranged as "OR days" and "office days," which also accommodates OR staff who want to work full days.

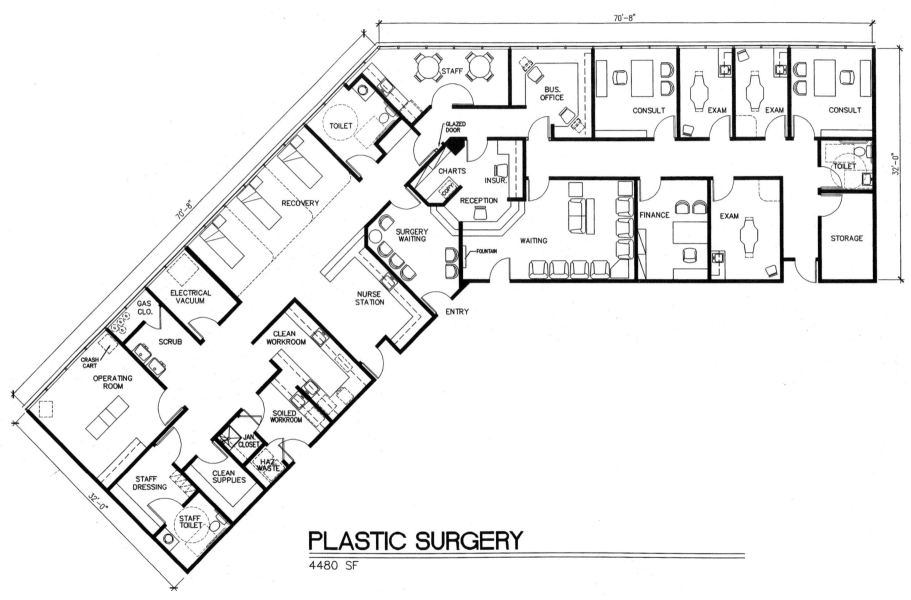

PLASTIC SURGERY

4480 SF

Figure 4-93. Space plan for plastic surgery, 4480 square feet. (*Design: Jain Malkin Inc.*)

PLASTIC SURGERY

6190 SF

Figure 4-94. Space plan for plastic surgery, 6190 square feet. (*Design: Jain Malkin Inc.*)

Secluded Entry

The composition of the plastic surgeon's practice will dictate the design features that need to be incorporated. A practice dedicated to cosmetic surgery may cater to an affluent clientele who expect a luxurious office. Of particular importance is a secluded entrance so that clients may park their cars and conveniently enter the office without being seen. After the procedure, they can slip out a private exit and elude others in the waiting room.

For this reason, plastic surgeons who specialize in cosmetic surgery frequently prefer a ground floor location, with a private driveway or turnaround so that patients need not walk through the lobby or public areas of the medical building (Figure 4-94). This is valid even when the practice is composed of a less affluent population. Patients who elect to have cosmetic surgery may be self-conscious about it and prefer privacy. It is very important to understand the practice's patient base and procedure mix. A common design mistake is to tailor it for the wrong target market. Today, plastic surgery has a wide middle-income base and, depending on the demographics, a high-profile design may be intimidating.

Concierge Reception Desk

A concierge-type reception desk is often preferred to a typical medical office reception window (Color Plate 10, Figure 4-22, and Figure 4-96).

Examination Rooms

Exam rooms in a plastic surgeon's office are quite different from those in other types of medical offices in that they generally use a motorized chair (Figure 4-97), or one room might be designed for examining hands (Color Plate 16, Figure 4-98). Note that the last example also doubles as a recovery room when the bed that stores in the wall is pulled down and the table pushed back into the cabinet, acting as a bedside table. The room also serves for patient

PLASTIC SURGERY
2415 SF

Figure 4-95. Space plan for plastic surgery, 2415 square feet. (*Design: Jain Malkin Inc.*)

Figure 4-96. Reception desk, plastic surgery suite. (*Interior design: Kelly Wearstler, Los Angeles, CA; Photo courtesy: Grey Crawford©.*)

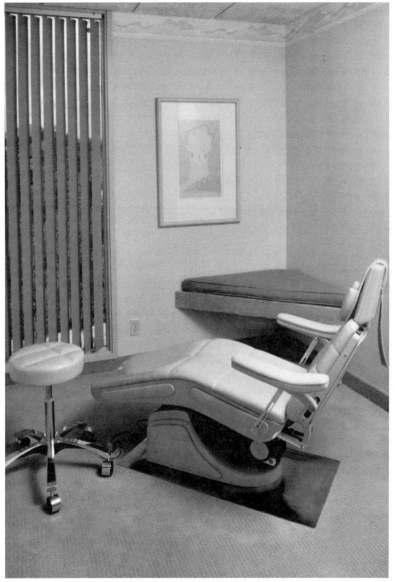

Figure 4-97. Examination room, plastic surgery suite. (*Design: Jain Malkin Inc.; Photographer: Michael Denny.*)

education, with a built-in VCR and TV monitor. Plastic surgery exam rooms may be large and elegantly designed, especially if used as the consultation room as well (Color Plate 17, Figures 4-99a and 4-99b). A clever treatment for the end of the exam room corridor (Figure 4-100) uses a mirror to give the illusion of an open-shelved divider with corridors on both sides. A different type of illusion is created by the trompe l'oeil mural at the end of the exam corridor in Color Plate 18, Figure 4-101, en route to the surgical suite in Figure 4-102. In this same suite, high ceilings make possible a geometry of intersecting planes complemented by cable lights that dance through clerestory openings (Color Plate 18, Figure 4-103).

Consultation Room

Patients considering surgery often interview more than one physician who may spend half an hour or more with a patient showing slides or photos of other patients who have had similar procedures, reviewing costs, and discussing the probable outcome. This initial consultation is an important element of a plastic surgeon's practice, because it is generally just this one meeting by which the patient decides whether he or she is comfortable with the surgeon's personality, qualifications, and results.

Plastic surgeons often use their private offices (consultation rooms) to make case presentations (Color Plate 17, Figure 4-99c), or a special room may be designed for this purpose (Figures 4-95 and 4-102). It is desirable to functionally and visually integrate the audiovisual (AV) presentation equipment (monitor, slide projector, or digital projector) into a custom-built wrap-around desk from which all elements, including dimming of room lights, can be controlled. New technology with digital photography means more surgeons will use presentation software. Monitor placement must consider this possibility. The new trend is multiple monitors displaying "before and after" photos located in exam rooms or wherever the surgeon prefers to do initial interviews/consults. Networked software allows photos to be accessed wherever there is a computer and monitor.

Figure 4-100. Clever treatment at end of corridor in plastic surgery suite uses a mirror to create the illusion of additional space. (*Interior design: Kelly Wearstler, Los Angeles, CA; Photo courtesy: Grey Crawford©.*)

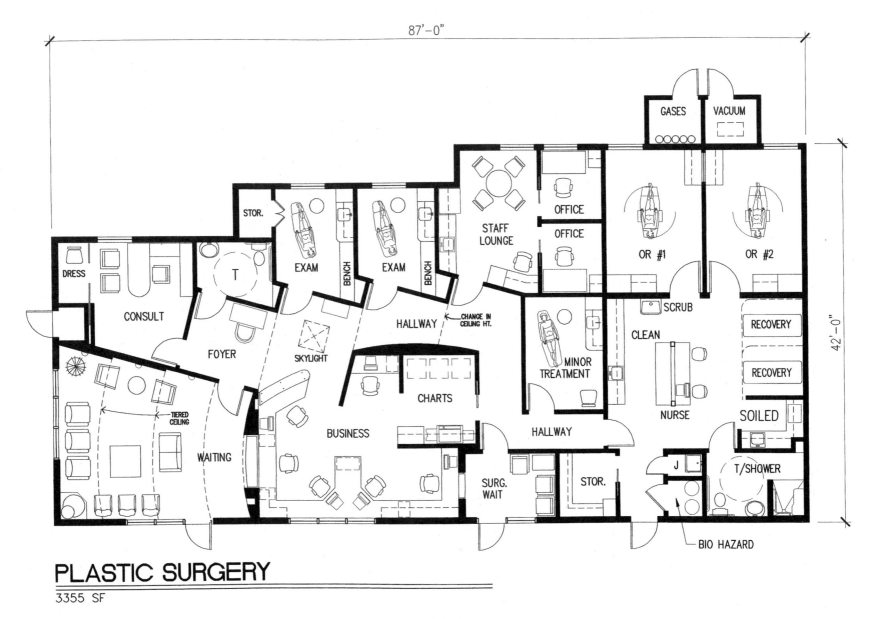

PLASTIC SURGERY

3355 SF

Figure 4-102. Space plan for plastic surgery, 3355 square feet. (*Design: Jain Malkin Inc.*)

Some physicians use a computer photoimaging system to demonstrate to patients possible outcomes from surgery. If this is to be used, the designer must plan well to accommodate it as the equipment, as well as the position of the patient and camera, require a certain relationship, specific countertop heights, and space allocation; otherwise, the process can be exasperating. This is often located in a small room, rather than in the physician's private office/consultation room.

The consultation room should convey a solid, successful image, but not be flamboyant or trendy. This room might be styled more conservatively than the remainder of the suite, although this is determined in large part by what would be appropriate for the patient population served. A plastic surgeon in Beverly Hills, to be competitive, would probably have a more lavishly designed office than one in Des Moines, Iowa. The space should be designed with the female consumer in mind although it should be noted that some plastic surgeons have perfected a specific procedure for men that brings them a higher number of male patients than the average.

The surgeon's diplomas and awards should be prominently displayed here in elegant frames and mats. Sometimes patient education is accommodated in the consultation room (a VCR and TV would be provided), or a dedicated room is created for this purpose.

Office-Based Surgery

Surgery performed within the physician's office is called *office-based surgery,* compared with that which is performed in a *freestanding* ambulatory surgical center. The latter is called freestanding, because it is not attached to or associated with a physician's office and is physically separate from a hospital. The reader is referred to Chapter 7 for additional information.

Any discussion of office-based surgery begins with the issue of reimbursement. Unlike surgery performed by ophthalmologists, most plastic surgery is elective in nature and, as such, would not be covered by third-party payers. Therefore, designing the surgery suite to meet the criteria

for reimbursement by third-party payers seems a moot point. Those cases that would be reimbursed (for example, reconstructive surgery to attach a severed finger or surgery to restore a burn victim's appearance) would be done outside the office in an ambulatory surgical center or hospital.

Most insurance companies and Medicare will pay the physician's fee for any covered procedures done in the physician's office, but if the surgery suite itself does not meet certain requirements, they will not reimburse for the use of the facility.

Accreditation, Licensing, and Medicare Certification

Major changes have recently occurred with respect to enhancing patient safety in the office-based surgery setting. While there are many differences among individual states, from the national perspective, the American Society of Plastic Surgeons and the American Society for Aesthetic Plastic Surgery mandated January 1, 2002 compliance for their members to operate in facilities that are accredited by one of the national accreditation organizations, or be Medicare certified (even a more rigorous standard), or be state licensed, also quite stringent.

What triggers compliance with NFPA fire codes is whether more than four persons are incapable of self-preservation at one time. If not, meeting occupancy codes will generally suffice. As most plastic surgeons (according to AAAASF) have only one operating room, it is unlikely that four or more persons would be in that condition. But this is certainly a gray area and open to interpretation. Common sense dictates that even one patient deserves the maximum in safety and protection, especially if you are that one person. But this explains why, for many years, plastic surgeons in some states have been able to get occupancy permits for undersized surgery suites that fall short, according to many criteria, of what would be expected today.

For those to whom this may be new, states license hospitals and all types of hospital-based surgery facilities, imposing what are generally regarded as the highest or most rigorous standards in terms of patient safety, minimum sizes of rooms, and a host of other issues. Most facilities that are state licensed will also have achieved Medicare certification. Medicare is a program under HCFA (Healthcare Financing Administration). Medicare uses NFPA 101 (Life Safety Code) and a local fire marshal—and sometimes an additional inspector who may be a retired surgeon—to inspect for compliance. With either licensing or Medicare certification, a fee for the use of the facility may be billed. Of the national accreditation associations, the AAAASF (American Association for Accreditation of Ambulatory Surgery Facilities), located in Mundelein, Illinois, considers itself to have the most rigorous standards with very tough quality assurance and, according to the director, is the only organization that requires semiannual peer review. The AAAASF accredits facilities for all surgical specialties as listed by the Board of Medical Specialties, including OB-GYN, urology, ophthalmology, ENT, plastic surgery, and orthopedics. It should be noted that AAAASF excludes dermatology because it is not listed as a surgical specialty. Nor will it accredit endoscopy facilities, but AAAHC (Accreditation Association for Ambulatory Healthcare) will.

It is not possible to print a definitive guide to negotiating the minefields of accreditation, certification, or licensing because one will encounter codes that are contradictory, gray areas that are ambiguous, and local inspectors whose personal experience leads them to make demands that are not stipulated in the code manuals, yet they are in a position to deny certification if their requests are not satisfied. All of this is nasty business for the designer or architect who wants to turn over a successful project and meet the client's expectations. To add complexity to these matters, one agency might use a different version of the code than another. Medicare might require the 1985 NFPA and this is what AAAASF uses, as of this writing; however, the latter anticipates going to the 1997 version, according to a discussion (April 2001) with an official at that organization. In the 1985 edition, back-up emergency power might be battery operated or use a generator. However, the 1997 edition provides for a generator only with no grandfathering of what was formerly acceptable.

The state of Nevada, on the other hand, requires, as of this writing, the 1999 NFPA code. In general, where there is a discrepancy, the more stringent code applies. Some states require a CON (Certificate of Need) for Medicare certification, whereas other states require state licensing as a precursor to Medicare certification, and some states don't require either of these. In California, dermatologists must be accredited in order to do surgery. AAAASF does not preempt local or federal codes and the facility must always be in compliance with OSHA. AAAASF requests written documentation to prove that the physician has "like" privileges at a local hospital to do the kinds of procedures that will be performed in the office-based setting.

As a general statement, according to the executive director, AAAASF prefers not to give minimum sizes of rooms or be draconian in terms of facility design, but rather to be flexible in order to allow the physician to meet the objective of safety in a variety of ways. This is what it means by "adequate" when it states that "a separate and adequate recovery room must be maintained free and clear of litter." AAAASF specifes that there must be 4 feet of open space around all sides of the OR table for patient safety during resuscitation. This is stated as, "needs sufficient space around OR table for emergency personnel to get access to the patient." Separate clean and soiled rooms are required, without giving sizes. Instead, it might read, "instrument prep and assembly area must be separated by a wall from the space where instrument cleaning is done or, if not, a policy to disinfect the area each time must be in place." Corridor widths are required to be "adequate" for movement of gurneys.

The standards imposed by these various agencies with respect to facility design and architectural issues are accompanied by standards and protocols for processing of tissue samples, peer review, number of kits of Dantrolene on hand for malignant hypothermia (general anesthesia is the triggering agent), all issues that have nothing whatsoever to do with design but protect patient safety.

The reader is referred to Chapter 7 for additional discussion about accreditation and, specifically, the Accreditation Association for Ambulatory Healthcare (AAAHC). However, as a closing thought about accreditation possibilities for office-based practices, state medical licensing boards (licensing of physicians) can often recommend state accreditation agencies, which may have less rigorous standards with regard to facility design.

American Association for Accreditation of Ambulatory Surgery Facilities

The American Association for Accreditation of Ambulatory Surgery Facilities publishes three booklets that will guide both the designer and the facility's staff if they wish to meet the *voluntary* accreditation standards of this organization. One booklet is the *Inspector's Manual,* another is the *Standards Manual,* and the third is the *Checklist/Questionnaire.*

The major determinant of design criteria relates to the type of anesthesia used. This, in turn, relates to the types of procedures that can safely be done in the office. The AAAASF standards classifications used in the manual are as follows:

Class A—performed under local or topical anesthesia; applies to minor plastic surgical procedures.

Class B—performed under intravenous or parenteral sedation, regional anesthesia, analgesia, or dissociative drugs without the use of endotracheal or laryngeal mask intubation or inhalation general anesthesia, including nitrous oxide.

Class C—performed under general anesthesia with endotracheal mask intubation or inhalation anesthesia (includes nitrous oxide); external support of vital body functions.

The AAAASF standards cover the environment of the surgery facility, general safety, medical records, quality assessment and improvement, policies and procedures for the OR and recovery room, blood and medications, personnel, and governance. An on-site inspection of the facility is made the first year, followed by self-evaluation the second and third years, and another on-site inspection the fourth year.

Although accreditation by AAAASF is voluntary, it does certify to the medical community and the community at large that the surgery facility meets nationally recognized standards such as those set for members of the American Board of Plastic Surgery. The AAAASF recommendations are not considered codes, but they are guidelines (standard of care issues) for the safe handling of patients.

Operating Suite Design

After a thorough discussion with the physician about goals for certification, accreditation, and/or licensing, appropriate code references must be consulted. The reader is referred to Chapter 7 for a discussion of these issues.

The *minimum* size of an operating room, in terms of function, number of personnel, and equipment (based on doing Class A procedures), is 14×16 feet clear, which may include one full wall of built-in cabinets for supplies. Outside the room, provide a scrub sink; storage for linens, gowns, caps, disposable supplies, and surgical dressings; drawers or carts for sterilized surgical instruments; clean and soiled utility rooms; a sterilization area; and male and female staff dressing area with lockers if space permits. Note that ORs may not have sinks in them as this compromises infection control.

Utility Areas

One often finds, in plastic surgery offices, attempts to save space by combining rooms like clean and soiled into a common "prep" area. It may even open off of the operating room as in Figure 4-95. Note in this plan that the scrub is alongside the nurse station and the latter is a "galley" nurse station against a wall. This is typical of many office-based facilities that try to cram two pounds of program into a one-pound space. In Figure 4-102, the soiled utility is quite small and recovery beds are undersized. Space is tight throughout the surgery suite. In the latter case, the surgeon found the "perfect" location, a high-profile freestanding building, with the ideal address, but the suite was locked in on all sides with no additional space to be acquired. To be functional, and meet business plan objectives, no rooms could be eliminated. High ceilings, however, allowed for dramatic interior design (Color Plate 18, Figures 4-101 and 4-103). Full-height maple doors have wood transoms and custom flush door jambs to direct the eye to the ceiling treatments.

As regulations tighten, the common "prep" room will be replaced by separate soiled and clean utility rooms as in Figures 4-93 and 4-94. However, if a common prep room is indicated, it should be designed similarly to a large nurse station. It should be a minimum of 10×12 feet, lined with cabinets and work surfaces. Instruments will be sterilized and wrapped here; dressings and medications are prepared. Do not underestimate the amount of space required for sterilizers and work space and also a rather sizable piece of equipment, a blanket warmer. Clinic service sinks and standard sinks in the prep or cleanup area should have plaster traps.

Falling in Love with a Space That's Too Small
One may note considerable variation in these space plans with respect to the composition of the operating room suite. Typically, a plastic surgeon finds an "ideal" lease space in terms of location, views, the "right" building, and it invariably has less space than required to design an optimum operating room suite. If the surgeon does not intend to seek accreditation to be able to bill a facility use fee, and does not intend to allow other "outside" surgeons to use the facility, there is considerable leeway in terms of minimum sizes of rooms, minimum sizes of recovery bays, separation of clean and soiled, and numerous other factors that are highly controlled in state-licensed facilities and those accredited by Medicare. Refer to Chapters 7 and 15 for more specific information on codes.

Occasionally, a surgeon may request a large OR with two tables and only a cubicle drape separating them, but regulatory agencies do not allow this due to risk of cross-contamination and also lack of privacy. In a busy practice, while the nurse is prepping one patient, the surgeon may be completing surgery on another, and a nurse may be applying a dressing on the third before moving the patient to a nearby recovery room. On this basis, three operating tables could be in use simultaneously, sometimes even

with just one plastic surgeon working, but it would be very expensive, in terms of space, to build three ORs in a one-physician practice. Some plastic surgeons design a large operating room that is divided into two separate rooms by a wide cabinet that can be accessed from either side but this is no longer allowed.

Design of the OR
An OR will have a motorized operating table and ceiling-mounted surgical lights (which require support above the ceiling) overhead. A crash cart containing resuscitation equipment and a defibrillator (Figure 3-55) must be in the room as well as an anesthesia machine. Oxygen and suction (vacuum) can be either piped into the room or portable, but most plastic surgeons would want central (not portable) medical gases. Some prefer that they be piped through the ceiling to keep cords off of the floor (Figure 4-104). The designer must check local fire code requirements for storage of anesthetic gases. (See Chapters 7 and 14 for additional discussion.)

If Class B and Class C anesthetic procedures are to be done, there will be a number of pieces of monitoring equipment, plus the anesthesia machine, in the room. There will also be an anesthesiologist or nurse anesthetist, one or two nurses, and the physician. This is the reason that operating rooms are often16×18 feet or 18×18 feet in size. Access to supplies within the OR is necessary. Often, a full wall (full height) of 15-inch-deep cabinets with adjustable shelves and glass doors is either recessed into the wall or, if not, designed with a sloped top to avoid collecting dust. Prefab metal cabinets specifically for ORs are available or they can be custom plastic laminate casework.

Lasers are often used in plastic surgery. Refer to a discussion, and photos of lasers, in the Dermatology and Ophthalmology sections of this chapter and in Chapter 7.

Interior Finishes
The operating room must be easy to clean. Walls should have an eggshell enamel paint finish. This does not preclude, however, having an artist stencil or paint a decorative border around the room to make it less intimidating to patients. A floor with a minimum of joints is desirable—a

hospital-quality sheet vinyl with self-coved base and heat-welded seams. Refer to Chapter 12 for recommendations.

Access by Vendors

A lot of linen is used in a surgery facility, and accommodation must be made for large carts of soiled linen and storage of clean linen. It is ideal if the linen supply company can enter the soiled workroom directly, pick up the dirty linen, and drop off the clean (Figures 4-93 and 4-94). Similarly, vendors picking up biohazardous waste or delivering medical gas cylinders should be able to do this without walking through the surgery suite.

Emergency Power

An essential element is the emergency back-up power system. Some states and localities, as well as accreditation bodies, allow a battery-powered source but the trend is to require a generator. There are very specific requirements as to the capacity of the generator and the number of items that must be tied to it as well as the number of hours it must be able to function in an emergency. Obviously, all of this relates to the number of ORs, recovery beds, type of anesthesia used, and average length of procedures.

Dressing Area/Recovery Room

A dressing room, with lockers for valuables, may be provided for patients. This is a moot point, however, since patients are told not to bring valuables and must have someone drive them home. Often, one's clothing and shoes are placed in a basket on the lower portion of the gurney, which travels with the patient, both eventually ending up in the recovery room. Sometimes the dressing area is combined with the recovery room. The recovery area should be located immediately adjacent to the operating room and nurse station so that staff can keep a watchful eye on the recovering patient (Figures 4-93, 4-94, and 4-102). Each recovery bed must have suction, oxygen, and electronic monitoring equipment.

Typically, recovery beds are wheeled transport gurneys (often called Stryker carts), 2×6 feet. A patient would be

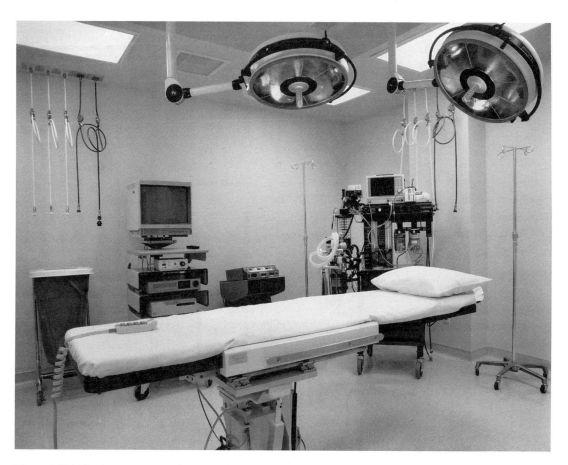

Figure 4-104. Plastic surgery operating room. (*Interior design: Kelly Wearstler, Los Angeles, CA; Photo courtesy: Grey Crawford©.*)

moved off the operating table onto a gurney and wheeled into the recovery room, so room layouts must allow for easy maneuvering of gurney carts without bumping into walls. One must be certain that all turns can be navigated.

Other Considerations

A busy plastic surgeon who specializes in cosmetic procedures may wish to have separate waiting rooms for male and female patients. A hairstylist may be on hand

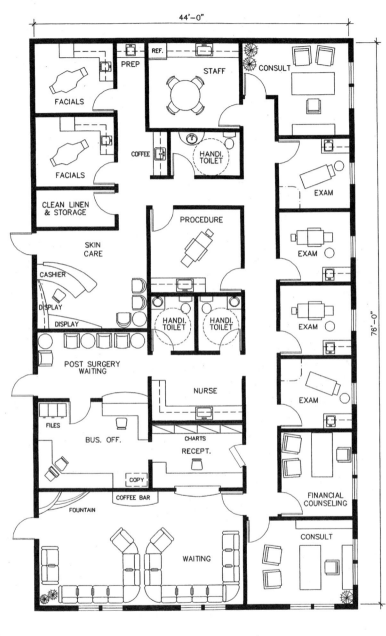

PLASTIC SURGERY

3344 SF

Figure 4-105. Space plan for plastic surgery with skin care services suite, 3344 square feet. (*Design: Jain Malkin Inc.*)

several afternoons a week to shampoo and style the hair of patients who have just had bandages removed after a facelift. Patients recovering from facelifts will have dried blood and scabs on their scalps, or even staples, which can make some hairstylists squeamish. Such patients may, understandably, be timid about visiting their own stylist in public until the bruises subside.

A small room should be set aside for this purpose with a standard beautician's shampoo chair, professional hair dryer, and good-quality mirrors (Figures 4-94 and 4-95). A gray-tinted mirror will downplay bruises, yet still provide enough reflection. Attractive wallpaper and accessories will help lift the patient's spirits. The color of the room should be complimentary to skin tones.

A plastic surgeon may also offer the services of a professional makeup artist for patients recovering from facial plastic surgery. This could be done in the same room as hairstyling (Figures 4-94 and 4-95).

Plastic surgeons who specialize more in reconstructive surgery—skin grafts for burn victims, surgery of the hand, repair of cleft palate, trauma—may not have strong sentiments about providing privacy and anonymity for their patients, and they may be less interested in the appearance or image of their offices.

Skin Care/Spa Services

Whether a plastic surgeon does or does not have a surgery center associated with the office, he or she may wish to have a suite of rooms that can be used for skin care or spa services. This requires at least two rooms 10×12 feet; an 8-×10-foot room with a sink for prep, storage of clean linen, and a hamper for soiled; a reception area with three or four chairs; and display cases for cosmetics and private-label skin care products that are available for sale. A laundry facility is useful if it can be located so that the noise of the washer and dryer cannot be overheard in the treatment rooms. These rooms, plus circulation space and a restroom, will total approximately 500 square feet, which, if not professionally managed, can result in a loss rather than profit when compared to the additional rent for the space. In many cities, spas have sprung up on every block, which means there is a lot of competition. However,

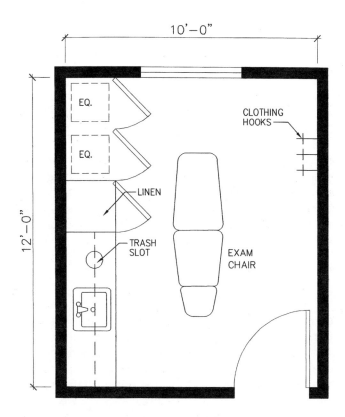

DUAL-USE EXAM ROOM AND SKIN CARE

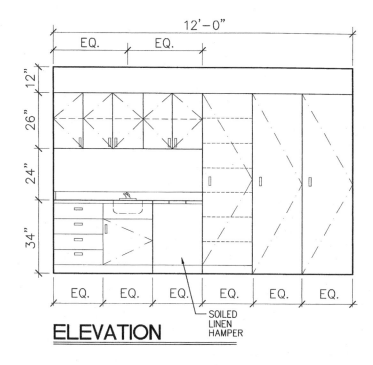

ELEVATION

Figure 4-106. Dual-use examination room that can also be used for skin care. Elevation shows design of casework wall accommodating both usages. (*Design: Jain Malkin Inc.*)

a busy plastic surgery practice can generate many referrals with patients having a higher level of confidence about the efficacy of the procedures than they might have in a commercial setting not associated with a physician's office. The ambience of a spa or skin care salon is very important. Color, music, fragrance, burning candles, and an environment that appears clean and bright, with exquisite lighting that flatters skin tones and highlights products to be sold, optimize the experience for patrons and increase sales. Treatment rooms should have soft lighting and feel soothing. Figure 4-105 shows

a spa services suite associated with a plastic surgery office.

It should be noted that one can design a dual-use exam room that will also work for skin care services, optimizing use of the room even when the physician is out of the office. The room must be 10×12 feet, larger than the standard exam room and have a full wall of cabinets in the long dimension. This results in a 6-foot-wide base cabinet with sink and upper cabinet and a 6-foot-wide full-height cabinet with three tall doors that conceal equipment and provide linen storage (Figure 4-106).

Interior Design

Since this is a low-volume medical practice, ease of maintenance and durability in finishes and furnishings are generally not an issue outside the surgery suite. Materials used may be residential in character (Color Plates 17 and 18, Figures 4-99a–d, and 4-101 and 4-103, respectively). The plastic surgeon trades in the quest for an aesthetic ideal and the eternal fountain of youth. The office is an expression of his or her attention to detail and an indication of aesthetic awareness; the image the surgeon projects is very important. People want to deal with a surgeon who appears to be successful—this amounts to third-party endorsement of the plastic surgeon's skills.

The plastic surgeon who spends a considerable sum on office design and furnishings will generally reap the rewards. No medical specialty benefits more from a high-profile image. Even the plastic surgeon's letterhead and business card, as well as brochures, should be striking and imaginative and coordinated with the office design.

All rooms of this suite may be carpeted, except for the surgery suite and a treatment room for small in-office procedures. Office design should be stylish but comfortable, and lighting should be soft and flattering in all rooms, except the exam rooms and operating suite. Incandescent and halogen lighting, as well as table lamps, are preferable to fluorescent in the waiting room (Color Plate 17, Figure 4-99d), corridors, and consultation room. The waiting room especially benefits from a low level of illumination to mask bruises resulting from surgery and to keep patients out of the spotlight.

The color temperature of fluorescent lamps is critical in examination and consultation rooms. A color temperature of 3500 kelvins with a high CRI (85 or more) is desirable. Consult Chapter 13 for more detail on lighting.

Bathroom design is important in this specialty. Large gray-tinted mirrors and interesting lighting may be incorporated into the vanity cabinet. Walls and ceiling may have an attractive wallcovering, and bathroom accessories (tissue boxes, paper towelette holders, soap dishes) should be elegant and residential in character. Other items a patient might use in light grooming before or after medical consultation ought to be provided. Grab bars, required by the ADA, should not be aluminum—highly institutional—and cold to the touch. Those by HEWI, which are nylon and can be matched to blend into the wall, are preferable.

Today, many people consider having plastic surgery to correct physical imperfections. Taboos about vanity have all but disappeared, and society places greater emphasis on self-expression, personal fulfillment, and an internal state of well-being. There is an increased exposure to the benefits of plastic surgery in the media, which has given more people the confidence to obtain treatment. Plastic surgery is no longer just an option of the rich; many persons of modest income also consider it a viable option, as do an increasing number of men.

DERMATOLOGY

A dermatologist treats diseases of the skin. It is not uncommon to find a one-physician practice. Since dermatologists rarely make hospital rounds or emergency house calls, their appointment schedule is strictly adhered to without the sort of interruption that plagues many other physicians. A one-physician suite would be composed of three examination or treatment rooms, a waiting room to accommodate eight to ten persons, a small lab, a toilet room, a business office, a consultation room, a minor surgery, and a large storage closet for drug samples (Figure 4-107). Larger practices may include a surgery facility, as well as offer ancillary services such as laser hair removal, chemical peels, facials, Botox (botulinum toxin) injections, sclerotherapy, Endermologie®, and massage. The reader is referred to Chapter 6 for a decentralized plan of a group-practice dermatology suite and to Figure 4-108 for a centralized plan. Figure 4-109 shows the relationship of rooms.

Procedures

The procedures performed in a dermatology office vary widely, depending on the number of providers, their entre-

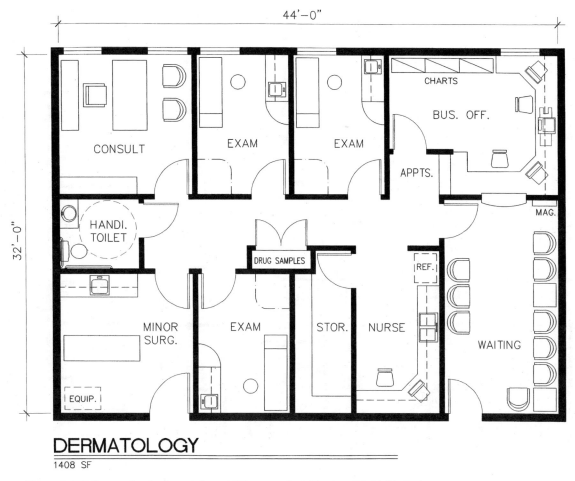

44'-0"

32'-0"

CONSULT

EXAM

EXAM

CHARTS

BUS. OFF.

APPTS.

MAG.

HANDI. TOILET

DRUG SAMPLES

REF.

MINOR SURG.

EXAM

STOR.

NURSE

WAITING

EQUIP.

DERMATOLOGY

1408 SF

Figure 4-107. Space plan for dermatology, 1408 square feet. (*Design: Jain Malkin Inc.*)

preneurial inclinations, and their training. Those having a more cosmetically oriented practice may do a considerable amount of plastic and cosmetic surgery and would need an office-based surgery facility similar to that used by plastic surgeons (see the Plastic Surgery section for details). The types of procedures would include brow lifts, liposuction, and facelifts.

Perhaps one of the physicians in a group practice may have been trained to do Mohs' surgery (more fully explained later in this section) for skin cancer. One of the physicians may be known for sclerotherapy techniques (treatment of varicose and spider veins) or perhaps hair transplantation.

Dermatologists, especially those with a cosmetically oriented practice, use many different types of lasers to remove unwanted hair, to do facial peels, and to remove tattoos, port-wine stains, birthmarks, red or brown spots, and freckles.

The more entrepreneurial practitioners sell skin care products, employ a number of estheticians or cosmetolo-

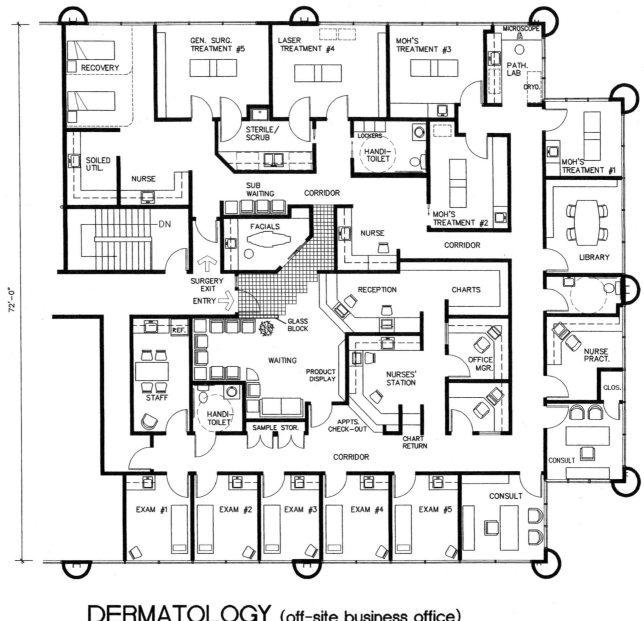

DERMATOLOGY (off-site business office)

4735 SF

Figure 4-108. Space plan for dermatology with off-site business office, 4735 square feet. (*Design: Jain Malkin Inc.*)

DERMATOLOGY.

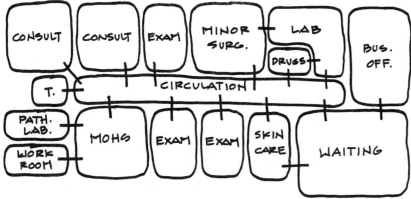

Figure 4-109. Schematic diagram of a dermatology suite.

gists to do facials, acne therapy, massage, cellulite therapy, facial chemical peels, and may even have a satellite suite for spa services (Figure 4-110). It is easy for a busy practice to generate many skin care referrals, and since most of these treatments require multiple visits, the volume of patients is steady and the profit can bolster sagging reimbursement for the clinical dermatology practice. Each state regulates the types of procedures estheticians can do under their licenses; some practices employ a registered nurse to oversee this type of enterprise.

Explanation of Procedures

Hair Restoration. Accomplished by laser micrografts, transplanting hair from one area of the scalp to another.

Sclerotherapy. Can involve injections into affected spider veins; removal of veins through small incisions (performed under local anesthesia); or "stripping" of larger vessels, a more involved procedure requiring general anesthesia or conscious sedation plus a local anesthetic.

DERMATOLOGY ESTHETICIAN'S SUITE

1126 SF

Figure 4-110. Space plan for dermatology esthetician's services. (*Design: Jain Malkin Inc.*)

Table 4-6.
Analysis of Program.
Dermatology

No. of Physicians:	1			2		
Exam Rooms	3@	8 × 10 =	240	6@	8 × 10 =	480
Minor Surgery		12 × 12 =	144		12 × 12 =	144
Toilets	2@	7 × 8 =	112	2@	7 × 8 =	112
Business Office		12 × 16 =	192		16 × 18 =	288
Staff Lounge		10 × 12 =	120		10 × 12 =	120
Waiting Room		12 × 16 =	192		14 × 18 =	252
Consultation Rooms		12 × 12 =	144	2@	12 × 12 =	288
Lab/Nurse		8 × 10 =	80		10 × 10 =	100
Facials/Chemical Peels		—			10 × 10 =	100
Storage		6 × 8 =	48		6 × 8 =	48
Subtotal			1272 ft^2			1932 ft^2
20% Circulation			254			386
Total			1526 ft^2			2318 ft^2

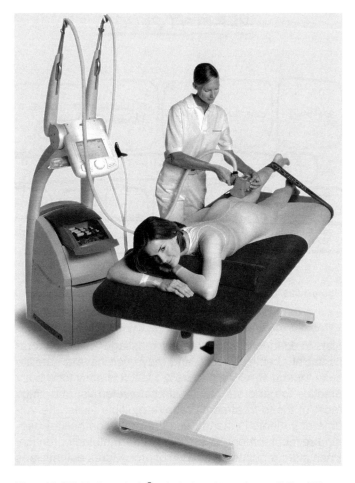

Figure 4-111. Endermologie® unit designed to reduce cellulite. (*Photo courtesy: LPG® USA.*)

Botox Injections. A form of botulinum toxin is used to smooth out and soften wrinkle lines. It causes temporary paralysis of the muscles so that they are unable to contract. An injection lasts several months.

DermaPeel. A skin resurfacing technique using microscopically abrasive crystals under highly controlled pressure to gently remove damaged cells from the outer layer of the skin.

Chemical Peel. A blend of retinoic acid and alphahydroxy acids to smooth the skin.

Cellulite Therapy. The newest technique is called Endermologie® and uses a device patented by LPG Systems (Figure 4-111). It requires a 10-×12-foot room as there is a corner photographic station (for before and after photos), a hydraulic lift massage table, and a large machine.

Tumescent Liposculpture. Localized fat deposits are removed by a high-pressure vacuum through tiny incisions through which a small cannula (hollow "tube") is inserted. Liposculpture uses a smaller cannula than liposuction and is performed with local anesthesia with oral and/or conscious sedation, rather than general anesthesia. These procedures are done in a surgery room with resuscitation equipment on hand.

Laser Surgery. Laser stands for *Light Amplification by the Stimulated Emission of Radiation.* The laser beam can cut, seal, or vaporize skin tissue and blood vessels. Lasers produce one specific wavelength (color) of light, which has variable intensity and pulse duration. When the laser light hits skin tissue, its light energy is absorbed by water or pigments in the skin, all of which absorb laser light of different wavelengths. A variety of lasers are used in dermatology because they are highly specific: The pulse of light that will vaporize a black tattoo will not affect red pigmented spider veins, for example.

Examination Room

Exam rooms can be 8×10 feet instead of the standard 8×12 feet. The exam table used is often a flat physical therapy table, 24 inches wide×78 inches long×36 inches high, which may be placed against the wall. When placing the table in this room, the head of the table should be positioned so that the physician can work on the patient's right side. Natural light (a window) is important in dermatology exam rooms. The room should have a sink cabinet and perhaps a dressing area, as well as a high level of illumination, free of shadows, supplied by full-spectrum fluorescent lamps. Adequate lighting is essential in all exam rooms.

One exam room may have a Dermascope (Figure 4-112), a diagnostic videoscope for examining the skin surface microscopically. It provides a printed photo for the patient and also digitally downloads the information onto an electronic medical record or transmits the image, provided broadband cable is available, to a remote location for a real-time consultation. The unit does not require a dedicated circuit but does need to plug into a surge suppressor.

Lab

The lab will have a microscope and an autoclave for cleaning instruments. In a small office, the nurse station may be combined with the lab (Figures 4-107 and 4-113). In a large suite (Figure 4-108), the pathology lab serves the Mohs' surgery area, and decentralized nurse stations are adjacent to exam rooms, surgery, and recovery.

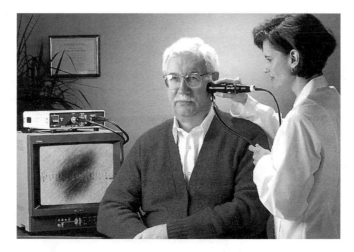

Figure 4-112. Video diagnostic Dermascope enables patient or family member to see what the physician sees and facilitates telemedicine consultation. (*Photo courtesy: AMD Telemedicine, Lowell, MA.*)

Surgical Procedures

The minor surgery room is 12×12 feet, with a long sink cabinet along one wall. Medical equipment to be accommodated in this room would depend on the scope of the procedures. However, the equipment would include an operating table or chair that adjusts to different positions (Figure 4-114) and a ceiling-mounted surgical light over the table. If an office-based surgery suite is required, consult the Plastic Surgery section of this chapter.

Dermatologists perform many surgical procedures in the office. Surgery may be done to improve the skin's appearance, to biopsy tissue to establish a diagnosis, or to prevent or control disease. Different types of surgical procedures include:

Curettage—scraping the tissue with a sharp surgical instrument called a curette.

Excision—cutting into the skin surgically, removing the tumor or growth, then closing the wound with stitches.

Cryosurgery—using liquid nitrogen sprayed on the tissue to freeze it and thereby destroy the unwanted cells.

66'-0"

32'-0"

EXAM　EXAM　EXAM　EXAM

CONSULT

DRUG SAMPLES

EXAM

WAITING

HANDI. TOILET

PATIENT EXIT

LAB/NURSE

CONSULT

DRUG SAMPLES

EXAM

MULTI-PURPOSE RM. (CHEMICAL PEELS, FACIALS)

STG.

HANDI. TOILET

BUS. OFFICE

EXIT CORRIDOR

APPTS.

MINOR SURG.

CHARTS

Figure 4-113. Space plan for dermatology, 2112 square feet. (*Design: Jain Malkin Inc.*)

DERMATOLOGY

2112 SF

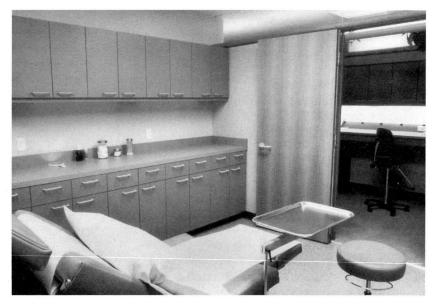

Figure 4-114. Minor surgery room, dermatology. (*Architecture/interiors: Richard Deno, Cardiff, CA; Photographer: Kim Brun.*)

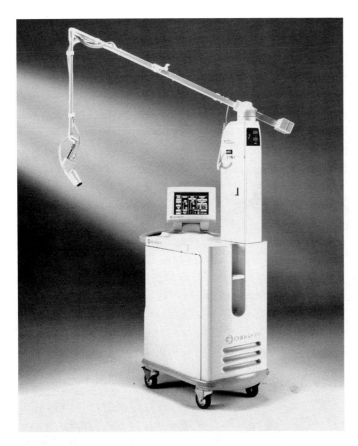

Figure 4-115. UltraPulse® 5000C aesthetic CO_2 laser system for dermatology. (*Photo courtesy: Coherent Medical Group, Santa Clara, CA.*)

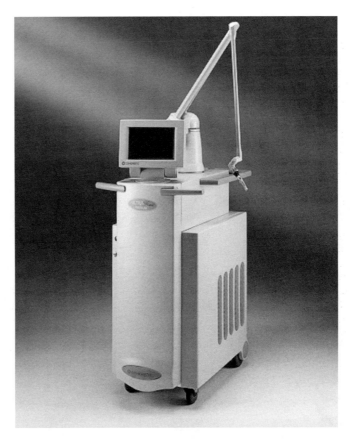

Figure 4-116. Ultra Fine™ erbium laser used for skin resurfacing. (*Photo courtesy: Coherent Medical Group, Santa Clara, CA.*)

Dermabrasion—a "sanding" of the skin using an abrasive rotary instrument to remove scars, acne, or damage done by exposure to the sun.

Laser Surgery—using a highly concentrated, focused beam of light to eradicate unsightly skin abnormalities such as tattoos, port-wine stains, birthmarks, and broken blood vessels. The CO_2 laser is the most common type used in dermatology practice. The unit shown in Figure 4-115 requires a standard 110/115-volt electrical outlet and is air cooled. Another commonly used laser is the erbium:YAG (Figure 4-116). The diode laser in Figure 4-117 is used for hair removal. (The reader is referred to a discussion of lasers under the Ophthalmology section of this chapter and also to Chapter 7.)

Mohs' Histographic Surgery—a specialized surgical technique developed by Frederic Mohs, M.D., some 50 years ago, it is a method of detecting the root of the tumor through the use of a sequential examination of tissue with a microscope immediately after the tissue has been excised. Because the microscope guides the physician in how much skin needs to be removed, tak-

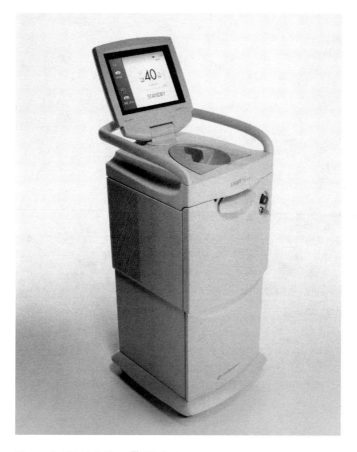

Figure 4-117. LightSheer™ EP diode laser system. Used for permanent hair reduction. (*Photo courtesy: Coherent Medical Group, Santa Clara, CA.*)

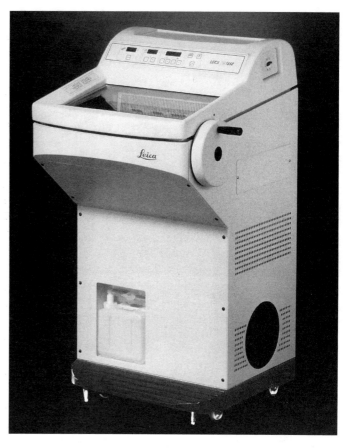

Figure 4-118. Cryostat used for sectioning tissue. Leica CM1900. (*Photo courtesy: Leica Microsystems Inc., Bannockburn, IL.*)

ing "extra margins" of tissue just for safety's sake is unnecessary. This technique is used especially where cancers have occurred or where they are at high risk of recurring.

This differs from other surgical techniques because the excision of tissue is guided by the use of diagrams, dyes, microscopes, and special surgical techniques. A local anesthetic is used during this procedure. The suite plan in Figure 4-108 shows a Mohs' suite with adjacent scrub

and prep area, pathology lab, and sub-waiting area. Note that surgical patients have a direct route to the surgery suite, without walking through the examination area.

Pathology Lab
The layout of the pathology lab is important. The three main pieces of equipment are the cryostat (Figure 4-118), which freezes the tissue specimen and slices thin sections to be examined under the microscope (the second piece of equipment), and the autostainer, which uses colored dyes

to stain the tissue. The cryostat should be opposite the autostainer to save steps, and the autostainer must be next to the sink as it connects, through a hole in the countertop, to water and drain (see layout in Figure 4-108). A stainless steel counter and sink are best as the dyes stain badly. The autostainer needs an electrical outlet and fume hood; some require a water source. Autostainers come in various sizes, which allows for considerable flexibility in tight spaces. Some are 60 inches long but only 6 to 10 inches deep, which means they can be placed on a 6- to 10-inch-deep shelf over the countertop (allow clearance for the hinged lid to open) to save space (Figure 4-119). Excellent lighting is essential. Other room requirements are an undercounter refrigerator for meds, considerable storage for gallon bottles of fixative and reagents for the autostainer, and a low countertop (less than 30 inches high) with knee space to support a heavy microscope without incurring vibration. The microscope should be close to the cryostat. The sequence is that the tissue goes first to the cryostat, then to the stainer, and, finally, to the microscope.

Storage and Surgery
Both the general surgery room and the Mohs' room require a full wall of cabinets to store many supplies and disposables.

Patient Flow
A diagram or map is made during Mohs' surgery to guide the excision and examination of tissue. While each sequential specimen is stained, frozen, and examined under the microscope, patients may leave the office and return 45 to 60 minutes later.

Psoralen Ultraviolet Light

Psoralen ultraviolet light, type A (PUVA), is used for treatment of severe psoriasis that cannot be controlled by conventional therapies, including ultraviolet light, type B. Psoriasis is a noncontagious skin disease characterized by elevated red patches on the skin, covered by a dry scale. The disease is the result of an excessive buildup of

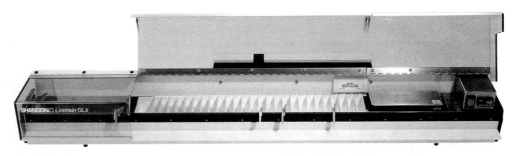

Figure 4-119. Tissue staining device used in Mohs surgery pathology lab. Linistain™ GLX Random Access Stainer. (*Photo courtesy: Thermo Shandon, Pittsburgh, PA.*)

skin cells. PUVA reduces this cell reproduction and temporarily clears symptoms for anywhere from a few weeks to a couple of years.

PUVA involves a combination of long-wave ultraviolet light (type A) and a prescription oral medication. Patients usually require three treatments a week for a total of approximately 30 treatments.

Most dermatologists do not do PUVA treatment in their offices because PUVA equipment is fairly expensive, requires a dedicated area, and would need a high volume of patients to make the investment worthwhile. The equipment generates a great deal of heat, and a separate air-conditioning unit is required for the PUVA treatment room.

Other Design Considerations

Dermatologists dispense a lot of drug samples, salves, ointments, and shampoos. A specialized closet should be provided in a convenient location in the corridor for storage of drug samples. The closet might have doors fitted with compartments or bins for sorting and making accessible frequently used products (Figure 4-120).

Interior Design

There are no special interior design considerations in a dermatology suite. However, lighting is critically important

Figure 4-120. Drug sample cabinet. (*Design: Jain Malkin Inc.*)

Figure 4-121. Sub-waiting area, dermatology suite. Note effect of planters used to divide room and to create privacy. (*Architecture/interiors: Richard Deno, Cardiff, CA; Furniture: Kathy Burnham; Art: Richard Fitzpatrick, M.D.; Photographer: Kim Brun.*)

in all areas. Full-spectrum lamps are best for evaluating skin tones. Refer to Chapter 13. Patients are all ages and in relatively good health. Exam rooms are often used for treatment; therefore, a hard-surface floor is preferable to carpet. The use of planters to provide privacy for sub-waiting areas (Figure 4-121) is an interesting space-planning device.

ORTHOPEDIC SURGERY

An orthopedic surgeon deals with diseases, fractures, or malformations of the bones, as well as arthritis, birth defects, industrial accidents, and sports injuries that affect the bones and joints. Some orthopedic surgeons specialize in hand surgery. With a tendency to group in large practices, it is not uncommon to find six or seven physicians working in the same office (Figure 4-122).

ORTHOPEDIC SURGERY

7260 SF

Figure 4-122. Space plan for orthopedic surgery, 7260 square feet. (*Design: Jain Malkin Inc.*)

Table 4-7.
Analysis of Program.
Orthopedic Surgery

No. of Physicians:		1		2		3	
Consultation Rooms	2@	12 × 12 = 288	4@	12 × 12 = 576	6@	12 x 12 = 864	
Exam Rooms	2@	9 × 12 = 432[a]	8@	10 × 10 = 800	8@	10 × 10 = 800[b]	
Cast Rooms		12 × 12 = 144	2@	12 × 12 = 288	2@	12 × 12 = 288	
Business Office		14 × 16 = 224		20 × 20 = 400		20 × 26 = 520	
Office Manager		10 × 10 = 100		10 × 10 = 100		10 × 10 = 100	
Toilets	2@	7 × 8 = 112	2@	7 × 8 = 112	3@	7 × 8 = 168	
Staff Lounge		10 × 10 = 100		10 × 12 = 120		14 × 16 = 224	
Waiting Room		16 × 20 = 320		24 × 30 = 720		24 × 30 = 720	
Physical Therapy (Optional)		—		—		20 × 25 = 500	
Tech Workstation		6 × 8 = 48		6 × 8 = 48	2@	6 × 8 = 96	
Radiology		12 × 14 = 168		12 × 14 = 168		12 × 14 = 168	
Darkroom		6 × 8 = 48		6 × 8 = 48		6 × 8 = 48	
Storage and Film Filing		10 × 12 = 120		10 × 16 = 160		12 × 16 = 192	
Film Viewing		8 × 8 = 64		8 × 8 = 64		8 × 8 = 64	
Subtotal		2168 ft²		3604 ft²		4752 ft²	
20% Circulation		434		721		950	
Total		2602 ft²		4325 ft²		5702 ft²	

[a]Assumes one physician is seeing patients while the other is in surgery.

[b]In a six-person practice, it is unlikely that more than three or four surgeons would be in the office at the same time.

Schedules may be arranged so that each doctor performs surgery two days a week, is off one day, and is in the office the balance. Therefore, all the surgeons are seldom in the office at once.

Required Rooms

A two-physician practice would typically have four exam rooms, one cast room, a small nurse or tech station, two consultation rooms, a large business office, a large waiting room, a radiology room with darkroom and tech workstation, a toilet room, and a large storage and film filing room (Figure 4-124). A larger practice might also have a

physical therapy room, additional cast rooms and exam rooms, and a sit- down film viewing area adjacent to the radiology room (Figure 4-122). Orthopedists typically do not have conventional nurse stations; it is more a workstation for the techs who assist the physician in the exam rooms.

Physical therapy (PT) is an ancillary service affected by the Stark legislation, designed to eliminate conflict-of-interest self-referral opportunities for physicians. This has reduced the number of PT facilities associated with physicians' offices, as has managed-care contracting, which may dictate that patients go to specific facilities for physical therapy services. If an orthopedist has a facility adjacent to the suite, it must have its own entrance (Figure 4-122).

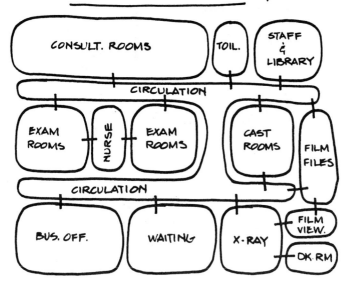

Figure 4-123. Schematic diagram of an orthopedic surgery suite.

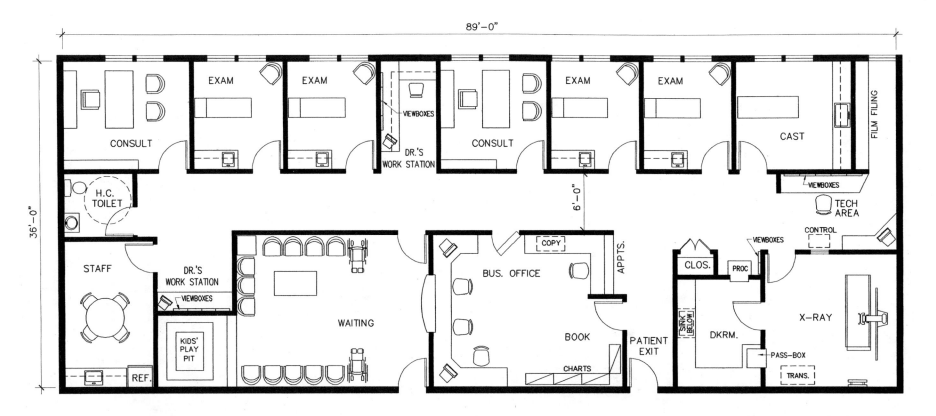

Figure 4-124. Space plan for orthopedic surgery, 3204 square feet. (*Design: Jain Malkin Inc.*)

ORTHOPEDIC SURGERY

3204 SF

Examination Rooms

Exam rooms may be 9×12 or 10×10 feet since an orthopedist uses a 24- to 27-inch-wide×78-inch-long table (sometimes custom built), which may be placed against the wall to save space (Figure 4-125). Some orthopedists prefer to place the head of the table per-

pendicular to the wall so that they can walk around three sides of it (Figure 4-126), in which case the room needs to be 10 feet wide.

The table will frequently have pull-out leaves for examination of limbs, and the lower portion of the table may be enclosed for bulk storage. Sometimes a row of drawers is provided alongside the bulk storage portion of the cabinet.

Digital Technology

A workstation with computer central to the exam rooms, at stand-up height, makes it easy for techs and physicians to retrieve lab results and, with the proper type of monitor, view digital X-rays (Figure 4-127). View box illuminators (preferably recessed into the wall) should also be provided for viewing film-based X-rays. There is considerable interaction between physicians and techs in the examination area and this centralized hub facilitates communication. The suite in Figure 4-127 is set up for digital X-ray but accommodates film filing storage for historical films prior to conversion to a digital system.

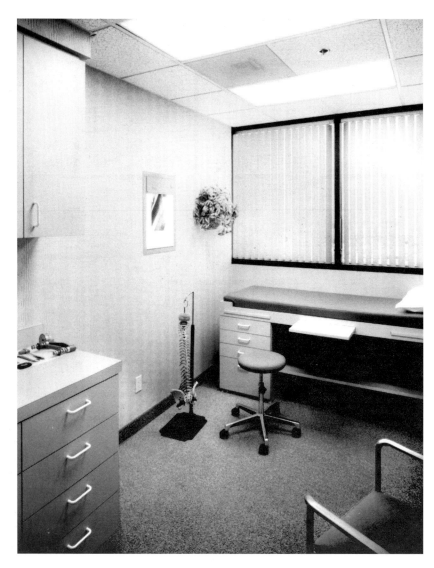

Figure 4-125. Examination room, orthopedic surgery. (*Design: Jain Malkin Inc.; Photographer: John Christian.*)

Figure 4-126. Examination room, orthopedic surgery. (*Design: Jain Malkin Inc.; Photographer: Michael Denny.*)

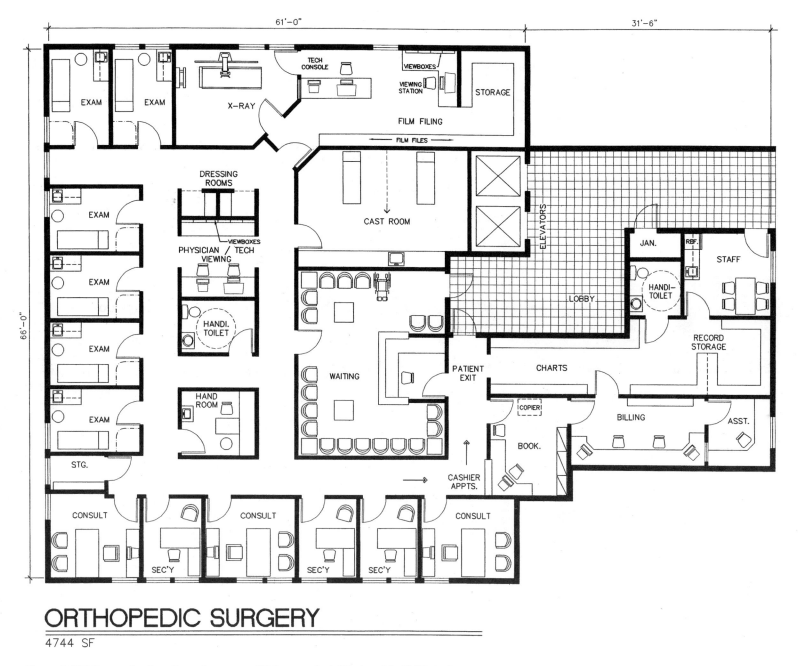

ORTHOPEDIC SURGERY

4744 SF

Figure 4-127. Space plan for orthopedic surgery, 4744 square feet. (*Design: Jain Malkin Inc.*)

Hand Surgeon

A hand surgeon works at a T-shaped desk (Figures 4-128a and 4-128b). The patient is seated on one side of the stem of the "T" and the surgeon on the other. Drawers and a flip-top countertop hold instruments and tools. This room may be as small as 8×8 feet.

A hand surgeon also requires a treatment room or cast room (Figure 4-129) for dressing wounds and building casts. Removal of sutures can be done in the hand room. Each exam room and cast room must have a double-panel X-ray film illuminator (Figure 4-130) recessed into the wall or surface mounted, at a stand-up height (see the Appendix). As digital X-rays become more standard, flat-panel monitors and keyboards will need to be accommodated.

Cast Room

The cast room will have one full wall of cabinets designed precisely to accommodate the numerous splints, bandages, plaster, and required tools (Figure 4-131). The design of a cast cabinet is extremely important to the efficiency of the room. Plaster comes in rolls in widths of 2, 3, 4, and 6 inches. Slots in the face of the cabinet allow the rolls to feed through easily, when pulled. Stockinette may be fed through other slots. Drawers hold padding; open bins hold elastic bandages; and a drawer contains cast tools. Each orthopedist seems to have a preferred arrangement of drawers, slots, and bins on the cast room cabinet, but all cast cabinets are composed, in one arrangement or another, of the above components. Sometimes a prefabricated cast cart is used for this purpose.

A large hinged trash bin should be built into the cabinet, if space permits. If possible, this bin ought to be vented to the outside, since cast cutoffs have a foul odor. If this is not possible, the room should have an exhaust fan. The sink in the cast cabinet should have wrist blade faucets, or foot-pedal control, a gooseneck spout (so a bucket can be put under it), and a plaster trap.

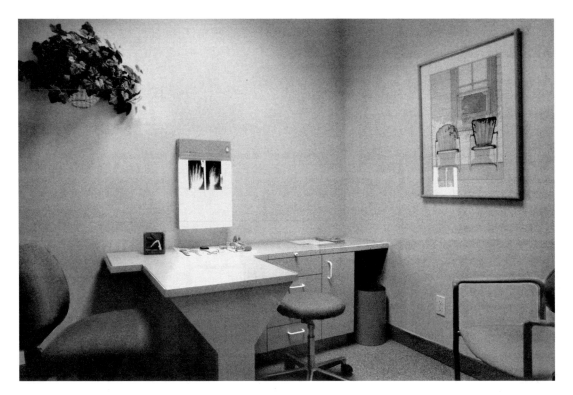

Figure 4-128a: Hand room, orthopedic surgery. (*Design: Jain Malkin Inc.; Photographer: John Christian.*)

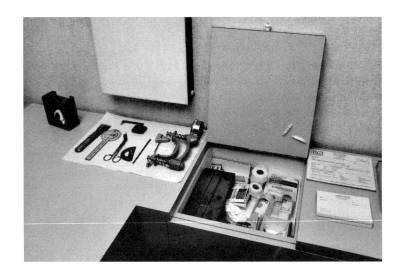

Figure 4-128b: Hand room, detail of cabinet. (*Design: Jain Malkin Inc.*)

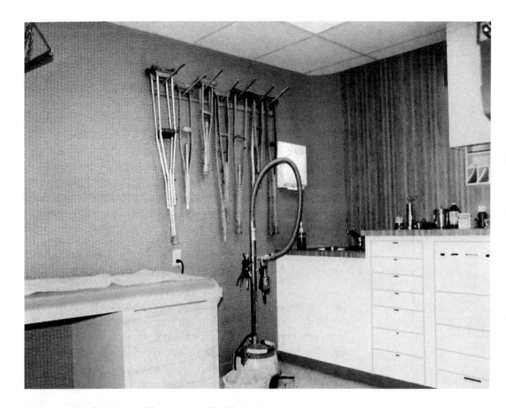

Figure 4-129. Cast room. (*Design: Jain Malkin Inc.*)

Figure 4-130. Double-panel view box. (*Photo courtesy: GE Medical Systems, Waukesha, WI.*)

One must bear in mind that surfaces of the cast room must be washable since the room is exposed to plaster dust when casts are sawed off and wet drippings when new casts are built. A sheet vinyl floor and vinyl wallcovering are recommended.

Orthopedists often use Fiberglas casts. This requires no special accommodation in the cast room as the Fiberglas comes in rolls, like the plaster. The rolls come sealed in foil packets in varying widths. The same type of padding is used for both plaster or Fiberglas casts. Private cast rooms (Figure 4-122) are preferable to multi-station cast rooms (Figure 4-127) as they can also be used as exam rooms.

Minor Surgery

Some orthopedists use a minor surgery room for procedures such as removing foreign bodies or removing toenails, for example.

Consultation Room

The consultation room will usually be used as the doctor's private office and as a place to return phone calls and review X-ray films. For this purpose, a four-panel illuminated film viewer should be located to the side of or

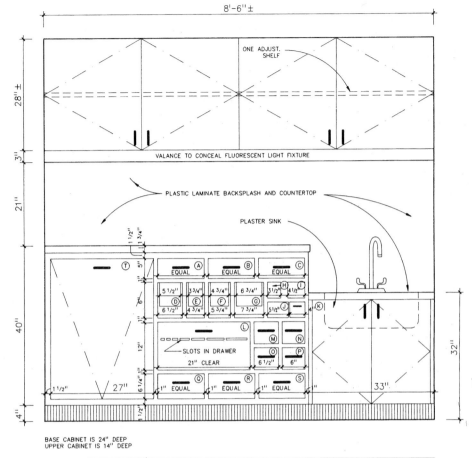

8'-6"±

ONE ADJUST. SHELF

VALANCE TO CONCEAL FLUORESCENT LIGHT FIXTURE

PLASTIC LAMINATE BACKSPLASH AND COUNTERTOP

PLASTER SINK

28"±   3"   21"   40"   4"

1 1/2" 1 3/4"

5" (T) EQUAL (A) EQUAL (B) EQUAL (C)

5 1/2" 3 3/4" 4 3/4" 6 3/4" 3 1/2" (H) 4 1/2"
(D) (E) (F) (G)
6 1/2" 4 3/4" 5 3/4" 7 3/4" 5 1/2" (J) 4" (K)

(L)

SLOTS IN DRAWER   (M) (N)
21" CLEAR   (O) (P)
                   6 1/2" 6"

1 1/2"   27"   6 1/4"   1" EQUAL (Q) 1" EQUAL (R) 1" EQUAL (S)   33"

32"

BASE CABINET IS 24" DEEP
UPPER CABINET IS 14" DEEP

DOOR AND DRAWER SCHEDULE

(A) (B) (C) (Q) (R) (S)	DRAWERS WITH SIDE ROLLERS, A, B & C MUST HAVE CLEAR DEPTH OF 4" INSIDE.
(D) (E) (F) (G)	NO SIDE ROLLERS. BOTTOM DRAWER GLIDE ONLY. THESE DRAWERS ARE RARELY OPENED.
(H) (I) (J)	OPEN SHELVES FOR SPINTS (CUBBY HOLES).
(K)	DRAWER FOR 4" BIAS. DRAWER GLIDE ON BOTTOM.
(L)	STOCKINETTE DRAWER. SLOT OPENINGS MUST BE SANDED VERY SMOOTHLY. (NO SNAGS).
(M) (N) (O) (P)	DRAWERS FOR PADDING.
(T)	TILT-OUT TRASH BIN. (HOLDS LARGE PLASTIC TRASH CAN).

CAST CABINET

Figure 4-131. Cast cabinet. (*Design: Jain Malkin Inc.*)

behind the physician at a sit-down height, usually mounted over the credenza (Figure 4-132).

Adjacency of Rooms

Cast room(s), radiology, and the film viewing area should be located in proximity to each other (Figures 4-122, 4-124, and 4-133). There should be a tech work area near the cast room and radiology room (Figure 4-134 and see Figure 5-18). It would have a 6-foot-long countertop and X-ray view boxes and be close to the darkroom and film processor. Sometimes the X-ray tech assists the physician in the cast room.

Radiology Area

The reader is directed to Chapter 3, Family Practice, for design of an X-ray room, control area, and darkroom. Open shelves (or deep chart file cabinets) must be provided for film filing. Shelves should have vertical dividers every 18 inches, since films are heavy and unwieldy and tend to slump over if not packed tightly between divider supports. X-ray jackets (the paper storage envelopes) are 14½×17½ inches, and shelves should be shallow enough so that about 2 inches of the film jacket hang over the edge of the shelf for ease of access.

One must be sure that the door to the X-ray room is large enough to move in the equipment. The ceiling height of this room must be at least 9 feet high.

Digital X-Ray

Predictions are that digital X-ray will not become widespread in orthopedic offices for a number of years due to the expense of conversion. When new equipment is purchased, it will likely be digital but orthopedists who have been in practice awhile will still require storage of films and conventional film illuminators in addition to a digital workstation for reviewing X-rays (Figure 4-127). And there would be a need to print digital images on opaque or transparent paper. Along with this, monitors to receive digital X-rays may be located in the consultation room, cast room, and tech workstation. Swissray International (Elmsford, New York) offers a software package called OrthoVision to enable an orthopedic practice to convert to digital imaging.

Other Considerations

Corridors of the suite should be 5 to 6-foot wide for easy passage of patients on crutches and in wheelchairs. The corridor is also used as a gait lane. Sometimes a patient education room is included (Figure 4-135). Surgeons find it time saving to purchase videotapes explaining certain frequently performed procedures to patients (joint replacement, arthroscopy, etc.).

Toilet rooms in this suite, as in any other, must accommodate the handicapped (see the Appendix).

Interior Design

The interior design of the suite must please patients of all ages. Artwork might include sports photos or perhaps educational exhibits dealing with prevention of sports injuries or other orthopedic topics. All floors except cast rooms and the X-ray room can be carpeted with a level-loop commercial carpet glued to the slab without a pad. Any other type of installation will be unsuitable for wheelchairs and people on crutches. A firm feeling under foot is desirable here.

The waiting room needs to be large enough to accommodate people in wheelchairs without ambulatory patients tripping over them. Chairs should be firm, with high seats, and have arms to help arthritic patients, for example, raise themselves out of the chair. Chairs should be well balanced, to avoid tipping when patients lean on them for support. It is practical, in an orthopedic waiting room, to offer several types of seating to provide comfort for the widest number of people. In Color Plate 19, Figure 4-136, a large saltwater aquarium is the focus of the room. It is serviced from a closet behind it.

If the budget allows, walls (at least corridor walls) should be covered with commercial vinyl wallcovering, since wheelchairs and crutches can damage paint.

Figure 4-132. Consultation room, orthopedic surgery. (*Design: Jain Malkin Inc.*; Photographer: Michael Denny.)

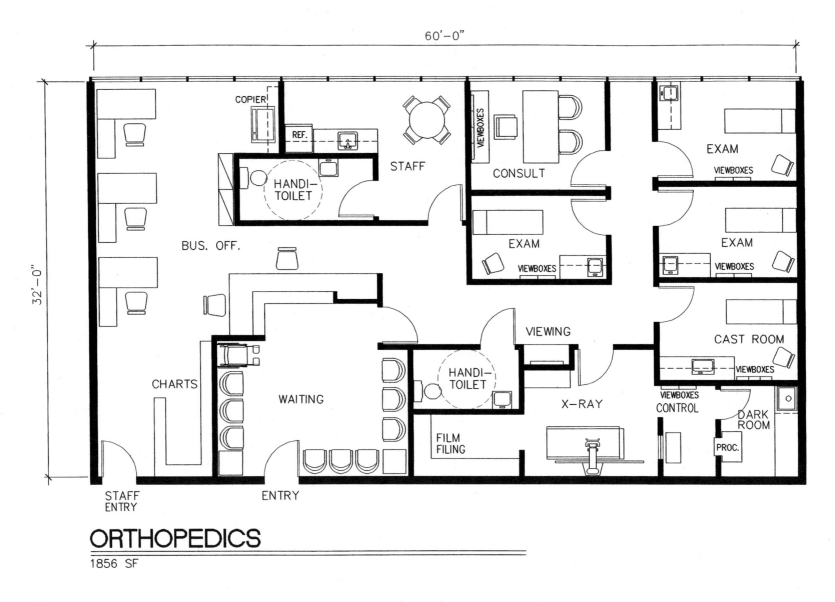

60'-0"

32'-0"

COPIER

REF.

HANDI-TOILET

STAFF

VIEWBOXES

CONSULT

EXAM

VIEWBOXES

BUS. OFF.

EXAM

VIEWBOXES

EXAM

VIEWBOXES

VIEWBOXES

CAST ROOM

CHARTS

VIEWING

HANDI-TOILET

WAITING

X-RAY

VIEWBOXES
CONTROL

DARK ROOM

FILM FILING

PROC.

STAFF ENTRY

ENTRY

ORTHOPEDICS

1856 SF

Figure 4-133. Space plan for orthopedic surgery, 1856 square feet. (*Design: Jain Malkin Inc.*)

Figure 4-134. Tech work area. Control (generator) for X-ray unit is outside room. Lead glass window provides view into X-ray room. Emergency electrical shutoff panel located here. Automatic processor and tech viewing area can be seen in rear. Note: This photo shows an older-model film processor, but it is illustrative of a film-based tech work area. A brochure rack makes it easy for tech to distribute relevant literature to patients. (*Design: Jain Malkin Inc.; Photographer: John Christian.*)

Figure 4-135. Patient education room, orthopedic surgery. (*Design: Jain Malkin Inc.; Photographer: John Christian.*)

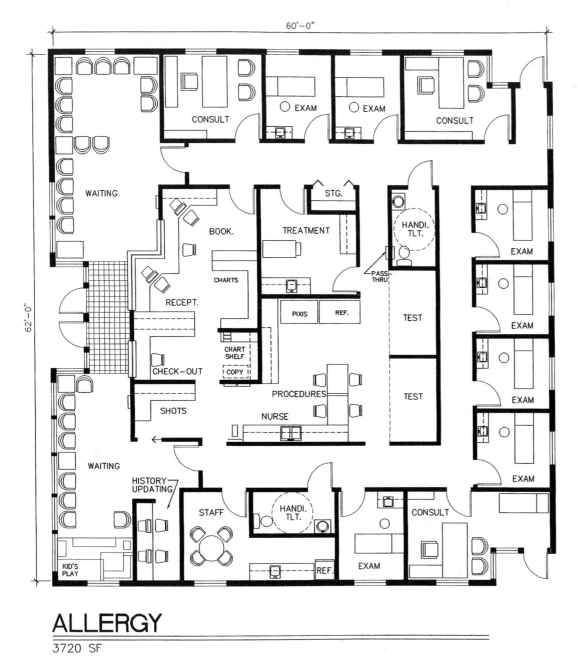

60'-0"

62'-0"

WAITING

CONSULT

EXAM

EXAM

CONSULT

STG.

HANDI. TLT.

EXAM

BOOK.

TREATMENT

PASS THRU

CHARTS

RECEPT.

PIXIS

REF.

TEST

CHART SHELF

COPY

CHECK-OUT

PROCEDURES

TEST

EXAM

SHOTS

NURSE

EXAM

WAITING

EXAM

HISTORY UPDATING

STAFF

HANDI. TLT.

CONSULT

KID'S PLAY

REF.

EXAM

ALLERGY

3720 SF

Figure 4-137. Space plan for allergy, 3720 square feet. (*Design: Jain Malkin Inc.*)

ALLERGY

Patient Histories

Allergy is defined as an overreaction in some individuals by a specific defense mechanism of the body responding inappropriately to certain environmental substances and resulting in annoying and sometimes debilitating reactions. The substances to which these reactions occur are called allergens. A methodically detailed patient history is a part of any preliminary examination or interview. Often, a lengthy printed questionnaire is given to the patient prior to the first visit to be filled out at home. In some situations, patients may fill out a history, or update it, while sitting in the waiting room with clipboard in hand. Several alcoves with countertop writing surface, chair, and light may be included in or near the waiting room (Figures 4-137 and 4-138). Computers will increasingly be used for patient histories. A patient may be able to log on to a physician's Web site, answer the questions on line, and email the completed questionnaire to the physician's office where it can be downloaded into the patient's electronic medical record, if such exists. Software to handle this type of confidential information in the medical setting is already available to safeguard patients' privacy during transmission, as explained in Chapter 3. (See Figure 4-139.)

Providing carrels or alcoves in the waiting room allows patients to update information on their electronic medical record to reflect changes since their last visit. They can also be used for accessing information about allergies on the Internet; the physician may have set up on the home page icons for Web sites with the best medical resources. These carrels, if equipped with TV monitor and VCR, can also be used to view videotapes.

Frequently, a combination of staff interview and printed questionnaire will be used. In this situation, an alcove may be created off of the corridor for a number of tablet arm chairs; however, privacy must be considered and the area should be located where patients in the waiting room cannot overhear the conversation. The suite plans in

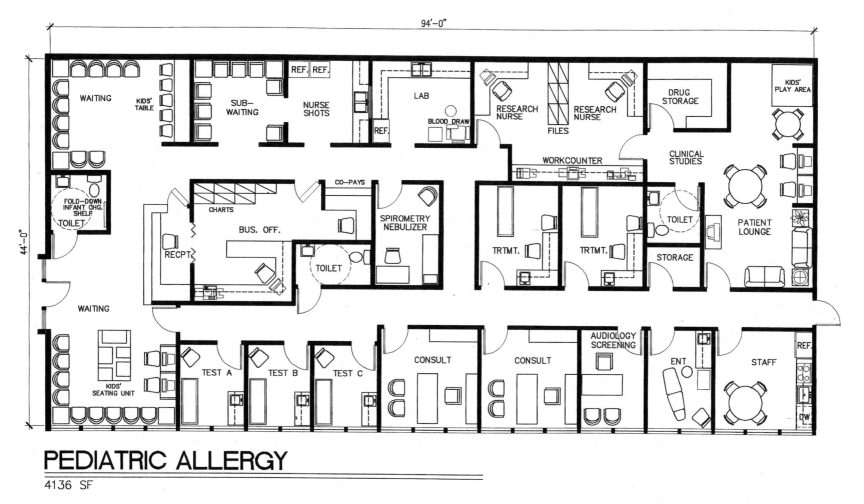

PEDIATRIC ALLERGY

4136 SF

Figure 4-138. Space plan for pediatric allergy, including research area for clinical studies, 4136 square feet. (*Design: Jain Malkin Inc.*)

Table 4-8.
Analysis of Program.
Allergy

No. of Physicians:		1		2		3
Exam Rooms	2@	8 × 12 = 192	4@	8 × 12 = 384	7@	8 × 12 = 672
Treatment Rooms		12 × 12 = 144	2@	12 × 12 = 288	2@	12 × 12 = 288
Consultation Rooms		11 × 12 = 132	2@	11 × 12 = 264	3@	11 × 12 = 396
Waiting Room		16 × 16 = 256		16 × 26 = 416		20 × 25 = 500
Sub-Wait (shots)		10 × 10 = 100		10 × 15 = 150		12 × 20 = 240
Storage		6 × 8 = 48		6 × 8 = 48		8 × 8 = 64
Nurse Station/Lab		12 × 16 = 192		12 × 14 = 168		10 × 32 = 320
Toilets	2@	7 × 8 = 112	3@	7 × 8 = 168	3@	7 × 8 = 168
Shots		(Combined w/lab)		8 × 10 = 80		8 × 10 = 80
Recovery/Reaction		6 × 8 = 48		8 × 10 = 80		8 × 10 = 80
History Alcoves		—[a]		8 × 10 = 80		8 × 10 = 80
Test Rooms[b]		(2 persons) 96		(3 persons) 144		(4 persons) 192
Audiology		—		8 × 10 = 80		8 × 10 = 80
ENT Exam (optional)		8 × 12 96		—		—
Staff Lounge		10 × 10 = 100		10 × 12 = 120		12 × 14 = 168
Business Office[c]		12 × 20 = 240		12 × 24 = 288		14 × 22 = 308
Subtotal		1756 ft²		2758 ft²		3636 ft²
20% Circulation		351		552		727
Total		2107 ft²		3310 ft²		4363 ft²

[a]History-taking alcoves may be worked into the circulation area or waiting room or be located in a dedicated room.
[b]May be one room with cubicle drape separation or individual rooms with pocket doors.
[c]Includes reception, appointments, bookkeeping, and insurance.

Note: The above spaces may vary greatly, depending on the location of shot, test, and recovery/reaction rooms and how they are combined.

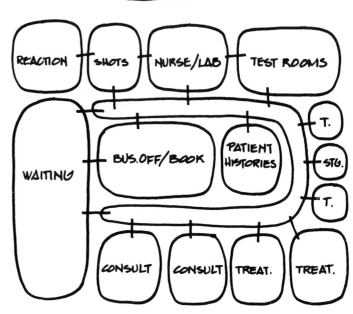

ALLERGY

Figure 4-139. Schematic diagram of an allergy suite.

Figures 4-137, 4-138, and 4-140 indicate various options for handling patient histories. If the practice includes a large number of pediatric cases, the interview room will have to accommodate one or both parents, the child, and the interviewer, since the parents will usually answer questions for the younger child.

Some allergists prefer that the patient history be taken by the staff. In this case, small rooms (6×8 feet) may be provided with a desk (2×4 feet is adequate) and a chair for both the patient and the interviewer, and perhaps one for a companion (Figure 4-137). The nurse can also take the history in a standard exam room. Sometimes allergists may take the patient history themselves, using the consultation or exam room.

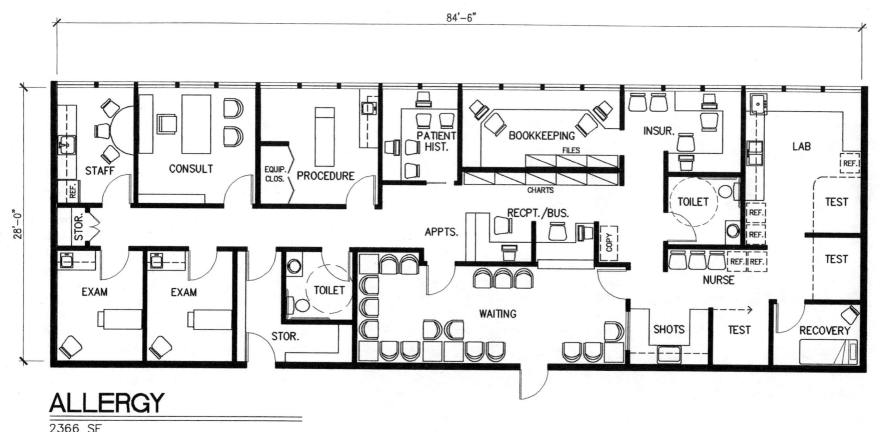

ALLERGY

2366 SF

Figure 4-140. Space plan for allergy, 2366 square feet. (*Design: Jain Malkin Inc.*)

Pediatric Allergy

There are pediatric allergists whose entire practice focuses on children (Figure 4-138). These offices should be designed according to the needs of an allergist, but with design and color palette suitable for a pediatrician's office (Figures 4-141 and 4-142). The treatment or test rooms, instead of having number designations, may have large animals or cartoons painted alongside them so that staff can tell the child to go to the "butterfly" or the "frog" room. However, one must take care to not make it too pediatric, which may offend adolescent patients. A digital technology theme, with interactive art, would appeal to children of all ages. It should be noted that, in a pediatric practice, there will be a high volume of shots after school.

Patient Flow

Allergy patients generally fall into several categories in terms of flow and treatment.

Figure 4-141. Waiting room for pediatric allergist. (*Design: Jain Malkin Inc.; Photographer: John Waggaman.*)

nesses, will visit an allergist to evaluate these problems and develop a treatment plan. These patients will review their medical histories with the nurse and physician, have a physical examination, and often undergo various tests, which may include skin tests, pulmonary function tests, screening audiology, tympanometry, and, in some practices, rhinolaryngoscopy and inhalation challenge tests. After the physician's examination of a new asthma patient, spirometry (measuring lung capacity) is part of the routine work-up. It can be done in the lab or the procedure room. Afterward, a nebulizer treatment with a bronchodilator medication may be administered for diagnostic or therapeutic reasons. Established asthmatic patients periodically undergo spirometry as part of their ongoing care. Providing a room for this purpose near the lab (Figure 4-138) is useful. Allergists perform tympanometry and audiology screening to diagnose middle-ear disease. Rhinolaryngoscopy is performed in an exam room with a specialized equipment cart (refer to the discussion in the Otolaryngology section) to evaluate the condition of the sinuses, the nasal cavity, larynx, and throat. If a fiber-optic scope is used with a tiny camera on the end (connected to a video monitor), the internal structures can be visualized in color on the monitor, which can be helpful to both the physician and the patient.

Acutely Ill
These patients proceed to a treatment room immediately upon entering where they are evaluated by a nurse and the physician who will make a decision about the immediate intervention required. This may include treatment with an aerosolized nebulizer, the placing of an IV line in the patient's arm, delivery of oxygen, or administration of systemic medications. The procedure room would be used for the more acutely ill patients, most often those with more severe acute exacerbations of asthma.

Initial Evaluation
Individuals experiencing a variety of respiratory tract, skin, and miscellaneous other reactions, or chronic ill-

Desensitization Injections (Allergy Shots, Immunotherapy)
A series of injections may be given once or twice per week for a period of months, eventually reaching a four-week interval that may continue for several years. Patients check in at the reception desk and proceed immediately to the nurse station for the shot. Afterward, the patient will sit in a sub-waiting area, in view of the nurse, for a period of 20 to 30 minutes to check for an adverse reaction. It is necessary to find out how many patients come in for shots at one time to make sure that the sub-waiting area will accommodate them.

Follow-Up Visits
From time to time, patients will return to report new symptoms or to have a tuneup. These are routine visits such as

might be encountered in any primary-care or specialist's medical office. The patient would be seen by the physician, nurse practitioner, or medical assistant in the exam room, followed by any procedures deemed necessary by the doctor or nurse practitioner.

Inhalation Challenge Tests

In some practices, patients suspected of having asthma, or those participating in research studies, undergo the serial inhalation of chemicals or allergens known to induce asthma in the procedure room. A dosimeter and spirometer are used to provide exact dosages and to measure effects, respectively.

Clinical Research

Some allergists are involved in clinical research studies. Patients participating in these investigations may be present 10 to 12 hours, or more, in the physician's office where they are given medications and have their lung functions tested periodically. It's important to have a lounge setting for this purpose and a pediatric playroom (for pediatric research), as well as a kitchen to prepare food for patients and their companions (Figure 4-138). This involves a considerable outlay of space, which, when patients are not present, may double as a staff lounge. However, it is unlikely the research office could be shared by other personnel due to the amount of records, paperwork, and experimental drugs stored there during ongoing clinical trials.

The clinical research nurse does a lot of teaching in this room. There is a great deal of paperwork and mail, both received and sent out, which requires a work counter with postage meter, letter opening machines, copier and fax machine, printers and computers. In the evening, the waiting room or research lounge area can be used to explain the study to groups of 20 people or more to interest them in participating. Lots of file cabinets and bookshelves are required for binders, journals, paperwork, and study drugs.

Each research nurse needs desk and file space as well as shelves for manuals and binders. Files cannot be stored where patients can access them. An 18-inch-deep

Figure 4-142. Secondary waiting room, pediatric allergy. (*Design: Jain Malkin Inc.; Photographer: John Waggaman.*)

storage area (cabinets with locking doors) is needed for drug samples involved in the studies. Opposite this cabinet, a shelf or work counter should be available to place a box while it is being accessed. It is clear, from looking at Figure 4-138, that a sizable area is required for clinical studies. Since this is a lucrative endeavor, however, resulting in sizable fees from pharmaceutical companies, the cost of the lease space is usually not an issue.

Patient Volume

An allergy practice has a high volume of patients (as high as 50 to 60 per doctor per day), which falls into two categories: short visit (to receive an injection or have a follow-up visit) and long visit (patient interview, procedures). Of the 50 patients per day per physician, 20 to 25 will be shots, which means they likely will not see the physician. Due to the high volume of patients, an efficient layout is of utmost importance. A large number of patients come once or twice a week, and others at various intervals up to four to six weeks, to receive allergy shots. Thus, the nurse station where injections are given should be located off the waiting room or just inside the suite near the waiting room so that these patients do not have to mingle with the long-visit patients (Figures 4-137 and 4-140). Functions requiring quiet, such as audiology screening, as well as the research area (if it exists), should be at the rear of the suite. Look at the nurses' principal functions and activities and group them together to avoid needless steps.

Injection Protocol

After receiving the injection, as just explained, the patient will return either to the main waiting room or to a sub-waiting area off of the nurse station to sit for a period of time (typically 20 to 30 minutes) to check for an adverse reaction. The waiting room must be large enough to accommodate the high volume of patients. One may wish to include a small "reaction" room furnished with a cot and chair so that a patient after receiving an injection may lie down and be observed by the nurse (Figure 4-140).

Skin Tests

After the physician has reviewed or completed the initial history taking and the physical examination, the patient frequently has skin tests administered by a nurse or technician. Two types of skin tests are used, either alone or in combination. If both are used, the doctor usually starts with prick tests on the back or upper extremities on a patient who is sitting or lying down. This may be followed by intradermal tests, in which a small amount of an allergen is injected just under the skin, on the upper extremi-

ties. Skin tests may be performed in small procedure rooms, 8×8 feet or 8×10 feet in size, or in a large room that has been divided into 6×8 foot or 8×8 foot areas by way of a ceiling-mounted cubicle drape or, if more privacy is desired, low partitions, closed off with a drape on the open end. The patient lies on a physical therapy–type flat table that is often placed against a wall. The technician sits alongside the patient, working off of a cabinet or a mobile cart. A rack of small vials containing allergens is carried from room to room and placed on the cart. This can also be done in standard exam rooms.

Treatment or Procedure Room

Patients who are in no immediate physical danger are seen in test rooms or exam rooms, but patients who are experiencing severe symptoms such as asthma or vomiting may be examined in a treatment room where the staff has access to IV equipment and respiratory equipment such as nebulizers, oxygen (usually portable), and medications that may need to be injected.

After a diagnosis has determined to which agents the patient is sensitive, desensitization treatment begins. The injections and tests are done by nurses and aides; therefore, one doctor may have several aides.

Audiometry

A small number of otolaryngologists also do allergy. Full audiometry testing as well as testing for hearing aids may be provided. (Refer to the Otolaryngology section for photos of an audio testing booth.) Trained allergists may perform simple audiometry *screening* and/or tympanometry. Although this type of test equipment is, for the most part, digital, pediatricians or allergists who wish to do basic screening may use a low-cost manual audiometer (Figure 4-143) that sits on a table, with the patient (wearing headphones) on one side and the staff person on the other. The room should be as soundproofed as possible to screen any extraneous noise and to enable the patient to totally concentrate on the sounds being generated by the machine. A tympanometer (Figure 4-144) is sometimes combined with the audiometer in one piece of equipment. The tympanometer diagnoses middle-ear disease, which may indicate eustachian tube dysfunction.

Other Considerations

The physician needs a fairly large consultation room with a desk since not only will the results of the testing and the prescribed treatment often be discussed there, but the doctor's reference materials, books, and files will be stored there. The nurse station/lab in this suite must be large and have space for two or more full-size refrigerators for storage of injectables and allergen extracts for testing and desensitization.

Interior Design/Construction Issues

Heavy textures, irregular surfaces (e.g., some acoustic ceiling tiles), "shag" carpeting, and many fibers (wool, in particular) collect dust and can cause problems for those with allergies and are to be avoided in the office. Similarly, draperies, because they collect dust, are to be avoided in favor of PVC vertical blinds. All materials in this suite must be easy to dust or sanitize, and they must be as hypoallergenic as possible. Avoid dust shelves—any nonfunctional surface that might collect dust. Upper cabinets, for example, should continue to the ceiling. An electronic filter on the HVAC system can be useful.

There are certain building materials that are known to off-gas VOCs, the most formidable of which is formaldehyde for many individuals. Particle board, often used as the substrate for plastic laminate in cabinets and casework, is made with formaldehyde. At considerable additional expense, one may buy domestic particle board—made without formaldehyde—but if it is stored even for a period of days in a millwork shop alongside conventional particle board, it will quickly pick up the odor like a sponge. An alternative to plastic laminate casework is

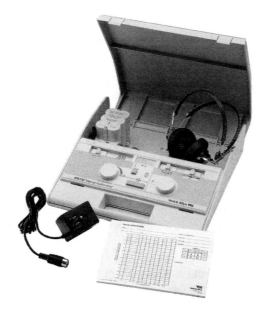

Figure 4-143. Manual audiometer for screening hearing. (*Photo courtesy: Welch Allyn®, Skaneates Falls, NY.*)

Figure 4-144. Tympanometer for diagnosing middle-ear disease. (*Photo courtesy: Welch Allyn®, Skaneates Falls, NY.*)

solid hardwood cabinets with solid surface tops such as Corian. Moreover, the contact cements used with plastic laminates are high in VOCs. The water-based equivalents tend not to be as effective and often will invalidate a warranty by the fabricator. The EPA (Environmental Protection Agency) publishes excellent literature listing the VOC content and period of years one can expect these potentially hazardous agents to off-gas. There are numerous excellent resources and books that have been written on the topics of "sick building syndrome" and "green design."

There are individuals who are so highly sensitive to the components of most construction materials, as well as fibers used in textiles and agents used in housecleaning solutions, that life from day to day is almost unbearable for them, as they try to figure out how to limit their exposure. An allergist may develop a subspecialty in treating patients of this type, in which case the office should be designed as "green" as possible. It may be more practical for an allergist to rent an old house (assuming it is free of asbestos) whose contents may have off- gased may years ago, as opposed to renting space in a new medical office building. Even in a new building, there are a couple of things that can be controlled. Carpet should be unrolled and exposed to fresh air to off-gas for a week prior to installation. Vinyl wallcovering should be avoided in favor of low-VOC, or no VOC, paint, which is readily available from most manufacturers. Forbo Marmoleum® is a linoleum sheet goods product containing only natural materials. It does not need waxing and may be a good choice for rooms that are not appropriate for carpet. Finally, if operable windows exist, the suite should be fully ventilated for at least one week after all finishes have been installed, prior to tenant occupancy. Fans are often placed at strategic locations in the suite to direct the flow of air (which may contain petrochemicals) to keep it moving toward the windows.

HVAC Issues

Being able to monitor and control the relative humidity, especially in humid locales such as Florida and Hawaii, will reduce mildew and mold and retard the growth of other fungi, bacteria, and dust mites. Keeping the relative humidity below 50 percent (which may require dehumidi-fication) minimizes these allergens and their irritating by-products, which flourish in moist environments. In addition, exceeding the standard number of room air changes in the HVAC system can keep the air cleaner, as can meticulous attention to changing air filters on a regular schedule.

NEUROLOGY

Neurologists diagnose diseases of the nervous system and brain. Their patients are always referred by other physicians. Patients may complain of headaches, epileptic seizures, damage suffered as a result of a stroke, or perhaps a cerebral palsy condition that has resulted in facial distortion—a distended jaw or a drooping mouth. Neurologists manage progressively degenerative diseases such as Parkinson's disease, Alzheimer's disease, multiple sclerosis and Lou Gehrig's disease (amyotrophic lateral sclerosis, ALS), which involves considerable "trial and error" manipulation of drugs. Responsibility for diagnosing tumors of the brain and spine falls to the neurologist, who also manages the patient's care postsurgically, if indicated.

This is a low-volume specialty, with the taking of a preliminary history and an interview in the physician's consultation room or exam room requiring 20 to 45 minutes for new patients. Occasionally, there may be a small exam room opening off of the consultation room (Figure 4-145). Two exam rooms per physician is generally adequate.

A patient education room with TV and VCR and CRT with Internet access is useful for patients and their families to learn about neurodegenerative diseases.

Planning for patients in wheelchairs is mandatory in this specialty. Individuals with spinal cord injuries may have large motorized wheelchairs possibly with attached portable ventilators. The waiting room and exam rooms must easily accommodate wheelchairs; a corridor width of 5 feet is optimal.

Diagnostic Procedures

Neurologists used to do numerous diagnostic tests within the office, but as reimbursement has steadily decreased, in some locales, there is a trend toward sending the patient to the hospital for tests. This means the physician need not invest in the equipment or bear the cost of additional space to accommodate it. Moreover, the increased availability of MRI and CT (computer tomography) scans —the gold standard in neurological diagnosis—has greatly reduced the number of EEGs (electroencephalograms) performed although they are still used for epilepsy. It is necessary, nevertheless, for space planners to be familiar with this test and equipment. Figure 4-145 shows a suite designed to accommodate in-house testing.

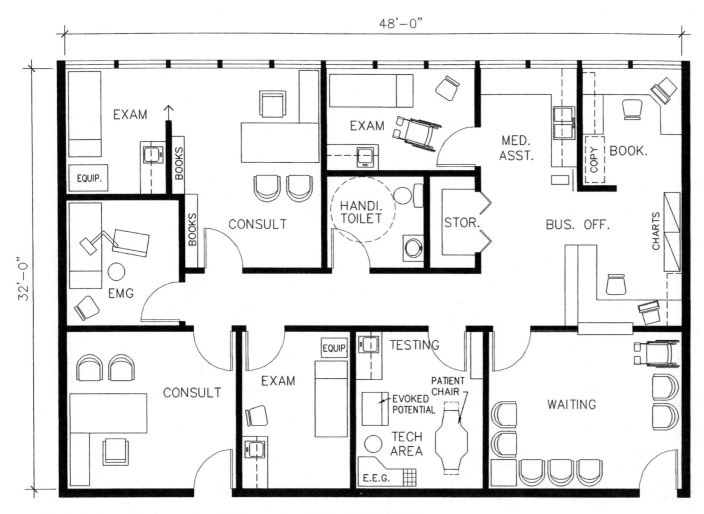

Figure 4-145. Space plan for neurology, 1536 square feet. (*Design: Jain Malkin Inc.*)

After the patient interview, a series of tests may be performed. The most common test is the *electroencephalogram* (charting of brain waves), commonly known as EEG (Figure 4-147). This can be performed in a room as small as 8×10 feet if the technician does not remain in the room with the patient, but sits in an adjoining control room.

There are two schools of thought on this point. Some neurologists feel that the patient is comforted by the technician's being in the same room, and others feel that it is distracting to the patient. However, most prefer to have the tech in the room with the patient. In either case, the patient usually sits in a comfortable recliner chair, since this seems to make the patient less apprehensive and

Table 4-9.
Analysis of Program.
Neurology

No. of Physicians:	1		2	
Consultation Rooms	12 × 14 = 168	2@	12 × 14 =	336
Exam/EMG	10 × 10 = 100		10 × 10 =	100
Exam Rooms	8 × 12 = 96	3@	8 × 12 =	288
Business Office	12 × 14 = 168		14 × 16 =	224
Waiting Room	12 × 14 = 168		14 × 16 =	224
Toilets	7 × 8 = 56	2@	7 × 8 =	112
EEG/Control	10 × 12 = 120		10 × 12 =	120
Med. Asst./Tech	8 × 8 = 64		8 × 8 =	64
Storage	4 × 6 = 24		6 × 6 =	36
Subtotal	964 ft²		1504 ft²	
20% Circulation	193		301	
Total	1157 ft²		1805 ft²	

NEUROLOGY

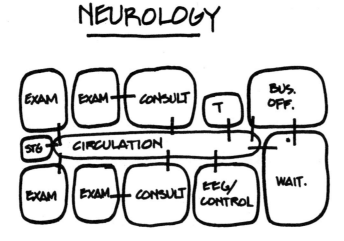

Figure 4-146. Schematic diagram of a neurology suite.

more relaxed. It is not essential but it is helpful to have a sink in the EEG room for hand washing.

There are two ways to administer the EEG. One method requires the application of conductive paste at the temples before the leads are attached. The paste is messy and the patient must have access to a sink or a bathroom to wipe it out of his or her hair afterwards. A thoughtful designer would provide a vanity counter in the bathroom with a paper towel dispenser, a soap dispenser, and a place to hang a coat or handbag. While one does not wish to encourage the patient to shampoo his or her hair in the office, it is necessary to remove the paste at least partially.

The second method is generally considered the simplest for both the tech and the patient. It involves the use of an electrode cap that resembles an old-fashioned swimming cap. With this method, there is very little paste to wipe off the hair. The EEG procedure takes about 40 minutes to perform.

Another commonly performed test is *evoked potential,* which tests the different pathways to the brain (auditory, visual, and somatosensory) (Figure 4-148). Both EEG and evoked potential testing are done by a technician, and both units may be located in the same room (Figure 4-45). A room 10×12 feet would be adequate. With the EEG unit, the tech sits at the computer keyboard during the procedure. If the neurologist prefers that the technician be in an adjoining control room, there must be a large window so that the patient can be observed at all times.

In the test room, locked storage is needed for drugs used to sedate patients. Test equipment is all digital. Therefore, computer printouts are stored in the patient's chart, and compressed digital storage of data is standard. Lighting in the test room should be able to be dimmed.

Frequently, a neurologist will perform EEGs for other physicians but have no personal consultation with the patient. The EEG technician would perform the test, and the printout would be read or interpreted by the neurologist, with a report mailed to the patient's physician. However, the neurologist would not consult with the patient unless the physician, after receiving the report, felt the referral was necessary for treatment of the

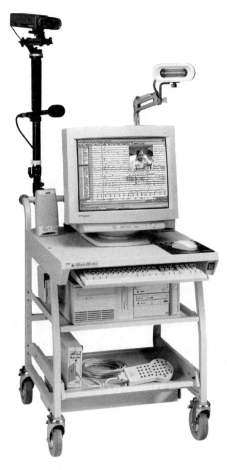

Figure 4-147. EEG machine. (*Photo courtesy: Nicolet Biomedical Limited, Warwick, United Kingdom.*)

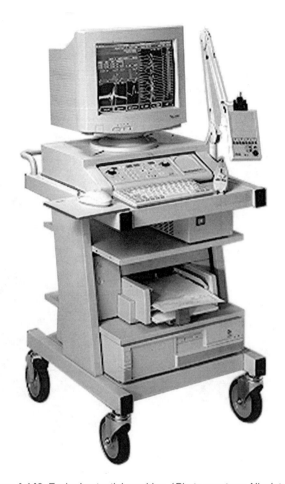

Figure 4-148. Evoked potential machine. (*Photo courtesy: Nicolet Biomedical Limited, Warwick, United Kingdom.*)

patient's condition. Therefore, a good location for the EEG room is near the front of the suite so that these patients do not have to pass the consultation room or exam rooms in order to reach the test room.

A neurologist may also perform a *spinal tap* (to drain off fluid) in the office. For this procedure, the neurologist would use an exam room with the patient lying on an exam table, which is usually placed against a wall.

Another office procedure is EMG, *electromyography,* which shows if a muscle is deteriorating or can be reha-

bilitated. It measures the strength of a muscle and indicates if the nerve has been affected. This test is performed by the physician, in a dedicated room, with a table placed against the wall. The procedure takes about half an hour, and the reason for putting it in a dedicated room is that it saves time in moving the equipment around and in setting up each patient. The room need only be 10×10 feet. The equipment is on a mobile cart so that the physician can move it around the patient (Figure 4-149).

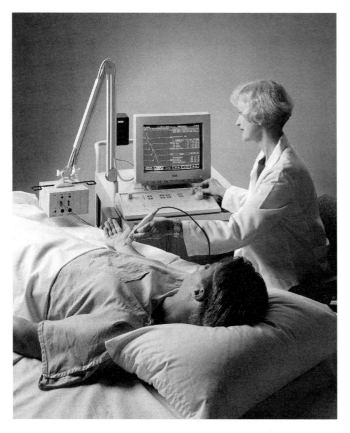

Figure 4-149. EMG machine. (*Photo courtesy: Nicolet Biomedical Limited, Warwick, United Kingdom.*)

Other examination rooms will have a physical therapy–type table, a small sink cabinet, and a wall-mounted diagnostic instrument panel (Figure 3-42) with ophthalmoscope, blood pressure cuff, and otoscope. In addition, these rooms may have an eye chart and perhaps an X-ray view box. Some neurologists like a scale in each exam room. The patient's evaluation of his or her weight helps the physician gauge a patient's touch with reality.

Maximum soundproofing is essential in the test rooms. Do not locate the door to a bathroom opposite the door of a test room and do not place plumbing for an adjacent room on a wall contiguous with walls of test rooms. See Chapter 14 for soundproofing construction details.

Interior Design

The consultation room should be large and comfortably furnished, since patients may be interviewed here. Furnishings in this room, and the remainder of the office, should be tasteful but understated. All colors and patterns should be selected for their restful quality—anything bold is to be avoided. One must be particularly aware of patterns that have a figure-ground reversal or that have a visual rhythm. Such patterns may cause seizures in people with certain types of neurological disorders.

All rooms in this suite may be carpeted. Most carpet has sufficient antistatic properties to avoid interference from static electricity that might affect electronic testing equipment. Lighting should be rheostatically controlled so that it can be dimmed when patients are relaxing and being tested.

NEUROSURGERY

A neurosurgeon's office is often smaller than a neurologist's office and does not include diagnostic testing equipment. All of the tests would be performed in the neurologist's office, and the neurosurgeon would mainly see patients for preoperative and postoperative consultations. Therefore, a small number of examination rooms is necessary, in addition to a business office, a bookkeeping area, and a consultation room for each physician (Figure 4-150). One exam room per physician is usually adequate since the surgery schedule rarely permits all physicians to be there at the same time. Each physician may have a private secretary to schedule surgeries and handle correspondence. The interior design of the waiting room should be soothing with careful attention to avoidance of geometric patterns or elements that may cause a figure-ground reversal or may "vibrate" or cause dizziness or possibly seizures in sensitive individuals (Color Plate 20, Figure 4-151).

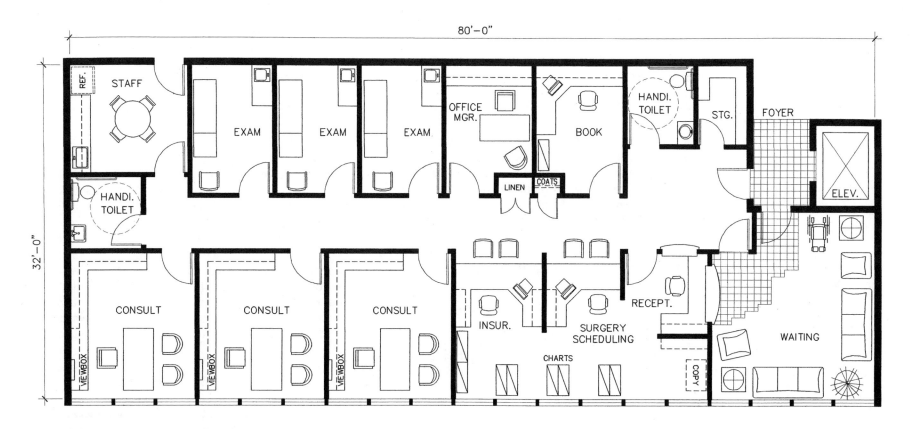

NEUROSURGERY

2560 SF

Figure 4-150. Space plan for neurosurgery, 2560 square feet. (*Design: Jain Malkin Inc.*)

PAIN MANAGEMENT CENTERS

These are hybrid-type suites that are becoming increasingly common. They involve a multidisciplinary approach to the treatment of pain. Frequently, one will find neurologists, nutritionists, deep-tissue massage therapists, chiropractors, psychologists, and biofeedback technicians working together in a holistic manner to change the patient's behavior or symptoms. Some neurologists may have one or more biofeedback rooms and physical therapy massage rooms incorporated into their offices.

In recent years, anesthesiologists have become involved in pain management of persons suffering from intractable pain. Anesthesiologists who specialize in pain management are physicians who have received additional training in this area after completion of anesthesiology training. According to the American Board of Medical Specialties, certification in pain management recognizes that these physician anesthesiologists have demonstrated competence to provide a high level of care either as a primary physician or as a consultant to patients experiencing either acute or chronic pain.

Procedures Performed by Anesthesiologists

Fluoroscopic-guided injections into the epidural space can be carried out in a minor procedure room but are more commonly done in a hospital or ambulatory surgical center setting as the cost of radiographic equipment would go beyond what most physicians would want to invest in their offices. All injections, however, are not fluoroscopically guided. Sometimes a local anesthetic is injected into soft tissue, joints, and the spine. Fluoroscopy is used where the space is anatomically small and hitting the target may be difficult without the help of fluoroscopy. Often, there is a recovery area because patients can get up after the procedure and fall. How patients feel after the procedure is very important and they might be interviewed in a consultation room or exam room after recovery.

Measuring the Problem

Chronic and intractable pain is a huge problem in that it affects approximately 50 million Americans and results in considerable loss of productivity and time away from work. In the inpatient setting, only recently has pain been documented as one of the vital signs. Patients are asked to rate their level of pain, which is recorded in their chart, along with vital signs. For those with terminal illnesses, there's currently much discussion about the appropriate use of morphine and other narcotics to end suffering.

For others, chronic pain—defined as that which no longer serves a biologically useful function—is terribly debilitating and, according to researchers, can actually change the wiring in the brain, spinal cord, and nerve cells by triggering the release of proteins that cause tissue damage. Pain can actually become a disease in itself. Treating it is often a trial-and-error process in which sufferers consult numerous physicians and therapists trying to find the magical cure. Low-back pain is second only to the common cold as the most common cause of illness. Other common causes of pain are migraine headaches, fibromyalgia, arthritis, cancer pain, and that which results from traumatic injuries and degenerative disk disease. Table 4-10 shows the impact and extent of the problem caused by chronic pain.

Table 4-10.
Impact and Extent of Chronic Pain

Number of Americans who have chronic pain	**48 million**
Adults who routinely take prescription painkillers	**21.6 million**
Number who can't do routine activities because of pain	**13.6 million**
Proportion of employees who take time off from work because of pain	**14%**
Number of work days lost yearly to pain	**4 billion**
Annual loss in productivity due to pain	**$65 million**
Annual sales of over-the-counter analgesics	**$3 billion**
Amount Americans spend annually on pain care	**$100 billion**
Most common types of chronic pain that physicians treat	**Cancer pain, lower back pain, arthritis, headaches, fibromyalgia**

Source: *Wall Street Journal,* October 18, 1999, p. R-6; National Institutes of Health; Louis Harris & Associates Inc.

Defining the Program

Because pain treatment providers vary so widely in their specialties, skills, and approach to pain management, the following questions may be helpful in defining the program:

1. What types of patients do you see and do you have a subspecialty in treating certain types of conditions?

2. What is the patient flow after patients have checked in?

3. Where does the initial history taking and interview take place? Who performs it?

4. What is the frequency of visits or treatments for each type of patient and/or condition?

5. Is anesthesia or conscious sedation used?

6. What do the treatments consist of?

7. What is the type of coordination with the patient's primary-care provider, neurologist, neurosurgeon, physi-

atrist (physician specializing in rehabilitation medicine), oncologist, rheumatologist?

8. What type of recovery is generally required after treatment? If required, what is the length of stay in the recovery room?

9. Is there any equipment used that requires specific or unique utilities?

10. What is the ideal type of lighting in your examination and procedure rooms? Do you require a surgical light?

The plan in Figure 4-152 was developed for an anesthesiologist. It does not accommodate a massage therapist, psychologist, chiropractors, or others who sometimes work together in a coordinated, integrated approach to pain management.

Figure 4-152. Space plan for pain management center, 2950 square feet. (*Design: Jain Malkin Inc.*)

PAIN MANAGEMENT

2950 SF

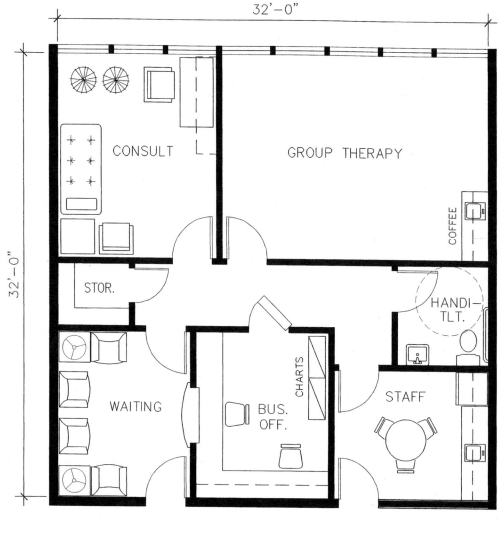

PSYCHIATRY

1024 SF

Figure 4-153. Space plan for psychiatry, 1024 square feet. (*Design: Jain Malkin Inc.*)

Types of Treatments

There are many treatments for chronic pain such as physical therapy, massage, chiropractic, electrical therapy, nerve injections and blocks, implantable pain devices, neuromuscular conditioning, biofeedback, and group and individual psychotherapy.

Design Features

People who suffer from chronic pain need a relaxing, comforting environment in which to receive medical treatment. Lighting is especially important. All attempts should be made to do away with 2-×4-foot fluorescent lighting in favor of indirect lighting around the perimeter of the room or from wall sconces or other semiconcealed sources.

Temperature control is very important, especially in a biofeedback room, physical therapy room, or massage room. When patients are relaxing and/or undressed, if they are too warm or uncomfortably cold, their discomfort will defeat the treatment. With respect to the mechanical system, it is important to zone this suite very carefully and locate thermostatic controls in appropriate rooms.

Depending on the types of specialists represented, the interior design of a pain management suite may run the gamut from clean and clinical, for suites that are more procedure oriented, to "New Age"—serene spaces with soft lighting, soothing music or nature sounds, perhaps a fountain, nonclinical style of furniture—reflecting the practitioners' desire to balance mind, body, and spirit.

PSYCHIATRY

This is the easiest medical suite to design. The consultation room is the key element in this suite. Each psychiatrist will have a preferred method of working, depending on his or her treatment philosophy. Some prefer a casual living room decor where doctor and patient sit next to each other in lounge chairs. Others offer the patient a sofa or chaise (Figure 4-153). Still others prefer a formal

PSYCHIATRY

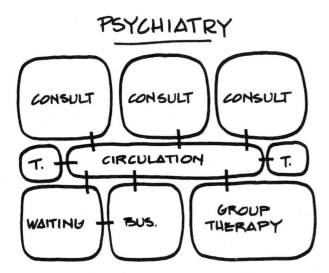

Figure 4-154. Schematic diagram of a psychiatry suite.

directive approach, with the doctor behind the desk and the patient across from it. Those who practice hypnosis often choose to have the patient relax in a recliner chair that rocks back to elevate the patient's legs.

Regardless of counseling style, the consultation room should be a minimum of 12×14 feet and preferably 14×16 feet. Psychiatrists usually house their professional libraries in this room, so adequate bookshelf storage should be planned. Diplomas can be framed creatively and hung as artwork in the room.

Some psychiatrists prefer a consultation room with a window; others find it distracting to the patient's concentration. Illumination should be rheostatically controlled so that it can be dimmed.

Sometimes solo practitioners share an office suite. Each would need a consultation room, but the business office, waiting room, and group therapy room would be shared. There should be two or three seats per doctor in the waiting room. Since each psychiatrist can see only one patient per hour, this is a very low-volume specialty. The group therapy room should accommodate about 12 persons. Chairs that stack are best, but they must be

comfortable. The room should have a sink cabinet for preparation of coffee and perhaps a coat closet.

Interior Design

The waiting room may be residential in character. Patients are often nervous before therapy; thus, the waiting room ought to have a relaxing color palette and feel comfortable, yet afford individuals some degree of privacy. Sound control is very important in this suite. All walls of consultation rooms and the group therapy rooms should have sound-attenuating construction (see Chapter 14).

The ambience of this suite is of utmost importance. Colors and design should be tranquil and serve as a background rather than be stimulating enough to be distracting. Sharp contrasts in color or pattern should be avoided in favor of mellowness (Color Plate 21, Figures 4-155a and b).

Table 4-11.
Analysis of Program.
Psychiatry

No. of Physicians:	1	2	3
Exam Rooms	14 × 16 = 224	2@ 14 × 16 = 448	3@ 14 × 16 = 672
Toilets	7 × 8 = 56	7 × 8 = 56	2@ 7 × 8 = 112
Group Therapy	16 × 18 = 288	16 × 18 = 288	16 × 18 = 288
Staff Lounge	10 × 10 = 100	10 × 10 = 100	10 × 10 = 100
Business Office	12 × 14 = 168	12 × 14 = 168	14 × 16 = 224
Waiting Room	12 × 10 = 120	12 × 10 = 120	12 × 16 = 192
Storage	4 × 6 = 24	4 × 6 = 24	6 × 8 = 48
Subtotal	980 ft²	1204 ft²	1636 ft²
15% Circulation	147	180	245
Total	1127 ft²	1384 ft²	1881 ft²

Figure 4-156. Examination/observation room, child psychiatry. (*Design: Jain Malkin Inc.; Photographer: John Christian.*)

Child Psychiatry

Child psychiatrists prefer to observe patients in a natural setting, necessitating a room for play therapy. Typically, this room would have a one-way glass observation window, a play table with chair or carpeted platforms, and an assortment of dolls, games, and other toys (Figure 4-156). If an easel and paints are provided, a sink should be included in the room. An attractive cabinet may be

designed to house all the toys in an orderly fashion. If appropriate space is available, a secured outdoor play area can be developed to allow the psychiatrist to study children playing naturally without their realizing they are being observed.

The room in Figure 4-156 has been carefully designed for discreetly videotaping the child's activity, a necessary step for prosecuting child abuse offenders.

UROLOGY

A urologist treats diseases of the genitourinary tract. Thus, each patient must submit a urine specimen before being examined. The toilet room should be located close to the laboratory and have a specimen pass-through to the laboratory. Sometimes a toilet room is located between two exam rooms. Urologists perform most of their own lab work in the suite, and a minimum of 12 lineal feet of countertop should be provided in the laboratory. In addition, a solo practitioner would need two examination rooms, at least two toilets, a cystoscopy (cysto)

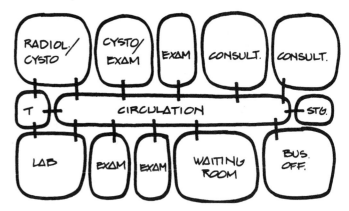

Figure 4-157. Schematic diagram of a urology suite.

Cystoscopy

In a cystoscopic procedure, the patient lies on a specialized table (Figure 4-158) with feet placed in stirrups. The patient is usually lightly sedated with conscious sedation, perhaps Valium via an IV in the arm. An endoscope with fiber-optic light (and optional tiny camera) is inserted into the urethra to diagnose the problem. If the scope has a camera connected to a video monitor, the procedure can be viewed in real time and, with a printer, images can be captured for future reference. Men who have prostate cancer or enlarged prostates, common as men age, routinely have this examination to monitor their conditions. Bladder tumors and kidney stones can also be discovered with this type of procedure. Sometimes the capacity of the bladder

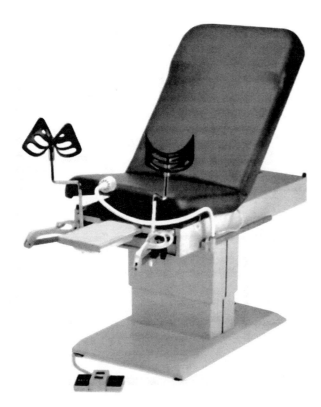

Figure 4-158. Cystoscopy table. (*Photo courtesy: Hamilton Medical Furniture Corporation, Milwaukee, WI.*)

room, a business office, a waiting room, and a consultation room. This is a surgical specialty and therefore patients will have pre- and postsurgical consultations, which may occur in the urologist's private office or consultation room. Figure 4-157 shows the relationship of rooms.

Patient flow is from the waiting room to the bathroom to the exam room and then to the cysto room, if necessary. The components of this suite are standard, with the exception of the cysto room. A patient with an inflammation of the urinary bladder or prostate would be diagnosed by a cystoscopic procedure to determine the presence of an obstruction or an infection in the urinary tract.

Table 4-12.
Analysis of Program.
Urology

No. of Physicians:		1		2		3
Business Office		12 × 14 = 168		16 × 18 = 288		16 × 20 = 320
Office Manager		10 × 12 = 120		10 × 12 = 120		10 × 12 = 120
Waiting Room		14 × 16 = 224		14 × 20 = 280		14 × 20 = 280
Toilets	2@	7 × 8 = 112	3@	7 × 8 = 168	3@	7 × 8 = 168
Staff Lounge		10 × 12 = 120		10 × 12 = 120		12 × 12 = 144
Storage		6 × 8 = 48		6 × 8 = 48		8 × 8 = 64
Consultation Room		12 × 12 = 144	2@	12 × 12 = 288	3@	12 × 12 = 432
Exam Rooms[a]	2@	8 × 12 = 192	4@	8 × 12 = 384	6@	8 × 12 = 576
Nurse Station		8 × 10 = 80		10 × 10 = 100	2@	8 × 10 = 160
Cysto/Exam (no X-Ray)		—		12 × 12 = 144	2@	12 × 12 = 288
Cysto (with X-Ray)[b]		12 × 24 = 288		12 × 24 = 288		12 × 24 = 288
Dressing Rooms	2@	12 SF = 24	2@	12 SF = 24	4@	12 SF = 48
Recovery		6 × 8 = 48		8 × 8 = 64		8 × 8 = 64
Laboratory		8 × 10 = 80		10 × 10 = 100		10 × 10 = 100
Subtotal		1648 ft²		2416 ft₂		3052 ft²
20% Circulation		330		483		610
Total		1978 ft²		2899 ft²		3662 ft²

[a]If three exams per physician plus cysto rooms are required, as in Figure 4-159, suites will be larger.
[b]Includes darkroom, control, film filing, and dressing cubicle.

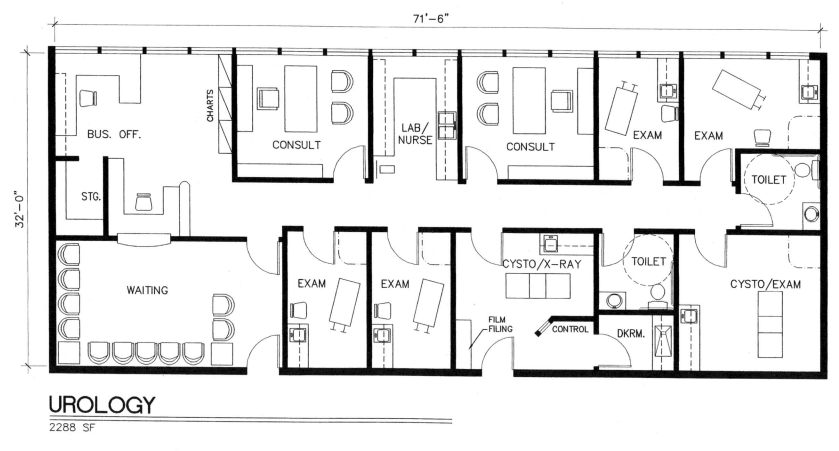

71'-6"

32'-0"

BUS. OFF.

CHARTS

CONSULT

LAB/
NURSE

CONSULT

EXAM

EXAM

TOILET

STG.

TOILET

CYSTO/X-RAY

WAITING

EXAM

EXAM

FILM
FILING

CONTROL

DKRM.

CYSTO/EXAM

UROLOGY
2288 SF

Figure 4-159. Space plan for urology, 2288 square feet. (*Design: Jain Malkin Inc.*)

is evaluated by inflating it with water. The cysto table has a tray to catch fluids that are voided during the procedure. A kick bucket on casters may also be used. Cysto rooms used to have ceramic tile floors and floor drains; however, current thought is that a floor drain can be a bacterial reservoir and should therefore be avoided.

Certain procedures require X-rays. A urologist will typically have a large cysto room for retrograde cystoscopic examinations (with X-rays) and a smaller room for cysto procedures not requiring X-rays (Figures 4-159 and 4-160). X-rays are used for dye procedures. For example, dye introduced into each ureter allows the urologist to

visualize the upper kidney tract to see a stone. Dye is also used to image bladder tumors. Iodinated dye is used in a cystogram to show how a woman's bladder may have dropped downward with gravity. The patient's bladder is X-rayed while lying down (with the table flat) and in an upright position (Figure 4-158 shows exam table tilt). If the X-ray unit has fluoroscopy, the bladder can be imaged as it fills and empties to see the configuration of the bladder.

After the procedure, the patient is able to get off of the table but may be a bit woozy or unstable as the sedation wears off. A recliner chair for brief recovery (Figure 4-159) is useful. Patients have to undress for this procedure.

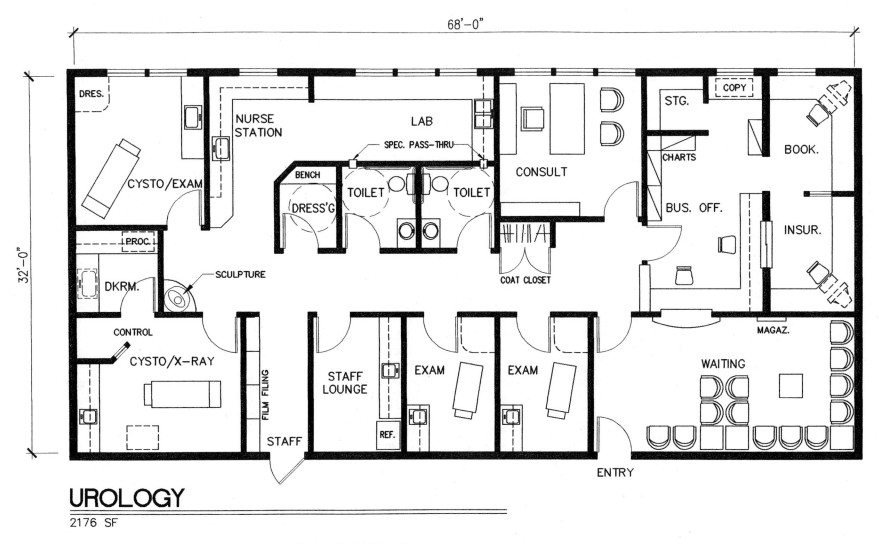

UROLOGY

2176 SF

Figure 4-160. Space plan for urology, 2176 square feet. (*Design: Jain Malkin Inc.*)

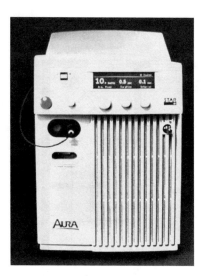

Figure 4-161. Aura portable laser. (*Photo courtesy: Laserscope, San Jose, CA.*)

Dressing rooms may be inside or outside the cysto room (Figures 4-159 and 4-160). It's important to have toilet rooms nearby as patients have the urge to urinate after the procedure.

Design of the Cysto Room

If designed to accommodate X-ray, the cysto room will have a darkroom, control area, and lead-shielded walls. The reader is referred to Chapter 3, Family Practice, for design of an X-ray room. The smaller cysto room can also be used for vasectomies, excisions of scrotal cysts, and minor surgical procedures. A portable laser may be used in this room (Figure 4-161).

Good-quality sheet vinyl flooring with a self-coved base is recommended. A cysto room not equipped with X-ray may be as small as 11×12 or 12×12 feet. With X-ray, it will be about 12×24 feet, including the darkroom, and the room should have a 9-foot ceiling height. Open-shelf filing of X-ray films may be located in the corridor adjacent to the cysto rooms (Figures 4-159 and 4-160). Cysto rooms may have a 5-foot-high ceramic tile wainscot on all walls or other easily cleaned surfaces, and may have a wall-mounted urinal. (There is a strong urge to urinate after a cystoscopic procedure.) Furthermore, the room should have an exhaust fan. The examination table used in this room is pictured in Figure 4-158.

It should be noted that the X-ray film plate pulls out from the right side of the table; therefore, the optimal layout of the room would place the table with ample room on the right side, which should also be closest to the darkroom (Figures 4-159 and 4-160). The sink cabinet would be to the left of the patient.

Lab

The lab is used for semen examination and for simple dipstick tests such as urinalysis to measure sugar or blood in urine, or to measure pH. A centrifuge on the counter would be used to spin-down blood. An undercounter refrigerator and a sink are required. A specimen pass-through in the wall between the lab and toilet prevents patients from having to carry a urine specimen through the corridor. The lab may have a CRT and printer for running off labels for urine or blood specimens.

Nurse Station

The nurse station is typical in this specialty. It will have a wet area with sink and an autoclave for sterilizing instruments (many of which are reusable) and a "dry" area for charting and making phone calls. Storage for frequently used forms and for instruments, a CRT for receiving lab results, and an undercounter refrigerator are also required.

Interior Design

Because this is a surgical specialty, physicians often run late, necessitating a larger than average waiting room. In addition, many elderly patients are accompanied by a spouse or escort.

There are no special requirements in this specialty in terms of interior design. However, there are some urologists who have built a large practice in a subspecialty, namely, male sexual dysfunction. If this is the case, one may want to design the suite in a more masculine style, perhaps using artwork with a Western theme or a sports or hunting theme.

As regards finishes, the walls and floors of cysto rooms must be easily cleanable. Exam rooms should not have carpet. A wood-look sheet vinyl like Toli® is functional as well as aesthetically appealing. Note that the recovery room should have hard-surface flooring as the urge to urinate frequently is strong after cysto procedures. A restroom should be nearby.

CHAPTER 5
Diagnostic Medicine

Author's Note: Writing this chapter has been a challenge in that digital imaging at this moment is a work in progress and, to describe it, is somewhat akin to shooting at a moving target. I gathered information from many sources to educate myself about the topic so that I could explain it to others. I contacted knowledgeable sources representing five perspectives: an architect friend and colleague whose expertise and passion about diagnostic imaging is well known; manufacturers, who understandably are proud of their new products and anxious to promote them; chief technicians with 20 to 30 years of experience installing a variety of imaging modalities and systems during their employment with major equipment manufacturers; regional vendors of X-ray equipment, accessories, and supplies; and radiologists. All of these resources have experience with film-based as well as digital imaging, realizing, however, that the latter is still in its infancy. What has been vexing is the difference of opinion on how quickly digital imaging will overtake the industry; the reliability of the interface—called DICOM compatibility—between equipment by different manufacturers; and what the final digital imaging system will look like 5 or 10 years from now when, one would assume, film has gone the way of the horse and buggy and a darkroom can only be found in the studio of a fine-art photographer.

My architect friend, who works for a national architectural firm and often plans diagnostic imaging departments for academic medical centers and 250,000-square-foot ambulatory-care centers, suggested that references to film and darkrooms should be cut to an absolute minimum, that in a very brief period one will not find even a view box illuminator in most settings. I got a different picture, however, from several radiologists I interviewed and from regional vendors

of equipment and supplies. A number of the vendors said they are selling as much film now as they did five years ago and the conversion to digital will happen more slowly than some estimate because the financial analysis has to be favorable to enable radiologists to make the conversion, which, of course, involves many factors. If reimbursement for orthopedic films is low and since digital radiography equipment costs considerably more, the number of procedures one could feasibly do within the workday may provide a poor return on investment, although one also has to factor in the expectation that digital imaging enables higher throughput (patient volume) than a film-based machine.

Although most radiologists recognize the value of ultimately converting to a totally digital system, which will enable them to send and retrieve images over a network throughout the enterprise, they are dealing with the tremendous financial commitment as well as the risk of selecting the best manufacturers to partner with whose systems will ultimately prove to be the most reliable and the most flexible as the technology evolves. I also received a lot of practical tips and advice from the technical experts who are charged with installing the equipment and systems, keeping it maintained, and troubleshooting when there are problems. Oblivious to the marketing hype of "how DICOM compatible every item is," they will tell you that a lot of black boxes (electronic pieces of equipment that create an interface between non-DICOM-compatible items), switches, patch panels, and converters are required to make it all work at the current time. Clearly, this industry is changing rapidly and the plethora of products introduced every couple of weeks to manage and store digital data is staggering. As in any field when rapid change takes place, eventually a number of leading products emerge, while others fall by the wayside. What

I've presented in this chapter represents all the viewpoints I've heard from respected sources and I've tried to present an unbiased view of the industry today. However, I was limited as to the number of equipment photos I could use and I regret I could not include selections from all major manufacturers.

I was pleasantly surprised to see, compared with 10 years ago when the second edition of this book was writ-ten, how dramatically product design has improved. Every manufacturer has CT, MR, and nuclear imaging equipment that is so sleek and sculptural—which is hard to imagine for items of such large mass and weight. Compared to equipment available 10 years ago, it seems as if design and aesthetics were not even factored into the equation at that time.

DIAGNOSTIC IMAGING

What's new in diagnostic imaging? Everything. Nowhere in healthcare has the digital revolution had more impact. The goal is seamless transfer of images throughout the enterprise—total connectivity among physicians, radiologists, and hospitals. Referring physicians and specialists who previously had to wait many hours to several days for a film to be retrieved and delivered now have instant access to patient information. No misplaced or lost films; no need to carry films from one location to another; elimination of X-ray retakes (exposing the patient to more radiation) to compensate for errors in technique; and elimination of the cost of film. Of course, to accomplish this massive undertaking, eventually all diagnostic imaging equipment has to be digital so that images go directly to a network where they can be reviewed, analyzed, distributed, and, ultimately, stored. GE's PathSpeed™ is an example of a PACS (Picture Archiving Communication System) that manages data. Many manufacturers are developing PACS, each offering certain commonalities as well as distinctive proprietary features to give them a marketing edge. Once one recovers from the trauma of conversion from film to digital, the day-to-day ease and speed of working with images on a monitor, and being able to send an image to a remote specialist for consultation (by a teleradiology connection), no doubt the expense and discomfort of learning and mastering a new system will be justified. Certainly, there are various steps that can be taken to ease into a fully digital work environment. The easiest conversions, of course, are CT and MRI because they are digital modalities to begin with. Ultrasound is also digital, which leaves—in the basic radiology suite—a general radiography room, a radiography and fluoroscopy (R/F) room, and mammography. As new equipment is purchased, these investments will most likely be digital and, over time, the entire enterprise will be a totally integrated digital environment.

Goal: Acquiring Better Diagnostic Information in Less Time

The overarching goal in the transformation from analog/film images to digital is the hope of acquiring better diagnostic information in less time. Conventional X-ray film and chemicals are being replaced by silicon detectors and images that are displayed almost instantaneously on a high-resolution monitor. With such systems, a physician is able to send an image electronically to colleagues for discussion and evaluation in real time, all looking at the same image on their respective monitors.

Currently, pulling a reference film from five years ago to compare it with a new one can be a challenge, requiring the time of a file clerk to find it and someone to transport it to the referring physician or radiologist, and then reversing the process to get it back to the hospital. Many steps, many people. Ideally, when hospital images are all digital and there is total interconnectivity within the enterprise, the images should be available within moments, rather than days or weeks. The overall goal is not just to move film images, but to integrate them with patients' laboratory test results and the electronic medical record and, with powerful databases, to code procedures for processing insurance claims, send reports and thumbnail images to referring physicians, and offer to rural medical centers and clinics the expertise of radiologists at distant major medical centers.

The new diagnostic imaging equipment showcased at RSNA (the Radiological Society of North America) each November is often startling in its innovation. Perhaps responding to a somewhat flat market for certain imaging modalities, manufacturers seem to have recently worked diligently to differentiate their products, especially true in CT, MRI, and a hybrid CT/PET (positron emission tomography) that is truly an astounding accomplishment. For those who may not be familiar with it, RSNA is "Mecca" for anyone associated with any aspect of diagnostic imaging. Held each November or December at McCormick Place in Chicago, it attracts 65,000 attendees worldwide. Magazines like *Diagnostic Imaging and Medical Imaging* publish a preview issue prior to the event and a new product review afterward, both of which are very informative.

PACS

Picture Archiving Communication Systems are being developed to manage digital data and images. Each vendor offers somewhat different system design, user-friendly interface, and certain proprietary features. PACS is a generic term for these data acquisition and image management systems, which generally have the following four components: image acquisition, image storage, image transfer (over a network), and image retrieval. PACS refers, in a generic sense, to any electronic substitute for film, but PACS can be based on direct ray (DR)* transfer of images or computerized radiography (CR), which is explained below. PACS may further be defined, according to Data General, as:

---

*It should be noted that DR, as a term, is interchangeably used to refer to direct ray, digital radiography, and direct radiography.

- Mini-PACS—connecting single or multiple imaging modalities using viewing stations with or without soft reading and/or digital storage archiving.

- Full PACS—connecting all modalities, viewing/reading soft copy/enlarged digital storage. It is integrated with both the hospital and the radiology information systems and distributes data and images throughout the healthcare network.

- Teleradiology—connecting the radiology service to the radiologist's home, emergency department, intensive-care unit, or rural clinics.

Computed Radiography

Computed radiography (CR) is a more advanced form of radiography that uses electronic media instead of film. The cassettes typically look like standard film cassettes but they don't have film in them; they have a phosphor plate that records the image and gets reused. The tech takes the plate out of the unit and puts it in a plate reader, which reads the image and simultaneously erases the plate for reuse. This has several additional workflow steps associated with it compared with a more direct method of recording the image. The image that has been read is stored on an internal hard drive, which can then send the image to a PACS or print it on paper or film.

Direct Radiography

Direct radiography (DR) bypasses the phosphor plate; it is a direct transfer of the image to a PACS. One can potentially do many more procedures per room because the tech has fewer workflow steps. Presently, DR is considerably more expensive and the "Holy Grail" for the future will be less expensive direct-transfer systems.

Converting Film to Digital Images

There are several ways of transitioning from film to a digital system and the major radiographic equipment manufacturers have recognized the need for a transitional strategy to help make this conversion by developing systems that achieve filmless imaging in phases, over a period of time, working with existing diagnostic equipment.

There are several methods of converting film to digital images: One can take the X-ray and digitize it; images from modalities that cannot output digitally can be converted into digital images by video capture systems (multifrequency video capture boards installed in PC controllers can be equipped with barcode readers to facilitate quick entry of patient details and identification data).

DICOM Compatibility

Most manufacturers are making products that are DICOM compatible, which facilitates interconnectivity among pieces of equipment purchased from different vendors and assures that all images will reach the server without degradation or loss. Digital Imaging and Communications in Medicine (DICOM) is the standard for compliance developed by the American College of Radiology and the National Electrical Manufacturers Association. DICOM provides a format for how files are created to make it possible to move information from one system to another. The goal is total interface among the equipment of various manufacturers.

Image Storage

It is a challenge to keep pace with the vast amounts of graphical data (radiographic images) and the need for short-term and long-term storage, as well as quick retrieval of old files to compare with new imaging studies for a specific patient. Data may be stored in a main server with storage capacity enhanced by RAID (redundant arrays of inexpensive disks), which provides more immediate-access on-line data. *On-line storage* of images — perhaps 30 to 90 days of studies — would be on the RAID (although it is possible to configure a RAID-centric PACS model to accommodate more than a year's studies available on line). From there, they will likely go to *near-line storage,* which may constitute a 6- to 12-month period, and this storage may be on an ultra-high-capacity tape or digital videodisc (DVD) library or "jukebox." After that, images would go to off-line storage for long-term archiving. It should be noted that the library or jukebox relies on a mechanical process to locate the proper piece of media and load it into the drive in order to retrieve the data.

DVDs hold much more data than CDs (compact discs) and offer 30 to 50 years' shelf life. Realizing the size of these graphical files, which must handle large images, the demand for large memory configurations and vast storage capacity is staggering. To be able to store and retrieve such large amounts of data in a matter of seconds requires high-speed, broadband networks and high-resolution displays. Jukebox technologies may be optical, DVD, tape, or CD. These are designed for mass storage of data. A rack (Figure 5-1), located in a secure storage room, can hold the UPS (uninterrupted power source),

Figure 5-1. Mass-storage unit/archive library for radiologic images. (*Photo courtesy: Rorke Data, Eden Prairie, MN, a subsidiary of Bell Microproducts, Inc.*)

RAID, server, and long-term archive library. Multiple archival libraries can be connected using pass-through technology. Images move from on line (the server) to near line (the jukebox or archival library), and then off line, which may be in a remote location. Redundancies are built into all of these archiving systems to account for power failures, loss of data, fire, and so forth. Some PACS are designed to automatically route data, at certain preestablished intervals, to three to five redundant storage locations. Of course, the cost of storage media is a large contributor to total costs. Optical storage, also known as MOD Magneto Optical Storage, is a disk read by laser and considered the most reliable for long-term storage but is currently the most expensive.

Jukeboxes or archive libraries must be placed in a secure, restricted-access, storage room, which may be within the facility or located remotely. There are no special HVAC requirements for this room as the storage "racks" have internal cooling fans. Some are accessed only from the front, others from the rear, but none should be placed too close to a wall as there is considerable cabling and one must have access to it for maintenance. Once a library archive or jukebox is operational, it cannot easily be moved.

Data Storage. Off-line images and data can be stored in large data repositories and "warehouses," the digital equivalent of sending aged medical charts to a Beacon's warehouse for storage.

For hybrid suites, there will still be a need for conventional film filing, discussed later in this chapter. For a fully digital operation, film filing is replaced by a room for the server and archives (jukebox) although, theoretically, the jukeboxes (and even the server) may be at a remote location. Film files used to require a tremendous commitment of space, whereas now perhaps a room 10×12 feet may store 10 years of data.

Application Service Provider

It should be noted that the PACS can be outsourced to an application service provider (ASP). This represents a way of financing the endeavor, which, much like lease pay-

ments, comes out of an operating budget rather than capital investment. And, much like a lease, as equipment becomes obsolete it is replaced because the equipment is owned by the ASP. This option is often priced on a per-patient (procedure) basis.

ASPs grew out of the recognition that financing the conversion to digital imaging out of capital budgets constituted a big hurdle for many organizations. There is great variety in what ASPs offer. Basically, they buy software and hardware from a variety of vendors and customize a system to meet an individual enterprise's needs. Some of these are proprietary models that use Web-based architecture to enable a number of data and image management tasks to be executed from scheduling and registering patients to processing and interpreting diagnostic studies to archiving images to distributing these data to referring physicians.

Getting from Here to There

The challenge in writing this chapter is that it needs to reflect the hybrid nature of what designers will be encountering whether designing a one-room radiology suite for an orthopedist or general practitioner or a radiology suite in a medical office building. The focus of the discussion, and the market for this book, is the non-hospital-based facility, which, in this case, means a radiology suite that serves tenants in a medical office building or that may be freestanding. A recent trend in some regions of the nation is the freestanding radiology enterprise that contracts with physicians and hospitals. It frees hospitals from having to make an investment in expensive equipment, keep it maintained, and employ technical staff. Although it would seem cumbersome and costly to transport inpatients to an off-site facility, apparently this is occurring in some regions.

The hybrid nature of what an architect might encounter implies that there will be some film-based modalities and others that are digital within the same facility. In this case, a conventional darkroom, or daylight processors, will be needed, or a dry view laser imager may be used for CT or MRI, which requires no darkroom, or one may encounter a new, fully digital environment. As reliable sources differ in their forecasts of when all imaging equipment will be filmless, this chapter will, of necessity, address all of the above.

Conventional Radiology

General principles are commonly understood. A limb is exposed to X-rays, which penetrate body tissues, exposing film mounted on a cassette (film holder) positioned on the other side of the limb. Since body tissues absorb different amounts of radiation, bones, fat, gas, and so on make different exposures compared with surrounding tissues, which allows the observation of internal body parts without pain and with small exposures to radiation.

In addition to examination of limbs, diagnostic imaging is used to diagnose the presence of gallstones and kidney stones, tuberculosis, arthritis, and bone tumors; to discover foreign bodies in soft tissue; to detect enlarged or malfunctioning glands; to scan the brain; to reduce tumors (radiation oncology); to monitor a child in the womb (ultrasound); and to diagnose scores of other diseases. Some forms of diagnostic imaging, such as ultrasound, do not involve radiation.

Making an X-ray film of a leg or the chest requires no special preparation, but filming organs such as the gallbladder or the gastrointestinal tract requires that the patient fast before the procedure and then drink a special liquid or receive an injection that makes the organs visible to the radiologist. Since the designer must understand these procedures in order to plan an efficient suite, a brief outline of diagnostic radiology modalities follows.

Diagnostic Imaging Modalities

Fluoroscopy
Fluoroscopy enables the radiologist to watch internal body structures at work. The patient swallows or receives an injection of a contrast medium—air, barium sulfate, or organic iodine compounds—which causes the soft-tissue systems of the body to be outlined. X-rays passed through the body strike the input phosphor of an image intensifier tube, and that image is intensified electronically and can be viewed on a TV monitor. (TV monitors may be ceiling or wall mounted, or portable, on the floor.) Hard copies (X-ray films) can be made at this time. With a video camera, screen images can be converted into real-time studies for future reference.

A contrast medium injected into a blood vessel (angiography) travels with the blood supply to a specific organ and allows the radiologist to examine that organ. For a study of the large intestine, a patient is given a barium enema. The radiologist makes sequential spot film (or digital) radiographs while the barium travels through the large intestine. To study the digestive system, a patient drinks barium and the radiologist films it traveling down the esophagus into the stomach, following it through the small intestine. Of course, endoscopy has greatly reduced the number of gastrointestinal barium studies.

Digital fluoroscopy is the technique for converting X-rays into visible images without film. Photographic film is replaced by an electronic image tube that produces a direct image of a broken bone, lung, brain, or other body organ being studied. This eliminates photographic processing.

Ultrasound
Ultrasound does not involve radiation. A high-frequency sound, much like sonar, bounces off internal body structures. Ultrasound is particularly useful in examining soft pelvic tissue masses, gallbladders, or a fetus in the wom—procedures where even low doses of radiation might be dangerous. Ultrasound is also commonly used to image the heart (echocardiography) and for studies of blood flow in arteries and blood vessels. It is commonly used to analyze suspicious breast lesions, and tissue can also be biopsied using ultrasound. Physicians who do in vitro fertilization use ultrasound routinely during a variety of procedures.

Nuclear Medicine

Nuclear medicine deals with the diagnosis and treatment of disease with radioactive isotopes—chemicals that are unstable and break down, giving off radioactivity. The isotope may be given to the patient orally or by intravenous injection. The substance is specific to a particular gland or organ (e.g., iodine travels to the thyroid gland). The amount of the isotope absorbed by the gland permits the radiologist to determine the function of the organ and to trace its outline. Nuclear scans are useful for diagnosing brain tumors and malfunctioning of the kidneys, pancreas, and thyroid. Positron emission tomography (PET) scanners are considered one of the best modalities for detecting cancer lesions. One of the most stunning advances in technology is the CT/PET combination, which allows a fusion of CT's rendering of anatomy with PET's imaging of critical metabolic processes.

Computed Tomography

Computed tomography (CT) allows physicians to see cross sections of internal body structures, enabling the radiologist to discover tumors embedded in soft tissue or organs that formerly could not be seen by radiographic procedures. Thus, CT scans have eliminated much exploratory surgery and offer the patient greater safety by reducing the need for more dangerous, often painful, tests.

The patient lies on a table that slides through a rotating doughnut-like enclosure called the gantry. X-rays scan narrow cross sections of the body in a painless, noninvasive procedure. For example, 180 scans just 1 degree apart may be taken of an area. The numerous images are collected by a detector and reconstructed by a computer into a composite scan of the organ or tissue. CT scanners represented a major breakthrough in diagnostic imaging technology when they were introduced in 1977. The newest CT scanners are multislice, six times faster than traditional single-slice scanners. During the scan, three-dimensional (3-D) images are built in real time and are completely constructed by the time the scan ends. Potential future uses include measurement of cerebral blood volume and flow, used in evaluation of stroke.

Mammography

Low-dose mammography, an X-ray of the breast, is considered to be the most accurate and safe means of detecting breast cancer at an early, usually curable stage. The American Cancer Society claims that 1 out of 10 women in the United States will get breast cancer at some point in her life. Therefore, screening mammographies are recommended on a regular basis for women over the age of 40 and perhaps even earlier for those who have a family history of breast cancer. As of this writing, mammography is more commonly film based, although the Food and Drug Administration (FDA) recently approved a full-field digital mammography system.

Radiation Oncology

Through use of a linear accelerator, tumors are bombarded by very narrowly focused, high doses of radiation in an attempt to kill cancer cells. The course of treatment is carefully plotted and monitored by a radiation physicist and the radiology team. The normal course of treatment runs six weeks, during which time the patient reports five times per week.

Magnetic Resonance Imaging

Magnetic resonance imaging (MRI) has been heralded as a major innovation in diagnostic imaging and, today, it represents 20 percent of the medical imaging market, according to *Medical Imaging* magazine. It provides exceptional soft-tissue contrast and is especially good for imaging the central nervous system and, in particular, the brain. It permits early and accurate diagnosis of a wide variety of conditions, including brain tumors, strokes, hemorrhage, and multiple sclerosis. Spinal cord compression is more effectively shown by MRI than by other imaging techniques. A pinched nerve or the effects of arthritis can be graphically demonstrated and may prevent the need for a myelogram or CT study. MRI is also effective for diagnosing knee injuries and cancers of the musculoskeletal system.

MRI does not use X-rays, but rather depends on the interaction of radio waves and small particles within the body, called protons, in the presence of a strong magnetic field generated by the MRI equipment. A simplified explanation of a very complex process follows.

Inside the body, protons absorb energy from incoming radio waves of various frequencies and, in turn, give off energy in the form of radio waves. These outgoing signals are recorded by a highly sophisticated computer and reconstructed into an image similar to that produced by CT, but generally with higher resolution, showing more detail and an enhanced view of diseased tissues.

Advantages to the patient are that no special preparations are required before the procedure, no injections of contrast media are generally required, and it does not use radiation. Although currently MRI examinations are expensive and take longer than a similar CT procedure, this may change as the technology advances. Other applications of MRI include in vivo spectroscopy and study of living tissues, providing information on processes occurring inside the cell. A single example of the derived benefit of this is diagnosing a tumor without resorting to biopsy, based on the fact that tumors are known to affect cell metabolism. There are many applications of MRI continually in development.

Planning Considerations

The purpose of this chapter is to introduce the reader to the most common diagnostic imaging modalities and to explain the general parameters of designing rooms to accommodate this equipment. Clearly, one could write an entire chapter on each of the modalities if one wanted to cover thoroughly all aspects of design and construction. The focus of this discussion is the *outpatient radiology facility* that would commonly be found in a medical office building, as opposed to one located within a hospital.

Before a space planner can begin to lay out the suite, a program must be developed. There is a difference in how this is accomplished when the client is an independent radiology group developing a tenant space in an MOB versus a client that represents a radiology department that will serve a 250,000-square-foot ambulatory-

care center affiliated with a hospital. In the former case, the radiology group will generally detail for the space planner the number and type of diagnostic imaging rooms that will comprise the suite. There is no way a space planner can second-guess this, as it depends on a number of considerations. First, if the radiology group has CT at another office not too far away, it's unlikely they will duplicate this equipment. Second, the number of physician tenants in the building and their respective specialties will influence the type of equipment the radiologists buy. Third, the medical building's proximity to a hospital and the type of imaging modalities available at the hospital may influence the selection of equipment for the facility, especially if the same radiology group staffs the department at the hospital.

In the other example (the radiology department serving a large ambulatory center), the programming will be done by the architect or planner who will do workload analysis to determine the number and type of procedure rooms required. This must be done in collaboration with the radiologists as throughput (volume on each imaging modality) will be influenced by decisions to purchase new equipment and the extent of overall digital integration in the enterprise. If the medical center with which the ambulatory facility is affiliated has a high-profile cardiology, oncology, or neurosciences center, a high enough volume of patients in one of these areas may warrant the purchase of specialized imaging equipment. All of these issues must be considered and factored into the workload analysis and ultimate program that is developed.

These are the six basic planning considerations:

1. Equipment

2. Patient flow

3. Staff flow

4. Information flow

5. Function

6. Flexibility

Equipment

A number of manufacturers offer equipment for each imaging modality. Room size and critical dimensions vary considerably, as do utility requirements. There are numerous accessory or ancillary items that may be added to each major piece of equipment. The space planner, therefore, may be faced with a number of possible combinations of equipment for an individual room. The radiologist will make these selections, but the space planner must obtain from each manufacturer a planning guide and specifications for each unit. Clearly, equipment dictates the size of each room, with function and future requirements being the two important considerations. It should be noted that manufacturers usually offer planning services to lay out a department and often produce almost a full set of construction documents. One must remember, however, that their goal is to sell equipment and to make sure it fits in the room. These services should be relied on only to provide technical assistance to the space planner or architect, who is much more likely to produce a functional layout that considers overall patient flow, business office activities, and the relationship of each room to the whole.

When equipment is placed in the room, function is achieved when proper clearances are preserved for items that swivel, extend, or tilt and for travel of the tabletop. Other aspects of function are patient access and staff ability to move around the room (e.g., if a patient needs to be transferred from a stretcher or gurney alongside the X-ray tabletop). Finally, each procedure room must have an area within it, or outside of it, for controls. Within the room, the control area is a lead-lined partition with a window in it. The tech stands behind it to operate the generator that controls the equipment in a film-based set-up. Note that the window must have a minimum 18 inches of wall on the leading or open end to protect the tech. The control unit is not very large as shown in Figures 5-3 and 5-4; however, in a digital set-up, the control room is somewhat larger and will have a stand-up- or sit-down-height countertop approximately 4 feet wide for the operator's control console in addition to a quality-control computer, which, in the future, may be integrated into one unit (Figures 5-7, 5-8, and 5-10).

It is optimal, when designing major radiography or radiography/fluoroscopy rooms (abbreviated R&F or R/F), to size them generously in order to accommodate future technology and anticipation of more interventional procedures requiring more staff. Radiographic rooms are very expensive to remodel due to lead shielding and other construction features.

Patient Flow

The overall layout of the radiology suite is driven by a desire to separate patient circulation from the staff work area (Figure 5-2). In Figures 5-3 and 5-4, patient dress-

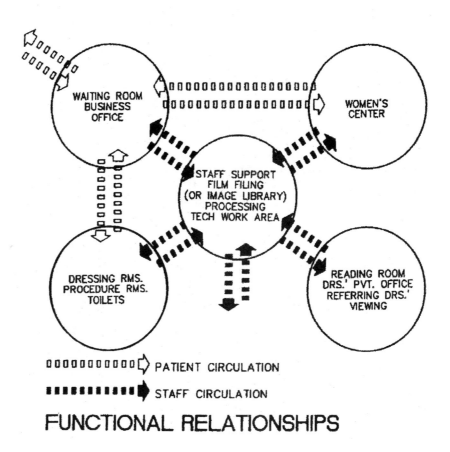

Figure 5-2. Functional relationships, diagnostic imaging.

Table 5-1.
Analysis of Program.
Diagnostic Imaging

No. of Physicians on Site:		1–2		2–3
Waiting Room		14 × 18 = 252		16 × 18 = 288
Women's Center, Sub-waiting[a]		10 × 12 = 120		10 × 12 = 120
Business Office		14 × 16 = 224		16 × 20 = 320
Dressing Cubicles	6@	4 × 4 = 96	10@ 4 × 4 = 160	
Handicapped		6 × 7 = 42	2@	6 × 7 = 84
General Radiography		14 × 16 = 224		14 × 16 = 224
Radiography/Fluoroscopy		16 × 18 = 288	2@	16 × 18 = 576
Toilet		7 × 8 = 56	2@	7 × 8 = 112
Ultrasound		10 × 12 = 120		10 × 12 = 120
Mammography	2@	10 × 12 = 240	2@	10 × 12 = 240
Nuclear Medicine		—		
Hot Lab		—		6 × 8 = 48
Procedure Room		—		16 × 19 = 304
Patient Prep		—		8 × 10 = 80
Sub-Waiting		—		10 × 12 = 120
Toilet		—		7 × 8 = 56
CT Scanner Suite[b]		—		14 × 28 = 392
MRI Suite[c]		—		23 × 51 = 1173
Toilets	3@	7 × 8 = 168	5@	7 × 8 = 280
Darkroom/Processing (optional)		10 × 10 = 100		10 × 12 = 120
Tech Work Area		Varies 120		Varies 150
Film Filing (Optional)[d]		Varies 300		Varies 400
Private Office (Radiologist)		12 × 12 = 144	2@	12 × 12 = 288
Administrator		10 × 12 = 120		10 × 12 = 120
Physicians' Viewing Area		6 × 8 = 48		6 × 8 = 48
Storage		8 × 10 = 80		8 × 10 = 80
Staff Lounge		12 × 16 = 192		14 × 16 = 224
Subtotal		2934 ft²		6127 ft²
25% Circulation		733		1532
Total		3667 ft²		7659 ft²

[a]Optional

[b]Includes procedure room and control room.

[c]Includes procedure room, control, and electronic equipment room; layouts and room sizes vary per manufacturer and model/type of magnet.

[d]If totally digital, a film filing area is not needed; an on-site storage room for the digital library and data communications equipment would replace it (requiring much less space).

Note: The above sizes are an approximation, since radiography rooms must also have control areas, which may be inside or outside the room. Many radiologists will have both a private office and a reading room, while others may share a private office. There are many variables, depending on whether the radiologists rotate among several locations or remain at one. Tech work areas will vary in a digital versus film-based setting.

ing rooms are toward the front of the suite but also near procedure rooms. Patients circulate around one side of the procedure rooms, while the staff work corridor is on the other side of those rooms in Figures 5-4 and 5-5. However, it is not always possible to do this (Figure 5-3). The staff work area includes film (if used) processing, film (or digital image) reading, tech sorting (if film based) and viewing area, staff lounge and restrooms, and radiologists' private offices. In Figure 5-5, the control area for each procedure room is outside the room in the control corridor. This suite plan keeps patients out of staff work areas and, additionally, prevents them from overhearing staff conversations and from casually seeing X-ray films on view boxes in the tech area. It is desirable to protect the patient from overhearing or seeing anything that might cause anxiety or discomfort or constitute a breach of privacy. This has also been accomplished in the breast center plan in Figure 4-19. In Figure 5-4, the control areas are within the procedure rooms. Film cassettes are passed back and forth to the darkroom by cassette pass boxes in the wall. If Figure 5-4 were to be all digital, the area where the darkroom is located would be the control console, the view box illuminators would not be needed, and the "film" reading room would have, in addition to a conventional view box illuminator, a PACS monitor(s) for reading and interpreting images (Figure 5-6). There may be an additional viewing station (Figure 5-7) designed for passive viewing and for sending and receiving images to remote locations. This viewing station may also be used by referring physicians in the medical office building who may not be set up in their offices to receive this type of data.

The suite in Figure 5-5 separates traffic to the women's center, which is typically a high-volume unit. The sub-waiting area is dedicated to the women's center. This unit functions independently from the rest of the suite and has its own daylight film processor located in the tech work area. In Figure 5-4, a mammography room with a private entry vestibule accommodates patients of a neighboring OB-GYN office.

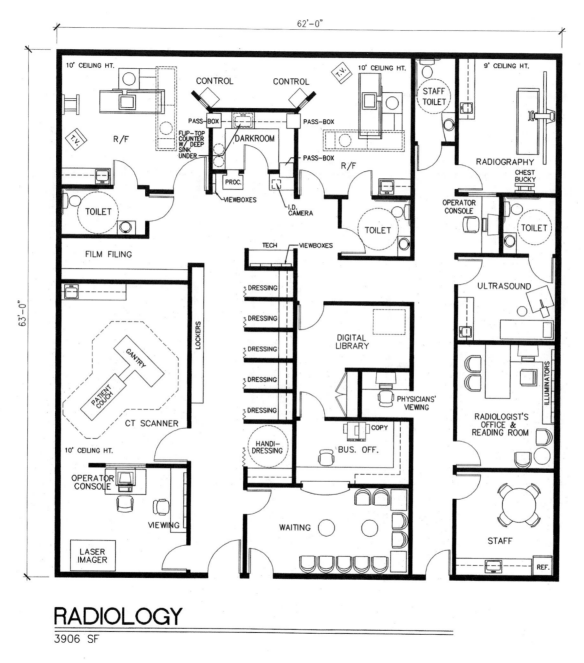

RADIOLOGY

3906 SF

Figure 5-3. Space plan for radiology, 3906 square feet. (*Design: Jain Malkin Inc.*)

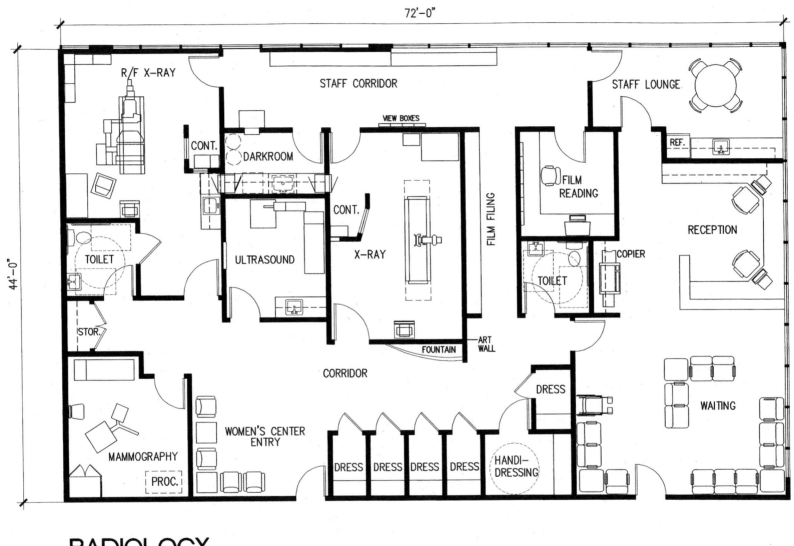

72'-0"

44'-0"

R/F X-RAY

STAFF CORRIDOR

STAFF LOUNGE

VIEW BOXES

CONT.

DARKROOM

REF.

CONT.

FILM READING

ULTRASOUND

X-RAY

FILM FILING

RECEPTION

TOILET

COPIER

TOILET

STOR.

FOUNTAIN

ART WALL

CORRIDOR

DRESS

MAMMOGRAPHY

WOMEN'S CENTER ENTRY

DRESS   DRESS   DRESS   DRESS   HANDI-DRESSING

WAITING

PROC.

RADIOLOGY
3168 SF

Figure 5-4. Space plan for radiology, 3168 square feet. (*Design: Jain Malkin Inc.*)

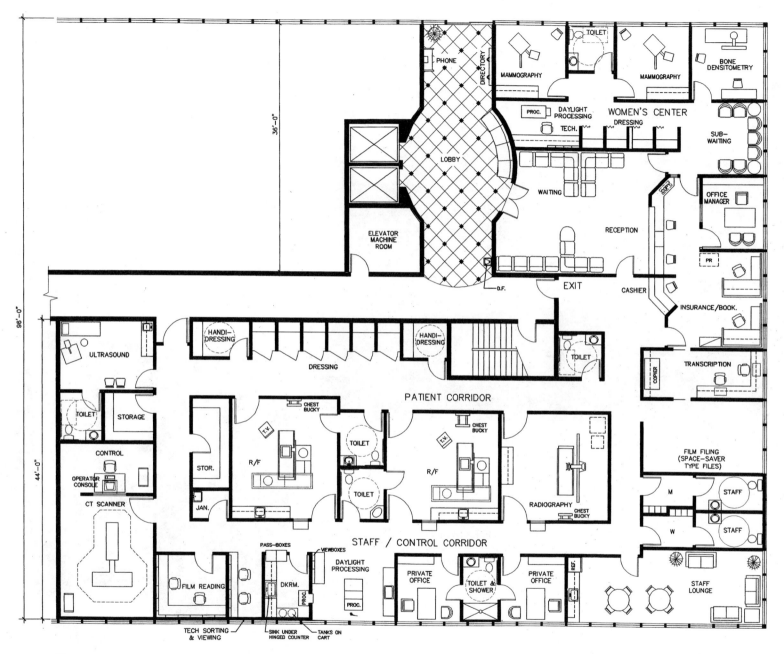

RADIOLOGY (FILM BASED)

7400 SF

Figure 5-5. Space plan for film-based radiology suite, 7400 square feet (*Design: Jain Malkin Inc.*)

The facilities in Figures 5-8 and 5-9 also show separation of patient and staff flow into each procedure room. Both of these facilities are totally digital with no darkroom, yet the imaging rooms look quite the same as film-based rooms with the exception that the control area is a bit larger and has a countertop. Figure 5-10 shows a central control area that serves four general radiography rooms that are not direct digital, but use computed radiography (CR), which can be viewed through the PACS.

Staff Flow

Staff flow must be planned carefully with the X-ray technologists who will work in the clinic. Certain imaging modalities such as CT, ultrasound, and nuclear medicine may have dedicated technologists. There must be ample space for all of these technologists to pass one another in

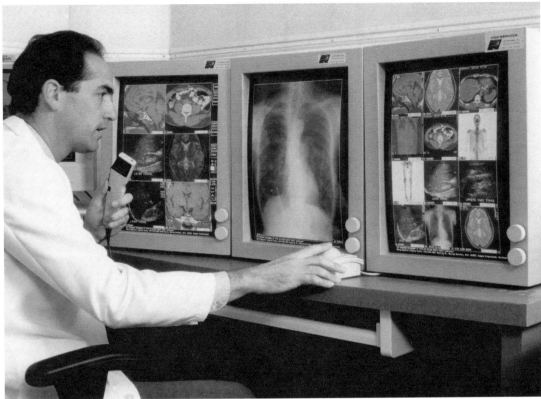

Figure 5-6. Radiologist's diagnostic console. (*Photo courtesy: DR Systems, Inc., San Diego, CA.*)

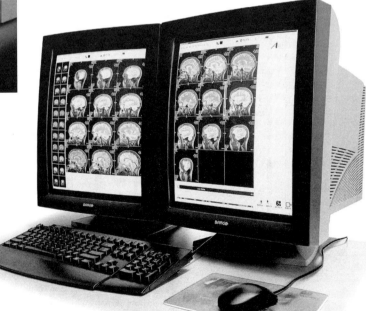

Figure 5-7. GE RadWorks™ 5.0 PACS image distribution system. (*Photo courtesy: GE Medical Systems, Waukesha, WI.*)

corridors and process their films without bumping into one another, as well as a place to sort and view films (in a film-based setup). In a digital setting, the same amount of tech work space is needed but it may be configured differently.

Figure 5-11 presents a schematic layout for a radiology suite, indicating separate entries to procedure rooms for patients and for techs as well as other functional adjacencies. Figure 5-4 shows a small radiology suite with the tech work area behind the darkroom. In this plan, patients have no access to the tech area, nor do they have opportunity to overhear conversations or see other patients' images on view boxes or monitors.

It is desirable to provide a separate staff bathroom because patient bathrooms are often in use, and those serving the R/F rooms can get messy. Front office staff function as they would in any medical practice, although the high volume of patients in a radiology suite may necessitate a larger waiting room and a wider reception transaction area (Figures 5-12 and Color Plate 22, Figure 5-13).

Information Flow

Information flow is dictated by PACS and network system design rather than by space planning. A typical PACS configuration is illustrated in Figure 5-14. Individual system configurations will be as varied and unique as the enterprises they serve. However, Figure 5-14 explains the general flow of data. Physical space allocation doesn't differ demonstrably from film-based settings or any contemporary office for that matter because the same general components can be found such as multiple numbers of monitors, servers, and printers. These happen to be specialized for diagnostic imaging but in terms of space allocation, there isn't much difference. The one area in which there is a huge saving of space, when comparing film-based and digital settings, occurs in storage. With film, huge storage capacity is required (as well as structural accommodation to support the weight), whereas an enormous amount of imaging data can be stored digitally in components placed in a small room.

What differentiates one PACS from another is (as with any software) the way it's configured to meet specific needs in the most user-friendly manner. The flow chart in

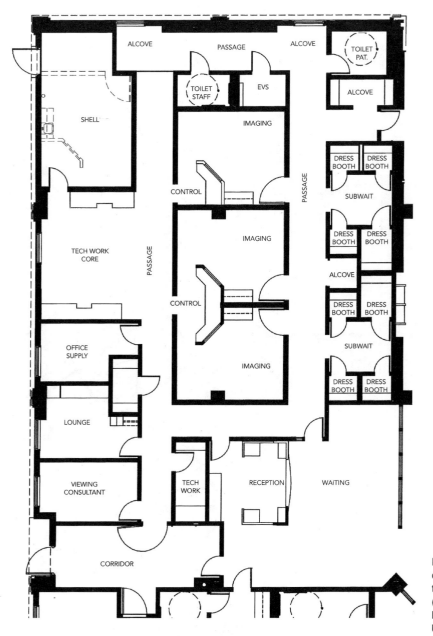

KAISER UNION CITY MOB

5000 SF

Figure 5-8. Outpatient diagnostic imaging center, 5000 square feet (fully digital). Kaiser Permanente Health Plan Union City MOB. (*Architecture and interior design: SmithGroup, San Francisco, CA.*)

STAFF LOUNGE/
CONFERENCE

EQUIPMENT/SUPPLY
STORAGE

STORAGE/STAFF CORRIDOR

SOILED
HOLDING

PATIENT
PREPARATION
RECOVERY ROOM

DRESS

GOWNED
SUBWAIT

VIEWING/
RADIOLOGIST
OFFICE

VESTIBULE

TOILET

COMPUTED
TOMOGRAPY

COMPUTER
CONTROL

TOILET

TOILET

DRESS

FLUOROSCOPY

TOILET

TOILET

ULTRA
SOUND 2

STORAGE

STORAGE

CHIEF TECH.

BLOOD
DRAW
ROOM

DRESS

ULTRASOUND

DRESS

HAMPER

CONTROL

WORK
AREA
(COPIER/
FAX)

TOILET

RECEPTION

TOILET

DRESS

TOILET

GENERAL X-RAY

HARD COPY
FILE

REGISTER

DRESS

DRESS

CONSULT/
FUTURE
MODALITY

GOWNED
SUBWAIT

UCLA Outpatient Imaging Center   7,500 SF

Figure 5-9. Outpatient imaging center, 7500 square feet (fully digital). Santa Monica/UCLA. (*Architecture and interior design: SmithGroup, San Francisco, CA.*)

Figure 5-14 was provided by DR Systems to visually describe how its multicomponent modular system employing proprietary software (as well as hardware components) functions to input, display, archive, transmit, and print radiographic images and, at the same time, manage patient demographic, scheduling, and reporting information. It was designed by radiologists. One component is an Intranet server that frequently polls the main central image server to update, compress, and reformat files and data so that images can be viewed using a standard Internet browser. The Intranet access serves referring physicians or radiologists who are able to log on from remote sites using a password, which then enables them to pull images and view them on a PC. The recipient can be located in a remote office and access the system via a dial-up service or a local-area network (LAN) or wide-area network (WAN). The reference to HL-7 refers to the standard interface between HIS (hospital information systems) and RIS (radiology information systems). Each PACS offers different features with the overall goal of enterprise-wide connectivity, eliminating the need to redundantly enter data.

Function

A functional layout is one that separates patient and staff flow, as discussed above, and one that has a logical placement of rooms based on patient volume and other considerations. For example, the patient dressing area should be near the procedure rooms.

The general radiography room for chest films is best located near the front of the suite as these are short examinations, but can be high volume, necessitating a number of dressing rooms nearby. The radiologist's private office and reading room, on the other hand, should be located in the most remote and quietest part of the suite.

A functional construction issue relates to the size of studs around procedure rooms. Six-inch studs are a wise choice to accommodate all the conduit for cabling. Since imaging is such a technologically driven space, 6-inch studs should be considered for other areas, as appropriate.

Figure 5-10. Control area for general radiography rooms. Santa Clara Valley Medical Center. (*Architecture: Anshen+Allen, San Francisco, CA; Photographer: Robert Canfield Photography.*)

Flexibility

Flexibility is desirable in any healthcare facility because technology is advancing so quickly that it is hard to forecast space needs 5 or 10 years in the future. As diagnostic imaging rooms are very costly to construct, planning for future expansion is critical, knowing that optimal patient and staff flow can be maintained and the addition of new procedure rooms will not create awkward adjacencies. Flexibility can also be achieved by making rooms larger than the manufacturer's minimum requirements.

RADIOLOGY

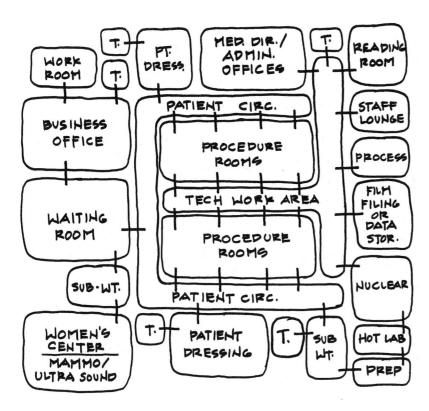

Figure 5-11. Schematic diagram for diagnostic imaging.

Components of a Diagnostic Imaging Suite

These are the basic components of a radiology suite, and each will be discussed in detail:

1. Waiting room
2. Business office
3. Patient dressing
4. Tech work area
5. Reading and consultation (may be film or digital image)
6. Film filing (if digital, data storage room for server and archives)
7. Film or digital image processing (darkroom, daylight, or PACS)

The various types of radiography and imaging rooms will be described separately.

Figure 5-12. Radiology registration desk has "friendly" appearance. (*Design: Jain Malkin Inc.*)

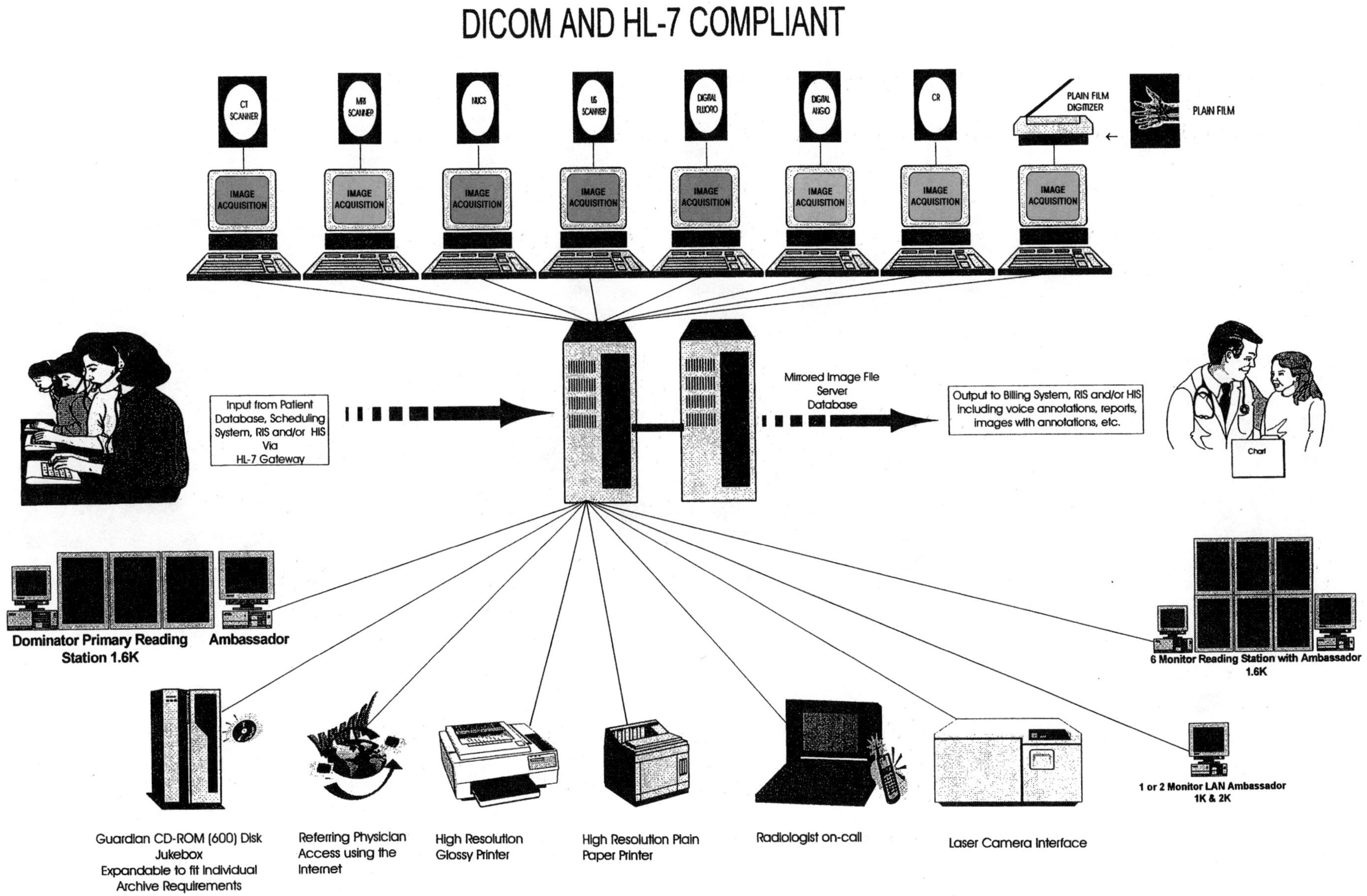

DICOM AND HL-7 COMPLIANT

Figure 5-14. Diagram of PACS system design. (*Illustration courtesy: DR Systems, Inc., San Diego, CA.*)

Figure 5-15a. Radiology waiting area uses low walls to create privacy groupings. (*Design: Rita St. Clair Associates, Baltimore, MD; Photographer: Gordon Beall Photography.*)

Figure 5-15b. Diagnostic imaging waiting room divides seating into privacy groupings. (*Architecture and interior design: Loebl Schlossman & Hackl, Chicago, IL; Photographer: Bruce VanInwegen.*)

Waiting Room

Allow 2.5 waiting room seats per procedure room and provide a suitable space out of the traffic lane for a patient in a wheelchair. (In a digital setting, there is more throughput or higher volume, necessitating more seats per procedure room.) At times, a patient may be brought in on a stretcher or gurney. This should be taken into account when laying out the space, but it is desirable for the stretcher to be brought through a private staff entrance (rather than the waiting room), through the corridor and into a procedure room, without causing damage to walls or needlessly jostling the patient.

In a large radiology facility, the number of chairs in the waiting room can make it look like a bus station. It is preferable to divide the seating into privacy groupings, providing several styles of seating to accommodate individual comfort (Figure 5-15a). Figure 5-15b portrays an excellent solution as the wood grid partition provides privacy without sacrificing the ability of staff to monitor the room. Ceiling design and lighting offer variation and interest. The use of light and dark woods gives this area a warm, inviting appearance.

Business Office

The business office is generally not large in a radiology suite, because this is a referral practice, and the patient's medical record remains with the referring physician. The radiologist stores only the X-ray films and a brief report on each patient. Billing and bookkeeping may be done within the suite or at another location. In a fully digital setting, an integrated data management system can handle billing and insurance claims, inventory of supplies, reports to referral physicians, as well as manage all the radiographic digital images. Radiographic images for the recent week would, of course, be on line, accessible from the server for the radiologist in writing reports.

It is common for radiology groups to sign contracts with hospitals to staff their radiology departments. It is not unusual for one large radiology group to staff three hospitals in a city, in addition to staffing and owning a number of outpatient radiology clinics in various medical buildings throughout the city. If such is the case, bookkeeping and billing might be done off site at a centralized location for all of the clinics. Likewise, archiving of near-line and off-line images may also be at a central location.

Patient Dressing

Allow two dressing rooms for each procedure room. Rooms may be as small as 3 feet wide×4 feet deep, but they should have a chair or built-in bench, mirror, shelf for disposable gowns, and one or two hooks for clothing (Figure 5-16). A proportional number of dressing rooms must be handicapped accessible. Sometimes dressing rooms have an emergency buzzer for summoning staff. In

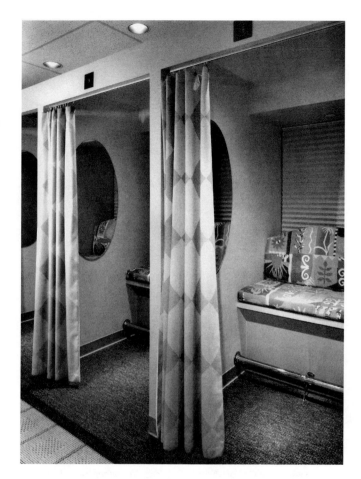

Figure 5-16. Radiology dressing rooms. (*Design: Rita St. Clair Associates, Baltimore, MD; Photographer: Gordon Beall Photography.*)

a clinic with a sufficient number of dressing rooms, patients may leave their personal effects in the dressing rooms, which should have a lockable compartment for handbags, briefcases, or jewelry if the room cannot be locked.

In other clinics, patients are asked to store their clothing in lockers outside the dressing room, so that others may use the room as in Figure 5-17, which also serves as a sub-waiting area. The dressing area should be carpet-

Figure 5-17. Radiology sub-waiting and locker area. University of California San Francisco. (*Architecture and interior design: Anshen+Allen, San Francisco, CA; Photographer: Robert Canfield Photography.*)

technologist initiated by the change in name of the American Registry of X-ray Technicians to the American Registry of Radiologic Technologists. The term "technologist" recognizes the evolution of education and skills—the X-ray technician has become a radiologic technologist.

Many diagnostic procedures are performed entirely by the X-ray technologist, without the radiologist being present. The tech greets the patient, gives instructions for the examination, sets up the equipment, positions the patient, makes the exposure, processes the film (or manipulates the digital image), and places the finished films in the radiologist's reading room or, in the case of digital images, routes them to the network.

The darkroom (if any) should be located close to the procedure rooms to save steps for the tech who walks back and forth, picking up unexposed film cassettes from pass boxes located in the darkroom wall, and, later, returns to the pass box the exposed film to be fed into the processor from the darkroom. This, of course, applies to a film-based setting.

A suite with three or more procedure rooms will generally have a dedicated darkroom technician who continually replenishes the pass boxes with film cassettes and feeds the exposed film into the processor. The processed film drops out of the processor on the daylight side, where the tech picks it up, checks it on the view box, sorts a series of films, puts it in X-ray film jackets, and later delivers it to the film viewing room for the radiologist to interpret. Note that techs need access to film filing, as they often have to pull older films for the radiologist to compare with new ones. In the digital setting, a passive viewing station (Figure 5-7) can be used by the tech to locate prior diagnostic studies to route them, along with the new images, for comparison and interpretation by the radiologist.

Before the film is fed into the processor, it must have patient identification placed on it. The patient identification camera could be on the countertop outside the darkroom or may be inside the darkroom. In a digital setting, patient identification is bar-coded and executed by the PACS software.

In a film-based setting, each tech requires a stand-up-height countertop work surface for sorting and viewing

ed, since patients may be walking barefoot. Sometimes one dressing cubicle is made double-width so that the built-in bench may serve as a recovery cot in case a patient feels ill. This oversized dressing room also accommodates a patient in a wheelchair.

Tech Work Area

A discussion of the technologists' work space must begin with a clarification of terms. Although often used interchangeably, there is a difference between *technician* and

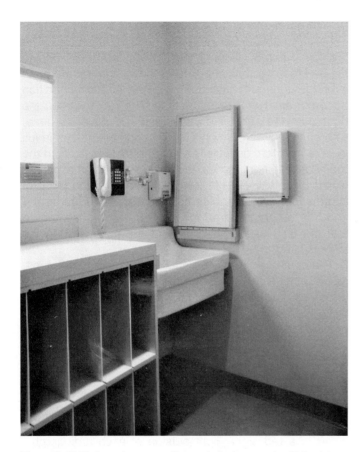

Figure 5-18. Tech work area, sorting and viewing counter. Note sink under hinged countertop. (*Design: Jain Malkin Inc.; Photographer: John Christian.*)

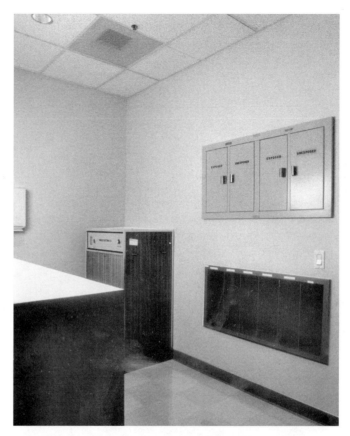

Figure 5-19. Tech work area (opposite side). Note pass boxes to darkroom and automatic processor (outdated model) and film sorting bins under pass boxes.

films. Mounted over the countertop would be a four- to six-panel view box illuminator and, below, a rack with a number of vertical dividers for sorting films (Figures 5-18 and 5-19). In addition, a double-panel view box must be provided immediately adjacent to the processor on the daylight side for checking films as they exit the processor. (See the Appendix for mounting heights of view box illuminators.) The tech work area in Figure 5-19 depicts cassette pass boxes in the wall contiguous with the darkroom. When the cassettes have been loaded with unex-

posed film, they are removed from the "tech side" if the darkroom is not contiguous with the radiography room, as is the case here. In a fully digital environment, the tech work area would be a viewing station (Figure 5-7), at either sit-down or stand-up height, with one or more printers. Hard copies of diagnostic studies may be printed on paper or film and sent to the referring physician along with a report.

The control area, discussed in detail below, is also the tech's work area.

Figure 5-3 shows a frequently used layout with a control area that runs between two radiography rooms. The problem with this, although it is convenient with respect to the darkroom and pass boxes, is that a right-handed and a left-handed room have been created. And this condition does not differ in a digital setting. The R/F room on the right puts the control area behind the patient's head, whereas the R/F room on the left keeps the patient in full view of the tech, especially when the table is tilted. In the room on the right, when the table is tilted, the patient would be totally out of view of the tech. (As a point of information, all R/F tables tilt.) Note that in Figures 5-4 and 5-5 the control area for the R/F room is located so that the tech has a good view of the patient when the table is tilted.

The control area may be outside the radiography room as in Figure 5-5 (the operator or technologist looks through a lead-shielded window at the patient), or it may be in the radiography room (Figures 5-4, 5-8, and 5-9), provided the control partition and window are lead-shielded (Figure 5-21). Prefabricated, lead-lined control partitions and lead-shielded windows may be purchased from X-ray supply dealers.

If the control area is outside the room, a method of verbally communicating instructions to the patient may be required. As a safety precaution, the control console is wired to a red signal light outside of each radiographic room to prevent entry when the machine is in use.

The facility in Figure 5-3 has been designed as a hybrid facility with two film-based R/F rooms and a digital general radiography room and a digital CT room. Were it to be converted to a totally digital environment, the control area between the two R/F rooms would be the same except a countertop would span the two wing walls and the control equipment would sit on the countertop. What is currently the darkroom would become a tech work alcove with a passive viewing station and printer.

Reading and Consultation
Reading Room—Film. The film reading room is where the radiologist interprets the films. It is approximately 10×12 or 10×14 feet in size, with a countertop along one

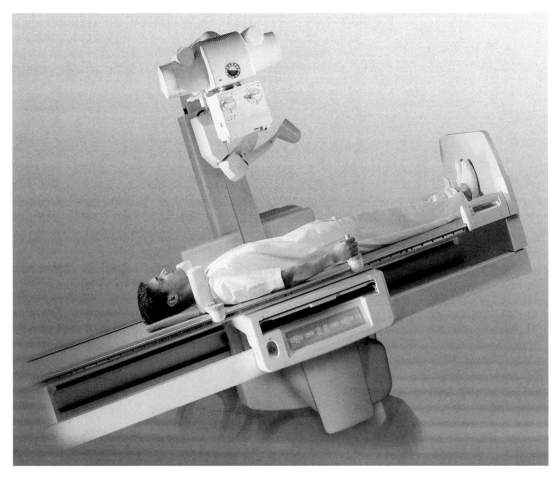

Figure 5-20. Prestige II digital radiography/fluoroscopy unit. (*Photo courtesy: GE Medical Systems, Waukesha, WI.*)

Control Area. Note that, when laying out radiographic fluoroscopy rooms, the *tables tilt so that the right side goes down, and the left up, when one is standing on the working side* (Figure 5-20), although some newer tables tilt in *both* directions. The control area, therefore, should be on the right end so that the technologist can see the patient at all times. General radiography tables do not tilt, making this issue less critical, but it is still optimal for the technologist to have the patient in view. It is surprising how often this planning error occurs.

or two walls at sit-down height. Above the countertop are two tiers of view box illuminators lining the room, wall to wall. The countertop needs to be completely clear underneath so that the radiologist can move freely from side to side. A cantilevered countertop can be accomplished with steel reinforcement inside the wall, extending underneath the countertop.

Ideal room lighting would be a perimeter valance (with dimmer control) running along two or three walls of the room. This would provide glare-free indirect illumination. This room should be located in the staff work area or at the rear of the suite where it is quiet. It should not be in the front of the suite or in the hectic patient circulation area.

Occasionally, radiologists view films on an alternator (Figure 5-22), which rotates a series of films that have been preloaded, as opposed to manually mounting a series of films on view boxes. Alternators are quite large and, like film illuminators (which will also be in the room), need to be positioned to avoid glare. Mammography films are often reviewed on an alternator, which may be supplemented by an additional monitor and software that acts like a spell checker to identify microcalcifications and masses. As an example, R2 Technology, Inc., has loaded detection algorithms and a large database into its ImageChecker® software for screening mammography. The processing unit that does the scanning is often placed in the tech work area and the display unit (CheckMate™) located in the reading room.

Reading Room—Digital. A reading room in a totally digital setting can be smaller than one used for reading films, but there are numerous environmental issues that must be addressed. The following information is based on an article by Bill Rostenberg, FAIA.* Reading workstations for radiologists must be designed with great care, working closely with the individuals who will work there. Issues of privacy if more than one radiologist will use the room simultaneously loom large because distraction must be

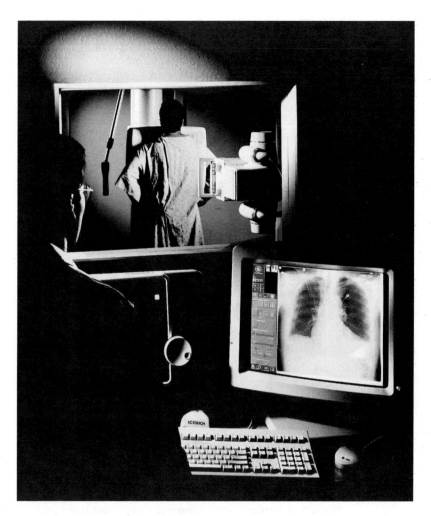

Figure 5-21. GE Revolution XQ/i digital tech console. (*Photo courtesy: GE Medical Systems, Waukesha, WI.*)

avoided; as voice recognition systems become more common, extraneous noise can be a problem and, if one individual is looking at films on a view box (which produces very bright light compared with a computer monitor), this can create glare on the other individual's monitor. PACS workstations may be configured differently, reflecting individual preferences, which includes the num-

---

*Bill Rostenberg, 1998. "Success by Design: Maximizing Your Digital Environment." *Advance for Administrators in Radiology and Radiation Oncology* 14.

Figure 5-22. Film alternator viewing unit. (*Design: Jain Malkin Inc.; Photographer: Glenn Cormier.*)

ber of monitors, the depth of the countertop, and the location of the keyboard tray (if any). In addition to reading and interpreting radiologic images, the radiologist may dictate, talk on the phone, do handwritten paperwork, or bar-code entry.

Lighting. Lighting in a reading room should be indirect, able to be dimmed, and divided into several zones so that one workstation can be controlled or dimmed independently of others. Because conventional film illuminators produce an average of 880 footlamberts and a CRT offers 20 to 180 footlamberts, designing an environment that accommodates both is tricky. The level of luminance also relates to the amount of reflected glare.

Ambient lighting for computer workstations should minimize contrast between the monitor and surrounding surfaces in order to avoid eyestrain, yet the room must be sufficiently dark—and without glare—for the image on the screen to be readable. A relationship of 1:1 between ambient light and that of the display terminal is recommended. Task lighting can be used to supplement ambient lighting where more light is required for handwriting or illuminating a keyboard. If task lighting is to be used, consider electrical outlet locations so that they are convenient and electrical cords are not running to distant outlets.

Anyone who works at a computer terminal knows the problems caused by glare from overhead lighting, white walls parallel to the screen, windows, and other monitors on a parallel wall. In the reading room, glare on a screen is far more than an annoyance and a cause of eyestrain: It can make it difficult to interpret an image. Flat-screen monitors that don't use cathode ray tubes and minimize glare are becoming increasingly popular. To minimize reflection on the screen, walls should be a medium tone, never white. Plastic laminate countertops should be dark as should any shelves or other casework in the room that might reflect on the screen.

Task lighting may also be accomplished by narrow- or wide-beam halogens mounted on tracks or cables that allow for quick and easy repositioning. Room lights may alternately be controlled on a panel at the radiologist's workstation, so that lights may be turned on or off in various zones without leaving one's chair.

Ergonomics. As in any computer workstation, it is desirable to be able to adjust the height of the work surface to accommodate tall or short individuals, and, of course, the chair should be a quality ergonomic design that provides adjustment of arm height, rake of the back, and seat height. Fixed countertops do not afford flexibility; howev-

Plate 1

Figure 3-9. Reception room, Planned Parenthood League of Boston, Massachusetts, provides a secure environment for patients and staff (built after the fatal shooting of two employees) as well as privacy at the reception desk for those who are registering. Colors, shapes, and forms create a dignified environment with a sense of whimsy. (*Architecture and interior design: Tsoi/Kobus & Associates, Boston, MA; Photo courtesy: Steve Rosenthal.*)

Plate 2

Figure 3-10. A fountain greets patients as they enter the Center for Executive Health, La Jolla, CA. See Figure 3-70 for space plan of this facility. (*Interior architecture and design: Jain Malkin Inc.; Photographer: Steve McClelland.*)

Plate 3

Figure 3-19. Clinic check-out stations provide patient privacy as well as a place for physicians and clinical staff to write notes or fill out forms. Montefiore Medical Center in the Bronx. (*Architecture and interior design: Guenther Petrarca, New York City; Photographer: © Christopher Lovi.*)

Figure 3-15. Reception desk, primary-care community clinic. High portion of desk conceals cubby-hole slots for storing forms (see Figure 3-16), and lowered portion provides a more welcoming interface with patients. (*Interior design: Jain Malkin Inc.; Photographer: Steve McClelland.*)

Plate 4

Figure 3-82. Waiting room, cardiac surgery suite. (*Design: Jain Malkin Inc.; Photographer: John Christian.*)

Plate 5

Figure 3-96. Corridor in pediatrics area of community clinic. (*Interior design: Jain Malkin Inc.; Photographer: Steve McClelland.*)

Figure 3-99. Pediatric examination room in community clinic, with lowered desktop for provider. (*Architecture: Moon Mayoras Architects, San Diego; Interior design: Jain Malkin Inc.; Photographer: Steve McClelland.*)

Plate 6

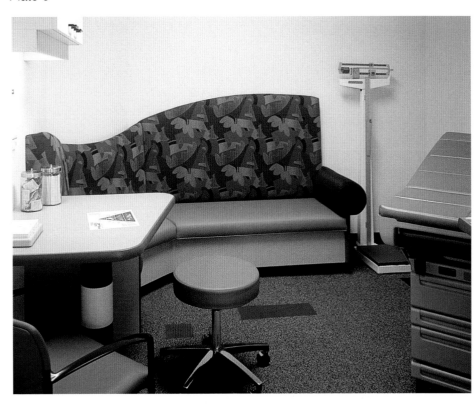

Figure 3-98. Pediatric examination room with built-in seat for parent and child. Victor Yacktman Children's Pavilion, Park Ridge, IL. (*Architecture and interior design: Watkins Hamilton Ross Architects, Inc., Houston, TX; Photographer: Jud Haggard.*)

Figure 3-97. Destination treatment. Victor Yacktman Children's Pavilion, Park Ridge, IL. (*Architecture and interior design: Watkins Hamilton Ross Architects, Inc., Houston, TX; Photographer: Jud Haggard.*)

Plate 7

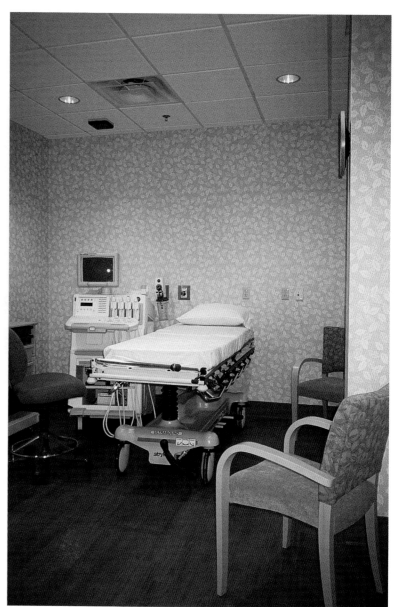

Figure 3-108. Reception window, pediatrics clinic. (*Design: Jain Malkin Inc.; Photographer: John Christian*

Figure 4-10. Ultrasound examination room. (*Interior design: Jain Malkin Inc.; Photographer: Jain Malkin.*)

Plate 8

Figure 4-13. Waiting room, OB-GYN suite. (*Photo courtesy: Janet Richardson, ASID, Annapolis, MD; Photographer: Ron Solomon.*)

Figure 4-14. Women's center reception desk. St. Elizabeth's Medical Center, Brighton, MA. (*Architecture and interior design: TRO/The Ritchie Organization, Newon, MA; Photographer: Richard Mandelkorn.*)

Plate 9

Figure 4-16. Corridor, women's clinic. (*Design: Jain Malkin Inc.; Photographer: Kim Brun.*)

Figure 4-20. Corridor with trompe l'oeil mural. Scripps Breast Care Center, La Jolla, CA. (*Interior architecture and design: Jain Malkin Inc.; Photographer: Glenn Cormier.*)

Plate 10

Figure 4-22. Waiting room with concierge desk. Scripps Breast Care Center, La Jolla, CA. (*Interior architecture and design: Jain Malkin Inc.; Photographer: Glenn Cormier.*)

Plate 11

Figure 4-23. Rotunda with mural of Hygeia and Panacea (goddesses of prevention and treatment), daughters of Aesclepius, the god of healing in 4th century B.C. Greece. Scripps Breast Care Center, La Jolla, CA. (*Interior architecture and design: Jain Malkin Inc.; Photographer: Glenn Cormier.*)

Figure 4-24. West of the Moon Lounge (gowned waiting). Scripps Breast Care Center, La Jolla, CA. (*Interior architecture and design: Jain Malkin Inc.; Photographer: Glenn Cormier.*)

Plate 12

Figure 4-25. Waiting room. Hoag Hospital Breast Care and Imaging Center. (*Architecture and interior design: Taylor & Associates Architects, Newport Beach, CA; Photographer: Farshid Assassi.*)

Plate 13

Figure 4-31. Waiting room. Smotrich Center for Reproductive Enhancement, La Jolla, CA. (*Interior architecture and design: Jain Malkin Inc.; Photographer: Glenn Cormier.*)

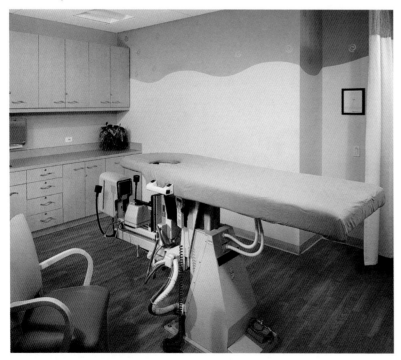

Figure 4-27. Stereotactic procedure room. Scripps Breast Care Center, La Jolla, CA. (*Interior architecture and design: Jain Malkin Inc.; Photographer: Glenn Cormier.*)

Plate 14

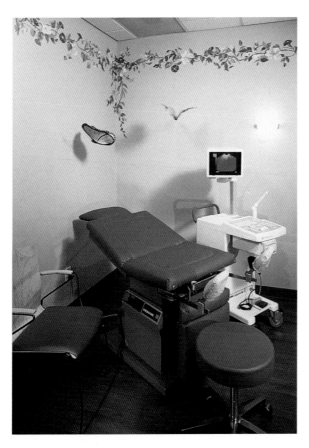

Figure 4-36. Examination room, reproductive medicine. Smotrich Center for Reproductive Enhancement, La Jolla, CA. (*Interior architecture and design: Jain Malkin Inc.; Photographer: Glenn Cormier.*)

Figure 4-54. Reception/waiting room for vascular surgery suite. (*Interior architecture and design: Jain Malkin Inc.; Photographer: Steve McClelland.*)

Plate 15

Figure 4-88. Waiting room, ophthalmology suite. (*Photo courtesy: Ann Asher, Inc., Los Angeles, CA; Photographer: Ron Solomon Photography.*)

Plate 16

Figure 4-98. Plastic surgery examination room for hands; also serves as recovery room. (*Design: Sue Walling, SW Design Inc., Minneapolis, MN; Photographer: P. R. Siegrist.*)

Figure 4-89. Reception window, ophthalmology suite. (*Photo courtesy: Carmel Repp, ASID, IDA, San Diego, CA; Photographer: Kim Brun.*)

Plate 17

Figure 4-99a: Consultation/exam room, plastic surgery (see Figure 4-99b for opposite side of room). (*Interior design: Kelly Wearstler, Los Angeles, CA; Photo courtesy: Grey Crawford©.*)

Figure 4-99b: Consultation/exam room, plastic surgery. (*Interior design: Kelly Wearstler, Los Angeles, CA; Photo courtesy: Grey Crawford©.*)

Figure 4-99c: Plastic surgeon's private office. (*Interior design: Kelly Wearstler; Photo courtesy: Grey Crawford©.*)

Figure 4-99d: Waiting room, plastic surgery. Note that Figures 4-99a–d are same project. (*Interior design: Kelly Wearstler; Photo courtesy: Grey Crawford©.*)

Plate 18

Figure 4-101. Trompe l'oeil mural at end of corridor, plastic surgery suite, expands the space and creates the illusion of an outdoor portico. (*Architecture and interior design: Jain Malkin Inc.; Photographer: Steve McClelland; Artist: Jean Karam.*)

Figure 4-103. Corridor of plastic surgery suite with view of check-out desk. Note custom-designed, black wrought iron chart rack. (*Architecture and interior design: Jain Malkin Inc.; Photographer: Steve McClelland.*)

Plate 19

Figure 4-136. Waiting room, orthopedic surgery. (*Design: Jain Malkin Inc.; Photographer: Michael Denny.*)

Plate 20

Figure 4-151. Waiting room, neurosurgery suite. *(Interior architecture and design: Jain Malkin Inc.; Photographer: Steve McClelland.)*

Plate 21

Figure 4-155a: Consultation room, psychiatry. (*Photo courtesy: Marna L. Sherman, Interiors, New York, NY; Photographer: Peter Vitale.*)

Figure 4-155b: Consultation room, psychiatry (opposite view). (*Photo courtesy: Marna L. Sherman, Interiors, New York, NY; Photographer: Peter Vitale.*)

Plate 22

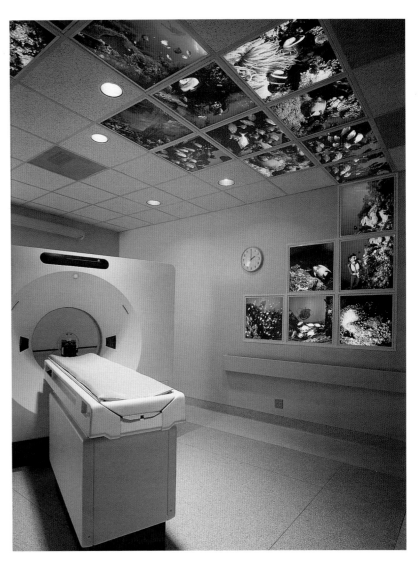

Figure 5-55. Back-lit film images of scuba divers exploring the ocean depths provide a pleasant diversion for patients undergoing CT scans. Note that the equipment in this photo is an older-model CT. (*Interior design: Jain Malkin Inc.; Photographer: Steve McClelland.*)

Figure 5-13. Outpatient imaging waiting area. Santa Monica/UCLA. (*Architecture and design: SmithGroup, San Francisco, CA; Photographer: John Edward Linden.*)

Plate 23

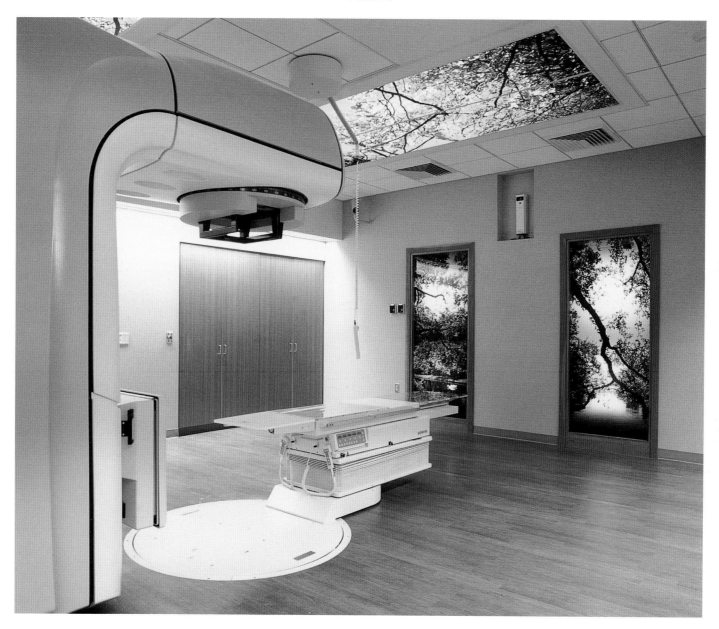

Figure 5-57. Radiation therapy room with linear accelerator. Back-lit film transparencies of views of nature "open" the room, providing a psychological escape for patients and a stress-reducing diversion. (*Photo courtesy: Art Research Institute—Joey Fischer ©2001.*)

Plate 24

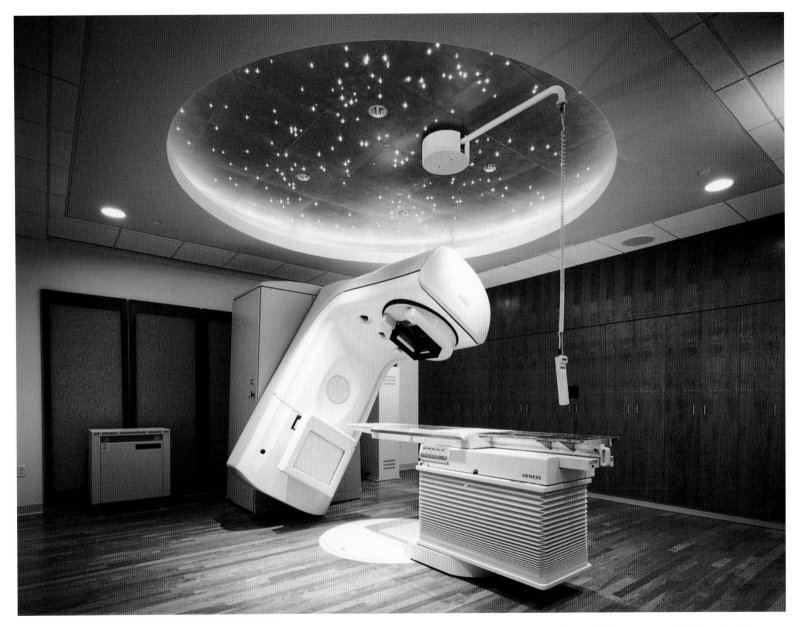

Figure 5-58. Linear accelerator vault room. University of California San Francisco, Mount Zion Comprehensive Cancer Center. (*Architecture and design: SmithGroup, San Francisco, CA; Photographer: Michael O'Callahan.*)

Plate 25

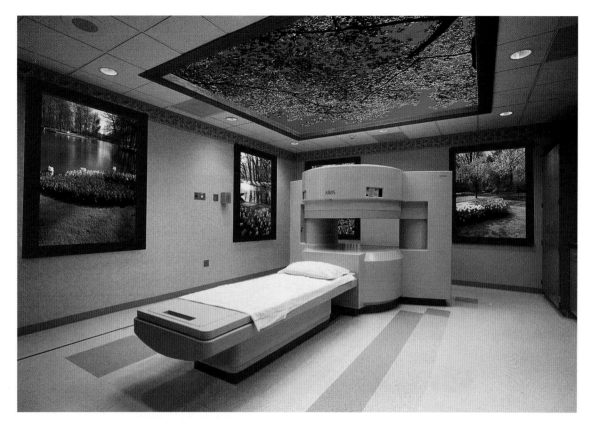

Figure 5-60. Open MRI unit. Room offers patients extraordinary views of nature via back-lit film transparencies, giving the appearance of windows and a skylight overhead. (*Photo courtesy: Art Research Institute—Joey Fischer ©2001.*)

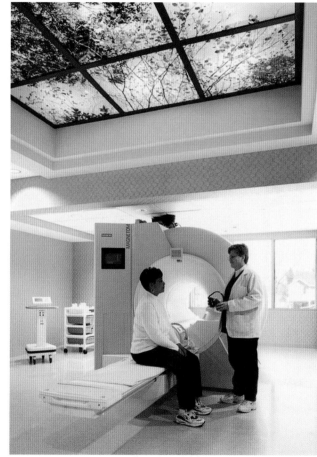

Figure 5-70. Siemens Magnetom 1.0T MRI. Back-lit film transparencies are a stress-reducing diversion for patients. Valley Hospital, Ridgewood, NJ. (*Photo courtesy: Shepley Bulfinch Richardson and Abbott, Boston, MA; Photographer: ©Peter Mauss/Esto.*)

Plate 26

Figure 6-8. Breast center waiting room. Torrance Breast Diagnostic and Family Center. (*Architecture and interior design: Boulder Associates, Inc., Boulder, CO; Photographer: Daniel O'Connor.*)

Figure 6-7. Entry/registration area, St. Francis Hospital Primary Care Medical Center, Morton Grove, IL. (*Architecture and interior design: Mekus Studios, Chicago, IL; Photographer: Jon Miller® Hedrich Blessing.*)

Plate 27

Figure 7-7. One section of the waiting room focuses on a coffee bar and fireplace with comfortable Stickley arm chairs and view into courtyard with garden. (*Design: Jain Malkin Inc.; Photographer: Philip Prouse.*)

Figure 7-12. Trellis with air-brushed sky above creates outdoor feeling as patients proceed toward registration. This is the same facility as depicted in Figure 7-11. (*Interior architecture and design: Jain Malkin Inc.; Photographer: Steve McClelland.*)

Figure 7-11. Ambulatory surgical center greeter's desk. Waiting area showcases Mexican folk art and hand-woven textiles as a counterbalance in an otherwise high-tech setting. Large photos of Mexican street scenes and a bold color palette complement the theme. Scripps Memorial Hospital, Encinitas, CA. (*Interior architecture and design: Jain Malkin Inc.; Photographer: Steve McClelland.*)

Plate 28

Figure 7-14. Patients in ambulatory surgical prep and recovery bays benefit from view of nature overhead; back-lit film transparency. (*Design: Jain Malkin Inc.; Photographer: Corey Hobbins.*)

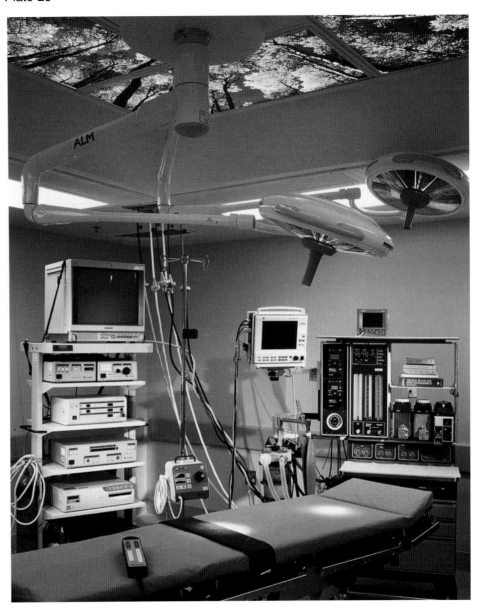

Figure 7-15. Operating room conveys the illusion of a view of sky and treetops. Alpine Surgery Center. (Architecture and interior *design: Boulder Associates, Inc., Boulder, CO; Photographer: Daniel O'Connor.*)

Plate 29

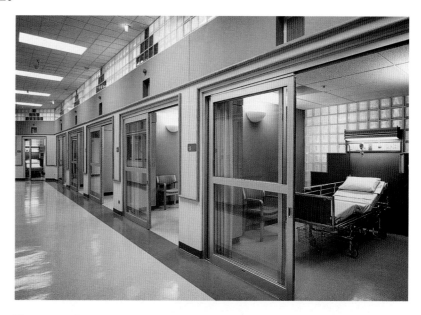

Figure 7-17. Recovery area with view into private recovery rooms. Note use of color, glass block, and oak detailing. (*Photo courtesy: Anderson Mikos Architects, Ltd., Oak Brook, IL; Photographer: Jay Wolke.*)

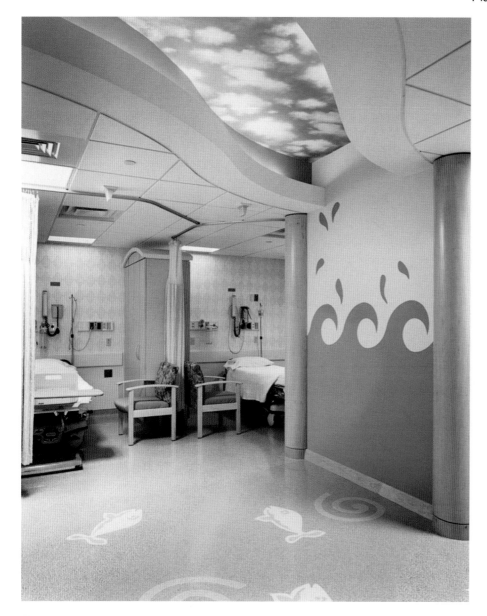

Figure 7-16. Pediatric postanesthesia recovery area introduces wood, playful clouds air-brushed on the ceiling, and colorful graphics on walls and floor. The Valley Hospital, Ridgewood, NJ. (*Architecture and interior design: Shepley Bulfinch Richardson and Abbott, Boston, MA; Photographer: ©Peter Mauss/Esto.*)

Figure 7-29. Private recovery bay has nonclinical ambience with wood detailing, light wells, and back-lit film image of nature. Alpine Surgery Center. (*Architecture and interior design: Boulder Associates, Inc., Boulder, CO; Photographer: Daniel O'Connor.*)

Plate 30

Figure 8-3. Pool and spa. Note interesting architectural features, lighting, and use of color. (*Photo courtesy: Eisenman & Enock, Inc., New York, NY; Photographer: Roger Bester.*)

Plate 31

Figure 8-8. Trompe l'oeil mural expands, and adds dimension, to the room. (*Photo courtesy: Maxion Design, Sausalito, CA; Photographer: Peter Hendrix.*)

Figure 8-9. Sophisticated mural gives illusion of looking through panes of glass at the bay. (*Photo courtesy: Maxion Design, Sausalito, CA; Photographer: Jeff Weissman.*)

Plate 32

Figure 10-3. A living room environment, focusing on a fireplace, creates a comfortable waiting experience for patients. (*Design: Janice Thayer-Johnson, Kristin Harleman, and Susan Barrett; Photographer: Marshall M. Johnson.*)

Figure 10-4. Casual furniture and residential-style accessories create a relaxed waiting environment for patients; note the built-in hot and cold water dispenser. (*Design: Signature Environments, Inc., Seattle, WA; Photographer: Marshall M. Johnson.*)

Plate 33

Figure 10-35. Treatment room corridor has interesting architectural features as well as sliding glass door access to upper cabinet at 12 o'clock wall of treatment room for supply of clean tray set-ups: (*Space planning and interior design: Janet Pettersen, IIDA, Design Wave, Fallbrook, CA; Space planning collaboration and dental equipment engineering: Lee Palmer, Burkhart Dental, San Diego; (Photographer: J. T. MacMillan.)*

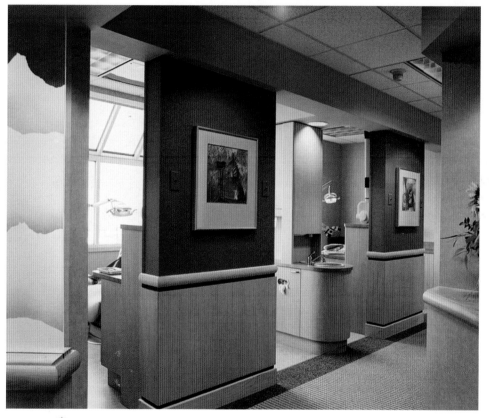

Figure 10-36. Corridor has attractive wrap-around wood detailing that continues into treatment rooms. (*Casework for dental operatories: Stelte Dental Systems, Mukilteo, WA; Interior design: Signature Environments, Inc., Seattle, WA; Photographer: Marshall M. Johnson.*)

Plate 34

Figure 10-45. TV monitor in ceiling over patient's head can be used for a variety of educational or entertainment programming. The stress-relieving benefits of nature programming, in this case, contrasts sharply with the headline news running along the bottom of the screen. Although the patient controls the programming with a remote control, even briefly reading messages like this can be quite unnerving during dental treatment. (*AV consultant: Mr. Hookup, San Diego; Photographer: Jain Malkin.*)

Figures 10-39 and 10-40. Treatment rooms feature custom-designed casework and unique design details. (*Architecture and interior design: Lawrence Man, AIA Los Angeles, CA; Photographer: ©1989 Lucy Chen.*)

Plate 35

Figure 10-88. A well-appointed bathroom pleases both patients and staff. (*Photographer Jain Malkin.*)

Figure 10-101. Orthodontic treatment bay. (*Photo courtesy: Sue Wailing, SW Design, Inc., Minneapolis, MN; Photographer P. R. Siegrist.*)

Plate 36

Figure 10-103. Operatory bay, orthodontics. Note: Suite was designed prior to enactment of practice standards for sterilization; therefore, pliers are exposed, unbagged, on instrument trays. (*Interior architecture: Jain Malkin Inc.; Photographer: John Christian.*)

Plate 37

Figure 10-105. Waiting room, children's dental clinic. (*Architecture/interior design: Margo Hebald, Architect, Pacific Palisades, CA; Photographer; Marvin Rand, Marina del Ray, CA.*)

Figure 10-106. Preflight check-in, children's dental clinic. (*Architecture/interior design: Margo Hebald, Architect. Pacific Palisades, CA; Photographer: Marvin Rand, Marina del Ray, CA.*)

Plate 38

Figure 10-107. Pedodontic bay. (*Architecture/interior design: Margo Hebald, Architect, Pacific Palisades, CA; Photographer: Marvin Rand, Marina del Ray, CA.*)

Figure 10-108. Corridor, orthodontic office. (*Interior architecture: Jain Malkin Inc.; Photographer John Christian.*)

Plate 39

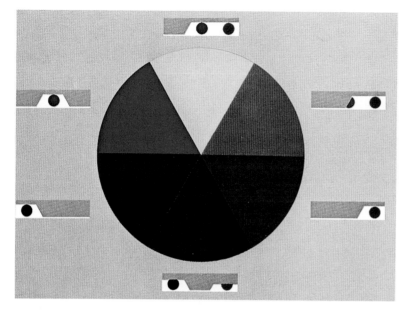

Figure 11-1. The old color wheel. (*Reprinted from* The Theory and Practice of Color, *by Frans Gerritsen, by permission of Van Nostrand Reinhold, New York, 1974, p. 172.*)

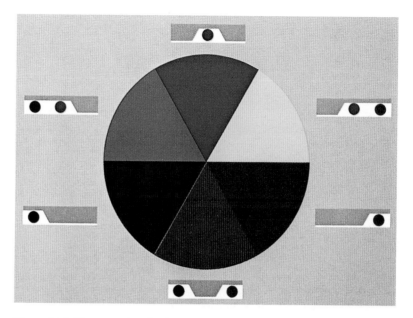

Figure 11-2. The new color wheel. (*Reprinted from* The Theory and Practice of Color, *by Frans Gerritsen, by permission of Van Nostrand Reinhold, New York, 1974, p. 173.*)

Figure 11-3. Simultaneous contrast. (*Reprinted from* The Theory and Practice of Color, *by Frans Gerritsen, by permission of Van Nostrand Reinhold, New York, 1974, p. 128.*)

Figure 11-4. Successive contrast/afterimage. (*Reprinted from* The Theory and Practice of Color, *by Frans Gerritsen, by permission of Van Nostrand Reinhold, New York, 1974, p. 146.*)

Plate 40

Figure 13-1. Corridor, dermatology suite, indirect lighting. (*Architecture and interior design: Richard Deno, Cardiff, CA; Photographer: Kim Brun.*)

Figure 13-8. Interesting ceilings and imaginative lighting complement the architectural geometry of the space. (*Architecture and interior design: Taylor & Associates Architects, Newport Beach, CA; Photographer: Farshid Assassi.*)

er, a number of manufacturers offer freestanding workstations with maximum ergonomic adjustment. Refer to Chapter 3 for a detailed discussion and illustrations of ergonomic issues, some of which may apply to a reading room.

HVAC. Thought should be given to zoning the film reading room independently as PACS workstations and numerous monitors give off considerable heat. The radiologist should be able to control the temperature from a thermostat in the reading room.

Electrical. The key to any high-functioning digital system is an uninterrupted power supply. Disturbances from other equipment, inadequate system capacity, and inadequate grounding can cause fluctuations that are devastating to electronic instruments. Newer electronic instruments are far more sensitive to power line disturbances than their predecessors. Even minimal amounts of electrical noise can affect the dense digital circuitry of these advanced microprocessors. UPS units can be attached to each electronic instrument or be built into the infrastructure of the facility.

Summary. For now, reading rooms may need to accommodate conventional film-based "hard copy" reading along with "soft copy" reading in a hybrid transition phase until fully digital soft-copy reading is commonplace. This is expected to change quickly. CT and MRI, because they are already inherently digital, will be the first modalities to come on line with R/F and general radiography following along. A resource, for keeping in touch with these issues, is the Society for Computer Applications in Radiology (SCAR) in Great Falls, Virginia (www.scarnet.org).

Referring Physicians' Viewing. This is generally an alcove off of the corridor (see Figure 5-8, where it is labeled "viewing consultant," and Figure 5-3), to which referring physicians may come to review their patients' X-rays in a film-based (or digital) setting. A four-panel view box is generally sufficient. This would usually be at a sit-down height, but could be a stand-up consultation area

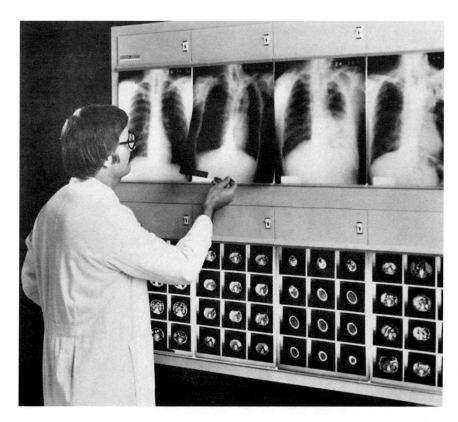

Figure 5-23. Six-over-six view boxes. (*Photo courtesy: GE Medical Systems, Waukesha, WI.*)

(Figure 5-23). This room should be positioned in the suite so that physicians' discussions will not be overhead by patients. If located near the front of the suite, or the staff entry, doctors would not have to intrude upon patients in the examination area. In a fully digital setting, the physicians' viewing area may be fairly small (Figure 5-3) and would have a passive viewing station as in Figure 5-7. Increasingly, referring physicians will be viewing patients' radiographic images via the Internet in their own offices.

Radiologist's Office/Consultation. The radiologist usually does not consult with patients, but does consult with referring physicians. This may take place in the private office or in the referring physicians' viewing area. (Those

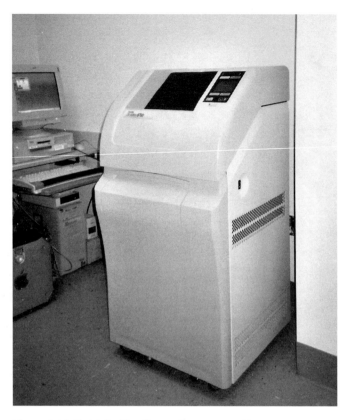

Figure 5-24. Kodak DryView™ 8700 laser imager. (*Photo courtesy: Jain Malkin Inc.*)

Film Filing

Sufficient storage for X-ray films must be provided in special-sized lateral file cabinets. Films are placed in color-coded paper jackets and stored on open shelves for easy retrieval. (X-ray film jackets are 14½×17½ inches in size.) Many radiology suites use space-saving movable aisle-type filing systems, which may be manually operated or motorized. A word of caution: The weight of these file cabinets, loaded, must be carefully calculated in order to design the floor to support it.

Digital Data Storage

This was explained under the PACS section at the beginning of this chapter. A facility may or may not have a storage room to accommodate a large server and jukebox tower for archival storage. The facility in Figure 5-8, for example, is part of a 250,000-square-foot building that has telecommunications equipment rooms disbursed throughout it. The facility in Figure 5-9 is also part of a larger facility. An independent radiology suite as in Figure 5-3 (although this one is not fully digital), located in a medical office building, does need a room for data storage equipment.

Film Processing

Film processing may be done in a darkroom or by a daylight process that does not require a darkroom or by a dry view laser imager (can be used with CT and MRI). However, daylight processing also requires a small darkroom, which does not need plumbing—just literally a *dark* room with a light seal on the door and a countertop for loading film into magazines. The dry view laser imager does not require a darkroom; the machine contains a cartridge that holds a quantity of film. For this type of processing, one must be able to send a digital image directly to the laser imager (Figure 5-24). As film may be used in many facilities for a number of years, film-based processing systems will be discussed. The large central darkroom that necessitates long travel routes has been replaced, in large facilities, by a number of processing areas distributed in a *decentralized* fashion throughout the suite, adjacent to procedure rooms. An individual

who do consult with patients would use the private office.) In a film-based setting, most radiologists will have view box illuminators in their private offices (four-over-four or perhaps eight-over-eight panels) mounted on the wall behind and to the side of the desk, with a sorting shelf underneath. In a digital setting, the film illuminators would be replaced by a PACS workstation as in Figure 5-6 or possibly a passive viewing station (Figure 5-7). This room should be located in the quietest part of the suite. Expectations are that telephone consultations supported by images sent over the Internet will replace face-to-face encounters between radiologists and referring physicians.

procedure room such as mammography or MRI might have a dedicated film processor (daylight for mammography or dry view laser for MRI) that does not require a darkroom.

The advantages of decentralized darkrooms and processing are several. They free the tech from carting cassettes back and forth, which can be tiring. Shorter walking distances allow the tech to spend more time with patients who, in turn, have a shorter wait because films are processed more rapidly. This improves the operational efficiency of each procedure room, thereby generating more revenue.

From the planning point of view, there are four different possibilities for routing exposed film to the processor.

1. Single-film cassette

2. Transportable film magazine

3. Daylight system

4. Integrated (attached) film processor

The *single-film cassette* is used in all conventional fluoroscopic and radiographic procedures. Single cassettes are loaded and stored in lead-lined cassette pass boxes (Figure 5-25).

The *film magazine* accommodates a large quantity of exposed films that are processed sequentially, together, in the processor.

Daylight systems (used for general radiography and mammography) allow the film processor to be located in a lighted room. Advocates of this system claim that daylight processing saves 20 percent of the total patient examination time, allowing the tech to spend more time in the room with the patient, rather than running back and forth to the darkroom. There may be some savings in utilization of space as well. A darkroom can be used only for opening and processing film, whereas a daylight area is all usable space. A daylight processor may be placed in the procedure room itself if it is internally shielded from radiation but most units are not. This type of processing is indicated in Figure 5-5 and described more fully later in this section.

Darkroom. Film-based radiology suites contain one or more darkrooms unless they are dedicated to daylight film processing.

The size and design of the darkroom and processing area depend on the equipment, the number and arrangement of radiographic rooms around it, whether there is one central darkroom or several decentralized ones, and the volume of film to be processed. In any case, there would be a "wet" side and a "dry" side. The wet side is where the automatic processor and the replenishment (developer and fixer) tanks are located. Either inside the darkroom or in the tech work area outside, there needs to be a large sink (size 18×24×9 inches deep) for washing the roller racks of the processor. This sink should have hot and cold water as well as a sprayer attachment. Since it is not used on a daily basis, it is advisable to put it under a hinged countertop (Figures 5-5 and 5-18) to preserve more working space.

The dry side of the darkroom is where the film storage bin (which requires an electrical outlet) is located and where cassettes are loaded with film. One or more cassette pass boxes will be built into the wall for the transfer of unexposed and exposed film cassettes. Since these are very heavy lead-lined boxes, the wall in which they are supported will require reinforcement. Pass boxes will be located in the wall of the darkroom closest to, or contiguous with, the radiography rooms (Figures 5-3 and 5-4). If the darkroom is not contiguous with the radiography rooms (Figure 5-5), pass boxes would be located on a darkroom wall accessible to the radiography room corridor. Daylight processing systems do not require pass boxes.

The automatic processor (Figure 5-26) is typically located outside the darkroom, feeding through a light-sealed opening in the wall into the darkroom. (The unit is outside the darkroom with the feed tray extending into the darkroom.) Exposed film is fed from inside the darkroom into the tray, and the processed film is delivered on the daylight side of the tech work area (Figures 5-3, 5-4, and 5-19).

Processors require only cold water as temperature is controlled within the unit. The processor shown in Figure

Figure 5-25. Cassette pass box. (*Photo courtesy: GE Medical Systems, Waukesha, WI.*)

Figure 5-26. Kodak X-OMAT 3000RA film processor. (Photo courtesy: Eastman Kodak Co., Rochester, NY.)

Figure 5-27. Safelight. (*Photo courtesy: Eastman Kodak Co., Rochester, NY.*)

Figure 5-28. Safelight. (*Photo courtesy: GE Medical Systems, Waukesha, WI.*)

5-26 is the standard in the industry; therefore, its planning requirements will be noted. It needs 36 inches clear on three sides for maintenance and repair. The unit requires a floor drain or, preferably, a floor sink inside the darkroom near the processor and a vent to the outside for exhaust. Exhaust comes out of the processor from the rear, which can be handled by connecting a flexible duct that runs exposed along the inside darkroom wall, or it can be run concealed inside the wall at the proper location to connect with the vent hold exhaust pipe at the rear of the processor. The unit requires 120/208 volts ac, single- or three-phase, 30-ampere service with a 30-ampere breaker.

Two 50-gallon replenishment tanks of developer and fixer can be located under the countertop on the wet side of the darkroom, close to the processor. These tanks may also be placed on a rolling cart. Tanks may also be placed in a closet adjacent to, but outside the darkroom (Figure 4-19) and preferably near a service entrance so that vendors need not enter the tech work core to service the tanks. The area under the processor, including the path between the processor and the sink used for washing rollers, must have hard-surface flooring, preferably sheet vinyl. Carpet should not be used in the tech work area outside the darkroom.

A darkroom needs two sources of light. A 100-watt incandescent fixture, either recessed or surface mounted to the ceiling, will serve for general illumination, but a red safelight must be provided for work with exposed film. The safelight can be plugged into an outlet at 60 to 72 inches off the floor, and it can work by a pull chain or be wired to a wall switch (Figures 5-27 and 5-28). If the latter, the switch should be located away from the incandescent light switch, so that the technologist does not accidentally hit the wrong switch while working with exposed film. The safelight shown in Figure 5-28 can sit on a countertop or be bracketed to the wall. Any recessed light fixtures and the exhaust fan must have light sealed housings. Similarly, the darkroom door must have a light seal. Codes in some cities require a lightproof louver ventilation panel in the darkroom door. Note that ceilings should be drywall to minimize dust.

Countertop work surfaces in a darkroom may be at a height of 34 or 42 inches, depending on personal preference; however, the ADA has a limit of 34 inches high. Open shelves may be provided above the countertop for storage of various items. There is no need for closed storage in a darkroom. As for color of walls, some techs prefer dark walls, while others prefer a light color.

An option for a darkroom door is that shown in Figure 5-29, which is also available in a wheelchair-accessible version. This revolving door provides lightproof entry into the darkroom, allowing one tech to enter while another is working with exposed film. If this type of door is not used, it is important to have a red warning light over the door that is automatically activated (tied into the film bin) whenever cassettes are being loaded or unloaded.

Figure 5-29. View of tech work corridor showing through-the-wall film processor ("daylight" side) and revolving darkroom door. (*Design: Jain Malkin Inc.; Photographer: Glenn Cormier.*)

Figure 5-30. Silver recovery unit. (*Photo courtesy: GE Medical Systems, Waukesha, WI.*)

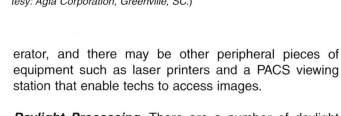

Figure 5-31. Compact E.O.S. daylight processor system. (*Photo courtesy: Agfa Corporation, Greenville, SC.*)

The darkroom water supply must be filtered, and the processor may need a silver recovery unit (Figure 5-30), depending on local codes. When disposing of waste chemicals or water, regulations of local agencies must be followed. If used liquids are allowed to be fed into the sewer system, piping must be of polyethylene up to the main line (vertical disposal pipe). Additionally, waste lines must have vacuum breakers.

Digital Processing

This has been discussed previously under PACS and Computed Radiography. The tech work area in a fully digital environment can be quite large (Figure 5-8), if centralized, depending on the volume of films and the number of procedure rooms served. For example, the plate reader (for phosphor plates) might be the size of a refrig-

erator, and there may be other peripheral pieces of equipment such as laser printers and a PACS viewing station that enable techs to access images.

Daylight Processing.

There are a number of daylight processing systems as well as options within each system. As with any selection of equipment, it depends on an analysis of needs. The layout of the suite, availability of space, number and type of radiology examinations, anticipated workflow, availability of personnel, and, of course, cost must all be factored into the decision. Manufacturers' literature must be consulted for suggested equipment layouts, critical distances between various components, weight, and utility requirements.

The daylight processing system shown in Figure 5-31 (size 37 inches deep×28 inches wide×55 inches high) can be placed in a daylight processing area or immediately outside a procedure room such as mammography, both illustrated in Figure 5-5. The processor depicted is intended for general radiography and R/F but, with special developer racks, accommodates mammography films.

Today, it is popular to create a women's center within a radiology suite. For marketing purposes, this area is generally located near the front of the suite and may even have a private entrance (Figures 5-4 and 5-5). This means that the tech would have quite a distance to walk to a central darkroom or processing area; therefore, a daylight processor may be a solution. In Figure 6-6, six mammography rooms are supported by daylight processing.

Certain issues need to be considered with daylight processing systems. All machine functions are monitored and controlled by microprocessors; therefore, manufacturers' recommendations for relative humidity and ambient temperature must be heeded. There are two methods of discharging waste, water, and chemicals (fixer and developer): central discharge into the sewer system, or collection of waste into storage tanks. If local codes allow for chemicals to be discharged into the public sewer system waste liquids would be run straight to the drain through a hose. Polyethylene piping will be needed for the drain as far as the main riser (vertical downpipe). An alternative to this is a waste disposal trolley with containers to collect the chemicals.

There are a number of critical plumbing connections required with daylight processors. Manufacturers' technical planning manuals should be reviewed. For the unit depicted in Figure 5-31, a floor drain is required close to the machine, and a sink must be provided for maintenance work. This is a large, deep sink such as would be found in a darkroom for washing the roller rack of a processor. Plumbing connections can be made through either the bottom or the back of the machine. These include an exhaust connection (with flexible hose) and connections for water, intake and discharge of fixer and developer. Flexible hoses are used because it may be necessary to move the machine for repair work and for this reason connections through the floor must be

placed behind the machine, not under it. The processor in Figure 5-31 requires minimum clear access of 20 inches to the rear, 24 inches to the right side, 40 inches to the left side, and 28 inches in front. A countertop is needed nearby for items such as a patient identification camera.

Additional accessory items that may be internally integrated into the processing system (or may be accessory attachments) are a water filter, replenisher tanks, a silver recovery unit, or a chemical mixer. Most daylight processors require a dedicated circuit, good ventilation in the processing area, controlled water pressure, and a 3- to 4-inch-diameter exhaust connect from the processor, vented to the plenum or to the outdoors, as local codes dictate.

To avoid too high a concentration of chemical fumes, the air exchange should be 10 times the room volume per hour. Consider noise levels when locating these machines. In standby mode expect 36 decibels (dB(A)) and in film processing mode 51 decibels. Also, the machine must not be exposed to direct sunlight. It should be noted that some daylight processors can also be located contiguous to a darkroom with a film feed tray through the darkroom wall.

General Radiography Rooms and Radiography and Fluoroscopy Rooms

Not all radiography rooms are equipped for fluoroscopy. A diagnostic imaging facility may have two general radiography rooms plus one radiography and fluoroscopy (R/F) combination room or perhaps one general radiography room and two R/F rooms. The R/F rooms should be a minimum of 14×16 feet in size and may even be 16×18 feet.

The size of the radiography room will vary in accordance with the size of the X-ray unit and the ancillary equipment. As the room is equipped for taking radiographs of all parts of the body in standing, sitting, or angled positions, the room will have freestanding, wall-mounted, and ceiling-suspended equipment. Because there are a certain number of variables from one manufacturer to another, the space planner must obtain sug-

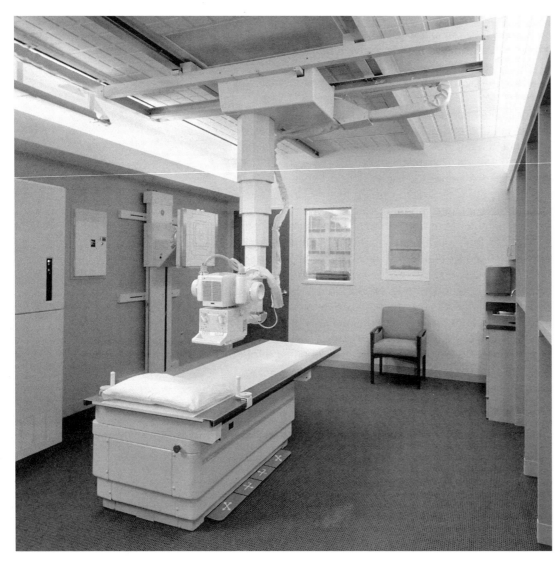

Figure 5-32. General radiography room. University of California San Francisco. (*Architecture and interior design: Anshen+Allen, San Francisco, CA; Photographer: Robert Canfield Photography.*)

gested room layouts that note critical distances between various components, along with specifications of required utility connections from each manufacturer. Technical planning guides should be requested.

To begin with, electrical cables connect the control unit (generator) to the X-ray tube stand and the transformer. The most unobtrusive way of handling this is to trench the floor and bury them under a coverplate. Conduit or cabling can also be run, exposed, at the base of the wall. (The transformer is generally located in one corner of the radiography room.)

An R/F room must have a toilet attached to it. The toilet often has one door to the R/F room and another to the corridor as shown in Figures 5-3 and 5-4. The patient needs to immediately discharge the barium enema after the lower GI (gastrointestinal) procedure.

The patient exits the bathroom via the corridor door, adjacent to the dressing area. If he or she needs to use the bathroom again, the patient may enter from the corridor side, as the next patient would not be using it immediately. (A certain amount of cleanup time and prep is required before examining the next patient.)

In older facilities, one may find a barium prep area, which is a countertop with sink and plaster trap for preparation of barium or contrast media and an under-counter refrigerator. However, barium now comes prepackaged and requires no preparation.

The fluoroscopy room is the workroom for the radiologist. He or she will watch the TV monitor as the patient is turned in different positions, and the contrast medium moves through the organs.

The size of the fluoroscopy room is largely determined by the amount of ceiling equipment. The ceiling tube mount moves on ceiling-mounted tracks, supported by a Unistrut® system above the finished ceiling as in Figure 5-32, although, technically, this is not a fluoro room. When a room has a table that tilts (Figures 5-20 and 5-33) and a ceiling-mounted tube stand, a 10-foot ceiling height may be required. Of course, the weight of the equipment must also be considered, which, for fluoro, is about 3000 pounds for the table.

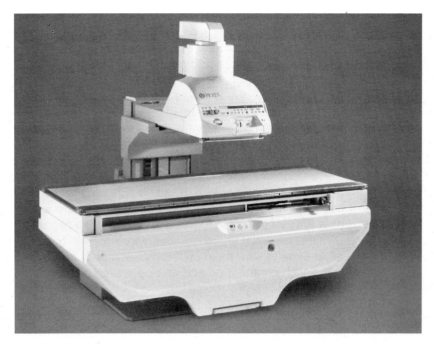

Figure 5-33. Clinix™-RF Plus digital radiography/fluoroscopy unit. (*Photo courtesy: Marconi Medical Systems, Cleveland, OH.*)

Radiography Room Without Fluoroscopy

A radiography room without fluoroscopy may be as small as 12×16 feet, although 12×16 feet would be recommended only for a compact table that might be used by an orthopedist. Always err on the side of a larger, rather than a smaller, room. In these compact units, the X-ray tube column may be mounted directly to the table, negating the additional space required for ceiling mounting. If a radiography room is used by a technologist only (as is often the case), the room may be smaller than if it is used by the radiologist, who may be doing special procedures requiring more than one person to be in the room and perhaps the use of additional portable equipment.

Chest films would typically be done in a general radiography room, although Figure 5-34 shows digital equipment specifically for chest films. In a general radiography

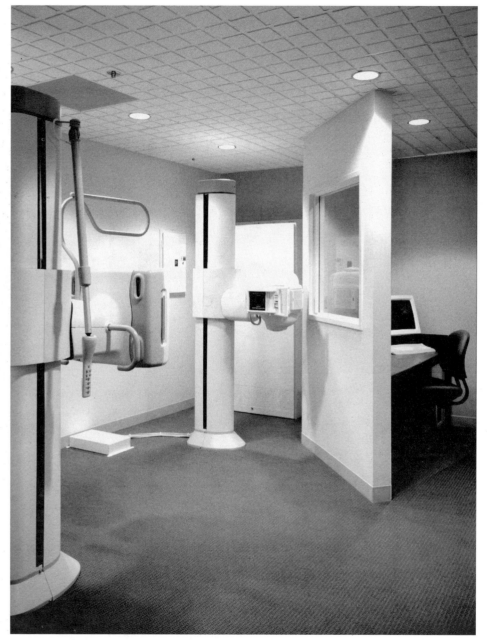

Figure 5-34. Digital chest room. University of California San Francisco. (*Architecture and interior design: Anshen+Allen, San Francisco, CA; Photographer: Robert Canfield Photography.*)

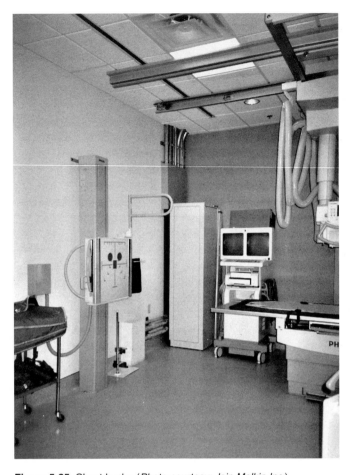

Figure 5-35. Chest bucky. (*Photo courtesy: Jain Malkin Inc.*)

patient positioning devices such as sandbags and foam wedges and for disposable items needed for procedures.

The door to a radiography room must be large enough to move equipment in and out. It should be noted that a lead-lined door is very heavy and will require a heavy-duty closer. Figure 5-3 shows a 42-inch-wide door on the R/F rooms, but movement of equipment can also be accommodated by a 3-foot-wide door placed in a 4-foot-wide frame with a 1-foot dead panel (lead lined) that can be removed as needed.

The four general radiography rooms and the control area depicted in Figures 5-10 and 5-36 are not direct digital; they use CR, explained previously, which can viewed on a PACS. The unit in Figure 5-37 converts traditional X-ray films to digital (in lieu of scanning films with a digitizer) in order to view them on a PACS. This may be located in the tech control area and can be shared between two general radiography rooms.

Lead Shielding. Once a radiology suite is designed, a radiation physicist must be consulted to prepare a study of lead-shielding requirements. In order to do this, the physicist will need to know full specifications on the equipment for each room, the anticipated volume of films, the location of a particular X-ray room with respect to adjacent rooms in the suite, and the location of the suite itself within the medical office building.

For example, if a radiology room is on the third floor of a building and has two exterior walls, the lead-shielding requirements would be considerably different than if the room were contiguous with an office where someone sits at a desk all day. If the suite is located on the ground floor of a building and the radiography room is on an exterior wall, with passersby walking to a parking lot, the physicist evaluates the volume of foot traffic and the amount of exposure in order to "protect the genes of future populations." Of course, placement of equipment in the room will determine the direction of radiation scatter.

The lead-lined control partition in Figure 5-36 is viewed from the opposite side in Figure 5-10. The leading edge must have at least 18 inches of wall to the side of the window to protect the tech.

room, a wall-mounted film holder, called a *bucky,* would be located generally at the "head" end of the X-ray table (Figure 5-35), but it may be placed to the side of the table (Figure 5-32). Another common procedure, an IVP (intravenous pyelogram), used to study the kidneys, uterus, and bladder, is performed in a general radiographic room that has tomographic capabilities but these are more commonly done with CT. For these studies, a bathroom must be nearby, but need not be attached to the room.

Radiography rooms without fluoroscopy need not have sinks, but do require a cabinet and shelves for storage of

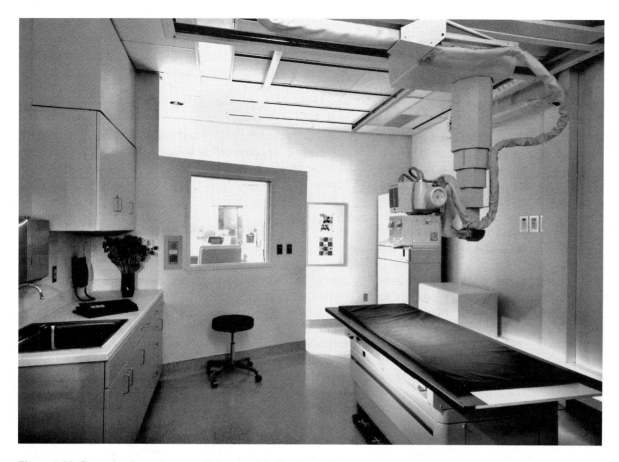

Figure 5-36. General radiography room. University of California San Francisco. (*Architecture and interior design: Anshen+Allen, San Francisco, CA; Photographer: Robert Canfield Photography.*)

Figure 5-37. SmartCR™ computed radiography plate reader with flat-panel touch screen and information processing unit. (*Photo courtesy: Fujifilm Medical Systems USA, Inc., Stamford, CT.*)

Odor Control. To prevent the spread of odors from the darkroom, the ventilation system should be designed so that negative air pressure, relative to adjoining corridors, is maintained. This can be accomplished by exhausting more air from this room than is supplied to it. This is only an issue if the fixer and developer replenisher tanks are located in the darkroom. As always, local codes must be followed. Similarly, bathrooms that serve R/F rooms (in consideration of the lower-GI examinations) deserve consideration with regard to exhaust of odors and recirculation of air.

Emergency Precautions. When laying out a radiology suite, thought must be given to the possible evacuation of a patient on a stretcher. Since most radiology suites are located on the ground floor, this may be accomplished by a secondary exit that leads directly to the parking lot, enabling an ambulance to pick up a patient without the patient having to be carried through the waiting room or the building lobby. Resuscitation equipment on a crash cart should be readily available to the procedure rooms. Radiologists sometimes request emergency call buzzers for procedure rooms, patient dressing rooms, and toilet rooms. The annunciator panel would be located at the reception desk.

Whenever working with chemicals or reagents, OSHA recommends an eyewash device, which can be a diverter attached to a faucet, as in Figure 3-50, or a dedicated unit wall mounted or placed in a countertop. The issue with an eyewash diverter is that, in a panic, one may turn on hot water to wash the eye, whereas a dedicated eyewash unit prevents this. Bear in mind that an eyewash unit should be located within a 10-second walk of where the accident might occur. Although historically it has not been common to locate an eyewash device adjacent to darkrooms or daylight processing units, it may be prudent to do so.

Lighting. There should be two types of lighting in a general radiography or R/F room: overhead fluorescents and indirect perimeter lighting, switched separately (Figure 5-32). Perimeter lighting should be able to be dimmed, as fluoroscopy procedures are done in a dark or dimly lit room. Note the upgrade to the acoustic ceiling tile in Figure 5-32, which adds considerably to the ambience of the room, as opposed to seeing exposed ceiling grid and the ubiquitous 2-×4-foot acoustical tiles.

ULTRASOUND

Since ultrasound does not use radiation, there is no need for lead shielding. The room should not be smaller than 10×12 feet in size. The patient lies on an examination table and the technologist typically works to the right side of the patient. The equipment is portable (Figures 3-60, 4-10, and 4-30), approximately 27 inches wide×34 inches deep×54 inches high, and consists of a microprocessor, videotape recorder, and monitor. Images may be sent to a PACS or a laser camera or a video recorder. Enhanced ultrasound units provide instantaneous 3-D images of anatomical structures including the liver, kidneys, thyroid, breast, and fetuses. Ultrasound equipment has no special electrical requirements, except for a dedicated circuit. However, the room is darkened for the procedure, and an ideal type of lighting would be indirect perimeter lighting that can be dimmed.

An ultrasound room must have a toilet immediately adjacent to accommodate voiding studies of the bladder. A cabinet with sink should be provided in the ultrasound room.

NUCLEAR MEDICINE

Historically, nuclear imaging equipment was found primarily in hospitals, rather than in the outpatient setting, because of its availability to both inpatients and outpatients and due to environmental issues of safely handling and disposing of radioactive materials. Statistics indicate that 75 percent of nuclear medicine imaging is hospital based; however, it is increasingly appearing in outpatient settings. Nuclear imaging also includes PET (positron emission tomography) scanners that image metabolic and biological functions of the body. An impressive new hybrid CT/PET scanner that combines the best of both modalities in one unit reveals exquisite images of internal anatomy (CT) and images of metabolic processes (PET).

Although there are numerous variables in equipment, these are the basic components:

1. Operator's console/workstation

2. Detector gantry (single, dual, or triple head)

3. Collimator

4. Patient bed (may be part of detector stand)

A nuclear imaging room does not require lead shielding, as the gamma camera emits no radiation; it picks up the small amount of radioactivity released by the organ being imaged. The patient ingests or is intravenously injected with a small amount of a radiopharmaceutical that travels through the bloodstream to the specific organ being studied. The patient prep room should be close to the hot lab where the radioactive material is prepared so that the tech never has to walk through patient circulation corridors carrying radioactive material. Having a nuclear scan can be an all-day process for a patient as explained below. In the interim, while they are radioactive, they should not mix with other patients in the waiting room as there is a risk, for example, of birth defects should this patient sit next to a pregnant woman in the first trimester who is waiting for an ultrasound. Sometimes patients leave the facility for a couple of hours and then return. A sub-waiting area near the nuclear imaging procedure rooms is practical, as is a dedicated toilet since human waste discharged from patients who have ingested radioactive materials could splash on the floor or toilet seat. Because the type (and amount) of radioisotopes used in *diagnostic studies* (as opposed to *treatment*) is minimal and decays quickly, the toilet waste can generally be discharged into the sewer system without being diverted to a holding tank; however, local codes should be consulted. The radioactive material dissipates quickly in the patient after the examination has been completed.

There are many types of nuclear medicine scans, including bone, liver, thyroid, lung, and gallbladder scans, to name a few. The time between administering the radioactive compound and taking the scan may vary, depending on the compound used and how long it takes to accumulate in the part of the body being studied. Some scans are performed a few hours after the injection, while others may be performed immediately. The scan itself may take anywhere from 30 minutes to two hours, again depending on the part of the body being studied. Gamma cameras may have single, dual, or triple detectors. A dual or triple head cuts the scan time because scanning is done from several locations at the same time. Collecting the data is vastly increased. Figure 5-38 shows the manufacturer's suggested layout for equipment shown in Figures 5-39 and 5-40. Because layout options for nuclear imaging equipment can vary considerably in

Room Layout Examples

E.CAM with left side patient access shown in large room.

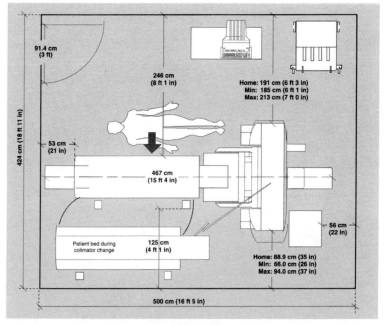

E.CAM with right side patient access shown in small room.

Figure 5-38. Suggested room layouts for Siemens e.cam™ nuclear medicine gamma camera. See Figures 5-39 and 5-40 for equipment depicted in this site plan. (*Illustration courtesy: Siemens Medical Systems, Inc., Hoffman Estates, IL.*)

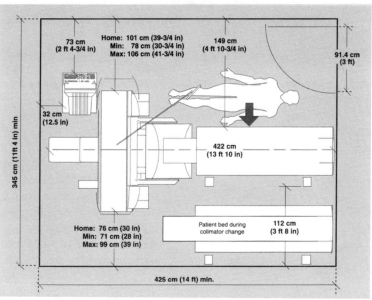

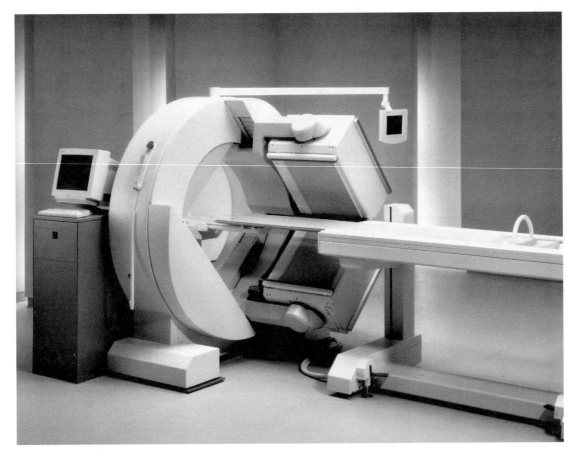

Figure 5-39. Siemens e.cam™ dual-detector-head nuclear medicine gamma camera. (*Photo courtesy: Siemens Medical Systems, Inc., Hoffman Estates, IL.*)

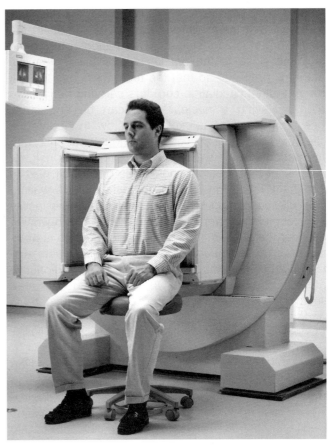

Figure 5-40. Siemens e.cam™ dual-detector-head nuclear medicine gamma camera, posterior seated view. (*Photo courtesy: Siemens Medical Systems, Inc., Hoffman Estates, IL.*)

shape and size, manufacturers should be contacted for suggested room layouts. As with any radiographic equipment, weights that exceed 3000 pounds require careful structural analysis as does the path of travel into the room and through doors. An example of a nuclear imaging workstation is depicted in Figure 5-41. The operator's console is in the procedure room and does not require lead shielding or enclosure.

The space planner may encounter the terminology *SPECT* in regard to nuclear imaging procedures. It

refers to *single-photon emission computed tomography* capability.

Nuclear Stress Test

This is used in conjunction with a dynamic ECG. The room may have a nuclear cardiology scanner (or a "general purpose" gamma camera), a workstation for the tech, and possibly a treadmill, although cardiac stress can also be imposed pharmacologically. This equipment may be accommodated in a dedicated room or it may be performed in a larger multipurpose nuclear imaging room.

Positron Emission Tomography

PET is a nuclear technology that offers intimate glimpses of molecular functioning (Figure 5-40). The volume of PET scanners in the total marketplace nationally is low due to the significant cost and licensing issues regarding technical staff who administer the scans. The PET market was given a boost in mid-1999 when HCFA decided to allow

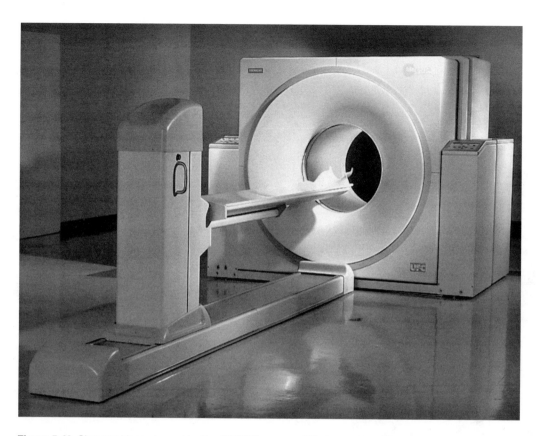

Figure 5-42. Siemens biograph combination CT/PET scanner. (*Photo courtesy: Siemens Medical Systems, Inc., Hoffman Estates, IL.*)

Figure 5-41. Siemens e.cam™ nuclear medicine operator's console. (*Photo courtesy: Siemens Medical Systems, Inc., Hoffman Estates, IL.*)

reimbursement of PET scans for five types of cancer, including cancer staging (a method of evaluating tumor growth), based on a number of clinical studies demonstrating that PET was considerably more accurate than conventional CT imaging for patients with certain types of cancers. HCFA is expected to expand its coverage of PET, which will most likely energize the market, but the combination PET/CT (Figure 5-42) is expected to constitute the state of the art for cancer diagnosis and management. In some regions, entrepreneurial radiologists have joined together in a business venture to purchase a PET scanner and contract with hospitals. Sometimes these are dedicated PET centers with no other imaging modalities.

Figure 5-43. Clear-Pb nuclear medicine mobile barrier. (*Photo courtesy: Nuclear Associates, Carle Place, NY.*)

Figure 5-44. Lead-lined refrigerator, hot lab. (*Photo courtesy: Nuclear Associates, Carle Place, NY.*)

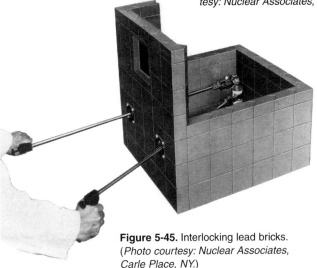

Figure 5-45. Interlocking lead bricks. (*Photo courtesy: Nuclear Associates, Carle Place, NY.*)

It should be noted that PET scan rooms do require lead shielding and that PET involves higher levels of radioactivity than with the standard nuclear gamma camera. The techs are in a separate room, similar to the layout for an operator's console in CT or MRI.

Tech Shielding

When tech shielding is required, the nuclear medicine mobile barrier in Figure 5-43, featuring lead-impregnated acrylic, may be used. The oversized window permits unobstructed viewing of the patient. This barrier (which comes in many sizes) may be positioned close to the patient table, and it shields the tech from patient-emitted radiation.

Hot Lab

This is a room, perhaps no larger than 6×8 feet, where radiopharmaceuticals are prepared. This is best located in a part of the suite where there is not a lot of traffic. It should be noted that unit-dose, freeze-dried "kits" specific to each study (e.g., lung kits, bone kits, etc.) have greatly reduced the amount of prep required and the amount and type of storage needed. With unit dose, a refrigerator and the various bins depicted in Figure 5-46 are not required, but as the use of unit dose is not universal, these items are pictured. The room would have 34-inch-high countertops with a single-compartment sink, and may have a lead-lined undercounter refrigerator (Figure 5-44), with some open shelves and hinged-door storage under the countertop. Note that the countertop must be steel reinforced in order to support the interlocking lead bricks (Figure 5-45) that will be placed on it. These may total as much as 1000 pounds. It may be more practical to buy a prefabricated workbench designed specifically for handling, storing, and disposing of radioactive materials (Figures 5-46 and 5-47). The modules of these workbenches are lead lined and encased in steel. Stainless steel countertops allow for easy cleaning and decontamination.

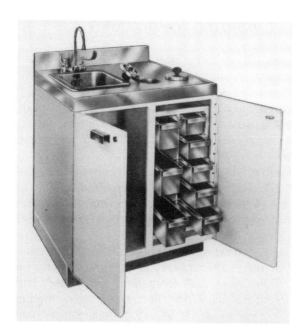

Figure 5-46. Workbench for handling radioactive materials. (*Photo courtesy: Nuclear Associates, Carle Place, NY.*)

Figure 5-47. Workbench for handling, storing, and disposing of radioactive materials (stainless steel countertop). (*Photo courtesy: Nuclear Associates, Carle Place, NY.*)

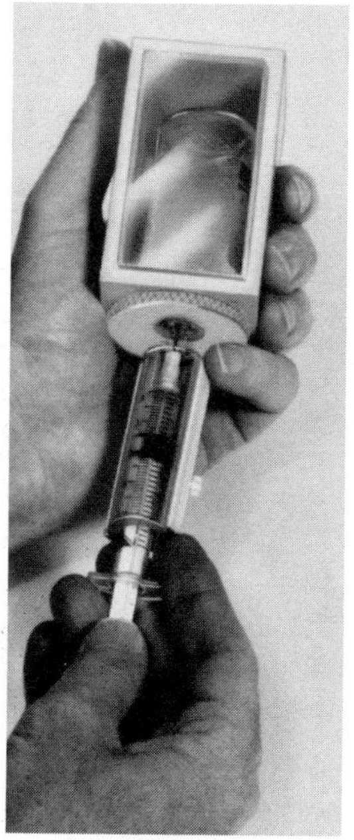

Figure 5-48. Vial shield for viewing, handling, and dispensing radioactive liquids. (*Photo courtesy: Nuclear Associates, Carle Place, NY.*)

Radioisotopes are stored in *vial shields* (Figure 5-48) from which the contents are dispensed. Vial shields of radiopharmaceuticals are stored in a small *safe* made up of interlocking lead bricks or in a lead container such as that shown in Figures 5-49 and 5-50. These containers may be placed on the countertop or on a shelf under it— one with enough space to lift the lid and access the contents of the safe.

Remember that safes range from 125 to 200 pounds in weight. Figures 5-51a and 5-51b show clear *benchtop shields* that provide a protective lead barrier from radiation exposure when working with radionuclides.

Electrical outlets are required over the countertop for radioisotope calibrators (Figure 5-52), the wipe test counter (Figure 5-53), and other accessory items. There is a need for storage of items used to mix agents such as vials and syringes, for gloves, and for gripping tools.

Figure 5-49. Square lead container for storing radioactive materials. (*Photo courtesy: Nuclear Associates, Carle Place, NY.*)

Figure 5-50. Lead storage container (safe) for storing radioactive materials. (*Photo courtesy: Nuclear Associates, Carle Place, NY.*)

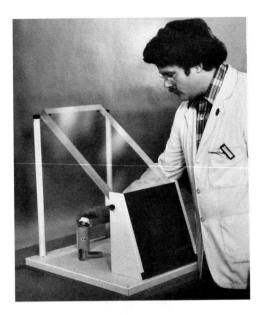

Figure 5-51a. Protective lead barrier for benchtops, hot lab. (*Photo courtesy: Nuclear Associates, Carle Place, NY.*)

Figure 5-51b. Protective lead barrier for benchtops, hot lab. (*Photo courtesy: Nuclear Associates, Carle Place, NY.*)

Figure 5-52. Computerized radioisotope calibrator. (*Photo courtesy: Nuclear Associates, Carle Place, NY.*)

Figure 5-53. Wipe test counter. (*Photo courtesy: Nuclear Associates, Carle Place, NY.*)

COMPUTED TOMOGRAPHY

The CT suite consists of a scanner or procedure room and a room with an operator's console. Manufacturers will supply engineering data sheets with alternative suggested layouts, critical dimensions, floor loading, and utility requirements. Some of the new multislice scanners require an electronics closet, which can be in the procedure room.

Although there are slight differences between different models of CT scanners, generally a procedure room 18 feet long by 14 feet wide and an adjoining room for the operator's console 8×14 feet will suffice (Figures 5-3 and 5-5).

The space planner should note that these are minimum space requirements, and larger spaces may be desirable. Remember that, for patient safety, sufficient access around the scanning unit must be maintained in case a patient becomes ill to allow the resuscitation team unobstructed access.

The procedure room is where the scanner gantry is located. The patient is positioned on a table that slides back and forth under a rotating doughnut-like enclosure; some units have a gantry that tilts. The room needs a built-in cabinet and sink and storage for clean linen, patient positioning devices, contrast media, and IV materials. A cart for soiled linen is also required. An 8-foot-long base cabinet with a wall cabinet or shelves above would be adequate. A couple of drawers might be partitioned for storage of alcohol preps, disposable syringes, injectables, contrast media, tubes, tape, and emesis (vomit) basin.

The ceiling of the room is normally 9 feet 6 inches high and the door should be at least 48 inches wide, with a heavy-duty closer. The walls and door will have to be lead shielded according to recommendations of a radiation physicist.

Room lighting must be controlled by a dimmer. Indirect lighting around the perimeter of the room will keep glare out of the patient's eyes. The massive size of this equipment can be frightening to patients, even though it does not have exposed cables and is quite streamlined in

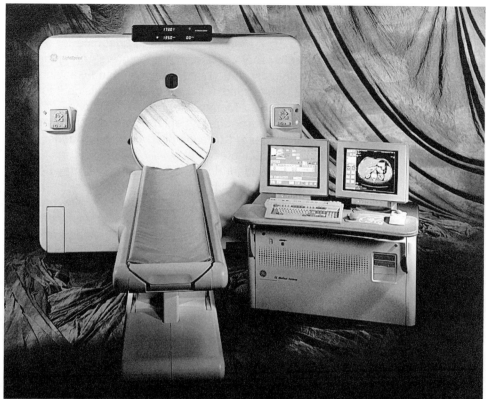

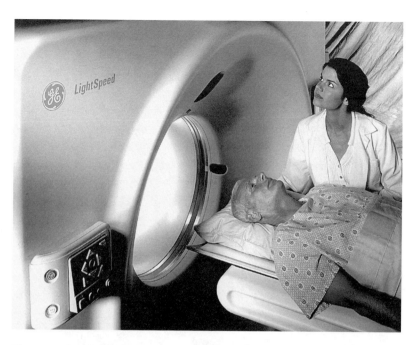

Figure 5-54b. GE LightSpeed OX/i multislice CT scanner. (*Photo courtesy: GE Medical Systems, Waukesha, WI.*)

Figure 5-54a. GE LightSpeed™ OX/i multislice CT scanner. (*Photo courtesy: GE Medical Systems, Waukesha, WI.*)

appearance (Figures 5-54a and 5-54b). A room with cheerful colors and a mural or back-lit film images of nature on the walls and/or ceiling can be quite effective in relaxing patients as in Color Plate 22, Figure 5-55. [Note that this is an old model of a GE CT scanner.]

The room with the operator's console is where the technologist sits during the procedure. It must have a lead-shielded window facing the procedure room so that the patient is always in view. A typical operator's console is depicted in Figure 5-54a. The dimmer control for procedure room lighting should be accessible from this room; however, this room also benefits from dimmer control to eliminate glare on computer monitors. A wall-mounted injector control is wired to the ceiling-mounted IV injector in the procedure room that allows the tech to manually time injections of contrast medium to alter the appearance of vascular structures so that they can be imaged.

Digital images are constructed during the scan (the multislice concept was explained previously) and images go to the network where they can be accessed by the radiologist for interpretation. Although older CT units that construct images on X-ray film may still be in use, totally digital formats are the norm.

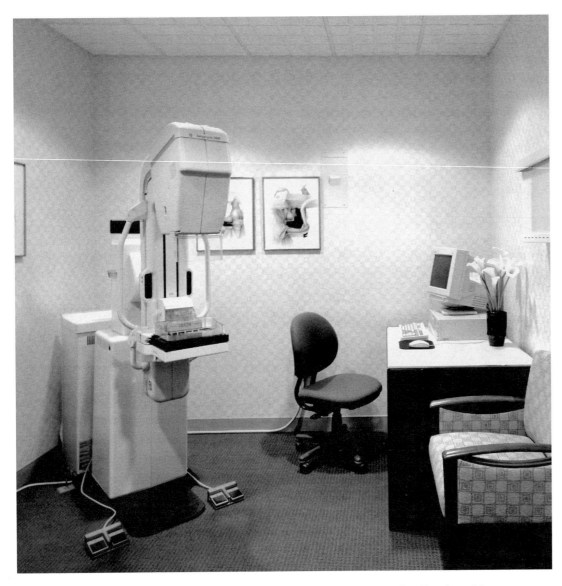

Figure 5-56. Mammography room, GE equipment. (*Photo courtesy: Anshen+Allen, San Francisco, CA; Photographer: Robert Canfield Photography.*)

MAMMOGRAPHY

A room 10 ×12 or 12 ×12 feet is adequate for a mammography room. Most manufacturers' equipment is approximately the same size. A hand-washing sink should be provided in the room or just outside it to serve several rooms. Mammography examinations are often performed in a women's center or breast center, and the reader is referred to a detailed discussion under these headings in Chapter 4.

An independent daylight processing unit may be used here so that the tech does not need to leave the patient and travel to the darkroom to process the film; however, in a few years it is expected that mammography units will be digital. Mammography equipment incorporates an attached leaded-glass protective screen behind which the operator stands. There are no unusual utility requirements for this equipment, and sometimes the walls may not need to be lead shielded. As with any diagnostic imaging equipment, however, a radiation physicist must be consulted.

An imaging suite having two or more mammography rooms may have equipment from more than one manufacturer, which may alter somewhat the orientation of the equipment in the room.

Indirect lighting is optimal for this type of room, and decorative wallpaper, carpeting, and attractive artwork make the patient's experience more pleasant (Figures 4-28, 4-29, and 5-56).

RADIATION ONCOLOGY

Also known as radiation therapy, radiation oncology is designed to bombard tumors with high doses of radiation. This is usually an outpatient-based modality found in large ambulatory-care centers and sometimes in a medical office building. It is mandatory that this tenant be identified while the building shell is being planned.

The room containing the linear accelerator (Figures 5-57 and 5-58) will have concrete walls of varying thickness anywhere from 24 to 60 inches. The amount of concrete can sometimes be reduced by the addition of steel or other materials. Sometimes this room can be situated on the site where the ground slopes (or below grade), to enable the room to be either partially or totally underground, reducing somewhat the radiation shielding requirements.

The radiation therapy space plan in Figure 5-59 illustrates the required ancillary rooms. Patients arriving for therapy may be ambulatory or may arrive on a gurney; therefore, both types of traffic must be accommodated. If the radiation therapy suite is part of a diagnostic imaging center, it is desirable to have a dedicated sub-waiting area for radiation therapy so that those patients need not wait with diagnostic radiology patients.

The design of a radiation oncology facility is worthy of an entire chapter as there are so many psychological issues associated with the treatment as well as innovative design solutions. The author's book *Hospital Interior Architecture* devotes an extensive chapter to these facilities; however, the two projects included in this text are illustrative of the highest level of design and patient amenities. Color Plate 23, Figure 5-57 features a floor that has the warmth and appearance of wood and suggests—in what is truly a concrete bunker or tomb—that there are windows with beautiful views of nature as well as skylights with cherry blossoms overhead. These back-lit film images are extraordinarily beautiful and provide a much needed diversion for patients undergoing radiation therapy. The equipment in Color Plates 23 and 24, Figures 5-57 and 5-58 is by Siemens. The unit in Figure 5-58 is the new Primus dual energy with multileaf collimation, which means a computer in the machine programs the setting, thereby performing the function of what lead blocks and molds would have done. This will change the design of linear accelerator rooms because it eliminates the need for shelves or racks for lead molds and the requirement for a room where molds are poured.

In the Mount Zion installation (Color Plate 24, Figure 5-58), a PermaGrain real-wood floor (has a clear acrylic coating and meets all fire codes) is complemented by a wall of wood casework that conceals the positioning light, plumbing, and electronic equipment. As patients enter the room, their eye is drawn to back-lit panels of fabric that have the feeling of shoji screen. Clearly, the most dramatic aspect of the room is the ceiling designed with fiber-optic lights and indirect uplighting around the perimeter of the circle. There are five different lighting settings that change the color at the patient's request.

The layout of the vault is innovative in that it addresses psychological issues of the patient as well as functional issues to reduce the weight of the shielded door which, in turn, affects the time it takes for the door, to open and close. There is a double-door entry so that the patient walks through a wooden architectural door that has a "soft" appearance. The gigantic, thick shielded door is out of view and, by the time a patient encounters it, it is in the fully open position and the eye is drawn to the beauty of the ceiling. Typically, linear accelerator vaults have a maze design to deflect the radiation. The entire layout of this department deserves commendation for excellent space planning: the separation of male and female gowned waiting, functional adjacencies of rooms, and corridors without jogs to make wayfinding easy.

Dressing rooms and examination rooms need to be provided, along with the radiation physicist's office, which has a large computerized workstation, and a tech work area. The tech work area has TV monitors that allow techs to view patients in the therapy room. A large conference room is needed to enable the entire treatment team to meet to plan treatment for each patient. The physicians who work in this specialty are called radiation oncologists.

Most rooms of this suite, including the linear accelerator room, may be carpeted. Other design options for the vault include a full-wall trompe l'oeil (fool the eye) mural (Color Plates 9 and 18, Figures 4-20 and 4-101, respectively), which provides a psychological escape for the patient.

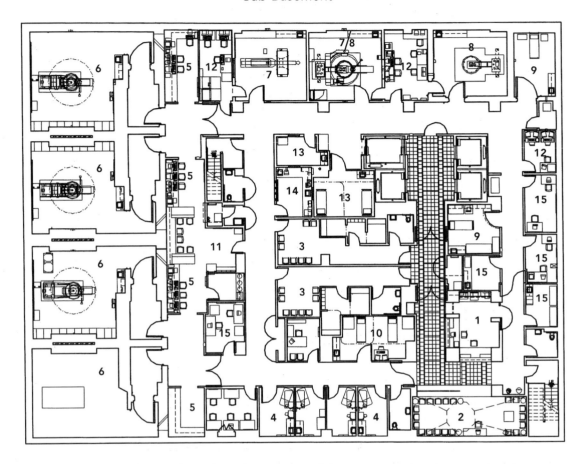

MOUNT ZION COMPREHENSIVE CANCER CENTER

RADIATION ONCOLOGY

1.	Reception	6.	Linear Accelerator	11.	Image Review
2.	Family Waiting	7.	CT Simulation	12.	Control
3.	Gowned Waiting	8.	HDR Imaging	13.	Patient Holding
4.	Exam	9.	HDR Procedure	14.	Nurse Station
5.	Linear Accelerator Control	10.	Hyperthermia	15.	Work Area / Support

Figure 5-59. Space plan, radiation oncology. University of California San Francisco, Mount Zion Comprehensive Cancer Center. (*Architecture and design: SmithGroup, San Francisco, CA; Photographer: Michael O'Callahan.*)

MAGNETIC RESONANCE IMAGING

Magnetic resonance imaging (MRI) is considered by many to be the most revolutionary imaging technology of the century. Manufacturers of radiology equipment have committed large sums of money to engineering, research, and product development to continually expand the capabilities of MRI. For example, advances in magnet technology have continually reduced the area of magnetic field influence (the Gauss field) surrounding the equipment to the point where it is for the most part contained within the room itself.

This discussion will acquaint readers with the basic principles of MRI facility planning and design. Each manufacturer's equipment will vary somewhat in terms of room layout, depending on magnet weight and strength. Manufacturers will supply technical manuals to aid the architect or designer in planning the space.

MRI uses computers and magnetic fields to provide noninvasive images of human anatomy. It does not involve radiation but, rather, uses powerful superconducting magnets to generate magnetic fields 8000 times stronger than that of the earth.

High-strength magnets (which were the only ones available until a few years ago) constitute a problem for those who are claustrophobic. The magnet—essentially a cube 8 feet in size—has a fairly narrow channel (the bore) in the center through which the patient's body travels. The "bed" that the patient lies on slides through the bore. It gives some individuals the feeling of being buried alive. As the typical scan may last 45 minutes and one is instructed to lie perfectly still with arms and hands folded across one's chest, it can be a torturous experience that occasionally results in panic attacks, causing the study to be aborted and the patient sedated. Manufacturers have worked hard to solve this problem by developing open MRIs that are lower in strength, and although they cannot be used in lieu of the superconducting magnets for some patients, they are very popular with consumers and frequently marketed to the public in local newspaper and TV ads (Color Plate 25, Figure 5-60, and Figure 5-61). Initially, when first introduced, open MRIs were weak, required longer scanning times, and could not perform

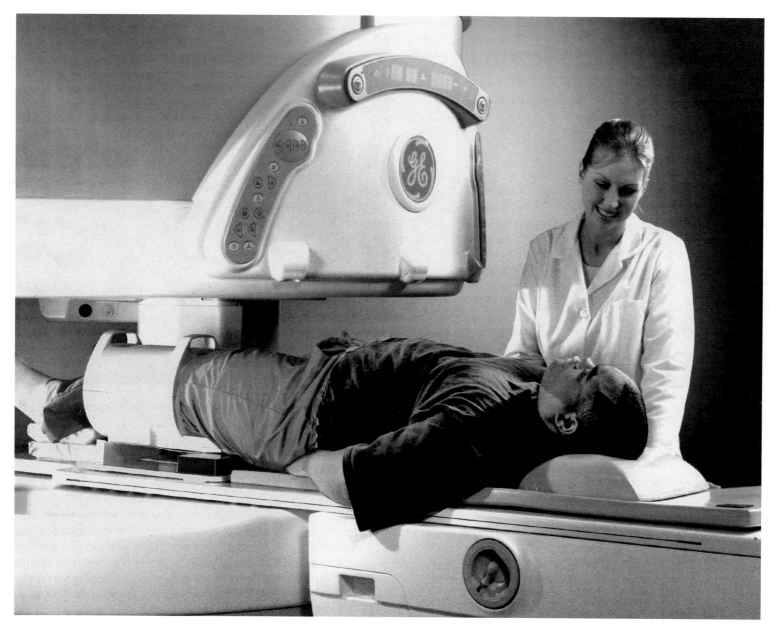

Figure 5-61. GE OpenSpeed™ MRI. (*Photo courtesy: GE Medical Systems, Waukesha, WI.*)

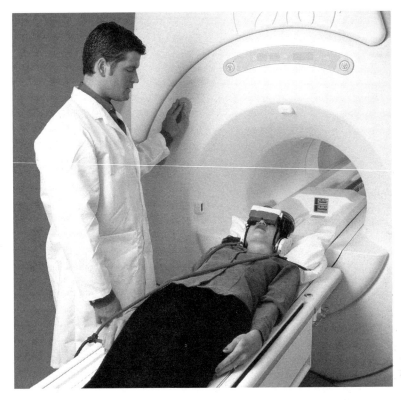

Figure 5-62. Patient wearing visor watches 3-D video to ease claustrophobia during MRI procedure. Figure 5-63 illustrates the view. (*Photo courtesy: Resonance Technology, Inc., Northridge, CA.*)

Figure 5-63. Diagram of video view seen by patient. (*Photo courtesy: Resonance Technology, Inc., Northridge, CA.*)

certain applications. The unit in Figure 5-61 is a 0.7 tesla—one of the higher-strength open magnets—but these can be difficult to site as they are highly sensitive to vibration. They are also incredibly heavy (in excess of 29,000 pounds) as open magnets are steel and run on electricity. Cryogens are not required. Some of the higher-strength open magnets in development are expected to weigh 90,000 pounds. Open magnets are used for imaging the knee, shoulder, ankle, spine, and brain, and they can also be used to monitor stroke therapy.

The trend is toward superconducting magnets with shorter bores such as the 1.5-tesla magnet in Figure 5-64, which is just 54 inches in length, and even this is visually reduced by the flared opening at both ends. The

reduced size also results in reduced weight, which, in this case, is 6000 pounds. However, many of the older MRI units (with deep bores) will still be in service as there are no moving parts and the software can continually be upgraded. How the data are processed is the important issue. A dedicated phone line into the system allows the software to be upgraded (or remote diagnostic troubleshooting to be carried out) during the night without disruption of patient scheduling during the day.

Feelings of claustrophobia can be lessened in the large-bore magnets through the use of virtual reality. A patient can wear a visor that delivers 3-D video at a resolution of 180,000 pixels (Figure 5-62). Obviously, it's difficult to capture a view of the video from the patient's perspective inside the magnet, but Figure 5-63 simulates it. It would be in vibrant color, of course, and integrated with an audio system. Soothing images and sounds of nature deal with another vexing aspect of MRI, namely, the noise generated by the machine (when current is applied to the copper gradient coils), which sounds like an air hammer. Acoustic wall treatments help to provide a quieter environment when the patient enters the room, which may lessen the patient's anxiety. Once the study is under way, the noise increases, and the acoustic attenuation in the room may not lessen the noise for the patient inside the bore. If this is frightening to many adults, imagine how traumatic it can be for children, although parents can be in the room for comfort, and diversions such as the virtual-reality video with cartoons may help.

Innovation in MRI is continually advancing as digital technology enables ever higher levels of sophistication in imaging. For example, interactive software allows radiologists to pan around the patient's anatomy in real time to find the most appropriate locations to image. It can also measure how long it takes for a contrast agent to travel from the point of injection to the blood vessel being studied—physicians can do studies in real time as patients breathe and move.

Planning Considerations

Large superconductive magnets (Figures 5-64 and 5-65) are 1.5 teslas and higher in strength. A number of issues must be evaluated before choosing the site for an MRI facility.

1. Magnet's effect on the surrounding environment

2. Environment's effect on the magnet

3. Corridor/door sizes for transport of magnet during installation

4. Convenient access for delivery of dewars for magnet cryogen replenishment and for servicing the equipment

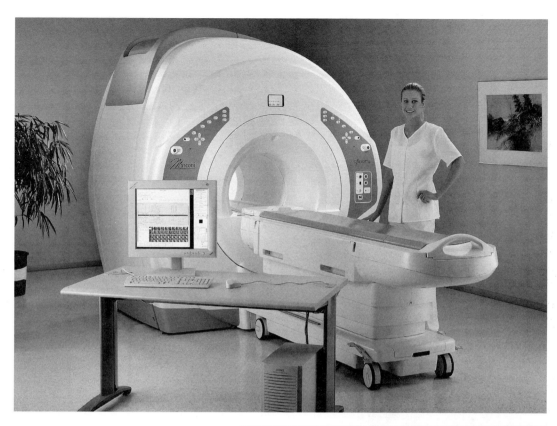

Figure 5-64. Marconi Infinion™ short-bore superconducting magnet. (*Photo courtesy: Marconi Medical Systems, Cleveland, OH.*)

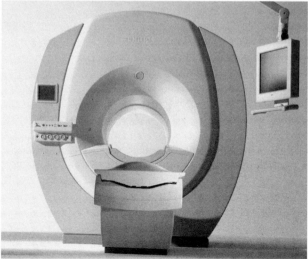

Figure 5-65. Philips GYROSCAN Intera 1.5T MRI. (*Photo courtesy: Philips Medical Systems North America, Shelton, CT.*)

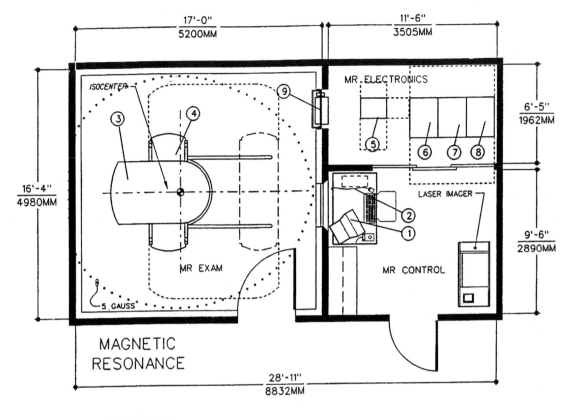

Figure 5-66. Typical room layout (475 square feet) for Marconi 0.23T Proview open MRI. See Figure 5-67 for equipment depicted in this layout. (*Illustration courtesy: Marconi Medical Systems, Cleveland, OH.*)

MAGNETIC RESONANCE

EQUIPMENT

1 OPERATOR CONSOLE
2 COMPUTER MODULE
3 MAGNET ENCLOSURE
4 MOBILE COUCH/LONG TRACK
5 TEMP. CONTROL UNIT
6 POWER AMPLIFIER
7 ELECTRONICS SCAN
8 POWER DISTRIBUTION UNIT
9 RF PENETRATION PANEL

5. Area of magnetic field influence

6. Radiofrequency interference (RFI) shielding

7. HVAC

8. Power requirements

9. Floor loading

10. Storage of accessory items

11. Interior design

Magnet's Effect on Environment

The influence of a strong magnetic field upon the surrounding environment must be considered, although today's magnets are internally shielded and the Gauss field is contained principally within the room as illustrated in Figure 5-66, which depicts the layout for the open MRI in Figure 5-67. For the most part, fringe fields are within the room, but looking at Figures 5-68 and 5-69a for superconducting-strength magnets, portions of the 5-gauss field may fall outside the room. Figure 5-69b is a layout for a 3.0-tesla superconducting magnet, which requires a considerably larger area (1156 square feet) compared to the 1.5-tesla magnet in Figure 5-69a (470 square feet). Notice that the 5-gauss field in Figure 5-69b is contained within the MRI suite of rooms. Note also that Figure 5-69a is the layout for the magnet in Figure 5-64. The 5-gauss field is the FDA recommendation for safety with respect to individuals who have pacemakers. The Gauss field is measured from the center of the magnet in all directions. If the 5-gauss line extends outside the room, the area must be secured and a sign posted notifying passersby of the high magnetic field. If the area extends outdoors, it must be secured with a chainlink fence. When the magnet is up and running, the 5-gauss field must be measured and a report filled out and filed with regulators.

Magnetic fields are three dimensional, extending outward on all sides, above and below, measured from the exact center of the magnet. Related to the magnet's maximum operating field strength, the fringe magnetic field (the measurable stray field around the magnet) decreases in strength the farther one is from the center of the magnet.

People with heart pacemakers are especially vulnerable, as are any sort of electronic or electromagnetic systems. Information on credit cards or magnetic tapes may be erased. Even more sensitive are cathode ray tubes, image intensifiers, or other types of electronic equipment commonly found in diagnostic imaging systems. These must be kept out of the 1-gauss line. (As a point of information, gauss and tesla are units of measurement of magnetic field strength. 1 tesla = 10 kilogauss.)

An assessment of all adjacent areas within the influence of the magnet is required to carefully identify the presence of equipment, people, or materials that may be sensitive to the magnetic field.

Environment's Effect on Magnet

The presence of ferrous material within the vicinity of the magnet can adversely affect the equipment's performance. Ferromagnetic material may be either stationary or moving. Moving objects may include an elevator in the vicinity of the magnet, a passing automobile, or a piece of garden maintenance equipment. Structural steel beams and reinforced concrete in floors, ceilings, or walls are examples of stationary materials that may interfere with a distortion-free image.

The negative effects of stationary material can sometimes be minimized by positioning the magnet symmetrically between and/or parallel to the ferromagnetic objects. *Shims* (energized coils that provide a magnetic field opposite to the one causing the disturbance) are another method of compensating for stationary ferrous objects. The most critical area is the floor immediately under the magnet. Each manufacturer has a specification on the allowable number of pounds of steel in a 10-foot-square area under the magnet. The next area of concern is immediately above the magnet, namely, the direction of the I-beams running overhead. If diagonal, it constitutes a problem. The magnet should be parallel and perpendicular to the steel in order not to disturb the magnetic field. High-tension power lines can also affect the magnet. However, one can evaluate the site with a Gauss meter to read the magnetic fields in the vicinity to see how best to site the unit. All metals have a maximum saturation, which

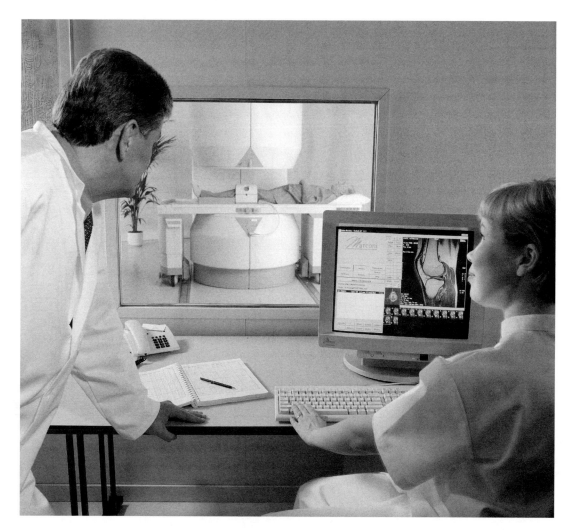

Figure 5-67. Marconi 0.23T Proview open MRI. (*Illustration courtesy: Marconi Medical Systems, Cleveland, OH.*)

means there is a limit as to how magnetized they can become. Stainless steel, for example, is at the low end with little potential to affect a magnet. An elevator in a corridor outside the MRI unit constitutes a large magnetic field that can interfere with the magnet, especially since it is a moving object.

Figure 5-68. Suggested room layout for GRYOSCAN Intera 1.5T MRI. See Figure 5-65 for equipment depicted in this layout. (*Illustration courtesy: Philips Medical Systems North America, Shelton, CT.*)

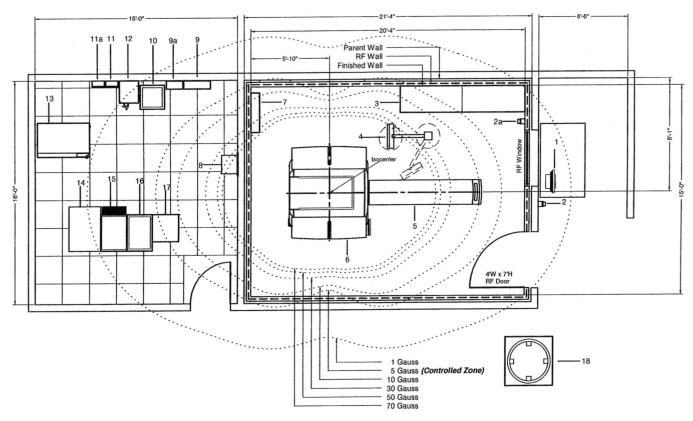

PREFERRED ROOM LAYOUT

GYROSCAN Intera 1.5T Power

(1)	Operator Console	(10)	Power Distribution Cabinet
(2) (2a)	Emergency Run-Down Button	(11)	System Circuit Breaker
(3)	RF Coil Storage Cabinet	(11a)	Chiller Circuit Breaker
(4)	Interactive Display	(12)	Cryocooler Compressor
(5)	Patient Support	(13)	Neslab HX750 Chiller
(6)	Magnet Assembly	(14)	Gradient Amplifiers 274
(7)	System Filter Panel	(15)	NT Data Acquisition Cabinet
(8)	Patient Ventilation Fan	(16)	RF Amplifier Cabinet
(9)	Main Distribution Unit	(17)	Gradient Heat Exchanger
(9a)	Main Distribution Extended	(18)	Helium Dewar

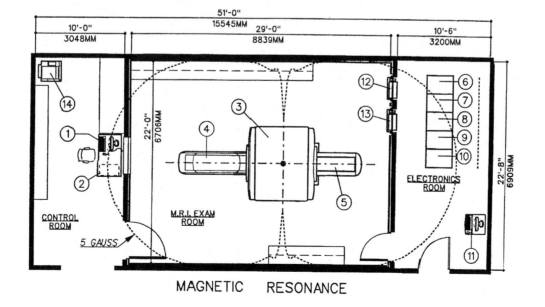

Figure 5-69a. Typical room layout (470 square feet) for Marconi Infinion™ 1.5T MRI; equipment depicted in Figure 5-64. (*Illustration courtesy: Marconi Medical Systems, Cleveland, OH.*)

Figure 5-69b. Typical room layout (1156 square feet) for Marconi Infinion™ 3.0T MRI. (*Illustration courtesy: Marconi Medical Systems, Cleveland, OH.*)

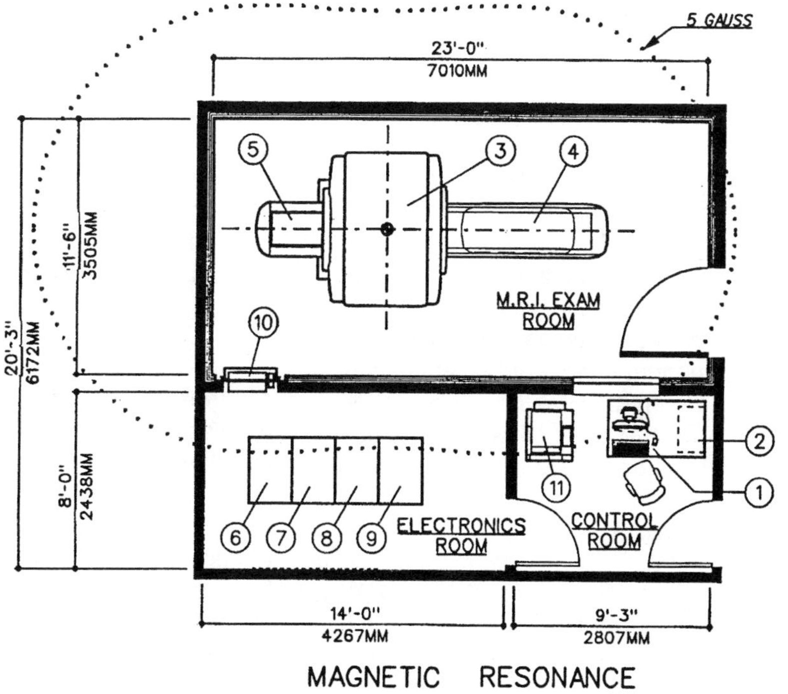

EQUIPMENT

1   OPERATOR CONSOLE
2   COMPUTER MODULE
3   MAGNET ENCLOSURE
4   PATIENT COUCH
5   BLOWER/ COUCH EXTENSION
6   CRYO. REFROG./ H.E.
7   SCAN RCON/RF AMP/PDU
8   GRADIENT CABINET #1
9   GRADIENT CABINET #2
10 RF PENETRATION PANEL
11 LASER IMAGER

EQUIPMENT

1   OPERATOR CONSOLE
2   COMPUTER MODULE
3   MAGNET ENCLOSURE
4   PATIENT COUCH
5   BLOWER/ COUCH EXTENSION
6   CRYO. REFROG./ H.E.
7   SCAN RECON/RF AMP/PDU
8   SHIM CABINET
9   GRADIENT CABINET #1
10 GRADIENT CABINET #2
11 I−FMRI PC RACK (OPTION)
12 RF PENETRATION PANEL
13 RF PENETRATION PANEL
14 LASER IMAGER

MAGNETIC   RESONANCE

MAGNETIC   RESONANCE

It is critically important to estimate, by taking physical measurements of the site, the influence of moving ferrous objects that may produce an image artifact. Each manufacturer supplies an overlay grid that indicates, in concentric circles, the Gauss field and indicates the distance, in feet, moving away from the center of the magnet.

There are a number of other issues that should be considered. Light fixtures within the 5-gauss field must be of nonmagnetic material. Fluorescent lighting must not be used within the R/F shielded room containing the magnet. Incandescent lighting with rheostatic-type light dimmers may be used within the magnet room, but SCR-type dimmers may not be used. Commonly used medical accessory items such as oxygen cylinders, IV poles, and gurneys may not be used within the 5-gauss line. Framework for suspended ceilings must be of aluminum. Metal studs, however, may be used in walls.

Magnet Transport Access

Consideration must be given to the transport of a magnet during installation. Corridor and door sizes, as well as floor strength, must be adequate to handle a 13,000-pound superconducting magnet or 29,000-pound open magnet. This piece of equipment cannot be broken down into smaller components. One might wonder how it arrives at the room. It is often brought through the roof or the side of the building. An MRI site should be planned at the time the medical office building is designed so that issues of access can be considered. It's important not just to get it into the room initially, but to think about how one would remove it through a roof hatch or an access panel in the exterior wall. If traveling down a corridor, the load is spread on 2-×12-×16-foot-long planks of wood.

Cryogenic Replenishment

Superconducting magnets carry electrical current free of resistance only at cryogenic temperatures, necessitating cooling by liquid helium and nitrogen. Storage cylinders containing liquid helium and liquid nitrogen are called dewars. Facilities no longer store dewars on site because newer units don't need to be replenished as frequently and the dewars are delivered by a service as needed. It should be noted that although they do not show in the manufacturers' marketing photos, there is a cryogen replenishment "chimney" or turret at the top of the magnet and some cabling. In some models, the cryogen tube folds and is recessed into the machine housing (Figure 5-64). There is also an electronic box for the gradient and shim coils on the side.

Magnetic Field Influence

As discussed previously, the extent of the magnetic field of influence would be determined by the size of the magnet. A superconducting magnet of 1.5 tesla has a larger field of influence than a less powerful one. Minimum safety distances for objects in the magnetic fringe field must be carefully assessed. Inside the facility, a strict protocol regarding patient screening, the use of metal detectors, and architectural barriers can be used to protect visitors, as well as protect the magnet. A ferrous object in a person's pocket can become a lethal projectile if too close to the magnet. For this reason, it's important to provide lockers for patients' valuables, as all jewelry, wristwatches, wallets, and so forth must be stowed.

Radiofrequency Interference Shielding

There are two types of shielding in an MRI facility. One is shielding to contain the magnetic field (however, machines are currently internally shielded); the other is shielding from radiofrequency interference (RFI). Noise generated by stray radiofrequencies distorts the image. Any penetrations in the room, such as doors, windows, light fixtures, or mechanical ductwork, must be filtered to prevent radiofrequency interference. Some brands of equipment are internally shielded from RFI, thereby eliminating the cost of shielding the room. There are many variables here; sometimes just half the room requires RFI shielding.

HVAC

A careful analysis of the heat output of the equipment must be made, and each area must be individually environmentally controlled so that the heat load in one room does not adversely affect the temperature and humidity of other rooms. An audible thermal alarm may be required in the computer room to alert the operator if the ambient temperature exceeds operating limits. An air filtration system may be required in the computer equipment room. Some units need chilled water for cooling the power supply, while others are air cooled, eliminating the need for water.

A vent system must be provided to exhaust helium and nitrogen to the outside of the building. Precautions must be taken to ensure that the exit end of the exhaust duct does not allow gases to be vented into a closed area or allow access to passersby within 10 feet of the duct in order to protect people from cold burns.

Power Requirements

A power conditioner unit is a component of most MRI systems to assure a clean, continuous power source with minimum fluctuation. A power management system or power conditioner controls electrical surges and spikes, which are the principal causes of computer malfunction.

Floor Loading

MRI magnets (superconducting) average 13,000 pounds, concentrated in a relatively small area. The floor space immediately under the magnet is of critical concern with respect to allowable amounts of ferrous material used in construction of the slab. Manufacturers' recommendations must be carefully followed in this regard.

Storage of Accessory Items

A 24-inch-deep closet should be considered in the procedure room for storage of the body coil calibration kit and for breast and head coils, which are heavy to carry around.

Interior Design

When MRI was first introduced, it was thought that any ferrous substance would negatively affect image quality. Very expensive construction techniques using totally nonferrous materials were standard procedure. Wood beams, glued connections, stainless steel nails, Fiberglas, copper, and aluminum were considered appropriate construction materials. Now, however, manufacturers generally agree that shimming of the magnet is able to compensate for *static* ferrous building materials. The use of conventional construction techniques and materials greatly reduces the expense of constructing an MRI facility.

Carpeting may be used in the examination (magnet) room, although it has the potential to create dust and contribute fiber particles to the air that may affect the equipment. If used, manufacturer's specifications must be checked to verify that the carpet has the proper amount of static control. The computer room will generally have computer-access-type flooring, making this an optimum condition for the installation of carpet tile.

The ceiling height of the magnet room will generally be 9 or 10 feet for a superconducting magnet. Ancillary areas will usually be 9 feet in height.

A view of the outdoors or a garden can occasionally be achieved in the siting of the unit as in Color Plate 25, Figure 5-70. A simulated view of nature can be achieved with back-lit film transparencies overhead. Considering the cost of this equipment and the inherent fear and anxiety that many patients experience, it is tragic to find these units placed in rooms with no interior design amenities—with vinyl composition tile (VCT) flooring, painted walls, and a 2-×4-foot acoustic tile ceiling with direct lighting overhead. A wallpaper border does not constitute interior design and does nothing to relax patients. Bland, clinical diagnostic imaging environments are created all too often. It is hoped that the photo images in this book will stimulate a desire to go beyond this.

CLINICAL LABORATORY

Laboratory tests are a vital tool in diagnosing disease. A basic part of a thorough examination, these studies may be performed in a small room within the physician's office or in a sophisticated clinical laboratory located within a medical office building, in an adjacent hospital, or in a distant laboratory. A physician may take a blood or urine specimen from a patient, but send it out for testing to a reference laboratory. Others will do simple tests in the office, but send out the more complicated ones. The i-STAT handheld analyzer (Figure 5-71) is an example of what may become more commonplace in coming years for tests performed in physicians' offices. The instrument performs the following "waived" tests: prothrombin times, blood gases, electrolytes, glucose, and creatinine but does not do hematology. Refer to Chapter 3, CLIA Compliance, for a discussion of waived and nonwaived tests and how CLIA has affected what tests physicians ordinarily do in their offices. Currently, government agencies are establishing new regulations for physician-operated laboratories.

The designer of a medical office building will most often encounter small clinical labs. Large labs, employing a pathologist, will usually be designed by a lab specialist experienced in the planning of such facilities. It is unlikely that a large clinical lab will be included in a medical office building if that building is adjacent to a hospital. Sometimes a "drawing station" will be provided in an MOB with specimens processed and tested at another location (Figure 5-72). This discussion, then, is limited to introducing the reader to basic laboratory processes and space requirements—some of which will occur in a small laboratory facility.

Figure 5-71. i-STAT handheld analyzer. (*Photo courtesy: Abbott Diagnostics, Abbott Park, IL.*)

CLIA and Other Regulations

The Clinical Laboratory Improvement Act (CLIA), reported in the *Federal Register,* imposes strict regulations on laboratories, some of which may affect design but mostly deal with processes and procedures, safety, billing, record keeping, and the like. At the outset of a project, it's important to understand the requirements for accreditation and licensing by a potential number of agencies. In addition, as can be expected, OSHA has many standards and regulations that assure the safety of laboratory personnel.

Development of the Requirements

As with all medical suites, the success of a well-designed laboratory is dependent on a thorough understanding of needs—a written description of all requirements that must be incorporated into the design.

The following checklist will serve as a guide:

1. List the procedures that are to be performed. They will vary with the medical specialties of the building's tenants.

2. Analyze the space in terms of projected equipment and personnel in three areas:
   a. Administrative.
   b. Technical.
   c. Support (includes washing, sterilization, biohazardous waste storage, reagent and supply storage, computer hardware, clean and dirty lab coats, lockers, and laboratory records). Storage is required at workbenches for manuals, disposables, and constantly used items. Open shelves and closed storage are required.

3. Review sizes and specifications of major pieces of equipment. Tabulate the lineal feet of high and low countertop space required for each item or area and note required adjacencies. Determine if equipment will have special plumbing, electrical, and temperature requirements.

4. Determine which procedures may be combined in the same work area and which require separate areas (Figure 5-73).

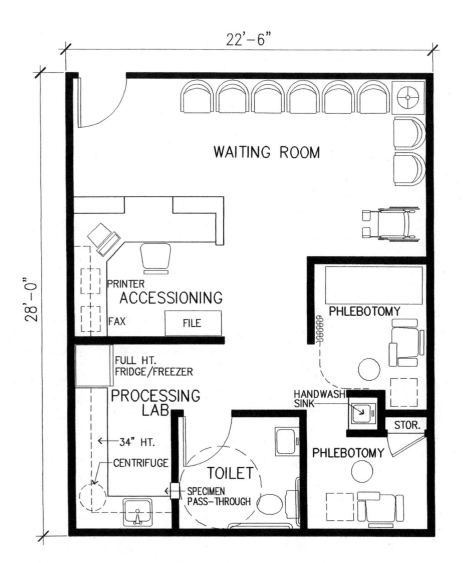

LAB BLOOD DRAWING STATION

630 SF

Figure 5-72. Space plan for laboratory blood-drawing station, 630 square feet. (*Design: Jain Malkin Inc.*)

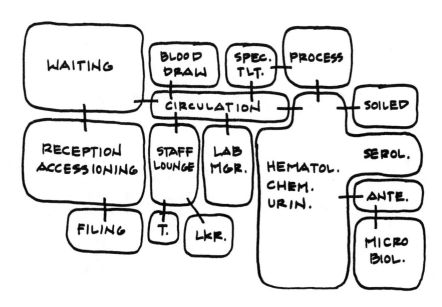

Figure 5-73. Schematic diagram of clinical laboratory.

5. Divide technical areas by functional units: hematology, chemistry, microbiology, urinalysis, serology, but the trend is to avoid (except for microbiology) enclosing them with walls; an open area is more flexible.

6. Estimate the volume of tests in each functional unit in order to determine the number of tech workstations required.

7. Review desirable functional adjacencies. For example, urinalysis can be combined with either chemistry or hematology. Hematology can be located near the blood drawing area since those specimens do not require additional processing prior to analysis. Due to the prevalence of disposables and premade reagents, the amount of glassware has been greatly reduced. If the laboratory does need a glass-washing/sterilization area, it should be located near microbiology or chemistry. Small laboratories have a limited staff; therefore, technical modules need to be clustered together so that staff working in each unit can support each other.

8. Allow for future expansion. If any units are expected to expand in terms of physical space, they would best be located in the area of the suite adjacent to the laboratory and where expansion may easily occur without infringing upon existing critical office functions.

9. Review utility requirements for all equipment carefully. Separate electrical circuits are required for many instruments in order to avoid fluctuating voltage, which adversely affects the accuracy of the instruments. During construction, it is a good idea to leave room in the panel for future power requirements and potential need for a 220-volt circuit.

10. Determine which equipment and space, if any, will be shared among departments. Depending on the size and volume of testing performed in the laboratory, either common-use or dedicated refrigerators, freezers, computer terminals, and clerical space will be needed. In some space plans and based on workflow,

the refrigerators and freezers may be "banked" together in a location convenient to all departments. These may need to be anchored to the wall in earthquake-prone areas. The refrigerator is a wide, deep restaurant type with glazed doors, and the freezer an upright model.

11. Allot storage space for supplies used on a daily basis in each technical module. A storage room would be used for bulk purchase of supplies.

12. Consider environmental factors such as ventilation, light, and isolation of equipment that may be noisy or produce heat when used.

Technical Modules

The following descriptions of technical modules will familiarize readers with standard methods of processing samples. Electronic, automated clinical analyzers are widely used even by small labs. Instrument manufacturers in recent years have designed automated equipment specifically for this market, the price of which has been brought in line with what the small laboratory can afford. Newer equipment is often capable of performing a variety of tests that formerly required several instruments.

Hematology. This is the study of the cellular components of blood. Procedures performed in this area are those most frequently ordered by a physician such as CBCs (complete blood counts); thus, this module should be located close to the phlebotomy (blood drawing) station for most efficient workflow (Figure 5-74).

One half of the module should be set aside for procedures such as sedimentation rates (a level, stable work surface is needed), the hematology analyzer, and slide staining. Another portion of the work surface (at 30-inch height) should have knee space for sit-down work at the microscope. If there is a microhematocrit centrifuge

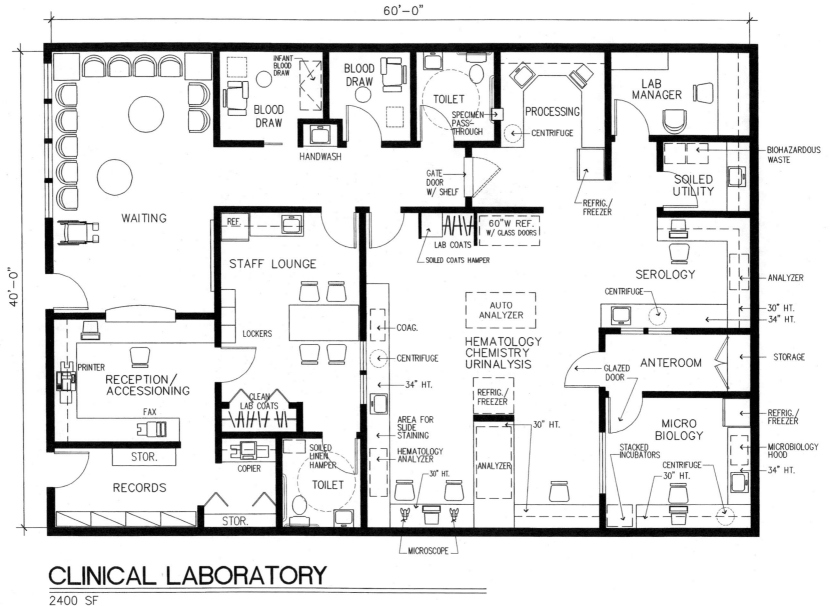

CLINICAL LABORATORY

2400 SF

Figure 5-74. Space plan for clinical laboratory, 2400 square feet. (*Design: Jain Malkin Inc.*)

Figure 5-75. SPINCHRON® DLX centrifuge. (*Photo courtesy: Beckman Coulter, Inc., Brea, CA.*)

Figure 5-76. Cell-Dyn® 3200 hematology analyzer. (*Photo courtesy: Abbott Diagnostics, Abbott Park, IL.*)

(Figure 5-75), due to its noise and vibration when in use, it should be placed in an area where it will not disturb anyone or interfere with the microscopic examination of slides. In a small-volume lab, a refrigerator/freezer, desk, and computer terminal (if applicable) should be centrally located for use by hematology, urinalysis, and chemistry. Critical adjacencies of equipment are dependent on staffing and whether one tech is doing a few tests in each area. If, because of the physician mix or the presence of an ambulatory surgical center, coagulation tests, such as prothrombin time, are to be done, they would be performed in this unit. Additional benchtop space would be needed for a coagulation instrument and a high-speed centrifuge. The hematology analyzer is often a benchtop instrument (Figure 5-76).

Chemistry. A variety of chemical procedures are performed here. Most manual testing is done at a 34-inch-high countertop, but a lowered knee-space area should be provided for seated procedures or benchtop instruments. There should be floor space for larger multitest instruments in laboratories supporting a large number of physicians (Figures 5-77 and 5-78). One countertop will

have open shelves above for chemicals used during procedures and for disposables and constantly used items. However, these shelves should have a protective barrier such as a 3-inch-high Plexiglas band at the edge to prevent the fall of items in case of an earthquake or accident. A sink is required in the chemistry work area, and built-in cabinetry would consist of drawers and hinged-door storage below the countertop. It is useful if the bottom drawers in a few locations are file drawers to keep frequently used references at hand. Ninety percent of the specimens are blood; 10 percent are urine.

An instrument table or countertop should be available for small instruments or manual tests. The area will require countertop space for a centrifuge. Depending on the volume of work performed in the laboratory, this centrifuge could be shared by specimen processing, if adjacencies exist.

Urinalysis. This unit may be located in the hematology or the chemistry module. One half of the urinalysis work counter is used for microscopic examinations and the other half for chemical procedures. The work surface should be 30 inches high and have a sink.

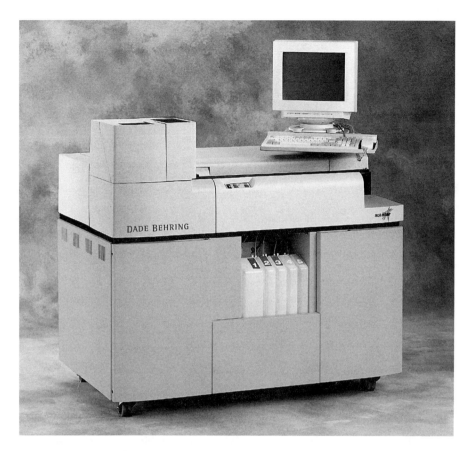

Figure 5-77. aca® Star™ chemistry analyzer. (*Photo courtesy: Dade Behring, Inc., Deerfield, IL.*)

Serology and Microbiology. Serology is the study of serum and the body's immunological response to disease. Microbiology is the study of infectious organisms. These units may be combined. Parasitology, the study of parasites (normally performed on feces), is included in the microbiology module. Since most work is done in a seated position, the countertop should be 30 inches high with a knee space for the technologist, space for a centrifuge, and open shelves above for reagents. A refrigerator is needed for the storage of purchased media and reagents. Floor or countertop space must be allocated for

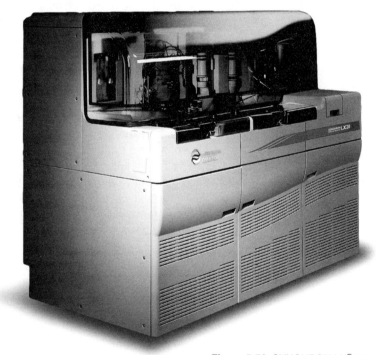

Figure 5-78. SYNCHRON LX® 20 chemistry analyzer. (*Photo courtesy: Beckman Coulter, Inc., Brea, CA.*)

both a 37 degree Celsius incubator and a CO_2 incubator. A sink is needed for staining slides and for hand washing. As with other technical modules, drawers and under-counter cabinets are necessary.

Although few small labs will do microbiology, it should be noted that a microbiological hood is required to prevent the spread of infection during preparation of specimens for tuberculosis, fungi, viruses, bacteria, or parasite isolation and identification. This HEPA-filtered biological safety cabinet (hood) may or may not require venting to the outside, depending on the model and health regulations. If at all possible, separate the microbiology module from other modules by full-height partitions to reduce contamination of air and the chance of infection being transmitted to other lab personnel. A window in the door is a good idea to see if someone is working in the room and to prevent the occupant from feeling isolated while in the room. A new law may require an anteroom or vestibule air interlock.

Histology. This is the study of tissues. Thin slices of diseased specimens are examined by microscope. During surgery, for example, sections of tumors would be sent to a hospital for a pathologist's report on possible malignancy or other cellular deformities. Small labs in a medical office building would not have a histology unit or a pathologist. Normally, this work would be performed in a hospital or reference lab. Thus, the requirements in equipment and work space will not be discussed here.

Automated Analyzers

Many laboratories now have microprocessor-based hematology and chemistry analyzers, which considerably reduce the number of technologists required and eliminate much of the equipment necessary for manual analysis. Automated analyzers vary considerably in their size and capabilities. All of them are aimed at speed and total automation, freeing the technologist to walk away while samples are being tested.

One may place a blood specimen into the machine, and in a few minutes, the analyzer will complete multiple tests on the specimen and produce a printed result form. Large analyzers can process upwards of 180 tests per hour with little manual intervention. Many analyzers have RS232 ports, which allow results to be sent directly to the laboratory computer. Some analyzers fit on a countertop (Figure 5-76), whereas others require floor space (Figures 5-77 and 5-78).

Accessioning of Specimens and Processing Area

The lab should have an area designated for accessioning (recording) of specimens and tests to be performed. Recording may be done manually or by computer. If done manually, there should be an area in each module for performing paperwork. This is where labels are printed for specimen vials with patient's name and identification number.

Generally, a laboratory will need an area for the processing of specimens that are to be tested later or sent to an outside laboratory. A countertop area large enough to accommodate a centrifuge, specimen containers, test tube racks, a computer, and clerical functions is necessary. This area is usually located near where the specimens first arrive in the laboratory. A refrigerator and freezer are also needed for specimen storage awaiting pickup.

Central Communication Center

The modern laboratory is directly linked by computer to physicians' offices and to reference laboratories. Communication into and out of the laboratory is of critical importance. Depending on the size of the laboratory, one or more phones should be available for reporting results. A personal computer may be used for laboratory record keeping. If the lab sends out a substantial amount of work to a reference laboratory, a CRT and printer allow quick access to specimen results from the reference laboratory. This is best located at a desk convenient to all of the technical modules. In Figure 5-74, it is located in the processing area. In the future, laboratories may use the Internet to connect with reference laboratories and physicians for ordering tests and reporting test results.

Administrative Area

The administrative area consists of waiting room, business office/reception room, staff lounge and locker room, and, sometimes in a large laboratory, a private office for the director or manager of the lab. These areas should be separated from the clinical areas so that non-lab personnel need not enter the clinical work space.

Dressing Area for Employees. A lab will often include lockers and a dressing area where technicians may change clothes. A staff toilet room at this location is convenient. The dressing area may be combined with the staff lounge. Since food cannot be stored or eaten in the lab, it is important to provide a room to be used for breaks and lunch. This area should also contain an area for clean lab coats and a linen hamper. There should be a location for hanging up coats being worn so that they are left outside the lunch room.

Specimen Toilet

The toilet room for collection of urine specimens should have a small pass-through in the wall (see the Appendix) that opens into the clinical area so that urine samples can be picked up by the technician without the patient having to carry the cup out of the bathroom. This toilet room, as in any medical or dental suite, should be designed to accommodate the handicapped.

Drug-Testing Toilet Design
If there is a need for the collection of "chain of custody" drugs of abuse urine specimens, a "dry" toilet needs to be created. This requires a mechanism for shutting off the water to the sink and toilet. A plumber can install shut-off

valves that allow the handles to be removed so the patient cannot dilute the specimen with water. A colored dye is also added to the water remaining in the bowl so it cannot be used.

Blood Drawing

Blood drawing (phlebotomy) can be performed in a small room or cubicle equipped with a straight chair and a 24-×36-inch table or a prefabricated specialized blood drawing chair (Figures 3-49 and 5-79). Privacy is important. If individual rooms or enclosures are not possible, a screen or cubicle drape will protect those waiting from the view of blood being drawn and provide privacy if

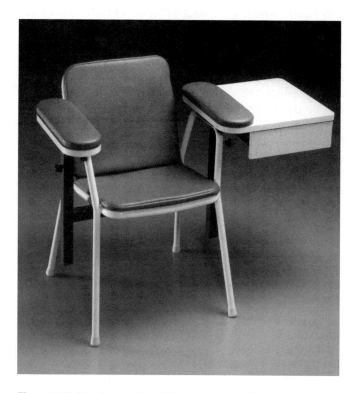

Figure 5-79. Blood draw chair. (*Photo courtesy: Midmark Corporation, Versailles, OH.*)

clothing needs to be removed to access the arm. If space allows, it is a good idea to have one private cubicle large enough to accommodate a built-in bed or bench for drawing blood of patients who may feel faint and for babies or small children. A sink is needed in the area so phlebotomists can wash their hands between patients. This is a good location for a rack to hold glove boxes (Figure 3-43).

Auxiliary (Support) Services

Disposal of Biohazardous Waste. Regulations for the disposal of biohazardous waste dictate that an area be allocated for the storage of laboratory specimens, disposable supplies, needles, syringes, and other items that may have come into contact with patient specimens until these contaminated items are collected by licensed disposal companies. Presently, OSHA standards require storage in sharps containers or red bags placed in leakproof secondary containers. A secured labeled area is required for storage until pickup. The soiled utility room can be used for this purpose.

The laboratory has the option, however, of autoclaving its infectious waste prior to its being picked up by the standard refuse collection agency. If the laboratory chooses this option, an additional space large enough to accommodate this equipment will be required in the sterilization room. Criteria for the handling of hazardous materials (i.e., potentially carcinogenic or infectious waste) must be reviewed before designing a laboratory that must meet certification and licensure requirements.

Glass Washing and Sterilization. Today, with the use of disposables and premade reagents, the need for a glass-washing and sterilization area has been almost eliminated. This area used to be larger when lab procedures were done manually. This module, if required, should be located near microbiology or chemistry. This unit may contain deionized water equipment, sterilizer, drying oven, and pipette washer, depending on the laboratory's test volume and mix of procedures. Storage of glass-

ware, chemicals, reagents, and paper supplies should be provided in cabinets. A ventilation hood over the sterilizers would exhaust heat and moisture generated by the equipment.

Record Storage. Due to the increased volume of records, which need to be maintained for several years, file cabinets and an area for storage of old records should be provided. These records include requisitions (as a backup for billing to Medicaid and Medicare), instrument printouts, equipment service records, and quality control reports.

Future Technology

As with any medical space, there should be some flexibility in the layout to allow for future space requirements as technology evolves.

Utilities

A clinical lab may require gas tanks. External cylinders of CO_2 are needed for the incubator in microbiology. Acid-resistant material for plumbing drains and the U-joint is recommended for sinks that will be used for reagent disposal. Also, sinks should have plaster traps. Depending on the volume, the substance, and local wastewater regulations, most laboratory waste can be discharged into the sewer. Devices to prevent backflow are required. It is important to know local codes regarding requirements for waste disposal. Laboratory sinks should be of a noncorrosive material and countertop work surfaces may be chemical-resistant plastic laminate or special ceramic lab tops.

Air Conditioning and Ventilation

The need for a well-planned, functional air-conditioning and ventilation system is critical in a laboratory. Chemical fumes, vapors, gases, heat from equipment, plus the impracticality of open windows, create a health hazard to those in adjacent medical suites as well as to the laboratory staff who suffer repeated exposure. It is not adequate simply to exhaust these vapors out of the roof of the building without considering the dispersion to nearby persons and buildings.

Ventilation requirements for each work unit must be studied so that airflow patterns can be regulated by proper location of supply and exhaust grilles. A competent mechanical engineer should be consulted to prepare this study. Exhaust air from fume hoods should be conducted through noncorrosive ducts to the roof of the building and not be recirculated. The microbiology module should have negative air pressure in relation to surrounding rooms. In addition, slightly negative air pressure between the lab and the medical building should be maintained in order to prevent odors and contaminants from spreading.

Power Requirements

A laboratory demands maximum flexibility; thus, each work surface countertop should have a continuous plug-mold strip and a separate circuit every 8 to 10 feet. Because certain pieces of equipment may draw as much as 15 amperes when warming up, a careful inventory must be made of the power requirements of each major piece of equipment. Automated analyzers are sensitive to voltage fluctuations and may require a constant voltage regulator as well as a separate circuit. [It should be noted that a centrifuge or shaker should not be put on a counter where the vibration may interfere with a computer screen.]

Work areas need shadow-free light, requiring that a fluorescent "shelf" light be mounted below the upper cabinets. Otherwise, light may be supplied totally by ceiling-mounted fluorescent luminaires in sufficient quantity to assure a level of at least 100 footcandles for close work and 50 footcandles for general illumination.

Consideration must be given, when designing and specifying lighting, to the elimination of glare from data management display monitors associated with clinical analyzers. This may necessitate indirect lighting that bounces off the ceiling for general illumination. The issue would be the same as that encountered in any office where computer monitors are in use.

Interior Design

For years, laboratories have been designed in a neutral color palette because the reflection of colors made it difficult to match samples to a standard or to analyze colors. Today, with automated equipment, matching of specimens to a standard is no longer done visually. Walls may be any pleasant color the technologist prefers, and subtle patterns may be considered for plastic laminate countertops. The floor might have an attractive design created with several colors of vinyl composition tile or it may be sheet vinyl with a confetti pattern.

In the laboratory area, there needs to be wall space for white boards and bulletin boards in the modules. These provide space for messages to other staff members, posting of quality control charts, and changes in test procedures.

In patient areas, provide a place where patients can hang their coats, handbags, and stow their packages or briefcases. This should be located principally in the blood-drawing area. The waiting room needs a secure place for hanging overcoats and umbrellas and for stowing boots.

Small Laboratory

The small laboratory, which may be part of a group-practice suite, would perform the more common and simple laboratory tests. (This is also known as a *stat* lab, because the tests are generally urgently required.) Specimens requiring complex bacteriological or chemical procedures would probably be sent to an outside laboratory. Biopsied tissue specimens would be sent to a

pathologist for diagnosis. Thus, the small lab (650 to 750 square feet) would have separate areas for hematology, chemistry, urinalysis, and possibly microbiology, allowing approximately 8 lineal feet of countertop for each, plus two blood draw cubicles, specimen toilet, small reception/waiting area, storage room, and glass-washing/ sterilization area. With the continuing development of small multipurpose analyzers and "waived" tests requiring minimal work space, small laboratories may require less space in the future. The small benchtop analyzer in Figure 5-80 does routine chemistry tests. It is low volume and hand-fed and may be found in physicians' offices in a stat lab. The i-STAT (Figure 5-71) may also be used in a stat lab.

Figure 5-80. Cobas MIRA Plus benchtop chemistry analyzer. (*Photo courtesy: Roche Diagnostics, Indianapolis, IN.*)

CHAPTER 6
Group Practice

The focus of this chapter is the small to medium-sized group practice—8 to 20 physicians. Large ambulatory-care networks, such as the Mayo or Cleveland Clinic or the 100,000- to 150,000-square-foot hospital-based ambulatory facilities that have become so common in the past 10 years on medical center campuses, are far too complex to cover in one chapter. These facilities grow out of a context of politics (relationships between physicians and hospitals as to what departments will be included and how the revenue is to be divided); an analysis of market share; and a sophisticated master planning process that involves workload analysis using computer programs to model various scenarios, analyze revenue stream, allocate space by department, and estimate construction cost. Nevertheless, this book will be helpful at the micro level, as each department is planned, since the basic composition of each specialty suite and the layout of typical rooms, as well as the equipment used, will be relevant. In addition, the many patient-centered features and design ideas will be useful. The reader is reminded to read Chapters 3 and 4 as background for Chapter 6. These include a discussion of digital technology.

The point of origin for all group practices is the Mayo Clinic. Founded in 1897, it became the prototype for others that followed, including the prominent Menninger Clinic in Topeka. The Mayo Clinic is reputed to be the world's largest medical clinic. While few aspire to this level of achievement, many of the principles upon which the Mayo Clinic was founded apply to smaller group practices as well. These include the sharing or pooling of knowledge, a division of labor that allows physicians to concentrate on their specialty, and a desire to stay on the cutting edge of new technology. It is a teamwork approach to the delivery of medicine.

There is an ever-increasing trend toward group practice. Economics and the threat of for-profit chains dominating the market have encouraged many solo practitioners to band together in groups to enhance their strength and presence. Moreover, group practice offers physicians better managed-care contract negotiation power. Although some physicians do not feel psychologically geared to practice in a large organization, and some fear a loss of individual authority in medical matters, group practice does increase a physician's productivity and may lower the cost of healthcare.

In theory, each physician can be made more productive by eliminating the waste and inefficiencies inherent in a solo practice. A solo practitioner may work a 60- or 70-hour week, but perhaps 20 percent of his or her time is spent on office management. A group practice provides a division of labor with sufficient personnel to perform these nonmedical tasks, thereby enabling physicians to concentrate solely on practicing medicine.

Another advantage of group practice is the convenience of having a fully staffed radiology department and clinical lab in the physician's own office. Equipment that might be too costly or underutilized in the small medical office can easily be justified in a large group practice. Other benefits of a group practice are greater freedom with regard to leisure time. Partners can cover for one another with no lack of continuity in care for the patient. And physicians in a multispecialty group provide one another with immediate access to specialists in other fields. This pooling of resources provides patients more efficient and complete professional services than each physician could provide individually.

Of course, economics plays a prime role in motivating physicians to practice together. Eight physicians in private practice would require eight business offices, eight waiting rooms, possibly six to eight X-ray rooms, six to eight minor surgery rooms—a great duplication of space and personnel. Together, as a group, the eight might have two minor surgeries, two X-ray rooms, one large waiting room, and one centralized business office. More efficient use of space and personnel means more take-home profit for physicians and perhaps lower costs for patients. In addition, certain lab tests or X-rays that might otherwise be sent out could be done within a properly equipped suite, netting extra fees for the group practice to reduce office overhead, providing CLIA regulations are met. Refer to Chapter 3 for a discussion about why physicians currently do little lab work within their offices, and to the Introduction for information about HIPAA.

As healthcare approaches the status of a commodity, the pressure on group-practice physicians to meet revenue goals (with compensation often tied to productivity) has steadily increased. The group-practice model that once sheltered physicians from some of the minutiae of private practice has imposed its own sort of tyranny, which, as reimbursement steadily decreases, enslaves them to "beat the clock," seeing ever greater numbers of patients and enjoying it less. In past years, the billing of ancillary services helped to compensate for declining professional fees as managed care continued to dominate the marketplace. However, CLIA regulations and the Stark statute (relates to physician self-referral regulations) have made it difficult to vertically integrate ancillary services to enhance physicians' income without tripping over conflict-of-interest issues and ever more complex compliance requirements.

STARK STATUTE

Stark I

Named after California senator Pete Stark, this statute creates penalties for physicians who engage in self-referral of Medicare patients to clinical labs in which they have a financial interest. Known as Stark I, the legislation was enacted by Congress in 1989.

Stark II

Stark II, enacted by Congress in 1993, prohibits self-referrals for radiology, hospital inpatient/outpatient, and eight other services. Proposed regulations on Stark II, issued in 1998, were considered by many to be confusing and ambiguous, prompting the Health Care Financing Administration (HCFA) to issue important changes in the Stark II final rule as a response to formal hearings and criticism. The definition of group practice has been broadened in terms of what qualifies as a "single legal entity," and productivity bonuses and profit-sharing rules have been revised. Significant changes were made to the "in-office ancillary services" exception to ownership and compensation arrangements. The final rule, divided into Phase I and Phase II, is reported in the January 4, 2001 *Federal Register.* Phase I became effective January 4, 2002.

ACCREDITATION

At the start of programming, the space planner must determine the type of certification, accreditation, or licensing the group is seeking. Some regulatory agencies have requirements that affect space planning and design (Medicare certification, for example), while others deal with issues of governance, credentialing, quality management and improvement, and clinical records. Periodic on-site surveys and peer review occur. These agencies may include JCAHO (Joint Commission on Accreditation of Healthcare Organizations), AAAHC (Accreditation Association for Ambulatory Health Care), and a number of organizations that accredit managed care enterprises. Refer also to Chapter 4 and Chapter 7 for additional discussion of these issues.

TYPES OF GROUP PRACTICES

There are four types of group practices in terms of space-planning considerations. The *single-specialty group* consists of physicians (rarely more than eight) who are all of the same medical specialty. This type of group permits a physician a great deal of freedom since patients usually will accept treatment from any member of the group. This allows for better utilization of all the doctors' time. The single-specialty group represents two-thirds (67 percent) of the market.* This includes family practice and internal medicine.

The *multispecialty group* (33 percent of the market)† might typically be a large clinic offering internal medicine, OB-GYN, urology, pediatrics, family practice, ENT, or any combination of medical specialties. A group such as this could potentially offer many of the outpatient services provided by a hospital: clinical lab studies, diagnostic radiology, physical therapy, chemotherapy infusion, endoscopy, and multiphasic medical screening. A multispecialty group might consist of 20 physicians to several hundred physicians as in an HMO.

The *internal medicine group* might be a group of general internists plus those with various subspecialties: pulmonary medicine, cardiovascular disease, hematology, oncology, gastroenterology, or endocrinology. A large enough group could support its own clinical lab, radiology department, cardiovascular rehabilitation, and pulmonary function testing.

The *family practice group* enables primary-care physicians to expand beyond their individual resources in purchasing equipment and staffing an office. Large family practice groups are often found in small towns, and sometimes they have one or more specialists on staff in an effort to offer the community a wider range of services.

PRIMARY-CARE CLINICS

The primary-care clinic is an extension of the family practice group, which, depending on the extent of ancillary services, can be quite large and self-sustaining. As an example, both of the primary-care clinics in Figures 6-1 and 6-2 and 6-3 and 6-4 have been set up to contract with insurance companies to provide total care for patients on a capitated (fixed amount per month) basis. There is every incentive to keep patients out of the emergency (ER) and

out of the hospital, since that cost comes out of the medical group's profit. Therefore, both of these clinics have an urgent-care unit to observe and treat patients who might otherwise go to the ER. They also offer fairly extensive diagnostic imaging and lab services. Physicians in these clinics are salaried employees, a number of whom would have a financial interest in the enterprise.

In Figure 6-1, registration, ancillary services, and urgent care are on the first floor with direct gurney access from urgent care to the exterior. Radiology has a direct entry into urgent care. On the second floor (Figure 6-2), generic clinic modules accommodate a variety of practitioners. The clinic is designed for after-hours security when everything is locked except access to urgent care, radiology, and lab.

In Figure 6-3, the first floor includes central registration, medical records (with a dumbwaiter to urgent care above), staff lockers and lounge (also serves for in-service training, conferences, classroom), and three generic primary-care modules. The second floor, Figure 6-4, has urgent care, lab, diagnostic imaging, pediatrics, OB-GYN, and administration. [One might wonder why urgent care is not located on the first floor. In reality, neither floor is on grade—they are the second and third floors of an MOB.]

The hybrid nature of primary-care clinics can be illustrated by Figures 6-5 and 6-6, which, in addition to the expected components, feature, respectively, a medical oncology unit and a diagnostic breast center. A unique example of adaptive reuse, the 30,000-square-foot freestanding St. Francis Hospital community health center (Figure 6-5) was converted from a 30-year-old former supermarket. Exploiting the high ceilings with a playful trellis and colorful fabric panels, it has an upbeat ambiance (Color plate 26, Figure 6-7). The reader may wish to refer to Figure 4-50 for a view of the medical oncology waiting area and resource center in this facility.

Centralized waiting and registration areas lead directly to four primary-care pods and to diagnostic imaging in Figure 6-6, while the breast center has its own entry and well-appointed waiting room (Color Plate 26, Figure 6-8).

SMG Market Letter, January 2000, Chicago.
†Ibid.

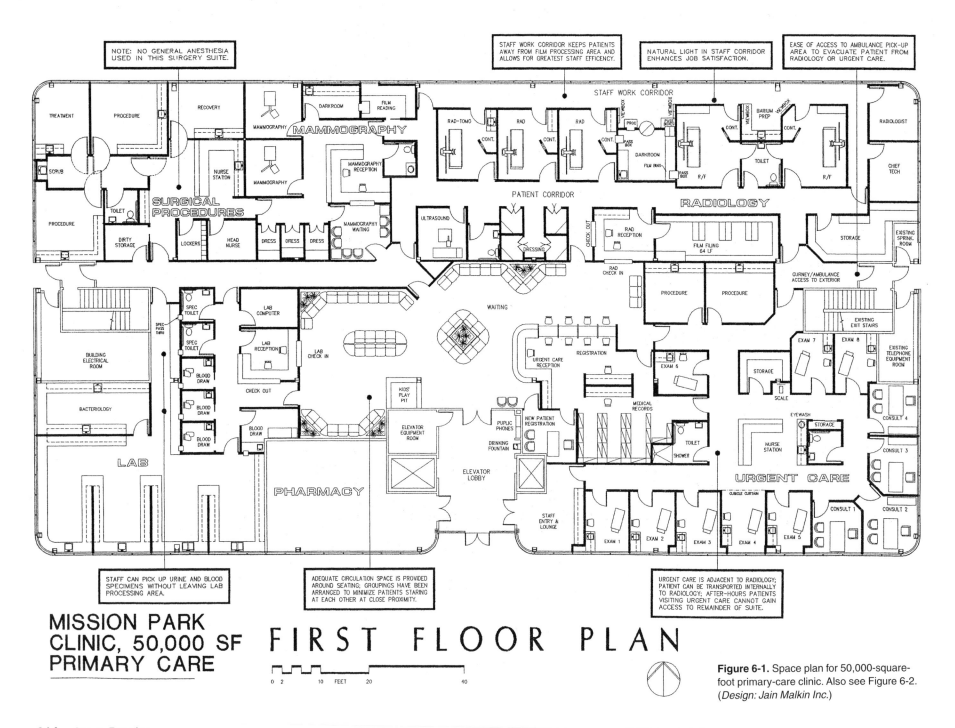

NOTE: NO GENERAL ANESTHESIA USED IN THIS SURGERY SUITE.

STAFF WORK CORRIDOR KEEPS PATIENTS AWAY FROM FILM PROCESSING AREA AND ALLOWS FOR GREATEST STAFF EFFICENCY.

NATURAL LIGHT IN STAFF CORRIDOR ENHANCES JOB SATISFACTION.

EASE OF ACCESS TO AMBULANCE PICK-UP AREA TO EVACUATE PATIENT FROM RADIOLOGY OR URGENT CARE.

STAFF CAN PICK UP URINE AND BLOOD SPECIMENS WITHOUT LEAVING LAB PROCESSING AREA.

ADEQUATE CIRCULATION SPACE IS PROVIDED AROUND SEATING; GROUPINGS HAVE BEEN ARRANGED TO MINIMIZE PATIENTS STARING AT EACH OTHER AT CLOSE PROXIMITY.

URGENT CARE IS ADJACENT TO RADIOLOGY; PATIENT CAN BE TRANSPORTED INTERNALLY TO RADIOLOGY; AFTER-HOURS PATIENTS VISITING URGENT CARE CANNOT GAIN ACCESS TO REMAINDER OF SUITE.

MISSION PARK CLINIC, 50,000 SF PRIMARY CARE

FIRST FLOOR PLAN

0 2   10 FEET 20   40

Figure 6-1. Space plan for 50,000-square-foot primary-care clinic. Also see Figure 6-2. (*Design: Jain Malkin Inc.*)

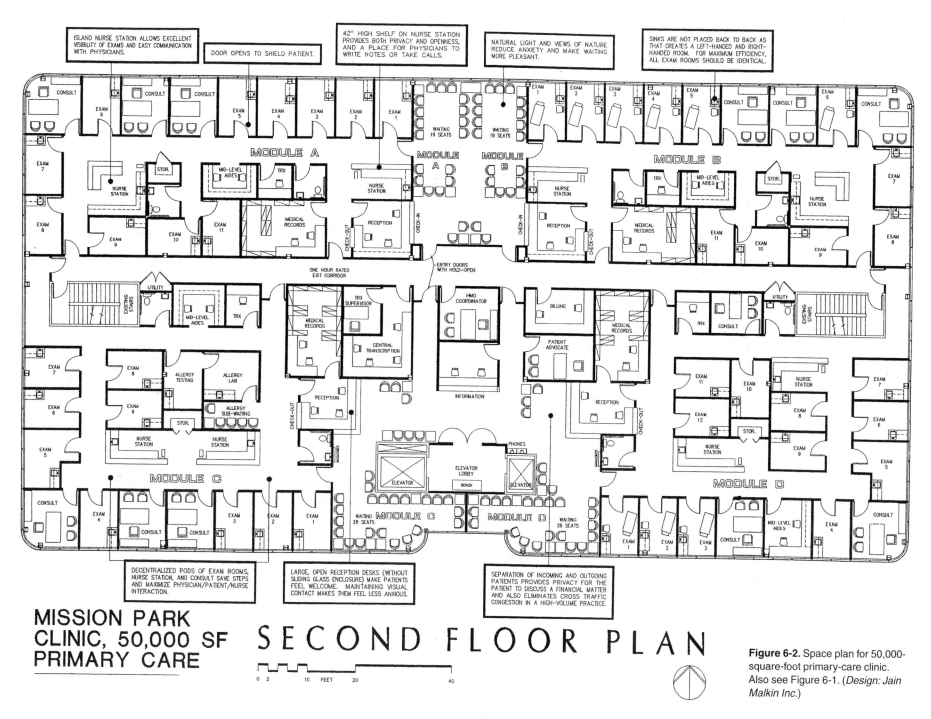

ISLAND NURSE STATION ALLOWS EXCELLENT VISIBILITY OF EXAMS AND EASY COMMUNICATION WITH PHYSICIANS.

DOOR OPENS TO SHIELD PATIENT.

42" HIGH SHELF ON NURSE STATION PROVIDES BOTH PRIVACY AND OPENNESS, AND A PLACE FOR PHYSICIANS TO WRITE NOTES OR TAKE CALLS.

NATURAL LIGHT AND VIEWS OF NATURE REDUCE ANXIETY AND MAKE WAITING MORE PLEASANT.

SINKS ARE NOT PLACED BACK TO BACK AS THAT CREATES A LEFT-HANDED AND RIGHT-HANDED ROOM. FOR MAXIMUM EFFICIENCY, ALL EXAM ROOMS SHOULD BE IDENTICAL.

MODULE A

MODULE B

MODULE C

MODULE D

ONE HOUR RATED EXIT CORRIDOR

ENTRY DOORS WITH HOLD-OPEN

ELEVATOR LOBBY

DECENTRALIZED PODS OF EXAM ROOMS, NURSE STATION, AND CONSULT SAVE STEPS AND MAXIMIZE PHYSICIAN/PATIENT/NURSE INTERACTION.

LARGE, OPEN RECEPTION DESKS (WITHOUT SLIDING GLASS ENCLOSURE) MAKE PATIENTS FEEL WELCOME. MAINTAINING VISUAL CONTACT MAKES THEM FEEL LESS ANXIOUS.

SEPARATION OF INCOMING AND OUTGOING PATIENTS PROVIDES PRIVACY FOR THE PATIENT TO DISCUSS A FINANCIAL MATTER AND ALSO ELIMINATES CROSS TRAFFIC CONGESTION IN A HIGH-VOLUME PRACTICE.

MISSION PARK CLINIC, 50,000 SF PRIMARY CARE

SECOND FLOOR PLAN

0 2   10   FEET   20   40

Figure 6-2. Space plan for 50,000-square-foot primary-care clinic. Also see Figure 6-1. (*Design: Jain Malkin Inc.*)

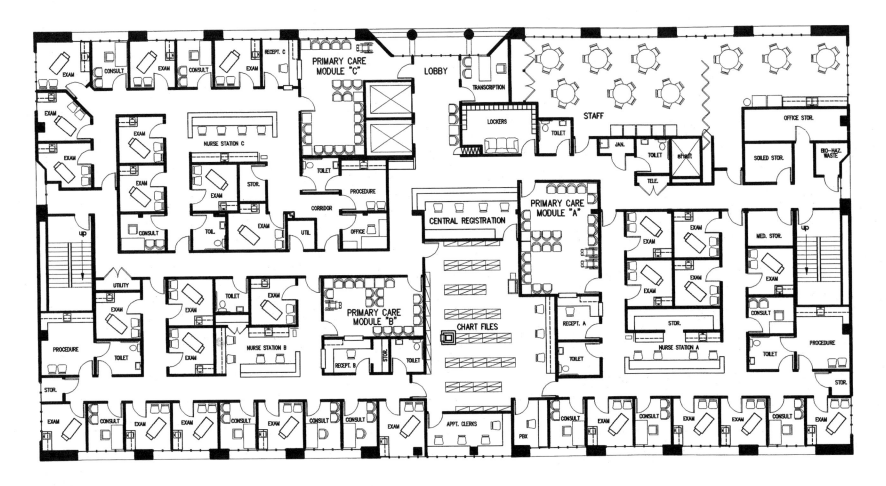

PRIMARY CARE CLINIC – FIRST FLOOR

30,000 SF ON TWO FLOORS

Figure 6-3. Space plan for 30,000-square-foot primary-care clinic. Also see Figure 6-4. (*Design: Jain Malkin Inc.*)

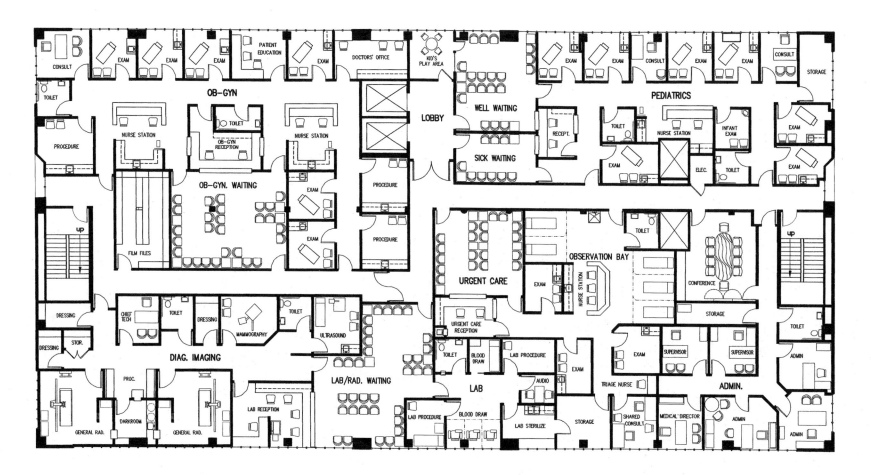

PRIMARY CARE CLINIC – SECOND FLOOR

30,000 SF ON TWO FLOORS

Figure 6-4. Space plan for 30,000-square-foot primary-care clinic. Also see Figure 6-3. (*Design: Jain Malkin Inc.*)

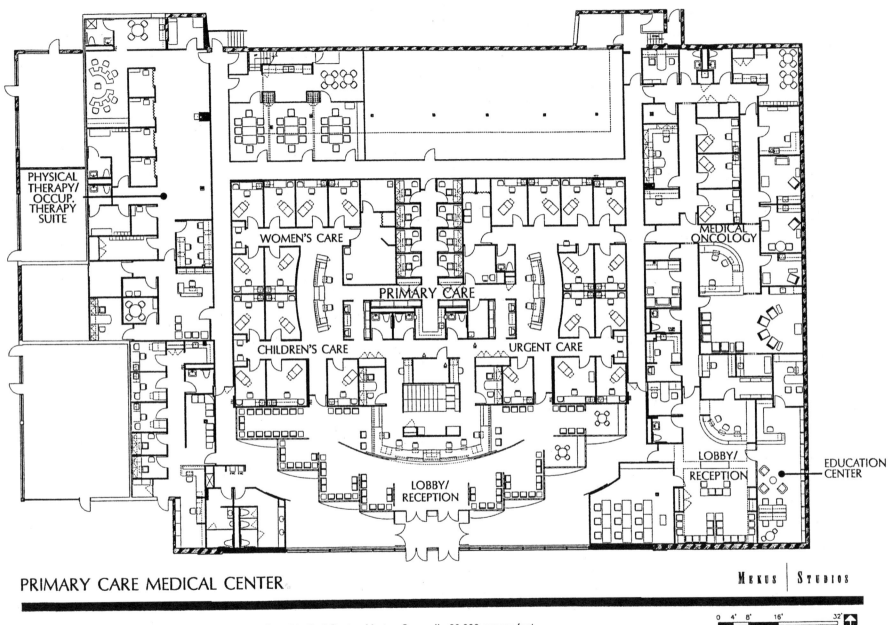

Figure 6-5. Space plan, St. Francis Hospital Primary Care Medical Center, Morton Grove, IL, 30,000 square feet. (*Architecture and interior design: Mekus Studios, Chicago, IL.*)

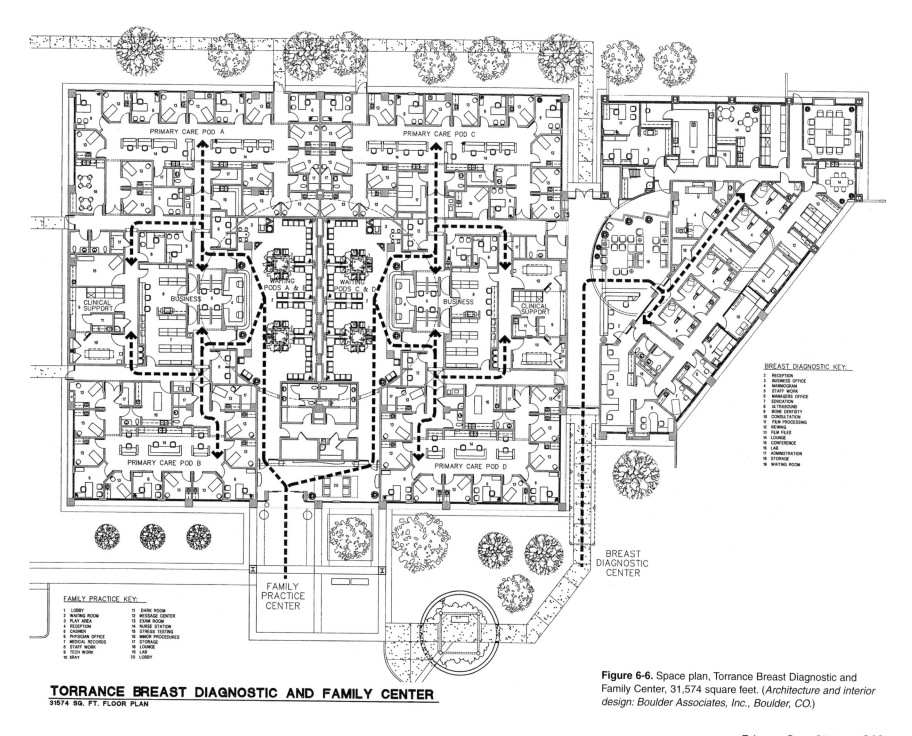

PRIMARY CARE POD A

PRIMARY CARE POD C

WAITING PODS A & B

WAITING PODS C & D

CLINICAL SUPPORT

BUSINESS

BUSINESS

CLINICAL SUPPORT

PRIMARY CARE POD B

PRIMARY CARE POD D

BREAST DIAGNOSTIC KEY:

2 RECEPTION
3 BUSINESS OFFICE
4 MAMMOGRAM
5 STAFF WORK
6 MANAGERS OFFICE
7 EDUCATION
8 ULTRASOUND
9 BONE DENTISTY
10 CONSULTATION
11 FILM PROCESSING
12 VIEWING
13 FILM FILES
14 LOUNGE
15 CONFERENCE
16 LAB
17 ADMINISTRATION
18 STORAGE
19 WAITING ROOM

FAMILY PRACTICE CENTER

BREAST DIAGNOSTIC CENTER

FAMILY PRACTICE KEY:

1 LOBBY
2 WAITING ROOM
3 PLAY AREA
4 RECEPTION
5 CASHIER
6 PHYSICIAN OFFICE
7 MEDICAL RECORDS
8 STAFF WORK
9 TECH WORK
10 XRAY
11 DARK ROOM
12 MESSAGE CENTER
13 EXAM ROOM
14 NURSE STATION
15 STRESS TESTING
16 MINOR PROCEDURES
17 STORAGE
18 LOUNGE
19 LAB
20 LOBBY

TORRANCE BREAST DIAGNOSTIC AND FAMILY CENTER
31574 SQ. FT. FLOOR PLAN

Figure 6-6. Space plan, Torrance Breast Diagnostic and Family Center, 31,574 square feet. (*Architecture and interior design: Boulder Associates, Inc., Boulder, CO.*)

HEALTH MAINTENANCE ORGANIZATIONS

In theory, any of these groups can be organized as a health maintenance organization although, since the obligation of an HMO is to provide a full range of health services to its members, it would most likely be only the large multispecialty group that would be prepared to do this. Kaiser is the best-known HMO of this type, referred to as a *staff model* because its providers are employees of the HMO. More commonly, HMOs contract with medical group practices, individual physicians, and other healthcare providers to provide services for their members who prepay a monthly fee, in addition to a fee or co-pay at the time the service is rendered. For many individuals, this arrangement centralizes and simplifies their healthcare and eliminates debates with insurance companies over what is covered and not covered, and it eliminates having to pay bills and write checks to a number of physicians. Members are issued an embossed identification card that is presented to the receptionist upon checking into the clinic. This saves time in heading up a form for each patient visit, and the identification card has the patient's billing code and other pertinent information on it. Increasingly, these transactions, patient identification, and records will be digital. Thus, although an HMO may have more subscribers than a similar-sized multispecialty group that charges a fee for service, billing procedures are often less complicated (there are no insurance claims to file) and are facilitated by sophisticated electronic data-processing and computer systems.

Large multispecialty group HMOs like Kaiser have historically stressed health maintenance on the basis that it is less costly to keep people healthy than to treat them when they are sick. An HMO that follows this principle should be designed to accommodate many more patients than would a multispecialty group of the same number of physicians, and many more physician extenders will be employed in an HMO to provide health screening and other procedures aimed at preventive medicine. Having said that, it should be noted that the HMO of today differs from the somewhat idealistic model of yesteryear—one that promised to keep people healthy. Spending money to keep enrollees healthy only pays off if members stay with the plan a number of years. If they switch plans, the new HMO realizes the benefit. This has forced many HMOs to make tough decisions about how much they can offer at a capitated rate. Responding to inadequate government reimbursement, many HMOs pulled out of the Medicare program in January of 2001, dropping over a million elderly and disabled individuals. The number of HMOs showing profitability dropped from 83 percent in 1993 to 41 percent in 2000[*].

An HMO based on the staff or Kaiser model will usually have a large physical therapy department, chemotherapy, cardiopulmonary lab, and allergy department—all of which may process a large volume of patients daily who do not have to see a doctor.

HMO Models

The three main types of HMOs are the *independent practice association* (IPA), the combination model, and the *network* model. The IPA represents 58 percent of all HMOs, followed by combination models with 23 percent and network models with 12 percent. Staff and group models, together, total approximately 7 percent of the market[†]. In all but the staff model, the HMO contracts with medical groups or individual physicians to provide care to its enrollees and, in turn, contracts with employers to provide services to their employees. In addition, HMOs enroll individual members and families. Following is a description of the various HMO models.

Independent Practice Association
In this model, the HMO either develops or contracts with an existing association of individual physician practices to provide services to enrollees. Physicians are paid on a negotiated fee-for-service basis, or on a per capita basis, or a flat-fee retainer. IPAs allow physicians to remain in

[*]Ibid.
[†]Ibid.

private practice and to treat subscribers in their own offices. Patients select from a list of providers, which includes hospitals, physicians, physical therapists, and others, to meet their healthcare needs. An HMO may employ a "gatekeeper" system that requires patients to select a primary-care physician who makes referrals to specialists, although some HMOs permit patients to self-refer to a specialist.

Combination Model
In this model, HMOs may combine two or more of the plan models.

Network Model
The HMO, in this model type, contracts with several multispecialty group practices to provide services to enrollees residing in a single large service area or several noncontiguous service areas with physicians commonly reimbursed on a per capita basis.

Group Model
Consisting of one or more medical group practices, care is delivered in one central facility, supported by several satellite facilities. The group practice is paid on a negotiated per capita rate, and physicians receive a salary plus incentive payment. Patient care is usually managed by a primary-care physician who controls referrals to specialists.

Staff Model
In this model, physicians and other healthcare providers are full-time employees of the HMO and as such receive a salary. Care delivery is centralized in one or more locations, typically in large clinics. Care is managed by a primary-care physician who controls referrals to specialists.

HMO Statistics

Health maintenance organizations are regulated by the state and are subject to close scrutiny by various health-planning regulatory agencies to ensure that they have met strict requirements with regard to their clinical services, quality management and improvement, utilization of personnel, and schedule of fees. As of January 2000, there were 906 HMOs nationwide, with an enrollment of 104 million individuals.* However, consumer backlash against HMOs' stringent controls and restricted choices has resulted in significant increases in enrollment in PPOs (Preferred Provider Organizations), which offer greater choice and give the consumer more control.

POINT-OF-SERVICE (POS)

In the late 1990s, an alternative to the HMO emerged. called the Point-of-Service plan. It has many similarities to HMOs in that it provides prepaid, comprehensive health coverage for both hospital and physician services and it requires members to select a primary-care physician. The difference is that enrollees may select a provider outside the plan's network and receive coverage at a discounted rate.

SINGLE-SPECIALTY GROUP

This suite is composed of the same elements as a standard medical office for a solo practitioner except on a larger scale. (The reader is referred to Chapter 3, Family Practice.) The functions of administration, patient care, and support services remain the same. It is the *relationship* of rooms that becomes critical as the suite becomes larger. It is no longer possible for all rooms to be close to each other as they are in a small suite. Administrative and support services may be *centralized* or *decentralized*—that is the major decision to be made at the outset. With a centralized plan (also known as an "island" plan), the business office, nurse station, lab,

---

*Ibid.

Table 6-1.
Analysis of Program.
Group Practice—Single Specialty (Nonsurgical)

	Internal Medicine 8 Physicians			Family Practice 8 Physicians		
Waiting Room(s)		$35 \times 35 = 1225^a$			$24 \times 36 = 864$	
Exam Rooms	20@	$8 \times 12 = 1920$		24@	$8 \times 12 = 2304$	
Consultation Rooms	8@	$12 \times 12 = 1152$		8@	$12 \times 12 = 1152$	
Nurse Stations	3@	$10 \times 12 = 360$		3@	$10 \times 12 = 360$	
Toilets	4@	$7 \times 8 = 224$		4@	$7 \times 8 = 224$	
Storage	2@	$8 \times 10 = 160$		2@	$8 \times 10 = 160$	
Staff Lounge		$12 \times 16 = 192$			$12 \times 16 = 192$	
Laboratory[b]		$24 \times 32 = 768$			$24 \times 32 = 768$	
Minor Surgery		—		2@	$12 \times 12 = 288$	
Cast Room		—			Use Minor Surgery	
ECG/Treadmill		$12 \times 12 = 144$			$12 \times 12 = 144$	
Radiology[c]		$12 \times 26 = 312$			$12 \times 12 = 312$	
Flex Sig Room[d]		$12 \times 18 = 216$			—	
Pulmonary Function Testing (Optional)		$14 \times 16 = 224$			—	
Business Office[e]		$24 \times 24 = 576$			$24 \times 24 = 576$	
Office Manager		$10 \times 12 = 120$			$10 \times 12 = 120$	
Medical Records		$12 \times 16 = 192$			$12 \times 16 = 192$	
Insurance/Collections		$14 \times 16 = 224$			$14 \times 16 = 224$	
Subtotal		8009 ft²			7880 ft²	
25% Circulation[f]		2002			1970	
Total		10,011 ft²			9,850 ft²	

[a]Includes calculation of late factor; see Chapter 3. Internal medicine physicians are often called to the ER or must visit hospitalized patients, which can account for delays.
[b]Includes lab waiting, blood draw, and toilet. This assumes lab work done in house.
[c]Includes darkroom, control, film filing, film viewing, and dressing area. (Radiography room not equipped for fluoroscopy.)
[d]Includes prep area and toilet.
[e]Includes reception, bookkeeper's office, transcription, and workroom.
*Allows for 5- to 6-foot-wide corridors.

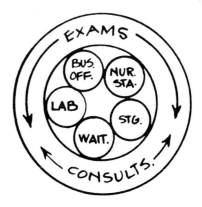

CENTRALIZED PLAN SINGLE SPECIALTY GROUP

Figure 6-9. Schematic diagram of a centralized plan for a single-specialty group.

and supply room would be grouped together, forming the core of the suite, with patient areas (exam and treatment rooms, consultation and waiting rooms) grouped around the perimeter of the core (Figures 6-9 and 6-10).

The suite in Figure 6-10 enables seven providers (six physicians and a nurse practitioner) to see patients simultaneously, each having three exam rooms. It is assumed that two of the eight physicians on any given day will either have a day off or be in surgery off site. In this high-volume specialty, the plan provides separate paths for patients entering and exiting the suite.

With a decentralized plan, administrative and support services would be divided into units, each serving a certain number of exam and treatment rooms. Exam and treatment rooms would be grouped into pods (three to six exam rooms to a pod) with an adjacent nurse station/lab

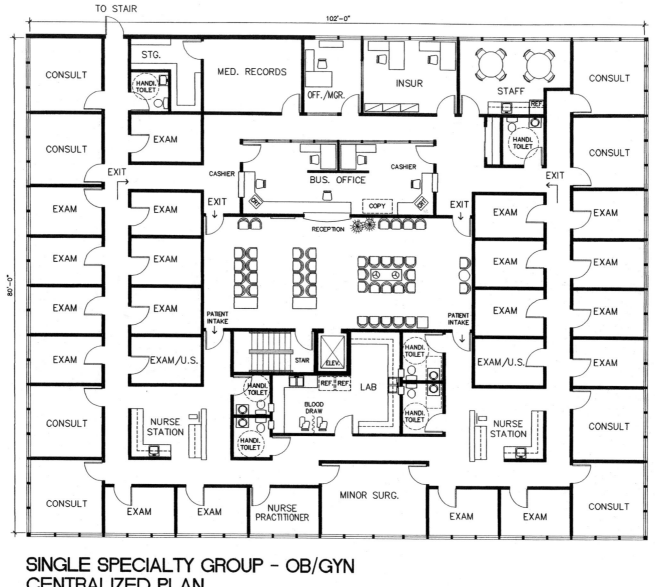

SINGLE SPECIALTY GROUP – OB/GYN
CENTRALIZED PLAN

8160 SF

Figure 6-10. Space plan for single-specialty group (OB/GYN) accommodates eight physicians and one nurse practitioner, 8160 square feet. (*Design: Jain Malkin Inc.*)

Table 6-2.
Analysis of Program.
Group Practice — Single Specialty (Surgical)

	OB-GYN 8 Physicians			Orthopedics 8 Physicians	
Waiting Room(s)[a]		$26 \times 30 = 780$		$20 \times 22 = 440$	
Exam Rooms	19@	$8 \times 12 = 1824$	12[b]@	$8 \times 12 = 1152$	
Exam/Ultrasound	2@	$10 \times 12 = 240$		—	
Consultation Rooms	8@	$12 \times 12 = 1152$	8@	$12 \times 12 = 1152$	
Nurse Stations	3@	$8 \times 10 = 240$	3[c]@	$8 \times 10 = 240$	
Toilets	6@	$7 \times 8 = 336$	4@	$7 \times 8 = 224$	
Storage	2@	$8 \times 10 = 160$	2@	$8 \times 10 = 160$	
Staff Lounge		$12 \times 16 = 192$		$12 \times 16 = 192$	
Lab		$12 \times 16 = 192$		$12 \times 14 = 168$	
Minor Surgery		$14 \times 16 = 224$		$12 \times 14 = 168$	
Cast Rooms		—	2@	$12 \times 12 = 288$	
Radiology[d]		—		$12 \times 34 = 408$	
Business Office[e]		$16 \times 30 = 480$		$16 \times 30 = 480$	
Surgery Scheduling		$10 \times 10 = 100$		$10 \times 10 = 100$	
Office Manager		$10 \times 12 = 120$		$10 \times 12 = 120$	
Insurance/Collections		$14 \times 16 = 224$		$14 \times 16 = 224$	
Medical Records		$12 \times 16 = 192$		$12 \times 16 = 192$	
Nurse Practitioner Office		$10 \times 10 = 100$		—	
Physical Therapy (Optional)		—		$20 \times 30 = 600$	
Subtotal		6556 ft²		6308 ft²	
25% Circulation[f]		1639		1577	
Total		8195 ft²		7885 ft²	

[a]Includes children's play area.
[b]Assumes no more than four physicians seeing patients in the office at one time.
[c]Tech workstations.
[d]Includes darkroom, control, film filing, and film viewing.
[e]Includes reception, bookkeeping, transcription, and workroom.
[f]Allows for 5- to 6-foot-wide corridors.

and one or two consultation rooms (Figures 3-2, 6-11, and 6-12). It would be impractical to have more than one business office, medical records area, or insurance office, so these services would have to be located so that a patient exiting from any pod of exam rooms would follow a path leading him or her past the cashier's desk and appointment desk and back into the central waiting room. In a large clinic, proper circulation must be reinforced by strategically placed, easy-to-read signage (Figures 6-13 and 6-15) and even unique destination entries (Color Plate 6, Figure 3-97). Inset carpet designs can be effective as wayfinding cues (Figure 6-14).

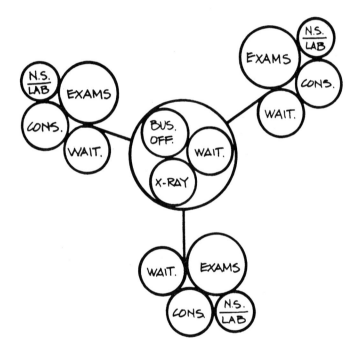

DECENTRALIZED PLAN
SINGLE SPECIALTY GROUP

Figure 6-11. Schematic diagram of a decentralized plan for a single-specialty group.

SINGLE SPECIALTY GROUP - DERMATOLOGY -DECENTRALIZED PLAN

4752 SF

Figure 6-12. Space plan for single-specialty group (dermatology), 4752 square feet, accommodates four providers: three physicians and one nurse practitioner. (*Design: Jain Malkin Inc.*)

Figure 6-13. Clinic signage system: Each medical specialty has a color identification. (*Design: Jain Malkin Inc.; Photographer: Jain Malkin.*)

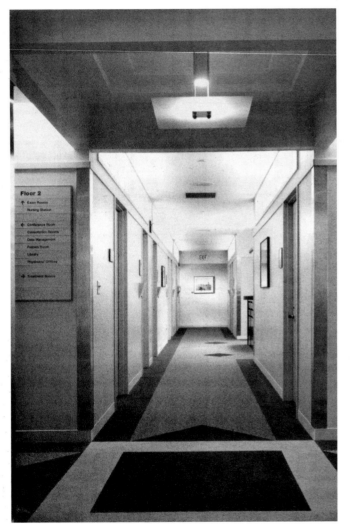

Figure 6-14. Corridor intersection with good wayfinding cues. Saint Francis Hospital, Hartford, CT. (*Photo courtesy: TRO/The Ritchie Organization, Newton, MA; Photographer: Warren Jagger.*)

Figure 6-15. Modular signage panel alongside doors is both functional and attractive. Frisbie Memorial Hospital, Rochester, NH. (*Photo courtesy: TRO/The Ritchie Organization, Newton, MA; Photographer: Edward Jacoby Photography.*)

MULTISPECIALTY GROUP

This type of clinic offers the greatest challenge to a designer. The space to be planned may be vast, and each specialty must be carefully analyzed for its relationship to other specialties (Figures 6-16 and 6-17). Large multispecialty clinics tend to grow and change a good deal. Physicians leave, and others join the group. Departments are sometimes shuffled around to realign them according to new priorities. The facility should be designed for expansion with anticipation of which departments may outgrow their present limits.

Radiology, for example, tends to expand. New equipment is introduced, and due to the scale of the machinery, a single piece may require its own room. Thus, it is a good idea to locate the radiology department on the perimeter of the suite adjacent to the area allocated for expansion. Radiography rooms are very costly to build due to special electrical, plumbing, and lead-shielding requirements; therefore, it would not be economically fea-

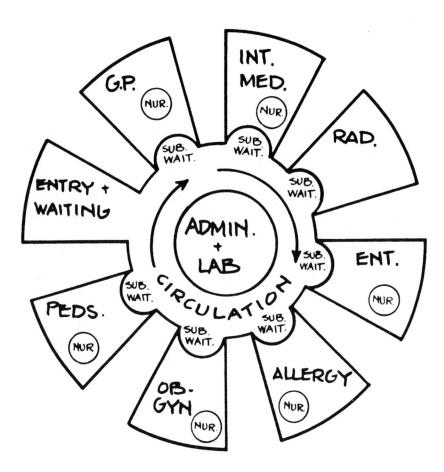

Figure 6-16. Schematic diagram of a satellite plan for a multispecialty group.

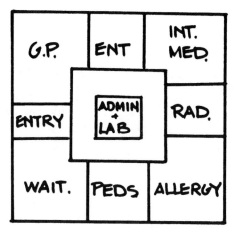

MULTI-SPECIALTY GROUP

Figure 6-17. Schematic diagram of a multispecialty group, showing the relationship of specialties for optimum function—keeping the highest volume toward the front, pediatrics close to allergy, radiology close to internal medicine, lab and business office central to all.

Table 6-3.
Analysis of Program.
Group Practice — Multispecialty — 9 Physicians

This program assumes the following: two internists, three family practitioners, three pediatricians, and one otolaryngologist; a central business office and lab will serve all; in addition to the central supply, several small storage rooms would be scattered throughout the facility.

Waiting Room(s)				$24 \times 30 =$	720
Children's Play Area					120
Peds Sick and Well Waiting					600
Pedo Exam Rooms	2@	8×12	& 8@	$8 \times 10 =$	832
Pedo Nurse Station				$10 \times 12 =$	120
Pedo Consultation Rooms				$10 \times 12 =$	360
Pedo Minor Surgery				$12 \times 12 =$	144
ENT Exams			3@	$8 \times 12 =$	288
Audio Room				$10 \times 12 =$	120
ENT Minor Surgery				$12 \times 12 =$	144
ENT Consultation Room				$12 \times 12 =$	144
ENT Nurse Station				$8 \times 10 =$	80
IM Exam Rooms			6@	$8 \times 12 =$	576
IM Consultation Rooms			2@	$12 \times 12 =$	288
IM Nurse Station				$8 \times 10 =$	80
Flex Sig Room[a]				$12 \times 18 =$	216
ECG/Cardiopulmonary Lab				$16 \times 20 =$	320
Family Practice Exam Rooms			9@	$8 \times 12 =$	864
Family Practice Consultation Rooms			3@	$12 \times 12 =$	432
Family Practice Nurse Station			2@	$8 \times 10 =$	160
Cast Room				Use Minor Surgery	
Minor Surgery/Procedures				$12 \times 12 =$	144
Staff Lounge				$16 \times 18 =$	288
Central Supply				$12 \times 16 =$	192
Medical Records				$16 \times 18 =$	288
Administrator				$10 \times 12 =$	120
Lab[b]				$24 \times 32 =$	768
Radiology[c]				$12 \times 26 =$	312
Toilets			7@	$7 \times 8 =$	392
Business Office					
Reception				$12 \times 14 =$	168
Bookkeeping				$16 \times 20 =$	320
Insurance/Collections				$16 \times 20 =$	320
Transcription				$10 \times 12 =$	120
Workroom				$10 \times 10 =$	100
Subtotal					10,140 ft²
25% Circulation[d]					2,535
Total					12,675 ft²

[a]Includes prep area and toilet.
[b]Includes lab, lab waiting, blood draw, toilet, and storage. This assumes lab work done in house.
[c]Includes darkroom, control, film filing, viewing areas, and dressing area.
[d]Allows for 5- to 6-foot-wide corridors.

sible to abandon existing radiology rooms, tearing them down to remodel for less specialized use such as additional examination rooms or an expanded waiting room. By locating the radiology department contiguous to the area of the proposed future expansion, existing radiology rooms need not be altered and new rooms could be added.

Medical records is another area that often has to be expanded. However, since this would typically be located in the core of the suite, it is usually difficult to enlarge it. It is better to project a realistic number of charts and growth for a seven-year period (physicians generally keep medical records for seven years) and make the room large enough to begin with.

If the building is designed for and owned by the doctors, the architect can take liberties with the design and make the structure of the building really conform to the spatial requirements of the group's practice. A large clinic may be laid out with the administrative and support services in the core, with each specialty department radiating out from it like spokes of a wheel. Each "spoke" would have its own nurse station and waiting room, but the clinical lab, medical records, insurance, business office, and so on would be in the core area (Figure 6-18). This is also known as a *satellite* plan.

If the square footage of each specialty department is not great, one large waiting room may be designed near the reception and business office. Patients would be called from there to the various departments. More often, each specialty department would function independently with its own waiting room, reception desk, nurse station, and other support facilities. There may be a central reception desk and waiting room at the entrance of the clinic, where an aide may prepare a form that the patient carries to the sub-reception desk located at the specialty department. Upon checking out, the patient may book a future appointment either at the sub-reception desk or at the central reception desk, depending on how the flow is set up. Payment for services would usually be made at the central reception desk or cashier's counter, if one exists, rather than at the specialty department.

The multispecialty group-practice clinic shown in Figures 6-19a, b, c is 30,000 square feet in size and located on 2½ floors of a large medical office building. The clinic includes internal medicine, family practice, radiology, pharmacy, vascular lab, cardiopulmonary testing, clinical lab, and a large endoscopy suite. Medical records, conference room/staff lounge, and the clinic administrator's office are on the lower level. Medical charts are brought up from the lower level to the circulation point on each floor via a dumbwaiter.

The clinic functions as a *group-practice model* HMO, a preferred provider organization (PPO), and also accepts fee-for-service patients. On the first visit, the patient registers on the first floor, near the family practice reception desk, where an embossed card is dispensed, paperwork is handled, and a medical chart is prepared. The patient is then referred to the appropriate decentralized reception desk to check in prior to receiving treatment. On subsequent visits, the patient proceeds directly to the reception desk at the respective department and does not need to stop at the registration desk.

This is an example of a *decentralized* plan where each specialty department has its own reception and waiting area, with nurse stations, exam rooms, and private offices arranged in pods.

Great attention was paid to circulation patterns in order to minimize the possibility of patients leaving without passing the cashier's desk. On the first floor, inset carpet designs and unique signage properly placed lead patients past the principal cashier station, while radiology patients exit through the radiology waiting room. On the second floor, all exiting circulation is directed past two cashier stations.

INTERNAL MEDICINE GROUP

This is a single-specialty group, but due to the many internal medicine subspecialties, more specialized rooms and a larger clinical lab and radiology suite are required than with most single-specialty groups.

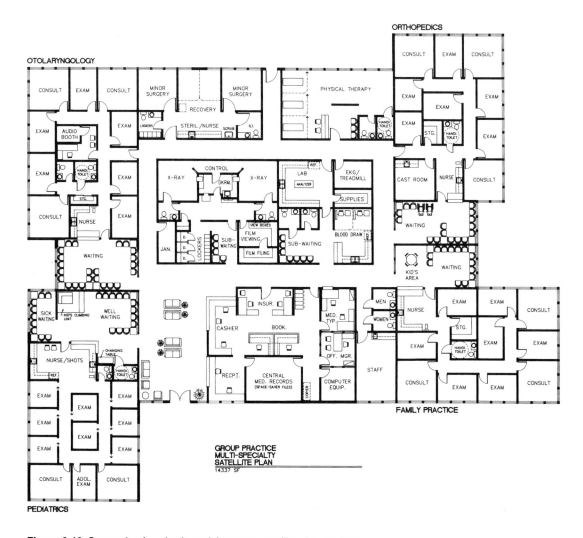

Figure 6-18. Space plan for mixed-specialty group, satellite plan, 14,337 square feet. (*Design: Jain Malkin Inc.*)

MULTI-SPECIALTY GROUP PRACTICE CLINIC, 30,000 SF
MAIN LEVEL FLOOR PLAN

Figure 6-19a, b, and c. Space plan for multispecialty group, 30,000 square feet. (*Design: Jain Malkin Inc.*)

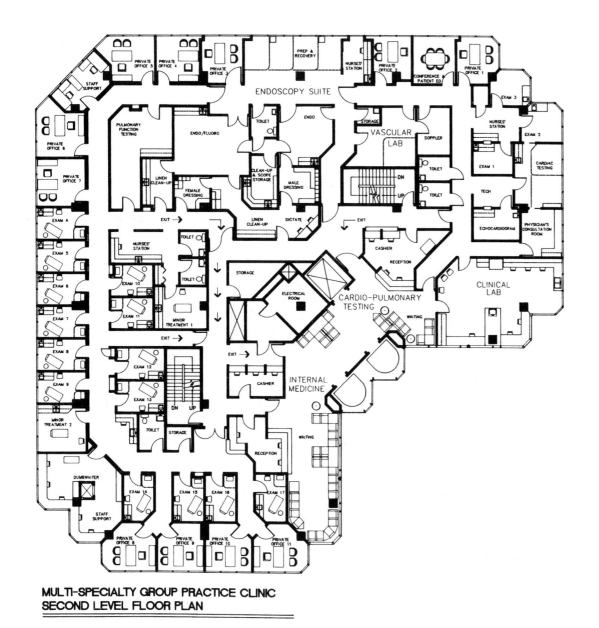

**MULTI-SPECIALTY GROUP PRACTICE CLINIC
SECOND LEVEL FLOOR PLAN**

Figure 6-19b.

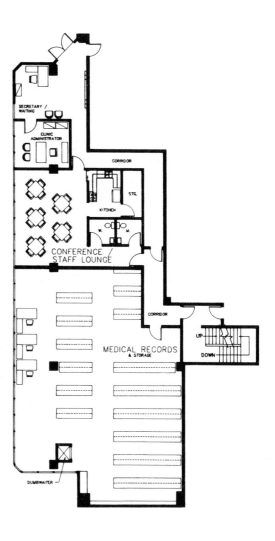

**MULTI-SPECIALTY GROUP PRACTICE CLINIC
LOWER LEVEL FLOOR PLAN**

Figure 6-19c.

An internist specializing in cardiology or in pulmonary disease would need an ECG room and a cardiopulmonary lab. One who specializes in gastroenterology would require a sigmoidoscopy room and perhaps an endoscopy suite. Endocrinologists, on the other hand, order many lab studies—some of which require patients to report to the lab in the morning and remain nearby for four to six hours, with blood being drawn every hour. Thus, the lab must be of sufficient size to accommodate a high volume of work and should have a comfortable lounge for waiting patients.

The suite for a group practice of internists would typically have three exam rooms for each doctor, a consultation room for each physician adjacent to his or her pod of exam rooms, a toilet, and a nurse station. The flex sig room, ECG treadmill, cardiopulmonary lab, clinical lab, and radiology suite would be located in the core area central to all exam rooms. The business office, insurance office, cashier's desk, and waiting room would be located at the entrance to the suite so that each patient, upon entering and leaving, must pass by the reception and cashier's desks (Figure 6-20).

A large group practice will have a business manager or an administrator who will require a small private office preferably with a window wall (starting at 48 inches off the floor) facing the business office so that he or she can keep an eye on operations at all times.

Patients may at times report to the lab without having to see a physician, so the lab should be located at the front of the suite, enabling a patient to enter and leave without mingling with patients waiting for visits with a physician. In fact, there might be an entrance from the street (or public corridor of the medical building) directly into the lab. The reader is referred to Chapter 5 for space-planning requirements of a clinical lab.

The waiting room must accommodate one hour's patients per doctor. Thus, if each doctor can see an average of four patients per hour and each has three examining rooms, an eight-physician group would need seating for approximately 40 persons in the waiting room or elsewhere within the suite when all doctors are seeing patients simultaneously. A formula for estimating the required number of seats is

$$2P \times D - E = S$$

where

P = *Average number of patients per hour per physician*

D = *Number of doctors*

E = *Number of exam rooms*

S = *Seating*

The formula assumes that each patient arrives with one other person, a friend or relative.

Allowing that some patients will arrive unaccompanied by a friend and some will be directed to the lab, X-ray, procto room, or ECG room, the 40 required seats might be reduced to 35 at the absolute minimum. Figuring 18 square feet per person, a waiting room that will accommodate 40 persons will have to be approximately 800 square feet in size, allowing extra space for wheelchairs. Include additional space for a children's play area.

FAMILY PRACTICE GROUP

The suite for a family practice group would be an expansion of a suite for a solo practitioner (refer to Chapter 3). It would also include an X-ray facility, lab, private office for a business manager, and maybe a small allergy suite. Often, a group of family practitioners includes a general surgeon. The formula discussed above for estimating the number of seats in the waiting room applies here, except that a family practitioner can see up to six patients an hour, and each physician should have the use of three exam rooms.

Note: Medical Group Management Association (Englewood, Colorado), known as MGMA, is the oldest and largest member organization for group practices, founded in 1926. According to a January 2001 news release, MGMA represents 6000 healthcare organizations and 176,000 practicing physicians. It is an excellent resource for a variety of statistics and information. SMG Marketing Group (Chicago, Illinois) is another good source of statistics and forecasts published in a newsletter format.

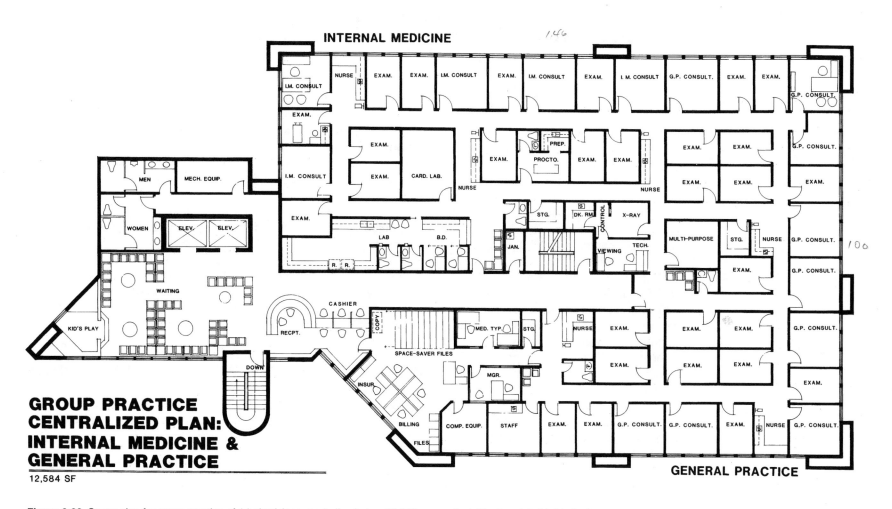

INTERNAL MEDICINE

GROUP PRACTICE CENTRALIZED PLAN: INTERNAL MEDICINE & GENERAL PRACTICE

12,584 SF

GENERAL PRACTICE

Figure 6-20. Space plan for group practice of 14 physicians, centralized plan, 12,584 square feet. (*Design: Jain Malkin Inc.*)

CHAPTER 7

Ambulatory Surgical Centers

OVERVIEW

Ambulatory surgery refers to scheduled surgical procedures provided to patients who do not require overnight hospitalization. Ambulatory surgery may be provided in a physician's office—in which case it is called *office-based surgery*—or in a freestanding, independent facility specifically organized to provide scheduled ambulatory surgery. In this chapter, the acronyms FOSC (freestanding outpatient surgery center) and ASC (ambulatory surgical center) are used interchangeably.

The practice of ambulatory surgery is not a new concept. The British Medical Association in 1909 reported 7320 operations performed by a Scottish physician on ambulatory patients at the Royal Glasgow Hospital for Children.* The results were reported to be as successful as those for inpatient surgery. However, the interest in ambulatory surgery declined somewhat until the early 1960s when the development of new fast-acting anesthetics made ambulatory surgery more practical.

The first successful freestanding ambulatory surgical center is generally recognized to be the Phoenix Surgicenter®, which began operations in February 1970. Anesthesiologists Wallace Reed and John Ford established the facility that has become the model for other non-hospital-based ambulatory surgical centers.

The freestanding ambulatory surgical center may be organized according to a variety of operational models that vary according to type of ownership and sponsorship, affiliation with hospitals, and types of services offered. The term

*Thomas O'Donovan, *Ambulatory Surgical Centers,* Aspen Systems Corp., Germantown, MD, 1976, p. 4.

freestanding may be used to refer to a facility that is physically separate from another, such as a hospital, or it may mean a facility whose program and ownership are independent and legally distinct from any other organization.

Ambulatory surgical centers may be located within a hospital, may be a separate building located on the hospital campus, or may be a satellite facility located off campus. Some ambulatory surgical centers are entrepreneurial enterprises owned and operated by a group of anesthesiologists or surgeons and have no affiliation with a hospital. These facilities are commonly located within a medical office building, or they may be physically freestanding in a single-tenant building. It is this last example that is the focus of this chapter—a facility not owned by a hospital and located in a medical office building, or freestanding.

ADVANTAGES OF AMBULATORY SURGERY

There are many advantages to ambulatory surgery from both the patients' and the physicians' viewpoints. Some of these advantages follow.

1. Hospitals are geared to traditional inpatient surgery protocols, which are often inappropriate for ambulatory patients, whereas a facility organized for the sole purpose of ambulatory surgery would have a staff trained to meet the specific needs of these patients. Hospitals sometimes find it difficult to merge new protocols with existing systems.

2. Ambulatory surgery patients are not sick; they are candidates for elective procedures. In a hospital, their families may have to share a common surgery waiting room with

inpatients' families, which can have a devastating psychological effect. Imagine the stress of sitting next to someone whose husband may be having open heart surgery.

3. Patients often experience psychological stress when entering a hospital. Fear of the unknown is heightened by unexpected sights, such as a view of a patient arriving in an ambulance or seeing a patient on a gurney with an IV in the arm. Patients are generally less apprehensive when arriving for surgery in a facility located in a medical office building.

4. Physicians and staff often experience greater satisfaction in an FOSC because they can tailor operational systems as they wish, with no bureaucratic red tape.

5. There is much greater flexibility in scheduling procedures in an FOSC. In a hospital, ambulatory patients will be bumped to open up the schedule for urgent or emergent patients. Both physicians and patients find ease of scheduling an advantage in an FOSC.

6. Ambulatory surgery provides better utilization of hospital beds and costs considerably less than doing the same procedure in a hospital. The major savings is due to elimination of a hospital stay, and insurance payers often stipulate they will pay for certain procedures only if done within an ambulatory surgical center.

7. Ambulatory surgical patients receive less medication both pre- and postoperatively, and they often return to work sooner than people who have those same procedures as inpatients. Perhaps this is due to the fact that FOSCs promote a wellness philosophy, treating patients as if they are healthy, and allowing them to take responsibility for a large part of their own care.

OWNERSHIP AND AFFILIATION

A great many mergers and acquisitions in 1999 resulted in 69.6 percent of FOSCs being independently-owned, 27 percent owned by multifacility chains, and 3.4 percent

hospital owned. HealthSouth of Birmingham, Alabama, is the nation's largest FOSC multifacility chain, owning 8 percent of the total market with 229 facilities. Columbia/HCA Healthcare Corp. is the second largest chain with 123 facilities.* If the HCFA ambulatory payment classification (APC) system reimbursement rates are more favorable to hospital-based outpatient facilities, this may tip the scale in that direction.

ECONOMIC AND REGULATORY ISSUES

Prior to designing an FOSC, it is necessary to understand the facility's goals with respect to licensing, certificate-of-need (CON) requirements, accreditation, and reimbursement by Medicare/Medicaid and commercial insurance carriers.

Ambulatory surgery centers (ASCs) are highly regulated at the federal, state, and peer level. Most facilities will be state licensed, have Medicare certification, and JCAHO or AAAHC accreditation. AAAHC has been granted "deemed status" by HCFA (Health Care Financing Administration) to certify ASCs for Medicare participation as can JCAHO.

The American Association of Oral and Maxillofacial Surgeons (Web site aaoms.org) offers a state-by-state summary of requirements for licensure and Medicare certification for operation of ambulatory surgical centers.

Licensure

A facility owned and operated by a physician group practice generally need not be state licensed, provided that non-owner surgeons are not allowed privileges. However, the state business and professions Code in some states, such as California, does require even solo practitioners to obtain licensure, certification, or accreditation if they administer general anesthesia "in doses that place

---

*SMG Marketing Group Inc. FOSCs Database, June 1999 edition.

patients at risk for loss of life-preserving protective reflexes." In other states, a physician's license to practice his or her specialty may meet the requirements. Surgical procedures are usually done on a small scale and are performed within the context of the physician's practice. State agencies often do not regulate office-based surgery, although there is increasing pressure for greater regulation. The American Society for Aesthetic Plastic Surgery, for example, mandated that, by January 1, 2002, practitioners must be accredited by one of the national organizations such as AAAASF (American Association for Accreditation of Ambulatory Surgery Facilities), which accredits all surgical specialties. Office-based surgery facilities are discussed in greater detail in Chapter 4 under Plastic Surgery.

When a facility is organized specifically for the purpose of ambulatory surgery, and a surgeon need not be an owner to be awarded privileges, then licensure of the facility is an issue. Licensing is often a requirement for receiving state reimbursement, and insurance payers may require that a facility be licensed for their participation. Furthermore, licensed facilities may be eligible for rate discounts from liability carriers.

NFPA 101 Life Safety Code and state building codes are the standard for all licensing and certification requirements. The designer must check with the state fire marshal, state facilities' development agencies, the local building department, and the local department of health services to ensure that all requirements are identified. The cost of designing a facility initially to meet licensing requirements will be comparatively small compared with trying to retrofit it later to achieve compliance. Licensing offers a certain amount of economic security in that it assures the facility of receiving the maximum amount of reimbursement offered by payers. Currently, 41 states require state licensure of ASCs, making them the most highly regulated type of ambulatory medical facility.

CON/Health Systems Agency Review

Each state is unique in its approach to regulating FOSCs. The Health Planning and Resources Development Act of 1974 mandated that state governments establish Certificate-of-Need (CON) programs to regulate healthcare facilities and services. In some states, a CON may be required for an FOSC, whether it be owned by a hospital or another entity. The purposes of the CON are to prevent duplication of highly specialized facilities and equipment and to keep a lid on rising healthcare costs. Some states exempt facilities from the CON process if they are not owned by a hospital.

In many states, the CON process starts with a review by the local health systems agency (HSA), which must endorse the project and make recommendations to the state. Early in the planning stages of an FOSC, it is essential to ascertain whether a CON may be required and whether HSA endorsement is mandatory. If a local HSA does not exist, there may be another areawide health planning agency that should be consulted. It should be noted that many states have abandoned their CON programs since the federal government ceased funding them. The national trend toward deregulation allows FOSCs a much easier path to their goals. Currently, 36 states have some type of CON regulations.

Accreditation

The Joint Commission of Accreditation of Healthcare Organizations (JCAHO) can accredit freestanding ambulatory surgical centers that are not owned by hospitals; however, accreditation by the Accreditation Association for Ambulatory Health Care (AAAHC), established in 1979 (located in Wilmette, Illinois), is more common. This is a voluntary accreditation program aimed at quality assurance in all aspects of patient care. The agency publishes a handbook of standards for ambulatory healthcare as well as a code checklist for ambulatory surgical facilities based on compliance with NFPA 101 Life Safety Code. In summary, accreditation is a voluntary assessment process whereby industry experts and peers define conformity standards by which surveyors evaluate and rate the organization's performance. It's a means of identifying and validating for the consumer quality facilities that meet recognized standards.

It should be noted that there is a national nonprofit association for freestanding ambulatory surgical centers called FASA (Federated Ambulatory Surgery Association), with national headquarters located in Alexandria, Virginia. FASA publishes a bimonthly journal and an annual bibliography on ambulatory surgery issues with the goal of improving the delivery of outpatient surgery. FASA helped organize the AAAHC.

Certification

Medicare certification is a requirement for receipt of federal reimbursement for patients eligible to receive these benefits. Medicare and Medicaid are programs administered by HCFA. With respect to the physical plant, Medicare does not stipulate sizes of rooms or number of scrub sinks per operating room, but rather relies entirely on compliance with NFPA 101 Life Safety Code. Medicare engages a local state fire marshal to conduct the survey of a new facility to verify compliance. Medicare certification paves the way for approval by other reimbursement agencies and insurance payers. It constitutes the seal of approval, so to speak. In reality, there is little difference between licensure and certification with respect to design criteria, because both rely on compliance with the Life Safety Code. Ninety percent of ASCs are Medicare certified.

HCFA Definition of ASC
HCFA defines an ASC as "any distinct entity that operates exclusively for the purpose of providing surgical services to patients not requiring hospitalization." *

Reimbursement Policies

The total charge for a surgical procedure has two components. One is the anesthesiologist's and surgeon's pro-

---

*Title 42, Vol. 2., Sec. 416.2 Code of Federal Regulations, revised Oct. 1, 1999.

fessional fees, and the other is the facility fee—the charge for the surgical suite, operating room staff, and supplies. Third-party payers vary in their reimbursement policies with respect to these two components.

Physicians are generally reimbursed a "reasonable and customary" fee for their services regardless of whether the facility is licensed or certified; however, third-party payers will not pay for the use of the facility unless it meets certain criteria. These usually involve a strict adherence to the Life Safety Code. Therefore, Medicare certification and/or state licensure assure that the FOSC will be reimbursed for the use of the facility.

MARKETING CONSIDERATIONS

An appealing aspect of surgery in a freestanding facility is the element of choice. A physician may have privileges at several facilities and may offer the patient the opportunity to choose the preferred setting. Along with that choice comes the expectation of convenience and care delivered in a small-scale, noninstitutional, friendly environment. Patient satisfaction is necessary for a facility's success, and many ASCs are keenly aware of guest relations. Both patients and physicians benefit from the fact that, according to a study by Arthur Andersen, more than 82 percent of cases start on time in ASCs.

The interior environment is a critical element of patient satisfaction. The entire facility should use color to relax and soothe patients, and texture may be introduced in carpets and wallcoverings, whenever appropriate (in terms of maintenance and infection control). Artwork and accessories should not be overlooked as a means of distracting patients and making the facility less threatening.

However, patients and their families are not the only ones who benefit from a well-designed environment. To attract top-quality physicians and nursing staff and to keep morale high, staff areas must be properly designed so that they are functional and they should look as attractive as patient areas.

SURVEY OF SURGICAL PROCEDURES

Advancements in medical technology such as lasers and endoscopic surgery enable an increasing number of procedures to be carried out in a minimally invasive manner, safely, in an outpatient facility. According to FASA, over 50 percent of all surgery is performed in an outpatient setting at lower cost, greater convenience, and quality that meets or exceeds that of hospital-based surgical facilities.

It is helpful to understand, prior to designing a facility, the types of procedures that are normally performed in an FOSC. A survey of facilities nationwide is represented in Table 7-1, indicating that 66 percent of procedures fall into four specialty categories.

HCFA-Covered Procedures

Covered surgical procedures defined by HCFA are those that can be safely performed in an ASC; are not commonly or safely performed in physicians' offices; require a dedicated operating room and post-op recovery room (not overnight); can generally be executed in 90 minutes in the OR and do not exceed 4 hours' recovery time; do not result in extensive blood loss; do not require major or prolonged invasion of body cavities; do not directly involve major blood vessels; and are generally not life-threatening or emergency in nature. In addition, general anesthesia must not exceed 90 minutes duration.

TRENDS AND INNOVATION

Advances in Pharmacology

Pharmaceuticals have changed outpatient surgical practices. These include new short-acting anesthesia agents that wear off in minutes, fast-acting agents for pain and postoperative nausea, and anesthetic agents that enable "fast-tracking"—bypassing the recovery room by transferring the patient directly from the OR to the second-stage recovery area. Fast-tracking is expected to result in significant cost savings; however, it is appropriate primarily for patients who have had uncomplicated procedures and only if they meet physiological discharge criteria. The patient is actually awakened while still in the OR and allowed to recover there (which requires only a few minutes) prior to being moved to second-stage recovery.

Minimally Invasive Surgery

Surgery performed in ways not requiring large open incisions—for example, laparascopically—is revolutionizing outpatient surgery. There is less scarring, shorter recovery times, less disability, lower medical risks, better clinical outcomes, and reduced costs. Endoscopic surgery has become so popular that "videoscopy suites" are being developed across the nation.

Harmonic Scalpel

Using ultrasound technology, the Harmonic Scalpel® by Ethicon Endo-Surgery cuts tissue and seals blood vessels at the precise point of impact, resulting in minimal lateral thermal tissue damage. Instead of burning the tissue,

Table 7-1.
Specialty Surgical Procedures Performed in Ambulatory Surgery Centers in 1998

Type of Procedure	Percentage
Ophthalmology	26.8
Gastroenterology	18.8
Gynecological	9.5
Orthopedic	9.8
ENT	6.9
Plastic Surgery	7.7
Other (pain block, urology, podiatry, dental, neurology)	20.5
	100%

Source: ©1999 by the SMG Marketing Group, Inc.

the scalpel's vibration clots the blood to stop the bleeding. Lasers, on the other hand, operate at very high temperature to vaporize or burn tissue.

FACILITY DESIGN

An enormous amount of careful planning precedes the establishment of an ambulatory surgical center. Feasibility studies analyze the demographics of the area and determine the demand for such a facility. In terms of codes and regulatory agency review, an FOSC is certainly the most complicated of any outpatient facility.

Location

The feasibility study will identify, among other things, the geographical area from which patients will be drawn. Travel time factors heavily into the equation. FOSCs, after all, are designed to be convenient for patients and physicians; therefore, driving distance and site accessibility are important. Traffic patterns near the location, parking availability, visibility from the street, and building appearance all require consideration.

What makes an FOSC so sensitive to these factors is that the best marketing efforts cannot create an increased demand within a given area for surgical services. Business must be generated from within the existing demand of the area served. Marketing studies will reveal whether there is excess demand, whether existing facilities are underutilized, or whether projected growth will support the additional service.

Transfer Agreement

The preference for a facility to be located near a hospital is a matter of individual consideration. The incidence of need for patient transfer to a hospital following outpatient surgery has been much lower than was originally anticipated. Those transfers that have occurred were nearly always for pain control or for persistent bleeding. Transfer for life-threatening conditions has been rare according to studies done by the FASA. This is the result of careful patient screening to determine potential risks and careful selection of types of procedures. Nevertheless, a transfer agreement with a local hospital is required.

Codes

The FOSC has many characteristics of a hospital inpatient surgery unit and must comply with many, but not necessarily all, of the same requirements imposed upon hospitals. To receive certification and/or licensure, state administrative codes and NFPA 101 Life Safety Code must be followed. Federal guidelines focus almost entirely on operational policies and procedures of the facility, and they make no demands above state requirements for the built environment.

Explosion/Fire/Electrical Shock. Codes are designed to prevent a variety of hazards in the operating room and recovery areas and to reduce fire hazards elsewhere. The National Electrical Code (NEC) is widely used across the nation to set standards for the use of electricity. This code, like the others described here, is implemented through adoption by state and local jurisdictions, and exact requirements vary somewhat from region to region. For instance, explosive anesthetic gases, which might be ignited by a stray spark, are no longer in use, yet some states require that conductive flooring and isolated electrical power be used. Other states recognize that this is unnecessary.

NFPA 101 concentrates on fire protection and prevention. NFPA 99 is the industry standard for storage and distribution of hazardous gases, vacuum systems, essential electrical systems, and respiratory therapy.

Power Failure. Emergency power for certain medical equipment and for egress lighting is required. The capacity and intended use are described in the NEC, Section 517. It gives requirements for ORs and recovery areas and defines which features are required to enhance life safety.

Infection Control. The most pervasive risk in the surgery setting is that of infection. This involves two issues: contamination of the open wound and staff exposure to HIV or hepatitis virus. Facility design, internal protocols for handling infectious waste, and proper protection during surgery are the three principal ways of reducing this hazard.

Patient and staff circulation patterns bear significantly on the spread of infectious microorganisms. This often poses a challenge for the space planner, since program requirements often exceed available space, sometimes reducing circulation alternatives. State building codes usually establish standards for smooth and washable finishes and for special ventilation requirements within specific areas, but there is little of a definitive nature in the way of regulatory codes to assist the designer in laying out the suite to minimize the spread of infection. Common sense, experience, and guidance of the OR supervisor often dictate best practices.

Today, the risk of acquired immune deficiency syndrome (AIDS) and hepatitis B and C is the major health hazard to be encountered whenever working with blood or body fluids. Extreme care must be taken in the surgery setting to protect both patients and staff. The Centers for Disease Control in Atlanta and the Association of periOperative Registered Nurses (AORN) in Denver offer written guidelines on facility design and patient handling to control the risk of infection.

OPERATIONAL PROTOCOLS

FOSCs adhere to very strict procedural protocols. To assure life safety and quality of care, and to move patients and supplies through the facility with ease and efficiency, it is imperative that each task be performed routinely, in the same manner, by all personnel. The AAAHC guides facilities on protocols for medical record keeping, patient discharge procedures, quality assurance/peer review, patients' rights, and so forth.

Every aspect of patient handling is based on a protocol developed by the individual facility, to assure that nothing is forgotten or overlooked. While many of these protocols do not actually have an impact on the physical design of the facility, it is important for a successful project to include in the planning process representatives of all staff functions, including anesthesiologists, surgeons, nurses, and administrative staff. The space planner must avoid making any assumptions about a center's operations that could inadvertently defeat operational effectiveness.

PATIENT FLOW

There are seven stages of patient flow through the facility: *preadmitting, arrival, patient prep, induction, recovery, postrecovery,* and *discharge.* The patient's first encounter with the facility may be a day or two prior to surgery, to complete preadmission forms, undergo laboratory tests, and receive dietary instructions. Sometimes this is handled by phone and lab tests are not always necessary.

This may be the first time the patient has ever had surgery, or perhaps the first time the patient has had ambulatory surgery, and he or she may have no frame of reference upon which to rely to combat fear and anxiety. Therefore, it is important that the preadmitting process give the patient confidence about the experience. After all, a patient truly cannot evaluate the quality of the clinical care or the surgeon's competence, but patients do make judgments nevertheless, based on interactions with staff and an assessment of the interior environment.

A patient's confidence can be bolstered by an understanding of exactly what to expect on the day of surgery. Nursing staff, anesthesiologists, and surgeons all play a significant role in educating and reassuring the patient. If the facility is designed well, circulation patterns will be predictable and convenient, allowing easy access for patients, staff, and family. Good design should make it easy for staff to do things right.

The patient arrives on the day of surgery approximately one and one-half hours prior to the scheduled surgery time, accompanied by an escort. Some facilities, it should be noted, do the lab work on the day of surgery, which means patients may have to arrive a little earlier. The patient is next directed to a preparation area where street clothes are exchanged for surgical apparel. This may be handled in a number of ways. Some facilities have dressing rooms and lockers for storage of the patient's belongings (Figure 7-1), while others have the patient undress in a private prep/exam room (Figure 7-2), and belongings may be placed in a container that is stored in a secured area. In the recovery room, belongings are returned to the patient prior to dressing for discharge. In many states, regulators insist that patient belongings be stowed in lockers.

Some facilities do not have individual patient prep rooms and, instead, use a large room (called pre-op holding) similar to the recovery room, with gurneys separated by cubicle drapes for privacy (Figure 7-3). In this situation, patients sometimes change clothes within this enclosure, or they may use a dressing/locker room. It should be noted that JCAHO and state surveyors are especially interested in visual *and auditory* privacy for patients in pre-op and postanesthesia recovery units (PACUs). New facilities should not consider cubicle drape separation as an option but should construct private bays for each patient to address these standards (Figure 3-75).

After the patient is undressed, the operative site is scrubbed, shaved, and prepped for surgery. The anesthesiologist will interview the patient in the prep room or in the preoperative holding area, discussing the alternatives for anesthesia and answering any questions the patient may have.

Most FOSCs do not use preoperative sedatives, as they increase recovery time. Therefore, patients may read or visit with their families prior to being taken to surgery. The patient may walk or be wheeled on a gurney into the operating room. Some facilities prefer to have patients walk in order to enhance their perception of being healthy and undergoing an elective procedure.

Anesthetic induction almost always takes place in the operating room, although an intravenous fluid may be started in the preoperative holding area. Following surgery, the patient is transferred to the postanesthesia recovery area until he or she is conscious and stabilized. Many facilities use a second-stage recovery area that has recliner chairs and lounge seating (Figures 7-1 and 7-4). Patients remain here after they are dressed, have some juice or tea, and leave when they feel well enough for discharge or when their escort has arrived. Often, the escort is allowed to sit with the patient in the secondary recovery area. Instructions for postoperative care may be delivered here or in a private office, adjacent to the discharge area.

FACILITY ACCESS

Handicap Requirements. Barrier-free access is a code requirement throughout the nation, and although patients are accompanied by staff in almost all areas of an ambulatory surgical center, the facility must be designed to accommodate the disabled.

Vehicular Access—Patient Pickup/Emergency. As the term ambulatory surgery implies, patients are able to walk into the facility without assistance. However, patients often leave a facility in a wheelchair, due to protocols established by insurance carriers and regulatory agencies. The patient will be met by transportation at the facility's entrance or pickup area, which is often a private driveway located near the surgical center's discharge area. Optimally, patients and families should never have to backtrack through the facility. As the patient progresses through the facility and ultimately to the secondary recovery and discharge area, the escort proceeds from the waiting room to the discharge area to greet the patient, and then goes to pull up the car at the patient pickup exit.

When designing a medical office building with an ambulatory surgical center as a tenant, it is advisable to plan for a vehicular turnaround or drive-through, separate from the medical building lobby. This driveway must be large enough to accommodate an ambulance or a van.

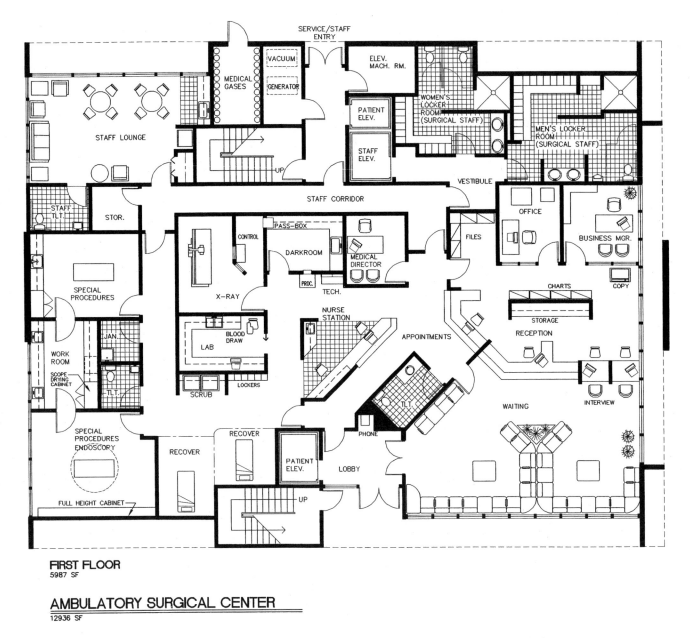

FIRST FLOOR
5987 SF

AMBULATORY SURGICAL CENTER
12936 SF

Figure 7-1. Space plan for ambulatory surgical center on two floors, 12,936 square feet. (*Design: Jain Malkin Inc.*)

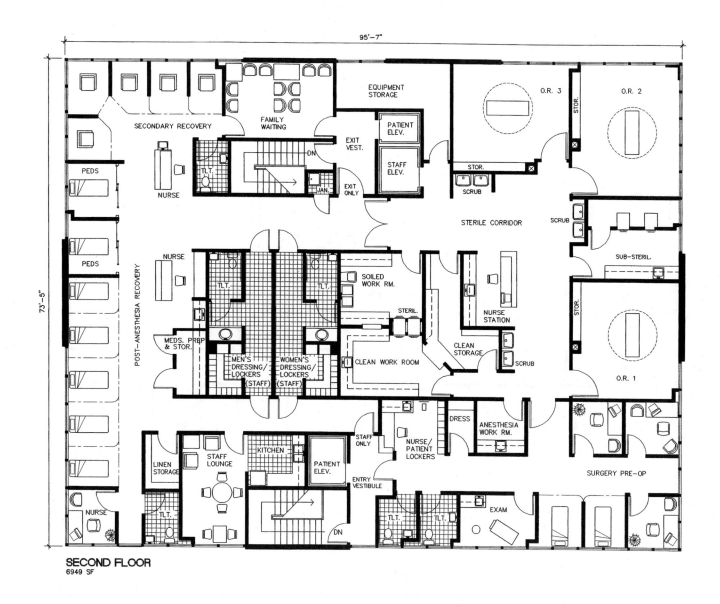

95'-7"

73'-5"

SECONDARY RECOVERY

FAMILY WAITING

EQUIPMENT STORAGE

O.R. 3

O.R. 2

PEDS

PEDS

NURSE

TLT.

DN

EXIT VEST.

PATIENT ELEV.

STAFF ELEV.

STOR.

STOR.

SCRUB

SCRUB

STOR.

SUB-STERIL.

POST-ANESTHESIA RECOVERY

NURSE

TLT.

TLT.

SOILED WORK RM.

STERIL.

NURSE STATION

CLEAN STORAGE

SCRUB

O.R. 1

MEDS. PREP & STOR.

MEN'S DRESSING/LOCKERS (STAFF)

WOMEN'S DRESSING/LOCKERS (STAFF)

CLEAN WORK ROOM

NURSE

LINEN STORAGE

STAFF LOUNGE

KITCHEN

PATIENT ELEV.

STAFF ONLY

NURSE/PATIENT LOCKERS

DRESS

ANESTHESIA WORK RM.

SURGERY PRE-OP

NURSE

TLT.

DN

ENTRY VESTIBULE

TLT.

TLT.

EXAM

STERILE CORRIDOR

EXIT ONLY

JAN.

SECOND FLOOR
6949 SF

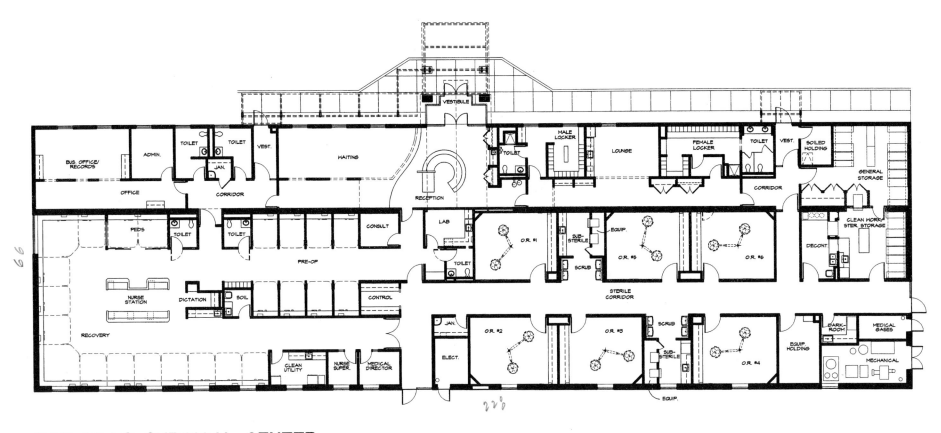

FAR HILLS SURGICAL CENTER

14813 SQ. FT. FLOOR PLAN

Figure 7-2. Space plan for ambulatory surgical center, 14,813 square feet. (*Design: Boulder Associates, Inc., Boulder, CO.*)

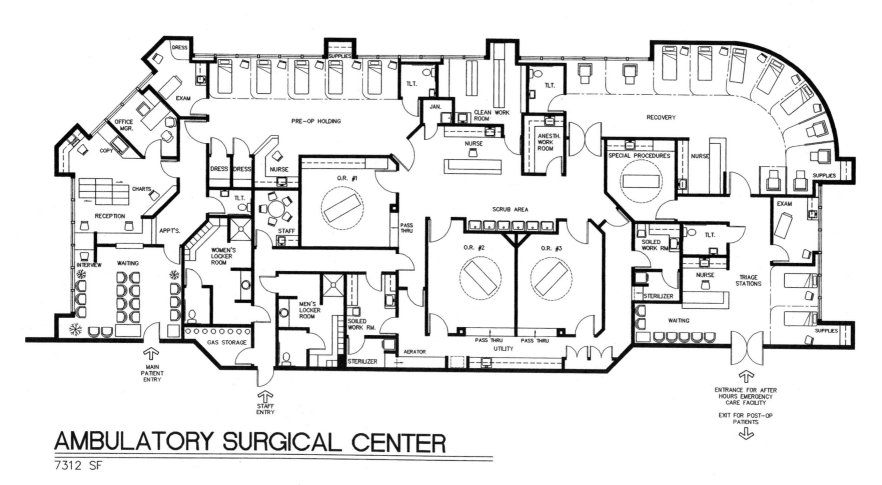

Labels within the floor plan:

DRESS

EXAM

OFFICE MGR.

COPY

CHARTS

RECEPTION

APPT'S.

INTERVIEW

WAITING

SUPPLIES

PRE-OP HOLDING

TLT.

JAN.

CLEAN WORK ROOM

NURSE

ANESTH. WORK ROOM

TLT.

RECOVERY

SPECIAL PROCEDURES

NURSE

SUPPLIES

EXAM

DRESS DRESS

NURSE

TLT.

O.R. #1

STAFF

PASS THRU

SCRUB AREA

O.R. #2

O.R. #3

SOILED WORK RM.

TLT.

NURSE

TRIAGE STATIONS

WOMEN'S LOCKER ROOM

MEN'S LOCKER ROOM

SOILED WORK RM.

STERILIZER

AERATOR

STERILIZER

PASS THRU PASS THRU

UTILITY

WAITING

SUPPLIES

GAS STORAGE

MAIN PATIENT ENTRY

STAFF ENTRY

ENTRANCE FOR AFTER HOURS EMERGENCY CARE FACILITY

EXIT FOR POST-OP PATIENTS

AMBULATORY SURGICAL CENTER

7312 SF

Figure 7-3. Space plan for ambulatory surgical center with emergency-care facility, 7312 square feet. (*Design: Jain Malkin Inc.*)

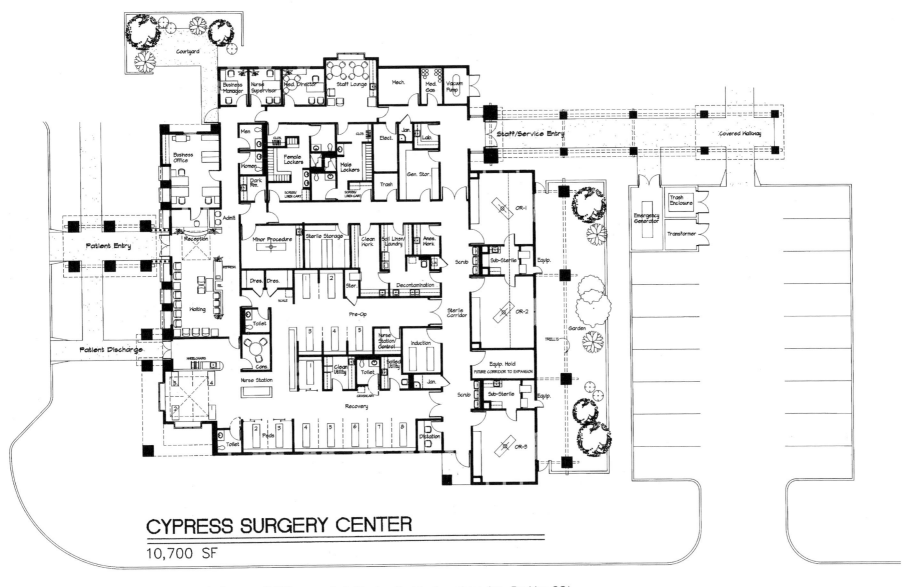

Courtyard

Business Manager | Nurse Supervisor | Med. Director | Staff Lounge | Mech. | Med. Gas | Vacuum Pump

Staff/Service Entry

Covered Walkway

Business Office

Men | Women | Dark Rm. | Female Lockers | Male Lockers | CLOS. | Elect. | Jan. | Lab. | Gen. Stor. | Trash

SCRUB/ LINEN CART

Patient Entry

Admit

Reception

REFRESH

Minor Procedure | Sterile Storage | Clean Work | Soil Linen/ Laundry | Anes. Work

Scrub | Sub-Sterile | Equip. | OR-1

Emergency Generator | Trash Enclosure | Transformer

Waiting

Dres. | Dres. | 2 | Ster. | Decontamination

SCALE

Pre-Op

Sterile Corridor

OR-2

Garden

Toilet

Cons.

3 | 4 | 5 | Nurse Station/ Control | Induction

Patient Discharge

WHEELCHAIRS

Clean Utility | Toilet | Soiled Utility | Jan.

Equip. Hold
FUTURE CORRIDOR TO EXPANSION

TRELLIS

Nurse Station

CRASHCART

Scrub | Sub-Sterile | Equip.

Recovery

Toilet | 2 | 3 | Peds | 4 | 5 | 6 | 7 | 8 | Dictation

OR-3

CYPRESS SURGERY CENTER

10,700 SF

Figure 7-4. Space plan for ambulatory surgical center, 10,700 square feet. (*Design: Boulder Associates, Inc., Boulder, CO.*)

Facility Entrance. The building or facility entrance and passage to the reception area should be easily identifiable, and should be pleasant and welcoming. If the patient has to hunt for the entrance, if signage is poor, or if the entry is poorly illuminated, it undermines the patient's confidence about the surgical experience.

The building lobby or the waiting room of the FOSC must have a public telephone and a drinking fountain. Comfortable seating and current reading material should be provided for the patients' escorts. An outdoor courtyard or garden, accessible to the patients' companions, is a pleasant addition to the facility. If the FOSC is located on an upper floor of the building, at least one of the elevators must be large enough to accept a gurney and must have an override call button for emergencies.

Physician/Staff Access. A physician/staff entrance should be provided near the staff lounge and locker area. Patients should not observe the coming and going of personnel. Dedicated physician parking close to the staff entry will be expected and appreciated by physicians.

Service Access. Thought must be given to service access for pickup and delivery of laundry and for disposal of infectious waste and trash. Boxes of disposable supplies might be purchased in bulk lots and stored outside the surgical suite, replenishing the clinical area as needed.

Figure 7-5. Registration area provides privacy. (*Architecture and interior design: Shepley Bulfinch Richardson and Abbott, Boston, MA; Photographer: ©Peter Mauss/Esto.*)

INDIVIDUAL COMPONENTS OF AN FOSC

The outpatient surgical facility is divided into three designated areas—unrestricted, semirestricted, and restricted—defined by the activities performed there. Intermediate and major surgical procedure rooms must be located in the restricted area, whereas a minor surgical procedure room may be located in the restricted or unrestricted area. This is discussed in more detail under Surgical Core.

Waiting/Reception Area

The patient's first impression of the surgical center will be formed in the waiting room. The patient should be able to reach the receptionist easily and be able to speak with a certain amount of privacy. The registration area, where scheduling and financial arrangements are made, must be private, quiet, and comfortable. Figures 7-1 and 7-5 show a registration area divided into privacy carrels. There is increasing awareness of the importance of patient privacy

Figure 7-6. Family/escort waiting area has appearance of library/lounge with slate-clad fireplace and wall of bookshelves. (*Design: Jain Malkin Inc.; Photographer: Philip Prouse.*)

and confidentiality resulting from HIPAA (Health Insurance Portability and Accountability Act of 1999), which deals with electronic transmission of data. However, JCAHO and other accreditation agencies have extended this to the built environment in terms of acoustic and visual privacy. In addition, a public telephone, drinking fountain, restrooms, and wheelchair storage are required.

The design of the waiting room enables the surgical center to demonstrate visually to patients its concern for their comfort. Colors should be cheerful, furniture comfortable, and lighting appropriate for reading and/or relaxing. Natural light and views of the outdoors should be exploited whenever possible. Figure 7-6 shows a waiting

room with a fireplace, bookshelves, and seating arranged more like a living room, while Color Plate 27, Figure 7-7, has a coffee bar. Seating arranged in privacy groupings (Figure 7-8) is preferable to that which lines the perimeter of the room. Providing options and choices, according to a large body of research, reduces stress. Consider providing a choice of environments such as a quiet room where family can read, another that has a TV built into an armoire or cabinet so that it doesn't dominate the room (Figure 7-9), and one with a protected play area for children with a built-in aquarium that can be viewed from the pediatric area as well as an adult lounge. A refreshments area with coffee and tea is welcomed by escorts dropping off patients for early-morning surgeries. Research also indicates that pleasant diversions greatly relieve stress—items such as water elements, aquariums, interactive art—things that distract the mind and cause relaxation.

An ASC that is part of a large ambulatory-care center has the potential to provide, by virtue of scale, a number of attractive alternatives for waiting families.

An outstanding design with an interior that provides numerous pleasant diversions, dynamic architecture, natural light, and connects people to nature—even during robust Michigan winters—can be seen in Figure 7-10.

Regional design features can flavor the decor. In San Diego, where residents are much enamored of Mexican culture, the high-tech aspects of ambulatory surgery were tempered with handcrafted folk art, colorful ceramic tile, and exuberant color (Color Plate 27, Figure 7-11). The ceiling of the registration area with a trellis and blue "sky" creates an outdoor ambience indoors (Color Plate 27, Figure 7-12).

In some surgery centers, family are issued a beeper that enables them to shop, leave the facility to enjoy a meal, or sit in the garden, knowing that they will be "beeped" when the patient is in second-stage recovery.

Waiting Room Capacity

Waiting room capacity will be determined by the facility program. Most patients will be accompanied by a com-

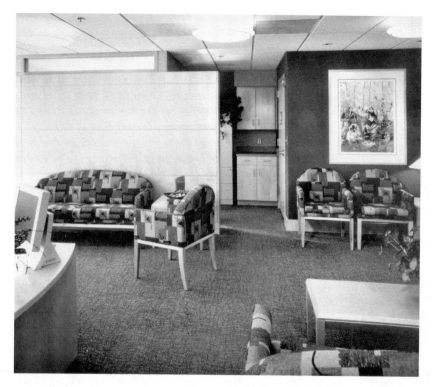

Figure 7-8. Ambulatory surgical waiting area features privacy groupings and coffee bar at rear. Alpine Surgery Center. (*Architecture and interior design: Boulder Associates, Inc., Boulder, CO; Photographer: Daniel O'Connor.*)

panion. Scheduling practices in an individual facility may cause last-minute rescheduling, necessitating a one- to two-hour patient wait in the waiting room. Turnover in an individual OR can be quite high, when taking into account that some procedures may only be 30 to 40 minutes in length. This means that a substantial number of patients and their companions may be in the waiting room at any one time, especially at peak scheduling periods. For example, patients who work often tend to schedule surgery on a Thursday or Friday so that they have the weekend to recover. Sometimes a small secondary family waiting room is provided for family or escorts near the secondary recovery area and discharge exit.

Figure 7-9. One area of the waiting room has a TV built into a cabinet with sloped magazine shelves alongside. This is the same facility as depicted in Figure 7-6. (*Design: Jain Malkin Inc.; Photographer: Jain Malkin.*)

Figure 7-10. Light-filled atrium with horticultural garden and koi pond provides a delightful waiting experience for families and escorts of ambulatory surgery patients. (*Architecture and interior design: Shepley Bulfinch Richardson and Abbott, Boston, MA; Photographer: ©Peter Mauss/Esto.*)

Business Office

The size of the business office will depend on the program established by the FOSC. The reader is referred to Chapter 3 for a discussion of the business office and related areas. Medical record storage is less extensive than in a physician's office since the patient's chart is retained by the referring physician, and only a brief medical history and a report of the surgical procedure are kept at the facility. Medical records must be protected from fire and unauthorized access.

Scheduling is an important aspect of this enterprise. Scheduling staff use sophisticated computer software that is linked to a physician referral network, whereby patients' histories and preadmitting information are transmitted by computer, eliminating the need for the patient to be present prior to the day of surgery. ASCs often schedule blocks of time for individual physicians who use the facility regularly.

Preadmit Testing

Although not specifically part of an ambulatory surgical center, hospitals often have a preadmit testing area located either in the hospital or in an ambulatory-care facility. Patients are directed to this unit several days prior to surgery for "one-stop" presurgical testing, which may include blood tests, chest X-ray, ECG, verification of insurance and preauthorization, and completion of patient histories.

Patient Examination/Prep Area

The patient examination and prep area should be close to the waiting room and have a direct path to the operating rooms. Patient prep areas have a nurse station nearby (Figure 7-3) where patients may be weighed and their vital signs recorded. The patient will be supervised by the charge nurse, who reassures the patient during the preparation process and answers questions.

In many facilities, the corridor leading to the patient prep area is clinical in appearance with portable medical equipment and gurneys stored there, all of which may contribute to the patient's anxiety. It is desirable to create a nonclinical ambience, devoid of medical equipment clutter, using attractive vinyl wallcoverings, colorful sheet vinyl with inset geometric designs, and artwork.

A preoperative or prep area needs a minimum of one bed per OR, varying as the facility program dictates. Individual prep rooms should be at least 8×10 feet in size (Figure 7-2). As discussed previously, a large room with privacy curtains dividing beds should not be considered in light of recent emphasis on patient visual and auditory privacy, but many existing facilities will have this (Figures 7-3 and 7-4). Refer to Figure 3-75 for an optimal example of private treatment bays. Waiting for surgery (the anticipation of the procedure) is the patient's time of highest anxiety; therefore, a chair for a family member should be provided.

A nice touch in the prep and recovery areas is colored bed linens, accompanied by color-coordinated cubicle curtains, wallcoverings, and upholstery. Don't be afraid of color. This area need not be bland. Research shows that views of nature greatly reduce stress. The pre-op holding area in Figure 7-13 has a raised garden at gurney level on three sides and, in addition, a 2-×4-foot back-lit film transparency of tulip gardens over each bed. Color Plate 28, Figures 7-14 and 7-15, illustrate this concept in a procedure room and an OR, respectively.

In many facilities, the preoperative holding area is used, later in the day, for recovering patients. If such is the case, each bed should be equipped with oxygen and suction as well as patient monitors.

Pediatric Patients

If the facility will serve a significant number of pediatric patients, a number of factors should be considered. It is important for the parent to be able to accompany the child through as much of the process as possible. Dedicated pre-op holding and recovery areas (Figures 7-2 and 7-4 and Color Plate 29, Figure 7-16) ensure that parents will not be infringing upon the privacy of adult surgical patients, nor will adult surgical patients be disturbed by the crying of children.

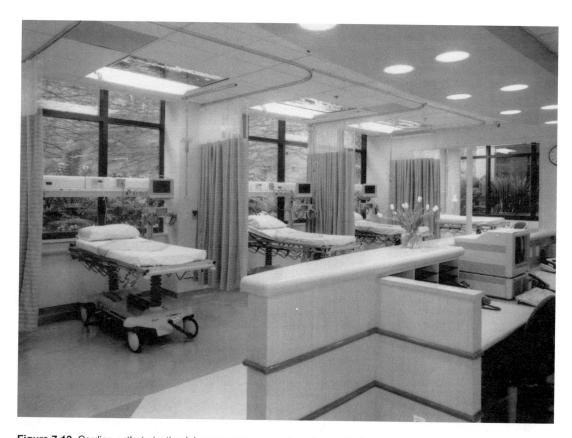

Figure 7-13. Cardiac catheterization lab prep area surrounds patients with the stress-relieving benefits of nature in a garden that starts at the height of gurneys, wrapping around three sides of the room. Overhead, patients look at back-lit film transparencies of tulip gardens in Holland. Scripps Memorial Hospital, La Jolla, CA. (*Architecture: Rodriguez and Park, San Diego, CA; Interior design: Jain Malkin Inc.; Photographer: Steve McClelland.*)

Surgical Core

The information in this section is largely based on the 2001 edition of the AIA/USDHHS *Guidelines for Design and Construction of Hospital and Health Care Facilities.* Substantial changes have occurred with regard to outpatient surgical facilities since the 1996–1997 edition of the guidelines, which was much more general and not nearly as detailed in regard to specific rooms and areas. The essay at the front of the 2001 *Guidelines* states: "There has been a concerted effort to level the playing field and to give patients the same level of protection for surgical procedures whether they are performed in an acute general hospital or in an outpatient setting." Two specific areas of change relate to the classification of operating rooms according to three levels of care as defined by the American College of Surgeons. This incidentally correlates with the three classifications (A, B, and C) of anesthesia used by AAAASF. Refer to Chapter 4, Plastic Surgery, for a description of these classifications. Another change in the new guidelines that should be noted relates to the soiled workroom, which can no longer have a pass-through to the clean assembly workroom.

American College of Surgeons Classification of ORs

The sizes of ORs stipulated in the 2001 AIA *Guidelines* are based on levels of care defined by the American College of Surgeons. The italics indicate the ACS class descriptions, followed by the *Guidelines* sizes for outpatient ORs.

Class A. *"Provides for minor surgical procedures performed under topical and local infiltration blocks with or without oral or intramuscular preoperative sedation. Excluded are spinal, epidural axillary, stellate ganglion blocks, regional blocks (such as interscalene), supraclavicular, infraclavicular, and intravenous regional anesthesia. These methods are also appropriate for Class B and C facilities."*

(Minor surgical procedure rooms) shall have a minimum clear area of 120 square feet, a minimum clear dimension of 10 feet, and minimum clear distance of 3 feet at each side, head, and foot of table. May be located within a restricted or unrestricted corridor.

Class B. *"Provides for minor or major surgical procedures performed in conjunction with oral, parenteral, or intravenous sedation or under analgesic or dissociative drugs."*

(Intermediate surgical procedure rooms) shall have a minimum clear area of 250 square feet with a minimum clear dimension of 15 feet, minimum clear distance of 3 feet, 6 inches on all sides of the table. Must be located within restricted corridors of the surgical suite.

Class C. *"Provides for major surgical procedures that require general or regional block anesthesia and support of vital bodily functions."*

(Major surgical procedure rooms) shall have a minimum clear area of 400 square feet, a minimum clear dimension of 18 feet, and minimum clear distance of 4 feet on all sides of the table. Must be located within restricted corridors.

The number of first-stage and second-stage recovery stations required is related to the number of each class level OR in the AIA *Guidelines.*

Control Station/Nurse Station

The nerve center of the surgical core is the nurse station. It provides visual surveillance of all traffic entering the restricted corridor and commands total visual control of the area, including OR doors and surgical core access. There may be another nurse station in the pre-op holding area and in the recovery room.

The nurse station should be large enough to allow adequate staff work space to monitor activities. It should contain a built-in blanket warmer in the casework and a sink and a locked drug storage cabinet or medications closet. The area will contain a crash cart (emergency resuscitation), wheelchair, and gurney storage.

Unrestricted, Semirestricted, and Restricted Areas

According to the 2001 edition of the AIA *Guidelines,* the *unrestricted* area includes a central control point (reception desk) established to monitor entry to the semirestricted and restricted areas. The *semirestricted* area includes the peripheral support spaces of the surgical suite and has storage areas for clean and sterile supplies, work areas for storage and processing of instruments, and corridors leading to the restricted areas of the surgical suite. Traffic here is limited to authorized personnel and patients who must wear surgical attire and cover head and facial hair. The *restricted* area includes operating and procedure rooms, the clean core, and scrub sink areas. Surgical attire and hair covering are required and masks must be worn where open sterile supplies are located and where contact with persons who have scrubbed may occur.

The path to the operating rooms should be direct and as aesthetically pleasant as possible, maintaining consistency with the aesthetic ambience of the prep area, which by now will have become familiar to the patient. Although a sterile (restricted) zone is far more limited in terms of allowable finish materials, color and detailing may still reiterate the theme. Careful attention to detail, the use of oak trim, and the colorful ceramic tile in Color Plate 29, Figure 7-17, reinforce an image of quality.

The sterile corridor functions as a transition, separating operating rooms from patient prep and recovery. It should never be entered in order to reach another destination. Surgical apparel must always be worn in this corridor, and unprotected street clothes are not permitted.

Scrub Area

Scrub sinks (with knee- or foot-activated controls) are located near the entrance to each OR (Figure 7-18). State codes establish the specific number of sinks per OR, which is usually two per OR for the first two and one additional sink for each additional OR beyond two. These should be positioned to prevent splashing of personnel or equipment. They are usually recessed in a niche lined with floor-to-ceiling ceramic tile or other stain-resistant material. A clock must be visible from each scrub sink, and the OR door should push into the room to prevent personnel from using their hands to pull it open. Additionally, doors into ORs should be visible from the control or nurse station (Figure 7-2).

Operating Rooms

Operating room design requires the consideration of many factors, as described below.

Size. There seems to be a rule of thumb for economic viability of an FOSC, which necessitates at least three ORs. With required support services, this translates to approximately 10,000 square feet. The sizes for Class A, B, and C ORs in the *AIA Guidelines* were stated previously. In other codes and standards, the minimum size of a minor OR is 270 net square feet, with a 15-foot minimum dimension across the room. The minimum

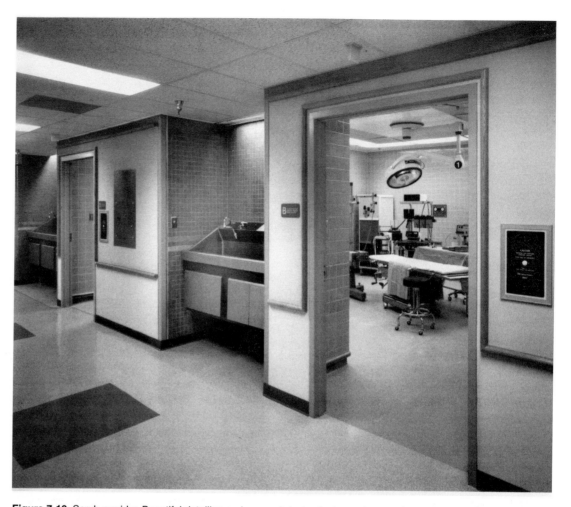

Figure 7-18. Scrub corridor. Beautiful detailing and unusual design features characterize this facility. Also see Color Plate 29, Figure 7-17. (*Photo courtesy: Anderson Mikos Architects, Ltd., Oak Brook, IL; Photographer: Jay Wolke.*)

size for a major OR is 350 net square feet, with an 18-foot minimum dimension across the room. It is prudent to size ORs larger than may have been anticipated in order to accommodate additional portable equipment such as microscopes for ophthalmic surgery, arthroscopes, lasers, video monitors, C-arm X-ray, and robotic devices that are becoming standard as ambulatory

Room shape should be as close to square as possible for convenient placement of mobile and ceiling-mounted equipment around the table. Figures 7-19 and 7-20 show typical ASC operating rooms. The extraordinary ceiling design in Color Plate 28, Figure 7-15, connects patients to nature, distracting and relaxing them prior to anesthesia induction. Operating rooms in an FOSC should be designed to the same exacting standards as hospital inpatient ORs. Precautions for infection control, fire safety, equipment performance, lighting design, airflow, gas shutoff, and electrical back-up power should all be carefully considered.

Planning Issues. Operating room features that affect turnaround time between procedures deserve careful examination. The typical inpatient OR may be used for three or four procedures per day, each of which may last two to four hours, whereas an FOSC OR may be used six or seven times per day for procedures lasting 30 to 90 minutes. In an FOSC, surgery generally terminates by 2 P.M. to enable patients to recover and leave by closing time.

In this regard, the route between the operating rooms and sterilization and the manner in which instruments and sterile supplies are delivered to the room become significant. Some facilities have a separate sterile corridor (Figure 7-3) around the operating room for flash sterilization and for quickly supplying the operating rooms. This is a matter of individual consideration, based on the surgical program and available space. (Note that the facility in Figure 7-3 functions as an after-hours emergency-care facility.) Staff input on design of the OR is critical in laying out the rooms so that gas lines, suction, electrical, and computer access are properly placed. Location of the sterile field should be part of this discussion.

Casework in operating rooms either should be recessed in the wall (Figure 7-19) or, if freestanding, should have a sloped top to avoid a shelf that becomes a dust collector. Operating room casework usually has glass doors for viewing the contents (Figure 7-19).

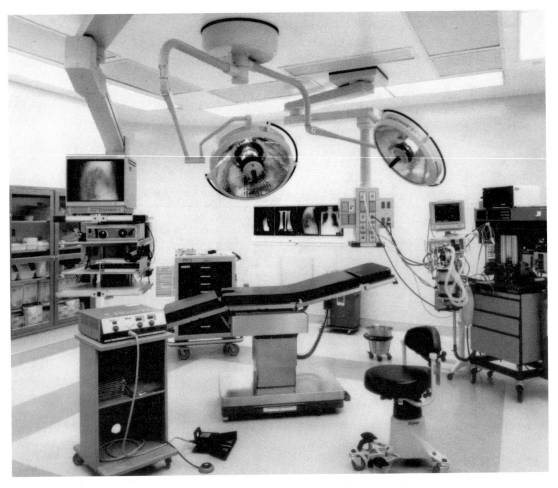

Figure 7-19. State-of-the-art operating room uses ceiling-mounted articulating arms to facilitate quick repositioning of equipment. Ambulatory Care Center at Bronson Methodist Hospital, Kalamazoo, MI. (*Architecture: Shepley Bulfinch Richardson and Abbott, Boston, MA; Photographer: ©Peter Mauss/Esto.*)

surgery takes on an expanded role. As time goes on, more procedures will be done on an outpatient basis and more complicated types of surgery will be performed in an FOSC.

Hospital inpatient ORs are generally 400 net square feet or larger. That size allows for great flexibility and space for a number of OR personnel and equipment.

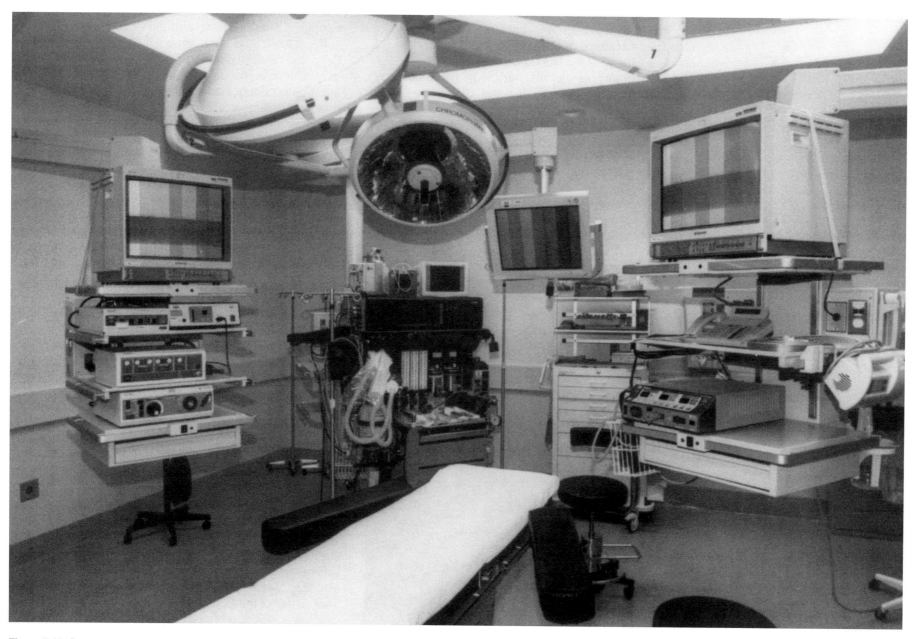

Figure 7-20. State-of-the-art laparoscopic operating room equipped with video-laparoscopic surgery "towers" suspended from the ceiling by power booms (articulating arms) to keep floor clear of clutter. (*Photo courtesy: Hacksensack University Medical Center, Hackensack, NJ*)

Equipment. The operating room is on its way to becoming an ultra-high-tech environment, integrating voice recognition systems, robotics, and PACS, and there will be more blurring of the line between interventional radiology and surgery as vascular radiology, neuroradiology, and cardiology become more invasive. CIMIT (the Center for Innovative Minimally Invasive Therapy, a partnership between the Massachusetts Institute of Technology, Massachusetts General Hospital, and Brigham and Women's in Boston) is currently designing a minimally invasive surgery suite using remotely controlled robots to execute the procedures laparoscopically. As an example, a coronary artery bypass graft (CABG), in the conventional procedure, involves opening the rib cage. But, when executed robotically, it can be performed endoscopically through a small opening and the patient can be playing golf just three days later, without the pain, loss of productivity, and rehabilitation required with the standard procedure. CIMIT is evaluating, among other things, whether the robotic control station for the surgeon should be in a remote location or within the room. In these high-tech ORs, the pieces of equipment will "talk" to each other. A nurse's desk for computerized charting also needs to be accommodated.

It is likely that ambulatory surgery centers associated with academic medical centers may well be the first to embrace and invest in this level of technology. The Hackensack University Medical Center, at the end of 1998, opened a new ASC featuring 10 state-of-the-art laparoscopic surgery operating rooms. Each is equipped with video-laparoscopic surgery towers suspended from the ceiling by Berchtold Teletom® power booms, which neatly conceal electrical cables, gas lines, and video cables, removing the clutter of multiple cables and wiring as well as equipment, from the floor, mounting it on these articulating arms and shelves (Figure 7-20). In these ORs, various components of the electronic video equipment for laparoscopic operations are integrated through the use of a voice-activated robot called Hermes®. The surgeon wears a microphone and controls all of the equipment through various voice commands. The surgeon is assisted by a second voice-operated robot called Aesop®, which holds the video camera and points it in different directions (Figure 7-21). At Hackensack, patients are assigned a day accommodation room where they change gowns and are interviewed by the nurse and anesthesiologist prior to walking to the OR. After anesthesia recovery, patients return to this same dayroom to be rejoined by their family (Figure 7-22).

The new (opened in 2000) Ambulatory Care Center at Bronson Methodist Hospital in Kalamazoo, Michigan, also makes use of the Berchtold power boom, which allows for quick repositioning of equipment (Figure 7-19).

Electrical Systems. The electrical system must meet standards established by the National Electrical Code,

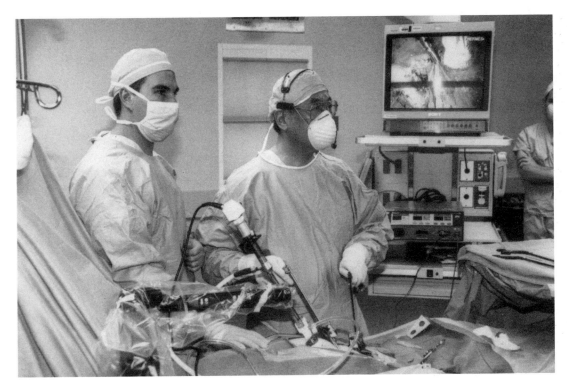

Figure 7-21. Surgeons at work in state-of-the-art operating room designed for minimally invasive surgery. Surgeons wear microphones to control voice-activated robots. (*Photo courtesy: Hacksensack University Medical Center, Hackensack, NJ.*)

NFPA 70; Essential Electrical Systems, NFPA 99; Use of Electricity in Patient Care, NFPA 99; and state codes. The AIA/USDHHS *Guidelines for Construction and Equipment of Hospital and Health Care Facilities* gives a brief description of requirements with references to the aforementioned codes.

The electrical system in any facility where general anesthesia is used is very complex and an electrical engineer experienced in healthcare design should be part of the design team. Code-mandated items include an alarm system, emergency power, ground-fault protection, nurse call and communication systems, and possibly an isolated power system. All ORs must have an emergency communication system connected to the control station.

Electrical outlets in the OR should be mounted at waist height, when located on the wall. Outlets overhead are practical as cords are less likely to become tangled.

Mechanical System. Air-handling systems (HVAC) in the OR and other areas of a surgical suite are very specifically regulated, and they require the technical expertise of a mechanical engineer experienced in healthcare design. The AIA/USDHHS *Guidelines* give a detailed description of requirements in various areas of the suite and refer the designer to applicable NFPA codes that form the basis for regional requirements.

Simply stated, airflow in an OR should be from "clean" to "less clean" areas. Air should enter the room at the ceiling, above the patient, and be drawn off at two or more widely spaced locations near the floor. Filtration, number of air changes per hour, volume, humidity, and temperature are specifically mandated. In some circumstances, where the potential for infection is high, a laminar airflow system may be used. This system sends a large volume of slow-moving, nonturbulent, filtered air down over the patient and the operating team, preventing any particles from settling on the wound.

An enhancement of this concept is the Steriflo® system by Krueger in Richardson, Texas. Forced sterile air, which is comfort conditioned to specific surgical requirements, creates a cube from ceiling to floor surrounding the patient and the surgical team. Contaminated air between

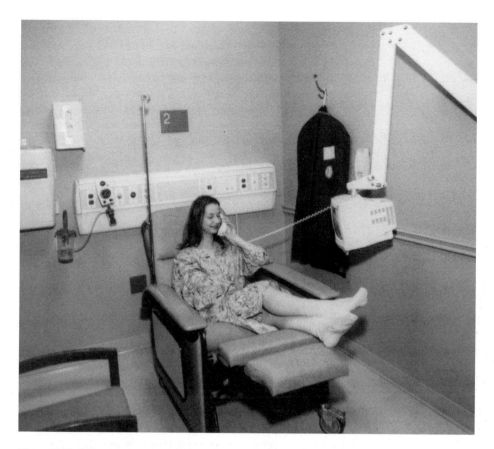

Figure 7-22. Private day rooms assigned to each surgical patient are used for changing clothing, clinical interviews, and second-stage recovery where patient is rejoined by family. (*Photo courtesy: Hacksensack University Medical Center, Hackensack, NJ.*)

the actual operating area and the four walls of the operating room impinges, but cannot penetrate, the curtain of sterile air and is immediately exhausted through the return air system. The curtain of sterile air is forced through pressure plenums and filtered downward through slot diffusers positioned in the ceiling around the operating table.

Operating rooms must maintain positive air pressure to keep contaminants from being sucked into the room when the door is open. Air inputs at the ceiling, with exhausts at the base, ensure that contaminants from the floor are not carried up to the sterile field.

Room temperature and humidity affect each other and therefore must be reviewed accordingly. Relative humidity higher than 60 percent with a temperature in excess of 72 degrees Fahrenheit can create condensation, while relative humidity lower than 50 percent at 72 degrees Fahrenheit can create static electricity.

Lighting. Recommendations for lighting levels have been established by the Illuminating Engineers Society in its publication, *Lighting for Hospitals and Health Care Facilities.* In an operating room, general room illumination is provided by flush-mounted fluorescent fixtures (with dimmer controls), which give 200 footcandles of intensity at the work surface. Fluorescent lamp color, to match the surgical light, should be at a color temperature of 4200 to 5000 kelvins with a CRI (color rendering index) of 85 to 90. Ceiling-mounted surgical lights must produce tremendous brightness (illuminance up to 260,000 lux), high color contrast for tissue definition, shadow-free lighting, and excellent color rendition with a CRI of 85 to 90.

The quantity of light is of equal importance to the quality of light, with reference to issues of glare, contrast, color rendering, surface reflectance, and dimming capacity.

Videoscopy is sometimes enhanced by the lowering of light levels. When using microscope illumination, fluorescents and operating lights may be dimmed. (The surgeon should be able to control room lights with a foot switch or voice command.) Auxiliary downlights, located where they will not be distracting, provide lighting for nurses and the anesthesiologist when surgical lights have been dimmed.

Medical Gases. Medical gases include oxygen, compressed air, vacuum (suction), nitrous oxide, and nitrogen (used for power instruments). These are centrally piped to each operating room and may be delivered by an outlet in the wall, through a fixed column extending from the ceiling, or via a movable track. Medical gases are used by both the anesthesiologist and the operating team; separate outlets are needed for each.

Oxygen and suction are also required at each recovery bed. The endoscopy procedure room needs oxygen, compressed air, and suction. The endoscopy workroom needs compressed air and suction. Refer to Chapter 3, Endoscopy, for details of workroom design.

A gas scavenging system to "clean" room air of any anesthesia gases is required in any OR using inhalation anesthesia. The AIA/USDHHS *Guidelines* list requirements for each area of the surgical suite.

Use of Lasers. Lasers have become standard equipment in operating rooms. Different types of lasers, and how they function, are explained in Chapter 4 under Ophthalmology. The holmium and Nd:YAG laser called the VersaPulse® Select™ by Coherent Medical Group is commonly used for urology, orthopedics, ENT, and other specialties. Figure 4-116 is actually an erbium laser used by dermatologists for skin resurfacing, but it looks, from the exterior, the same as this manufacturer's holmium Nd:YAG. The small laser in Figure 4-161 operates on standard electrical service and is used for ENT, gynecology, urology, and general and aesthetic surgery; however, many lasers have higher power requirements. The laser in Figure 4-115 is a CO_2 laser, commonly used by gynecologists, general surgeons, and plastic surgeons, although the specific model depicted is an aesthetic laser system used by dermatologists and plastic surgeons. The surgical CO_2 (by the same manufacturer) used in multiple types of surgery looks exactly the same, however. The laser in Figure 4-84 is a Nd:YAG type, commonly used by ophthalmologists and otolaryngologists.

The ability of lasers to cut precisely, vaporize tissue, and coagulate blood has revolutionized surgical techniques. Certain procedures that were routinely preformed in an operating room may now be done in a physician's office, which illustrates that lasers are very much a part of ambulatory care. Valuable though they are, lasers do require thorough understanding and respect for associated occupational hazards.

Two major occupational hazards associated with lasers are exposure to the eyes and skin and toxic fumes, especially the CO_2 laser plume, about which much has been

Figure 7-23. Laser smoke evacuation system with Fresh Aire ULPA filter. (*Photo courtesy: Stackhouse Inc., A Thermo Respiratory Company, Palm Springs, CA.*)

written. Standard surgical masks are ineffective as a precaution against inhaling the minute particulate matter in the laser plume. Standard surgical masks filter out particles down to 5 microns in size, whereas particulate matter in the laser plume goes down to 0.3 micron in size. The Association of periOperative Registered Nurses (AORN) and the National Institute of Occupational Safety and Health (NIOSH) have determined that laser and electrosurgical smoke is hazardous and may expose OR personnel to aerosolized infections, viruses, toxic gases, and vapors.

The laser smoke filtration system in Figure 7-23 suctions the laser plume and filters particles as small as 0.12 micron. It also helps to control the odor of vaporized tissue. This unit is designed for office-based surgery suites in physicians' offices but can also be used in an ASC. A new model, the VitalVac™ by Stackhouse®, has many useful features for the ASC OR. Note that in ORs the motor and blower may be placed in the power column and above the ceiling (not visible), while the filter and keypad are exposed on a shelf.

The American National Standards Institute (ANSI) document Z-136.1 (may be purchased from the Laser Institute of America in Florida, www.laserinstitute.org) describes four basic categories of controls that should be employed in laser environments. These involve *engineering controls, personal protective gear, administrative and procedural protocols,* and *special controls.* Personal protective equipment includes goggles, clothing, gloves, and laser masks, depending on the type of laser and the amount of laser radiation emitted.

All windows in operating rooms or glazing in doors must be covered during laser procedures, as some laser beams can pass through glass. Appropriate warning signs must be placed on doors to ORs when lasers are in use. Nondefeatable entryway controls may be required on OR doors to prevent people from entering when lasers are in use. Safety interlocks that disable the laser beam are standard on all laser systems. These allow an electrical connection to a door, for example, when it is opened during laser use to immediately put the laser into standby mode.

As infrared and ultraviolet laser beams are invisible, manufacturers must do something to make them visible. A red aiming beam is coaxially aligned with the invisible treatment beam to solve this problem.

Some lasers have special power requirements (208- to 220-volt, three-phase power), but many function with standard current. ANSI Z-136.3 specifically deals with the use of lasers in the medical environment. This is required reading for anyone designing facilities where lasers will be used.

Equipment Storage. An equipment room convenient to the ORs should be provided for the storage of lasers. If they are stored in the OR, one has to plan well in advance to move them to the OR where they will be needed next. If they are all kept in one OR, dedicated strictly to laser surgery, scheduling and flexibility can become a problem. Since only one procedure can be done at a time, the other lasers in the room would be unusable. Other types of equipment might also be stored in this room, such as a C-arm X-ray machine.

Accessory Items. Operating rooms will have two clocks with second hands (one for tracking elapsed time) and a recessed X-ray film illuminator. An individual room may have a C-arm fluoroscopic X-ray unit with TV monitor; there may be a number of ceiling-mounted monitors, a ceiling-mounted microscope, and a number of portable pieces of equipment, including an emergency resuscitation cart. Each piece of equipment has specific power requirements, which must be carefully coordinated between the equipment suppliers and the electrical engineer. A structural engineer should be consulted to ensure that all ceiling-mounted equipment is adequately supported. A Unistrut system above the finished ceiling is usually required.

Overhead Utilities. The designer must provide enough space above the finished ceiling to accommodate structural support, HVAC ducts, recessed fluorescent lighting, electrical conduits, and medical gas piping. The finished ceiling height in an OR should be 10 feet plus another 2 feet in the plenum above. It is sometimes difficult to achieve this height within the structure of the standard medical office building.

Interior Finishes. Finish materials used in the OR must be very durable and able to be cleaned with strong, germicidal agents. Materials should be monolithic and free of seams. Frequent, harsh cleanings tend to open seams, which then harbor microorganisms.

Floors. ORs often used to have terrazzo floors. This is an excellent material, but in today's market, it is expensive and not adaptable to remodeling. A high-quality cushioned sheet vinyl with heat welded or chemically welded seams is ideal for ORs. Attractive products are available that can be cut and inlaid with contrasting borders (Figure 7-19). Sheet vinyl should be installed with a self-coved, 6-inch-high base. Conductive flooring is not required unless flammable anesthetic gases are used.

The reason surgical scrubs (attire) are green is to neutralize the afterimage of blood, since green and red are opposite each other on the color wheel (see Chapter 11). After staring at the surgical field (red) when one looks away, the eye produces the complementary color (green). To avoid seeing green "spots," an 8-×8-foot inset of green sheet vinyl set into the floor neutralizes the afterimage and is also attractive.

Walls. For years, operating rooms had ceramic tile walls, usually in surgical green color. Largely for cost considerations, epoxy paint (specify dull sheen) has become more common in recent years. If ceramic tile is used, it must have a nonreflective matte finish and should be of a medium color value (less reflective for lasers), rather than light. Grout joints must be flush, and latex grout should be considered.

Ceilings. Operating room ceilings must be smooth and washable. Gypsum board with a washable, nonreflective finish in a light to medium color tone is recommended. Ceilings in semirestricted areas, such as clean corridors, central sterile supply, radiographic rooms, and minor procedure rooms, must be smooth, scrubbable, and capable of withstanding germicidal cleaning.

Pathology Prep Area

A small room with cabinet and undercounter refrigerator may be provided for storing tissue to be sent to a pathology lab. Prepared vials containing formalin to preserve the tissue are taken into the OR and later must be refrigerated until pickup. These can also be stored in a fridge in the soiled workroom.

Endoscopy and Minor Procedure Rooms

Ambulatory surgical centers often have an endoscopy suite (Figure 7-1). Specific design details are discussed in Chapter 3 under Internal Medicine. This room can be used for other types of minor procedures that require a clean, but not a sterile, environment.

A 12×12-foot or 12×14-foot procedure room is often used for procedures where minimal assistance is needed and where either no anesthesia, local anesthesia, or conscious sedation is indicated. In the *AIA Guidelines,* a Class A room need only be 120 square feet, but this would be too small for endoscopy procedures. The guidelines define a procedure room as having a clear area of 200 square feet exclusive of fixed cabinets and must have a freestanding hand-washing station nearby. This is the size room designated for endoscopy procedures.

Workrooms

The movement of clean and soiled instruments and materials through the surgical suite should be as efficient and economical as possible and must be carefully studied during the programming stage of design. There must be a continual flow of clean disposable supplies, linens, and instruments into, and removal of soiled items from, the OR. Provision should be made for computer monitors in workrooms to track instruments and manage a number of functions.

Soiled Workroom. Instruments leaving the OR go directly to a soiled workroom where they are decontaminated prior to sterilization. Here they are soaked, scrubbed, rinsed, and/or placed in ultrasonic cleaners to remove blood and debris. This room requires a clinic (flush) service sink, deep utility sink, built-in washer/sterilizer, countertop work surface, and storage for sorting soiled materials (Figure 7-24). A washer decontaminator that goes through the wall into the clean assembly workroom allows dirty instruments to be put in on one side and removed, after processing, on the other where they are put into peel packs for visualization or wrapped and labeled into kits prior to terminal sterilization (Figures 7-1 and 7-2). The lighting level recommended by the Illuminating Engineers Society is 100 footcandles.

It should be noted that the previous edition of the AIA *Guidelines* "allowed" pass-through doors, creating an opening between soiled and clean workrooms, but the 2001 edition eliminates this.

Soiled Holding. This is an area for the collection, storage, and disposal of soiled materials, including linen, and hazardous waste.

Clean Assembly/Workroom. This room is used for inspecting, assembling, and wrapping instruments after

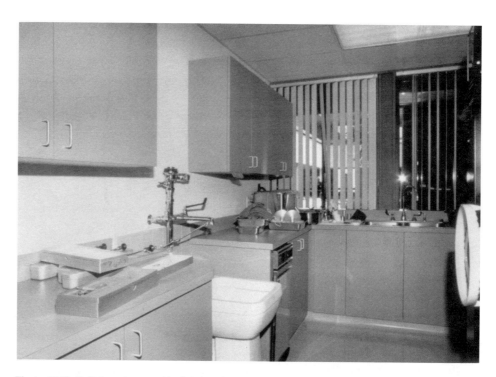

Figure 7-24. Soiled workroom with clinic service "flush" sink and sterilizer. (*Design: Jain Malkin Inc.; Photographer: Jain Malkin.*)

they have been washed and decontaminated, and for terminal sterilization of medical and surgical equipment and supplies. This room requires a handwash sink, adequate countertop work surfaces, and sufficient storage to accommodate supplies. Access should be convenient to the ORs. Smooth and washable floor and wall finishes are required.

Sterilization. Sterilization takes place in the clean assembly/workroom but may additionally be done in a *substerile* area, which is a small room adjacent to an OR, or sometimes between two ORs (Figure 7-2), with an autoclave for quick "flash" sterilization between procedures. Typically, there is a central location serving all ORs supplemented by decentralized sterilization (Figures 7-1 and 7-4), although, in Figure 7-3, the primary and only sterilization area wraps around the ORs. Substerile areas

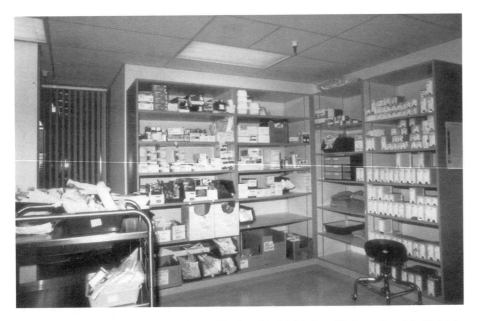

Figure 7-25a. Clean workroom and supply. (*Design: Jain Malkin Inc.; Photographer: Jain Malkin.*)

Figure 7-25b. Clean workroom and supply. (*Design: Jain Malkin Inc.; Photographer: Jain Malkin.*)

allow easy access for flash sterilization (pre-vac computerized sterilization takes only 3 to 10 minutes per cycle and is used between cases). It's a good idea to provide small blanket warmers in the substerile areas so that a warm blanket can be put around the patient as soon as he or she is settled on the operating table since ORs are always very cold.

Whatever the configuration, the sterilization room will contain a large, high-speed autoclave, a Steris peracetic acid sterilizer for heat-sensitive items (requires plumbing) that sterilizes items in 30 minutes, Chemiclave (steam autoclave that uses chemical solutions instead of water), dry heat sterilizer, sink, adequate countertop work surfaces, and storage of clean materials needed to restock the ORs. Cleaning, packaging, sterilization, and setup of surgical trays is done here. It should be noted that the ETO (gas) sterilizer releases toxic vapors that must be exhausted to the outdoors; however, ETO is being phased out. Ventilation issues should be examined carefully in a sterilization area. Wall finishes and flooring should be smooth and washable.

Clean/Sterile Supply Room. After instrument kits have been removed from terminal sterilization, they are allowed to cool before being stored in a clean environment convenient to the OR. Adequate open-shelf storage should be provided (Figures 7-25a and 7-25b), where humidity from the sterilizer is not a factor.

Anesthesia Workroom. A dedicated anesthesia workroom is required if Class C ORs exist. Anesthesia equipment is cleaned, tested, and stored in this room. At least one compressed-air outlet and one oxygen outlet are needed at the work surface.

A sink is required along with sufficient storage for separating soiled from clean equipment. All surfaces must be easily cleanable.

Housekeeping Room. The surgical core must have its own housekeeping room, even if one is located elsewhere in the suite. It will need a floor sink and storage for all cleaning supplies, materials, and equipment.

Storage of Medical Gases

Storage of medical gases must be evaluated in terms of convenient access, separation from other areas (fire hazards), and security. A room near the service entry is generally convenient. Gas storage may be outside the facility, if securely protected from vandalism. Building codes often require wall construction of two-hour fire rating around the room, one-hour duct protection, smoke-fire damper at air supply into the room, and a 90-minute rated door. Other requirements such as an alarm and automatic extinguishing equipment may be required, based on location and type of gases used. The room must be vented directly to the outdoors. Fire codes are very specific with respect to the storage and handling of medical gases. The designer is referred to NFPA 99C, Standard on Gas and Vacuum Systems (1999).

Vacuum and Compressed Air

Vacuum (suction) and compressed air are provided by compressors located on site. These may be remotely located, limited only by flow resistance in the supply pipe. Sometimes a basement, a rooftop, or an outlying utility pen may be utilized.

These compressors are very noisy and should be properly installed to isolate vibration and noise.

Staff Areas

The design of staff areas may vary. The main factors to consider are outlined in the following sections.

Dressing/Locker Rooms. Facilities for medical staff to change into surgical attire should have adequate space for storage of scrubs in various sizes, caps, and shoe covers as well as receptacles for soiled linen and disposable items (Figure 7-26). Separate male and female facilities must be provided, including lockers, showers, toilets, and handwash stations. The design should create a one-way traffic pattern so that personnel entering from outside the surgical suite can change and eventually exit into the restricted area.

Figure 7-26. Staff dressing area with storage for surgical apparel and a bin for soiled garments. (*Design: Jain Malkin Inc.; Photographer: Jain Malkin.*)

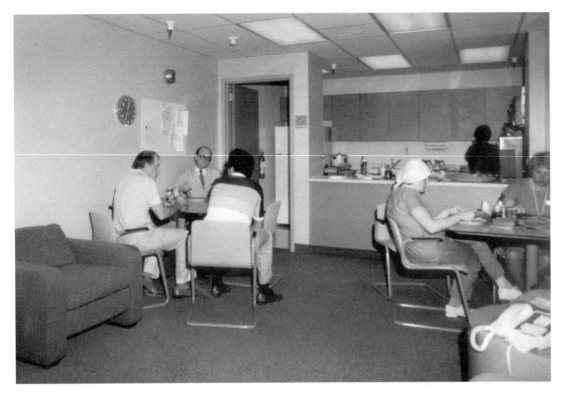

Figure 7-27. Staff lounge, with kitchen. (*Design: Jain Malkin Inc.; Photographer: Jain Malkin.*)

AORN recommends upholstered furniture and carpeting, provided a good maintenance program is enforced. Sometimes the lounge has carrels to enable physicians to dictate and chart. These functions can also be accommodated in a dictation room in the OR area.

The lounge should be a comfortable, softly illuminated room, with space for dining as well as lounging. Telephones are necessary, as well as a tackboard for posting notices of clinical or social importance to the staff. If natural light is available it should, by all means, be exploited. The surgical staff lounge in Figure 7-28 has clerestory windows, admitting light that is reflected by a mirror down into the room. The staff lounge is a high-traffic area used throughout the day.

Postanesthesia Recovery (Primary)

The patient's destination from the OR is the postanesthesia recovery room. This should be immediately accessible from the central sterile corridor. Economies, with respect to staffing, may be achieved by designing the pre-op holding area immediately adjacent to the recovery room, with a single large nurse station overlapping the two areas.

The AIA *Guidelines* define the number of recovery stations as follows:

Class A: minimum of one bed per OR with 2½ feet clear on three sides of bed

Class B: minimum of two beds per OR with 3 feet clear on three sides of bed

Class C: minimum of three beds per OR with 4 feet clear on three sides of bed.

Prior to the new *Guidelines,* two recovery beds per OR was common with an area allocated for each bed (inside the cubicle curtain), of at least 80 square feet, allowing at least 3 feet on all sides of the bed for work space and/or circulation. A patient is generally alert enough to be moved to second-stage recovery in about an hour. Theoretically, this would allow for two procedures per hour in each OR. Recovery room capacity may be adjusted higher or lower, depending on the program and the

Waste/Trash Disposal. A provision for fluid waste disposal (clinic flush sink) convenient to the ORs and postanesthesia recovery unit is required. The one in the soiled workroom may be used, provided, in addition, one toilet in the recovery area is equipped with a bedpan cleaning device.

Lounge. A staff lounge with kitchen should be provided for surgical personnel to allow them to relax between procedures without having to regown (Figure 7-27). This area is not considered "clean" in terms of maintaining sterile conditions such as exist in the surgical core. Walls may have vinyl wallcovering, and a suspended acoustical ceiling may be utilized. The type of furniture in this area is not specifically addressed in codes or guidelines; however, experience of the medical staff. Privacy between beds may be achieved by glass walls with cubicle drapes although glass will result in a noisier environment than standard gypsum board partitions.

The level of asepsis control measures applied in this area is based on licensing and accreditation guidelines. A sheet vinyl flooring is recommended for the high volume of wheeled traffic and also to facilitate cleanup if someone vomits.

Indirect lighting is ideal, adjusting light levels lower over recovery beds and higher at the nurse station. The area should be colorful, but avoid busy patterns or bold colors, which may cause discomfort if a patient is nauseated. Cubicle drapes are probably the best vehicle for accent color, as they are easily changed. The color of fluorescent lamps in this area is a critical factor, as skin tone is an indicator of the patient's condition. A color temperature of 3500 kelvins with a CRI of 85 to 90 is recommended.

The nurse station must have good visibility of all beds (Figure 7-2) and must have a handwashing sink, emergency resuscitation cart, lockable drug cabinet, wheelchair storage, and staff and patient toilets.

It is unlikely that an isolation recovery room for a single occupant would be required in an FOSC. However, occasionally facilities have private recovery rooms as in Color Plate 29, Figures 7-17 and 7-29, and Figure 3-76. To increase the perception of natural light in the basement-level recovery room, shown in Color Plate 29, Figure 7-29, faux window bays with art and colored glass, frosted glass, and quality indirect lighting were used. Foundation walls were penetrated to create basement window wells to maximize available natural light. In all OR (Color Plate 28, Figure 7-15) and procedure rooms, as well as behind each recovery bed, back-lit film transparencies are used to connect patients to nature. Natural maple woodwork and furniture add warmth and a soft glow. This is a welcome antidote to the "sterile" colorless settings typically seen. It also speaks of quality and attention to detail.

Pediatric Recovery. When the FOSC accommodates children on a regular basis, a pediatric recovery area

Figure 7-28. Staff lounge, with natural light from clerestory windows. Note the use of a mirror to reflect light. (*Architecture: Hope Consulting; Interior design: Jain Malkin Inc.; Photographer: John Christian.*)

should be provided that is separate from, but adjacent to, adult recovery. Space for a family member must be provided near each crib or bed, which means that more area per patient may be required than for adult beds. Sound control is very important here, as it is unpleasant for adults to hear children screaming and crying.

Pediatric recovery may receive the same interior finishes as the adult area, but could have a pediatric wallpaper border to make the environment a little less clinical. An environment that no doubt delights children and parents as well is shown in Color Plate 29, Figure 7-16.

Generally, this area would be monitored by the adult recovery nurse station. This can be accomplished by using glass walls to enclose each pediatric bed, allowing good visibility from the nurse station.

Recovery Lounge (Stage II)

As the patient becomes more alert, the staff evaluate his or her condition and, as soon as vital signs have stabilized and nausea (if any) has subsided, the patient would walk to the recovery lounge. This room accommodates the final stages of recovery in a more comfortable setting, where companions may sit with the patient (Figure 7-22). When the staff observe that the patient has been stable for at least half an hour, discharge instructions will be given to patient and family, and the patient will be formally discharged. Adequate space is needed to accommodate family, and the second-stage recovery would optimally be near the family waiting area.

The recovery lounge, equipped with comfortable recliner chairs and lounge seating, should be immediately adjacent to postanesthesia recovery. Observation by medical staff is still required, but it is more casual. The short duration of stay and the use of chairs, rather than beds, allow this area to be considerably smaller than postanesthesia recovery. The number of chairs depends on individual program requirements. For example, patients undergoing ophthalmic surgery with a local anesthetic may proceed almost immediately from the OR to a recliner chair in secondary recovery. The dressing area and toilets will be immediately adjacent to secondary recovery.

The 2001 edition of the AIA *Guidelines* requires the number of second-stage recovery stations to be one-half the minimum required total of first-stage PACU beds.

There is no restriction on the types of interior finishes that may be used in the recovery lounge, other than what good sense would mandate with respect to flammability and maintenance. Upholstery on recliner chairs must be washable. Carpet is an appropriate floorcovering, and vinyl works well on the walls. This area can be designed like a residential living room, with indirect lighting or table lamps. Natural light and views are highly desirable.

Administration

An ASC will need private offices for the medical director, the director of nursing or the OR supervisor, and the business manager or clinic administrator. The director of nursing's office should be adjacent to the surgical core or to the recovery room, where he or she can keep an eye on operations. Sometimes the office has a one-way glass window overlooking the nurse station in the surgical core.

RECOVERY-CARE CENTERS

Overnight recovery-care centers that provide extended observation following outpatient surgery exist in some states. These are defined by FASA as facilities that provide postsurgical care of the patient discharged from the postanesthesia care unit with a defined length of stay based on each state's regulation. According to FASA, the first extended postsurgical recovery-care unit in an ambulatory surgery setting was developed in 1984 in Coeur d'Alene, Idaho. The FASA 1996 recovery-care survey determined that 9.6 percent of surgery centers offer 23-hour postsurgical recovery care and 0.05 percent of all centers offer 72-hour recovery. Postsurgical recovery care represents one of the fastest growing trends of the ASC market with facilities existing throughout the United States with the exception of 15 states. Recovery care is currently not reimbursed by Medicare but the cost effectiveness of this option is being evaluated.

23 Hours and 59 Minutes of Care

The 2001 edition of the AIA Guidelines notes that, although most outpatient procedures do not require an overnight stay, some require extended patient observation for up to "23 hours and 59 minutes of care," which refers to recovery-care centers. The need for facilities for sleeping and nutrition services, and a communication system enabling patients to summon assistance, must be addressed. Also included are adequate waiting areas for family, including children and adolescents, adequate privacy for meetings between physicians and other professionals with the patient's family, and accommodation for translators or translation equipment.

Statistics

Sixty-eight percent of centers that provide extended postsurgical recovery care began offering 23- and/or 24- to 72-hour stays between 1993 and 1995. Recovery-care centers make it possible to perform more advanced and highly reimbursed procedures on an outpatient basis. According to FASA, the geographical distribution of surgery centers offering recovery care indicates a more favorable regulatory climate in the West. California leads the nation with 63 centers, followed by Texas and Colorado with 28 and 20 centers, respectively. There are currently 23 states that have 23-hour postsurgical recovery/surgery centers. Six states allow for greater than 24-hour stays in the surgery center setting, but they differ in exactly how they define and license recovery care. For example, in Arizona, the recovery-care concept grew out of a home recovery unit used by a surgery center. Eventually, the state passed legislation providing for a separate recovery-care license that enabled surgery centers to keep patients up to 72 hours. In Colorado, however, surgery centers may use a convalescence license that enables them to keep separate beds for patients who stay for indefinite periods. These specific beds may be located inside the surgery center.

TYPES OF PROCEDURES NECESSITATING EXTENDED CARE

Orthopedic procedures constitute the largest percentage of recovery stays with 35.9 percent of all patients. Plastic surgery and gynecology follow with 25.4 percent and 16.6 percent, respectively, according to FASA. Among the more common procedures that constitute extended recovery are anterior cruciate ligament repair, laparascopic vaginal hysterectomies, laparascopic cholecystectomies, abdominoplasty, and total facelifts.

SUMMARY

There are a number of models for designing ambulatory surgical centers. Each meets the goals of a specific program, and the final design of the facility is influenced by the available space, the shape of the building, the budget, and the personalities of the decision-makers. Success, however, can only be achieved by meeting the universal goals of ambulatory surgery: low cost, convenience for patients and physicians, and a high degree of safety.

CHAPTER 8
Sports Medicine

OVERVIEW

Sports medicine may be practiced from a sideline bench, a storefront therapist's office, or a multimillion-dollar facility employing highly sophisticated techniques appropriate for highly paid professional athletes. Programs for these facilities vary widely depending on the location of the facility, the client or patient population it serves, the treatment philosophy of those who have set up the practice, and the medical background or skills of those individuals. In spite of these disparate considerations, many issues and concerns are germane to all sports medicine facilities, large or small.

Sports medicine is a practice that focuses on the physiological health of athletes—professional, amateur, and recreational—and the problems and injuries athletes encounter. The medical practice most closely allied with sports medicine is orthopedics, and the medical director of these facilities is often an orthopedic surgeon. Physical therapy and fitness training are the other two disciplines integrated into this practice. Sports medicine endeavors to achieve four goals:

1. Maintenance of health and physiological function

2. Improvement of performance

3. Prevention of injuries through training and education

4. Treatment and rehabilitation from injuries

These goals are not unique to sports medicine, but the approach to achieving them may be. In the wake of ever-increasing investments in professional and collegiate sports and with technological advances in medical treatment capabilities, practitioners have developed techniques to allow athletes to recover from injuries more quickly and successfully. Treatment has gradually become more aggressive, and it is applied in a wholly integrated manner, taking into consideration the person's entire range of activities in relation to his or her strengths and deficits in body structure, musculature, and overall fitness. The objective is to transfer the responsibility and motivation for success to the athlete rather than to allow the person to be a passive recipient of treatment.

The success of these techniques has created public demand for access to testing, training, and treatment from sports medicine specialists. Practitioners have responded to this increasing demand by creating environments that offer services suited to the needs of a wide cross section of the public. A sports medicine facility may combine any number of services, including physical therapy, nutritional counseling, deep-tissue massage therapy, biomechanical analysis, and even prosthetic or reconstructive orthopedic surgery.

Marketing Plan

A sports medicine facility's marketing plan will have a direct effect on site selection and design. Location near a medical complex or hospital is very common for a source of patient referrals. Choice of facility, such as an existing space or a new building designed to suit, would be determined by the availability and flexibility of space and the complexity of the service program. Architectural detailing within the facility and interior design will be directly related to the desired public image.

User Mix

A sports medicine center's users are at any given time associated with one particular function of the center, be it physical therapy, fitness training, testing, or medical treatment. The client's activity may change from time to time from one function to another, such as from physical therapy to fitness, but normally users are focused on one major activity at a time. Thus, the same facility must accommodate a variety of needs simultaneously. As an example, a physical therapist rehabilitating a patient from an injury must be situated so as not to have difficulty communicating with the patient due to loud machine noise from the hydrotherapy area or disco music drifting in from the aerobics class around the corner. Each group of users expects to be treated with dignity and consideration, and designers must be aware and respond to these needs.

Providers of these services expect the facility itself—its physical layout—to support the goals they establish. The facility can do that successfully only if the designers clearly understand the practice program and if they meet users' expectations for a convenient, comfortable, and attractive environment.

Convenient Access

A center that is conveniently located, visible from the street, and easily accessible from the parking area will both enhance its marketing plan objectives and meet users' expectations for convenience. A physical therapy patient, who faces an intensive six- or eight-week course of treatment, may be discouraged by difficult access or parking that involves too long a walk to the building entrance. These facilities can attract very high volumes of users especially if they also sell memberships to the fitness gym and pool.

Internal Layout—Need for Visibility

In physical therapy, fitness, and medical treatment, visibility by staff is essential for safety and efficiency. In the physical therapy area, therapists may work with several patients, alternating from one to another. They may be applying a muscle stimulator to one person, cervical traction to another, setting up a patient on a Cybex™ machine, and placing another one in a hydrotherapy whirlpool. Each of these patients, once set up, needs no further assistance until the 10- to 20-minute cycle has ended. Therapists are constantly circulating among patients in an open-plan area set up with physical therapy tables, exercise bikes, large mat tables, and private physical therapy rooms or cubicles partitioned with a curtain (Figure 8-1).

In addition to circulating among patients, therapists often return to a central charting desk to record events on each patient's record. Visibility is essential to controlling these activities. Therapists also must be able to watch the entry area to greet new patients who have arrived, and keep an eye on the hydrotherapy area, which is generally a separate room positioned so that visibility can be maintained. The reader is referred to Chapter 9 for a more detailed discussion of physical therapy facilities.

The fitness area should be entirely open, so that staff can monitor use of equipment and weights and so that socializing can take place if users desire (Figure 8-2). An open plan enables exercise equipment to be arranged efficiently. It is important to have mirrors on any walls in the exercise area that do not contain wall-mounted equipment. Mirrors are not for vanity or for the purpose of expanding the room visually; they allow people using weight training equipment to make corrections in their form.

If there is a medical practice associated with the facility, the area would be partitioned into examination or treatment rooms, private offices or consultation rooms, a minor surgery room, and a nurse station, which should be located so as to command surveillance over all treatment areas. The reader is referred to other sections of this book for a discussion of efficient layout and requirements of orthopedic suites, physical therapy units, and family practice suites.

A pool and spa, if provided, could be either indoors or outdoors, depending on the locale's climate. The pool and spa generally command a high visual profile from an image-building standpoint (Color Plate 30, Figure 8-3), and they should be adjacent to the fitness area and locker/shower facilities.

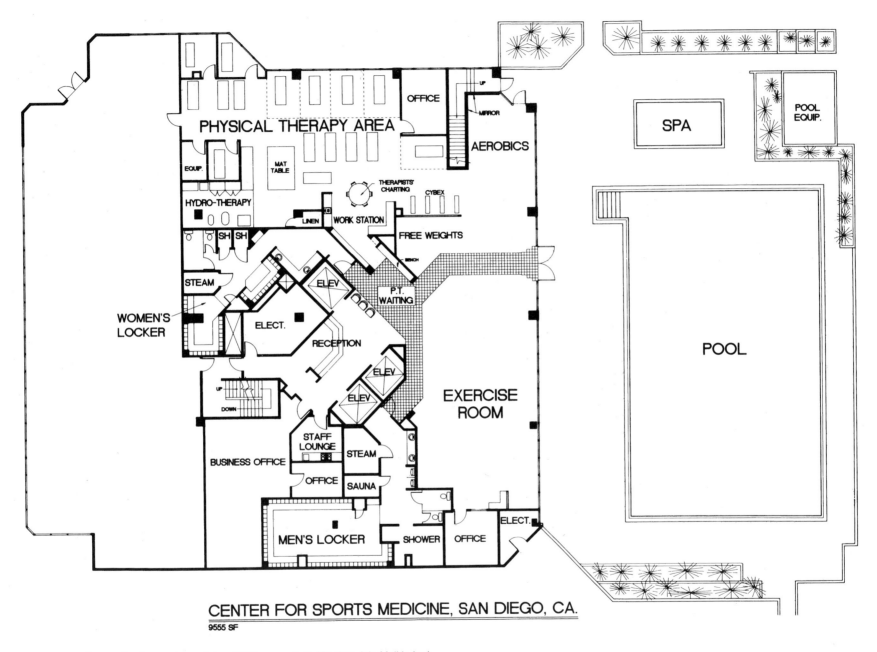

Figure 8-1. Space plan for sports medicine, 9555 square feet. (*Design: Jain Malkin Inc.*)

Figure 8-2. Fitness/therapy gym. (*Photo courtesy: Bert Moran, Montana Athletic Club Missoula, MT; Photographer: R. Mark Bryant.*)

The aerobics area can be separated completely, needing no direct visibility from staff other than the instructor conducting the session. Visual separation will avoid user self-consciousness caused by onlookers. The aerobics floor should be well cushioned. There are specific products designed for this purpose, but success can also be achieved with a very dense, thick foam rubber pad under an 88 ounce per square yard faceweight cut pile carpet. The pile need not be high, but must be dense.

Lockers and showers (Figures 8-4 and 8-5) will be used mostly by fitness and pool patrons, but should be convenient to other areas as well. These should be directly accessible from the lobby area to avoid unnecessary traffic through other activity areas.

The business office and reception desk need not necessarily be combined (Figure 8-6). As the reception area is so hectic, it is advisable to locate administrative and bookkeeping offices in a quieter area. Medical charts must

Figure 8-4. Attractive locker rooms are an amenity appreciated by patrons. (*Photo courtesy: Bert Moran, Montana Athletic Club Missoula, MT; Photographer: R. Mark Bryant.*)

Figure 8-5. Space-saving lockers are designed to provide space to hang a suit. (*Photo courtesy: Ideal Products, Ontario, CA.*)

be close to reception, but will still need to be accessible to the bookkeeping office for billing. In this or any medical practice, however, staffing does benefit from one person's ability to cover another's station if an absence is required. Depending on the size of the facility, there may be a need for anywhere from 6 to 12 seats in the reception area for those awaiting a physical therapy appointment, for a family member who accompanied a physical therapy patient, or for someone waiting for a friend, although those who plan to use the pool or work out in the gym generally go immediately to the locker room and change clothes.

Noise

Several functions cause considerable noise and should be separated by distance or mass (walls) without unduly restricting visual access where needed. Hydrotherapy generates some noise. This area may be separated by partially glazed partitions to reduce noise transmission to the adjacent physical therapy area. Jacuzzi pump noises can be reduced by surrounding pumps with an isolation closet.

The aerobics area should be fully separated by well-insulated partitions that run above the finished ceiling, since exercisers usually enjoy feeling the beat of the music. If the facility is not on the first floor, the designer must consider the effect of the aerobics activity on the tenants immediately below. The vibration caused by jumping and extremely loud music can be unbearable.

Aesthetics

The aesthetic character of a sports medicine facility depends on the marketing philosophy, target population, locale, and budget. A facility that draws patients from within a controlled environment, such as member-physicians, contracted service to sports teams or corporate clients, or from referrals within a tightly knit medical office environment, would not generally need to invest in a high-profile design or use expensive materials to be successful.

Figure 8-6. Elevator lobby/reception desk. (*Design: Jain Malkin Inc.; Photographer: Robinson/Ward.*)

On the other hand, a facility that concentrates on providing highly specialized services, which would draw from outside the immediate geographic area, or one that emphasizes memberships or establishes an exclusive character would be more likely to require an image-setting design treatment. Health clubs, for example, depend entirely on membership sales, and image is very important to their marketing effort. Generally, the higher the membership fee, the more elaborate the design treatment.

Wet Areas

Areas within the suite where significant moisture or wet activity is present should be carefully considered for moisture control, cross traffic, and noise. Obvious areas where moisture is present are spa areas, hydrotherapy, shower rooms, and steam rooms. Not so obvious, but significant, are the fitness gym and aerobics room, where high concentrations of vapor will occur due to heavy exertion and breathing. Without adequate ventilation, greater than needed for normal use, the area will seem "stuffy," and mildew odors are likely to occur over a period of time in carpets and in areas where cleaning is difficult.

With the exception of hydrotherapy, wet areas should be adjacent to one another or be connected by paths of moisture-resistant, slip-resistant flooring. Wet bodies or bare feet should not cross carpeting or areas of nonrelated activity. An outdoor pool may not be immediately adjacent to the locker/shower rooms, but a path of nonskid ceramic tile or slip-resistant rubber flooring can connect them and provide spatial definition between areas of different functions without wall separations (Figure 8-1).

Users of hydrotherapy usually are dry and dressed before leaving that area, so isolation may not be a problem. This must be evaluated on an individual basis to ensure proper adjacencies and traffic flow.

All wet areas, including locker and dressing rooms adjacent to showers, toilet rooms, spa, and hydrotherapy, should be supplied with floor drains. A slight, almost imperceptible slope of ⅛ inch per foot toward strategical-ly located floor drains may prevent a broken pipe or stuck valve from flooding carpet in adjacent areas.

Shower and steam rooms should have threshold water stops or dams of ½-inch maximum height (which must be beveled, maximum slope not to exceed 45 degrees) on the wet side of the entry, with a floor slope that directs water away from the entry. Some shower or steam room doors have water troughs at the bottom to prevent water from dripping off the door. This water must be delivered somewhere and usually winds up at the hinged edge, where floor slope is very difficult to control. At this point, water will go everywhere, including to the dry side, getting trampled into public areas by outgoing feet. One must pay special attention to wet floors.

Rooms housing steam equipment should be well drained and ventilated, since steam generators create heat and present a hazard of leaking. Ventilation of these same areas should be sized to prevent heat and moisture buildup.

Linen Storage

A designer must be aware of the copious amounts of linen used in the daily routine of a sports medicine facility. Clean and soiled towels must be accommodated in locker rooms (Figure 8-7), as well as the hydrotherapy area. The physical therapy area uses linen sheets on the tables, pillowcases, and towels. All of this linen must be delivered, stored before and after use, and later picked up by the linen service. The designer must be sure to provide adequate storage space for linen, plus additional ventilation to keep that which is soiled and damp from becoming a nuisance. However, ventilation alone cannot overcome an environment that is not kept clean and orderly with soiled linen stowed in the proper location.

Interior Finishes

The floor surface in wet areas should be slip resistant and consistent in texture. The user should not be challenged with changing from one material to another, because he or she will not be concentrating on the difference. The change could provide a hazardous surprise.

For wet areas, ceramic tile is the most favored flooring for design application, durability, and surface texture. However, contrary to public perception, ceramic tile is not always easy to clean. Light-colored grout is almost impossible to keep clean. The larger the tile, the fewer the grout joints. Sheet vinyl is an option of compromise to be used in damp areas when budget is a consideration. In hydrotherapy, sheet vinyl is quite suitable, preferably with a self-coved base. The designer should note whether heavy portable tanks will be used. They could compress and destroy a flooring material not designed for heavy loads. Vinyl composition tile, because of its many seams, is undesirable in high-moisture areas.

Vinyl wallcovering is ideal in a sports medicine facility because it offers great variety in texture as well as ease of cleaning. If paint is used, it must be semigloss or eggshell enamel, fully washable. Painted wallgraphics can be especially appealing in this type of facility. The reader is referred to Color Plate 31, Figures 8-8 and 8-9.

Lighting

Treatment areas within the facility normally require broadly distributed lighting of 30 to 50 footcandles. Under ideal conditions, the physical therapy area would have indirect or ambient lighting. Fixtures might be suspended from the ceiling, with the light shining on and bouncing off the ceiling, creating an overall high level of diffused illumination without casting glare in the eyes of patients lying on physical therapy tables. In the hydrotherapy area, fitness gym, and aerobics room, on the other hand, the standard 2-×4-foot fluorescent troffer with a parabolic low-brightness lens would be appropriate. The reception area, lobby, or corridors might benefit from accent lighting focusing on wallgraphics, special artwork, or educational exhibits. Other chapters of this book provide detailed information on lighting medical spaces such as exam rooms, minor surgery, and nurse stations. Specifically, refer to Chapter 13.

Figure 8-7. Clean and soiled linen storage, in locker room. (*Design: Jain Malkin Inc.; Photographer: Robinson/Ward.*)

CASE STUDIES

Several examples of sports medicine facilities serve as case studies to illustrate the concepts outlined above. Each illustrates a different approach to the practice of sports medicine. These facilities are clear reflections of their individual goals.

San Diego Sports Medicine Center: San Diego, California

The San Diego Sports Medicine Center has built its practice on high volume and a well-developed general referral system. Located near a 214-bed hospital owned by Tenet Health System, it occupies a ground floor location in one of a group of medical office buildings. It is surrounded by parking and has immediate access from a major freeway.

This 11,000-square-foot facility is operated by a group of osteopathic physicians with offices immediately adjacent to the center. These internal referrals, as well as those from practitioners in adjacent medical office buildings, contribute to the volume of this facility. In addition, contracts with local schools (athletic programs), municipalities, and corporations provide the largest source of referrals for both physical therapy and fitness programs. Of the four case studies, this facility most actively markets the fitness and testing program to a wide cross section of the public. As family practitioners, the osteopathic physicians encourage outside specialists' referrals for physical therapy relatively free of competitive conditions.

The center's programs focus on wellness—maximizing one's level of physical fitness and minimizing individual health risk factors. This involves assessment of one's fitness, education about wellness, and lifestyle evaluation. The center also offers worksite evaluation to employers, incorporating site walk-throughs to assess high-risk opportunities for injury.

Features include a 5500-square-foot physical fitness gym, separate aerobics room, physical therapy treatment area, and a four-lane lap pool, all contained within a large square surrounding a central locker and spa area. From the entry, one has immediate access to either the medical offices or the sports center administration area, through which one must pass to reach the locker rooms. Across the parking lot is a one-half-mile winding running track.

The 4000-square-foot medical office accommodates a staff of 10 physicians and clinicians, including radiology and a physiology testing lab. This area functions independently of the sports center.

The central location of the locker/spa area allows convenient access to other areas. Access control is easily maintained by staff in the business/administration area. Access to the track is located outside the immediate control of the center. The track is used frequently by staff from nearby medical offices, and this relationship facilitates outside use without unnecessary traffic in the sports center lobby.

The design character is low key and simple. The center prefers to project an understated image that allows the facility to remain low profile compared to the high-profile service provided. Since clients and patients represent a wide cross section of the population through referrals from a variety of sources, a straightforward unimposing appearance was considered most appropriate.

Center for Sports Medicine and Orthopedics: Phoenix, Arizona

The second case study incorporates many of the basic elements of other sports medicine facilities, but it is unique in that it is virtually self-sufficient, relying very little on outside physician referrals or recreational memberships to support it. The Center for Sports Medicine and Orthopedics is a $3 million (1985 dollars, when built), 40,000-square-foot medical treatment and diagnostic center that sits on a tiny site originally in the middle of a major metropolitan hospital campus (Figure 8-10). The freestanding building was raised one story to provide parking and to provide shelter for entry during periods of inclement weather. When it opened in February 1985, it won a Facility of Merit award in 1985 from *Athletic Business* magazine.

The center was the creation of three Phoenix orthopedic surgeons and a sports medicine specialist who, together, were team physicians to 18 professional and amateur sports organizations.

This facility provides contract services to local professional athletes and purposely integrates amateur and recreational athletes in the same treatment program. From a marketing standpoint, being able to converse with professional athletes during rehabilitation is a powerful

Figure 8-10. Center for Sports Medicine and Orthopedics, Phoenix, AZ. (*Architecture: Devenney Group, Ltd., Phoenix, AZ; Photographer: Michael Much.*)

attraction. The physical therapy program and fitness gym are designed to operate directly in conjunction with treatment and diagnostic programs. The 4000-square-foot physical therapy department is owned and operated by HealthSouth. All together, medical treatment, diagnostic testing, the physical therapy program, and the fitness area generate enough referrals to one another to make the center economically self-sufficient, relying little on outside physician referrals or recreational memberships in the gym. It should be noted that the Stark legislation enacted a few years ago to control physician referrals to ancillary services owned by those physicians changed

practice patterns, resulting in the physical therapy business being owned by HealthSouth, a large rehabilitation company, which, in fact, now owns the building.

It is interesting to see the changes that have occurred in this enterprise over the past 10 years, between the second and third editions of this book, as they are reflective of changes and stresses in the healthcare industry in general. The hospital and its campus went out of business and have been replaced by a grocery store. The last of the orthopedic surgeon founding fathers (all osteopaths) retired in 1999. The mix of providers has changed to include 5.5 osteopathic family practice physicians (all cer-

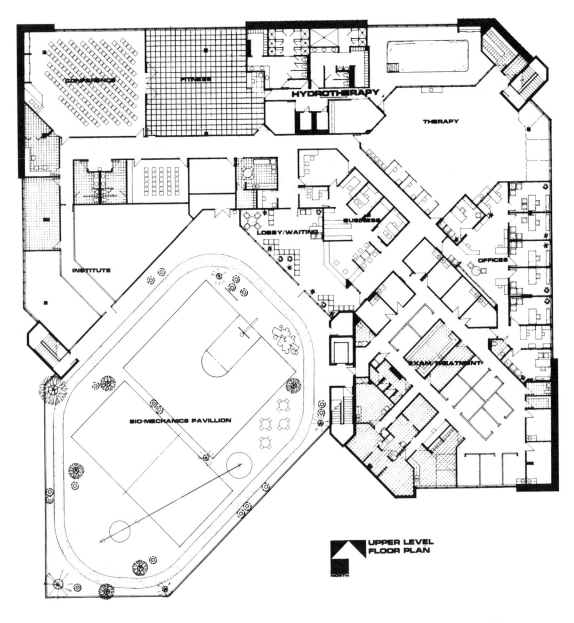

Figure 8-11. Space plan, Center for Sports Medicine and Orthopedics, Phoenix, AZ. (*Architecture: Devenney Group, Ltd., Phoenix, AZ.*)

tified in both sports medicine and family practice) and just one orthopedic surgeon. They are the team physicians for the Phoenix Suns, Phoenix Coyotes, Arizona Diamondbacks, and Phoenix Mercury (WNBA), as well as some junior colleges, high schools, gymnastics clubs, and many other sports groups, including the Seattle Mariners and Los Angeles Dodgers during spring training.

The center originally marketed to local employers a successful work-hardening program called the "Industrial Athlete," but has since replaced it with a program of executive wellness/physical assessment offered to individuals as well as employees of very large organizations with which it has contracted.

The overriding concept of the facility is that it is a medical facility first and foremost, as opposed to a membership fitness facility. The image is tailored to a center specializing in sports medicine treatment. As a result, an ever-increasing number of patients have been attracted to the facility from beyond the local service area.

As the facility was built to suit and freestanding, it was possible to express the program's concepts through the architecture, sculpting various activities around the 10,000-square-foot biomechanics pavilion.

What appears to be an open-air park (Figure 8-10) located above the covered parking area is, in fact, a sophisticated training field that allows athletes' motions to be captured on high-speed video so that experts can observe defects in technique that might lead to injuries. A basketball court, pitcher's mound, running track, and volleyball court are included, each with the type of flooring material typically found in a professional setting.

The entry and reception area form the facility's center to allow direct access to all areas, similar to the previous case study (Figure 8-11). The medical treatment center, fitness gym, administrative offices, physical therapy area, lockers, and swimming pool radiate around the reception station for visual control and convenient access.

Directly beyond the fitness area is the conference center, which includes a large auditorium, classrooms, separate restroom facilities, and entrance from the parking area below.

Athletic activity is the theme of an extensive collection of artwork displayed throughout the building, including a prominent, life-sized bronze sculpture of a gymnast. Interior finishes and furnishings are color-coordinated right down to the staff uniforms, to emphasize the discipline devoted to all details of the facility, reflecting consistency between the physical setting and manner of treatment. This sports medicine facility displays the design continuity that can be achieved when all objectives and goals are aligned in one program and expressed between the client and designers as an integrated whole.

The Center for Sports Medicine: San Diego, California

The third case study is an example of a facility that has become the centerpiece of an older, well-established medical office complex. The site consists of five sizable medical office buildings, the largest of which is a 90,000-square-foot, high-profile building with glass elevators. Located on the lower or plaza level of this building, just across the street, are a regional children's hospital and a 415-bed community hospital with a tertiary program in cardiac surgery. The site is accessed by two converging freeways.

The 9500-square-foot facility includes a physical therapy program, fitness gym, aerobics room, administrative and business offices, locker rooms, an NCAA-sized lap pool and large outdoor spa (see Figure 8-1).

The physical therapy area serves patients referred by physicians in adjacent medical buildings as well as by others off site. The fitness gym is used by physicians and staff of nearby medical offices who participate through private memberships. Some physicians offer employees memberships to the facility as an employment benefit.

This sports medicine facility was developed partly as a marketing feature to attract physicians to the medical buildings, to generate revenue for the physicians and others who own stock in the corporation, and to provide convenient treatment for patients at the same location as their physicians' offices. Design image was established as a high priority. Intricate ceramic tile designs were created

Figure 8-12. Aerobics area. (*Design: Jain Malkin Inc.; Photographer: Robinson/Ward.*)

for locker rooms and the path connecting the locker rooms to the pool (see Figure 8-6). Colorful soffitted ceilings, wallgraphics, and inset carpet borders were used to create an upbeat, stylish ambience.

Decorative lighting is used in the reception lobby. From the lobby, all other areas of the facility are directly accessible, arranged somewhat like spokes around a hub (Figure 8-9). The locker rooms, physical therapy area, administration offices, and fitness gym are accessible without any cross traffic. The aerobics area (Figure 8-12) is open and accessible from both the gym and the physical therapy area for overflow needs as one or the other becomes more or less busy throughout the day. Occasionally, there is some interference between the aerobics use and physical therapy due to loud music being played during the aerobics sessions. Early in the programming, however, it was determined that the availability of space to physical therapy would justify the occasional periods of possible conflict in the early morning and late afternoon, when therapy activity is light. The staff report that the tradeoff has proven worthwhile.

Through a team effort of the center's staff, the building owners, and local building officials, the designers were able to transform some rather unusual and challenging existing building conditions into assets. The resultant design was functional, flexible, and affordable, allowing the center to expand by 25 percent without remodeling existing features or suspending ongoing activities.

Figure 8-13. Montana Athletic Club, Missoula, MT. (*Photo courtesy: William Merci, Kessler, Merci and Associates, Chicago, IL; Photographer: Greg Merci.*)

Montana Athletic Club—Missoula: Missoula, Montana
Montana Orthopedic Physical Therapy: Missoula, Montana

Appearing to grow out of the earth, nestled in the mountains (Figure 8-13), this $4.6 million (cost in 1986, when built), high-tech facility has a threefold mission. It functions as a health club, it serves as a physical therapy clinic for the rehabilitation of sports injuries, and it supplies certified athletic trainers, on contract, to local schools and recreational sports teams.

The facility markets corporate memberships to employers as a perk for employees. A new Cardiac Phase III and Phase IV rehabilitation program addresses the large senior citizen population the center serves. Owner Bert Moran states that currently (year 2000) managed care accounts for 50 percent of the facility's business, which has eroded profits. Prior to managed care, 40 percent of gross revenue derived from physical therapy services; currently, it is only 20 percent and 80 percent of the revenue is from the athletic club, which is doing a brisk business. To assure greater financial viability, plans for a spa are under way.

Owned by a woman with a degree in finance, the facility employs an exercise physiologist as well as physical therapists and certified trainers. The indoor competition-sized track (Figure 8-14) was an important component of the design program, biomechanically designed to reduce the runner's potential for injury and to increase speed by as much as 3 percent. Windows offer runners a panoramic view of the valley. The 1500-square-foot physical therapy area includes a separate hydrotherapy room (Figure 8-15). Large locker rooms (see Figure 8-4), a fitness gym, basketball court, pool, snack bar/lounge, pro shop, conference room, classrooms, and administrative offices are arranged with great care in a layout that is both functional and aesthetically appealing (Figures 8-16, 8-17, and 8-18). Architecturally, this facility merits high marks for its high-tech design and careful detailing not often found in facilities of this type. It is easy to

Figure 8-14. Indoor track, biomechanically designed to reduce runner's potential for injury and to increase speed. Windows offer panoramic view of valley. (*Photo courtesy: Bert Moran, Montana Athletic Club Missoula, MT; Photographer: R. Mark Bryant.*)

Figure 8-15. Hydrotherapy room. Note that whirlpools have been built in. (*Photo courtesy: William Merci, Kessler, Merci and Associates, Chicago, IL; Photographer: Greg Merci.*)

see why it was named a "Facility of Merit" by *Athletic Business* in 1987.

One of the innovations of the design involves the mechanical system which integrates, through a highly sophisticated computer, all the HVAC components of the building in order to achieve energy conservation. The pool, for example, serves as a heat dump for the rest of the building.

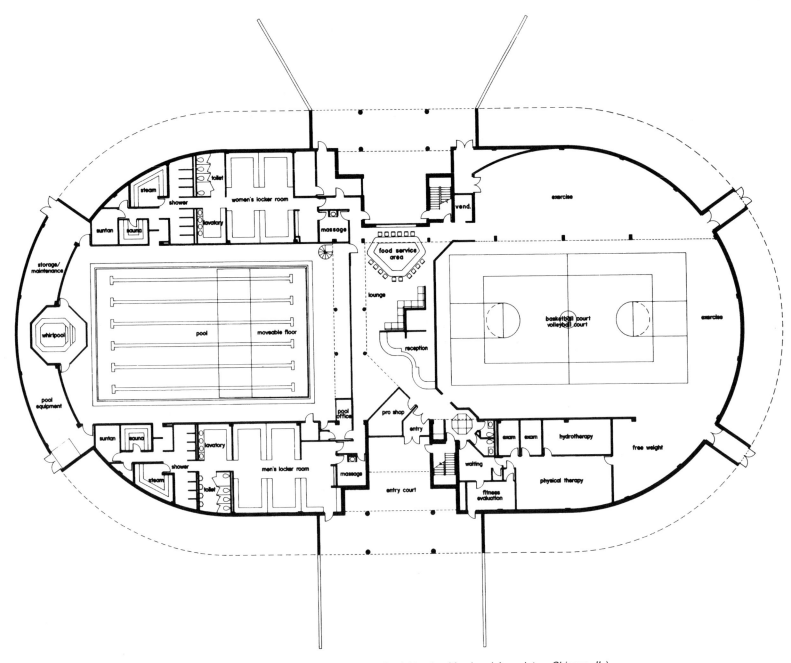

Figure 8-16. Main floor, Montana Athletic Club, Missoula, MT. (*Design: William Merci, Kessler, Merci and Associates, Chicago, IL.*)

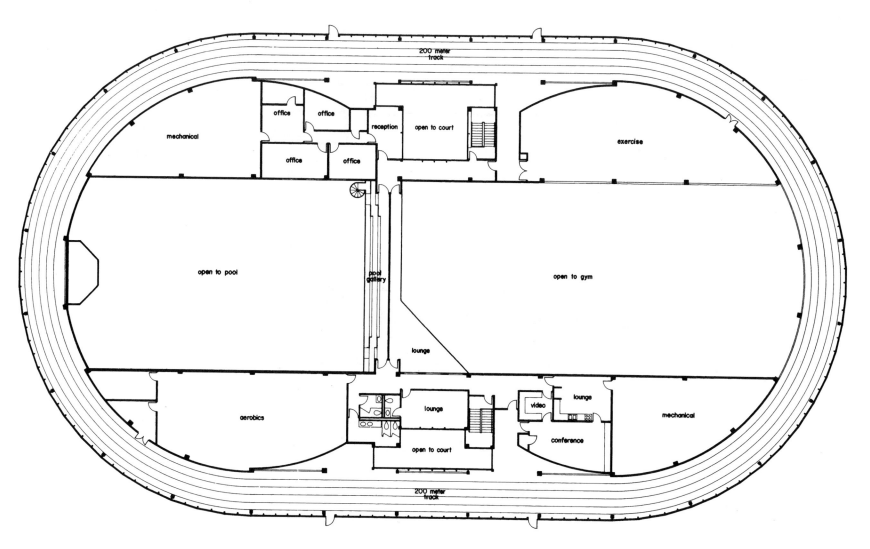

Figure 8-17. Second floor, Montana Athletic Club, Missoula, MT. (*Design: William Merci, Kessler, Merci and Associates, Chicago, IL.*)

Author's note: Track has been reduced to two lanes because the turns were too steep, resulting in injuries. It is noted for being the fastest and largest indoor track in the Northwest. Also, the offices have been replaced by a cardiac rehab space.

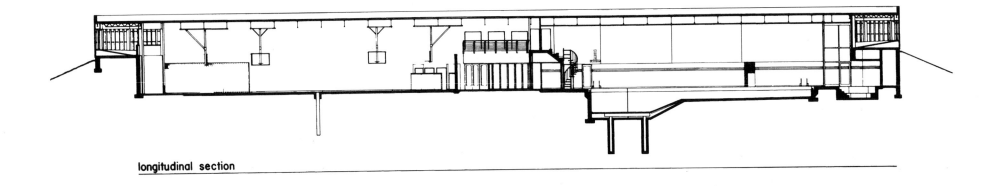

longitudinal section

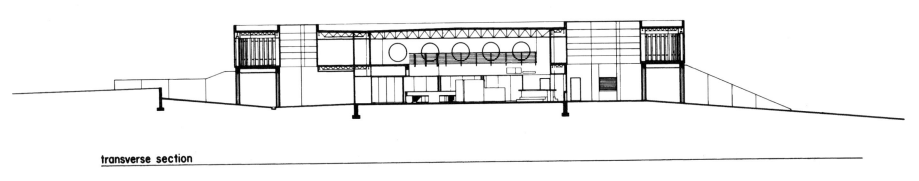

transverse section

Figure 8-18. Sections through building, Montana Athletic Club, Missoula, MT. (*Design: William Merci, Kessler, Merci and Associates, Chicago, IL.*)

CHAPTER 9
Paramedical Suites

Two types of paramedical suites, physical therapy and pharmacy, will be discussed in this chapter.

PHYSICAL THERAPY

Patients requiring physical therapy may need rehabilitation following surgery, stroke, trauma, or a work-related injury ranging from carpal tunnel syndrome to cervical problems associated with lifting heavy items or frequent twisting or bending movements. Usually referred by a physician, patients arrive for an initial evaluation, followed by a series of visits that may range from one to three times per week. For each patient, a routine is established that quickly becomes familiar. Some patients have to warm up by riding an exercise bike for 10 minutes prior to starting therapy and, after checking in with the receptionist, they proceed to the gym and set themselves up without the therapist greeting them. First-time visitors will wait in the reception room until called by the therapist.

Patients are usually asked to wear shorts or other garments that expose the injured limb, which means that the therapist can often treat them in an open, nonprivate area, working on a massage table, bending or massaging a limb to achieve better flexibility or range of motion, perhaps applying electrical stimulation to a muscle and, at the end of the session, applying ice to reduce swelling.

The gym floor must have sufficient open space to be used as a gait lane to visualize patients' ambulation and also to provide room for patients to exercise with elastic ankle bands or straps or other devices. A quieter, or less active, part of the gym should have one or more small rec-

tangular tables for a hand therapist who sits across from the patient. A nearby work area will provide space to fabricate braces to immobilize the hand. This requires storage for the Velcro® straps and other splint materials as well as a small device to heat the material so it can be molded.

Visibility by staff is essential for safety and efficiency in the physical therapy area. Therapists may work with several patients, alternating between them. They may be applying an electrical muscle stimulator to one person for 10 minutes, cervical traction to another for 20 minutes, setting up a patient on a Cybex machine, and placing another in a hydrotherapy tank for 20 minutes. Once set up, each of these patients needs no further assistance until the 10- to 20-minute cycle has ended. Therapists continually circulate among patients in an open plan arrangement set up with physical therapy tables, exercise bikes and other equipment, large mat tables, gait lanes, and private physical therapy rooms or cubicles partitioned by a curtain. The many activities going on simultaneously can make the treatment area very hectic. For this reason, natural light, ample window area, and views of nature are essential to both the therapists' and the patients' well-being. The open-plan workstations in Figures 9-16 and 9-17 work well.

Physical Therapy Modalities

There are eleven basic modalities of physical therapy:

1. Hydrotherapy

2. Heat or cold

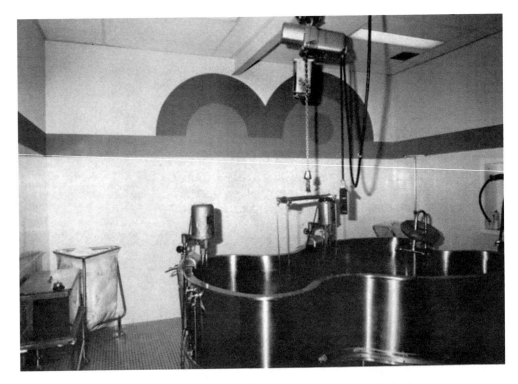

Figure 9-1. Full-body immersion hydrotherapy tank. (*Photo courtesy: Jain Malkin Inc.*)

Table 9-1.
Analysis of Program.
Physical Therapy

Waiting Room		14 × 16 =	224
Business Office		10 × 16 =	160
Tech Work Area/Charting		8 × 12 =	96
Gym		20 × 36 =	720
Whirlpool Rooms	3@	6 × 8 =	144
Treatment Rooms	5@	8 × 9 =	360
Toilet		7 × 9 =	63
Laundry		10 × 12 =	120
Private Office or Staff Lounge		10 × 12 =	120
Storage		8 × 10 =	80
Subtotal			2087 ft²
20% Circulation			417
Total			2504 ft²

3. Massage

4. Exercise

5. Ultrasound

6. Traction

7. Electrical stimulation

8. Transcutaneous electrical nerve stimulation (TENS)

9. Iontophoresis

10. Continuous passive motion

11. Mobilization

Hydrotherapy

Hydrotherapy involves immersion of a limb or, at times, even the entire body, in water. The tank may be a portable whirlpool or a full-body Hubbard tank (Figure 9-1). The latter is more apt to be found in a hospital physical medicine department. Mobile whirlpool tanks (Figure 9-2) may be filled and drained with a hose. The patient sits in a high chair such as that shown in Figure 9-4 and swings a leg over into the whirlpool. The full-body whirlpool in Figure 9-3 requires permanent water and waste connections. Since large amounts of hot water release a lot of steam, the walls of rooms with large tanks should have at least a 5-foot-high ceramic tile wainscot with commercial vinyl wallcovering above. The preferable flooring material is ceramic tile or else commercial-quality sheet vinyl.

Occasionally, physical therapy suites have built-in whirlpools, but most will have a couple of small portable tanks suitable for an arm or a leg. Floor sinks must be provided for portable tanks, which have to be drained and filled for each patient. A hose connection to a nearby tap may suffice for filling the tank. Whirlpool rooms or enclosures are usually 6×8 feet in size and may be closed off on the open side by a cubicle drape. Depending on the location of walls and circulation between hydrotherapy tanks, in order to accommodate ADA access, larger spaces may be needed.

Figure 9-2. Mobile arm, foot, and knee whirlpool. (*Photo courtesy: Ferno-Washington, Inc., Wilmington, OH.*)

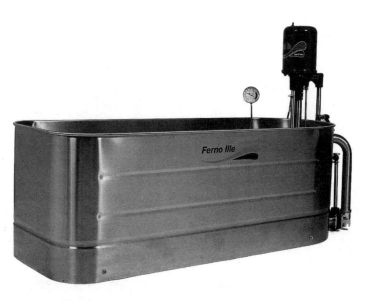

Figure 9-3. Full-body stationary whirlpool. (*Photo courtesy: Ferno-Washington, Inc., Wilmington, OH.*)

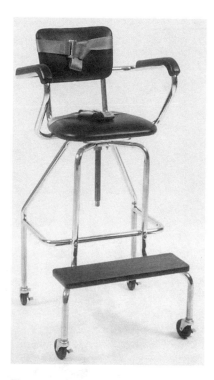

Figure 9-4. Mobile adjustable high chair. (*Photo courtesy: Ferno-Washington, Inc., Wilmington, OH.*)

There are several ways of designing the hydrotherapy area.

1. A large hydrotherapy room can be designed to accommodate several portable whirlpools, plus the Hydrocollator® units (steam packs), the cold pack unit, and the ice machine.

2. Individual privacy cubicles can be created as in Figure 9-12, each having a sloped ceramic tile floor with drain and plumbed for hot and cold water to fill the mobile whirlpool tank.

3. Fiberglas or stainless steel mobile whirlpool tanks may be enclosed to appear built-in as in Figure 8-15. They may be placed in either a large open room or individual privacy cubicles.

If whirlpool tanks are placed in privacy cubicles, the walls of these enclosures should have a 3- or 4-foot-high wainscot of ceramic tile, and the wall above the tile must have a waterproof enamel finish or commercial vinyl wallcovering.

Heat or Cold

Heat is produced by a variety of methods, ranging from a simple electric heating pad to hot steam packs to soaking the affected part of the body in hot water or placing it in hot paraffin (Figure 9-5). Figure 9-6 shows two models of heating units. The unit must be filled with water by a hose from a nearby faucet. It plugs into a standard 120-volt ac grounded outlet. Figure 9-7 shows what the steam packs look like, and Figure 9-8 shows optional terrycloth covers for wrapping the steam packs. If these covers are not

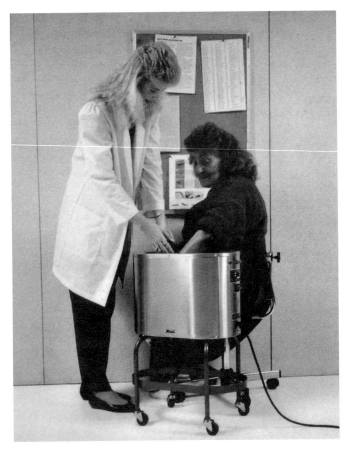

Figure 9-5. Mobile arm, hand, and foot bath. (*Photo courtesy: Ferno-Washington, Inc., Wilmington, OH.*)

Figure 9-6. Hydrocollator (hot pack) units. (*Photo courtesy: Chattanooga Group, Inc., Hixson, TN.*)

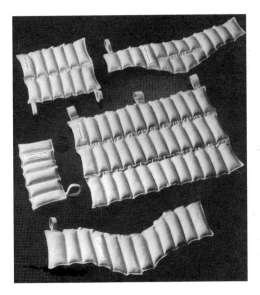

Figure 9-7. Steam packs. (*Photo courtesy: Chattanooga Group, Inc., Hixson, TN.*)

Figure 9-8. Terrycloth covers for steam packs. (*Photo courtesy: Chattanooga Group, Inc., Hixson, TN.*)

used, the steam packs must be wrapped in several layers of terrycloth towels.

A good deal of laundry is generated here. Suitable storage must be provided for clean linen, a large hamper for soiled linen, and a drying rack in a ventilated louver-door closet for drying wet towels until the linen service picks them up.

Cold is normally produced by cold packs or ice, which are applied to the affected part of the body. Figure 9-9 shows various sizes of chilling units. Figure 9-10 shows what the cold pack looks like. These units have the same electrical requirements as the steam pack units. Both the cold pack and the steam pack units may be positioned immediately adjacent to built-in cabinetry in order to provide a large countertop area for wrapping steam packs. The average height of these units is 33 inches.

The steam pack and cold pack units, along with an ice machine (Figure 9-11), may be located in the hydrotherapy room with the portable whirlpools, or it may be located

Figure 9-10. Cold packs. (*Photo courtesy: Chattanooga Group, Inc., Hixson, TN.*)

Figure 9-11. Ice dispenser on stand. (*Photo courtesy: Hoshizaki America, Inc., Peachtree City, GA.*)

Figure 9-9. Chilling units. (*Photo courtesy: Chattanooga Group, Inc., Hixson, TN.*)

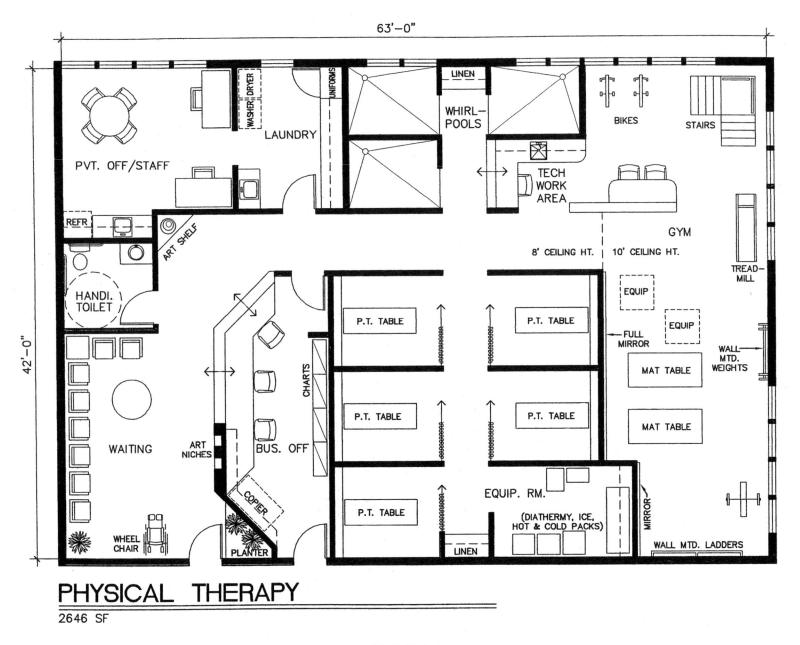

PHYSICAL THERAPY

2646 SF

Figure 9-12. Space plan for physical therapy, 2646 square feet. (*Design: Jain Malkin Inc.*)

Figure 9-13. Physical therapy treatment table. (*Photo courtesy: Hausmann Industries, Inc., Northvale, NJ.*)

in a separate equipment room, as shown in Figure 9-12. This equipment room might also contain a storage area for small pieces of portable equipment when not in use, such as muscle stimulators, the ultrasound cart, and the TENS unit.

Massage

Massage is the oldest form of physical therapy. It is generally performed in private cubicles, which may be constructed of standard gypsum board partitions on three sides with a ceiling-mounted drape on the fourth side (Figure 9-12), or treatment cubicles may be contained in one large room, each one separated from the others only by ceiling-mounted cubicle drapes. In either case, the treatment modules need to be approximately 8 feet wide by 9 feet long. A physical therapy treatment table (Figure 9-13) is 27 to 30 inches wide and 78 inches long. It would be placed in the center of the room, with space for the therapist to access either side of the patient. The room may also have a chair, wall mirror, hooks for patient's clothing, and a shelf for creams and ointments that may be used during the massage. Various types of portable equipment, such as a muscle stimulator or ultrasound unit, may be wheeled into the cubicles as needed (Figures 9-14 and 9-15).

Figure 9-14. Ultrasound unit and muscle stimulator, Sonicator® 730 and Sys*Stim®, on mobile cart. (*Photo courtesy: Mettler Electronics Corp., Anaheim, CA.*)

Figure 9-15. Standard physical therapy mobile equipment cart. (*Photo courtesy: Chattanooga Group, Inc., Hixson, TN.*)

Figure 9-16. Open physical therapy treatment area with therapists' charting station in rear. (*Design: Jain Malkin Inc.; Photographer: Jain Malkin.*)

Subdued, indirect lighting is optimal for these rooms. One would not want to subject the patient to the glare of overhead lighting. The interior finishes and color of these spaces should be soothing and restful, not stimulating.

It should be noted that some physical therapists prefer that at least 50 percent of the treatment tables be arranged in an open area (Figures 9-16 and 9-17) and that the therapists' charting and workstations be similarly open, with an unobstructed view of the gym floor. A 42-inch-high partition with a 34-inch-high work counter on the other side meets this goal.

Exercise

A good deal of physical therapy involves the use of gym equipment. A large exercise room should be provided for exercise equipment, some of which is wall mounted and some of which stands on the floor. Although windows and a nice view make exercising very pleasant, considerable

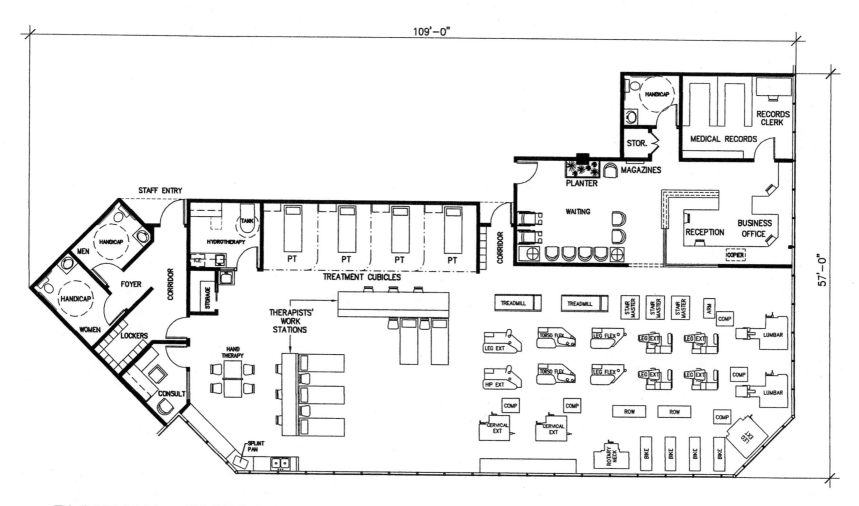

PHYSICAL THERAPY

4200 SF

Figure 9-17. Space plan for physical therapy, 4200 square feet. (*Design: Jain Malkin Inc.*)

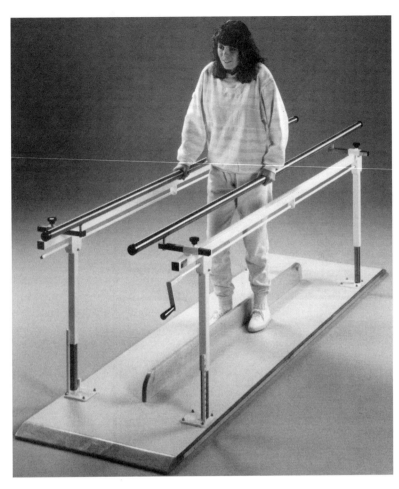

Figure 9-18. Parallel or gait bars. (*Photo courtesy: Hausmann Industries, Inc., Northvale, NJ.*)

Figure 9-19. Cybex exercise bike. (*Photo courtesy: Cybex International, Inc., Medway, MA.*)

Figure 9-20. Ambulation staircase. (*Photo courtesy: Hausmann Industries, Inc., Northvale, NJ.*)

wall space will be required for positioning wall-mounted equipment such as stall bars, weights, and pulleys.

The room may also have gait bars (Figure 9-18), exercise bicycles (Figure 9-19), barbells, an ambulation staircase (Figure 9-20), pulleys (Figure 9-21), and a shoulder wheel (Figure 9-22), as well as other gym equipment and mat tables (Figure 9-27). Note that physical therapy facilities sometimes have very sophisticated electronically integrated exercise equipment that can be calibrated to measure slight changes in a patient's progress (Figure 9-17). This equipment is designed to increase strength, flexibility, and range of motion and records resistance and other measures of muscle function, often printing out a chart or graph for the patient's medical record. Cybex and Med-X™ are two examples of this equipment.

Wall-mounted equipment must be located before construction begins, since the walls will require plywood reinforcement to support the additional weight. The room should have a 9-foot ceiling height and large mirrors, which must be positioned so that people can see them-

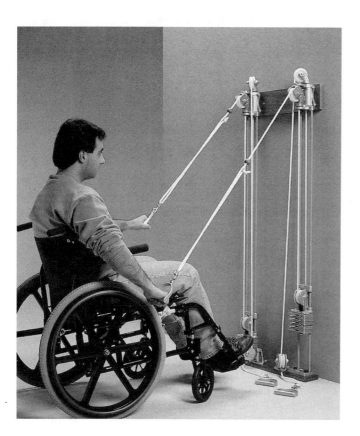

Figure 9-21. Chest pulley weights. (*Photo courtesy: Hausmann Industries, Inc., Northvale, NJ.*)

Figure 9-22. Shoulder wheel. (*Photo courtesy: Hausmann Industries, Inc., Northvale, NJ.*)

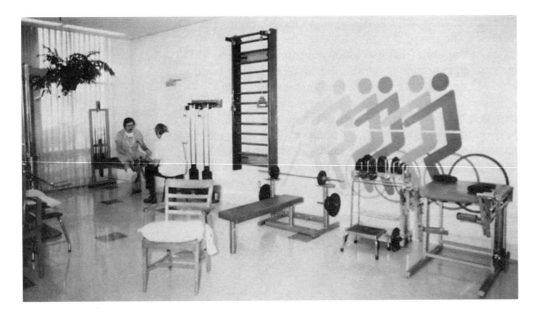

Figure 9-23. Physical therapy gym. (*Design: Jain Malkin Inc.*)

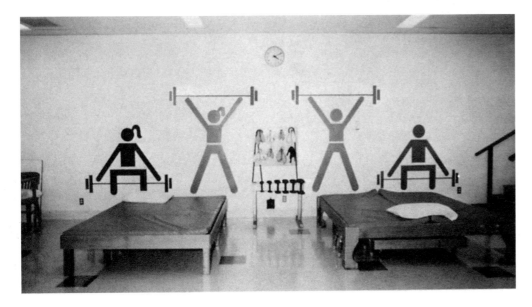

Figure 9-24. Physical therapy gym. (*Design: Jain Malkin Inc.*)

selves using the equipment. Stylized wallgraphics of people exercising add vitality to the room (Figures 9-23 and 9-24). Color Plate 31, Figures 8-8 and 8-9, are examples of graphic design. Carpet is the preferred flooring for the gym and treatment bays. Functionally, it softens the blow if weights are dropped and absorbs noise; visually, it softens the geometry of the equipment. Carpet should be very dense, low pile, directly glued to the slab without a pad. Vinyl-backed carpet, commonly used in hospitals, is a good choice as it's firm and prevents spills from reaching the slab.

Consider the use of indirect lighting in the gym and exercise areas. It is especially appropriate when people are lying on their backs looking up at the ceiling. The glare from standard fluorescent fixtures is unpleasant. Refer to Chapter 13 for examples of pendant and recessed fixtures that direct light to the ceiling, from which it reflects, to provide ambient illumination.

Ultrasound

Ultrasound involves an acoustic high-frequency vibration that is used to produce deep heat in muscle tissues. The ultrasound unit is small (see Figure 9-14) and can be wheeled on a mobile cart to a room as needed. It requires no special accommodation.

Traction

Traction can be applied to various parts of the body. The procedure removes pressure from the muscles, ligaments, and tendons of the area being treated to allow the return of proper nerve flow and blood flow through the area, as well as to promote normal joint mobility patterns. A traction table is shown in Figure 9-25. The electronic control unit is affixed to the end of the table.

Electrical Stimulation

Electrical impulses in milliamperages are delivered into the muscle to elicit external control of the muscle. Ranges of control extend from slight muscle tension to complete and extended muscle contraction. Electrical stimulation may be used to fatigue a muscle for treating spasm, for muscle re-education, to strengthen muscles,

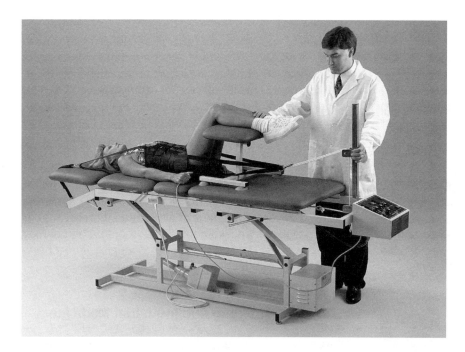

Figure 9-25. Table used for mobilization adjustments with traction device attached. (*Photo courtesy: Chattanooga Group, Inc., Hixson, TN.*)

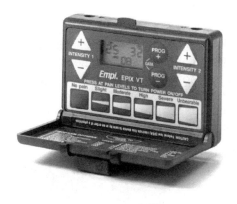

Figure 9-26. TENS unit neurostimulator. (*Photo courtesy: Empi, Inc., St. Paul, MN.*)

to stimulate debilitated muscles, and for pain management. Figure 9-14 features a neuromuscular stimulator on a mobile cart.

Transcutaneous Electrical Nerve Stimulation

Transcutaneous Electrical Nerve Stimulation (TENS) is the procedure of applying controlled, low-voltage electrical impulses to the nervous system by passing electrical current through the skin via electrodes placed on the skin. TENS therapy has been shown to interrupt or break the pain cycle, which facilitates control of spasms, inflammation, and pain. The TENS unit is shown in Figure 9-26.

Iontophoresis

Iontophoresis is the process of driving medication topically through the skin by means of an ion transfer device. This is a small unit that may be stored in a cabinet.

Figure 9-27. Exercise mat table. (*Photo courtesy: Hausmann Industries, Inc., Northvale, NJ.*)

Continuous Passive Motion

Continuous passive motion (CPM) is a technique for rehabilitating a joint or muscle group that has become inhibited, weak, tight, or otherwise injured. These devices would typically not be used in an outpatient physical therapy setting but would, rather, be used postsurgically to keep the limb in motion after a total knee replacement, for example.

Mobilization

Mobilization is a chiropractic-type manipulative therapy that mobilizes vertebral segments and other joints of the body to realign them to proper positioning and to restore normal joint motion. These procedures are sometimes called *adjustments.* A special segmented, adjustable table is used (see Figure 9-25) for these treatments.

Other Areas

A physical therapy suite will also contain a business office, a waiting room that accommodates wheelchairs and people on crutches, toilets that serve the disabled, one or more private offices for administration, a staff lounge, perhaps a laundry room with washer and dryer, convenient storage for clean and dirty linens, and a therapists' charting station.

The charting station may be a large circular table with four or five chairs on casters for the therapists. It should be placed in the large exercise room so that therapists may keep an eye on patients while completing paperwork and also have a good view of all treatment areas.

A small men's and women's locker room/bathroom may be provided to facilitate patients changing into shorts prior to their treatment.

Work Hardening and Industrial Medicine

Work hardening is goal-oriented clinical treatment geared to return people to the work force in a timely manner following an injury. Real or simulated job tasks, coupled with conditioning, are included in the treatment plan for each patient. A series of workstations allows systematic clinical evaluation of a patient's functional capacity and endurance, postinjury conditioning, and rehabilitation needs. The factory or workroom training module would be designed and equipped for tasks inherent in industries representative of the hospital's service area. Module task simulators may include a stud wall simulator, which is an open stud wall with predrilled holes at a variety of angles and heights permitting plumbing and electrical wiring simulations. A bending/range-of-motion simulator is fully adjustable for complete range-of-motion exercises. A shelf system is designed to evaluate the ability to lift or reach, required for certain industrial tasks. Weighted containers in assorted sizes and shapes are also provided.

The work-hardening environment in Figure 9-28 is particularly effective because equipment modules are placed in a simulated industrial environment where appropriate visual cues make the training experience

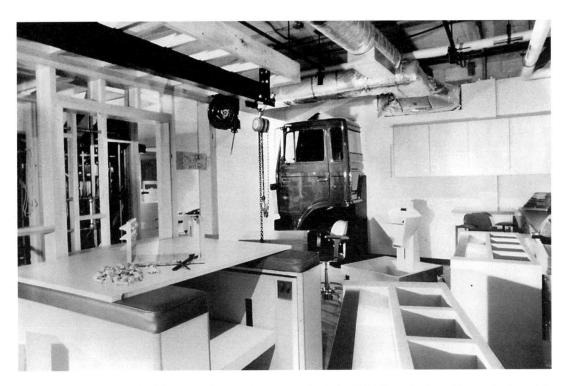

Figure 9-28. Work-hardening laboratory allows patients to practice industrial skills under the guidance of a therapist. (*Designer: David Guynes, Phoenix, AZ; Photographer: David Guynes.*)

more realistic. This concept has been highly regarded by employers who are motivated to rehabilitate injured workers quickly. As a preventive measure, training new employees to use muscles properly for specific tasks makes sense.

Industrial medicine (also called occupational medicine) practices fall into two broad categories. Both are geared to treating work-related injuries. Clinics, the first type, triage all types of injuries that might occur in the workplace, including lacerations, burns, and spine and joint injuries. Patients may avail themselves of these services without a prior referral. The other type of industrial medicine practice, often run by an orthopedic surgeon, signs contracts with large employers to handle workers' compensation referrals. Before a patient can be treated, the visit must be approved by the claims adjustor. This is an area where reimbursement is lucrative, unlike the situation that exists today in many types of medical practices.

Special Issues

Structural support for freestanding equipment as well as hydrotherapy tanks (if large) must be evaluated with respect to floor load. Occasionally, specialized rehab equipment has such concentrated loads that the floor must be reinforced. Evaluating the final fixed positions of each piece of equipment, their individual and combined weights, against the structural system of the building looking at locations of beams, stairs, and sheer walls, is not only practical but essential.

All electrical outlets must be grounded, and codes usually require ground-fault interrupters on whirlpool tanks.

PHARMACY

This discussion will be limited to pharmacies located in medical office buildings. Since the pharmacy's primary (and in some cases, total) source of business is the ten-ants in the buildings, it is wise not to plan the pharmacy's space until the tenants and their respective specialties are known. If the medical office building is isolated and not adjacent to neighborhood foot traffic, the pharmacy's referrals will come exclusively from the medical office building. However, if the pharmacy was in business in the neighborhood before moving into the new medical building, chances are a certain amount of outside business will follow the pharmacist to the new location due to loyalty or to prior business arrangements.

Thus, it is necessary to analyze the source and number of prescriptions, both new and refills. Once the tenant population is known, the volume of prescriptions can be analyzed. A general practitioner or internist will see 25 to 35 patients per day, and perhaps two-thirds of those patients will be given a prescription. Certain specialties tend to generate more prescriptions than others. When the estimated number of prescriptions (or "scripts") to be derived from the tenant population has been determined, one must speculate on what percentage of those scripts will end up at the building's pharmacy. If physicians in the building like the pharmacist, if the pharmacist provides a comfortable place for patients to wait while a prescription is being filled, and if the pharmacy is located so that patients have to pass it upon exiting the building, one may anticipate a certain percent of the building's scripts will be filled at the building's pharmacy. Maintenance drugs are often ordered through mail-order pharmacies under contract to insurance companies.

If the pharmacy is part of a group practice, it is anticipated that perhaps 40 percent of the group's prescriptions will be filled at its own pharmacy. If the pharmacy happens to be located in a medical complex, but it is in a separate building and the patient has to walk outdoors to reach it, perhaps less than 30 percent of the building-generated prescriptions will be filled there. Some patients will remain loyal to local pharmacies near their homes or use ones that will deliver. Pharmacies in supermarkets and discount superstores offer the convenience of grocery shopping while the script is being filled, further siphoning business away from the traditional pharmacy setting.

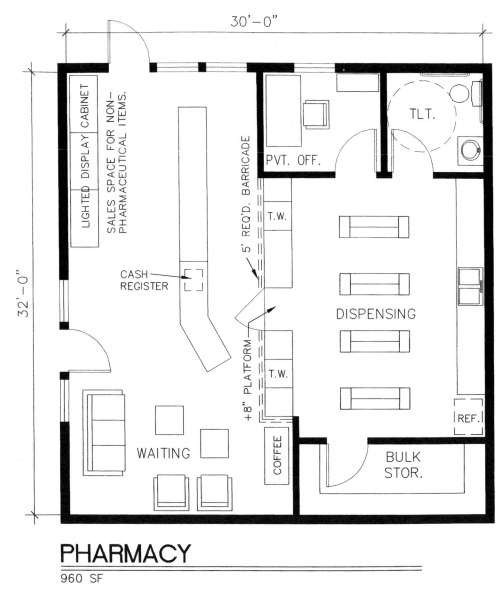

PHARMACY

960 SF

Figure 9-29. Space plan for a pharmacy, 960 square feet. (*Design: Jain Malkin Inc.*)

After the volume of prescriptions is determined, display space must be defined. If the pharmacy will sell prosthetic devices (crutches, braces, artificial limbs, colostomy supplies, etc.), a fitting room and a large storage room should be provided. Undoubtedly, a certain amount of display space will be required, even in a professional pharmacy, for toothpaste, special soaps, first-aid items, personal hygiene supplies, nonprescription drugs, candy and chewing gum, and perhaps a limited line of cosmetics.

One pharmacist can usually fill 50 prescriptions in a day, including compounding, packaging, and dispensing. If he or she can prepackage certain frequently used medications, scripts per day can be boosted to 70 per pharmacist. That is, certain physicians who are major sources of scripts may routinely prescribe certain medications in standard dosages. If the pharmacist knows this, he or she can, during slack periods, prepackage these items and store them on a shelf. When a patient requests them, only a label need be typed, and the script is complete.

Each pharmacist requires 4 to 5 feet of countertop work surface for compounding and another 2 to 3 feet of countertop for typing and labeling. Space is also required for a computer, printer, and fax machine. Each workstation needs a phone. A full-size refrigerator and a built-in cabinet with a double sink should also be provided. Adjustable open shelving 8 to 10 inches deep is all that is required for storage of pharmaceuticals. Twelve lineal feet (6 feet high) of shelving is a minimum, with an additional 4 lineal feet per pharmacist.

The dispensing area often has a raised-platform floor (8 inches above the display and sales area floor), a required 5-foot-high security wall separating the dispensing and sales area, a required bathroom, and a bulk storage room. Sometimes a small private office is included. The bathroom is a code requirement based on the reasoning that the pharmacist should never have to leave the store unattended to use a public restroom. A professional pharmacy will occupy anywhere from 800 to 1200 square feet of space (Figure 9-29).

CHAPTER 10
Practice of Dentistry

The modern dental office is truly a high-tech/high-touch environment. As a professional group, dentists have, for years, been well attuned to marketing and customer satisfaction. This may be due to the fact that, as the incidence of tooth decay and gum disease decreases, many dental procedures have become elective in nature unlike medical procedures, which are generally not elective. In dentistry, with the exception of oral surgery, endodontics (root canal), and sometimes periodontics (gum surgery), many treatments are done less for curing disease and restoring health than for *quality of life.* For this reason, cosmetic (esthetic) dentistry has been on the rise in recent years.

Dentists were among the first to advertise; to use color-coordinated uniforms; open offices in shopping malls; and to attend seminars on office design, stress reduction, and the psychology of dealing with patients.

Some dentists have what is called a *values-driven practice,* in which the staff have been trained to redefine their roles. The practice philosophy of "drill, fill, and bill" is replaced with one of bringing wellness to patients and improving the quality of their lives. Staff are trained to listen to patients, interpret behavior, and respond positively to confrontation and problems. Employees learn pleasant telephone manners and how to discuss financial arrangements without offending patients. Dental teams are aware of their self-image. They practice time management and stress reduction, and they set goals together. A values-centered staff makes it easier for patients to accept and want fine dentistry.

Progressive dentists with finely tuned management skills are a source of many satisfying design projects. These dentists want both their personnel and their physical environment to make people feel comfortable and confident about receiving care. To satisfy these dentists, the dental design specialist must be continually educated in changes in technology and in dental practice management. Fortunately, with the Internet, superb educational resources are available to anyone willing to spend the time visiting the Web sites of the professional dental associations and dental practice management magazines, as well as various Web sites developed by dentists for the benefit of their colleagues offering advice on incorporating technology into their practices. Dentists, as a group, have historically embraced new technology, rather than feared or resisted it. And the past two years have really kicked technology into high gear for dental practices.

HIGH-TOUCH PATIENT AMENITIES

Many adults fear and dread a visit to the dentist as a result of painful and frightening childhood experiences. When they enter the treatment room, their blood pressure becomes elevated, muscles constrict, and stress hormones are released into their bloodstream in a classic "fight-or-flight" response. This prevents many from seeking anything other than emergency care for an abscess, root canal, or periodontal disease that may have progressed to an advanced state. These individuals do not seek elective procedures or cosmetic dentistry. However, if they have a positive treatment experience that is relatively painless and interventions are in place to relax them and to reduce stress, it is possible to change their negative childhood associations. The overall ambience of the office from the time they enter the waiting room is the first line of defense (Figures 10-1 and 10-2). First impressions do matter. Interesting ceiling design, indirect lighting, art glass, an open and welcoming reception desk, and color palette can do much to put people at ease (Color Plate 32, Figures 10-3 and

10-4, and Figures 10-5 and 13-10). In the dental treatment room amenities such as DVDs or videos are very effective as pleasant diversions. Offering options and choices allows patients to feel more in control in a threatening situation.

There are no lengths to which dentists will not go to make patients feel comfortable and relaxed. Some of these amenities include an electric massage pad laid on the dental chair, heated aromatherapy pillows, a warm blanket, chairside CD player with headphones, virtual-reality glasses, ceiling-recessed monitor with video movies, hot towels and fruit juice at the end of treatment, a frozen-yogurt machine, the aroma of freshly baked bread for early-morning arrivals, and a great selection of magazines. Research shows clearly that having options and choices reduces stress and one of those choices should be "no bells and whistles." In the end, it is competent and caring staff and building relationships with patients that really results in financial success. Dentists' Internet Web sites are rife with anecdotal reports of imaginative things that have been implemented to comfort and entertain patients, but they usually end with the admonition: They did not increase revenue or patient base although that's really not the fundamental reason for doing them. They, as well as numerous practice management gurus who run seminars, advise that well-trained staff who are courteous and trained in understanding different personality types and how they react in stressful situations will prove to be a long-term asset. Nevertheless, it is worthwhile to distract and entertain patients in the treatment room as a considerable body of research demonstrates that such diversions are highly effective in reducing stress, especially in a clinical setting.

INTERVIEW QUESTIONNAIRE—AN IMPORTANT DESIGN TOOL

Dentistry allows for highly personalized practice methods, which must be set by the dentist before the space planner can begin. The interview questionnaire in the Appendix of this book is useful for documenting practice preferences and equipment. Prior to filling out the questionnaire, a general discussion should occur relevant to the doctor's long-term goals—perhaps a 10-year plan. Is the goal to bring partners into the practice, to get this one going and then open other locations, or to retire in 10 years and sell the practice? This information will influence the project budget, space allocation, room for growth, and equipment selections.

The information gathered from the questionnaire can be translated into an effective space-planning program. Occasionally dentists moving into new offices will bring outdated dental equipment with them, which might necessitate a less-than-optimal treatment room layout. Others buy sleek, state-of-the-art equipment that allows the designer to create an efficient treatment room. This chapter will acquaint the designer with the equipment and general requirements for the practices of general dentistry (including prosthodontics and cosmetic dentistry), pediatric dentistry (pedodontics), orthodontics, periodontics, oral surgery, and endodontics. While guidelines will be given, remember that the organization of dental offices is somewhat less standardized than that of medical facilities, owing to the number of options in size and design of the operatory or treatment room. The equipment, the location of casework, and the preferred style of delivery of instrumentation (rear, over the patient, or side) will determine the size and layout of the treatment room. As an aside, the preferred term for operatory is now "treatment room" unless surgery is performed there, as in oral surgery, although many dentists still use the term "operatory."

Therefore, although there is an optimal design of a treatment room, other choices will also be presented. That which is common to all dental suites will be discussed under General Dentistry. Modifications required for other dental specialties will be discussed thereafter.

PLAN THE SPACE BEFORE SIGNING A LEASE

Dentists tend to do the same thing that physicians do—namely, to lease a space prior to engaging a space planner.

COLUMNS SHOWN CUT AWAY
(TYPICAL)

Figure 10-1. Waiting area is furnished like a residential living room with seating grouped around the fireplace; architectural detailing complements the design. (*Rendering courtesy: Signature Environments, Inc, Seattle, WA.*)

Figure 10-2. Rustic detailing enhances the character of a dentist's waiting room/reception area. (*Rendering courtesy; Signature Environments, Inc., Seattle, WA.*)

While the dentist may know that he or she needs four treatment rooms to be functional, without a space plan, it will be impossible to know how that space will lay out and if it will yield four treatment rooms of optimal size. This is affected by the shape of the space, the location of structural columns, as well as the overall dimensions of the area and perhaps the desire to have north light in the treatment rooms. A wiser course of action is to meet with a space planner prior to committing to the space. If the configuration of the space results in an awkward layout, undersized treatment rooms, and poor adjacencies with respect to critical functions such as sterilization and overall flow through the office, it is better to recognize these conditions early rather than have to live with them for the next 10 years. Another space in the building may be available that would result in a better layout. As dentists know well, efficiency makes a tremendous difference, whether it is a convenient reaching distance while seated at the dental chair, the number of staff it takes to run the office, or the resulting stress inefficiency places on the dentist and chairside assistants as they move through a busy schedule.

Extraordinary Teamwork Required

The design and construction of a dental office require a level of team collaboration and coordination that has no parallel in the design of a medical office. A matter of inches can make a critical difference in the efficiency of a treatment room. The interior designer or architect's role is analogous to that of a symphony conductor, carefully timing and integrating all the instruments or, in this case, the work of the dental equipment planner, audiovisual media consultant, electrical and mechanical subcontractors, and dental equipment installers. A good general contractor experienced at building dental offices is essential. The complexity of this effort cannot be underestimated—precision is everything.

Figure 10-5. Waiting room features a built-in magazine rack and leaded glass windows reminiscent of Frank Lloyd Wright designs. (*Space planning and interior design: Janet Pettersen, IIDA, Design Wave, Fallbrook, CA; Photographer: Jain Malkin.*)

CODES AND REGULATORY AGENCY REVIEW

A review of codes should start with the State Business and Professions Code if one exists. The State Dental Board and Public Health Department should also be consulted. Any or all of the above may have policies and procedures relevant to infection control, pharmaceutical control log, calibration of equipment, patients' rights, and so forth, some of which have no impact on the physical design of the office. If the dentist uses general anesthesia (oral surgery, pediatric, or restorative/esthetic dentistry cases), this triggers many code issues as the patient is deemed "at risk for loss of life-preserving protective reflexes." In some states, the use of general anesthesia mandates licensing by the department of health services, Medicare certification, or accreditation by a recognized agency. These issues are explained in detail in Chapter 4 under Plastic Surgery, headings *Office-based Surgery* and *Accreditation, Licensing,* and *Medicare Certification.* See also Chapter 7, under Ambulatory Surgical Centers, heading *Storage of Medical Gases,* and Chapter 15, *Researching Codes and Reference Materials.*

ADA (Americans with Disabilities Act)

The ADA applies to medical and dental offices. Most architects and designers are very familiar with ADA regulations. Since there is no formal local enforcement of this national civil rights legislation, it is local building departments that review it during the plan check. Building inspectors can be quite rigorous about compliance to the point of taking out a measuring tape and not approving a door setback that is supposed to be 18 inches on the pull side, if it falls short by even an inch. The same is true for toilet rooms, *all* of which must be ADA compliant unless it has access only from the doctor's private office and that person is an owner of the building.

It seems, however, based on discussions with a number of architects and planners of dental offices, that the ADA is interpreted differently by building departments even within the same region with respect to treatment rooms and task areas such as sterilization. For example, since a person in a wheelchair may not be able to perform the tasks required of a dental assistant in the treatment room or sterilization area, the 36-inch clearance for a wheelchair on the assistant's side of the room may not be required, nor would the opening for room entry, in this case, be required to be 36 inches since the opening on the dentist's side would be 36 inches. Other jurisdictions require 36-inch clearance on all sides of the dental chair as well as wheelchair clearance under every sink in a treatment room. It has been reported to the author (but not verified) that OSHA has an interpretive newsletter that, in essence, states that task-oriented stand-up workstations at the ADA limit of 34-inch height can injure the worker's back. As a result, in some jurisdictions sterilization workstations are approved at 36-inch height.

Dentists are accustomed to packing a lot into small spaces. Tiny darkrooms, labs, or break rooms with doors opening into the room barely scraping the edge of the cabinet are no longer possible under the Americans with Disabilities Act design restrictions. All rooms must be wheelchair accessible and have an 18-inch wall area on the pull side of the door.

Building Codes and Construction Methods

Refer to Chapters 14 and 15 for relevant information on these topics. In most cases, these issues are the same for medical and dental offices.

OSHA (Occupational Safety and Health Administration) EPA (Environmental Protection Agency)

To avoid redundancy, the reader should refer to Chapter 3, heading *OSHA Issues* for a discussion of standards affecting medical and dental offices. What follows is a discussion of items specific to dental practices. It should be noted that around the country a number of OSHA compliance consultants are available to dentists and physicians to survey their offices for proper techniques and also to train staff. OSHA usually sends inspectors only if a complaint is filed.

EPA Disposal Requirements

Film Processing. The EPA is concerned with the capture and certified disposal of film-processing solutions or, at least, the fixer. This is in effect in almost all states, although some allow silver recovery systems to process fixer with disposal into the city sewer system. Of course, the darkroom will become extinct as digital imaging becomes widespread.

Amalgam and Mercury. In some states, old amalgam removed from patients and collected by traps in the office vacuum system must be disposed of through certified hazardous waste haulers. The amalgam also contains mercury, which is regulated as parts per million (ppm) in the air. Chances are more sophisticated gathering of amalgam and residual mercury will be available in the near future.

Lead from Film Packets. The storage of lead from intraoral X-ray film packets after processing and certified disposal is fairly common, but this does not affect design as several years' collection of wrappers can be compressed into a 1-cubic-foot box.

Hazardous Waste and Sharps. There is a gap between what OSHA considers biohazardous (medical) waste within the working environment and what the EPA considers hazardous waste during disposal. OSHA mandates that any material or waste that has contacted saliva or blood be stored within the office in marked waste containers declaring it as biohazardous. This is ostensibly to alert employees not to reach into these waste containers unprotected or to handle the waste during disposal without proper barriers in place. The EPA, however, does not consider the same waste, in general, as hazardous after it leaves the dental office. The concentration of blood and saliva is seldom significant enough to cause a health hazard. The problem lies in the misinterpretation of how to dispose of the waste. If it is red bagged, then the EPA and the waste haulers and landfill personnel must treat it as biohazardous medical waste. However, if it is disposed of properly, no special precautions are necessary during disposal.

Sharps can be stored in a new type of sharps container, called an Isolyser, which is filled with a high level of liquid disinfectant. Once the container is full, a catalyst powder is added and the solution becomes an impenetrable mass of polymer that seals all of the sharps from the environment. A label is applied over the original BioHazard emblem declaring the waste as treated and, as solid waste, it can be disposed of like any other trash. Refer to the *Casework and Modular Cabinetry* sections in this chapter for ideas to accommodate sharps containers and waste collection neatly and out of view in the treatment room. The designer needs to check local codes to see if the office needs a separate storage area (usually a small room or closet near the staff or service entrance) for biohazardous waste until the certified hauler removes it.

OSHA

It should be noted that OSHA has both state and federal agencies. National OSHA standards may be interpreted differently by state OSHA agencies. Both must be consulted.

Hazardous Materials Standard. All materials an employee comes into contact with must be examined for known health or safety hazards and labeled if found to be dangerous. This involves mandatory record keeping of an inventory of hazardous products and a readily available book of MSDS (Materials Safety Data Sheets) for reference in case of spills or contact with hazardous materials. Offices must have an eyewash diverter device or a dedicated eyewash in any area in which hazardous materials are used. It must be placed where an employee can reach it within 10 seconds of occurrence, which generally means placing it in the sterilization area, possibly the dental lab, and the darkroom. A faucet diverter device (see Figure 3-51) is often used, but it has the potential to cause additional injury if the injured worker accidentally turns on the hot water instead of the cold water. A permanent eyewash station has only a cold-water line. The types of hazardous materials that may be found in a dental office are phosphoric acid, sodium hypochloride, phenols, hydrofluoric acid, film developer and fixer. In the dental lab, fumes from methyl methacrylates and ethyl methacrylates need to be exhausted to the outdoors, not the plenum. This requires a good ventilation fan.

Bloodborne Pathogens Standard. This standard mandates that employees be educated as to the methods of transmission of disease, proper use of personal protective equipment, proper handling of waste and sharps, and the results of accidental needle sticks. Universal precautions should be taken with all patients. An often-overlooked design factor is the addition of a washer and dryer within the facility to launder barrier gowns. This also involves a storage area for clean gowns, which have either been laundered in the facility or sent out to a commercial laundry and subsequently delivered back to the dental office. A hamper is needed to collect soiled gowns until they can be laundered. Putting the washer and dryer or soiled-clothing hamper in the staff lounge is prohibited by OSHA. There must be a definite separation of food, cosmetics, and eye care products from items used in the clinical practice; likewise, one cannot take contaminated items into an area where food is prepared or consumed. A good location for the laundry area is near sterilization as the washer and dryer can be monitored during use. The hamper can be placed in the staff restroom if staff use this for changing clothing or it can be an isolated hamper next to the washer/dryer. If laundry is sent out to process, the hamper can be placed in the hazardous waste holding room (Figure 10-6).

Nitrous Oxide Scavenging and Monitoring. OSHA mandates that effective scavenging systems be used during nitrous oxide sedation to prevent overcontamination of the air for dental personnel. Nitrous oxide leaks from the face mask, putting female employees of childbearing age particularly at risk of miscarriage, premature births, and infants born with low birth weight. Some states have mandated that an electronic monitoring system be installed to alert staff when the acceptable level ppm (parts per million) of N_2O has been exceeded. Proper placement of this monitoring system is a design factor, which will also impact HVAC design. A high number of air changes per hour is essential in all treatment rooms. Air supply and return should be carefully studied to ensure adequate circulation.

Water Quality

This issue took center stage a couple of years ago as a result of investigative reports presented on several national TV news magazines. Water from a dental handpiece or syringe was declared to be considerably more contaminated than water samples taken from public restroom toilets when analyzed by an independent testing laboratory. As a result, many states have enacted legislation mandating that water used during treatment have no more than 200 CFUs (colony forming units) per milliliter of contamination. Dental equipment is now designed to incorporate containers that can be filled with distilled water and mounted on the assistant's cart or on the dental console (Figures 10-7 and 10-8a).

There are several methods for achieving good water quality in the dental office.

1. Design equipment to no longer use public water and instead use distilled water, reverse-osmosis water, or a new replacement solution. Even daily and weekly regimens for sterilizing or disinfecting the entire self-contained water system, using distilled water, do not guarantee that overcontamination will not occur with regular maintenance. This led to the development of an FDA-approved solution that can be added to regular drinking water to constantly kill microorganisms and prevent biofilm buildup in the water system without harming the patient or affecting the efficacy of dental materials. Several of these now exist.

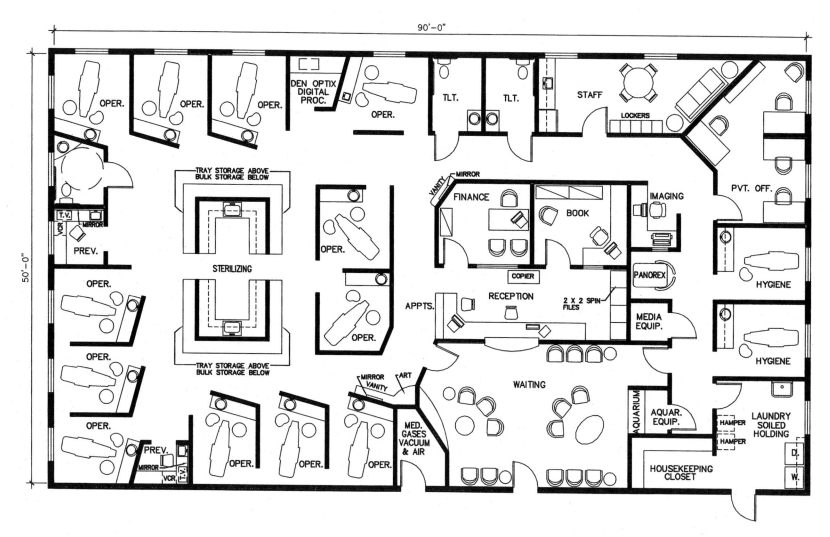

GENERAL DENTISTRY – GROUP PRACTICE
4500 SF

Figure 10-6. Space plan for general dentistry group practice, 4500 square feet. (*Design: Jain Malkin Inc.*)

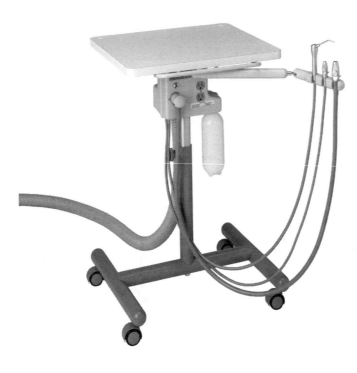

Figure 10-7. Chairside assistant's mobile cart. Note container for distilled water (*Photo courtesy: A-dec, Newberg, OR.*)

2. Some manufacturers have effected a solution by running the public water supply to the dental units through a device that meters in a product that kills microorganisms and prevents biofilm buildup.

3. Use public water but install an ultraviolet sterilization chamber and/or ozone treatment device on the water supply at each chair.

4. Use the public water system but install disposable filters on each water line to a dental unit just prior to the water being discharged into a patient's mouth.

All these methods must be approved by the FDA and the designer must establish which method the practitioner wishes to employ as it affects water supply design criteria.

It should be noted that almost all states and municipalities now require a separate RP (reduced pressure) backflow preventer on any public water line connected to a dental unit regardless of what devices the dentist has put in place to treat the water. This device is too large to put into the standard dental equipment junction box, so it must be mounted remotely. This can be either cost prohibitive or space prohibitive, in which case, the first solution listed above would be the most practical alternative as it does not require city water plumbed to the dental unit.

Exposure to Radiation

The safe use of X-ray machines is generally regulated by the State Board of Health and assigned to a radiological health subdepartment. OSHA only inspects facilities to make sure they are following these regulations as they pertain to the protection of employees. OSHA, itself, has no specific radiology standards. Regulations affecting the design of dental suites follow.

1. Most states require that a health physicist review floor plans and potential locations of equipment to determine proper radiation barrier materials and acceptable locations for operating controls. The physicist will need to know the specifications of the X-ray equipment with respect to radiation emitted and the anticipated usage or volume of films for each machine. The physicist will consider construction of walls, adjacent occupancies, and construction of floors and ceilings that separate this space from others above and below. Required barriers for dental X-rays are minimal compared with medical radiology equipment. The physicist's report must be submitted to the building department along with the construction documents.

2. The federal minimum barrier requirement for dental-type X-ray machines is a standard wall constructed with wood or metal studs and covered on both sides by one layer of ⅝-inch-thick gypsum board. An opera-

tor does not need to be behind an approved barrier as long as he or she is 72 inches or more from the source of the radiation and not in the primary beam trajectory. No one other than the patient can be in the primary beam trajectory, which means approved barriers must exist to prevent exposing staff or patients in adjacent areas during X-ray.

Typically, the only lead barrier requirement is immediately behind a cephalometric X-ray head holder and only if the space behind it is routinely occupied, although some states have more rigorous standards. This may include lead lining in modular dental furniture systems and/or in stud and drywall partitions. When a secondary entrance to the room exists, a photoelectric eye deactivation of the X-ray beam may be required if someone tries to enter during an exposure. Through-the-wall X-ray cabinets may be required to have switches on cabinet doors so that the X-ray will work only when one set of doors is fully closed.

A cephalometric X-ray device is generally found only in orthodontic and oral surgery practices, but may occasionally be found in general dentistry practices as well. State guidelines often require that the X-ray machine operator be able to see the patient during the exposure of a panoramic X-ray because the patient is essentially trapped inside a moving machine and can be injured if he or she tries to exit unexpectedly during exposure. Some states have misinterpreted this requirement and mandated that the operator be able to see the patient during any X-ray exposure. It is important to check requirements with the state agency and then provide a location for the operator that allows viewing of the patient from behind an approved barrier or from a distance 6 feet away from the radiation source and never in the primary beam trajectory. The use of leaded-glass operator viewing windows is probably the most common method for compliance. Refer to Chapter 5 for examples of protective barriers and resources. Nuclear Associates in Carle Place, New York, is a major supplier of lead-impregnated acrylic barriers.

3. Most states have laws that cover the design of the darkroom as well as the developing process and exposure. Poor technique forces a practitioner to take needless additional exposures. An absolutely light-proof room, but with good ventilation, is required. Refer to Chapter 3 for details on darkroom design and to Figure 10-78 for a diagram. The safelight must be filtered with a Kodak GBX filter or equal and must be located a minimum of 36 inches from the work surface and the input to the film processor. The EPA and local health regulations should also be checked with regard to disposal, treatment, or capture of chemicals.

NEW TECHNOLOGY TRANSFORMS THE DENTAL OFFICE

New technology is changing the fundamental way dentists practice, making it possible to achieve a level of integration and efficiency in practice management that is almost effortless once the proper software and hardware have been employed and networked. Think of the typical series of documentation and communication steps required for charting treatment, scheduling visits, discussing costs, documenting insurance codes, preparing lab slips, recording payments, filing insurance claims, and sending out statements. The same information is written or typed over and over with much repetition and little value gained. Think about a typical day's schedule and the total number of patients for which these multiple entries must be made and also consider the possibilities for error. One procedure for an individual patient can require as many as 15 entries, which results in high overhead and job security for office staff.

The Paperless Office

In the paperless office, there is total connectivity among all aspects of practice management and clinical care. Computers located at all workstations, including treatment

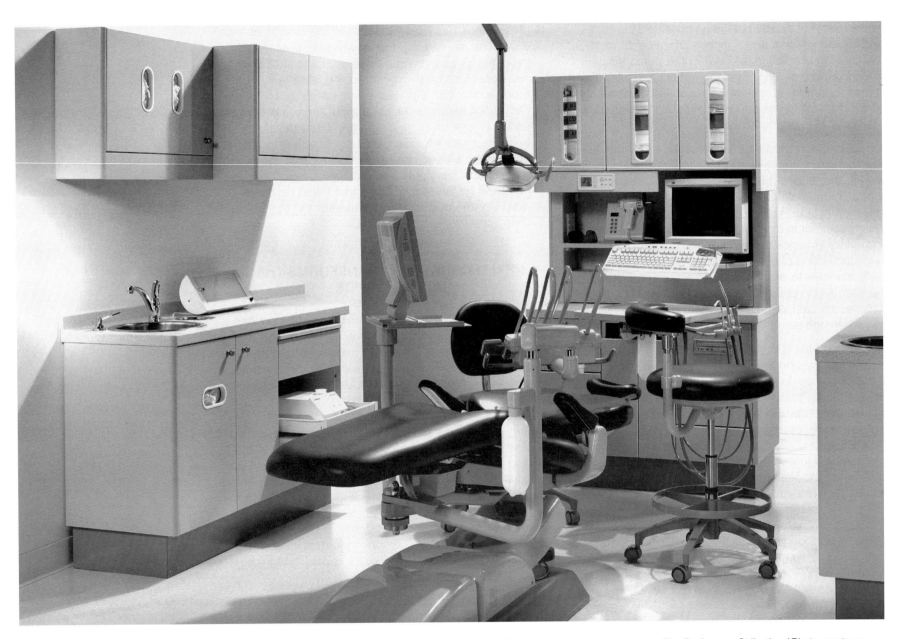

Figure 10-8a. Treatment room features practice management monitor at 12 o'clock wall and doctor/patient flat-screen monitor on radius arm. The Preference Collection (*Photo courtesy: A-dec, Newberg, OR.*)

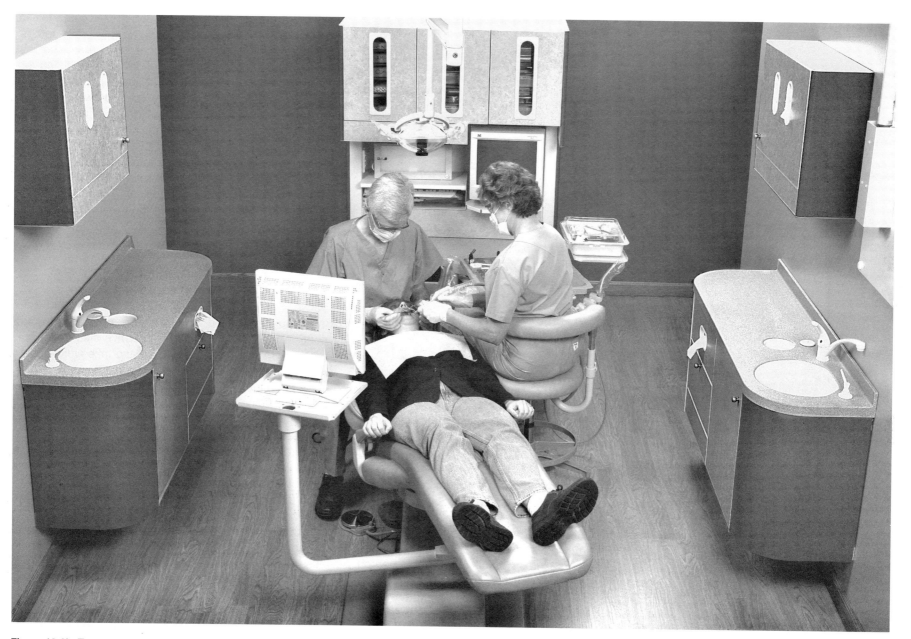

Figure 10-8b. Treatment room with dual cart rear delivery for doctor and chairside assistant. The Preference Collection (*Photo courtesy: A-dec, Newberg, OR.*)

payment right in the treatment room. This frees the front desk assistant to focus on sending marketing letters to patients and collecting accounts receivable and insurance, in addition to general overview of scheduling, posting payments, and handling in-office collections. There is another benefit to blurring the roles between front and back office staff who are sometimes critical of what they view as the others' shortcomings and lack of understanding of the importance of what they do. By having cross-trained staff who literally step into each other's shoes, it builds teamwork and uses everyone's time more effectively. Hygienists, for example, can schedule their own recalls as the patient is leaving the treatment room if they have a computer at their disposal.

Multiple Applications for Treatment Room Computers

In a paperless office, any notes or letters from referring dentists are scanned into the patient's electronic clinical record, which is easier to access and takes less space to store, can be transmitted to other locations, and is less likely to be lost, assuming proper back-up procedures are followed. Once the computer is in the treatment room, there is an array of peripheral items that can be added such as cosmetic imaging, digital X-ray, digital intraoral camera, and software for presenting complete treatment plans with estimates of cost, as well as patient education and entertainment programs (Figures 10-8b and 10-9). High-tech dental offices have totally integrated, multiple-application, seamless computer systems that result in improved practice management and enhanced diagnostic capabilities, giving patients a better understanding of necessary restorative treatment and what constitutes optimal dental health. Having a computer in the operatory provides greater ability to access, process, and store large quantities of data with instantaneous retrieval. The real benefit is that patients are being better served: Intraoral video cameras, digital radiography, and chairside microscope magnification improve the ability to find and treat problems earlier.

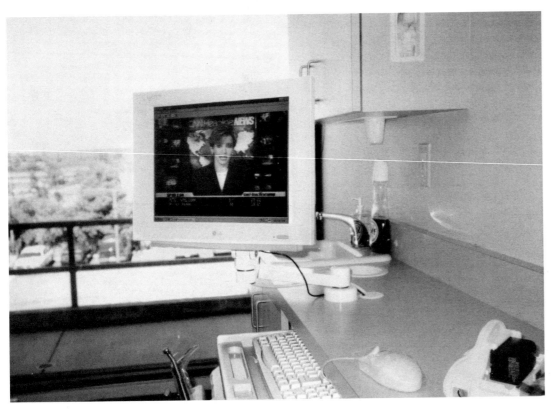

Figure 10-9. Treatment room depicting side delivery of instrumentation and doctor/patient flat-screen monitor on articulating arm secured to side cabinet. (*Photographer: Jain Malkin.*)

rooms, enable a seamless transfer of information that starts with scheduling the patient and ends with electronically processing insurance claims. Recall appointments can be scheduled from the treatment room without having to rely on one pivotal person at the front desk as the chief appointment maker. In small offices, the person seated at the front desk often runs the show, sending out statements as well. When he or she is absent, the practice may come to a grinding halt. Cross-training enables support staff to do several jobs, creating a situation sometimes known as "frontdesklessness." As chairside assistants become more comfortable with computers, they can post procedures, schedule, and even accept

The Technology Wave

Intraoral Video Camera

The intraoral video camera enables intraoral or extraoral visualization at magnification from 5× to 35×, depending on the mode. It is the greatest visual tool for dentists since the mirror. The system consists of a handpiece (which is actually a tiny lens) that looks like a pen, a docking station with fiber-optic system, and a video monitor (Figure 10-10), although the images can be displayed on any monitors in the room. An optional printer produces color hard-copy images for patient and insurance use. Figure 10-11 shows standalone and network configurations. A built-in freeze frame makes it easy to create a "show and tell" presentation for the patient, and, with appropriate software, images can be captured and downloaded to the patient chart or placed in a digital "photo album" for view at a glance of multiple images with dates, name, and patient identification. This software makes it easy to assemble case presentations by using the computer to search for images by type and then further refine the search by gender, age, tooth number, upper or lower, and so on.

The intraoral camera is a significant diagnostic tool that enhances the visibility of areas of the mouth that are difficult to see and it also makes it much easier to educate patients about restorative treatment. The docking station can be eliminated if the intraoral camera is integrated on the instrument console as it is in Figure 10-12. This system makes it ergonomically easy for the dentist to manipulate images or access data on the computer due to the convenient tray for a cordless mouse or an integrated touch pad. Freeze-frame images can be saved to the patient chart by tapping a foot pedal. Air and water are also controlled by foot pedal. While many dental equipment manufacturers have adapted their patient chairs and dental consoles to accommodate digital technology, the unit in Figure 10-12 is completely integrated without having to add separate items. Note also that the patient chair is cantilevered, creating a less bulky appearance.

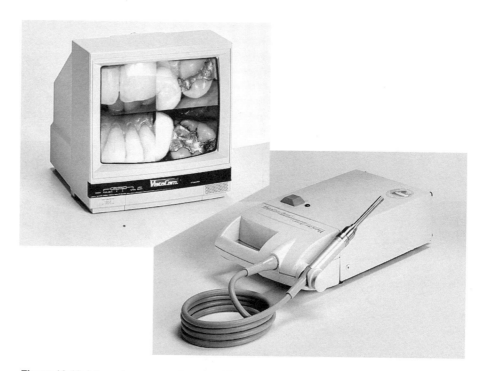

Figure 10-10. Intraoral camera and monitor. VistaCam OmniTM. (*Photo courtesy:Air Techniques Inc., Hicksville, NY.*)

Extraoral Cameras

Extraoral cameras are used to photograph the full face or smile. This can be used by imaging programs to show how the face will change after dental treatment. They are typically used in orthodontic practices and also in cosmetic or esthetic dentistry. If a digital camera is used, the image can be directly captured by a software program that morphs the face to show how it will change with the proposed dental treatment. Newer dental offices often have an imaging room (Figure 10-6) where photos are taken and in which an assistant trained to manipulate the software can prepare cosmetic dentistry case presentations. The imaging area needs a countertop work surface to accommodate the monitor and keyboard and to provide a place for the assistant to work. This room may also contain a panoramic or combination panoramic/cephalometric X-ray.

Stand-Alone Configuration

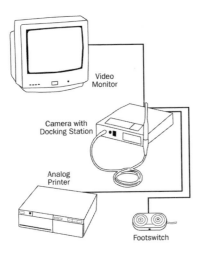

Video Monitor

Camera with Docking Station

Analog Printer

Footswitch

Network Configuration

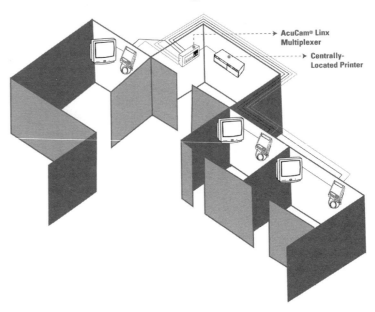

AcuCam® Linx Multiplexer

Centrally-Located Printer

Stand-Alone Configuration

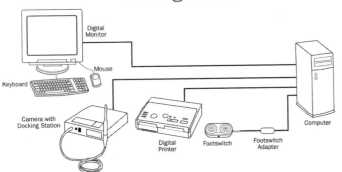

Digital Monitor

Mouse

Keyboard

Camera with Docking Station

Digital Printer

Footswitch

Footswitch Adapter

Computer

Network Configuration

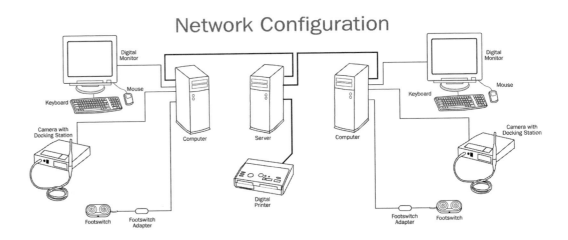

Digital Monitor

Mouse

Keyboard

Camera with Docking Station

Computer

Server

Computer

Digital Printer

Digital Monitor

Mouse

Keyboard

Camera with Docking Station

Footswitch

Footswitch Adapter

Footswitch Adapter

Footswitch

Figure 10-11. Diagram of intraoral camera configurations. (*Illustration courtesy: Dentsply International, Gendex Dental X-Ray Division, Des Plaines, IL.*)

Digital Radiography

The advantages of digital dental radiography are numerous. It eliminates the cost of film, chemistry, and processors. It eliminates the darkroom and the need to clean the processor roller rack as well as the need to dispose of the lead film packs and processor chemicals. In addition, it exposes patients to considerably less radiation, and issues of under- or overexposed film are resolved by being able to manipulate a digital image. Digital radiography is discussed in detail later in this chapter.

Operating Microscope

Ceiling- or wall-mounted microscopes in the treatment room are used by anyone who desires to see better: endodontists, prosthodontists, periodontists, general dentists, and, most recently, dental hygienists (Figures 10-13 and 10-14). The operating microscope enables dentists to work at high-level magnification ($2\times$–$21\times$) coupled with coaxial illumination. Telescopic loupes (eyeglasses only) provide 2- to 4-power magnification. The microscope may have accessories added such as video cameras, digital cameras, 35-mm film cameras, and/or a dental assistant's binoculars. Operating microscopes are being built into many offices today due to the significant ergonomic advantage of being able to sit up straight, looking forward at the microscope, rather than bending over the patient. This reduces head and neck injuries (Figure 10-14).

Networked Computer Systems

Networked multiple treatment room computer systems integrating clinical software, digital X-ray, and dental practice management software create a paperless office and a seamless transfer of information.

Dual Monitors

Each treatment room will have monitors for the patient and clinical staff.

Air Abrasion

Air abrasion is an alternative to conventional high-speed handpiece (drill) dentistry; however, it is appropriate only

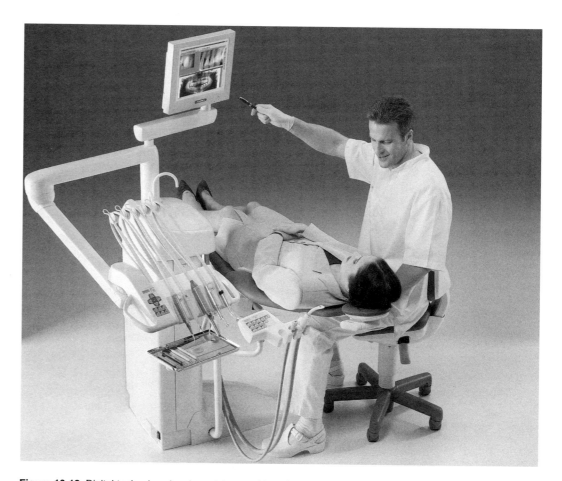

Figure 10-12. Digital technology has been integrated into the design of the Prostyle Compact dental unit, eliminating the need to connect a number of separate items. The intraoral camera is one of the handpieces. Air and water are controlled by tapping a foot pedal. (*Photo courtesy: PLANMECA, INC.,USA, Addison, IL.*)

for certain types of treatments. A small stream of particles (powder), under extremely high pressure, literally dissolves cavities. It generally does not require anesthesia and is therefore quite appealing for small children. When the decay is removed, a small tooth-colored filling is inserted. Air abrasion can also be used as a diagnostic tool to probe hidden decay in lieu of "watching and waiting" for a potential problem to get worse. It is minimally invasive and eliminates the vibration and microfracturing associated with rotary handpieces. It is often used with a rapid curing light that cures composite materials or bleaches quickly, compared with conventional methods. A large machine, on casters, the air abrasion equipment can be moved from room to room (Figure 10-15a), and some modular casework systems have created a recessed niche for it (Figure 10-43).

Cosmetic Imaging

With the advent of digital cameras, photo-quality ink-jet printers, and inexpensive image capture software, cosmetic imaging is taking center stage to help dentists demonstrate esthetic treatment results to patients. Cosmetic cases can involve extensive work and high fees. Dramatically changing someone's smile is professionally, as well as financially, rewarding compared with routine dentistry and discounted fees paid by dental plans.

Lasers

Lasers have been developed for both hard and soft tissue. They can be used to treat periodontal disease in a process called root planing. After tartar is removed using an ultrasonic scaler, the erbium laser is used to reduce bacteria associated with periodontal disease. A diode laser enables cosmetic dentists to sculpt the gum line. Not as common is the laser developed for hard tissue. These may be used for removal of tooth decay and cavity preparation as well as resin restorations. In the future, it is expected that they will be used in oral surgery and for cleaning out root canals in endodontic practices. Presently, research shows no differences in postoperative results compared with cavity preparation in the conventional air turbine/bur technique, except that laser treat-

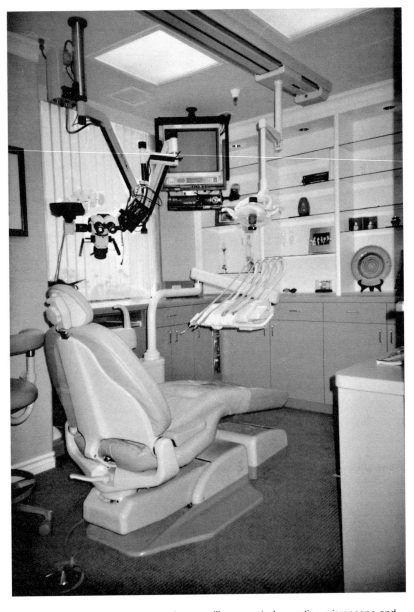

Figure 10-13. This treatment room has a ceiling-mounted operating microscope and TV monitor as well as centrally piped medical gases (note faceplates at toe of chair, left side). Glass shelves in front of patient display art objects. (*Photo courtesy: Cherilyn Sheets, D.D.S.; Photographer: Jain Malkin.*)

ment does not require local anesthesia. Lasers are somewhat controversial in dental practice: Some practitioners currently see no need for lasers and, in fact, have quite negative opinions about their usefulness, while others find them very useful for specific procedures. Many dentists prefer electrosurgery to lasers. For dentists who use them, there are no special space or design accommodations that need to be made. They are portable and can be moved from room to room. As the beam is narrowly focused in the mouth, it doesn't pose any environmental safety hazards; lasers are often used in treatment rooms without doors. The patient and clinical staff must wear goggles to protect their eyes and a sign must be posted when lasers are in use. Most states require that lasers be licensed like X-ray machines.

Chairside Patient Education/Entertainment

Patient education includes viewing images taken by the intraoral video camera, looking at digital X-rays, and watching DVD presentations on specific dental procedures or problems. CAESY®, an acronym for Clinically Advanced Education System (available from Dentistry Online, Inc., Vancouver, Washington), offers 2- to 3½-minute video presentations enhanced by clinical photos and computer animation and narration explaining periodontal disease, root canal, and dozens of other procedures. While the assistant is readying the treatment room or while waiting for the local anesthetic to take effect, the patient can be educated so that the dentist's time can be optimized by not having to explain the procedure. CAESY also supports the hygienist by eliminating repetitive treatment explanations, saving time, and it can be used by the treatment planning coordinator to prepare effective case presentations. The Smile Channel®, also available from Dentistry Online, in DVD format, can be used in the waiting room or the treatment room to stimulate a desire for cosmetic dentistry. In discussing topics like veneers, bonding, and teeth whitening, it demonstrates how the smile can be changed. It also has humorous programming for children using animals who "visit" the dentist to learn how to take care of their teeth.

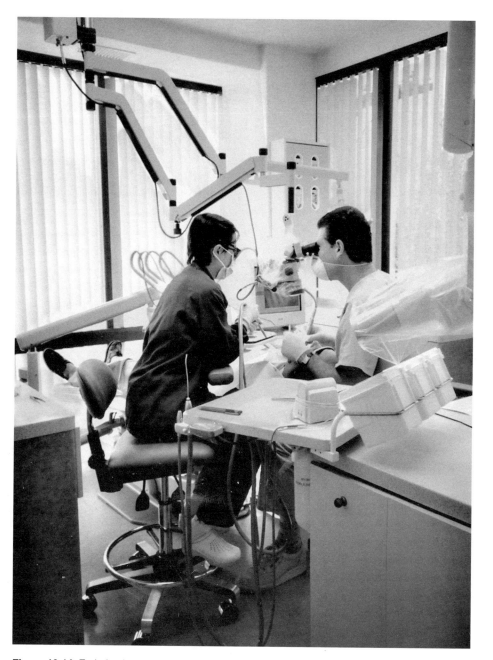

Figure 10-14. Endodontist using ceiling-mounted operating microscope, which enables the doctor to sit erect during the procedure rather than bent over the patient's head. (*Photographer: Jain Malkin.*)

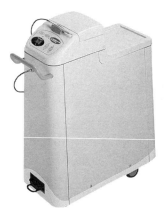

Figure 10-15a. Air abrasion system, AirDent II™ (11 inches wide × 24 inches deep × 28 inches high), can be moved from room to room. (*Photo courtesy: Air Techniques Inc., Hicksville, NY.*)

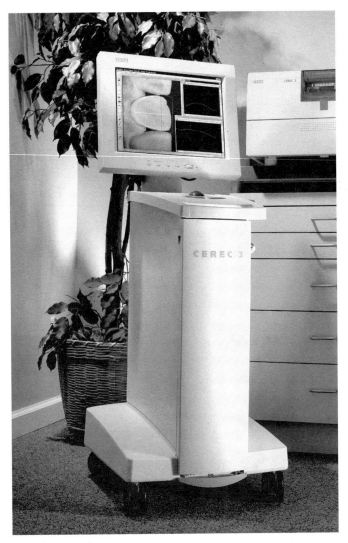

Figure 10-15b. The CEREC 3 (Chairside Economical Restorations of Esthetic Ceramics) produces, at chairside, fillings, veneers, onlays, and crowns. (*Photo courtesy. Sirona USA, LLC., Charlotte, NC.*)

For entertainment, virtual-reality glasses and programming may be more appropriate for children than adults as the nature of the device is somewhat of a barrier in establishing rapport between the patient and dentist. Making eye contact during treatment is important. Once the initial dialogue with the patient has ended and treatment begins, entertainment can be very useful in distracting patients to reduce anxiety. This includes videos of calming nature scenes (desert, tropical rainforest, beach and surf) as well as satellite TV and music, all of which can be controlled by the patient with a remote-control device.

Computer-Aided Restoration with Electronic Impressions

The CEREC 3 by Sirona uses CAD/CAM (computer-aided design/computer-aided manufacturing) to produce, at the chairside, fillings, veneers, onlays, and crowns (Figure 10-15b). Instead of several return appointments and temporary inlays or crowns, it can all be done in one appointment. The CEREC takes an electronic "impression" (no gooey impression material in the mouth), and the computer creates the restoration. Using an adhesive bonding technique, the dentist inserts the filling into the tooth or cements the crown. This eliminates having to send the impressions to a lab and waiting a couple of weeks for return of the crown. The conventional material for crowns is porcelain fused to metal, whereas the CEREC (chairside economical restorations of esthetic ceramics) uses ceramic material. There is some debate about whether ceramic crowns have the subtlety of coloration and artistry produced by the finest porcelain laboratories. Today, dentists have the capability of sending the laboratory a digital color photo of a patient's mouth with the standard tooth-matching color guide included in the photo as a visual reference to correct for differences in color reproduction on the monitor and/or printer receiving the image at the lab. Currently, the CEREC is not widely used in the United States because it takes considerable training and good technique to use it properly. In addition to chairside, it can also be used in an in-house dental lab.

Teeth Whitening

Increased awareness of beautiful smiles and white teeth has created demand for whitening or bleaching. This was formerly accomplished (and still is) at home by use of a bleaching gel that is injected into clear plastic molds, custom-made to fit the individual's teeth. Additionally, dentists can bleach teeth in their office by numerous methods, some of which have space implications. The large portable piece of equipment shown in Figure 10-16 requires that the patient sit still in a dental chair for approximately an hour and a half with mouth held open by a device to enable a bright light to reach the teeth, whereupon it interacts with a bleaching solution. During the procedure, the patient is distracted by watching a video. The unit may be kept in one of the hygiene treatment rooms.

Water Systems

Few dentists today use piped-in city water chairside in their treatment rooms due to awareness that microorganisms breed easily in standing water, which inadvertently exposes patients (especially those on Monday morning after water has been standing in the pipes all weekend) to health hazards. Manufacturers of dental equipment now routinely provide a container for distilled water mounted near the assistant's and/or dentist's handpieces (Figures 10-7 and 10-8a). Minerals in city water can also adversely affect the performance and longevity of handpieces, scalers, and syringes.

Sterilization Procedures

Sterilization techniques for instruments coming into contact with mucosal tissue during treatment must be processed, sterilized, and stored according to a higher standard of asepsis than has been common in the past. The CDC (Centers for Disease Control) suggests that all dental instruments be wrapped or bagged prior to sterilization and remain sealed until used. The Dental Board in each state or the Board of Public Health regulate asepsis. There are a number of states where it is not mandated by law that instruments be sterilized or packaged, but that number is diminishing as state regulators react to CDC guidelines by enacting legislation. The ADA (American Dental Association) has endorsed CDC regulations and made them the "standard of care," which has led many states to amend their practice acts accordingly.

Consumers would be surprised to learn how lax regulations have been with respect to sterilization of instruments and handpieces. There is no agency inspecting dental offices in this regard. Expect more regulation in the future, especially if dentists begin to seek accreditation by

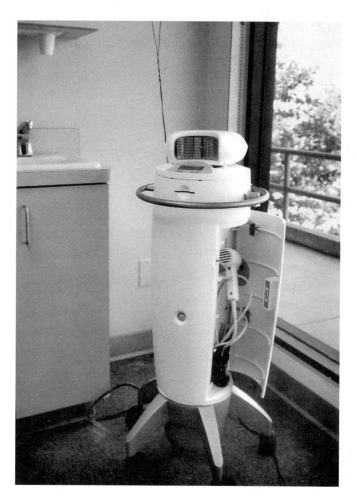

Figure 10-16. BriteSmile teeth whitening system. (*Photographer: Jain Malkin.*)

national agencies as many medical facilities must do in order for them to be eligible for Medicare and other third-party reimbursement.

Modular Cabinetry

Modular casework, as a generic item, is not new in dental treatment rooms, but the new generation of modular casework offers infinite possibilities for accommodating the numerous pieces of equipment that are now part of a high-tech treatment room, allowing for placement according to the practitioner's preference. Comparing the last generation of modular casework with the new generation (Figures 10-17, 10-18, and 10-19) tells the story. Also built into these units are dispensers for drinking cups, several sizes of gloves, and a tissue box, as well as the sharps container. The goal is to have everything out of sight when the patient enters the room and to open retractable and other doors and drawers after the patient is reclined in the chair. Note, in Figure 10-17, the pull-out shelf with keyboard and mouse and the ink-jet printer at the 12 o'clock wall.

Vacuum

There is a trend toward waterless (dry) vacuum systems because they save electricity, water, and sewage treatment costs; however, the greatest number of offices still use "wet seal" systems. Storage of old amalgam (silver fillings removed from patients) collected by traps in the office vacuum system must now, in many states, be disposed of through certified hazardous waste haulers. More sophisticated gathering of amalgam and residual mercury will be available in the near future. These systems exist throughout Europe, but thus far lobbying in the United States has stopped most state legislatures from enactment of similar legislation. Choice of vacuum system affects space requirements for the unit as well as piping requirements; consult the doctor's dental supplier for accurate information.

Safety Regulations

These have been discussed in detail earlier in this chapter and include standards issued by OSHA and the EPA regarding disposal of hazardous waste and sharps, the Bloodborne Pathogens Standard, the Hazardous Materials Standard, and tighter regulations for asepsis to prevent cross-contamination.

INFECTION CONTROL

People in a dental setting, whether staff or patients, are exposed to a wide variety of infectious microorganisms in the blood and saliva of patients. Proper infection control procedures used in the treatment room, sterilization, and dental laboratory prevent cross-contamination.

While much attention has been focused on AIDS, the dental team is much more at risk for hepatitis B and C. In 1982, the Council on Dental Therapeutics adopted a resolution recommending that all dental personnel be vaccinated against this virus. And, in 1988, OSHA began enforcing mandatory compliance with CDC/ADA (Centers for Disease Control/American Dental Association) recommendations developed to protect dental staff and patients from the risk of contracting HIV or hepatitis B virus from one another. As it is difficult to determine whether a patient is a carrier of one of these dangerous viruses, each patient must be considered potentially infectious and the same universal precautions should be implemented. The dental team is required to wear protective eyewear, masks, gloves, and uniforms or gowns to create a protective barrier between themselves and contact with blood, saliva, debris spatter, or aerosols. Head covers are recommended during invasive procedures that are likely to result in splashing blood or other body fluids. Laundry service or in-office washers/dryers are now the only options available to the dental practice for cleaning of barrier garments since OSHA forbids employees from taking or wearing home contaminated garments to launder them.

All surfaces within the treatment room must be able to be thoroughly cleaned and disinfected. The design of cabinetry should be simple and easy to clean, with few crevices. Wallcoverings, if used, should be smooth, and, although floors may be carpeted, a hard-surface floor will be easier to clean.

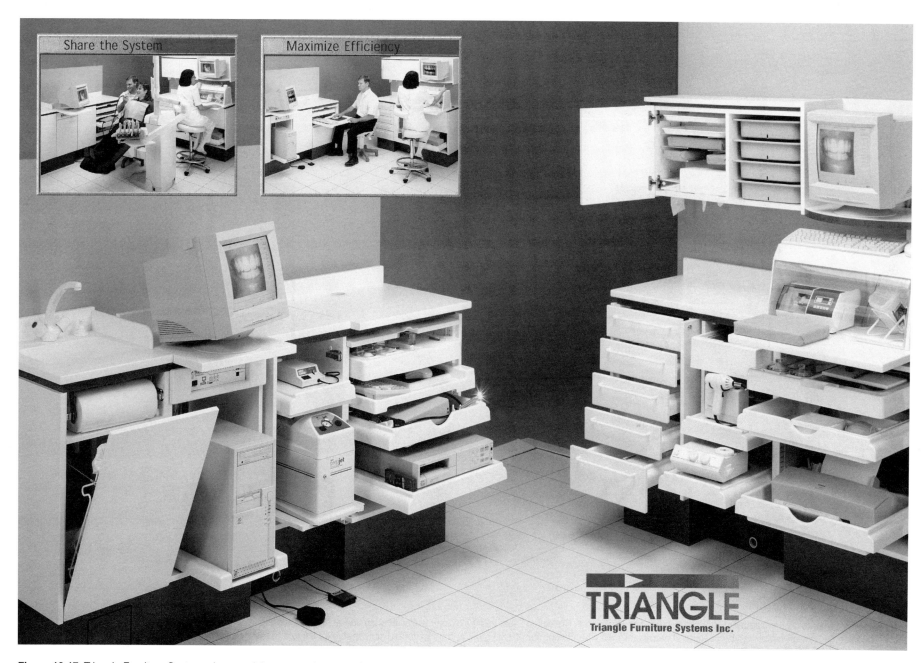

Figure 10-17. Triangle Furniture Systems, Inc., modular casework system for treatment room offers flexibility and storage for numerous individual pieces of equipment. (*Photo courtesy: Patterson Dental Supply, Inc., St. Paul, MN.*)

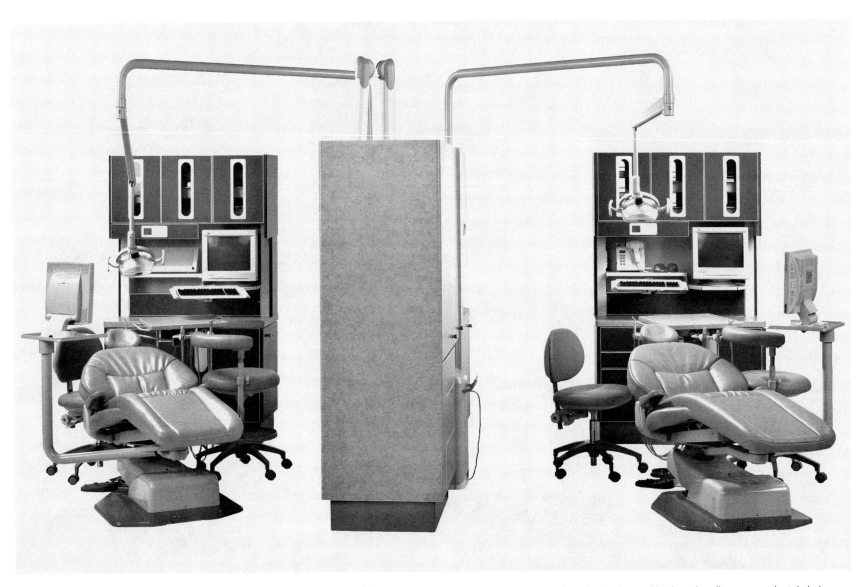

Figure 10-18. Modular treatment room casework, The Preference Collection™ features 12 o'clock wall with chairside assistant's monitor and keyboard; radius arm on dental chair enables flat-screen monitor to be positioned on patient's left when taking the X-ray image and on patient's right when explaining it to the patient. Note dental light is attached to casework. (*Photo courtesy: A-dec, Newberg, OR.*)

Dentists must cover any surfaces that may be contaminated by blood or saliva, such as the handle of the dental light or the X-ray head, with clear plastic film. This wrapping should be changed between every patient. Surfaces that cannot be covered or removed for cleaning and sterilization must be scrubbed and disinfected between each patient.

Select Finishes Carefully

Interior designers specializing in healthcare design are familiar with many attractive interior finish materials that have the illusion of texture but, in reality, can easily be cleaned. There are exquisite fabrics that have all the maintenance and durability properties of vinyl upholstery, yet are actually woven textiles that have the appearance of natural linen or other fine fabrics. Some of these can even be cleaned with bleach.

Upholstery fabrics, window treatments, wallcoverings, and flooring must be selected with asepsis in mind. Flooring in treatment rooms or operatories may be smooth sheet vinyl (the solid vinyl simulated woodgrain products are an attractive option). Many dentists prefer carpet for its acoustic properties and, contrary to popular wisdom, OSHA does not forbid carpet in treatment rooms as long as it is properly maintained. If carpet is used, it should be the type that has a laminated vinyl backing to prevent moisture from leaching up through the floor or, in the opposite direction, from the top through the backing into the slab or subfloor. Collins and Aikman and Mannington are two manufacturers that offer this option. Carpet should be directly glued to the slab. This provides a very firm surface on which to roll chairs.

A highly washable alternative to standard paint is a sprayed finish like Zolatone™, which has a speckled multicolor appearance that is quite attractive, and less expensive, than vinyl wallcovering. Consider polyvinyl chloride (PVC) vertical louver blinds as an easy-to-clean window treatment. A number of other interesting and practical window treatments have emerged in recent years using PVC mesh offered in different densities and a range of neutral

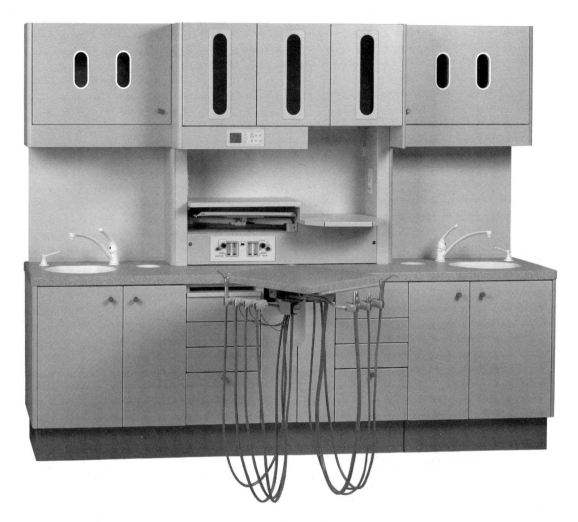

Figure 10-19. Modular casework configuration, The Preference Collection™, which may be used on rear wall of a private treatment room. Both doctor's and assistants instruments are delivered from the rear. (*Photo courtesy: A-dec, Newberg, OR.*)

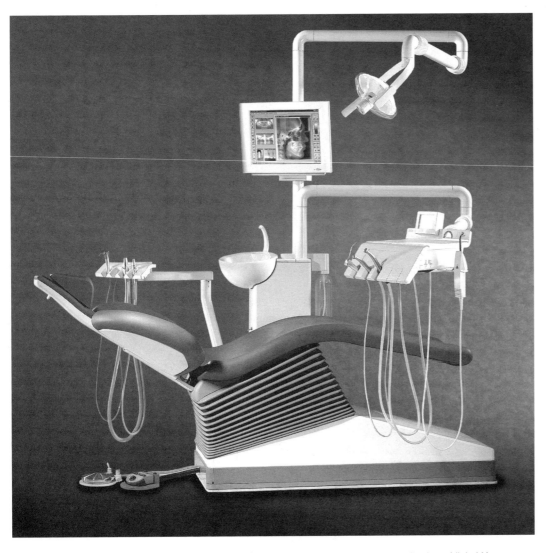

Figure 10-20. C8 Treatment Center with flat-screen monitor integrates patient communications (digital X-rays or intraoral camera images) with cabling concealed within the light post. (*Photo courtesy: Sirona USA, LLC., Charlotte, NC.*)

colors in the form of a roller shade or a pleated Roman shade. These fabrics are designed to control sun without blocking the view as well as to cut heat gain on southern and western exposures. Two manufacturers of these sun shade products are Mecho Shade (Phoenix, Arizona) and Solar Shade (Santa Ana, California). Chapter 12 provides a detailed discussion of appropriate finish materials for medical and dental offices and also discusses furniture.

Treatment Room Furniture and Equipment

Dental patient chairs, operator's stools, and equipment are designed with asepsis in mind using vinyl upholstery with a seamless, easy-to-clean design (Figure 10-20). High-speed evacuation (vacuum system), dry, oil-free compressed air, and proper patient positioning (made easier by having the right chair) all help to control cross-contamination. Sterilization of handpieces and air/water syringe attachments is required between each patient. This amounts to a lot of "spare parts," for each piece of equipment in each treatment room. Ample storage must be provided for disposables, and space for special waste containers must be planned in the treatment room. These containers are lined with plastic bags that can be sealed before being removed for disposal. Refer to the *Modular Casework* section for more detailed information.

No Routine Inspection of Asepsis

Contrary to what many individuals believe, OSHA does not regulate asepsis in regard to patients. OSHA's congressional charter limits it to issues affecting employees and their ability to carry out their tasks without exposure to hazardous products or serious injury on the job. Until the late 1980s when several patients were thought to have been infected with HIV by a dentist who had contracted the disease, most schools of dentistry did not teach asepsis and no state asepsis guidelines existed. Today, state dental boards and the public health department regulate asepsis in most states. In general dentistry, pedodontics, orthodontics, and endodontics, the goal is not to create a sterile field, it is to prevent cross-contamination. Obviously, there are oral surgery and periodontal procedures of an extensive and invasive nature where creating a sterile field is necessary and desirable, and some of those practitioners employ laminar-flow ventilation systems in their operatories. Refer to the *Sterilization* section for more specific information on procedures for processing dental handpieces and other tools.

GENERAL DENTISTRY

Office Circulation Patterns

Traffic flow within a dental office is from waiting room to treatment room, where the dentist greets the patient. After an interview about goals and objectives or dental problems, X-rays will usually be taken for new patients and, for return patients, at certain intervals (Figure 10-21). Intraoral X-ray is usually available in all treatment rooms but, occasionally, as in Figures 10-22 and 10-23, it may be located in a separate room. Panoramic and cephalometric X-ray is always located in a separate area. For subsequent visits during the course of treatment, X-rays may or may not be required. The patient should be able to enter the operatory and sit down on the right side of the chair (for a right-handed dentist) without walking around the chair or through the assistant's work area (Figure 10-24). At the end of the procedure, the patient walks to the reception area, repairs make-up, or combs hair at the vanity niche in the corridor (Figures 10-6, 10-22, and 10-25) or in the restroom, books a future appointment if required, and pays for services. Proper flow prevents exiting patients from interrupting the reception of incoming or new patients (Figures 10-26 and 10-99).

If the dentist does esthetic/cosmetic procedures, an imaging area may be provided where an assistant or treatment planning coordinator can take a 35-mm digital photo of the patient's smile, download the flash card into the computer, and prepare a case presentation or "photo album" demonstrating with "before and after" images how

the patient's smile can be improved through esthetic dentistry (Figures 10-6, 10-97, 10-99, and 10-102).

The dentist's circulation is from private office to treatment room and between treatment rooms or operatories. He or she should be able to enter the operatory without having to walk around the chair or through the assistant's work area, wash hands, and position him- or herself on the patient's right (if he or she is right handed), as in Figure 10-24. The assistant's path is from the treatment rooms back and forth to sterilization, laboratory, central X-ray room, and film-processing area. The X-ray processing area may be a separate darkroom, a film processor with a daylight loader attachment (Figure 10-79) in the lab or sterilization area, or a special niche, or it might even be a digital scanner in a dimly lit alcove such as is required by Gendex's DenOptix™ system (Figure 10-74) or Soredex's storage phosphor plate systems. The assistant also travels back and forth from the reception area to escort patients in and out of treatment areas.

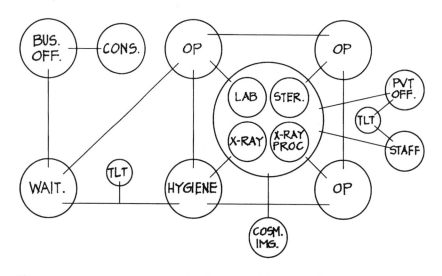

Figure 10-21. Schematic diagram of flow in a general dentistry suite.

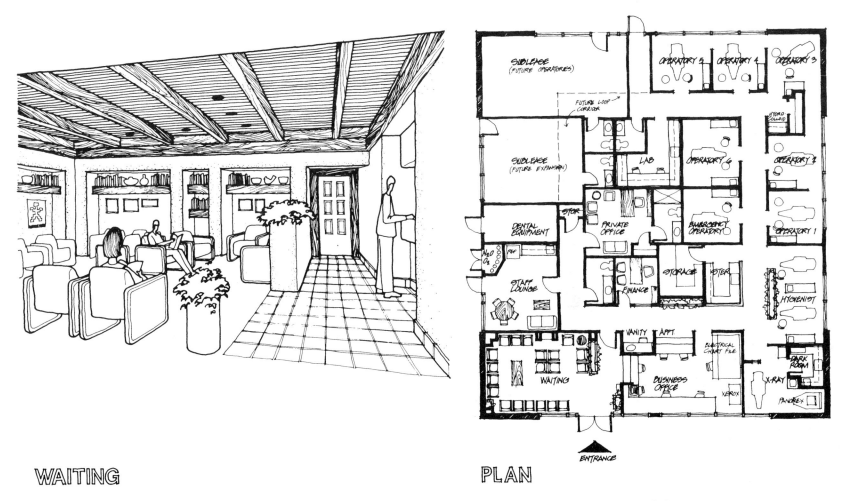

WAITING

PLAN

ENTRANCE

Figure 10-22. Suite plan for general dentistry (pre-ADA), 2516 square feet. (*Courtesy: T. Michael Hadley & Associates, AIA, Laguna Hills, CA.*)

Figure 10-23. Suite plan for general dentistry. (*Courtesy: T. Michael Hadley & Associates, AIA, Laguna Hills, CA.*)

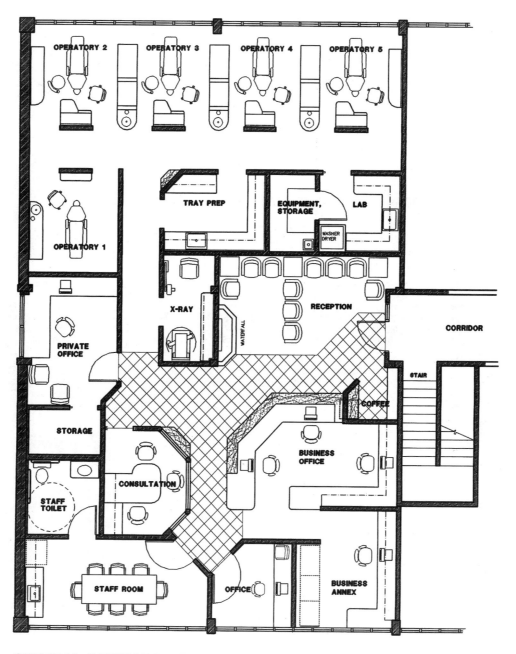

GENERAL DENTISTRY SUITE

2516 SF

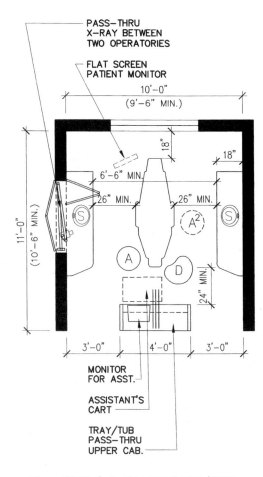

Figure 10-24. Optimal treatment room layout.

In the diagram:
- PASS-THRU X-RAY BETWEEN TWO OPERATORIES
- FLAT SCREEN PATIENT MONITOR
- 10'-0"
- (9'-6" MIN.)
- 18"
- 18"
- 6'-6" MIN.
- 26" MIN.
- 26" MIN.
- S
- A²
- S
- 11'-0"
- (10'-6" MIN.)
- A
- D
- 24" MIN.
- 3'-0"
- 4'-0"
- 3'-0"
- MONITOR FOR ASST.
- ASSISTANT'S CART
- TRAY/TUB PASS-THRU UPPER CAB.

OPTIMAL TREATMENT ROOM

ALLOWS FREEDOM OF MOVEMENT FOR STAFF AND MAXIMIZES EFFICIENCY. THE PRACTITIONER CAN CHOOSE ALMOST ANY KIND OF DELIVERY SYSTEM WITH THIS BASIC LAYOUT: CHAIR-MOUNTED DELIVERY, SIDE-MOUNTED DELIVERY, OR REAR (1 O'CLOCK) DELIVERY FROM A DUO CART OR WALL-MOUNTED DELIVERY SYSTEM. THIS ROOM CAN BE AMBIDEXTROUS WITH EITHER A CHAIR-MOUNTED RIGHT/LEFT SWITCHABLE DELIVERY AND REAR-MOUNTED ASSISTANT'S CART OR ARM, THAT SWINGS EQUALLY TO BOTH SIDES OF THE CHAIR AND ALLOWS SWITCHING THE SIDE OF THE CART THAT THE ASSISTANT'S INSTRUMEN-TATION IS DELIVERED FROM. THE PRACTITIONER CAN ALSO CHOOSE A DUO REAR DELIVERY CART OR ARM AND KEEP THE CHAIR FREE OF ANY CHAIR-MOUNTED DELIVERY. NOTE THAT THE OPTIONAL SECOND ASSISTANT (A²) WORKS TO THE RIGHT OF THE DENTIST.

Figure 10-25. Attractive vanity counter and mirror enable patients to check makeup or hair prior to exiting; it also makes a good first impression as one enters the office. (*Photographer: Jain Malkin.*)

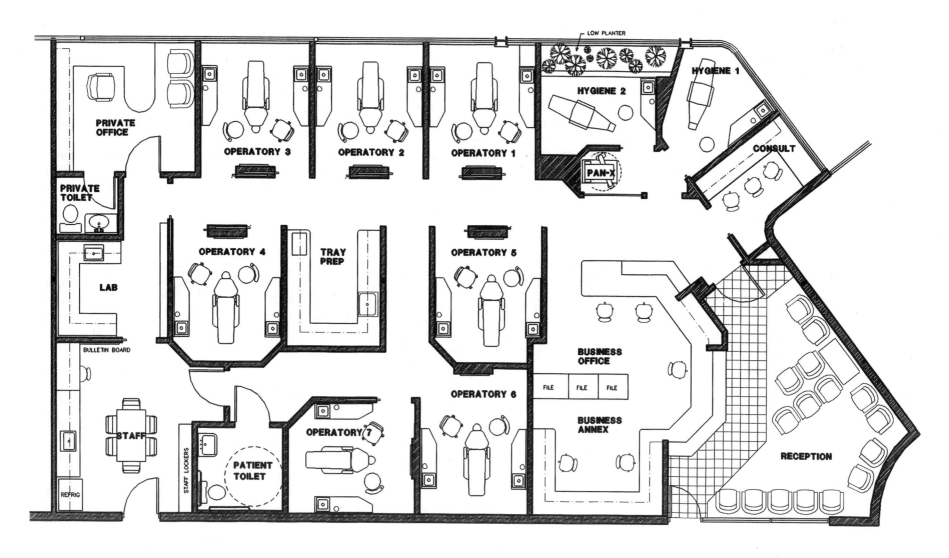

GENERAL DENTISTRY SUITE

2632 SF

Figure 10-26. Space plan for general dentistry, 2632 square feet. (*Courtesy: T. Michael Hadley & Associates, AIA, Laguna Hills, CA.*)

Depending on the treatment room layout, the chairside assistant (also called the auxiliary) may have to walk the greater distance in order to reach his or her work areas since it is more important for the dentist to have the shortest route (Figures 10-27 and 10-28). However, the operatory in Figure 10-29 has two entrances, one for the assistant and one for the dentist. This makes it easy for the assistant to enter and leave the room without walking behind the chair. Since the dentist and assistant are working in such confined areas, it is critical that these spaces be well planned and efficient. As with a medical office, a dental office should have a private entrance/exit for the staff and dentists so that they do not have to pass through the waiting room.

Table 10-1.
Analysis of Program.
General Dentistry

No. of Dentists:	1	2
Waiting Room[a]	12 × 14 = 168	16 × 18 = 288
Business Office/Reception	12 × 14 = 168	12 × 16 = 192
Operatories[b]	2@ 9½ x 11½ = 218	5@ 9½ × 11½ = 546
Lab	8 × 10 = 80	8 × 10 = 80
Sterilization Alcove or Room[c]	6 × 12 = 72	8 × 12 = 96
Darkroom (Optional)	4 × 6 = 24	4 × 6 = 24
Staff Lounge	10 × 10 = 100	10 × 12 = 120
Toilets	2@ 7 × 8 = 112	2@ 7 × 8 = 112
Hygiene Operatory	9½ × 11½ = 109	9½ × 11½ = 109
Panoramic X-Ray	5 × 8 = 40	5 × 8 = 40
Soiled Holding/Laundry	8 × 10 = 80	8 × 10 = 80
Housekeeping Closet	8 × 8 = 64	8 × 8 = 64
Private Office[d]	10 × 10 = 100	10 × 14 = 140
Storage	5 × 6 = 30	6 × 8 = 48
Mechanical Equipment Room	6 × 8 = 48	6 × 8 = 48
Subtotal	1277 ft^2	2027 ft^2
20% Circulation	255	405
Total	1532 ft^2	2432 ft^2

[a]A rule of thumb for estimating the number of seats in the waiting room is to allow 18 square feet per person.
[b]Size of operatories varies with doctor's practice preference for delivery of instrumentation and location of casework.
[c]Size depends on whether prefab modular system or custom casework.
[d]Shared in two-doctor office.

The Dental Assistant

The dental assistant or auxiliary performs many duties. Among them are cleaning the operatories, seating patients in the dental chair, preparing tray setups; taking X-rays; sterilizing instruments, loading anesthetic syringes, pouring impressions, mixing materials, charting conditions and treatment, handling suction handpieces and air/water syringes, and assisting the dentist in dozens of restorative and surgical procedures.

Dental assistants may have different levels of training. A certified dental assistant (CDA) is the first level of training, a registered dental assistant (RDA) is the next level, and, with additional training, an extended function certificate can be added to the RDA license. Extended-function assistants are able to perform tissue retraction, remove sutures, take impressions, change periodontal packing, and sometimes, depending on state practice laws, perform the more routine aspects of completing a procedure, thereby freeing the dentist to move to the next patient. In a state with an RDA-EF program, the doctor may need more treatment rooms because the assistant is using a room to perform part of the treatment functions while the doctor is using another.

The Dental Treatment Room or Operatory

This is the most important room in a dental office. Although analogous to the physician's examination room, it is far more critical to a dentist's practice than the medical exam room is to a physician's, as the physician has ancillary rooms for diagnosis, testing, and treatment, but the dentist has only the operatory. In terms of economics, the physician has the opportunity to enhance his or her income from laboratory tests, diagnostic imaging, and the use of medical aides to give injections, administer ECGs and EEGs, or perform various therapies. But the dentist has only the treatment room, the laboratory, and X-ray studies from which to derive income. Each treatment room should be thought of as a profit center. For this reason, many time-and-motion studies focusing on treatment room efficiency have been published in dental journals.

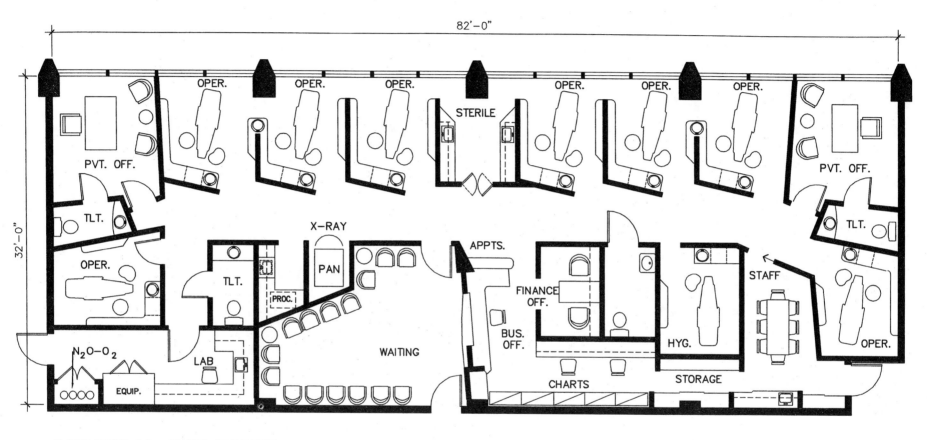

GENERAL DENTISTRY

2624 SF

Figure 10-27. Space plan for general dentistry (pre-ADA), 2624 square feet. (*Design: Jain Malkin Inc.*)

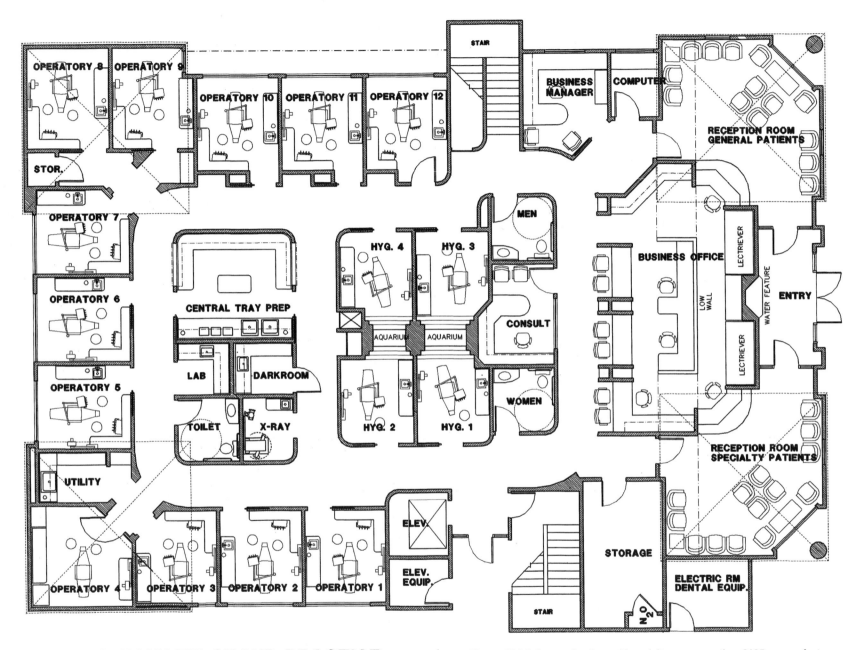

MULTI-SPECIALTY GROUP PRACTICE

6135 SF

Figure 10-28. Space plan for multispecialty group practice, 6135 square feet. Note pitched roof in four corners of the suite and aquariums between hygiene rooms. (*Courtesy: T. Michael Hadley & Associates, AIA, Laguna Hills, CA.*)

Over the years, changes have evolved as a result of these studies. Patients now recline in a contoured chair with the dentist working from a seated position at the side of the patient. If right handed, the dentist will be seated to the right of the patient and work in an area that could be designated as from 9 o'clock to 12 o'clock, imagining the area behind the patient's head as 12 o'clock and the feet as 6 o'clock.

Most dentists use an assistant, which is called *four-handed dentistry.* Some dentists use two assistants, which is called *six-handed dentistry.* While Figure 10-24 illustrates the optimum traffic flow pattern for an operatory, the structural features of the space, the location of windows, and other immutable factors have an impact on the layout of the space and may yield compromises in circulation.

Design for Flexibility

A right-handed dentist will work to the patient's right and a left-handed dentist to the patient's left. Traditionally, operatories were designed for either a right-handed dentist or a left-handed one. Today, flexibility is the key. New equipment is designed to accommodate change. In a practice composed of right-handed and left-handed dentists, an ambidextrous operatory can be achieved with the proper purchase of equipment. The equipment shown in Figures 10-8a and 10-18 has a dental light and a patient monitor (and may have dynamic instruments) mounted on an arm that swings around the toe of the chair to deliver these items to the other side. In an ambidextrous operatory, the X-ray head may be mounted on the rear wall (Figure 10-29) or, as is more common, on the side wall, which may take the form of a through-the-wall cabinet that allows it to swing between two treatment rooms (Figures 10-30 and 10-31). The assistant's cart can be ordered with a swing-away bracket to transfer the hoses to the other side of the cart when assisting from the right side of the chair.

Size of Treatment Rooms

Treatment rooms may be as small as 8½×8½ feet (Figure 10-32, Plan A) or as large as 10×11½ feet, but 100 square feet is the average size. Figure 10-24 shows the minimum distances among the dental chair, cabinetry,

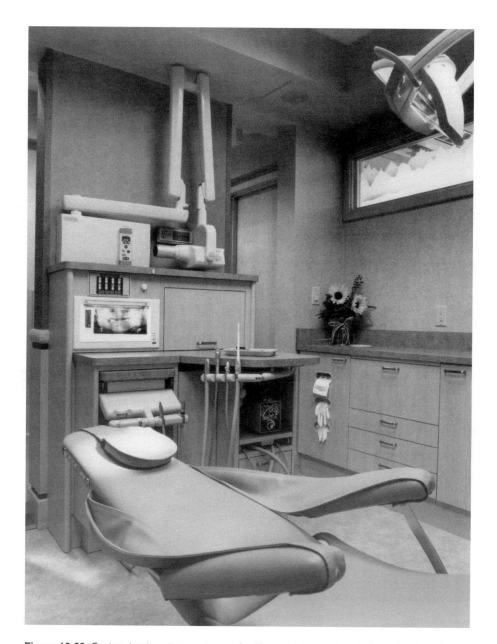

Figure 10-29. Custom treatment room casework with rear delivery of dentist's and assistant's instrumentation. (*Casework for dental operatories: Stelte Dental Systems, Mukilteo, WA; Interior design: Janice Thayer-Johnson, Signature Environments, Inc:, Seattle, WA; Photographer: Marshall M. Johnson.*)

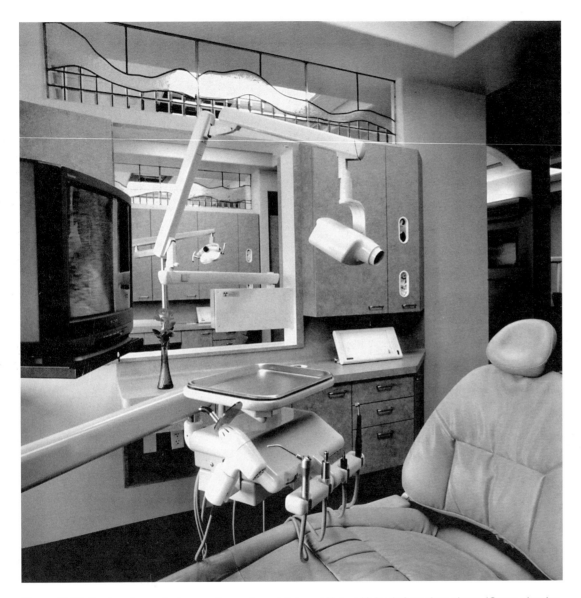

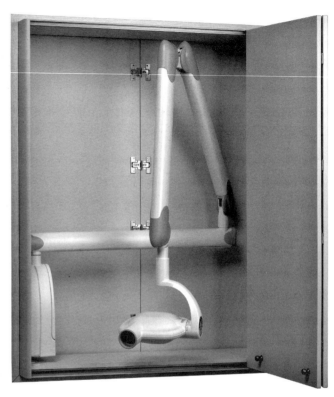

Figure 10-31. Intraoral X-ray, wall pass-through cabinet. (*Photo courtesy: A-dec, Newberg, OR.*)

Figure 10-30. Treatment room features wall pass-through intraoral X-ray with leaded art glass above. (*Space planning and interior design: Janet Pettersen, IIDA, Design Wave, Fallbrook, CA; Space planning collaboration and dental equipment engineering: Lee Palmer, Burkhart Dental, San Diego; Photographer: J. T. MacMillan.*)

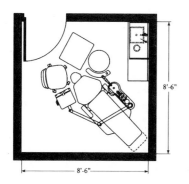

PLAN A - OVER-THE-PATIENT

CHAIR-MOUNTED DELIVERY FOR BOTH DENTIST AND ASSISTANT AND A MOBILE CART WORK SURFACE FOR ASSISTANT.

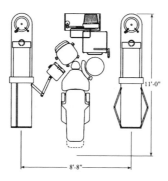

PLAN B - SIDE DELIVERY

SIDE WALL-MOUNTED DENTIST'S DELIVERY AND CART-MOUNTED ASSISTANT'S INSTRUMENTATION COMING FROM 12 O'CLOCK COLUMN.

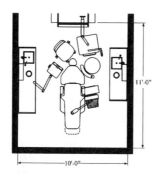

PLAN C - SIDE DELIVERY

DENTIST'S DELIVERY SIDE WALL-MOUNTED AND ASSISTANT'S REAR WALL-MOUNTED.

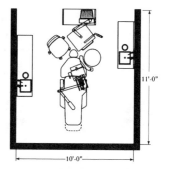

PLAN D - OVER-THE-PATIENT

DENTIST'S DELIVERY CHAIR-MOUNTED AND ASSISTANT'S REAR WALL-MOUNTED. 12 O'CLOCK WALL HAS PASS-THRU TRAY STORAGE.

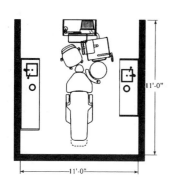

PLAN E - REAR DELIVERY

DUAL CART SHARED BY DENTIST AND ASSISTANT IS LEFT/RIGHT COMPATIBLE. 12 O'CLOCK COLUMN HAS PASS-THROUGH TRAY STORAGE.

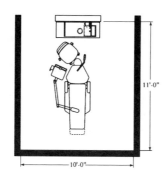

PLAN F - HYGIENE ROOM

INSTRUMENTATION IS DELIVERED FROM CHAIR-MOUNTED PIVOTING ARMS TO EITHER LEFT OR RIGHT SIDE. 12 O'CLOCK WALL STORES PERIPHERAL EQUIPMENT.

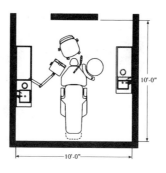

PLAN G - SIDE DELIVERY

DENTIST'S DELIVERY SIDE WALL-MOUNTED AND CHAIR-MOUNTED ASSISTANT'S.

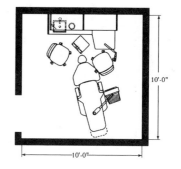

PLAN H - REAR DELIVERY

DELIVERY REAR WALL-MOUNTED FOR BOTH DENTIST AND ASSISTANT INTEGRATED INTO FREESTANDING CABINET.

ALTERNATIVES FOR TREATMENT ROOM LAYOUT

Figure 10-32. Alternatives for treatment room layout.

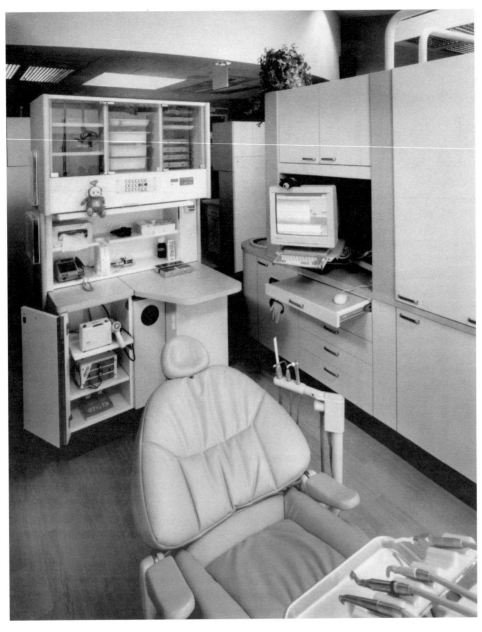

Figure 10-33. Treatment room with custom casework. (*Casework for dental operatories: Stelte Dental Systems, Mukilteo, WA; Interior design: Danix Design, Kirkland, WA; Photographer: Robert Weyrick— Perspective Image.*)

and perimeter of the room. There was a time when dentists worked alone and preferred small operatories so that, while seated (or standing), they could reach everything they needed. Now that dentists use a chairside assistant and the trend is toward longer appointments (it is more efficient to do a lot of work at one sitting), many dentists feel more comfortable working in a larger treatment room. However, the size is related to the use and location of fixed cabinets and to the number and locations of sinks and/or mobile carts.

Figure 10-32, Plans A through H, are but a few of the possibilities. The total number of options is related to the number of possible combinations of the following elements

Dentist's Instrumentation. Instruments may be delivered *over the patient,* or *trans thorax* (Figures 10-8a, 10-12, and 10-33), from the *side* (from a mobile cart, mounted onto a fixed cabinet, or wall mounted on an adjustable arm as in Figures 10-9 and 10-32, Plans B, C and G) or from the *rear* (sharing a mobile cart with the assistant) or mounted to a fixed cabinet behind the patient as in Figures 10-8b, 10-19, and 10-29).

Assistant's Instrumentation. Instruments may be delivered *over the patient,* from the *side* (post mounted on an articulating arm as in Figures 10-20 and 10-33, attached to a post-mounted cuspidor, or chair-mounted), or from the *rear* (a dual-purpose cart shared with the dentist as in Figures 10-8b and 10-19, or built into fixed cabinetry as in Figures 10-29 and 10-34. Ninety percent of all instruments and materials that a doctor handles are passed to him or her by the dental assistant. If the assistant's work area is not efficiently designed, it will affect the doctor's productivity and stress levels.

Work Surfaces. These may be mobile carts, fixed cabinets, or shelves that slide out of fixed cabinets to hold the tray of instruments and medicaments used during the procedure. For example, if the assistant's instrumentation is being delivered post mounted over the patient, the assistant will need an additional work surface, which would probably be a mobile cart placed near the head of the patient.

Mobile carts can be selected with both instrumentation and a work surface combined (Figure 10-14).

Number of Doors. A treatment room may have one, two, or three entrances, the third being an optional opening at the foot of the room between operatories (Figure 10-23). A solid-core hinged door helps to block the sound of high-speed drills, but is rarely used because it makes it difficult for the dentist and assistant to rotate quickly between operatories. Thus, many treatment rooms have no doors to facilitate movement. The ADA limitations on door sizes, clearances, and swings make it almost impossible to legally put a door on a treatment room.

Number of Sinks. A treatment room may have one or two sinks, wall hung or, more commonly, built into fixed cabinets. There is a trend toward one sink that functions for both the dentist and the assistant and can even serve two operatories as in Color Plate 33, Figures 10-35 and 10-36. In some regions, water and sewer fees are so high that it is more practical to use fewer sinks, placing them where they are convenient for several individuals, without compromising infection control. The dentist and assistant must wash their hands upon entering the room. Some dentists may prefer a foot-lever or wrist-action faucet (Color Plate 34, Figure 10-39), but many use a single-lever faucet (Figure 10-8b). Infrared faucets that activate when hands are placed underneath are another option for enhancing asepsis (Color Plate 33, Figure 10-35). Some modular casework manufacturers have placed a toe-kick faucet control in the base (Figures 10-63 and 10-64). Operatories may have an additional sink for the assistant in order to save steps and keep the assistant out of the dentist's path. Regardless of number, operatory sinks may be quite small and are usually round or oval in shape as they take less space than a square one in an 18-inch-deep countertop.

Casework. Casework may be custom built (usually clad in plastic laminate) by local cabinet shops, but first it must be meticulously designed and detailed, often necessitating several iterations of construction drawings and shop draw-

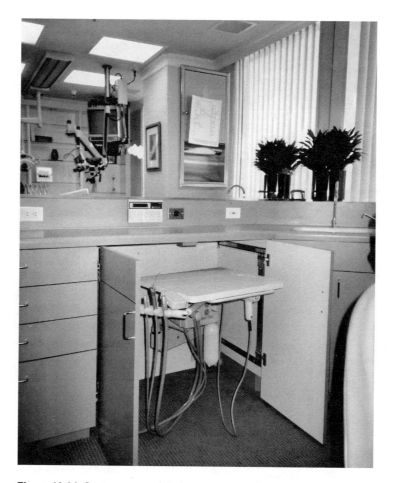

Figure 10-34. Custom casework in treatment room features retractable doors to conceal assistant's mobile cart. (*Photo courtesy: Cherilyn Sheets, D.D.S.; Photographer: Jain Malkin.*)

ings (Figure 10-37). This used to be a more viable option prior to the high-tech treatment room, which demands storage for an array of equipment in addition to computers and monitors. It is difficult for a local shop to be able to precisely accommodate all these items, including dispensers for gloves, drinking cups, and tissue boxes, unless it specializes in dental casework and is very familiar with these requirements which include accommodation of utilities.

Figure 10-37. Highly original design for treatment room corridor and lighting. Refer also to Color Plate 34, Figures 10-39, 10-40. (*Architecture and interior design: Lawrence Man, AIA, Los Angeles, CA; Photographer: ©1989 Lucy Chen.*)

In most cases, this type of casework requires a stud and gypsum board partition (wall) in which conduit carries electrical wiring and computer cables (Figure 10-30 and Color Plate 33, Figure 10-35). While this used to be considered a less expensive option than manufactured modular casework, there are other financial considerations. There is a considerably longer depreciation schedule for writing off tenant improvements compared with modular casework, which is considered furniture and can be written off over a five-year period. In addition, there is a considerable element of coordination when relying on a local casework fabricator. Casework is a long lead-time item; final measurements can't be taken until the partitions have been completed. The coordination of electrical and other utilities with the casework is the stuff that will invoke "Murphy's Law." And it all has to come together at the last minute. The dental equipment dealer has to wait until the casework is delivered to the job in order to fit the equipment and connect all the elements. Electrical, medical gas, and mechanical subcontractors also have to coordinate their work to bring wiring and utilities to outlets built into the casework. In short, it's not a smooth linear process with the assurance of perfection at the end of the road.

For dentists who wish to pursue this option, companies such as Greeno (Fresno, California) offer a variety of inserts to customize standard casework for the dental treatment room. These include recessed sharps containers (Figure 10-38), through-counter waste chutes with bag holders, and glove and tissue box dispensers. Sometimes, the shape of a treatment room or the practitioner's desire to create a totally unique design will necessitate custom casework (Figures 10-13, 10-37, and Color Plates 33 and 34, Figures 10-36 and 10-39, and 10-40).

Cabinets need only be 18 inches deep and, if they are going to be used as work surfaces while seated, should be at a 30-inch height although some dental planners prefer 33- or 34-inch heights. The most common use for upper cabinets in a dental operatory is for tray and tub storage and for boxes of disposable gloves, face masks, and patient bib towels. The depth of drawers must be carefully planned to accommodate the supplies that will be stored there (Figure 10-41). Most items used in treat-

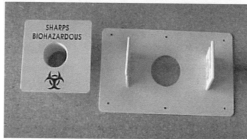

Figure 10-38. Accessory items for custom casework. (*Photo courtesy: Greeno, Fresno, CA.*)

Figure 10-41. Drawers must be carefully sized to accommodate specific supplies. Note protective lead apron hanging on door (draped over patient during X-ray). (*Photographer: Jain Malkin.*)

Figure 10-42. Custom casework in treatment rooms creates an attractive wood wall. Note monitor in ceiling over patient's chair. (*Casework for dental operatories:Stelte Dental Systems, Mukilteo, WA; Interior design: Janice Thayer-Johnson, Signature Environments, Inc, Seattle, WA; Photographer: Robert Weyrick—Perspective Image.*)

ment will be brought into the room on barriered tray or sterilized cassette and procedure tub setups. Unwrapped instruments to be used in the oral cavity may not be stored in drawers in the treatment room; they must be wrapped and packaged to maintain sterility.

Casework Fabricated by Specialty Shops. In various regions of the country, there are casework fabricators that specialize in dental offices such as Stelte Dental Systems in the Pacific Northwest (Mukilteo, Washington). They bridge the gap between basic casework from nonspecialty shops and prefabricated modular casework sold by dental equipment dealers by offering dentists a truly custom appearance and style as well as extraordinary craftsmanship and the knowledge of functional issues. Each dentist's personal preferences can be accommodated— it's analogous to ordering a custom suit from a Savile Row tailor. The 12 o'clock wall may be freestanding casework as in Figures 10-33 and 10-42 or it may be integrated with a standard stud and drywall partition as in Figure 10-29 and Color Plate 33, Figure 10-36. A custom feature of the Stelte system is a dry suction unit that tilts out from the cabinet to collect debris when making chairside adjustments.

Modular Casework. Some dentists prefer to buy prefabricated casework that takes the place of stud and gypsum board partitions, integrates utilities, and also accommodates whichever style of delivery the dentist and assistant prefer. The latest generation of these systems offers great flexibility in accommodating the monitors, computers, and sundry equipment items now part of a high-tech treatment room (Figures 10-8a, 10-8b, 10-17, and 10-43). Other niceties include wire management to conceal computer cabling, built-in clock/timer, slide-out drawers and shelves, doors with windows, through-the-wall tray storage, built-in accessory control panels, CPU base storage, dispensers for gloves and tissues, and foot-or knee-activated control of faucets. Hollow "columns" allow easy access to wiring and other service items (Figure 10-43). Task lighting is prewired and built in.

Equipment Drawer simplifies storage and delivery of ancillary devices like this amalgamator.

Equipment Drawer offers access to peripheral equipment.

Keyboard Drawer provides convenient delivery and storage of the keyboard.

Open Space Module allows two operatories to share large rolling equipment such as this air abrasion unit.

Medical Gas control panel.

Midsection Accessory Panel offers a location for items such as this X-ray viewer.

Column Service Access allows for quick and easy access to wiring, tubing, and other service items.

CPU Mounting Bracket secures to any vertical surface or countertop and simplifies access to the CPU.

Figure 10-43. A number of treatment column and central console features and options from The Preference Collection™. (*Photo courtesy: A-dec, Newberg, OR.*)

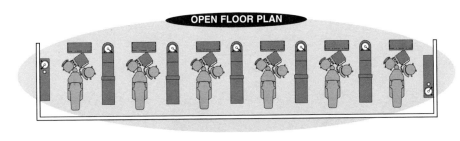

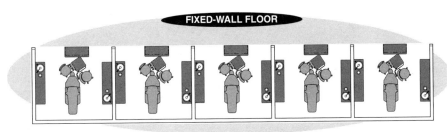

Open Floor Plan (top)
Open, unwalled layouts with freestanding central consoles can save enough space to add one operatory for every five fixed-wall operatories.

Fixed-Wall Floor Plan (bottom)
Preference offers wall-mounted, insert, and freestanding solutions with a number of different widths to accommodate a variety of fixed-wall operatories.

Figure 10-44. Diagram illustrates the space-saving feature of rooms divided by central consoles, as opposed to fixed walls. (*Illustration courtesy: A-dec, Newberg, OR.*)

In addition, one can eliminate X-ray and light mounts since they can be mounted on the modular casework as in Figure 10-18. Overall construction of the suite is facilitated by prefabricated casework as all it requires is an open room with utility stub-ins. One can predict with certainty where the cut-outs, raceways, and connection points will be in the casework. This cuts construction costs and time somewhat, but modular systems are not inexpensive.

Another consideration is that the "walls" and casework can move with the dentist to a new location. Dentists who don't own their own buildings may not want to make a large investment in a rented office. For them, modular partitions and casework would be a solution. Aesthetically, it has a much more open appearance

because the units are usually not full height. Some dentists like this, and others find there is a lack of acoustical privacy with a patient in one operatory being able to overhear the other patient's description of a toothache. Modular systems have always been popular in Europe, where space is at a premium. In fact, a series of operatories with modular walls can save enough space to add one operatory for every five fixed-wall treatment rooms as illustrated in Figure 10-44.

Number of Treatment Rooms

There is no rule governing the number of operatories per dentist since the dentist's temperament and practice methods dictate size and design. A dentist who works slowly or does a lot of restorative work with long appointments may be comfortable with two treatment rooms. A dentist with many short appointments will need four treatment rooms in order not to lose time during the change of patients and preparation or cleanup of treatment rooms. *A rule of thumb is three operatories per dentist in a general practice.*

Optimal Treatment Room Layout

In recent years, concern for infection control, reduction of stress on chairside assistants and dentists, as well as optimum efficiency, has resulted in the treatment rooms depicted in Figures 10-18 and 10-29. This allows for total freedom of movement for the staff and comfort for the patient since nothing is delivered over the patient's chest. The instrumentation is behind the patient and therefore out of sight, and the auxiliary has a minimum of twisting and turning. The auxiliary faces forward working off a mobile cart, which, when pushed back against the wall, is completely out of the path of the patient and staff.

Additionally, there are no unsightly utility umbilicals in view of the patient; thus, a clean, uncluttered appearance in the operatory is created. Some dentists might want a countertop on the rear wall, over the mobile cart to place an ultrasonic scaler or other occasionally needed equipment. If this is the case, the length of the operatory would have to be extended to 11 feet or, possibly, 11½ feet. The

X-ray head in this operatory may be mounted on the rear wall (Figure 10-29), usable by a right-or left-handed person or may be on the side wall. Each operatory will require a view box illuminator, located to allow easy visibility by a seated dentist (Figures 10-8a, 10-29, and 10-30) although, increasingly, all X-rays will be digital, viewed on a monitor.

The critical distances shown in Figure 10-24 are based on ergonomic data regarding proper positioning of both the dentist and the assistant to avoid back strain, fatigue, bending, twisting, turning, and reaching beyond limits. Everything the dental team needs is within easy reach. The operatory in Figure 10-24 also accommodates a dentist who prefers either over-the-patient or side delivery of instrumentation.

Instrumentation. There are four categories of instrumentation.

Handpiece Delivery System. This describes the drills (rotary tools) with drill bits that are used to cut and shape teeth.

Evacuation System. Blood, debris, and water are removed from the mouth, usually by suction. The vacuum system commonly used is a "wet" system that empties into a waste pipe. The evacuation system typically has high-speed suction for rapid debris removal and a low-speed saliva ejector positioned in the patient's mouth. Both are the responsibility of the dental assistant.

Handheld Instruments. These tools include probes, scalers, forceps, and intraoral camera.

Three-Way Syringe. Used by both the dentist and the assistant for spraying water, compressed air, or a combination thereof. The assistant will have his or her own three-way syringe for drying or moistening preparations as well as for washing debris from the patient's mouth.

Methods of Delivery. The dynamic instruments (drills, suction, syringes) can be delivered to the oral cavity

of the patient by four methods. There are advantages and disadvantages to each method of delivery listed below, and each has its proponents. Most practitioners will continue to work in the manner to which they have become accustomed, even if another method seems more efficient.

The dentist's handpieces may be delivered chair-mounted, side-wall-mounted, rear-wall-mounted, or cart-mounted. Regardless which of these four options is selected, the assistant's instrumentation may be delivered rear-wall-mounted, chair-mounted, or cart-mounted.

Chair-Mounted System (Dentist). Dynamic instruments are delivered either over the patient's chest or from the patient's left or right side. The systems are mounted on an arm, which is attached to a post. The post may be attached to the floor or to the chair. If the latter, as the chair is adjusted up or down, the relative position of instruments with respect to the oral cavity remains constant (Figures 10-14, 10-20, 10-30, and Figure 10-32, Plans A and D). Statistics show that over-the-patient delivery is the most popular system, favored by nearly half of all practicing dentists.

> *Advantages.* Functions for two-or four-handed stand-up or sit-down dentistry; requires minimal floor space; offers ambidextrous option; reduces eye fatigue as minimal adjustments in focus are necessary; handpieces are presented with easy access to the oval cavity and little handpiece tubing pullback; maximum flexibility in positioning instruments. (Tubing pullback occurs more often with coiled tubing than with non-coiled tubing.)

> *Disadvantages.* Instruments are in patient's view; assistant's access to dynamic instruments is reduced.

Chair-mounted System (Assistant). Instrumentation is placed near the patient's left shoulder if the dentist is working on the patient's right.

> *Advantages.* Requires least amount of operatory

space; single utility location; provides left-or right-handed operation.

Disadvantages. Limitations in instrument positioning; requires the addition of a work surface; may require a separate utility location; instrumentation located close to the patient.

Side Wall-Mounted System (Dentist). Dynamic instruments are wall mounted (Figure 10-32, Plans B and C), built into a side cabinet (Figure 10-9), or placed on a mobile cart that pulls out from the side cabinet.

Advantages. Good patient access to chair; dynamic instruments out of patient's view; mobile carts permit flexibility of movement; wall-mounted units require minimal floor space; easy-to-position handpiece controls.

Disadvantages. Reduces auxiliary's access to dynamic instruments; placement of umbilicals must be properly planned; may require a wider operatory; dedicated to left-or right-hand positioning; requires separate utility location.

Rear Wall-Mounted System (Dentist). Dynamic instrumentation is delivered from the 12 o'clock position, behind the patient's head, from a fixed cabinet (with the systems built into the face panel of the cabinet (as in Figures 10-18 and 10-19), from a wall mount (Figure 10-29), or from a mobile cart, which may or may not be shared with the assistant (called a dual cart if shared). Rear delivery can also be accomplished with what is called a *12 o'clock column* (Figure 10-33), which refers to the modular casework.

Advantages. Good patient access to chair; keeps dynamic instruments out of patient's view; dual cart gives assistant excellent access to dynamic instruments and a good work surface; ease of installation; requires minimal floor space. Accommodates left-and right-handed positioning; single utility connection for dual cart. 12 o'clock column also works for two-handed dentistry, has excellent work surface for assistant, and has controls integrated into the cabinet.

Disadvantages. Limited to sit-down use; integration into fixed cabinet may increase installation time or cost; hand fatigue due to handpiece tubing pullback; requires more body movement; requires a deeper operatory.

Rear Wall-Mounted System (Assistant). Instrumentation is placed at the 1 o'clock position (Figures 10-8a and 10-14).

Advantages. Instrumentation is out of patient's view; provides a large work surface; supports left-or right-handed operation; provides easy access to and optimal positioning of instrumentation; supports peripheral operatory equipment and makes it easy to see the practice management monitor if placed behind the patient.

Disadvantages. Requires separate utility connection if dentist does not use rear wall system; requires a deeper operatory; requires rear wall to mount it.

Cuspidors. Cuspidors (Figure 10-20) have the potential to create cleaning and asepsis problems, but they are favored by some practitioners and may be found in hygiene rooms as well as treatment rooms. They are available with or without attached assistant's instrumentation (suction, three-way syringe, and saliva ejector). Vacuum drain cuspidors are available for use with central vacuum systems.

Location of Computers and Ergonomic Considerations. There is general agreement that the ideal treatment room needs two computers and two monitors. A third monitor may be mounted in the ceiling for patient viewing in a reclined position. The first computer is usually located somewhere in the vicinity of the assistant with a screen not visible by the patient for the assistant to chart on, bring up management information, and record treatments. This computer can also be used to capture digital X-ray images and intra-or extraoral photographic images from digital cameras. The second computer is usually located where it is more convenient for the doctor or hygienist to manipulate, and the monitor is placed in as ideal a position as possible for patient viewing while sitting upright in the patient chair. This second system is used for patient education with DVDs of prepared topics, for screening of patient X-rays, for explanation of their personal conditions and possible treatments (using photographs), and sometimes just for entertainment purposes. The overhead monitor is usually slaved to the second computer and allows the same functions when the patient is reclined for treatment. This additionally allows patients to watch the actual examination of their oral conditions if they so desire.

Variables for Monitor Placement. Ergonomics are really important in the dental treatment room and yet dentists are often unaware of these issues when deciding where to place monitors. In theory, the dentist should focus on the oral cavity and, by merely looking up, be able to see the display on the monitor, pointing out problem areas to the patient (Figures 10-8b, 10-9, 10-12, and 10-13). Therefore, if the patient's monitor is placed on the left side, either near the foot of the chair (Figures 10-18, right side, and 10-24) or post mounted (Figures 10-12 and 10-20), it is positioned where it is convenient for both the patient and the dentist (assuming the dentist is right handed, or the reverse, if not). If it is post mounted or on a radius arm that moves around the toe of the chair (Figures 10-8b and 10-18), one has the flexibility of reorienting the monitor. The patient monitor (often a Sony TV) should be 17 or 20 inches in size so that it can be viewed from a distance. If it is post mounted, as in Figure 10-12, it can be smaller. One must be mindful of patients who wear bifocals and their ability to see images clearly or read text from a specific viewing distance.

Another option for a patient monitor is in the ceiling, immediately over the patient chair. Since the chair is laid almost flat while the dentist is working, this makes it quite easy for the patient to view educational or entertainment programming (Figure 10-42 and Color Plate 34, Figure 10-45). A competent audiovisual consultant or dealer can design a bracket to securely mount the monitor and handle all the installation. There needs to be a flange or a trim piece around it to provide a finished edge on the ceiling, whether it is gypsum board or acoustic tile.

Practice Management Monitor. The primary computer, used by the assistant, is best located at the rear of the chair in what is called the 12 o'clock position. This enables the assistant to see exactly what the dentist is seeing in the oral cavity, and it also has practice management software, providing full access to the patient's chart, notes, and radiographs. The monitor should be positioned so that the dentist can also view this information. During the procedure, the assistant will input data with a light pen, touch pad, pen and tablet, or wireless infrared keyboard and mouse. A second input device to the side of the dentist enables him or her to access information or manipulate X-rays without having to verbally ask the assistant to do it in the patient's presence. This also enables the dentist to review the treatment plan or read previous appointment notes discreetly on the assistant's monitor. The dentist in Figure 10-9 is using a monitor to his side with a keyboard and mouse in a slide-out tray. The patient shares this monitor.

Types of Monitors and Their Purposes. A computer monitor is specifically designed to process text and other information that is processed digitally. It has phenomenal clarity for text or computer-generated graphics. It also does a great job displaying digital X-rays or still photographs. However, it usually doesn't provide a good picture for "moving" video. The picture typically looks "pixelized" and somewhat dark. Flat-screen monitors typically look even worse, with washed-out pictures and diluted colors. Flat-screen monitors are usually LCD (liquid crystal display) screens and are much more costly than the CRT screens most of us are used to. Intraoral camera images are also usually washed out on a flat LCD-type computer monitor. Most computer monitors require the computer to process video through a video input card such as the ATI All-in-Wonder or Matrox. Some monitors (very few) offer inputs for both a computer and video. The video input on the monitor provides for additional flexibility, but, in most cases, still doesn't provide the same picture quality as a television monitor for video.

Television monitors typically provide a better picture for viewing video, but have unacceptable resolution for reading text or viewing some graphics. Intraoral cameras work very well on television monitors and digital X-rays are somewhat viewable. A television monitor should be used when the screen is primarily used for watching video, such as cable or satellite TV, background video, VCR, or a standalone DVD player. Most doctors feel that the television is adequate for showing digital X-rays to the patient, but not adequate for diagnosis. Computer monitors offer better detail for digital X-rays.

Like computer monitors, television monitors are also available as flat screens. Flat-panel displays are considerably more expensive than normal CRT-type screens and usually do not have a picture equal to CRT screens. Liquid crystal display screens are available up to about 22 inches. Screens larger than 5 inches diagonally increase dramatically in price as the size increases.

Video "glasses" are composed of two small LCD screens that are mounted on an eyeglass frame. The glasses provide a somewhat low-resolution picture for video and a totally unacceptable picture for computer. The glasses are typically equipped with stereo headphones that hang from the temples. Patients often find video glasses novel, but many feel claustrophobic or cut off from their surroundings. Doctors also sometimes feel cut off from the patient since they can't see the patient's eyes or expressions. The glasses need a source such as a VCR or DVD to provide a picture. Video glasses are affordable but may require maintenance, as they are constantly being handled, dropped, or tugged on by patients.

Other Ergonomic Considerations. An additional concern is eyestrain. Every time the dentist's eyes move from the oral cavity to the monitor, the pupil has to dilate or constrict (and this happens less rapidly with increasing age) to differing light levels and the focal length of the eye must adjust to the distance; eye muscles have to bend the lens. These physiological factors should be considered when placing objects in the treatment room. Note also, in considering ergonomics and back strain, that touch-pad programmable dental chairs are available to enable the dentist to quickly adjust the chair by presetting it for different positions. Operating microscopes, discussed previously, significantly reduce head and neck strain.

Audio and Video Possibilities. As a result of being one of those individuals who experienced frightening dental visits as a child, Keith Aderman, professionally known as "Mr. Hookup" (www.mrhookup.net), has developed what he refers to as "architectural electronics" specifically for the dental profession. He firmly believes that positive distractions relax patients and enable them to avail themselves of the dental care they need without the fear factor. He integrates, into a highly sophisticated system, a number of media elements that include satellite TV, music with no commercials, and a variety of educational programming, all remote controlled by the patient. Monitors are securely held in ceilings, over the patient's head, with a proprietary-designed bracket (designed to support considerably more weight than a TV for safety), while communication and media control panels are neatly recessed at the 12 o'clock wall (Figure 10-46). A satellite receiver for each treatment room is connected to a common 18-inch dish on the roof of the building, and stereo headphones provide the TV with quality sound. The picture shown on the TV can be duplicated on a computer screen for upright viewing (provided the computer screen is within the patient's view), which also works well for intraoral camera use. Competent execution of wiring and switching to integrate all the elements of the audio and video system to make it user friendly is essential.

Sometimes, large television monitors are used (Figure 10-30). However, new flat-screen computer monitors can display both analog video images from the intraoral camera, VCR, and broadcast TV and digital images in the form of DVD output and digital X-ray; both types of images can even be displayed simultaneously. Because they are closer to the patient, they don't have to be as large as wall-mounted monitors. In addition, the practitioner does not have to use a laser pointer, but can merely use his or her hand to direct the patient's attention to the image (Figure 10-12).

Central Media Station. A central media station or storage cabinet for the AV equipment and music system, as well as DVD player (for relaxing nature videos and the CAESY or

Figure 10-46. Communication system and AV control panel built into 12 o'clock wall. (*AV consultant: Mr. Hookup, San Diego; Photographer: Jain Malkin.*)

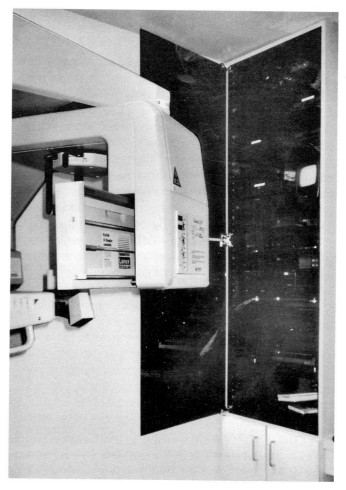

Figure 10-47. Central media station built into wall cabinet in X-ray alcove. (*AV consultant: Mr. Hookup; Photographer: Jain Malkin.*)

Smile Channel), is required, at least 24 inches wide×18 inches deep and 48 inches high, although it is best if it starts a distance off the floor to avoid bending. It may be recessed into a wall or perhaps tucked into the panoramic X-ray area as in Figure 10-47. Although it's hard to see in this photo because everything is black—the equipment, the cabinet interior, and the glass doors—it's an attractive element in the space when the doors are closed. The cabinet needs to be well ventilated. These items can also fit on open shelves in a small storage room as in Figure 10-6. Music can be provided throughout the office with high-quality speakers, each controlled by separate volume controls to adjust the sound level for each area. This is very important because each room has different acoustic qualities.

Prewiring During Construction. The wiring that connects computers to monitors, intraoral cameras, and communication devices, as well as audio and video media, is complex and requires carefully planned prewiring during construction to tie into the central media station, which may also be the equipment room containing the telephone system and central data hub. Of course,

it can also be done in existing offices, but it may not be as "clean" an installation. There is also wiring associated with satellite receivers and the speakers that may be located throughout the office. An optional feature is wiring for foot-pedal control of the printer, most likely located in a central area.

In offices that do not have computers in the operatories, the images are printed on a video printer. A switching network can allow one printer to be shared by numerous operatories. The network requires a special switcher and wiring specific to the brand of camera that is to be used. Intraoral camera printers are normally expensive and somewhat troublesome. Most offices use an ink-jet printer instead. The quality of print is actually better than that of a video printer, especially with photographic-quality paper. With the computer, one can add text explaining the picture or add a print of the X-ray, all on the same piece of paper. No printer switcher is required, nor is any special intraoral camera video wiring. One set of audio and video cables is required from the central media station for each source that is located there to be provided to each operatory. Sources that may be centrally located might include a satellite receiver, a VCR or DVD player dedicated to each operatory, a central DVD player shared among multiple operatories for interactive patient education, or a central DVD player shared among all the operatories for relaxing background videos accompanied by relaxing music.

Infrared wiring from each operatory goes to the central media station to link an infrared remote control to equipment such as interactive patient education systems, camera video printer, or entertainment electronics. An additional infrared link and sensor may connect the front desk to the media station to conveniently control the stereo or entertainment electronics from the front desk without the clutter of the actual components being located there.

Audio and video wiring from the central media station will run to the switcher location in each operatory (usually at the 12 o'clock wall) to support a TV location in front of the patient and a potential second TV location at the ceiling. Once the wiring is in, the TV can be installed at a later date. A switcher in the operatory is used to make selections among sources supplied to the TVs as depicted in Figure 10-46. In addition, stereo headphones are wired to each chair from the respective TV.

An AV link between the computer and the AV network must be wired to enable a computer equipped with certain accessories to display on the TV or for the computer to duplicate the TV picture. It also links the computer with both the intraoral camera and the foot-pedal wiring.

The DSS wiring for satellite TV and music requires secondary incoming feeds from the roof for each treatment room. Local cable TV is another option. This wiring comes into the central media station and is then distributed to remote locations.

Finally, high-speed data wiring must be run from a central panel to each treatment room or operatory and each computer workstation in the office, including each printer and the server. A separate data line for a high-speed DSL (digital subscriber line) modem may be run from the point of entry at the telephone room to the server. An enhanced category 5 wire (which some companies refer to as category 6 or 7) is desirable as it is capable of transferring data at 350 megabytes per second.

Competent System Design Essential

Dental software must be carefully chosen and computer systems skillfully designed and integrated, to be maximally effective. One should be able to control which data appear on which screen. Increasingly, developers of dental software are recognizing the need to design solutions for multiple monitors. *Dentrix®, EagleSoft, PracticeWorks®,* and Dentsply *SoftDent* are four of the most popular software systems. An excellent Web site resource for dentists making decisions about software and the integration of technology into the treatment room is hosted by Dr. Larry Emmott who lectures frequently on technology (www.drlarryemmott.com). The Web site has many practical tips for dentists.

Adapting Older Treatment Rooms

Dentists who buy new treatment room equipment can purchase casework and dental chairs that integrate new technology, but those with older equipment have to find a way to adapt their treatment rooms, which means that they may have fewer opportunities to place computer monitors where they are ergonomically most effective. Recognizing the need to adapt existing space to accommodate monitors, one vendor has developed an articulating arm that can be mounted in multiple ways, and in several locations, accommodating either a standard or a flat-screen monitor (Figure 10-48). One feature of the articulating arms depicted in this illustration is that the cabling

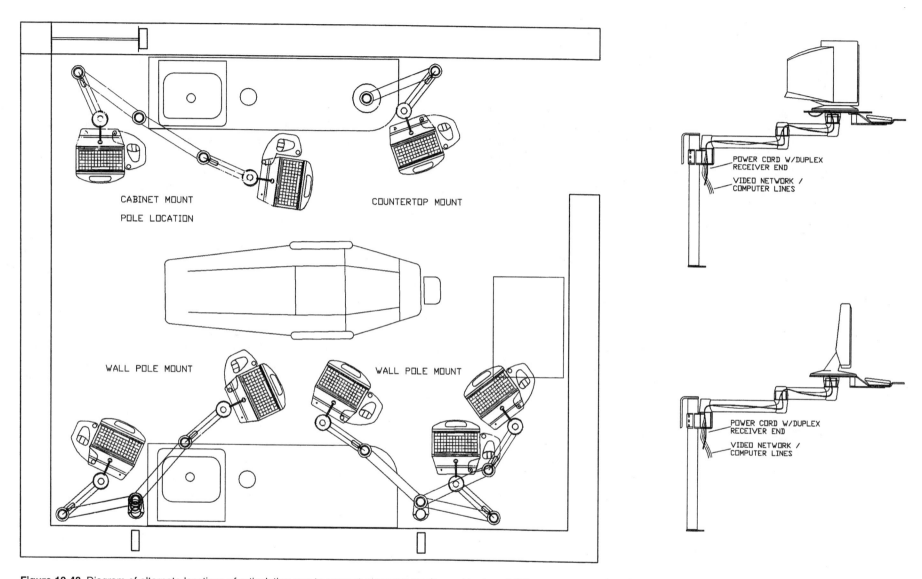

Figure 10-48. Diagram of alternate locations of articulating arm to support computer monitor and keyboard. (*Diagram courtesy: Imagin Systems Corp., San Carlos, CA.*)

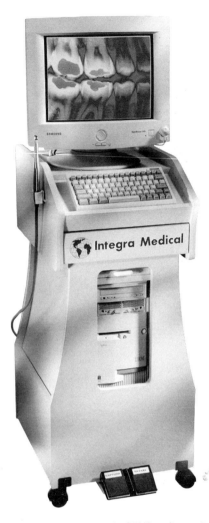

Figure 10-49. Portable CPU/monitor cart by Integra Medical. (*Photo courtesy: Sullivan-Schein Dental, Melville, NY.*)

is concealed within the arm. Another option is shown in Figure 10-9. Similar products can be found at Ergotron (www.ergotron.com), ICW (www.icw.com), or Lucasey (www.lucasey.com).

For dentists who aren't ready to commit to building computers into the treatment room, or who can't afford to make the financial investment, a unit on a mobile cart can be moved from room to room (Figure 10-49). This unit uses Vipersoft® 2000 software by Integra Medical that combines cosmetic imaging intraoral capture and digital X-ray software, creating an integrated system for the treatment room. It accommodates various types of digital X-rays such as the Schick CDR system using CMOS sensors, the Gendex DenOptix phosphor plate system, and the Trophy RVG CCD sensors.

Lighting

Good lighting is mandatory in a dental operatory. It is critical to use full-spectrum fluorescent lamps with a color rendering index (CRI) of 90 or more and color temperature (measured in kelvins) of 5500, sometimes referred to as "Natural Daylight." Refer to Chapter 13 for more details on the technical aspects of lighting and for photos of exemplary lighting solutions. The indirect "basket" recessed fluorescent luminaire referred to in Figure 10-50, Option A, represents a new option for dental treatment rooms, offering more brightness at the same wattage as the conventional fluorescent luminaire with standard acrylic prismatic lens that creates a lot of glare in patients' eyes. Lithonia's Avante series and Focal Point's Luna series are two options for this type of lighting (Figure 10-51).

The illumination should be free of shadows, and a *brightness ratio* of 4:1 should be maintained with the operating light or at least a minimum 10:1 ratio. The operating light may slide in a track mounted in the ceiling (Figure 10-13), or it may be post mounted to the dental chair (Figure 10-20) or side mounted on the wall (Figure 10-8b) or modular casework (Figure 10-18). The quartz halogen light delivers a concentrated 1200 to 2500 footcandles of illumination at the oral cavity.

Thus, the work counters and visual background of the room must receive 600 to 650 maintained footcandles measured at 30 inches from the floor to achieve a 4:1 brightness ratio with the 2500-footcandle operating light. Three four-lamp, recessed fluorescent luminaires arranged in a U shape around the chair (Figure 10-50, Option A) may meet this requirement, as may three recessed luminaires arranged side by side, as in Figure 10-50, Option B . The reflectance of the floor, walls, and ceiling has an impact on the amount of perceived illumination, as do the ceiling height, the size and shape of the room, and the location of upper cabinets, if any. It is difficult to achieve this level of illumination with restrictive energy codes that mandate the allowable number of watts per square foot throughout the office. Of course, having natural light in the operatory helps a great deal. A competent electrical engineer or lighting designer should be consulted for design and calculation of footcandle levels. The type of lens on the fixture, reflectors inside the fixture, and special characteristics of the lamp all affect its brightness. It is worthwhile to pay a premium for extended-life lamps that have the specific spectral distribution needed by dentists. These are listed in Chapter 13 and include the General Electric Chroma 50, the Aurora V, and the Spectralite.

For private treatment rooms with full-height walls, indirect fluorescent lighting around the perimeter of the room is aesthetically pleasing and keeps glare out of patients' eyes. However, the number of lamps must still yield the 4:1 brightness ratio or at least a minimum 10:1 ratio. Some of these fixtures have reflectors that enhance brightness. This lighting option requires a ceiling height of 9 feet and will most likely require an additional luminaire (fixture) recessed over the patient's head.

Handpiece fiber-optic illumination requires bright rooms to prevent "optical bounce," a term that refers to the continual opening and shutting of the iris of the eye due to extreme brightness differences. Optical bounce causes headaches and eyestrain as the dentist shifts focus from a bright mouth to an overly dark room.

Operatories should not have busy wallcoverings with intense colors because the rooms are small, and reflection of the colors will make it difficult to match shades of teeth. Soft colors and patterns with little contrast reduce eye

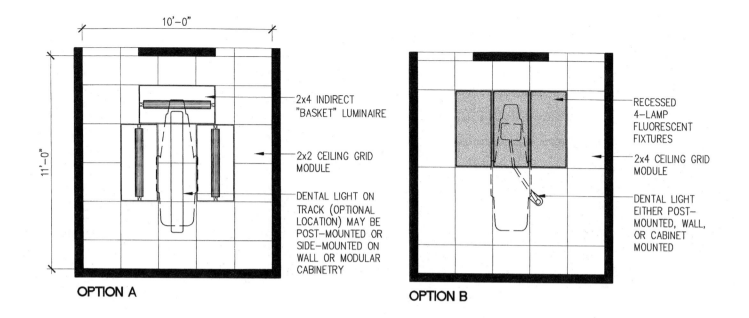

OPTION A

- 2x4 INDIRECT "BASKET" LUMINAIRE
- 2x2 CEILING GRID MODULE
- DENTAL LIGHT ON TRACK (OPTIONAL LOCATION) MAY BE POST–MOUNTED OR SIDE–MOUNTED ON WALL OR MODULAR CABINETRY

OPTION B

- RECESSED 4–LAMP FLUORESCENT FIXTURES
- 2x4 CEILING GRID MODULE
- DENTAL LIGHT EITHER POST– MOUNTED, WALL, OR CABINET MOUNTED

TREATMENT ROOM
REFLECTED CEILING PLAN

(Achieves 4 : 1 ratio between ambient lighting and halogen dental light)

Figure 10-50. Reflected ceiling plans in treatment room depict options for achieving a minimum 10:1 ratio (even better, 4:1 ratio) between ambient lighting and the halogen dental light. This is also influenced by the type of light fixture, the type of lamp, and the reflectance of interior finishes.

fatigue and make the room seem less confining. Many dentists prefer a northern exposure for shade matching in natural light. Refer also to the following section.

It's important to remember to consider the color temperature of all lamps in the office since light in the treatment rooms and light in the adjacent corridors flow into each other. If there is a disparity among the types of lamps and their color temperature, it creates visual disharmony. This doesn't mean that the corridor light should be 5500 kelvins as that would be very white and "cold," but a compact fluorescent wall sconce at 2700

kelvins (very pink) in the corridor would be a poor choice.

Design Considerations

In addition to functional requirements, the treatment room should meet certain psychological needs of the patient. A window is always desirable to give patients a psychological escape and a pleasant view. In lieu of a window, a photograph of a landscape may be installed. A small-scale mobile suspended from the ceiling, which the patient can see while reclined in the chair, is a diversion provided there is no monitor overhead. Other amenities in

Figure 10-51. An upgrade to standard lay-in fluorescent fixtures. Although it has considerable brightness, it provides indirect light. This is the type of fixture indicated in Figure 10-50, Option A. (*Photo courtesy: Focal Point, L.L.C., Chicago, IL.*)

the operatory include a hook for a handbag (located where the patient can see it) and a tissue box. Live plants and artwork add a nice touch to the operatory, but are an additional concern in terms of asepsis. Artwork, of course, can be framed with glass or Plexiglas to provide a cleanable surface.

Color as a Functional Tool. The dental chair and fixed casework and mobile carts should be selected in colors that coordinate with the room's interior design. Light, neutral colors used for cabinetry and dental units make them blend into the background and be less obtrusive. But there is a more important functional issue that should inform color selections in a dental treatment room, namely, reflectance. The previous section on lighting explained the optimal 4:1 ratio between ambient light and the bright halogen light at the oral cavity. It is increasingly difficult to achieve this ratio with energy restrictions on watts per square foot, which means that dark colors (which absorb light) should be avoided in favor of those that reflect light. This also avoids eyestrain since strong contrast forces the focal length of the eye to adjust rapidly. In practical terms, this means that the dramatic black or charcoal gray treatment room casework sometimes favored by dentists who want to make a design statement is creating a visually stressful environment in which to work. It's also harder to see dirt on dark surfaces and, therefore, to clean it. Select colors carefully for a treatment room, considering the color reflectance cast onto the patient's teeth.

Vision research indicates that there should ideally be little contrast among the casework color, the walls, and the floor. A dark floor with light walls and casework creates eyestrain. If carpet is used as flooring, select a medium to light value with a pattern that camouflages soil and spills.

Acoustics. There are many hard surfaces in the treatment room and few opportunities to absorb sound or stop its reverberation. Carpet and an acoustic ceiling tile with a high NRC (noise reduction coefficient) are the best solutions. Incidentally, one can achieve both noise reduction and high reflectance at the same time by selecting products like Armstrong's Ultima™ or Optima™, both with DuraBrite™ high-reflectance surface and an NRC of 0.85 to 1.00. High reflectance means that it maximizes the brightness of the ambient light. Acoustic tile is available in many textures and patterns such as raked sand, leaves, and geometric designs that provide visual interest for patients.

Accessories. Attractive chart holders and magazine racks are available from Peter Pepper Products (Compton, California). Refer to Chapter 12 for photos.

Installation Sequence. The flooring material should be in place and all decorating complete before dental equipment is installed.

Hygiene Treatment Room

The hygienist performs many duties. He or she takes and processes X-rays, performs dental prophylaxis, instructs patients on proper brushing and flossing techniques, discusses nutrition in regard to prevention of dental caries, and maintains the patient recall system.

Many dentists dedicate one or more treatment rooms to hygiene, while others schedule a hygienist perhaps two or three afternoons per week and use one of their standard treatment rooms. Figure 10-32, Plan F, depicts a hygiene room. A hygiene room almost always has a sonic or ultrasonic scaler and many times has a separate or combined air polisher unit. Additionally, more and more practices are installing irrigation devices for irrigating below the gums after the scaling and root planing. Check with the practitioner and dental supplier about requirements for these units. The hygienist often uses an intraoral camera and uses the computer-based DVD patient education system. He or she may also have a microscope in the room to check plaque samples for various bacterial infections. A dedicated hygiene room may be smaller than a standard treatment room because the hygienist works alone without an assistant, and it has considerably less equipment and instrumentation than a standard treatment room.

Since the goal is positive reinforcement of good dental hygiene, this room should be attractively designed so that a good impression lingers after the patient departs.

Utilities

The planning and design of utilities to serve dental treatment rooms and operatories requires considerable experience and coordination. Having previously reviewed issues such as a safe water supply, the variables involved in handpiece delivery of the dentists' and assistants' instrumentation, and the options of fixed or modular casework, these will not be discussed again here. What follows are some technical considerations.

Special Plumbing and Electrical Requirements

The many variables in laying out an operatory and in selecting equipment demand close attention to the proper location of plumbing and electrical service. The space planner should work closely with a qualified dental equipment dealer in order to coordinate the location of utilities. In fact, dealers will typically provide engineering services to specify and lay out utility requirements. As these are the individuals who will service the equipment after it is installed, it is wise to consider their advice.

In the treatment room, one can provide for current and future technology by coring the floor from the toe of the chair to the 12 o'clock wall and installing a 2-inch-diameter conduit to carry the many cables and wiring needed for equipment, computers, and monitors. If a 12 o'clock wall is not used and equipment is placed on the sides of the room, the conduit will run from the chair laterally to those locations.

Most dental units now have a self-contained water supply separate from the building's water supply unless they have a cuspidor/cup filler. Each treatment room should have shutoff valves for building water, if so equipped, and compressed air, so the equipment can be isolated for repair without shutting down other treatment areas. The ideal location for these shutoffs will vary according to the type of delivery system being provided; therefore, consult with the dental equipment supplier.

A central water control (solenoid valve) that will turn off all water throughout the suite should be located in the equipment room where it can be serviced. Since most of these systems have integrated filters, they must be accessible for changing. This assembly is usually supplied by the dentist's dental equipment supplier and comes ready for the plumber to install on the main water line serving the suite. It is low voltage activated and comes with a 120- to 240-volt transformer and remote switch panel, which should be located near the staff exit so that they may turn off all the water to the suite at night as they exit. This is usually a combined panel that also remotely turns off the vacuum pumps and air compressor.

Gas

Gas is used to heat certain impression materials. A portable propane or butane heater or torch is generally used for this purpose. Occasionally, a dentist may wish to have natural gas plumbed into the laboratory but this is not common.

Central Suction

The suction at each treatment room comes from a central vacuum system usually located in an equipment room as close as possible to the treatment rooms. It should not be located overhead because of the additional power required to lift up any liquid being aspirated against gravity, which would reduce the overall efficiency of the system. This does not preclude running vacuum piping overhead to treatment rooms from a pump located basically at the same floor level as the treatment rooms. While this is less desirable than running vacuum piping under the floor in question, it may have to be used in some instances. If your design requires overhead vacuum piping, be sure to consult the manufacturer's design specifications for piping to be connected to the pumps to ensure an efficient system. The vacuum pump shown in Figure 10-52 will accommodate up

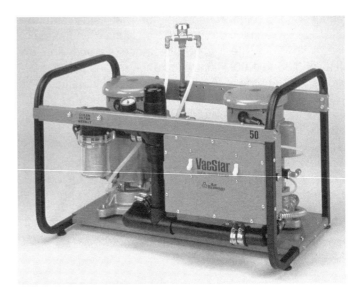

Figure 10-52. VacStar™ 50 dental vacuum system. (*Photo courtesy: Air Techniques Inc., Hicksville, NY.*)

to three high-volume evacuators (HVEs) plus up to six saliva injectors, all in simultaneous use. The vacuum system is sized according to the number of HVEs and saliva ejectors that might be in use at any one time. The space planner is advised to check with the manufacturer to verify the recommended maximum distances for vacuum piping and diameter of vacuum lines so as not to reduce efficiency. Additionally, it is desirable to enclose the vacuum pump and air compressor in a sound-insulated cabinet or room, as they can be quite noisy.

Quality vacuum systems provide consistent high-volume flow even when multiple users are on line. They not only evacuate the fluids building up from treatment, but aspirate potentially infectious aerosols from in and around the oral cavity. As stated previously, the "wet seal" vacuum pump is predominant, but there is a growing trend toward waterless pumps. As these usually require a different size piping than wet-seal systems, it is hard to make this change except in new construction. Dry or waterless vacuum systems can potentially save one-quarter million gallons of water annually in a single dental office, and, since

Figure 10-53. AirStar® 50 compressor. (*Photo courtesy: Air Techniques Inc., Hicksville, NY.*)

sewer charges are usually linked to water consumption for billing purposes, the more expensive dry systems will almost always pay for themselves in 3 to 5 years of utility savings. Take note of a new requirement for installing an air/water separator device on the waste output side of wet seal and some dry systems to separate the liquid discharge from the air discharge. This may be combined with a water recycling device with some manufacturers, but in any case this device must be vented outside of the building to an unoccupied area with a 2-inch i.d. (inside diameter) pipe separate from any sewer vent lines. The purpose of this is to vent scavenged nitrous oxide and contaminated air outside of the building.

Compressed Air

As with vacuum systems, compressed-air systems must be sized according to the number of users. The unit in Figure 10-53 is appropriate for five simultaneous users. Air compressors need more sound insulation than do vacuum pumps, and they can generally be located at a greater dis-

tance from treatment rooms than can vacuum pumps; however, it is common to find both located in the same equipment room. Some manufacturers offer a sound-reducing cover for the air compressor that purports to reduce noise by 70 percent. The best air compressors are oil-free, because oil-lubricated compressors distribute oil aerosols through the air syringe, which may jeopardize dental techniques that require an uncontaminated air stream.

It is important to monitor the amount of moisture in compressed air because a humid condition promotes the growth of bacteria and fungi, which increases the risk of infection when sprayed into the patient's mouth through the air syringe. Moisture can also prevent cohesion of composite restorative materials, cause permanent failure of handpieces (drill turbines), and cause water vapor damage to equipment. Figure 10-54 shows a remote-control panel for switching on the compressed air, the vacuum pump, and the moisture monitoring system. Twin-headed compressors are popular as they allow the office to continue to operate when one compressor head fails to function. Both vacuum and compressed air are regulated under the Uniform Fire Code and details of specific design requirements can be found in that code or NFPA 99.

Figure 10-54. Remote control panel for air, water, and vacuum. (*Photo courtesy: Air Techniques Inc., Hicksville, NY.*)

Central Air Abrasion

Air abrasion as a technique or technology has been discussed previously, but it should be mentioned that the portable units have their own on-board compressors typically functioning at 90 to 132 pounds per square inch. Typically, central office air compression is not high enough to run one of these units. However, it is possible to install a high-pressure compressor in the equipment room with lines running to each operatory. This enables one to have an air abrasion handpiece chairside, mounted on the standard handpiece delivery system. This is difficult to retrofit into existing offices but is an option for new construction. The remote-control head on each delivery system controls pressure and powder flow rates. It is possible to install this in an existing space if there is a crawlspace or basement. Air abrasion as a technique is sometimes maligned because of the powder overspray (the technique is similar to sandblasting), which creates considerable cleanup after the procedure. However, more expensive, top-of-the-line models meter the powder into the air stream with more precision. Education about proper evacuation and operating techniques is also important.

Emergency Power

Back-up generators may or may not be needed in general dentistry offices, depending on the reliability of electrical service. Severe shortages of electricity in some regions of the nation have created rolling black-outs that wreak havoc with computer systems and leave patients stranded, so to speak, in the middle of a procedure. State professional practice acts and local building codes generally dictate in what types of situations emergency power is required. For example, in most jurisdictions, oral surgeons would require emergency power. Generators cannot be used if they are not located on the ground floor, but high-capacity battery back-up may be used; however, one must be careful about what else is on that circuit. If planning for this option, a unit the size of a 3-foot cube will fit in a $4\times4\times8$-foot-tall room, which, by the way, needs good ventilation as it produces heat.

Equipment Room

One must think about where to locate the hot-water heater, telephone terminal panel, electrical subpanels, medical gases, air compressor, vacuum pump, and provision for natural gas, if required. If the dental suite is located in a medical office building, occasionally there is a central mechanical equipment room on each floor to serve tenants. This may allow the air compressor and vacuum pump to be housed in a remote location and piped to the dental suite, eliminating equipment noise and saving the tenant rent on square footage for a utility room within the suite. The building may also have provision for natural gas, saving the tenant the cost of running a gas line into the building. If the dental suite is located in a professional office building not specifically planned to accommodate physicians or dentists, the tenant usually has to allocate room within the suite for the installation of central equipment.

Analgesia and Anesthesia

The use of *analgesics* (medication that decreases sensitivity to pain but that does not put patients to sleep) is common in dental practice. Local anesthetics, injected into the tissue, make dentistry painless and require no special accommodation in the treatment room. However, analgesia that involves a mixture of nitrous oxide (N_2O) and oxygen (O_2) requires special consideration such as scavenging and monitoring, discussed previously in this chapter under OSHA Standards.

These gases may be stored in portable tanks that are wheeled into the treatment room as needed (Figure 10-55) or may be centrally located in a medical gas closet either inside or outside the suite and piped to each treatment room. The nitrous oxide conscious-sedation system in Figure 10-56 has a clean-air scavenging system mask. One tube of the mask brings the fresh gas supply to the patient, and the other tube allows the exhaled nitrous oxide to be removed from the treatment room by the central vacuum system. This reduces the concentration of nitrous oxide in the treatment room. The sedation system can be wall/cabinet mounted or flush mounted to a panel in the wall, as shown in Figure 10-57.

The use of *general anesthetics* (medication that puts patients to sleep) is confined mainly to oral surgeons, although intravenous sedation (also called conscious sedation) may be used by periodontists when doing implant surgery and, occasionally, by cosmetic or restorative dentists for lengthy and complex reconstructive procedures. Medical gas connections can be neatly designed into the casework at the foot of the chair where an anesthesiologist would work when administering and monitoring anesthesia during long procedures (Figure 10-58).

Figure 10-57. Flush-mounted flowmeter for centrally piped nitrous oxide and oxygen. (*Photo courtesy: Porter Instrument Co., Hatfield, PA.*)

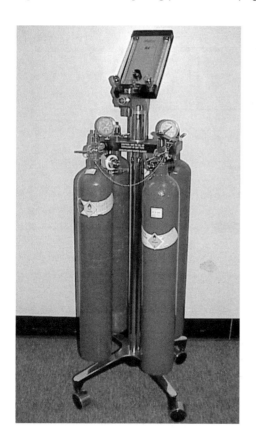

Figure 10-55. Dental analgesia flowmeter and gas cylinders on mobile stand. (*Photo courtesy: Littell Industries Inc., North Hollywood, CA.*)

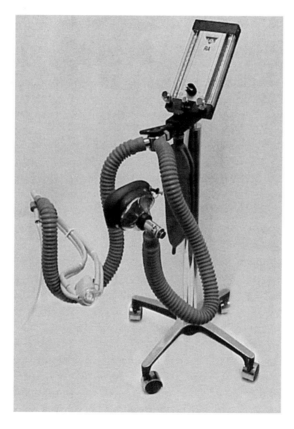

Figure 10-56. Nitrous oxide sedation system. (*Photo courtesy: Littell Industries Inc., North Hollywood, CA.*)

Figure 10-58. Outlets for medical gases at toe of dental chair, placed for convenience of anesthesiologist. (*Photo courtesy: Cherilyn Sheets, D.D.S.; Photographer: Jain Malkin.*)

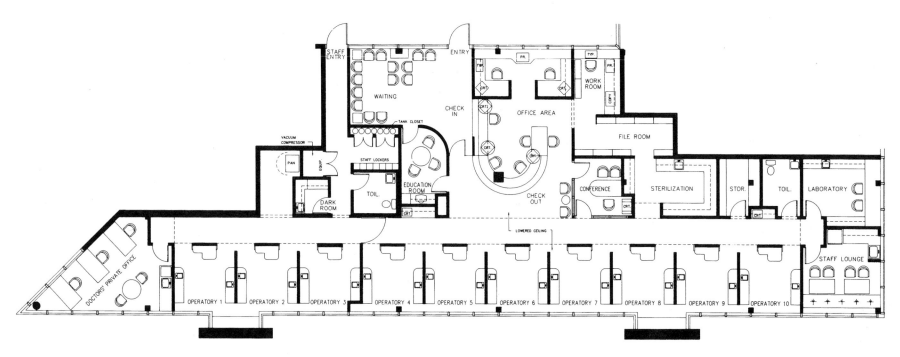

GENERAL DENTISTRY
3680 SF

Figure 10-59. Space plan for general dentistry (pre-ADA), 3680 square feet. (*Photo courtesy: Carmel Repp, ASID-IDA, San Diego, CA.*)

Storage of Medical Gases

Building and fire codes are very strict regarding where and how medical gases are to be stored. For information on the design of medical gas storage closets, consult Chapter 7 under the heading *Storage of Medical Gases.*

In addition, tanks should be stored in a place that is easily accessible for servicing. Locating them near the private or staff entrance to the suite (Figures 10-22 and 10-59) allows easy exchange of tanks without the service person walking through the rest of the office.

The Uniform Fire Code (UFC) requires that medical gases be stored in dedicated areas without other storage or uses. These enclosures may be a one-hour fire-rated exterior room, interior room, or gas cabinet constructed in accordance with UFC Standard 74-2 and the provisions of Article 74. These storage closets must be vented to the outdoors, have automatic sprinklers, and, if an interior room, have approved mechanical ventilation for exhaust and makeup air.

Medical gases stored in this manner are piped through degreased, sealed copper tubing (using only silver solder) to a flow meter in each operatory or surgery. If tanks are stored in a remote location outside the suite, a zone shutoff valve assembly and alarm system must be located within the suite to monitor the supply. The alarm panel monitors the gas pressure and provides both an audible and visual alarm if line pressure fluctuates more than 20 percent in either direction.

Communication Systems

Electronic Text Communication System
It is desirable, even in a small dental office, to have a digital communication system. This saves steps and enables the front desk to send messages to the treatment rooms without the clinical staff having to break asepsis to pick up a phone and without the patient overhearing messages. A communication panel integrated into the 12 o'clock wall is ideal (Figures 10-46 and 10-60). The keypad should have a membrane barrier that can be cleaned easily. Schedule changes, the caller's name, the priority of the next patient, utility reminders (e.g., clean vacuum traps), and communication with satellite offices can be responded to with the touch of a key and the keys are programmable with almost limitless uses.

Colored Signal Lights
A small panel of signal lights is mounted over treatment room doors, in the lab, and in the sterilization area, with a control panel in the business office and in the treatment

Figure 10-60. Communication system "Direct-Line"™. (*Photo courtesy: Amtel Systems Corp., Chester Springs, PA.*)

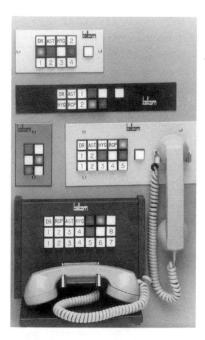

Figure 10-61. Communication system control panels. (*Photo courtesy: Kelkom Systems, Redwood City, CA.*)

rooms. This system can tell the dentist which room to go to next or whether a phone call or emergency is awaiting his or her attention. It also provides a light to signal that the dentist needs assistance. The limitation of this system is that the lights may go unnoticed. This is a far less sophisticated option than a digital text communication system.

Custom-Designed Systems
These are microprocessor-controlled custom systems that are designed, for example, to key the sequential order of patients in an orthodontic bay. A steady light indicates downstream patients, and a flashing light, the next patient. The microprocessor "remembers" which patient is next after a light is cancelled. It alerts staff to emergencies or phone calls and signals the number of patients awaiting each doctor (Figure 10-61).

Sterilization

Infection control has been discussed at the beginning of this chapter, and sterilization is one of the chief methods of preventing cross-contamination. The sterilization area should be close to the treatment rooms or operatories. If space permits, it may be a U-shaped arrangement (see Figure 10-6) with access from two sides, or it may have parallel 8- or 9-foot counters or an L shape (Figures 10-23 and 10-28). It should be large enough for two or three people to work in it simultaneously, depending on the number of treatment rooms served. An area that is too small will cause stress for those who have to work there, which, in some cases, is a dedicated sterilization technician who wipes down the operatories and handles instrument sterilization. Sterilization can also be performed in a large alcove off of the corridor (Figures 10-62 and 10-63). Casework may be custom built or a prefabricated modular system specifically designed for dental sterilization (Figure 10-64). A sterilization area or room is typically 8 feet wide×10 feet long; 16 lineal feet of countertop or work surface is considered the minimum to adequately perform the tasks of sterilization. Typically, with an engineered modular system, one can accommodate more equipment in less space.

A large, single-compartment sink, space for sterilization equipment, and sufficient countertop area for both a dirty and a clean side are needed. The dirty side of the sterilization area is where trays/cassettes are brought after a procedure to "break them down": Disposable items are removed and discarded. Then the instruments are presoaked to rid them of blood, debris, or extraneous material before it has dried, after which they are placed in an ultrasonic cleaner, then rinsed to remove dislodged debris and residual cleaning solution, placed in a dryer, and then bagged or packaged for processing in a chemical sterilizer (Figure 10-65) or autoclave (Figure 10-66). The sequence is always from dirty to clean. Dental handpieces, both high and low speed, are now separated from the instruments during the tray/cassette breakdown procedure and then processed through a cleaning/lubrication cycle before being washed externally, dried, and

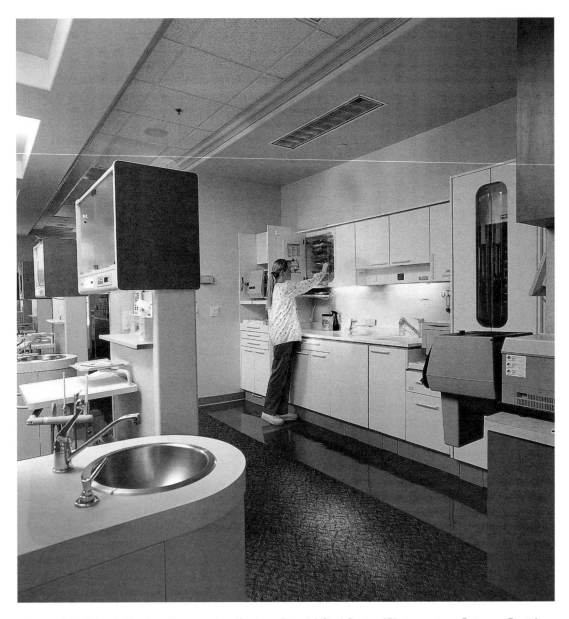

Figure 10-62. Triangle Furniture Systems, Inc. (Quebec, Canada) Steri-Center. (*Photo courtesy: Patterson Dental Supply, Inc., St. Paul, MN.*)

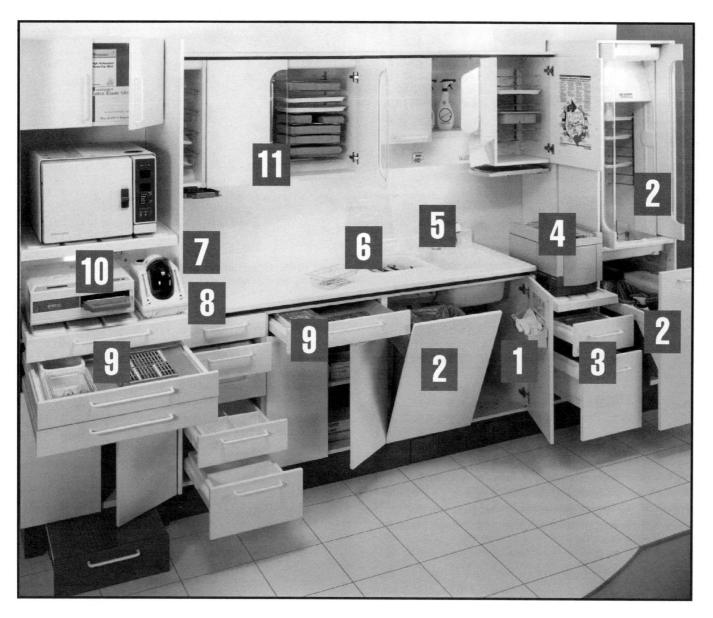

The 12' Steri-Center 9000X.3 shown features a systematic process of sterilization, from a red-lit contaminated instrument storage area to a blue-lit sterile instrument storage area. A clear acrylic floor-to-ceiling wall is also available.

Steri-Center Work Station:

1. Protective Equipment
2. Waste Management
3. Pre-soaking
4. Cleaning
5. Rinsing
6. Drying
7. Lubrication
8. Corrosion Control
9. Packaging
10. Sterilization
11. Storage

Figure 10-63. Triangle 12-foot Steri-Center 9000X.3 workstation. (*Photo courtesy: Patterson Dental Supply, Inc., St. Paul, MN.*)

Figure 10-64. Steri-Center modular casework. (*Photo courtesy: Midmark Corporation, Versailles, OH.*)

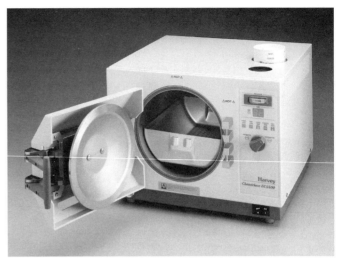

Figure 10-65. Harvey Chemiclave sterilizer. (*Photo courtesy: Barnstead/Thermolyne, Dubuque, IA.*)

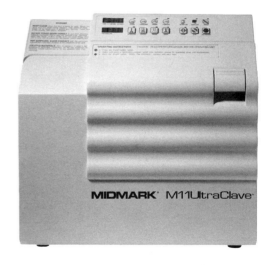

Figure 10-66. M-11 UltraClave™ steam sterilizer. (*Photo courtesy: Midmark Corporation, Versailles, OH.*)

packaged for heat sterilization. They are not usually put into the ultrasonic cleaner and may be added back into the instrument cassette just before it is wrapped for sterilization if the practice wishes. Note that an eyewash device (discussed previously under Hazardous Materials Standard) at the sink must be provided in a sterilization area (Figure 3-51).

The clean side of the sterilization area is used for setting up trays/cassettes of sterilized instruments (packaged and wrapped) for specific procedures. The sink is commonly located on the dirty side and requires a sprayer attachment, as well as suction for removing solutions from the ultrasonic cleaner and presoak basin,

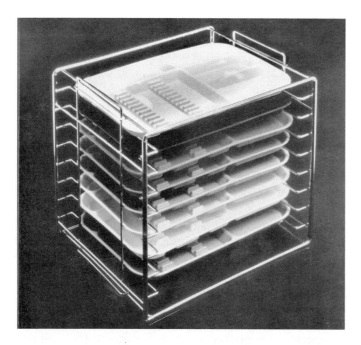

Figure 10-67a. Rack for tray set-ups. (*Photo courtesy: Clive Craig, Van R. Dental Products Inc., Oxnard, CA.*)

Figure 10-67b. Rack for tub set-ups. (*Photo courtesy: Clive Craig, Van R. Dental Products Inc., Oxnard, CA.*)

which have to be changed frequently. The CDC recommendations for processing dental instruments require large ultrasonic cleaners, large sinks, and large spaces for wrapping instruments and for breaking down dirty trays or cassettes.

The clean side may include a 3-foot-wide knee-space desk at a 30-inch height to allow the assistant to make phone calls to order supplies or do paperwork. A file drawer for forms and orders (or computer and monitor) and a shelf for binders containing policies and protocols, equipment maintenance records, and logs of various incidents (such as needle sticks) are required. Additionally, storage must be provided for clean and dirty linen, supplies, and disposables.

Tray/cassette setups can be stored in pass-through upper cabinets that open from both sides, making it unnecessary to enter the treatment room to stock it with clean trays or tubs. Slots can be created within the cabi-net to hold the trays or the cabinet can be designed to accommodate a prefabricated chrome rack to hold them (Figures 10-67a and 10-67b).

Universal Precautions
Staff must follow universal precautions when disinfecting and processing instruments. It is impossible to know if a patient has HIV or hepatitis; therefore, one should handle all waste and contaminated instruments with the same level of concern and protection. Heavy-duty utility gloves must be worn to protect hands and forearms when processing instruments. In addition, the lid should always be on the ultrasonic cleaner when in use to minimize pathogenic spray.

Distilled-Water Supply
Distilled water for the treatment rooms (to refill equipment-mounted containers) and for sterilization auto-

claves may be purchased in bottles (in which case it requires storage) or it can be distilled on site with a distiller located on the clean side of the sterilization room. Another alternative is the EzeeKleen (Oasis Dental Group) unit that uses reverse osmosis to produce a gallon of "purified" water in 4 minutes.

Understanding Sterilization Techniques

With the increased emphasis on sterilization explained earlier in this chapter, a number of manufacturers have developed research-based engineered modular systems such as the Steri-Center by Triangle (Quebec, Canada) and the Steri-Center by Midmark (Versailles, Ohio). Triangle offers an interesting fold-out brochure illustrating all steps of the disinfection and sterilization process.

Waste Management. There are three types of waste:

1. Regular trash

2. Medical solid waste (gauze with blood on it, gloves and masks); need not be red bagged

3. Biohazardous waste (sharps, blood-soaked gauze, tissue, bodily fluids); must be collected by a certified hauler

Providing appropriate storage of medical waste prevents access by unauthorized persons and protects waste from insects. Casework occasionally has knee-or foot-activated hands-free waste containers (Figure 10-63).

If the sterilization area is adjacent to treatment rooms, a sharps container may not be required in every room (verify state requirements) but may be located in the sterilization area. Sharps containers must be disposed of at least every six months (even if not full), which can be quite an expense for a dental office if one is placed in each treatment room in addition to sterilization.

Presoaking. Presoaking is used to remove blood and debris and to reduce the level of airborne contaminants by containing them in liquid. The goal is to prevent blood

and other particles from drying on the instruments. Although presoaking is a common practice, some infection control experts believe that skipping this step in favor of immediately putting the instruments in an ultrasonic cleaner removes the bioburden more effectively. A thermal disinfector is sometimes incorporated into the modular casework to disinfect instruments placed in cassettes (Figures 10-68 and 10-69).

Ultrasonic Cleaning. This step removes saliva, particles of tissue, and blood, which can interfere with the disinfection and sterilization process. The ultrasonic cleaner is often recessed into the countertop to make it easier to see into it and to suction out and refill with solution (Figures 10-64 and 10-70). It is sometimes put on a lowered counter as in Figure 10-63 (item 4).The sprayer hose on the sink may be used to refill it (Figure 10-70) and a suction hose to empty it. It should be noted that there are high-quality solutions that can be used in the ultrasonic cleaner that have a surfactant that rejects water and therefore eliminates the need to dry the instruments. Solutions that have a neutral pH do not damage instruments. According to a biomedical engineer, only 2 of the 50 ultrasonic solutions on the market have these characteristics; if they contain a germicidal agent, it changes the pH and one risks damaging the instruments.

Rinsing. After items have been removed from the ultrasonic cleaner, they are then rinsed in the sink (either in a basket or in a cassette) with the spray hose to remove debris, detergent, or residual cleaning solution unless the ultrasonic solution manufacturer recommends otherwise.

Drying. After cleaning, instruments are dried before being wrapped or packaged for sterilization. Moisture interferes with all methods of sterilization and, in addition, wet steam provides a fertile field for the growth of microorganisms. Drying also helps to prevent rusting, dulling, and corrosion

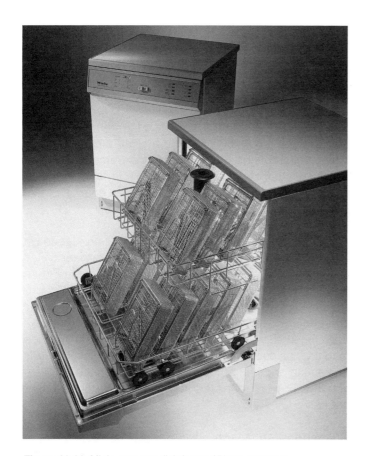

Figure 10-68. Miele cassette disinfector. (*Photo courtesy: Patterson Dental Supply, Inc., St. Paul, MN.*)

Figure 10-69. Sterilization workstation imported from Italy has sleek design and numerous pieces of equipment built into it; available through Patterson Dental Supply. (*Photo courtesy: Cherilyn Sheets, D.D.S.; Photographer: Jain Malkin.*)

Figure 10-70. Sterilization workstation in orthodontic office. (*Photographer: Jain Malkin.*)

of instruments. Transfer baskets or cassettes are used for placing instruments into the dryer, which may be recessed into the countertop or underneath it.

Lubrication. Lubrication helps to dislodge patient material from the internal surfaces of handpieces, enhances the effectiveness of the sterilization process, and protects handpieces from corrosion. One of the pieces of equipment used for this is the Assistina® (by A-DEC), which can be seen in Figure 10-63—it's the item with the black "bubble" cover.

Packaging. Instruments must be packaged in pouches (called bagging) or placed in cassettes wrapped with special paper prior to and during sterilization and remain sealed until use. Instruments that are used together as a set may be bagged as a set prior to sterilization, and later placed on tray setups to increase efficiency. Modular sterilization casework sometimes includes shallow drawers that, when open, function as surfaces for packaging instruments (Figures 10-63 and 10-64). Cassettes are wrapped with special paper and labeled for specific procedures.

Sterilization. The process of sterilization destroys all types of microorganisms, viruses, bacteria, and fungi and is required for critical items that penetrate bone or oral soft tissue. Semicritical items (those touching mucosa) should also undergo heat sterilization according to CDC guidelines. There are various methods of sterilization, each with advantages and disadvantages.

Steam Autoclaving. This is a common form of sterilization that uses live steam under pressure. Because steam is water saturated, it has the disadvantage of rusting and corroding certain metals and dulling the cutting edge of some instruments. Many ultrasonic cleaning solutions coat instruments with rust inhibitors and therefore should not be rinsed off before steam autoclaving.

Unsaturated Chemical Vapor. This method uses heat, a small amount of water, and chemicals under pressure. Because the resulting vapor is unsaturated with water, it does not harm cutting surfaces nor does it rust or dull instruments made of high-carbon steel. The disadvantage is that it cannot be used with certain plastics, agars, or items that cannot withstand a temperature of 131 degrees Celsius. The Harvey Chemiclave is a popular product of this type (Figure 10-65). It should be noted that there are potential health risks associated with the chemical vapor requiring adequate exhaust of fumes and, in some jurisdictions, the solution cannot be discharged down the drain. The doctor may have to actually prove to an OSHA inspector that the vapor is being adequately exhausted and sterilization staff may have to wear dosimetry badges to monitor exposure. As high-carbon instruments become less common, a steam autoclave may be all that is needed.

Dry Heat Sterilization. This procedure normally eliminates rust and corrosion caused by saturated steam, but it has limited usage because of the extremely high temperatures (350 degrees Fahrenheit) and long exposure times required for each cycle (generally an hour). It is also limited to sterilizing only metal instruments.

Flash Sterilization. When a few instruments are needed in a hurry between patients, a small steam sterilizer called STAT*IM*™ (often recessed into the casework as in Figure 10-71) processes instruments in a cassette in a 6- or 9-minute cycle but does not have an effective automatic drying cycle. The STAT*IM* uses distilled water and has a drain hose that attaches to a waste bottle outside the machine, placed below the level of the machine. It needs no venting and has an optional printer to print a sterilization log. The unit depicted in Figure 10-66 takes longer but has a full dry cycle.

Cassette Sterilization. Using cassettes reduces labor costs by eliminating wrapping and bagging and some of the handling that would otherwise be required. In addition, personnel have less risk of exposure to microorganisms. All the instruments for a specific procedure can be placed in one cassette, which then goes through the aforementioned processes. In theory, one never has to open the cassette until it is needed in the treatment room. For large practices with many treatment rooms, the Miele disinfector in Figure 10-68 holds multiple cassettes. It may not be practical for a small office because one wouldn't want to run the machine until it is full and this would require a considerable investment in cassettes and handpieces. Cassettes are wrapped and taped prior to sterilization, then brought into the operatory and opened with instruments being used directly from the cassette. At the end of the procedure,

Figure 10-71. STATIM 5000 cassette autoclave™. (*Photo courtesy: SciCan, Pittsburgh, PA.*)

dirty instruments are placed back into the individual compartments in the cassette, it is rewrapped in its original paper and carried back to the sterilization area where it goes through the various steps of the decontamination and sterilization process. Hu-Friedy® Corporation manufactures the cassettes.

Storage. Sterilized tray setups should be stored inside cabinets that are free of dust and moisture. They may be stored in a central location (Figure 10-6) or may be stored in each treatment room, typically at the 12 o'clock wall, which often has a pass-through cabinet to enable trays to be restocked in the room from the corridor (Figures 10-33 and 10-37 and Color Plate 33, Figure 10-35). Trays vary in size from 7×10 to 10×15 inches with 9½×13½ inches being the most common size.

Tubs, another organizational vehicle, may also be used with tray setups. Tubs are generally 9½×11½×2½ inches deep. Both trays and tubs stack on racks (Figures 10-67a and 10-67b) that fit into cabinets for storage. Trays and tubs are color coded or labeled by type of procedure for which they are intended, making it easy for staff to select

the proper tray or tub. During the procedure, the instrument tray is placed on a mobile cart or other work surface convenient to the assistant as is the tub containing medicaments and other supplies necessary for the procedure.

Prefabricated Modular Systems
The steps involved in disinfecting and sterilizing instruments can be traced in the modular system depicted in Figures 10-62 and 10-63. In Figure 10-62, a red light inside the cabinet on the far right side reminds staff that it contains dirty trays or instruments waiting to be processed and, at the far left end, an interior blue light indicates storage of clean trays.

Note, in Figure 10-62, the countertop film processor with daylight loader attachment (right side of photo), which eliminates the need for a darkroom. In Figures 10-62 and 10-63, the ultrasonic cleaner is on a lowered shelf and the sterilizers (STAT*IM* and autoclave) fit into open shelves on the left side. The system in Figure 10-64 has general and biohazardous waste drops in the countertop on the left side, pull-out shallow drawers for wrapping instruments, and foot-operated faucet control in the base of the cabinet.

Utility Considerations
A few construction issues should be noted. With respect to electrical service, many sterilizers require a separate circuit. Electrical outlets need to be carefully coordinated for the many pieces of equipment housed within the cabinets or placed on open shelves. Regarding ventilation, steam and condensation from the autoclave should be exhausted into the plenum or directly outdoors, if possible. The exhaust fan is best located over the autoclave with an adjacent timer switch. Consideration should be given to a solid-surface material like Corian for the countertop, backsplash, and integral sink to eliminate crevices that collect moisture and may harbor microorganisms. If a plastic laminate countertop is used, the sink should be one that fits under the countertop without a flange or stainless steel trim ring. The faucet with spray head should ideally be activated by knee or foot

pedal or, as in some prefabricated units, by a kickplate in the base.

X-Ray

Digital dental radiography is quickly replacing film. It has many advantages (discussed previously) and is equal to or exceeds film in all respects. It exposes the patient to considerably less radiation (and therefore requires less radiation shielding) and avoids the discomfort of bitewings. However, there are some patients who cannot tolerate the digital sensor (used with direct digital systems) in their mouth, which means that a dentist may still have to occasionally shoot film and perhaps use a chairside darkroom (a countertop "dip" for developing film) or use a system like DenOptix.

Two Competing Technologies

There are two competing technologies—direct digital and phosphor plate in which images are scanned into a computer. With either technology, an intraoral X-ray unit is required, which can be placed on the 12 o'clock wall (Figure 10-29) but more commonly is placed on a side wall or built into a pass-through cabinet that serves two treatment rooms (Figures 10-30 and 10-31). The integration of digital radiography with the treatment room computer and monitors has been discussed previously as has the advantages for practice management and case presentations to the patient.

Direct Digital. A sensor placed in the patient's mouth (attached to a cable) captures images in a direct digital system (Figure 10-72) and these are immediately available chairside as opposed to a film-based system, which requires leaving the room to process films. With film, a bad exposure must be redone, exposing the patient to more radiation, whereas, with digital, an almost infinite number of adjustments can be made with the computer. In addition, images can be enlarged to a macro size so that the patient can view them on a monitor (Figure 10-73). Direct digital is based on charged-coupled devices or CCD technology. Schick and Trophy are two of the more well-known manufacturers.

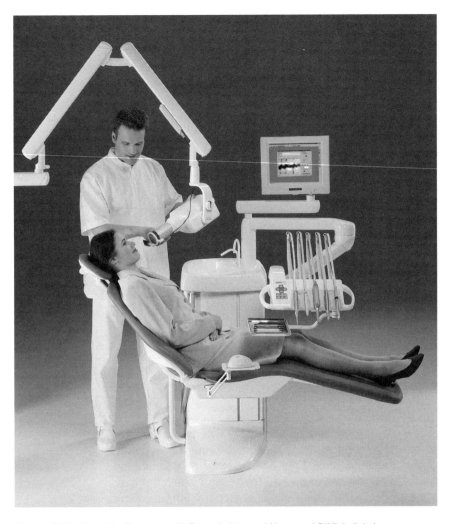

Figure 10-72. Prostyle Compact with Prostyle Intraoral X-ray and DIXI 2 digital sensor. Image capture is controlled by tapping a foot pedal. Note tray for mouse attached to side of chair. Intraoral camera is integrated as one of the five handpieces. (*Photo courtesy: PLANMECA, INC., USA, Addison, IL.*)

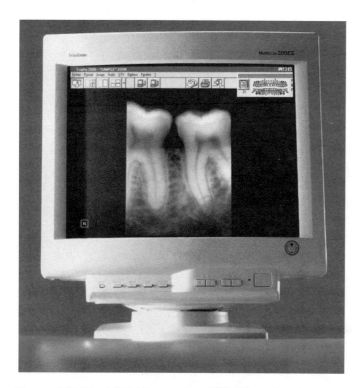

Figure 10-73. Direct digital X-ray system, RVG Ultimate Imaging System. (*Photo courtesy: Trophy Dental, Danbury CT.*)

Figure 10-74. DenOptix™ phosphor storage technology digital scanner system. (*Photo courtesy: Dentsply International, Gendex Dental X-ray Division, Des Plaines, IL.*)

Storage Phosphor Technology. This system mimics film-based radiography with reusable imaging plates in various sizes to accommodate intraoral, panoramic, or cephalometric images. Intraoral imaging plates are placed in a film positioning device similar to a bitewing. It does not employ cabled sensors as does direct digital, although the DenOptix system does offer a direct sensor option. After the images are taken, the imaging plates are loaded onto a carousel (Figure 10-74) and placed in a scanner where the information captured is digitized and sent to a computer or server. Images can be saved in many formats and, from this point, manipulated chairside as with direct digital, assuming one has a networked environment. In this case, a computer, monitor, and scanner

are placed in a central location. The DenOptix digital imaging system includes Windows-based VixWin image management software. Soredex is the other manufacturer of storage phosphor technology.

Erasing Imaging Plates. Scanning does not remove all of the image information from the imaging plates. This is performed by exposing them to intense light for 1 or 2 minutes, which can be accomplished by storing them under a view box illuminator with the light on.

Scanner Workstation. Once the imaging plates have been exposed, they are sensitive to light and should be handled in an area with a light level of 10 to 20 lux, which is

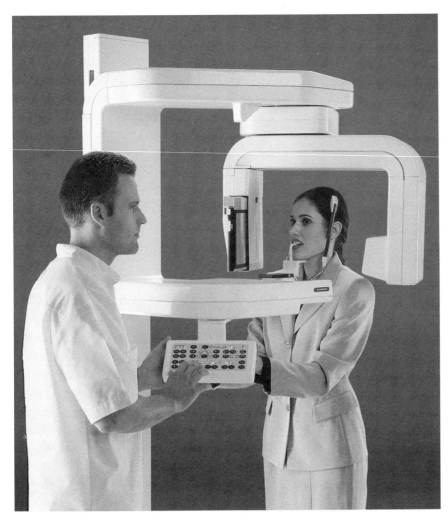

Figure 10-75. PM 2002 Proline digital panoramic X-ray unit. (*Photo courtesy: PLANMECA, INC., USA, Addison, IL.*)

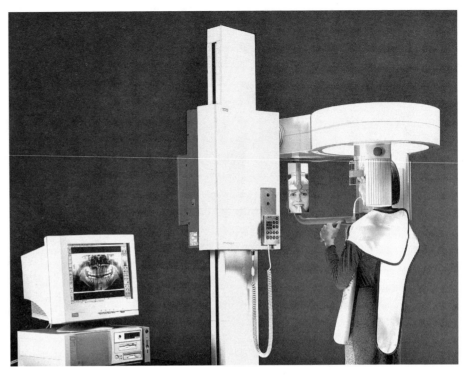

Figure 10-76. Orthophos 3 DS panoramic digital radiography system. (*Photo courtesy: Sirona USA, LLC., Charlotte, NC.*)

about 25 to 50 times brighter than a darkroom. Light levels can be checked with a photographic light meter. The scanner can be placed in an existing darkroom, leaving the lights off and the door open during loading of images onto the carousel. An alternate location for the scanner is an open niche off of the corridor, but the same issues exist with respect to light levels.

Direct Digital versus Storage Phosphor Technology.

Both systems eliminate the cost of film processors, X-ray film, mounts, toxic chemicals and heavy metals, and the weekly maintenance associated with film processing. Depending on a number of variables, both systems emit 60 to 90 percent less radiation than conventional film. Direct digital may require the purchase of a new DC-type intraoral X-ray machine to make the extremely short exposures, since many of the older AC-type are incapable of making very short exposures. Storage phosphor type X-ray systems are less sensitive to overexposure and will tolerate even old machines, making it easier to phase in digital without a large financial outlay. The downside is that it involves extra steps, which has a labor cost associated with it. However, DenOptix images are 150 percent larger than corresponding sensor images, which means that fewer X-rays must be taken to document the same area.

Panoramic X-Ray

Panoramic X-rays provide a view of the complete mouth rather than just the limited area of the intraoral X-ray series. This allows the dentist to assess abnormal bone configurations, cysts and tumors, impacted teeth, abscesses, temporomandibular joint (TMJ) problems, periodontal disease, and even sinus problems. The direct digital unit shown in Figure 10-75 requires an alcove 60 inches wide by 40 inches deep with an 87-inch minimum ceiling height. The unit can be adjusted to accommodate a patient standing or sitting or in a wheelchair. A similar unit, by another manufacturer, is shown in Figure 10-76. Check specific space requirements for the brand and model of X-ray to be used because these vary widely.

Cephalometric X-Ray

Cephalometric radiography is a comprehensive diagnostic device for facial views and lateral, posteroanterior, and oblique views. These are different images of the head and jaw than can be captured by panoramic X-ray although the two may be combined in a pan/ceph unit as in Figure 10-77, which just happens to be a film-based one. Cephalometric X-ray units are used primarily by orthodontists and oral surgeons. Although dimensions may vary somewhat among different models, a pan/ceph requires an alcove approximately 88 inches wide and 48 inches deep with a ceiling height of 87 to 92 inches.

Panoramic and cephalometric X-ray units are typically located in an alcove off of the corridor (Figure 10-6) and occasionally, especially in orthodontic offices, may be

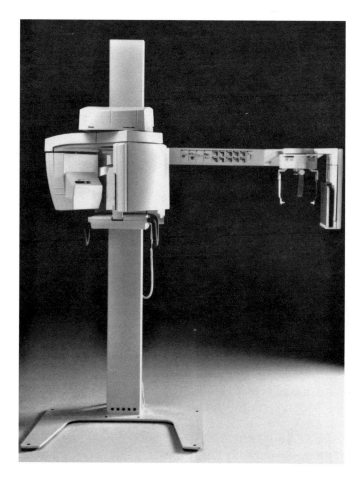

Figure 10-77. Orthoralix™ 9000 film-based panoramic/cephalometric wheelchair accessible X-ray system, digital compatible (*Photo courtesy: Dentsply International, Gendex Dental X-ray Division, Des Plaines, IL.*)

alongside a dental chair with intraoral X-ray, all together in one imaging area (Figures 10-22 and 23). Dentists sometimes refer patients to a dental X-ray lab.

Linear Tomography

Tomography provides cross-sectional imaging for successful dental implant placement to assess the quantity and quality of bone and to see other features. A combined panoramic/tomographic unit is manufactured by Instrumentarium Imaging, Planmeca, and Sirona.

Lead-Shielding Requirements

This has been discussed earlier under the heading *Exposure to Radiation.*

Miscellaneous Construction Details

The wall that supports the intraoral X-ray mount must have additional reinforcement to support the weight and longitudinal pull, starting at 36 inches off the floor and terminating at a height of approximately 60 inches. The designer must check with the manufacturer or dental equipment installer to determine the proper amount of bracing for the unit. Panoramic and pan/ceph units also require wall bracing but usually from 72 to 90 inches off the floor and on 16-inch centers.

Film Illuminators

If the X-ray modality is film-based, each operatory must be equipped with an X-ray film illuminator, also called a view box. It may be recessed in the wall over the fixed cabinet or it may be a portable tabletop model that sits on the counter (Figure 10-8a). In custom dental cabinets, a view box may be built into the cabinet (Figure 10-29). These view boxes are small—approximately 6×12 inches.

Darkroom

For film-based X-ray, an automatic processor is required. It sits on a 30-inch-high counter and is usually located in a darkroom, but most units are available with a daylight processing accessory, which allows film to be developed outside of a darkroom. In this case, the designer need merely provide a 4×5 foot alcove off of the corridor for film processing. A standard dental darkroom is depicted in Figure 10-78. Darkrooms will become obsolete as more dentists switch to digital imaging.

Automatic Processors. The Peri-Pro® (Figure 10-79) is a small unit 25 inches long×10 inches×8½ inches high, which only processes intraoral films. It does not require plumbing or a floor drain, because it is totally self-contained. It requires only a standard electrical outlet. The slightly larger unit, the A/T2000 (Figure 10-80), processes intraoral, panoramic, and cephalometric films and is also available with a daylight film loader option. This unit is 15 inches wide×25 inches deep×18 inches high and has a built-in replenisher unit. There are several other brands of processors for intraoral-only films and several for the combination of intraoral, panoramic, and cephalometric films.

It should be noted that the daylight loader portion of the processor hangs off the edge of the countertop, requiring that the countertop be 25 inches deep. This unit does require cold water (¾-inch-diameter male garden hose fitting) and an open vented drain. It does not require a floor drain, however, although local codes may require one whenever a processor has replenisher tanks. Codes vary widely with respect to waste drain requirements, and the designer must check local ordinances.

If the dentist starts out with a processor that does not require plumbing or a drain, it is advisable to plan for a future larger processor by installing a water line and drain during the general construction of the suite. It should be noted that the fixer and developer generally go down the waste drain, unless local codes prevent this. In some cities, the chemicals have to be collected in containers or, at the very least, the fixer must be processed through a silver recovery unit.

There should be a small area for storage in the darkroom or the processing alcove for bottles of developer and fixer. These plastic bottles are 1-quart size for the Peri-Pro and ½-gallon size for the A/T2000. There will also be a need to store packages of film. Unlike medical X-ray film, dental X-ray film is stored in lead-lined dis-

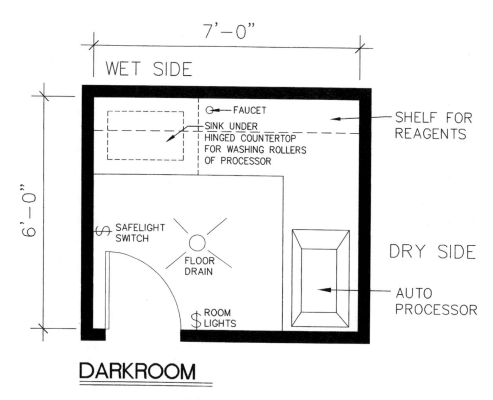

DARKROOM

Figure 10-78. Typical layout of darkroom for processing film. Can also be used as processing area for phospor storage technology scanner, which requires an area this size and a semidark room but does not require sink, floor drain, or plumbing connections.

pensing units, which are either wall-mounted in the operatory or stored in a drawer. Leave room below all larger processors for replenishing chemical containers and capture containers if required.

As with any processor, there needs to be a deep sink for occasionally washing the roller rack (Figure 10-78). The sink can be located under a hinged countertop, so that the sink is out of the way when not in use. The sink should be equipped with a sprayer. The daylight loader accessory is sometimes available with a film duplicator, providing a second copy at minimal expense.

Darkrooms often have a floor drain for overflow, but it really isn't needed with this type of automatic processor, although codes may require it for all processors.

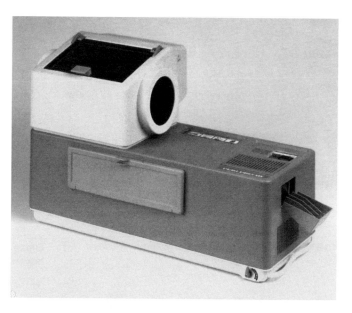

Figure 10-79. Peri-Pro® III countertop film-processing unit. (*Photo courtesy: Air Techniques Inc., Hicksville, NY.*)

Figure 10-80. AIT 2000® XR countertop film-processing unit. (*Photo courtesy: Air Techniques Inc., Hicksville, NY.*)

General Dentistry **475**

Figure 10-81. Dental lathe. (*Photo courtesy: Handler, Westfield, NJ.*)

Figure 10-82. Model trimmer. (*Photo courtesy: Handler, Westfield, NJ.*)

Figure 10-83. Vacuum porcelain furnace with quartz spiral muffle. (*Photo courtesy: Degussa-Ney Dental Inc., Bloomfield, CT.*)

exposed. *Any recessed light fixtures, as well as the exhaust fan, must have light-sealed housings.*

A small viewing and sorting area should be provided outside the darkroom. This may consist of only a shelf with a view box illuminator for the technician to check the films.

Manual Processing

Endodontists have a special need for manual processing of *working* X-rays. These are films made during the procedure to guide the dentist during treatment. Automatic processing takes too long to develop each of these single films, so the chairside assistant uses a portable chairside darkroom, dips the film into small jars of chemicals, and, in 30 seconds, has a processed film. This function can be replaced, however, by a digital system.

The darkroom or processing alcove should have an exhaust fan, and codes may require that the darkroom door have a lightproof louver ventilation panel. A darkroom door usually opens inward so that if someone tries to enter while developing is in process, the technician can put a foot against the door to prevent it. Darkrooms may have a red warning light over the door that is activated when the exhaust fan is started and the safelight goes on inside the darkroom. A darkroom door must be 36 inches wide per the ADA. However, if the room is designed to accommodate a wheelchair, it will be considerably larger than it functionally needs to be to carry out the processing function. The door must have a lightproof seal.

The darkroom must have two sources of light: a 100-watt incandescent light, either recessed or surface mounted to the ceiling for general work, and a safelight for working with exposed film. The safelight can be plugged into an outlet at 60 to 72 inches off the floor, and it can be activated by a pull chain or be wired into a wall switch. If the latter, the switch should be located away from the incandescent light switch so that the technician does not accidentally flip the wrong one while film is

Dental Laboratory

The size of the laboratory will vary, depending on whether the dentist sends out most of the lab work or employs in-office lab technicians. If two workbenches are arranged so that they face each other, a dental engine, lathe (Figure 10-81), model trimmer (Figure 10-82), porcelain oven (Figure 10-83), casting machine, and other tools can be shared. If the workload demands it, two separate workstations can be set up so that one person does not interfere with the other.

The porcelain station should be separated from the metal station to avoid contamination. Upper cabinets should be positioned so that they are accessible to seated technicians without too much stretching, and the sink should be in a central location. If space is not available elsewhere, the air compressor and vacuum may be located in the lab to supply the lab and the treatment rooms, unless it is located in a mechanical equipment room.

The type of vacuum used in the lab is a benchtop dust collector. Having no connection to the central suction used in the treatment rooms, this small portable vacuum is used for collecting dry grinding and polishing dusts produced by the lathe or the handpieces.

The lab requires compressed air, water, waste disposal (acid-resistant drainage lines and sink with plaster trap), a plaster bin, and many electrical outlets (continuous plug strips should be mounted above the countertops). If gas is required, it will most likely be a portable source rather than piped natural gas. It is important to design the electrical service to accommodate the high usage requirements of various pieces of equipment. The lab may be located near the operatories to meet demands of immediate impression pouring, but if many noisy procedures are performed, it is wise to keep the lab a distance from the operatories. Since labs tend to be messy, it is desirable to have a door on the room so that patients cannot see into it.

Vanity Area

A mirror and shelf or vanity cabinet may be located in the corridor near the reception area if space permits. Thus, a patient can comb hair or repair makeup while the receptionist is scheduling a future appointment (see Figures 10-6 and 10-25). A cabinet in the operatory corridor with attractive accessories takes little space but does much to enhance the office (Figure 10-84).

Patient Education/Consultation Room

Some dentists have small patient education rooms that consist of a countertop at 29-inch height, stools or chairs, and several electrical outlets for audiovisual equipment, which may be a TV monitor and VCR or DVD player (Figure 10-6). Patients may view presentations on how to floss teeth or learn about a complex dental procedure, although this type of programming is increasingly being offered in the operatory as discussed previously.

Patient education can also occur in a consultation room where a prosthodontist, periodontist, or cosmetic dentist may explain a course of treatment or specific procedures. This room is sometimes a combination operatory and office for a treatment coordinator. It will have a computer and monitors and should be attractively designed (Figures 10-85 and 10-86).

Figure 10-84. Operatory corridor can be enhanced by the placement of an antique or interesting cabinet with table lamp, small plug-in fountain, plant, and artwork. (*Photographer: Jain Malkin.*)

Figures 10-85 and 10-86.
Examination/consultation treatment room in prosthodontics office features cherry wood millwork and is set up to be multi-functional, offering a place to discuss financial arrangements in privacy, examine a patient and do a case presentation, and treat the patient in a fully equipped treatment room. (*Space planning and equipment engineering: Lee Palmer, Burkhart Dental, San Diego; Space planning collaboration/interior design: Janet Pettersen, IIDA, DesignWave, Fallbrook, GA; Photographer: J. T. MacMillan.*)

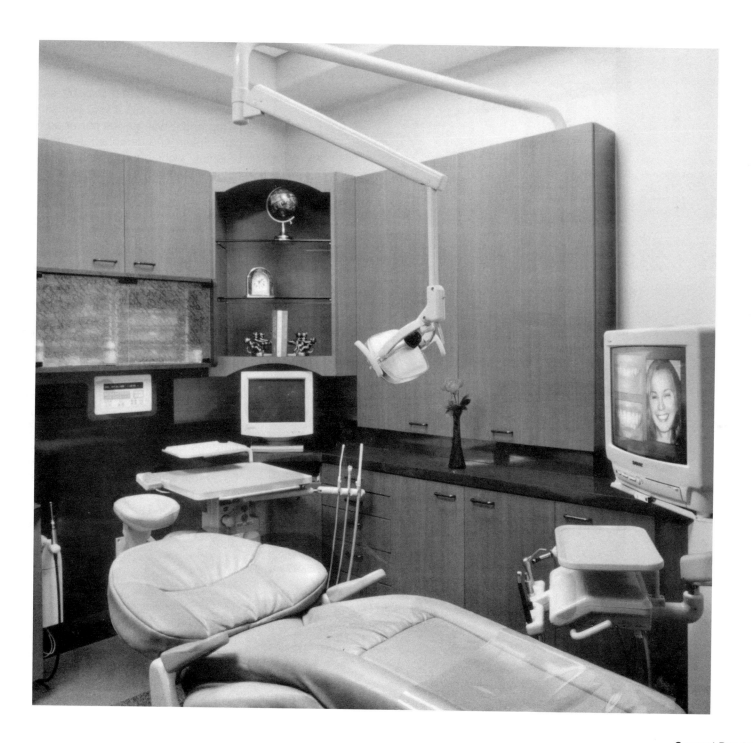

Plaque Control

A plaque control room is a combination patient education/hygiene room that may be set up in different ways. One way is to equip it with two sinks built into the countertop and a wall-to-wall mirror so that a dental assistant can explain and demonstrate dental flossing and proper brushing techniques, although this can also be carried out in a standard dental chair in a treatment room.

Staff Lounge

It is desirable to provide a staff lounge (preferably with windows) where the staff can relax, have a cup of coffee, or make a sandwich between patients. This is especially important in hectic, high-volume practices and in surgical practices, where staff may be involved in long procedures. Patients can rarely assess the quality of the clinical care they receive, but they judge it, to some degree, by the attitude of the staff and the attention to detail in the interior environment. Therefore, the staff must have their needs met in order to radiate good health and good cheer.

The staff lounge needs a built-in cabinet with sink and garbage disposal, undercounter refrigerator, microwave, and perhaps a cooktop (Figure 10-87). There should also be a table with chairs and perhaps some lounge seating. A closet for smocks or lab coats could be located here or in the corridor. The trend is for staff to wear uniforms only in the office; thus, dressing facilities may be a consideration.

Restrooms

Locate the staff restroom so that staff are not observed by patients when exiting. The restroom for patients may be located toward the front of the suite near the waiting room or perhaps in the treatment area. An attractive, nicely accessorized restroom is a pleasant amenity for patients and staff (Color Plate 35, Figure 10-88).

Figure 10-87. Kitchen/staff lounge is an important amenity that should not be overlooked. (*Space planning and interior design: Janet Pettersen, IIDA, DesignWave, Fallbrook, CA; Photographer: Jain Malkin.*)

Treatment Coordinator

Some offices have a treatment coordinator who handles patient relations and financial arrangements. In other offices, this person might be called the office manager or business manager. The duties vary, depending on the needs of the individual practice, but generally this person manages the staff, handles any patient problems or complaints, acts as an executive assistant to the doctors, handles patient financial arrangements, and acts as office administrator. An ideal location for this office is near the reception or business office, so that when the office door is open, the treatment coordinator can keep an eye on exiting patients. If a patient needs to discuss financial arrangements in privacy, the administrator's office is nearby. This office need not be large, but must accommodate a desk, file cabinet, computer and monitor, printer, fax machine, and two guest chairs. The ambience should be warm and nonthreatening. Attractive artwork and furniture should be provided.

Private Office

Dentists tend to have small private offices, sometimes as small as 8×10 feet. Patients rarely enter a dentist's private office, so it is used primarily to read mail, return phone calls, or relax between procedures. Sometimes, in order to save space, dentists will share a private office (see Figures 3-47 and 10-59).

Business Office

The business office of a dental suite is generally smaller than that of a similarly sized medical office, since the procedures are often fewer and do not require the large amounts of paperwork associated with batteries of lab tests and X-rays. Dental records are not as bulky as medical charts and X-ray films are considerably smaller. One can expect that dentists will commonly have electronic dental records and digital X-rays within the next couple of

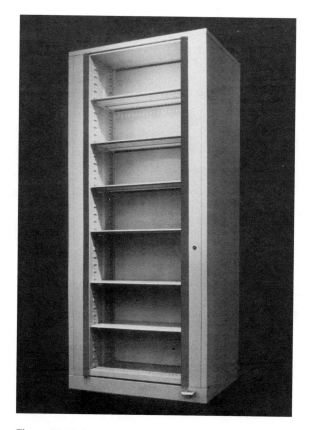

Figure 10-89. Space-saving chart file storage, Times-2 Speed Files. (*Photo courtesy: Richards-Wilcox Inc., Aurora, IL.*)

years if they don't already have them, which will eliminate the need for file cabinets to store large amounts of paper.

The increasing popularity of dental insurance plans, including HMO prepaid dental plans for subscribers, may necessitate a larger business office to accommodate additional insurance and bookkeeping functions, although electronic claims processing is increasingly common. A workroom off of the business office is practical for copier, fax machine, printers, and supplies (Figure 3-23 and 10-59). For those who do have paper charts, the file cabinet in Figure 10-89 works especially well in dental offices where it is desirable to make every

Figure 10-90. Computer monitors recessed into the countertop place screens at proper ergonomic viewing distance and keep them out of the way when greeting patients. (*Photo courtesy: Sullivan-Schein Dental, Melville, NY.*)

foot of space count. The unit spins around in place to access filing on the two long parallel sides. The dental suites in Figures 10-6 and 10-23 use this type of file cabinet.

Accommodation of computer monitors at the front desk needs careful planning. Figure 10-90 shows monitors semirecessed into the countertop, which is discussed more thoroughly, along with the topic of ergonomics, in the Business Office section of Chapter 3 (Figures 3-25, 3-26, and 3-27). Horizontal or slanted vertical slots for storage of forms beneath the 42-inch-high section of the transaction counter are convenient, provided they are sized to accommodate not just 8½-×11-inch paper, but oversized items such as clipboards as well (Figure 3-16). A section of counter should be at a 30-inch height as it is

friendlier and it accommodates individuals in wheelchairs (Color Plate 3, Figure 3-15).

Storage and Housekeeping

A common complaint from office managers is the lack of storage. A 6×8 foot minimum or, preferably, 8×8 foot room, lined with shelves, is essential as is a room approximately 6×6 feet for housekeeping supplies and equipment (Figure 10-91).

Figure 10-91. Housekeeping closet neatly stores supplies and cleaning tools. (*Space planning and interior design: Janet Pettersen, IIDA, DesignWave, Fallbrook, CA; Photographer: Jain Malkin.*)

Waiting Room

The reader is referred to the Waiting Room section of Chapter 3 for a general discussion of waiting rooms. Dentists tend to have smaller waiting rooms than medical offices of the same square footage since the patient volume is lower. A family practice physician may see upwards of four patients per hour, while the general practice dentist may see only two, depending on the procedure and whether the appointment is primarily for examination and diagnosis or for restorative work. In cold-weather climates where people wear coats and boots and use umbrellas, a coat closet or coat rack should be located where it can be supervised by the business office staff. A patient should be able to enter the waiting room, proceed to the reception window to check in, then select a magazine and be seated without tripping on furniture or patients' feet.

It is important to make the patient feel welcome, which means the reception desk should be open without glass and, perhaps, even without a door between the waiting room and the treatment area as in Figures 10-23 and 10-96. If a door is used, a French door with small lites of glass or a large panel of glass with sandblasted design would be appropriate. The reception desk should have a 42-inch-high stand-up-height transaction shelf to provide privacy for the receptionist's work area and to make it easy for someone to write a check, for example, but a 30-inch-high area should also be provided.

Some dentists prefer that patients enter through one door, circulate through the treatment area, and exit by another corridor, passing by a cashier/appointment desk on the way out. If this necessitates additional staff to separate the hello/good-bye functions, then it may not be advisable. The alternative is to provide a 42-inch-high stand-up-height shelf/desk in the exit corridor (Figures 3-22 and 10-26), allowing ample corridor width to accommodate this function. There should be a wall separating the reception area from the cashier/appointment area so that conversations about financial arrangements cannot be easily overheard by those in the waiting room (Figure 10-92). Note the privacy afforded this function in the large

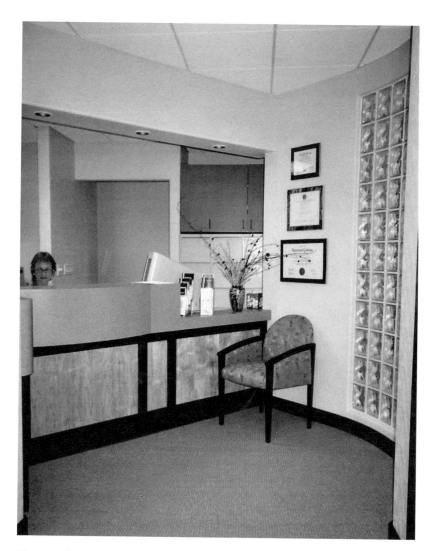

Figure 10-92. "Good-bye" and appointment desk, separated from the reception area, provides both auditory and visual privacy for patients. (*Space planning and interior design: Janet Pettersen, IIDA, DesignWave, Fallbrook, CA; Photographer: Jain Malkin.*)

group practice in Figure 10-28. A fountain greets patients at the entry; patients are directed left or right into waiting areas.

The designer must carefully consider sound attenuation. It is advisable not to locate an operatory too close to the waiting room, so waiting patients can avoid overhearing the sound of a drill. The waiting room and corridors should have carpeting and consideration should be given to sound-absorbing wall or ceiling treatments.

Even though modern dentistry is relatively painless, many people carry with them remembrances of former times when this wasn't true. A visit to the dentist still inspires terror in many people, and the interior design of the suite should be directed toward creating a relaxing, soothing environment (Color Plates 32 and 33, Figures 10-3 and 10-4, and 10-36). Note the aquariums built into the wall between hygiene rooms in Figure 10-28. A fountain built into the wall behind the reception desk creates visual interest (Figure 10-93) as does the tall fountain with sandblasted glass that acts as a room divider and is the first thing patients see as they enter the office (Figure 10-94). A children's corner (Figure 10-95) will be appreciated by children and parents alike. Also see Figures 3-12, 3-90, 3-91, 12-16, 12-17, and 12-18 for ways to accommodate children.

A patient wants to feel confident about being cared for by his or her dentist. If the office appears to be well organized and well cared for, with healthy live plants, and if it lacks visual clutter and has current, high-quality magazines, comfortable seating, and appropriate light for reading in the waiting room, chances are the patient will transfer that evidence of quality to the clinical setting.

As a rule of thumb, two seats in the waiting room should be provided for every treatment and hygiene room. High-volume practices such as orthodontics and pedodontics, which are characterized by many short appointments, should have three to four seats per dental chair, if space permits.

Figure 10-93. Small, plug-in fountains behind reception desk are recessed and framed to appear built-in. The vision of the shimmering water, as it cascades down the black "saw-toothed" panel, is soothing. (*Photographer: Jain Malkin.*)

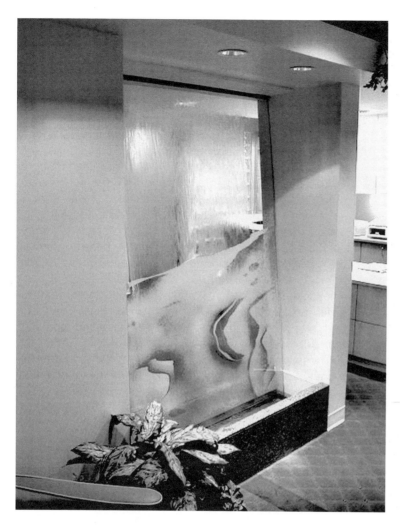

Figure 10-94. Glass water wall greets patients in reception room. Sandblasted design acts as a semitransparent room divider. (*Fountain by Harmonic Environments, www.harmonicenvironments.com; Photo courtesy: Andrea Huysing, Issaquah Dental Arts, Issaquah, WA.*)

Figure 10-95. Children's corner with recessed TV/VCR is welcomed by parents and children. (*Photo courtesy: Andrea Huysing, Issaquah Dental Arts, Issaquah, WA.*)

GENERAL DENTISTRY: PROSTHODONTICS EMPHASIS

Dentists may have a specialty in prosthodontics or maxillofacial rehabilitation, which requires additional postgraduate training. Additionally, general dentists may have an emphasis in the discipline of prosthodontics or maxillofacial rehabilitation. Prosthodontists specialize in complex dental and facial rehabilitation with a focus on fixed, removable, and implant-related prostheses. Even within the prosthodontist's office, there may be varying emphasis on geriatric patients or the oral care and management of patients undergoing radiation and chemotherapy treatment, or perhaps a younger esthetically oriented patient base. In terms of space planning, there are no special requirements except a large laboratory and perhaps a panoramic X-ray machine (Figure 10-96). Figure 10-30, Color Plate 33, Figure 10-35, and Figures 10-85 and 10-86 are the same prosthodontic office diagrammed in Figure 10-96.

ESTHETIC/COSMETIC DENTISTRY

There has been a dramatic increase in recent years in esthetic dental services performed by general dentists. Remarkable changes to an individual's smile can be achieved by skilled practitioners. Restorative dentists, enabled by new software, digital cameras, and photo-quality ink-jet printers, as well as the proliferation of computers and monitors throughout the dental office, are capable of letting patients see what can be accomplished. Imaging software features include image capture, storage, retrieval, manipulation, editing, and printing; some software programs are capable of integrating video and digital X-rays.

To capture the "before" photo, a photograph can be scanned or it can be taken with a digital camera. As previously discussed, an imaging alcove or niche is often created for this purpose. These digital images are stored in an electronic "photo album" for future reference. They can be altered by selecting options from the smile library, which consists of individual "ideal" teeth, several teeth, or the entire arch, and can demonstrate effects such as teeth whitening. Teeth can be rotated, lengthened, and reshaped. However, skill is required to carefully align the patient's actual smile with the replacement selections or "try-ins" to provide the patient with a realistic expectation of the proposed treatment.

Space-planning considerations include private operatories, as esthetic/cosmetic dentistry procedures are often lengthy (Figure 10-13), and a large lab (Figure 10-97). It is not uncommon to have a 4- or 6-hour procedure during which time an anesthesiologist will monitor and keep the patient sedated. Many anesthesiologists bring their own anesthesia equipment. Medical gas connections can be built into the casework near the foot of the chair on the left side (if the dentist is working on the right) as a convenience. Be aware that the use of conscious sedation involves additional code requirements, which are explained in Chapter 4 under Plastic Surgery and elsewhere under the topic "office-based surgery" (consult the Index).

Those who practice esthetic/cosmetic dentistry may be more aware of creating a high-profile image in their office interior design (Color Plates 32 and 34, Figures 10-3, 10-39, and 10-40). A number of dentists who have an aspect of their practice dedicated to teaching may build seminar facilities within their offices to train other dentists in specialized techniques. This involves a training room with computers, video monitors, and three projection screens side by side and may include a large laboratory and a kitchen for preparing or serving food.

TECHNOLOGY RESOURCE

A nonprofit research institute called CRA (Clinical Research Associates) in Provo, Utah (www.cranews.com), publishes a consumers' report of dental products and techniques in a newsletter format that is very useful in understanding and/or evaluating competing products. Clinical field trials and controlled laboratory tests are used in their research.

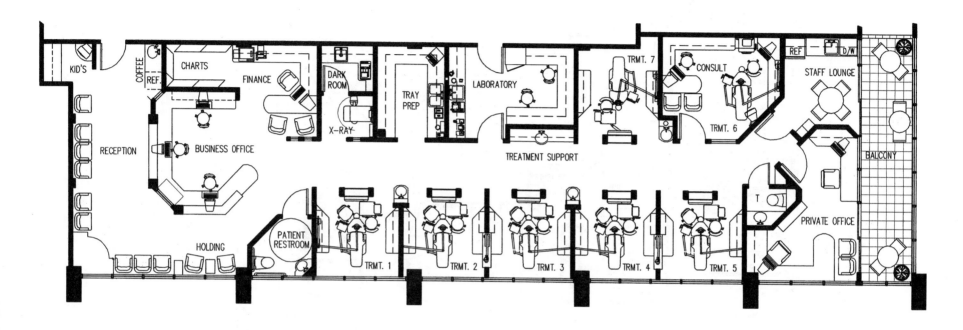

PROSTHODONTIST

2540 SF

Figure 10-96. Space plan for prosthodontist's office, 2540 square feet. (*Space planning and equipment engineering: Lee Palmer, Burkhart Dental, San Diego; Space planning collaboration/interior design: Janet Pettersen, IIDA, DesignWave, Fallbrook, CA.*)

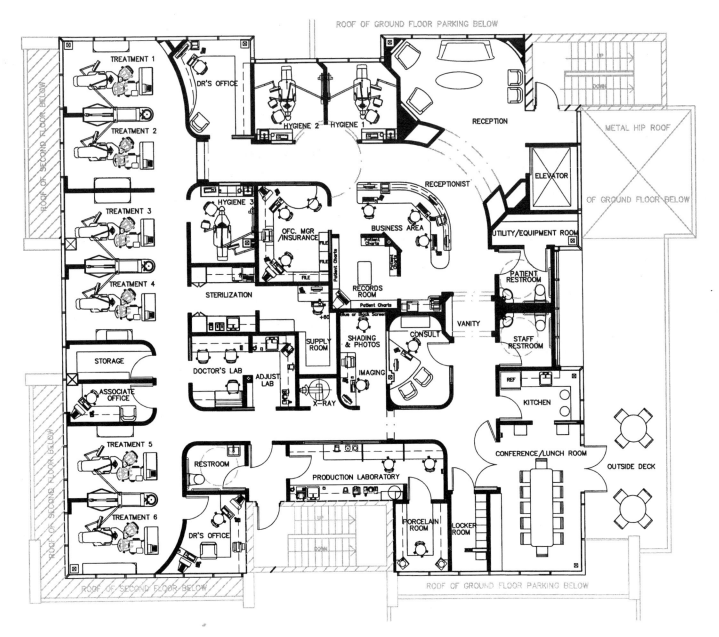

ESTHETIC/COSMETIC DENTISTRY PRACTICE
4044 SF

Figure 10-97. Space plan for esthetic/cosmetic dentistry practice, 4044 square feet. (*Space planning and equipment engineering: Lee Palmer, Burkhart Dental, San Diego.*)

RELEVANT INFORMATION IN OTHER CHAPTERS OF THE BOOK

To make it easier for dentists to find information relevant to dental practice in other chapters of this book, the following will serve as a guide. Use the Index to find the page(s).

Regulatory Issues/Codes

OSHA
Chapter 3

Accessible bathrooms
Appendix

Storage of medical gases
Chapter 7, Storage of Medical Gases

HIPAA legislation
Introduction and Chapter 1

Use of conscious sedation
Chapter 4, Surgical Specialties—Conscious Sedation/Minor Procedures and Office-Based Surgery; also see Chapter 4, American Association for Accreditation of Ambulatory Surgery Facilities (AAAASF), under Plastic Surgery, for classes of anesthesia

Oral Surgery: accreditation, licensing, and Medicare certification
Chapter 4, Office-Based Surgery, under Plastic Surgery

Construction Methods and Building Systems
Chapter 14

Lighting
Chapter 13

Color
Chapter 11

Business Office Design
Chapter 3

Ergonomic Issues
Chapter 3

Interior Design: furniture and accessories; interior finishes
Chapter 12

Miscellaneous

Dental interview questionnaire
Appendix

Darkroom design
Chapter 3, Darkroom

Research on reduction of stress
Chapter 4, Women's Health Centers, Translating Women's Primary Care Needs to the Built Environment; five bodies of research known to reduce stress are presented here but are by no means gender specific to women

ORTHODONTICS

Orthodontics is the branch of dentistry that deals with straightening teeth and improving incorrect bites (malocclusions). The majority of patients are children aged 12 to 18, although a sizable number of adults now avail themselves of these services. The orthodontic process is slow, often necessitating monthly visits for years. Pediatric practices may be combined with orthodontic practices because of the synergism and the obvious interface (Figure 10-102).

The Paperless Office

The previously discussed technology wave affecting general dentists includes orthodontists. Modern practices now often have electronic patient records, digital X-ray, and treatment room computers and monitors. Patients can sign in on a computer upon entering the reception area and this brings up their name, check-in time, and appointment time on a central monitor in the treatment room bay to alert staff about who has checked in and how long they have been waiting.

Circulation

On the initial visit, the child (or adult) is examined, and the orthodontist discusses the course of treatment with the parents. Some orthodontists have a well-designed exam/consultation room for making case presentations that includes the types of computers, monitors, and imaging software described in the General Dentistry section. It often includes, as in Figure 10-96 (Consult/Treatment Room 6), a patient dental chair. This is also shown in Figures 10-98 and 10-99 (Exams 1 and 2). Financial arrangements and future appointments may be discussed here or in an adjacent room, which frees up the exam/consult for the next patient. On subsequent visits, the patient proceeds to a tooth-brushing area and then to an "on-deck" area (often equipped with

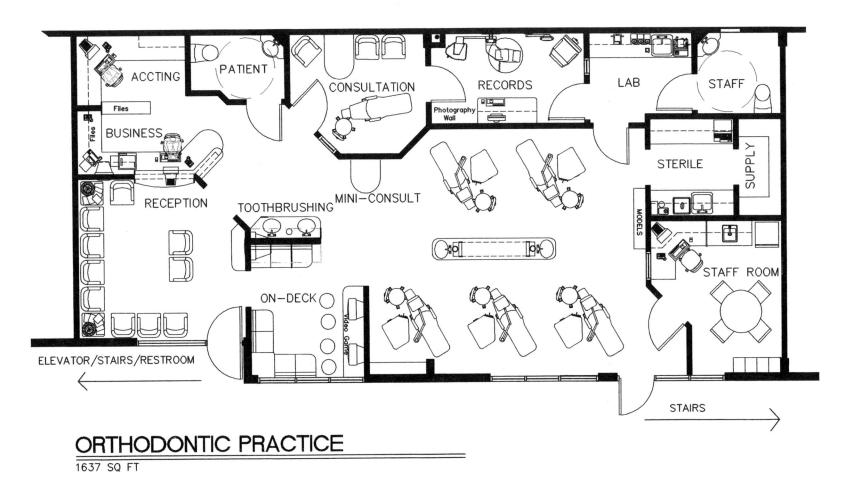

ORTHODONTIC PRACTICE
1637 SQ FT

Figure 10-98. Space plan for orthodontics, 1637 square feet. (*Space planning and equipment engineering: Lee Palmer, Burkhart Dental, San Diego.*)

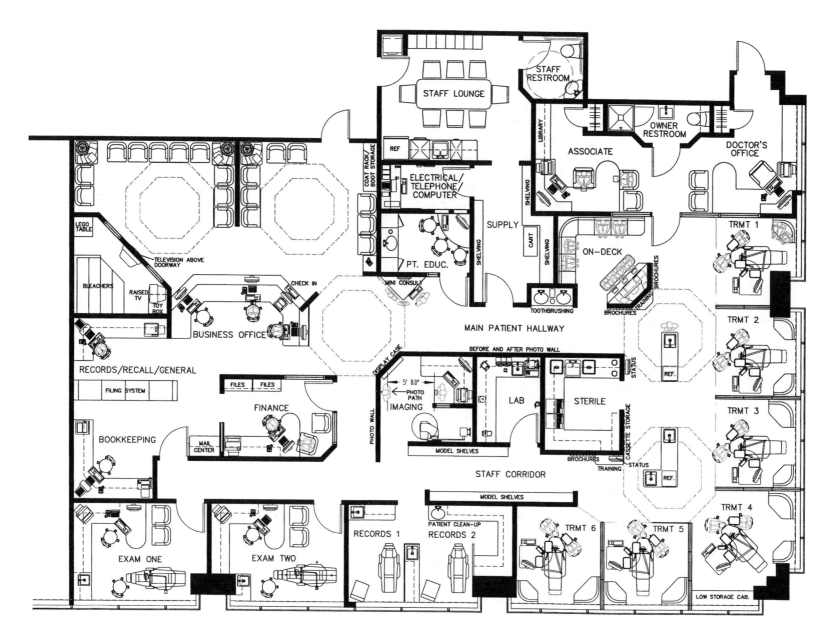

ORTHODONTICS

4021 SF

Figure 10-99. Space plan for orthodontics, 4021 square feet. (*Space planning and equipment engineering: Lee Palmer, Burkhart Dental, San Diego.*)

Figure 10-100. Time warp tunnel. (*Architecture/interior design: Margo Hebald, Architect, Pacific Palisades, CA; Photographer: Marvin Rand, Marina del Ray, CA.*)

video games and other entertainment) where he or she waits until proceeding to the treatment room. Figure 10-100 depicts the entry to the treatment room in an office with a space travel theme (see also Color Plates 37 and 38, Figures 10-105, 10-106, and 10-107). After the first few visits, during which the major work is done, monthly follow-up visits are short. Orthodontics is a high-volume practice that benefits from a waiting room able to accommodate a large number of patients. Three or four seats should be provided for each dental chair if space permits.

Sterilization

Orthodontists must now follow the same sterilization techniques outlined previously for general dentists. This has radically changed the support cabinetry in the bay as instruments are now brought to the chair on trays or in cassettes and chairside storage is limited to nonsterile items such as cements, brackets, elastics, and archwires.

The steam autoclave, chemiclave, and dry heat are all effective methods for sterilizing orthodontic instruments. Historically, many orthodontists have used a Dentronix or other brand dry heat sterilizer but, unless it's a recent model, it will not have the required protocol for packaged instruments, which involves a longer cycle. A steam sterilizer is considered the best overall alternative. The unit in Figure 10-66 is used by many orthodontists to sterilize pliers, a frequently used tool.

Treatment Bay

Orthodontists do most of their treatment in a large, communal treatment room called a "bay," in which three to eight chairs are arranged with no separating walls between them. Chairs may be arranged like spokes of a wheel (Color Plate 35, Figure 10-101) but, more often, are arranged in a row parallel to each other (Figures 10-98 and 10-102 and Color Plate 36, Figure 10-103).

(Note that in Color Plate 36, Figure 10-103, pliers are exposed, unpackaged, on trays as this photo was taken prior to the recent regulations on asepsis affecting orthodontists as well as general dentists.) Chairs should be 3 feet from the wall, with 4 feet separating them from one another. The large practice shown in Figure 10-99 uses all private treatment rooms with built-in corner seats for parents or a sibling. This enables parents to accompany the child during treatment in order to ask questions or listen to instructions being given. A bench at the foot of chairs in the open bay can be used for the same purpose, although it should be noted that some orthodontists prefer not to have parents in the treatment area but will use a small stand-up consult area between the treatment bay and the waiting room instead (Figure 10-99).

It should be noted that practitioners are converting from fixed-based treatment chairs to the fully motorized models found in general dentistry offices as these accommodate short and tall staff members more comfortably. There is also a trend toward standard dental lights mounted either on the chair or on the ceiling, providing better lighting with more variable positioning.

The location of fixed and mobile cabinets is critical to enable the orthodontist and assistant to move quickly from one patient to the next. Orthodontic treatment rooms have very little fixed cabinetry, compared to pediatric or general dentistry treatment rooms. Orthodontists do not use as many dynamic instruments as general dentists, and it is not uncommon to see custom-designed cabinets to the side or rear of the patient chair with instrumentation built in. The style of delivery is often over the patient, but could be rear delivery. Neither nitrous oxide nor oxygen is generally needed, only suction and air.

In addition to the treatment bay, the orthodontist usually has a standard individual treatment room, often referred to as a "quiet room," or an exam/consult, in which he or she may take X-rays, do the initial diagnostic examination, work on a noisy or obstreperous child, or treat an adult patient. This treatment room may have specialized equipment lacking in the orthodontic units in the bay.

Table 10-2.
Analysis of Program.
Orthodontics

No. of Dentists:		1		2
Waiting Room		$14 \times 20 = 280$		$16 \times 22 = 352$
Business Office/Reception		$12 \times 16 = 192$		$14 \times 16 = 224$
Bookkeeping/Business Manager		$10 \times 12 = 120$		$10 \times 12 = 120$
Operatory Bay (4 chairs)		$12 \times 24 = 288$	(8 chairs)	$12 \times 48 = 576$
On-deck Area		$10 \times 10 = 100$		$10 \times 10 = 100$
Consultation/Treatment Room		$10 \times 12 = 120$		$10 \times 12 = 120$
Quiet Room/X-Ray		$9\frac{1}{2} \times 11\frac{1}{2} = 109$	2@	$9\frac{1}{2} \times 11\frac{1}{2} = 218$
Patient Education		$6 \times 12 = 72$		$6 \times 12 = 72$
Lab		$8 \times 10 = 80$		$8 \times 12 = 96$
Sterilization		$8 \times 10 = 80$		$8 \times 10 = 80$
Darkroom (optional)		$6 \times 6 = 36$		$6 \times 6 = 36$
Staff Lounge		$8 \times 10 = 80$		$10 \times 12 = 120$
Toilets	2@	$7 \times 8 = 112$	3@	$7 \times 8 = 168$
Panoramic/Ceph X-Ray/ Imaging		$8 \times 8 = 64$		$8 \times 8 = 64$
Private Office		$10 \times 10 = 100$		$10 \times 12^a = 120$
Storage		$6 \times 8 = 48$		$6 \times 8 = 48$
Housekeeping Room		$6 \times 8 = 48$		$6 \times 8 = 48$
Mechanical Equipment Room		$6 \times 8 = 48$		$6 \times 8 = 48$
Subtotal		$1,977 \text{ ft}^2$		$2,610 \text{ ft}^2$
20% Circulation		395		522
Total		$2,372 \text{ ft}^2$		$3,132 \text{ ft}^2$

[a]Shared private office.

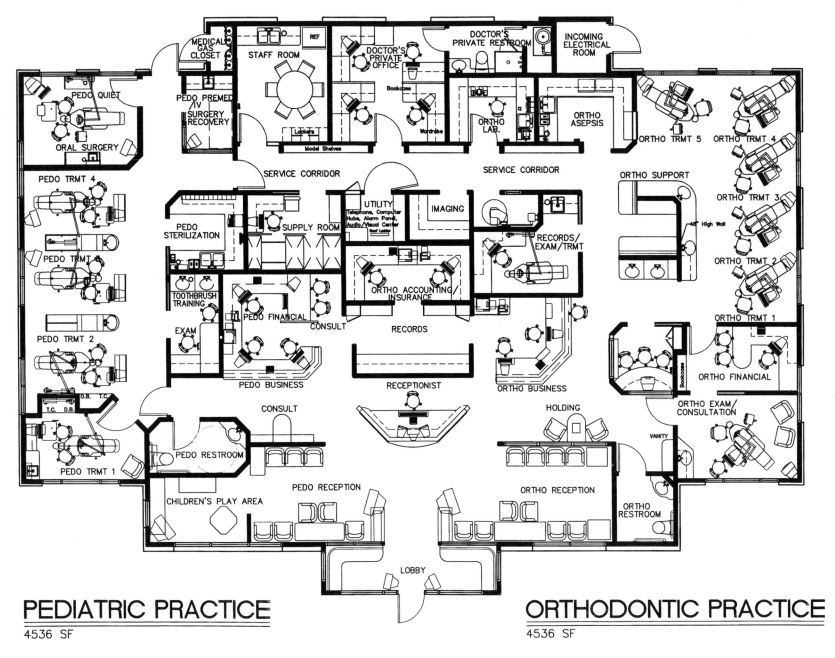

Figure 10-102. Space plan for pediatric/orthodontic practice, 4536 square feet. (*Space planning and equipment engineering: Lee Palmer, Burkhart Dental, San Diego; Interior design: Janet Pettersen, IIDA, DesignWave, Fallbrook, CA.*)

Laboratory

The laboratory should be large, with a storage bin for plaster and storage for the considerable number of plaster models accumulated. Sometimes as many as 4000 models, stored in cardboard boxes 3×3×10 inches, must be accommodated in the lab, or elsewhere in the suite, on shallow shelves (Figure 10-99 and Color Plate 36, Figure 10-103). The reader is referred to the General Dentistry section of this chapter for further discussion of a dental laboratory. As orthodontists shift to digital systems, the need to store models will disappear as will the need to take impressions. It will all be done electronically.

Other Rooms

An orthodontist's office will have a panoramic/cephalometric X-ray unit, a darkroom, if film-based (located near the central X-ray room), two toilet rooms, a fairly large business office, a patient education room, and, perhaps, a private office for a bookkeeper or office manager. The reader is referred to the General Dentistry section of this chapter for layout information on X-ray units, which may, as in Figures 10-98 and 10-99, be combined in one general imaging room, which also has a computer and monitor on a work surface for the creation of case presentation photo albums. This is where the computer for the digital X-ray is located. A photo wall, with a roll-down blue fabric panel, is used for taking conventional or digital photos of the patient.

Waiting Room

The waiting room of an orthodontic office may be treated with great imagination since the patients are, for the most part, preteens and teenagers who often appreciate an office designed around a theme.

Figure 10-104 shows a waiting room designed several years ago with carpet-covered plywood platforms instead of individual chairs to increase seating capacity in an undersized room and, at the same time, appeal to the teenagers' preference for lounging about, rather than sitting upright in a chair. The walls are Levi blue denim and carry photo blowups of children in various stages of orthodontia—before (with crooked teeth), during (with rubber bands and braces), and after (with straight teeth and beautiful smiles). The room, although unconventional, was a huge success and contributed to the orthodontist's popularity and the rapid growth of his practice. To add architectural interest to the room, an artificial skylight was centered over the platforms.

A truly imaginative office designed for children's dentistry is pictured in Color Plates 37 and 38, Figures 10-105, 10-106, and 10-107. The theme of space travel was expressed architecturally, not just cosmetically, as evidenced by the use of materials, the detailing, and the lighting.

Patients register for their space adventure at the *preflight check-in* counter (Color Plate 37, Figure 10-106) and then entertain themselves at the shuttle command center in the outer lobby. A spaceship control panel and electronic games with a space travel theme can be viewed on a large TV monitor. At the time of treatment, an automatic door springs open to admit the child to a shiny, metallic *time warp tunnel* (Figure 10-100) through which he or she must pass to reach the main treatment area (Color Plate 38, Figure 10-107). The patient is ushered into a "flight chair" complete with overhead TV monitor, stereo headphones, and personal, individual remote controls.

A totally different theme for an orthodontic office is shown in Color Plates 36 and 38, Figures 10-103 and 10-108. A tropical theme is expressed with bamboo detailing on the reception desk, blade fans, and stuffed tropical birds and iguanas perched in the soffit cut-outs and above the corridor "trellis" ceiling.

Patient Entertainment and Education

Many options exist for chairside education and entertainment using video, DVD, video glasses, and satellite music or TV. As most appointments are short, however, the expense of installing a monitor in the ceiling may not be worthwhile. These topics have been discussed in detail under General Dentistry.

Figure 10-104. Waiting room, orthodontics. (*Interior design: Jain Malkin Inc.; Photographer: Michael Denny.*)

PEDIATRIC DENTISTRY

Pediatric dentistry (sometimes called *pedodontics*) is the branch of dentistry that specializes in children (Figures 10-102, 10-109, and 10-110). It is based on a philosophy of prevention. If the child's teeth are maintained properly from an early age, there will be fewer problems as the child grows older. Thus, children from the ages of 2 to 18 visit pediatric dentists. Since the children are so young, much of the instruction and care of the child's teeth is entrusted to the parent. The parent must learn how to floss and brush the toddler's teeth, until the child is old enough to do it.

Thus, a patient education room is required and sometimes has a built-in bench so that the parent can be seated with the child's head in his or her lap and the child's body stretched out on the bench. The bench simulates a couch or bed at home, where plaque control is done with a dry toothbrush, without paste or water. The dental assistant sits near the parent and guides him or her during the procedure. The room should also have a built-in cabinet with sink, a large mirror, and good illumination.

Traffic Flow

A child and parent, on the initial visit, are escorted to the treatment room where the child's teeth are X-rayed and examined. As an alternative, there may be a centrally located intraoral X-ray machine as well as one in each "quiet" room. Then the parent may visit with the doctor in a consultation room, or perhaps remain in the treatment room, to discuss the course of treatment, followed by a stop at the finance office to discuss the cost. Pediatric dentists often do interceptive orthodontics on 5- to 12-year-olds using fixed and removable appliances to grow and shape the bones of the upper and lower jaw to fit the teeth into, rather than waiting until they stop growing and then extracting teeth to make room. This type of work involves case presentations similar to orthodontics.

Since visits are typically short, this tends to be a high-volume practice. Thus, the circulation of patients should

be direct and well planned, and things that little children should not touch should be behind closed doors. The waiting room must be large since each child is accompanied by one or both parents and, often, one or more siblings. A three-chair operatory bay may account for as many as 14 persons in the waiting room. The number of people in the waiting room is sometimes a function of the socioeconomic composition of the practice. Families with low incomes who cannot afford babysitters tend to bring all the children when one of them has to visit the dentist.

Table 10-3.
Analysis of Program.
Pediatric Dentistry

No. of Dentists:			1	
Waiting Room		$14 \times 20 =$	280	
Business Office/Reception		$12 \times 16 =$	192	
Operatory Bay (3 chairs)		$12 \times 18 =$	216	
Quiet Room/X-Ray		$9 \times 11 =$	99	
Sterilization		$8 \times 12 =$	96	
Lab		$8 \times 8 =$	64	
Darkroom (Optional)		$4 \times 6 =$	24	
Staff Lounge		$10 \times 10 =$	100	
Toilet Rooms	2@	$7 \times 8 =$	112	
Prevention/Patient Education[a]		$6 \times 12 =$	72	
Panoramic X-Ray		$5 \times 8 =$	40	
Private Office		$10 \times 12 =$	120	
Housekeeping Closet		$8 \times 8 =$	64	
Soiled Holding		$6 \times 6 =$	36	
Storage		$6 \times 8 =$	48	
Mechanical Equipment Room		$6 \times 8 =$	48	
Subtotal			1611	ft²
20% Circulation			322	
Total			1933	ft²

[a]May also be done chairside with DVD or videos.

Figure 10-109. Space plan for pedodontics, 1720 square feet. (*Courtesy: T. Michael Hadley & Associates, AIA, Laguna Hills, CA.*)

DECK

DENTAL BAY

QUIET ROOM

HYGIENE

STAFF

LOCKERS

FULL-HEIGHT CABINETS

STORAGE SHELVES

ELECT. PHONE, EQUIP.

TRAY PREP, LAB

VIDEO GAMES

ON-DECK

BENCH

STAND-UP CONSULT

EXAM / CONSULT

PATIENT TOILET

STORAGE

PROCESSOR WITH DAYLIGHT LOADER

PANELIPSE

PRIVATE OFFICE

FULL-HEIGHT CABINETS

RECEPTION

BUSINESS OFFICE

CHARTS

PEDODONTIC SUITE

1720 SF

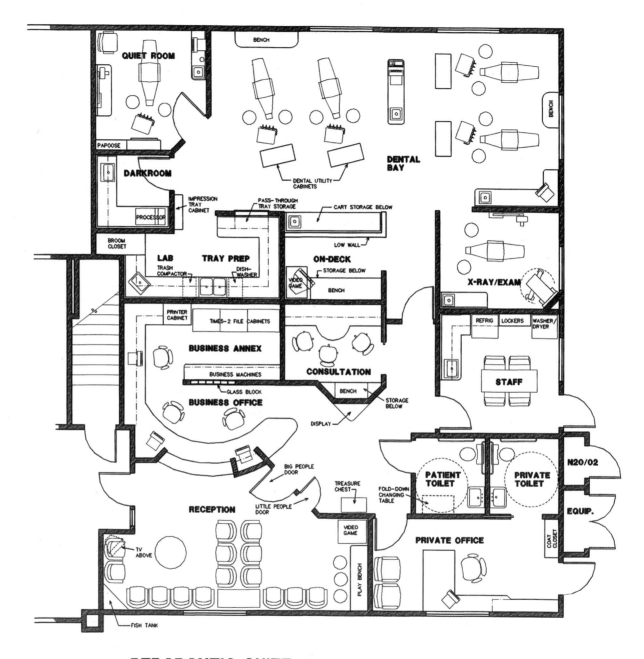

Figure 10-110. Space plan for pedodontics, 2266 square feet. (*Courtesy: T. Michael Hadley & Associates, AIA, Laguna Hills, CA.*)

QUIET ROOM

BENCH

BENCH

PAPOOSE

DARKROOM

DENTAL BAY

IMPRESSION TRAY CABINET

DENTAL UTILITY CABINETS

PASS–THROUGH TRAY STORAGE

CART STORAGE BELOW

PROCESSOR

BROOM CLOSET

LOW WALL

LAB

TRAY PREP

ON-DECK

TRASH COMPACTOR

DISH-WASHER

STORAGE BELOW

X-RAY/EXAM

VIDEO GAME

BENCH

PRINTER CABINET

TIMES-2 FILE CABINETS

REFRIG

LOCKERS

WASHER/DRYER

BUSINESS ANNEX

CONSULTATION

BUSINESS MACHINES

GLASS BLOCK

STAFF

BUSINESS OFFICE

BENCH

STORAGE BELOW

DISPLAY

N20/02

BIG PEOPLE DOOR

TREASURE CHEST

PATIENT TOILET

PRIVATE TOILET

FOLD-DOWN CHANGING TABLE

EQUIP.

RECEPTION

LITTLE PEOPLE DOOR

VIDEO GAME

PRIVATE OFFICE

COAT CLOSET

TV ABOVE

PLAY BENCH

FISH TANK

PEDODONTIC SUITE

2266 SF

Treatment Bay

The pedo chair is a bit smaller than a standard dental chair (Color Plate 38, Figure 10-107). It is common in pediatric dentistry, as in orthodontics, to have the chairs arranged in an open bay. Peer group pressure seems to keep crying to a minimum. The room should have cabinetry, sinks, and other features similar to a general dentist's treatment room, and the room may be gaily decorated with artwork that appeals to children, located where they can see it.

Pediatric dentists use the same dynamic instruments as general dentists. The delivery of instrumentation may be over the patient, from the side, or from the rear. There is no need for natural gas, except in the lab. Inhalation analgesia is fairly common in pedodontic practices. The gases are centrally piped to each chair, generally in the cabinet directly behind the patient's head.

New Technology

Pediatric dentists will have the same high-tech equipment as general dentists: chairside computer and monitor(s), digital X-ray, intraoral cameras, and so forth, discussed in detail previously. A monitor over the child's head, in the ceiling, can be useful to distract them with cartoons, Smile Channel programming for children on dental hygiene, DVD, or videos.

Other Rooms

The suite will require a business office and dental records area; darkroom (optional); panoramic X-ray unit (pan/ceph if interceptive orthodontics are done); storage room; sterilization area; lab; staff lounge; prevention/patient education room; private office; open treatment bay with at least three chairs to be used for examinations, hygiene, and minor treatment on children who are not afraid; and two quiet rooms (generally equipped with intraoral X-ray) as soundproof as possible.

Waiting Room

This room can truly challenge the designer's imagination. It can be as fanciful as a fairy tale. Children get bored very quickly in a conventional waiting room. Therefore, they should be treated to something that captures their imagination and lets them climb around and expend their enormous energies. This has an added benefit: The children will associate a pleasant experience with a visit to the dentist, thus forging what may be a lifelong positive relationship with good dental care.

A built-in toy bin or treasure chest just under the cashier/checkout counter is welcomed by children. While the parent is writing a check or arranging a future appointment, the child is kept amused by selecting a toy. If space permits, a toilet room may be provided in the waiting room area, in addition to the one in the treatment portion of the suite.

ENDODONTICS

This dental specialty is quite different from all the others in that much of the work is emergent in nature. Endodontists deal with the root of the tooth, and, therefore, all their treatment is within the tooth and difficult to see. Numerous working X-rays are taken during treatment to help guide the dentist.

Endodontists usually work four-handed except during surgical procedures, which are often done six-handed. One assistant handles the air, suction, and irrigation and hands instruments to the doctor; the other changes burs (drill bits) on the handpieces, reaches for items, and does the charting. Assistants also clean the room after the procedure and seat the next patient.

Perhaps more than any other specialty, endodontists use an operating microscope (Figure 10-14), the mounting of which is critical to its ease of use. It requires appropriate bracing in the ceiling; minimizing vibration is essential. Refer to the previous discussion of ergonomics, operatory design, operating microscopes, intraoral cameras, and the placement of computers and monitors in the

General Dentistry section. Endodontists are increasingly using a microscope with a high-quality digital camera with video output (often a Nikon), which enables them to see any tooth in great detail (aided by a mirror), and a computer or TV monitor. It provides a better image than an intraoral camera and this can be sent, with a digital X-ray and report, to the referring dentist by e-mail.

The operatory in Figure 10-24, called the *optimal operatory,* works well for an endodontic practice. The two openings in the room are essential since assistants occasionally leave the room during the procedure either to develop X-rays (if film-based) or to bring additional instruments. Sometimes, a third assistant may be present during the procedure to handle a fiber-optic light, if used, although the doctor may wear a fiber-optic headlamp. A solo practitioner would have two treatment operatories with a third one for post-op visits or emergency care; however, the solo practice shown in Figure 10-111 has only two operatories.

An endodontist has an intraoral X-ray unit in each operatory, but there is no need for a panoramic or cephalometric X-ray within the suite. An automatic processor is used for developing some X-rays, but it takes too long to process the working films done during treatment. For those, assistants use a portable chairside developer process, enabling them to develop a single film in 30 seconds, that is, unless they have switched to digital, which provides immediate images on the monitor. Digital imaging has become so widespread that the prior requirement for one darkroom for each dentist, unique to this specialty, will not be addressed. Some endodontists use an electronic device to measure the length of the root canal, thereby reducing the need for working X-rays during treatment. The reader is referred to the General Dentistry section of this chapter for additional discussion of X-ray and darkroom.

Endodontists use a lot of gadgets, perhaps more than any other specialty. In the process of doing routine root canal treatment, the following items are commonly used: an apex locator, an electric torque-control motor, an ultrasonic unit, a touch-n-heat unit, and an Obtura gutta-percha gun (or a System B heat source). These devices are in addition to the normal high- and low-speed handpieces

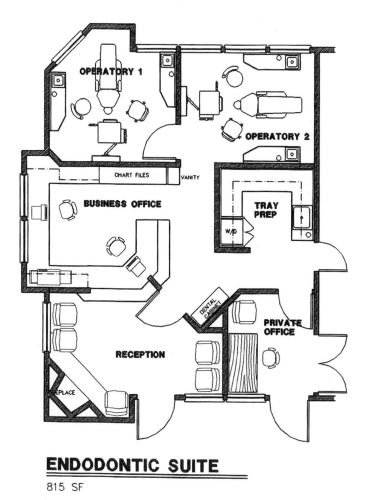

ENDODONTIC SUITE

815 SF

Figure 10-111. Space plan for endodontics, 815 square feet, solo practitioner. Note fireplace in reception room. (*Courtesy: T. Michael Hadley & Associates, AIA, Laguna Hills, CA.*)

and the air/water syringe. Each of these devices has a base and a handpiece that must be easily accessed as well as a separate electrical plug. Therefore, there is a space management issue. This has been addressed by various companies by incorporating all of these devices (including the regular handpieces) into a separate four-wheeled cart.

There is no need for a lab in an endodontic suite. The sterilization area should be designed as discussed under General Dentistry. The other rooms of the suite are similar to those required in general dentistry, including the business office, private office, staff lounge, waiting room, and so forth. There are no special requirements in terms of interior design other than those discussed under General Dentistry. As with any dental operatory, great care should be taken to control infection and follow OSHA guidelines explained in detail previously.

Table 10-4.
Analysis of Program.
Periodontics

No. of Dentists:		1		2
Waiting Room		12 × 14 = 168		14 × 16 = 224
Business Office/Reception		12 × 14 = 168		14 × 16 = 224
Financial Arrangements		10 × 12 = 120		10 × 12 = 120
Office Manager		10 × 12 = 120		10 × 12 = 120
Plaque Control/Hygiene Rooms	3@	9 × 11 = 297	5@	9 × 11 = 495
Surgical Operatories	2@	10 × 12 = 120	4@	10 × 12 = 480
Treatment/Exam		9½ × 11½ = 109	2@	9½ × 11½ = 218
Sterilization		8 × 12 = 96		8 × 12 = 96
Toilets	2@	7 × 8 = 112	3@	7 × 8 = 168
Recovery (Optional)		8 × 10 = 80		8 × 10 = 80
Darkroom (Optional)		6 × 6 = 36		6 × 6 = 36
Staff Lounge		10 × 12 = 120		12 × 12 = 144
Panoramic X-Ray[a]		5 × 8 = 40		5 × 8 = 40
Private Office		8 × 10 = 80	2@	8 × 10 = 160
Storage		6 × 8 = 48		8 × 8 = 64
Housekeeping Room		6 × 6 = 36		6 × 6 = 36
Mechanical Equipment Room		6 × 8 = 48		6 × 8 = 48
Subtotal		1798 ft²		2753 ft²
20% Circulation		360		551
Total		2158 ft²		3304 ft²

[a]May be off site.

PERIODONTICS

Periodontists are dental specialists in oral medicine, the treatment of gum diseases, and the replacement of teeth utilizing dental implants. Some of these procedures involve both soft-tissue and hard-tissue grafting. Plaque control and oral hygiene are the essential components of the periodontal practice for long-term predictable results. This is why periodontic offices may have several treatment rooms dedicated to hygiene and plaque control (Figures 10-112 and 10-113), typically located at the front of the suite so that patients need not walk through the area of the office dedicated to treatment and surgery. In Figure 10-112, hygiene patients, upon exiting, pass the cashier desk and exit through the waiting room. Surgical patients, on the other hand, have a separate circulation path. When exiting, they pass by a cashier/appointment desk and may exit either through the waiting room or, in Figure 10-113, at the rear of the business office.

Periodontic patients on the initial visit, after being examined, may meet with the office manager or treatment coordinator in the consultation room to discuss the course of treatment and make financial arrangements. Sometimes, the doctor discusses treatment options in a consultation room or private office where he or she may sketch the tooth and related tissue to explain to the patient what needs to be done. If the dentist has the CAESY software, the patient can learn more about gum disease and specific procedures by watching selected educational programs.

The suite shown in Figure 10-113 is for a solo practitioner, and that in Figure 10-114 is for two periodontists. A solo practitioner could function with two operatories, one for surgery and one for pre- and post-op examinations as in Figure 10-114; however, Figure 10-113 shows two surgery ops and one treatment/exam room for a solo practitioner. Many periodontists believe that all operatories should be equipped in the same manner, enabling them to do surgical implants in any one of them. Others create a large surgical operatory for performing implant surgery, based on design criteria recommended by Ingvar Branemark, a Swedish physician who pioneered the technique.

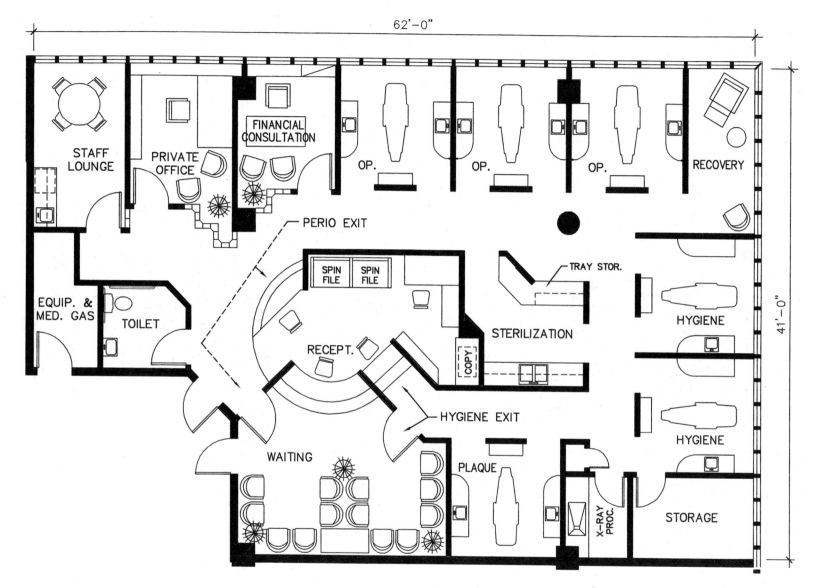

PERIODONTICS SUITE

2270 SF

Figure 10-112. Space plan for periodontics (pre-ADA), 2270 square feet. (*Space planning and design: Jain Malkin Inc.*)

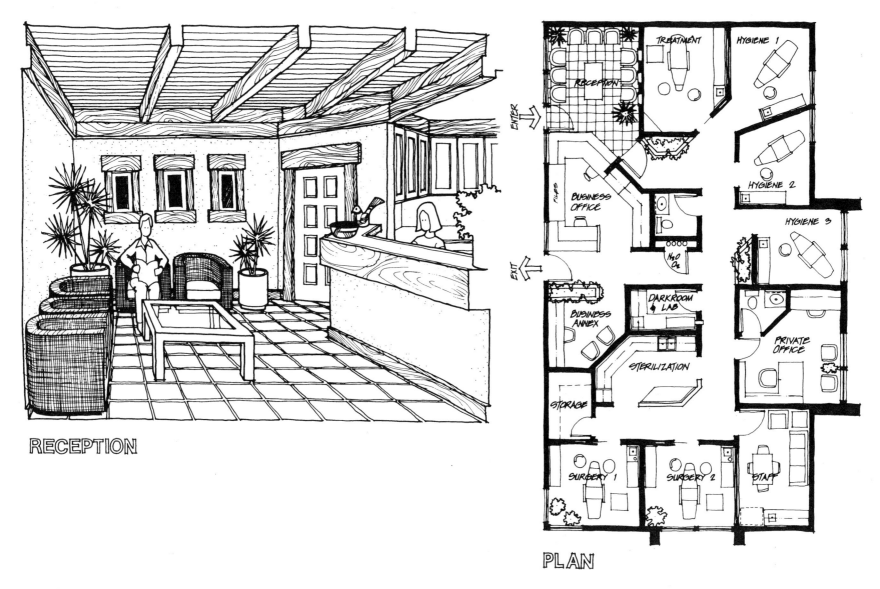

RECEPTION

PLAN

Figure 10-113. Space plan for periodontics (pre-ADA). (*Courtesy: T. Michael Hadley & Associates, AIA, Laguna Hills, CA.*)

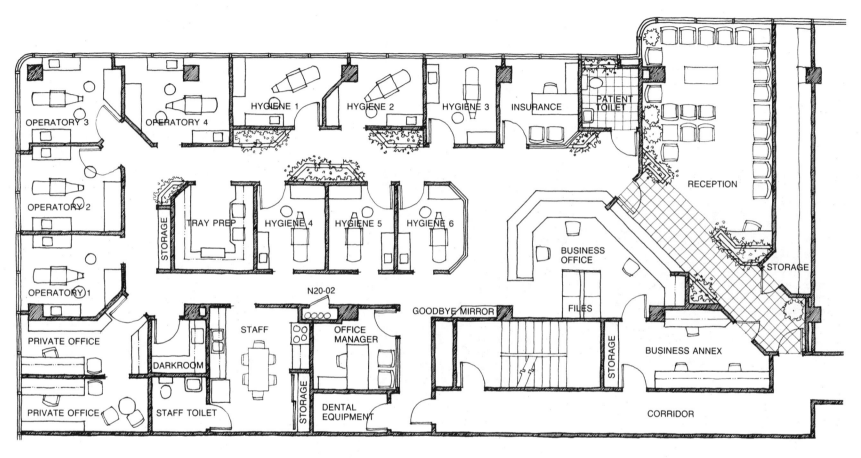

OPERATORY 3
OPERATORY 4
HYGIENE 1
HYGIENE 2
HYGIENE 3
INSURANCE
PATIENT TOILET
RECEPTION
OPERATORY 2
STORAGE
TRAY PREP
HYGIENE 4
HYGIENE 5
HYGIENE 6
BUSINESS OFFICE
STORAGE
OPERATORY 1
N20-02
FILES
PRIVATE OFFICE
GOODBYE MIRROR
STORAGE
BUSINESS ANNEX
STAFF
OFFICE MANAGER
PRIVATE OFFICE
DARKROOM
STORAGE
CORRIDOR
STAFF TOILET
DENTAL EQUIPMENT

PERIODONTICS
3782 SF

Figure 10-114. Space plan for periodontics (pre-ADA), 3782 square feet. (*Courtesy: T. Michael Hadley & Associates, AIA, Laguna Hills, CA.*)

Surgical Operatories

Surgical operatories are designed to meet hospital standards for sterility. Special consideration is given to smooth, cleanable surfaces (walls, floors, and ceilings); cabinets free of ledges to prevent the collection of dust; and an HVAC system that supplies the proper number of air changes per hour. Some doctors will have a scrub area, sterilization/clean utility room, recovery area, and soiled linen/cleanup room to support the surgery room. A dressing area may be required for changing into surgical attire and on-site laundry facilities are an option.

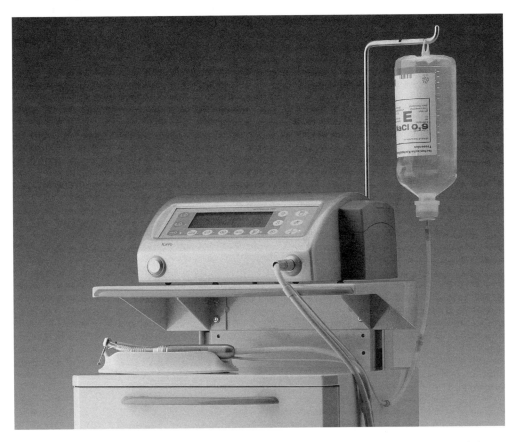

Figure 10-115. Electric surgery unit, INTRAsurg 500. (*Photo courtesy: KaVo America Corporation, Lake Zurich, IL.*)

Operatory Size

A 10-×12-foot room is the minimum for a surgery operatory as it typically involves six-handed dentistry (two assistants) and often involves a third assistant to circulate and bring items to the room during implant procedures. One assistant retracts and handles suction; another handles the instruments, which must be carefully separated as the titanium can be contaminated by the carbon steel instruments.

Blood may be drawn by a trained staff person or a contracted lab tech (phlebotomist) who brings a portable centrifuge, the purpose of which is to obtain autologous growth factor from platelet-rich plasma (PRP). This is added to bone graft material and becomes a gel, which is especially useful for sinus lifts with a bone graft. PRP enhances healing and bone formation.

There are numerous pieces of equipment that must be accommodated in the surgery operatory: a centrifuge for platelet preparation, dynamic handpieces, a laser, intraoral camera, computer and several monitors (explained below), digital X-ray, operating microscope (used by some doctors), and medical gases (N_2O and O_2), usually centrally piped. If intravenous sedation is used, blood pressure, pulse, and respiration must be constantly monitored. All emergency equipment, such as a defibrillator, should be behind the patient, out of view. The doctor may wear a fiber-optic headlamp, which is tethered to a battery pack or to an electrical outlet. If an operating microscope is used, a beam splitter and binocular eyepiece enable the assistant to see what the doctor is seeing. In addition, a video or 35-mm camera can be attached to the microscope.

A special electric surgery handpiece is used when doing implants. The unit is portable and has to sit on something either behind or to the side of the patient (Figure 10-115). It has a stainless steel hook that holds a saline bag. The unit is self-cooled and must be connected to electricity to drive it. In addition, standard handpieces are also used.

The dentist may select over-the-patient, rear, or side delivery of instrumentation. Ideally, the dentist would use rear delivery, and the assistant, working to the left of the patient, would either work off of her own mobile cart or use a dual cart, shared with the doctor. All operatories may be equipped with intraoral X-ray units.

Types of monitors and location alternatives have been discussed in detail under General Dentistry. In this setting, one would be used by the doctor, another by an assistant, and an optional one may be placed where the patient can see it overhead for entertainment and distraction, assuming the patient is not receiving nitrous oxide or other sedation.

HVAC Issues

Although some periodontists pay more attention to this than others, HEPA-filtered air, with the number of air changes required for medical surgery rooms or clean rooms, reduces the possibility of infection. Some doctors install a laminar-flow system to "bathe" the patient in clean air, which is drawn out of the room by return air grilles near the floor.

Surgical Attire

Surgical staff wear scrubs during procedures and typically wear disposable gowns over the scrubs. As has been discussed earlier, OSHA does not allow staff to wear contaminated linen out of the office. Clothes must be changed prior to leaving the office and soiled linen placed in a hamper for laundry pickup. There will be additional linen associated with patient drapes and bibs, which, alternatively, may be disposable. Lockers may be provided for staff street clothes and personal effects; the staff restroom is often used for changing clothes.

The Paperless Office

The paperless office and new technology, including changes in sterilization techniques, have been discussed extensively in the General Dentistry section and, therefore, will not be repeated here. This information applies equally to periodontists.

Other Rooms

All other rooms in the suite are similar to those required for general dentistry, including the business office, staff lounge, private office, and so forth. There are no special considerations with respect to interior design, but if the doctor does a lot of implant surgery, some of those patients will be elderly and may be more comfortable in an office that is calm and relaxing. A small recovery area may be provided with a recliner chair for the occasional patient who requires it (Figure 10-112).

ORAL AND MAXILLOFACIAL SURGERY

Oral and maxillofacial surgeons perform a variety of procedures: dentoalveolar surgery, oral and craniomaxillofacial implant surgery, correction of maxillofacial skeletal deformities, cleft and craniofacial surgery, trauma surgery, TMJ surgery, diagnosis and management of pathologic conditions, reconstructive surgery, and cosmetic maxillofacial surgery.

An oral surgeon's work consists primarily of *diagnosis* and *surgery.* On a patient's initial visit, a diagnosis will be made. Then the patient will be scheduled for surgery. However, the patient is often referred for surgery without a prior consultation. A medical history must be taken for each patient or filled out in advance. Some oral surgeons prefer to have the staff member take the patient history, perhaps in a private area in the business office, while others accomplish this in the consultation room. Most allow patients to complete their medical history while seated in the waiting room, using a clipboard. Similarly, some oral surgeons prefer to give postoperative instructions in the recovery room, while others like the patient and family members to sit near the front of the office to accomplish this prior to exiting.

Some oral surgeons use a consultation/patient education room located near the front of the suite to explain procedures to patients and to review X-rays (Figures 10-116 and 10-117). Depending on individual needs, the room may have a table or desk, a computer and monitor, a dental chair, and a cabinet with sink.

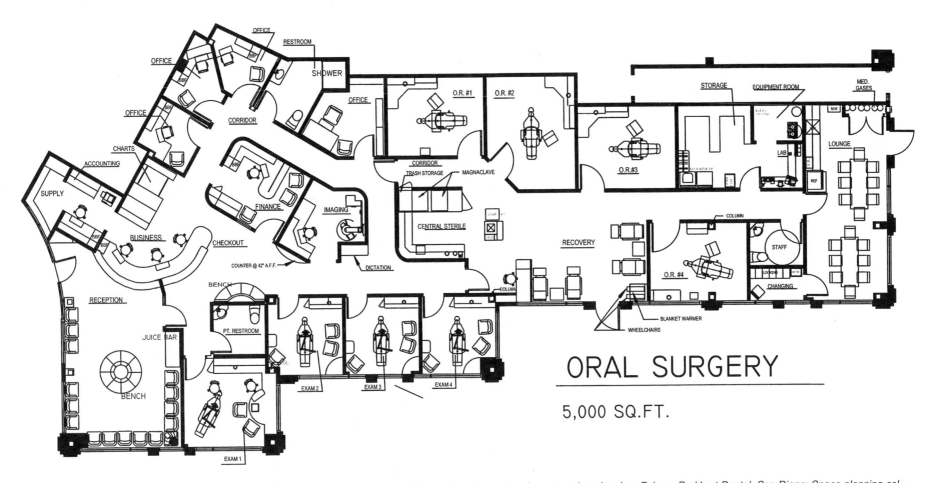

Figure 10-116. Space plan for oral surgery group practice, 5000 square feet. (*Space planning and equipment engineering: Lee Palmer, Burkhart Dental, San Diego; Space planning collaboration/interior design: Janet Pettersen, IIDA, DesignWave, Fallbrook, CA.*)

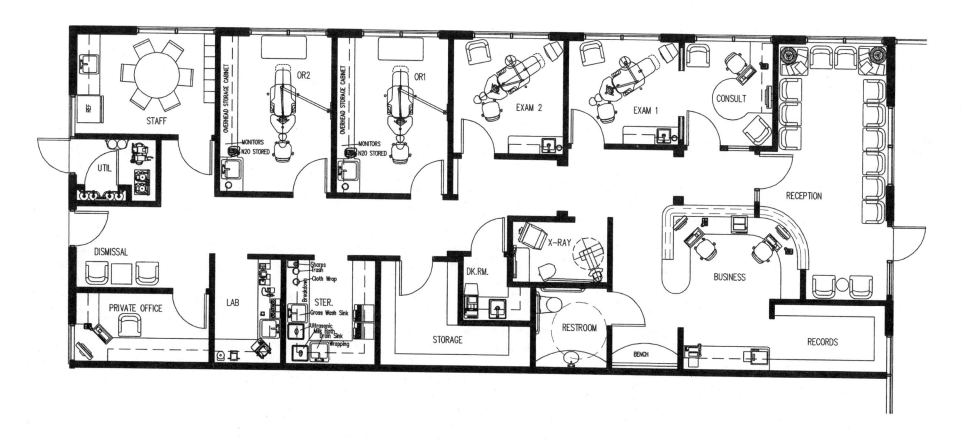

ORAL SURGERY PRACTICE (SOLO)
2077 SF

Figure 10-117. Space plan for solo oral and maxillofacial surgery, 2077 square feet. (*Space planning and equipment engineering: Lee Palmer, Burkhart Dental, San Diego; Interior design: Janet Pettersen, IIDA, DesignWave, Fallbrook, CA.*)

For a solo practitioner, two treatment rooms will suffice for examination and diagnosis, and may be used for post-operative procedures and checkups, as well. One or both of these rooms will be equipped for taking intraoral X-rays, although this may be done in a central imaging room as in Figures 10-116 and 10-118. In addition, there is an alcove for a panoramic/cephalometric X-ray unit unless located in the central room. A darkroom should be located near these treatment rooms if digital X-ray is not used. If these rooms are located at the front of the suite near the waiting room, only surgical patients need enter the rear. Ideally, traffic would be separated so that the exam/diagnosis/X-ray functions are near the front of the suite, and the doctors' private offices, sterilization, recovery, and surgical operatories are at the rear of the suite, perhaps with an exit for postoperative patients, so they don't have to walk through the waiting room (Figures 10-116 and 10-118).

A solo practitioner would generally have two surgical operatories in addition to the two exam/diagnosis treatment rooms (Figure 10-117). A larger suite for three oral surgeons, where no more than two are practicing simultaneously, is shown in Figure 10-116. Typically, such a suite would have four surgical operatories, four exam/treatment rooms, a small lab, two or three recovery beds, a staff lounge, a good-sized reception/business office, and a large sterilization area.

Some oral surgeons do not have a lab; others have a small one. If the suite lacks space for a dedicated equipment room, the air compressor and vacuum can be located in the lab.

Flow to Surgery

Practices vary in how they handle the flow to surgery, in terms of where they administer anesthesia. Some may do it in a prep area, then roll the patient into the operatory and back to the recovery area; others will administer anesthesia in the operatory. It is not uncommon for oral surgeons to administer general anesthesia as most have a general anesthesia permit and, in fact, oral surgeons occasionally have a medical degree as well as a dental degree.

X-Ray

Oral surgeons generally have X-ray machines in the pre-op exam rooms. In addition, an alcove for a pan/ceph X-ray is located near the front of the suite or examination area. A frequent oversight is lack of wheelchair access to the panoramic, and also intraoral, X-ray units.

Surgical Operating Rooms

Oral surgeons usually work eight-handed, using three assistants. One assistant handles the suction and retraction, another stabilizes the patient's head and manages the airway, while a third assistant circulates to bring instruments needed during the procedure. The doctor often wears a fiber-optic headlamp for additional illumination. It is tethered to a battery pack or electrical outlet that must be properly located to avoid neck strain. This outlet must be on the emergency power system in case of a blackout.

Surgical operatories are generally large, 10×14 or 12×14 feet in size. Many oral surgeons like the room designed with a full wall of base cabinets behind the patient's head or to the side, on a long wall. There is a large sink, outlets for oxygen and nitrous oxide, an open area for storing the anesthesia cart, and perhaps an area for storing the assistant's mobile cart. There are a number of electrical outlets that must be properly located. The sink has foot-pedal controls or wrist-action faucets for scrub. Other equipment in the room includes a pulse oximeter, an automatic blood pressure machine, and an ECG monitor, which may be combined in two compact stacked units (Figure 10-119). A defibrillator is also required. All these items may even be combined in one unit now. The assistant, whether working off of a mobile cart from the rear or using side delivery, needs suction.

Some oral surgeons use compressed nitrogen to drive high-speed surgical handpieces because it is a pure propellant, delivering very high, constant pressure. An electric surgery unit is an option to nitrogen-powered hand-

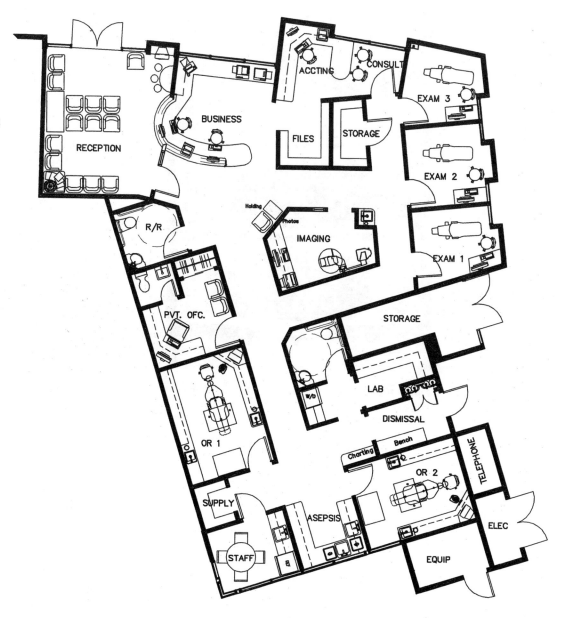

Figure 10-118. Space plan for solo oral and maxillofacial surgery, 2077 square feet. (*Space planning and equipment engineering: Lee Palmer, Burkhart Dental, San Diego, CA.*)

RECEPTION

BUSINESS

ACCTING

CONSULT

EXAM 3

FILES

STORAGE

EXAM 2

R/R

Holding

Photos

IMAGING

EXAM 1

PVT. OFC.

STORAGE

LAB

W/b

DISMISSAL

OR 1

Charting

Bench

TELEPHONE

OR 2

SUPPLY

ASEPSIS

ELEC

STAFF

EQUIP

ORAL SURGERY PRACTICE

2424 SF

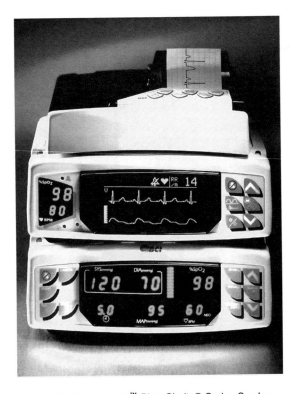

Figure 10-119. *Autocorr™ Plus,* Clarity® Series Combo, Pulse Oximeter/ECG/BP Monitor. (*Photo courtesy: BCI, Inc., Waukesha, WI.*)

pieces and is always used with implant surgery. Compressed air is generally used only to drive handpieces in the lab. The doctor may use a Mayo stand to hold the instrument tray or may work off of a mobile cart or a table that slides over the patient's chest.

Medical gases must be piped into the room through degreased, sealed copper tubing (using only silver solder) to a flow meter in each surgery. Building and fire codes are very strict regarding where and how medical gases are stored. The reader is referred to the General Dentistry section of this chapter for further discussion of this topic.

Oral surgeons may use a power procedure chair (Figure 10-120), an operating table, or occasionally, a standard dental chair with an armboard attachment for administering intravenous sedation. Oral surgeons often work standing up but this is not universal, so the chair must be able to be raised to the proper height. A resuscitation cart is nearby and close to electrical outlets to enable emergency equipment to be used immediately. Surgical operatories should have a nurse call buzzer.

A surgical light in the operatory is needed and should be easy to manipulate (Figure 10-121). It needs good color-rendition lamps for skin tones and a high color rendering index (refer to Chapter 13 and also Lighting under General Dentistry).

Recovery

Before planning an oral surgery suite, the space planner must determine how the doctor transfers patients from the operatory to the recovery area. Many oral surgeons walk patients with assistance, others use a wheelchair, and some may even use an operating room–type gurney. The patient may remain on the gurney in the recovery room or may be transferred to a recovery bed. Sometimes oral surgeons do long, complicated procedures in a hospital or an ambulatory surgical center, rather than in the office. If a gurney is used to transfer patients, then surgical operatories, corridors, and recovery rooms have to be large enough to accommodate maneuvering. In addition, a

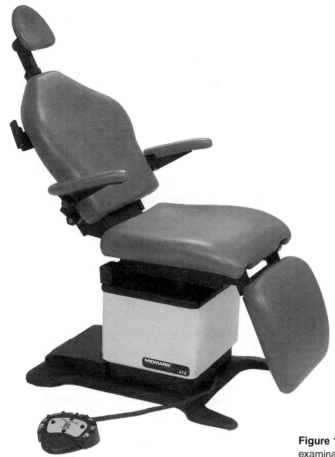

Figure 10-121. Dual halogen minor surgery light, Ritter® model 355; lamp has 4200K color temperature; provides 4000 fc at 36-inch focal length and 6200 fc at 24-inch focal length. (*Photo courtesy: Midmark Corporation, Versailles, OH.*)

Figure 10-120. Power procedure examination chair allows maximum access to head and neck for oral and maxillofacial surgery; available with a number of accessories, such as IV pole, armboard attachments, and an attached instrument tray. (*Photo courtesy: Midmark Corporation, Versailles, OH.*)

place to store the gurney or wheelchair is required. Consideration must also be given to access by paramedics to enter the suite, use the elevator, and evacuate a patient in an emergency. Note that patients from skilled nursing facilities often arrive on gurneys; therefore, it may be desirable to use 3½-foot doors on surgery operatories.

Alternatively, the patient may be allowed to recover in the surgery room while the staff are cleaning it up, or the patient may be walked to a recliner chair (Figure 10-116). If a recovery area is provided, there should also be a place for a companion to sit, a hook or locker for personal items, a toilet nearby, and a rear, private exit so that the patient does not have to pass through the waiting room after surgery. A certain amount of privacy should be provided for each recovering patient, either by fixed partitions or by a cubicle curtain. The recovery area must be located so that the staff can always observe patients while going about their cleanup and other duties.

Provision for oxygen delivery must be considered as well as appropriately located electrical outlets for monitoring equipment. Some oral surgeons may want centrally piped oxygen and suction in the recovery area.

Sterilization

The sterilization area for an oral surgery practice would not differ from that described under General Dentistry except that an area for storing clean linen and surgical supplies is required, as is a holding area for soiled linen, which should not be in the sterilization room.

Utilities

These have been discussed in detail under General Dentistry but a few additional comments are required. For obvious reasons, emergency back-up electrical power must be provided, adequate to enable the surgeon to complete the procedure. If on the ground floor, a diesel-powered generator may be used or, on an upper floor, a high-capacity battery back-up. Digital X-ray and computers should also be connected to it. This generator is about the size of a washing machine and needs good ventilation as it produces heat.

Another issue, relevant to HVAC, is that the surgical operatories should be zoned to be cooler than the rest of the office. A blanket warmer to comfort patients can be located in the sterilization area or prep workroom. Refer to Periodontics for a discussion of air filtration to reduce infection.

Regulatory Agency Review

Oral surgery suites are usually built to AAAHC (Accreditation Association for Ambulatory Health Care) or JCAHO (Joint Commission on Accreditation of Healthcare Organizations) standards, both of which are quite rigorous. JCAHO accredited its first oral surgery practice in March 2001 under its ambulatory-care voluntary accreditation program. The use of general anesthesia—usually conscious sedation—triggers a variety of fire and life safety codes that have become far more stringent even in the past year. This has been explained in great detail in Chapter 7 as well as in Chapter 4 under Plastic Surgery. Consult the Index for other listings such as "office-based surgery."

Other Rooms

A staff lounge is important due to the demanding nature of the work. The private office may be small, since patients usually do not enter. It is a place for the doctor to read mail, return phone calls, and take a break between procedures. The suite should contain at least two toilet rooms and a storage room. Due to the nature of the procedures, the volume of patients is low, so neither the business office nor the waiting room need be large, but remember that most patients arrive with at least one other person, and sometimes two. As with any surgical specialty, the office should be conservatively furnished using relaxing colors and avoiding flamboyance or frivolity. The surgeon's image should be that of a serious person, skilled and successful at his or her profession.

Consult the reference guide at the end of the General Dentistry section for links to other chapters of the book that may be of interest to dentists such as lighting, color, and interior design.

SUMMARY

Much has changed in the practice of dentistry in the last 10 years, causing many dentists to want to renovate their offices. Computers and monitors in dental treatment rooms enable patients to more fully understand their dental conditions and treatment options. Concern about infection control has mandated new criteria for sterilization of instruments. Consumers are more educated about healthcare and, in turn, are more selective about the professionals in whom they place their trust. Dentists, increasingly concerned about marketing, are engaging designers with special expertise in dental planning to help them create a functional office with an image that will appeal to their patients.

CHAPTER 11

Impact of Color on the Medical Environment

INTRODUCTION TO COLOR THEORY

In early civilizations, man made color holy. He saw intimations of life's mysteries in the spectrum, and assigned it power—so that each color became emblematic of divine forces in a world that so integrated art, ritual, and myths with everyday life that each was suffused with the other. Color was a language in itself; hieroglyphic paintings of vibrant blues, reds, greens, and purples could be interpreted as clearly as words are today. Recent comparative cultural studies have shown similar symbolic uses of color among peoples who could not possibly have had contact with one another. Birren,* a noted color historian, has reported that the points of the compass in China, for example, were represented by black for north, white for west, red for south, and green for east, and that the people of ancient Ireland and also the Indians of North America used identical designations.

Now the old myths have been dismissed as superstition; color has been stripped of its early and specific symbolism; we can no longer precisely "read" a color painting. It is the task of psychologists and mythologists to plumb the depths of the human consciousness from which came those primal myths, and from which our dreams still come, so that we may arrive at a greater knowledge of our common inner life. It is also important to learn how color has always held humankind in its sway—so much so that we hallucinate color if deprived of it too long—and most important, to gauge scientifically its specific influences upon our behavior. The color gold no longer carries the power of the Egyptian sun-god, but research indicates that its perception does have an effect upon the entire human organism, not only the optic nerve. And the implications of this—the differentiated influences of colors, real and measurable—are manifold in regard to environmental design and just beginning to be recognized.

The history of color theory and research is long and variegated, with most of the early work done by philosophers and artists. Aristotle was the first to pose a systematic theory of color, one that is no longer considered relevant. In the early part of the eighteenth century, the German poet Goethe expressed his views on color harmony and the symbolic values of color in his book, *Farbenlehre.* The most obvious weakness of Goethe's work was that of most color studies before the twentieth century; he dealt with hues, failing to consider saturation and brightness. Nevertheless, he did make an observation that—scores of studies and tests later—has been accepted as valid: that red, yellow, and orange—longer-wavelength colors at the warm end of the spectrum—are exciting and "advancing" colors; they seem to come toward one and draw one out, while blue, green, and purple—shorter wavelength colors at the cool end of the spectrum—are "retreating" colors and induce a more quieting, inward-drawing response.

Artists have had their own theories of color and its effect, and they have often been penetrating and insightful, but always based on one person's trial and error, or impression,

---

*Faber Birren, *Light, Color and Environment,* Van Nostrand Reinhold, New York, 1969.

rather than vigorous scientific investigation. Nineteenth-century artist Odilon Redon made dazzling explorations into color. Other artists famous for their research in color theory include Paul Klee, Wasily Kandinsky, and Josef Albers. Dozens of others—among the more well known are Munsell, Ostwald, Chevreul, Bezold, and Wundt—toward the close of the nineteenth century and the beginning of the twentieth, postulated color theories and laws of harmony along less subjective lines than the often empirical studies of the artists. In the first quarter of the twentieth century, investigators even began testing color preferences for many different groups of people.

COLOR PREFERENCE TESTS

The obstacles confronting all of these color preference enthusiasts, however, were considerable: Color samples were not yet standardized, nor were their backgrounds, nor the light of their viewing conditions similarly controlled. Furthermore, there is difficulty inherent in any test of color and "affect," or feeling—since an individual does not respond to a hue as pure color, but as something that evokes myriad and unique associations with objects and with experiences, which are psychological processes that resist measurement. It is hardly surprising, then, that in 1925 one well-known researcher reviewed the mass of contradictory preference findings in his own and others' studies and declared that all hope of finding consistent reactions to color would have to be abandoned.

It was not. In the 75 years since that pessimistic dictum, a great variety of studies on color responses has been conducted. The number of color preference studies—on normal people, mentally disabled people, psychotics, males, females, the old, the young, in all parts of the world—is probably equal to the total of all other studies on "color and affect" combined. While the findings are often contradictory, certain agreement has been reached among numerous investigators. The difficulty in testing for color preference lies in not being able to control the many variables. Too many articles have been published on the results of market research, and these findings represent current fads rather than scientific investigation. Many of the "conclusions" extracted from these spurious studies are either obvious or dubious.

Color preferences develop as a reaction to culture, education, experience, and genetics. People see the world in different ways and process the environment according to their own needs and drives. Thus, it has been postulated that there is a relationship between a person s color responses and his or her emotional state. But it is difficult to test reactions to color because so much depends on the subject's verbal assessment of what he or she sees, and colors are so symbolic, carrying highly personal connotations. If, as a child, a person had always been punished in a blue room, that person may dislike blue as an adult. Therefore, any studies of color preference on "normal" subjects must be based on large samples so that individual biases due to highly personal experiences do not bias the results of the study, which may have been designed to test cultural color preferences, age color preferences, or some variable other than pathologically based color preferences or aversions. There is also the physiological problem that people often do not see a color alike. One person may see a dark green as having more yellow; another may see it as having more blue.

Because the color preferences of adults are so much a result of learning, many researchers have preferred to work with children to minimize the effects of learning and experience. Various studies have corroborated that young children prefer the warm, exciting colors of red and yellow, but when they get older they prefer cool colors—blues and greens—as they become less impulsive and more reflective and intellectual.

The researcher Ellis, however, noted in primitive societies a continuing preference for the brilliant hues of red and yellow from childhood into adulthood—and hypothesized that "the apparent trend away from yellow as a revered color among early Greeks and Romans was largely due to the taboo placed upon it by the Christian church, as the symbol of sin and gaiety." Another researcher in the preference field, T. R. Garth, conducted tests among children of six different groups—white, Black, American Indian, Filipino, Japanese, and Mexican—and found that the preference differences were minimal among them; he concluded that the differences that do appear in adulthood are due to factors related to nurturing.

Eysenck, in a critical review of numerous other color preference studies conducted all over the world, and also of his own experiments, concluded that there is a high degree of agreement among investigators, and that a general order of preference is as follows: blue, red, green, violet, orange, and yellow. He furthermore concluded that there are no sex differences, apart from a slight preference among women for yellow over orange, and among men for orange over yellow.

How can such uniformity of color preference be explained? Researchers Guilford and Smith have attributed it to innate biological factors, while others have emphasized the role of culture, learning, and experience. The truth probably lies in a balance between the two, a combination of innate and cultural factors. In other words, it is not yet known exactly what determines color preferences, only that a marked similarity does exist among all peoples.

COLOR-FORM PREFERENCE

In child-development evaluation, various color-form preference categorization tests are among the most often used measures of the abstraction phenomenon—that ability to single out specific elements from a pattern on the basis of similar factors. The classic color-form preference of measure has been used mainly with young children, and it has demonstrated that most children reach the peak of color dominance around four and a half, that the median age of transition from color to form dominance is five, and that form dominance is usually established by the age of nine.

The Rorschach inkblot method has also been used, with its results consistently showing that pure color responses dominate among young children; color-form dominates in the older child; and from late childhood through adolescence and adulthood, form-color responses dominate. Explanations for the color-form dominance phenomenon include maturation, increased personality differentiation from the affective to the intellectual, increased meaningfulness of the environment in terms of utility, less concern for primitive characteristics, increased verbal skills, and introduction to reading and writing.

Furthermore, since 90 percent of the adult population is form-dominant, color-dominant persons have been considered deviates. One of the most commonly held theories is that since color is a primitive response, the adult color-dominant personality is impulsive, immature, egocentric, and less intelligent than his or her form-dominant and therefore mature, socially adjusted peers. Children who retain their color dominance after classmates have switched over, therefore, are considered regressive and are subjected to academic and cultural programs to change their orientation.

What is interesting, however, is that some recent studies of creativity have indicated that the color-oriented child is more likely to emerge as an artistic, creative adult, far more innovative than his or her form-dominant peers, who will tend to deal well with analytical work in the traditional mold. One of the ingredients of that creative ability is to be free of that mold, to see with fresh eyes and envision new relationships, untried combinations. If further studies support this theory, then it will be clear that a disservice has been done to those who have not fit the conventional mold, and who should be encouraged in their different way rather than pressed into a constricting and uniform shape.

One of the most interesting tests concerned with the connection between specific colors and emotion in children was performed by Alschuler and Hattwick at the University of Chicago. Noting that preschool children express themselves generally at the abstract, nonrepresentational level and reveal more of their affective lives than older children, they studied the expressive outlets of two-, three-, and four-year-old children in easel painting, crayons, clay, blocks, and dramatic play over an extended period of time. They concluded that color gave the clearest insights into the child's emotional life. Color preferences and color patterns gave clues to the child's emotional orientation. *Red,* found to be the most emotionally toned color, carried associations of both affection and love as well as aggression and hate. *Blue* was associated with drives toward control.

COLOR AND MENTAL DISORDERS

A variety of color tests—among them the Rorschach and the color pyramid test, devised by Swiss psychologist Max Pfister in 1950—are used as diagnostic tools in determining normality/abnormality. Because so many tests involving color preference, response, and placement have been performed on the mentally and emotionally ill, with such a plethora of conflicting results, it is clear that the data must be interpreted cautiously and in conjunction with those from other tests. The most abused area here is probably preference, as some have not hesitated to link preference for specific colors to specific disorders, in irresponsible and unproven attribution. Eric P. Mosse, as quoted in Birren, reveals:

> We generally found in hysterical patients, especially in psychoneuroses with anxiety states, a predilection for green as symbolizing the mentioned escape mechanism.... Red is the color of choice of the hypomaniac patient giving the tumult of his emotions their "burning" and "bloody" expression. And we don't wonder that melancholia and depression reveal themselves through a complete "blackout." Finally, we see yellow as the color of schizophrenia.... This yellow is the proper and intrinsic color of the morbid mind. Whenever we observe its accumulative appearance, we may be sure we are dealing with a deep-lying psychotic disturbance.

Birren, a noted color historian, disagrees. "Yellow may be looked upon as an intellectual color associated both with

great intelligence and mental deficiency." He claims that schizophrenics prefer blue. The contradictions are legion. A study done by Warner, in which 300 patients were tested, including diagnosed anxiety neurotics, catatonic schizophrenics, manics, and depressives, found in most cases no significant correlation of preference with psychiatric disorders.

How does the Rorschach contribute to clinical diagnosis? Rorschach's hypothesis was that color responses are measures of the affective, or emotional, state, and he noted that neurotics are subject to "color shock" (rejection), as manifested in a delayed reaction time when presented with a color blot. He also stated that red evoked the shock response in neurotics more often than did other colors. Schizophrenics also suffer color shock when presented with the chromatic or color cards (following the black and white cards) of the Rorschach. Birren postulates that color may represent an unwanted intrusion into their inner life.

In the realm of color research, however, nothing goes uncontested, and the Rorschach is no exception. Two major criticisms of it are the lack of work with normal subjects as a criterion against which pathological groups could be compared, and also the basic postulate that the way in which a person responds to color in inkblots reflects his or her typical mode of dealing with, or integrating, affect. In fact, researchers Cerbus and Nichols, in trying to replicate Rorschach's findings, found no correlation between color responsiveness and impulsivity, and no significant difference in use of color by neurotics, schizophrenics, and normals. Nevertheless, the weight of evidence still favors the Rorschach color-affect theory.

Color and Depression

Almost unanimous agreement exists regarding the depressive's total lack of interest in color. However, some studies indicate that depressed people prefer dark colors of low saturation, and others claim they prefer bright, deeply saturated colors. Probably both conclusions are accurate, since color can be either a stimulant or compensation for lack of excitement and dreariness as well as a reflection of one's inner state.

Seen in another manner, the depressive's attraction for bright colors may be an expression of homeostasis—the organism's subconscious striving for balance or equilibrium.

Compton Fabric Preference Test

Another test done with the mentally ill that deserves mention is the Compton fabric preference test. Sharpe* reports that Compton tested the fabric and design preferences of a group of hospitalized psychotic women, in terms of the relationship between concepts of body, image boundary, penetration of boundary, and clothing preference. It was anticipated that persons with mental and emotional problems would be likely to suffer some aberrated form of body image, and it was found that persons with weak body boundaries tended to reinforce them with fabrics of strong figure-ground contrasts and brighter, more highly saturated colors—thus allowing them to feel less vulnerable to penetration, in a sense armored by the "strength" of the color and pattern.

BIOLOGICAL EFFECTS OF COLOR

At the dawn of civilization, color was a biological necessity for locating food and observing predators. It is nature's survival kit for plants and animals—it attracts, camouflages, and protects them. Today color permeates our entire existence. Every aspect of our life involves color: Traffic is directed by color; instrument panels are regulated by color; electrical wires are color coded; advertising is printed in color; medicines and capsules are in color; office file folders have colored tabs; clothing has color; uniforms have color; the list is infinite.

---

*Deborah T. Sharpe, *The Psychology of Color and Design*, Nelson Hall, Chicago, 1974, p. 71.

Biological or physiological reactions to color are the most susceptible to testing and the most valuable from a pragmatic point of view, particularly in relation to design. Kurt Goldstein, a highly regarded researcher, attributes the ambiguity of so much research on color to the fact that the tests were not performed from a "biological point of view"; for color, he has stated, affects the behavior of the entire organism.

Goldstein is criticized primarily for having worked with a small sample of brain-damaged people, but he presumes—and later studies appear to support his position —that these sensations occur in "normals" also, but are brought to the fore in extremely sensitive persons, such as artists, or in psychotics or neurotics. One of his most famous examples of color and effect is that of a woman who had cerebellar disease and resultant disturbance of equilibrium; when she wore a red dress, her symptoms increased to the point of her falling down.

Other effects of *red* that Goldstein noted in other patients were myopic refraction, abnormal deviation of the arms when held out from the body, errors in cutaneous localization, and again, increased loss of equilibrium. In all of these cases, *green* had the opposite effect, that of reducing the already present abnormal conditions. Goldstein states, "The stronger deviation of the arms in red stimulation corresponds to the experience of being disrupted, thrown out, abnormally attracted to the outer world." Green stimulation resulted in withdrawal from the outer world and meditation.

Goldstein also noted a large variety of differential motor reactions displayed by his patients under the effects of red and green. Movements executed with the same intention were performed much more exactly in green than in red light; handwriting, for example, was nearer to normal with green ink than with red. And estimates of length, as well as weight and time, were better under green light than red.

Other investigators have noted that blood pressure and respiration increased during exposure to red light, but decreased in blue illumination. Red light has been said to reduce the pain of rheumatism and arthritis. It dilates the blood vessels and produces heat in the tissues. Birren postulates that the red color of mercurochrome may be effective in the healing of wounds due to its absorption of blue light. Blue light aids headaches and lowers blood pressure, and its tranquilizing effect may even aid insomniacs. Blue light is currently used with high success in the treatment of jaundice — bilirubinemia — in newborns. Yellow has been said to stimulate the appetite and to raise low blood pressure associated with anemia.

Finally, supporting the work of Goldstein and others, tests done with GSR (galvanic skin response, commonly called the lie-detector test) produced significant relationships between GSR and the colors that have been rated high in excitatory value, mainly reds and yellows.

COLOR AND PERSONALITY

Another major area of color research has focused on the interaction between color and personality. Many of these "tests" take the form of informal questionnaires in popular magazines — both irresponsible and exploitative. More serious tests include the Rorschach inkblot, and the color-form tests discussed previously. Although color has been associated with personal characteristics since antiquity, it was not until the publication of the Rorschach, in Switzerland in 1921, that a systematic exploration of the relationship between color responses and personality, or emotional pattern, was begun.

In Germany in the mid-1930s, Jaensch developed a personality-type theory correlating "systems of emotion" with "systems of color vision." Jaensch began by observing that in daylight vision there is increased sensitivity for red and yellow, and in twilight vision there is increased sensitivity for green and blue. He went on to classify individuals according to their predominance of warm or cold vision systems.

Persons of the "warm color type" supposedly meet the external world with warm feelings; those of the "cold color type" are closed off from their surroundings and inwardly integrated. Before puberty, Jaensch asserted, most individuals are of the "outward integration" type, but in maturity the distinction between Nordic and Mediterranean types appears: Nordic being of the cold system, Mediterranean of the warm. As spurious as Jaensch's theories seem, they have not been universally repudiated by those concerned with color research. Birren, noted author of dozens of books and articles on color, corroborates Jaensch's findings but substitutes "blond complexion type" for Nordic and "brunet" for Mediterranean, perhaps to make the "theory" seem more universal. Whatever the label, such notions seem far too generalized to be taken seriously.

Others have recognized the potential for opportunism and exploitation in color, since it strikes the public imagination, and its maze of contradictory research offers "scientific findings" to support practically any theory or commercial gimmick. In 1969, a book appeared by Max Luscher called the *Luscher Color Test,* which subsequently reached the ranks of the best-seller list, and which relates the various personality characteristics to a person's ranking of several series of colors. The reader is led to believe that through these projective devices he or she can determine his or her personality structure, his or her strengths or weaknesses, within just a few minutes.

Some believe that this kind of instrument, used in conjunction with many others, can be useful; others question any validity. What is inarguable, however, is that the *Luscher Color Test,* issued as a popular test, is grossly misleading, although Luscher's test seems to be highly regarded by many professionals in the field. His book, *The 4-Color Person,* tantalizes readers of the September 1979 *House & Garden* with an "intriguing color quiz" [sic], which promises to reveal the key to the reader's "four dominant feelings of self — self-confidence, self-respect, self-satisfaction, and self-development." Various categories (furniture, modern art, music, architecture, etc.) of preference are listed. Upon scoring the quiz, the reader becomes aware that the four preference choices of each category have been related to red, yellow, blue, or green, depending on the assumed "affect" qualities of each color. Thus, a preference for a "mobile by Calder" registers a point for yellow (self-development, imagination, independence); a preference for "Chopin," a point for blue (romance, trust, love, and peace); a taste for "cymbidium orchids" rates a point for green (self-respect, responsibility, persistence); and a preference for "riding a bike" over "joining a car pool" rates a red (passion, vitality, self-confidence).

Such personality quizzes are too simplistic and do not take into account those who have broad interests and diverse tastes. A gardener, for example, might prefer cymbidium orchids over daisies, because he or she has a greenhouse and has had good luck with that plant. Sometimes the questions on these tests are ridiculous: Would you rather read a book to a sick friend, eat in an Italian restaurant, or go dancing? Do you prefer filet mignon, duck flambé, imported cheeses, or homemade soup? Do you prefer florals, geometrics, or batik fabrics? A sophisticated person may like all of the choices equally depending on the proper context. Such examples of popularized color theory are analogous to newspaper astrology. Home-decorating magazines frequently carry articles that offer such illuminating clues to one's inner life as, "If you like red, you are a strong personality with a craving for action, and are compatible not only with other reds but 'sun yellow' and 'wild iris.'"

Researchers have even hypothesized that people express their personalities through the clothes they wear. Sharpe reports, "An overview of the research suggests that the more *secure* individual tends to favor colors that range from neutral to cool (green, blue, beige and gray), of medium value tending toward dull, whereas the more *insecure* individual tends to select warm, bright colors (red, yellow) that range from the extremes of light and dark."*

Such generalizations are narrow since they overlook many obvious reasons people dress as they do (education, upbringing, climate, budget, artistic expression, professional impact) and do not take into account the many people for whom clothing is completely unimportant, or those who economically cannot afford to express themselves sartorially, or that large group of people who wear anything that is "fashionable" at the moment regardless of whether it suits them. Perhaps those to whom clothing is unimportant are secure, since their self-image is not dependent on others' visual assessment of them. Those who cannot afford to buy the clothes they might like to buy may fall anywhere along the secure-insecure scale. Those who must continually buy and wear what is fashionable at the moment perhaps are the most insecure, since this expresses a strong desire to be accepted and to conform. Thus it seems that clothing is not a valid indicator of personality: There are too many variables.

COLOR AND HARMONY

In the last two decades, many of the old color taboos have been lifted, and the archaic "laws" have become obsolete—especially that of *complementary* colors (mainly, those diametrically opposite one another on the spectrally ordered color wheel)—as the only basis for color harmony. According to traditional colorists, complementary colors equaled harmony equaled balance; the modern school of colors added: noncomplementary colors equaled asymmetry equaled tension.

But adherence to such rigid formulas began to give way in the 1960s, when the color revolution, paralleling others, exploded in bursts of psychedelic light, furthering a lasting acceptance of a vastly wider range of color combinations, as well as more vivid, brilliant color. The psychedelic movement helped to create among designers a more eclectic approach, one that accepts the dictates of neither school but rather relies on creating the color environment most appropriate to the specific situation, taking into account the size of the space, its architectural form, the proposed use of the space, age of the occupants, natural light, and the tasks to be performed there.

Color harmony is not just a function of the relationship of hues but depends largely on the quantity of color, the intensity, balance, and weight. Certain color combinations create tension or movement. The goal of color is not always harmony; sometimes it is used to excite, stimulate, manipulate, create tension, or expand or contract a space.

---

*Sharpe, ibid., p. 69.

THE COLOR WHEEL

The old color wheel (Color Plate 39, Figure 11-1), based on arbitrary paint-mixing color qualities, has been replaced by a new color wheel (Color Plate 39, Figure 11-2) in which colors are based on the true color perception qualities of vision. The new color wheel has additional advantages in that it is accurate in explaining subtractive, additive, and partitive color mixing. Thus, in the new color wheel, the complement of yellow is blue, not violet. The complement of green is magenta, not red. Although it has been widely accepted (based on the old color wheel) that red is the complement of green and vice versa, this is usually incorrect. The afterimage of green is magenta and the afterimage of red is cyan (blue).

The three color mixing systems are defined as follows.

Subtractive. Transparent colors placed on top of each other or in front of each other form a third color. Yellow and blue mixed make green. The mixed color is always darker than any of the component colors.

Additive. The cumulative effect of colored lights mixed together. The mixed color is always lighter than the lightest component color. Yellow and blue light equal white.

Partitive. The averaging of several colors as in pointillism-style paintings. Adjacent spots in three-color printing and color TV are "mixed" by the eye and read as solid colors. The total effect of a fabric woven of different-color threads is a color different from any of the component threads individually. The mixed color has the average brightness of all the colors mixed.

It is not within the scope of this chapter to discuss in detail the highly technical aspects of color theory or the rationale that supports the development of the new color wheel. The reader is referred to an extraordinarily fine (but unfortunately out-of-print) book on the subject, *The Theory and Practice of Color,* by Frans Gerritsen (New York, Van Nostrand Reinhold, 1974).

LAWS OF PERCEPTION*

Sensitivity to Light and Color

The human eye can distinguish up to 9 million colors with normal vision and mutual combinations of the three eye primaries, blue, green, and red (short, medium, and long wavelengths, respectively) and the three eye secondaries, yellow, magenta, and cyan. Color is light energy after it hits the eye. *Rods and cones,* the light *receptors,* are located in the retina. There are many more rods than cones. The rods are clustered on the periphery of the retina and the cones in the center, generally speaking. Since the cones are concentrated in the center of the retina, color sensitivity *decreases* toward the periphery of the retina until it reaches the edge where only light and dark can be discriminated. *Translating this into a more practical application, the greatest values (brightnesses) and the warm, active colors (yellows, reds, and oranges) should be placed in the center of attention. Lower brightnesses and cool, unsaturated colors (dark green, dark blue, dark brown) should appear on the periphery of the visual field.* This knowledge is particularly important for the design of graphic signage, posters, large paintings, exhibitions, displays, and interior design. One may lead people from one room to another by the skillful arrangement of successive values and colors.

Simultaneous Contrast

Simultaneous contrast is the change in appearance of a color due to the influence of a surrounding contrasting color: Larger color masses influence smaller ones. If two spots of a neutral gray are surrounded by a larger area of white and black, respectively, the gray surrounded by

---

*A good deal of the material presented under Laws of Perception has been adapted from *The Theory and Practice of Color,* by Frans Gerritsen, Van Nostrand Reinhold, New York, 1974.

white will *appear* to have less brightness than the gray surrounded by black. This happens because the local adaptation of the eye is less sensitive to high brightness in a bright surrounding, thus more sensitive to low brightness or value. Against the bright white background, then, the gray will be evaluated as having less brightness than it actually has. However, against a black background, the eye will be less sensitive to low brightness and will evaluate the gray spot as being very bright. This is true not just of white and black but of most colors in which a strong contrast exists (Color Plate 39, Figure 11-3).

Successive Contrast and Afterimage

When the eye adapts to the value and color of an environment, this will influence the brightness and color of what is seen directly thereafter. For example, if the eye adapts to a blue background of a stage set, and a performer wearing a yellow costume suddenly appears, the costume will appear much brighter yellow than if the eye had not first adapted to yellow's complementary color, blue. If one concentrates on a green surface and then looks away at a white one, an afterimage of magenta will appear. One is, in effect, seeing the white surface *minus* the green to which the eye has already adapted. Looking at a certain color produces an *afterimage* of its complement (Color Plate 39, Figure 11-4). A practical application of this principle is the surgical operating room, where walls and garments are always blue-green because the eye is concentrated on a red spot (blood), and when surgeons look up from their work, they see afterimages of blue-green. If walls and garments were white, they would see green spots before their eyes every time they looked away from the surgical site. Thus, blue-green walls and gowns act as a background to neutralize these afterimages.

Another example of afterimage can be experienced if one walks through a corridor that has yellow walls, a warm-toned floor, and incandescent (warm) light—essentially a yellow-hued environment. When leaving the corridor, perhaps entering a lobby, one will see afterimages of blue, the complement of yellow. *This is very important for interior design.* An understanding of this concept can prevent a designer from creating undesirable color relationships.

Metameric Color Pairs

Metameric color pairs are those that are alike only under certain conditions. For example, if two color chips of turquoise blue paint fabricated by two different paint manufacturers seem identical under incandescent light, they may appear vastly different from each other under a different source of light, due to the absorption curves of the color surfaces. The vast number of chemical formulas and varying compositions of pigment and binder will produce colors that, although they may appear to match another color in a certain light, actually have different short- and long-wavelength areas. Thus, the colors would look quite different under a different source of light, due to the differences in absorption.

A practical application of this principle occurs daily in the offices of architects and interior designers. Frequently, the carefully selected paint colors specified by an architect or designer will be met by the contractor's request for a substitution of manufacturer. While seemingly harmless, provided the substituted manufacturer has a high-quality comparable product, the possibility of "mixing to match" the designer's original palette of colors is almost impossible.

It is highly unlikely that the two manufacturers would use the same chemical formula and exactly the same type of pigment. The colors will probably be "mixed to match" under cool white fluorescent light in the paint store. While they may appear to match perfectly there, they will not match the specific color temperature of fluorescents on the job site. *The pigment molecules of one formulation will be sensitive to and absorb different wavelengths than the other formulation.* Colors that have identical chemical formulations will look identical in all sources of light, even if the samples were mixed at different times. It is critical that colors always be evaluated under the lighting conditions where they will be used.

Reflectance

Colors of a room are influenced by the reflection of natural light entering the room as well as by electric sources of light. An example of the first condition is a room with a large expanse of window facing a garden. The green grass will absorb most of the long wavelengths of the daylight (the reds and oranges) and permit the short wavelengths (greens and blues) to be reflected through the window onto the walls of the room. If the walls are white, they will have a green tint. The green tint can be neutralized by painting the reflection wall a *complementary* color in the magenta or red family.

An example of the second condition (electric light) is a corridor with red carpet, white walls, and white ceiling, with recessed incandescent light fixtures. The carpet absorbs most of the wavelengths of the electric light except for the long waves of the red-orange spectrum. Thus, the floor reflects an intense red light on the ceiling, making it appear red. A way to avoid this condition is by lighting the ceiling from below.

Purkinje Effect

The Purkinje effect was named after its discoverer, a Czechoslovakian physician, who observed that at twilight, color impressions are shifted to favor the short-wavelength area of the spectrum. Thus, reds, oranges, and yellows become colorless, and darker, greens and blues become clearer.

Color Constancy

This phenomenon refers to the relationship between the eye and the brain to translate visual information in a constant manner. For example, if one looks at a piece of white paper while standing in front of a red wall under daylight, the paper will still appear white, but a colored photograph would show the paper to be pink. In other words, intellectually the brain knows the paper is white

and so translates it as white in spite of perceptual information to the contrary.

Advancing and Receding Colors

Goethe's observation, mentioned earlier, that warm colors seem to advance while cool colors recede, can be explained by optic laws. Red—being only slightly refracted by the lens of the eye—focuses at a point behind the retina, and the lens, in order to see it clearly, grows more convex, thus pulling the color forward. Blue, on the other hand, is more sharply refracted and causes the lens to flatten out, thus decreasing its size by pushing its image back.

Figure-Ground Reversal

This phenomenon is a principle of Gestalt psychology and refers to the optical illusion apparent particularly in geometric patterns in which the figure seems to be in front of the background. Obviously, both figure and ground are printed on the same surface. Warm colors (red, orange, yellow) tend to be seen as figure since they advance, and cool colors (green, blue, purple) as ground since they recede. But whether a color is seen as figure or ground also depends on the value (light advances, dark recedes) and the saturation (high advances, low recedes).

COLOR SYMBOLISM

Emotional evaluations of color are a function of time, place, culture, nationality, age, fashion, and even gender. Colors conjure up highly personal images and meanings, making it difficult to predict and understand preferences. Furthermore, emotional evaluations of colors are made in relation to an object. While "apricot" may be a fashionable color this year for residential interiors, it is unlikely to be considered tasteful in an automobile or a toaster. People usually like colors associated with pleasurable experiences. Those who like modern art usually like the brilliant colors found in such paintings. Those who prefer the old masters often favor a more subdued palette.

The symbolic nature of color is expressed in color names, which are often made up of the basic color plus an adjective: *black magic, snow white, spice beige, chocolate brown, shocking pink, red hot, true blue (loyal).* Paint manufacturers often express sheer whimsy in naming colors such as "persimmon" for an olive green or "touch of love," which tells one nothing about the color.

Colors, through the ages, have come to be associated with certain emotions or personality traits. Some of the more common follow.

Blue: Tranquility, cool, solitude, intelligence, soothingness, truth, divinity, quiet, melancholy, calm, sincerity, generosity, serenity, hope, conformity, control, suppression of feelings, constancy, accomplishment, devotion, introspection.

Yellow: Joy, gaiety, harvest, brilliance, morbidity, cowardice, disease, fruition, regality, hope, jaundice.

Orange: Warmth, glow, sociality, friendliness, good cheer, good nature, gregariousness.

Red: Heart, blood, tragedy, cruelty, war, heat, hatred, power, bravery, love of life, courage, fire, fury, purgatory, passion, beauty, truth, shame, destruction, anger, danger, stop, love, excitement.

Green: Peace, youth, hope, victory, jealousy, life, nature, immortality, safety, conventionality, good adjustment, balance.

Orange-Brown: Deceit, distrust, inconstancy, treachery.

Red-Brown: Strength, solidity, vigor, sadness, maturity, simplicity, sturdiness, reliability, rationality.

White: Truth, innocence, purity, virginity, chastity, modesty, humility, light, love, temperance, friendship.

Black: Evil, gloom, death, terror, horror, darkness, crime, melancholy, secrecy, mystery, wickedness, witchcraft, mourning, solemnity, potency, social status.

Gray: Penance, humility, sadness, age, sobriety, death, fear, dreariness, bleakness, sterility, maturity, emotionlessness, isolation.

PRACTICAL APPLICATIONS OF COLOR PSYCHOLOGY

Where does all this investigation—preference and personality, color shock and loss of equilibrium—bring us in terms of design? Clearly, much of the research that has been reviewed here is as yet inconclusive. Many conclusions propagated about the effect of color and its link to emotional patterns have not been scientifically proven; so the real investigation of the effect of color upon human behavior has only just begun. The early state of the science notwithstanding, however, certain practical applications in design do suggest themselves.

1. Reds and yellows, for example, should be used in settings where creative activity is desired; greens and blues in areas that require more quiet and extended concentration—and the appropriate combinations of these colors in classrooms, hospitals, and offices.

2. Cool colors should be used in the surroundings of the highly agitated, hypertensive, and anxious; red, in the depressive's environment. Highly saturated colors should be avoided with autistic schizophrenics, as should red with those afflicted—like Goldstein's classic case—with organic brain disease.

3. Rousing, bright colors should be used with the aged rather than pastels, which are barely visible to those with failing eyesight.

4. Strongly contrasting figure-ground patterns and extremely bright colors should be avoided in the rooms of psychotic patients since these—when not worn by the patients but impinging upon them from their environment—might be thought to have an overwhelming, even intimidating, and threatening effect.

5. The knowledge of color preference and usage can be

employed in cultural liaisons and trade with foreign countries. Knowing which colors are taboo and which carry religious or symbolic associations in each country is mandatory for expanded marketing and trade relations.

6. Under warm colors, time is overestimated; weights seem heavier; objects seem larger; rooms appear smaller. Under cool colors, time is underestimated; weights seem lighter; objects seem smaller; rooms appear larger. Thus, cool colors should be used where monotonous tasks are performed to make the time seem to pass more quickly, and red, for example, may be used in an employees' restroom to reduce the amount of time spent there.

7. Under warm colors with high illumination, there is increased alertness and outward orientation—good where muscular effort or action are required such as a physical therapy gym. Under cool colors and low illumination, there is less distraction and more opportunity to concentrate on difficult tasks, an inward orientation is fostered. Noise induces increased sensitivity to cool colors, probably because the tranquility of these colors compensates for the increased aural stimulation. One becomes less sensitive to warm colors under noise, since they offer additional stimulation rather than less.

COLOR AND ITS EFFECT ON OUR PERCEPTION OF SPACE

The various laws of perception discussed previously can be translated into the following guidelines for interior design and architecture.

1. To visually "prepare" people for the color of a room they are about to enter, the entry should be painted a *complementary* color.

2. Color modifies architectural form—it can expand, shorten, widen, lengthen, and give the illusion of lowering or raising a ceiling. Color can change the appearance of the environment to lift the individual out of reality.

3. Bright colors seem lighter in weight. Ordered from "heavy" to "light," they are: red, blue, purple, orange, green, yellow.

4. Bright objects are overestimated in size. Yellow appears the largest, with white, red, green, blue, and black in descending order.

5. A light object appears larger against a dark background. A dark object will appear smaller against a light background.

6. The wall opposite a window should generally be kept light, or it will absorb much of the daylight.

7. A window wall and frame should be light so as not to contrast too much with daylight sky—high contrast can result in headaches and eye strain.

8. If a red wall is placed next to a yellow wall, the yellow wall will appear greener than it actually is due to the afterimage of red: cyan. The blue afterimage of the yellow will cause the red to appear more purple.

9. Warm colors advance; cool colors recede.

10. Light colors and small patterns visually enlarge a space. Dark colors and large patterns make it appear smaller.

11. The absence of variety in the visual environment causes sensory deprivation. Those who are confined to nursing homes, hospitals, and institutions desperately need changes in lighting, accent walls, and artwork in order for their nervous systems to function properly. Monotonous white walls devoid of interesting graphics or artwork deprive the brain of the constantly changing stimulation it requires to remain healthy.

12. In low levels of light (under 30 footcandles), object and surface colors will appear normal when the light surface is slightly tinted with pink, orange, or yellow. As higher light levels are reached, a normal appearance for object colors will be found with cooler light; it

is best to stay warm at low levels and go cooler at high levels* (Kruithof's principle).

Since lighting and color influence each other greatly, the reader is referred to Chapter 13 for additional information.

SUMMARY

Today, considerable attention is being focused on the environment's vital influence and the powers inherent in design. In the past, different disciplines were rigidly separate; social scientists concentrated on the influence of the social environment; psychologists were absorbed with rat behavior and isolated stimuli in the confines of their laboratories; and designers and architects strove, in the main, for aesthetically pleasing functionality. What has emerged, however, is a more interdisciplinary, holistic approach, as we perceive people in their total environment and realize that behavior is influenced by space, structure, color, lighting, activity, and other participants, as well as by our own inner being—in sum, that everything has its effect in a process that works as a kind of circular feedback. With this understanding, design has the potential to stimulate learning or impair concentration; enhance recuperation or impede it; encourage social interaction or hinder it; improve mental and psychological well-being or increase anxiety. While an awareness of these influences through emerging research in the field is important for any design, be it private home or public facility, it is *crucial* in the planning of societal structures — schools, hospitals, mental and penal institutions, factories, office buildings — that contain large masses of people over sustained periods of time, thus giving shape to the moments and course of their lives.

---

*Faber Birren, *Light, Color and Environment,* Van Nostrand Reinhold, New York, 1969, p. 25.

CHAPTER 12

Interior Finishes and Furniture

The interior design of a medical or dental office is critically important to the patients' assessment of the physician or dentist and the level of anxiety patients experience. Patients can rarely assess the quality of the clinical care provided. Nevertheless, a judgment is made based on interactions with staff and an evaluation of the interior environment. Visible attention to detail in office design generates feelings of confidence about the healthcare professionals who work there and the services that are provided.

This chapter will discuss specifications of interior finish materials and furniture items that are particularly well suited to medical and dental offices. Photographs of individual rooms displaying a great attention to detail are scattered throughout the chapters of this book and in the color plates.

Occasionally, medical and dental interiors are designed to residential standards, with materials not intended to withstand the stress of a high-volume office. A door that, in a residence, may be opened and closed 3000 times a year, may be opened and closed 100,000 times a year in a medical office. Similarly, cut pile carpet designed for residential use does not hold up well. It is difficult to clean and may show wear sooner than a commercial carpet.

Certain high-profile suites such as plastic surgery may demand unusual interior finishes to achieve their marketing goals; however, sanitation and flammability considerations must not be overlooked. There are two issues here. First, if a product specified does not meet the minimum flammability standard for a particular usage, the physician may be denied Medicare reimbursement or the facility may be denied state licensing. For example, putting a hardwood floor in the operating room of an office-based surgery suite will prevent that physician from getting reimbursed for the use of the facility. In order to gain Medicare certification and reimbursement from many of the third-party payers, the surgery suite must meet NFPA 101 Life Safety Code, which stipulates fire ratings, among other things, for all areas of an office-based surgery suite.

The second issue is potential liability in case of fire faced by the designer who specifies interior finish materials. If, after a fire, it is determined that any of the materials within the office did not meet the minimum flammability requirements, the designer is certain to be included in the lawsuit. These are the two main reasons that designers should be extremely cautious and diligent in determining which, if any, local or state codes apply to the selection of interior finishes for their specific medical or dental project.

The Uniform Building Code (UBC), adopted in various states, classifies medical office buildings as Group B occupancy. As of this writing, interior finishes having a flame-spread index of 75 or less would be suitable for all areas within the suite (with the exception of surgery suites, where patients may be unconscious). Some areas of the suite may have finishes with a flame-spread rating in excess of 75, provided the area is not an enclosed vertical exitway (stairway) or an exit corridor. However, in the UBC, *textile* wallcoverings must be Class I (flame spread of 25 or less) in any part of a suite.

A suspended acoustic tile ceiling is more functional than a gypsum board ceiling because it gives access to the electrical and mechanical equipment above it and is easier to clean. Where sanitation is of extreme importance, a plastic-coated acoustic tile or an enameled gypsum board ceiling should be used.

HARD-SURFACE FLOORING

Flooring may be carpet, vinyl composition tile (VCT), sheet vinyl, ceramic tile, or a combination of all four. The least expensive flooring is VCT, which is very durable, but it does need to be waxed and buffed. Sheet vinyl is recommended for wet areas such as bathrooms if the budget does not allow for ceramic tile. Sheet vinyl is also recommended in minor surgeries or anywhere sanitation is a concern because it has fewer seams than VCT and may be installed with a self-coved base. Tarkett, a Swedish manufacturer, markets several high-quality sheet vinyl floorings suitable for operating room suites and other treatment areas where cleanliness is important. It also offers a cushioned sheet vinyl that does not compress under the weight of heavy equipment. The Tarkett products are extremely flexible and malleable, allowing them to be coved up and around inside and outside corners, pipes, floor sinks, or other obstructions, creating a seamless floor. Similar products by Mannington and Armstrong are also excellent. Seams may be either chemically welded or heat welded, depending on the degree of cleanliness required and protection against the penetration of dirt and moisture.

Sheet vinyl used in high-traffic areas or where considerable pivoting takes place, such as in an operating room, should have color that is integral throughout the entire thickness of the material, as opposed to a thin layer of color laminated to a backing material. Suitable products include Armstrong Medintech, Mannington BioSpec®, and Tarkett Eminent.

An attractive wood flooring product called GenuWood, manufactured by Perma-Grain Products (Media,

Pennsylvania) meets a Class A flame-spread rating. It has a 20-mil layer of clear vinyl over the wood veneer, making it easy to clean, although it is not a seamless installation.

A wood-look floor can be achieved at less cost with a solid vinyl sheet product called Toli Mature®; Amtico has a similar product. They look remarkably realistic and completely change the ambience of the exam room.

CARPET

It is not uncommon to find entire medical or dental offices carpeted. Apart from any considerations previously discussed regarding infection control, carpet, if selected properly, is easy to maintain and adds warmth to the office appearance. It provides a much-needed acoustic function as well, and it prevents serious accidents caused by people slipping. Acting as an air filter, carpet actually improves indoor air quality by holding on to dust particles, which might otherwise become airborne, until vacuum cleaners equipped with environmental airbags remove the dust from the carpet.

Performance Factors

When discussing carpet construction, it is important to keep in mind the fiber composition of a carpet style is only one of several performance factors to consider in the specification process. *Backing, yarn weight, pile height, camouflage, texture,* and *color* can have as great a combined impact on the suitability and performance of carpet as fiber selection. However, these factors can never compensate for a budget-priced fiber that lacks the physical structure or stain-resisting additives of quality healthcare carpet. Therefore, careful evaluation and comparison of all specifications should be made prior to selecting a specific carpet.

Nylon has continued to grow as the fiber of choice for most healthcare facilities. Superior performance characteristics such as resiliency, abrasion resistance, clean-ability, stain resistance, and texture retention have virtually eliminated other fibers such as polyester and acrylic.

Type 6.6 nylon (DuPont, Solutia) is approximately 17 percent harder than type 6 (BASF, Allied Chemical). All other things being equal, this could affect performance characteristics accordingly; however, pattern, camou-flage, color, and other factors can help to compensate. Piece-dyed and yarn-dyed solids or tonal colorations are often constructed with type 6.6 nylon.

In areas where the use of caustics and bleaching agents is common, solution-dyed nylons may be the best option. In solution-dyed fabrics, the color is integral to the manufacturing process when the fiber is extruded; hence, there is never a dyelot color matching problem. These yarn systems do not necessarily have better general stain resistance, but are substantially more colorfast than con-ventionally dyed nylons and permit the use of cleaning agents containing bleach. Some yarn-dyeing methods rival the colorfastness of solution-dyed yarns by using cationic dyes and other proprietary methods. Colorfastness warranties and stain-removal warranties are well worth consideration when evaluating the real benefits offered by these systems. Focus on the details of these warranties in this important area.

Carpets well suited to the maintenance and durability requirements of healthcare settings have never been more plentiful. The industry has reached a high state of achievement whereby extraordinarily beautiful carpets, in rich colors, that meet rigorous standards for flamma-bility, durability, and ease of maintenance are widely available and at moderate cost. Despite this, it is difficult for the consumer to evaluate the technical properties of carpet as thicker pile is not necessarily better. A wise buyer will consult a design professional or competent commercial (not residential) carpet dealer to evaluate and select an appropriate product. All too often, a resi-dential product is installed which gives disappointing per-formance.

Treatments to Inhibit Soiling and Microbial Growth

Antimicrobial treatments, such as Intercept® from Interface, Inc., inhibit the growth and reproduction of microorganisms and should be considered for most hos-pitals and other medical facilities where patients may be highly susceptible to these agents: allergists' offices, chemotherapy areas, surgery centers, oral surgery offices, pulmonary specialty clinics. When applied to car-pet yarn and backing, molds, mildew, fungi, and other microorganisms cannot multiply, cause odors, or discolor the carpet. Potential infection and allergic reaction to these organisms are significantly reduced. The control of odor and mustiness is perhaps the most visible advan-tage of these treatments.

Fluorochemical treatments, such as DuraTech® from DuPont and Protekt® from Interface, Inc., for enhanced soil resistance are an important aspect of any specifica-tion for carpet in a medical environment. These treat-ments, which may be effectively applied at several points in the manufacturing process, greatly reduce the surface tension of the fiber and thus its propensity to attract soil. This enhancement may be the most important in the medical environment, since much more carpet is replaced each year because of food and protein stains than for most other reasons combined. Remember, nylon fibers do not wear out; the appearance just deteriorates. Maintaining the appearance of the carpet through good maintenance can make a significant difference in the use-ful life of the carpet. Protekt comes with a 15-year prorat-ed warranty. DuraTech is available only on Antron® Legacy nylon and Lumena solution-dyed nylon.

Static Control

Static control "branded" nylons, such as Antron, Ultron®, and Zeftron, will contain a small percentage of conductive filaments capable of reducing static dissipation charge to below the level of human sensitivity (3.5 kilovolts). Some mills offer additional static control (1.5 kilovolts) by using a conductive backing and latex as well. This can be important for use with sensitive computer equipment.

Carpet Backings

Several commercial carpet backings offer improved seam strength, lamination integrity, moisture resistance, texture retention, and cleanability. It should be noted that there are two issues with respect to moisture: that which can wick up into the carpet from the concrete slab and that which penetrates the backing into the slab resulting from a spill on the *surface* of the carpet. When liquids seep through the backing into the slab, they are virtually impossible to remove when the carpet is cleaned and, over time, undesirable odors develop.

Enriched latex systems, usually 12 feet wide, such as Unitary or Unitary Actionback, offer improved tuft bind test results and often carry warranty protection against seam raveling and delamination. Note, however, that these water-based latex systems are susceptible to oxidation damage from excess moisture and require the use of chair pads. They are, however, an excellent approach to general office areas when the budget will not allow a more expensive backing structure. The premium for these backings is often less than 5 percent. Most styles and patterns are available with these options, and some running-line styles are available for cut orders.

Hot-melt plastic backings, usually 12 feet wide, such as Unibond from Lees, offer excellent tuft bind test results and carry warranty protection against seam raveling and delamination. The premium for these backings is about 10 percent, depending on the style. Moisture does not cause backing deterioration as with latex systems, and chair pads may be recommended to reduce accelerated texture loss, although they are not required with Lees Unibond specifically. Most styles and patterns are available with these backing options and running-line styles are available. These backings are generally not "moisture proof"; that is, they do not prevent water from penetrating

through the backing although Unibond creates a moisture barrier when it is installed. Other mills may have a similar product. These backings tend to be stiffer and a little more difficult to install.

Urethane backings, usually 12 feet wide, such as Enhancer from Dow Chemical, offer excellent tuft bind test results and carry warranty protection against seam raveling and delamination. The premium for these backings is about 20 percent, depending on the style. Moisture does not cause backing deterioration as with latex systems, and chair pads are not always required to maintain the warranty. Many styles and patterns are available with these options; however, some pattern matching may not be possible. Some running-line styles are available. Some of these backings are considered "moisture resistant" because they prevent water penetration from the surface leeching through the backing into the slab or subfloor. High-density cushion options are an excellent approach to areas requiring the benefits of padding. Urethane backings allow concrete moisture to readily escape from the slab.

Vinyl backings, usually 6 feet wide, or carpet tile, offer excellent tuft bind test results and carry warranty protection against seam raveling and delamination. The premium for these backings is about 30 percent, depending on the style. Moisture does not cause backing deterioration as with latex systems, and chair pads are not usually required to maintain the warranty. Many styles and patterns are available with these options; however, matching of large-scale patterns will not be possible. Many running-line styles are available. Most of these backings are considered "moisture proof" in the sense that they eliminate water penetration through the back. Vinyl backings *do not* allow concrete moisture to readily escape and require a low-moisture calcium chloride test score or concrete sealer prior to installation.

Pile/Texture

A *level loop* pile is the most serviceable for high-traffic areas, although a combination loop and cut pile will work well in many medical and dental facilities. A number of high-traffic commercial cut piles are available that perform quite well, although solid colors will not camouflage soil.

For maximum performance, consider these specifications:

| | Cut Pile | | Loop Pile |
	BCF[a]	Spun Nylon	BCF[a]
Yarn weight[b]	38 oz	42 oz	32 oz
Pile height[b]	0.375	0.375	0.250
Twist count[b]	5.5×5.5	5.5×5.5	—

[a]BCF, bulk continuous filament.
[b]Minimum requirements.

Installation

Carpet in a medical or dental office is usually glued directly to the slab with no pad. This provides a firm footing, making it less likely that people will trip. Direct glue-down is the recommended installation method in hospitals and many other commercial facilities as well. In offices, it sometimes eliminates the need for acrylic chair mats since it is firm enough to allow chairs and carts to roll freely. Where a pad is desired, as in a consultation room, a rubber slab pad is preferable to a foam waffle pad, which tends to "bottom out." Treadmor is a high quality brand of pad that works well where a pad is desired in a commercial facility. Urethane attached cushion backings, as mentioned above, have proven to be excellent where roller traffic is not a consideration. Attached cushion extends the appearance life of carpet by keeping the pile from packing down and losing texture. Ultra high-density attached cushion offers enhanced acoustics, ergonomics, thermal insulation, warmth, comfort, safety, and image. The best of these backings are "moisture resistant" and carry lifetime warranties. For installation specifications, reference the latest published guidelines for commercial carpet installation from the Carpet and Rug Institute. Proper maintenance is defined in detail by most manufacturers. Consider scheduling a meeting with the technical services representative from the mill and the senior maintenance managers involved.

WALL TREATMENTS

If budget permits, walls should receive commercial vinyl wallcovering (see Chapter 15 for classification characteristics), although, in high-profile-design offices, there are other more expensive options that are even more durable than vinyl and richer in texture and appearance such as Carnegie Xorel and Maharam Tek-Wall™. Gypsum board walls make a good substrate for application of vinyl wallcoverings, provided they have not been textured. A light texture is desirable, however, if the walls will be painted, since texture helps to conceal drywall taping and nail heads. A heavy stucco or sand finish texture is to be avoided since it collects dirt and is difficult to clean. Porous or excessively textured wall treatments such as wood paneling, grasscloth, or woven fabrics should not be used in examination or treatment areas, but may be used in limited areas such as consultation rooms and waiting rooms.

A class of woven wallcoverings made of polyolefin that carries a Class A flame-spread rating, is mildew resistant, remarkably durable, and has the luxurious appearance of fine linen fabric, is now widely available. These wallcoverings may even be used in patient areas of hospitals. Even though these fabrics appear to be delicate, they are extremely tough and some patterns may even be cleaned with a bleach solution. Maharam Tek-Wall, DesignTex Hardwear™, Wolf-Gordon Foundations™, and J.M. Lynne Olefin LX™ are products of this type.

FURNITURE

Offices located in cities with inclement weather must provide an area near the entrance to the waiting room for removing boots, rubbers, and winter apparel. An umbrella caddy and coat hooks (some low enough for children) are also necessary. For the comfort of those waiting, it is

Figure 12-1. Magazine rack. (*Photo courtesy: Peter Pepper Products, Inc., Compton, CA.*)

Figure 12-2. Magazine rack. (*Photo courtesy: Peter Pepper Products, Inc., Compton, CA.*)

Figure 12-3. Brochure rack. (*Photo courtesy: Peter Pepper Products, Inc., Compton, CA.*)

desirable that the coat area be visible from the waiting room. Offices in Southern California and other areas with a temperate climate usually do not have entry vestibules or coat closets.

To eliminate the clutter of magazines strewn about the room, waiting rooms ought to have a magazine rack. Wall-hung units are most functional. While these may be custom designed, those shown in Figures 12-1 and 12-2 are available in a number of options with respect to size and finish.

Most offices need to display and dispense many healthcare education pamphlets and brochures. The brochure rack shown in Figure 12-3 comes in various sizes and may be placed near the nurse station or in the waiting room. Custom-designed units (Figure 3-11) can be an attractive addition to a room.

The doors of medical exam rooms require a chart rack, which is often placed on the wall on the latch side of the door. Those in Figures 12-4 and 12-5 function well and are available in a number of accent colors. Some are sized for a standard medical chart, others for radiology films, and yet others are a combination size, with a pocket for each. It is a nice amenity to provide an individual

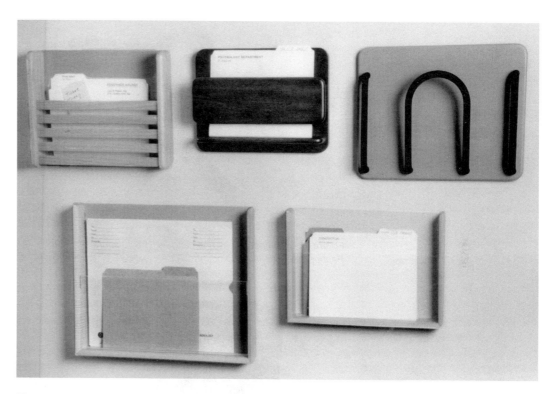

Figure 12-5. Medical chart racks come in various styles to complement any decor. (*Photo courtesy: Peter Pepper Products, Inc., Compton, CA.*)

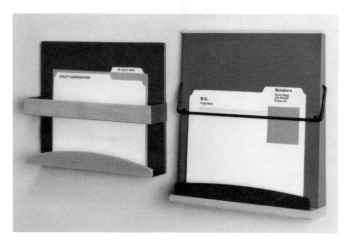

Figure 12-4. Medical chart racks. Larger one on right accommodates X-ray film jacket. (*Photo courtesy: Peter Pepper Products, Inc., Compton, CA.*)

magazine rack in each exam room such as that shown on the left-hand side of Figure 12-4. Exam rooms also require coat hooks and hangers. Those shown in Figure 12-6 come in attractive colors and are soft to the touch. Guest chairs may or may not have arms; they should be stable and accommodate overweight individuals (Figures 12-7 and 12-8).

Decorative accessories that are also functional add color to a business office or nurse station. The clock in Figure 12-9 is an example.

There is great latitude in selecting waiting room seating. The main criteria are that a suitable number of individual chairs with arms be provided and that the chairs

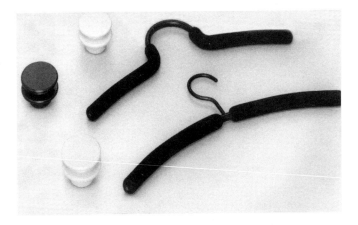

Figure 12-6. Clothes hooks and hangers. (*Photo courtesy: Peter Pepper Products, Inc., Compton, CA.*)

Figure 12-7. Zag chair works well in exam rooms: The sleigh base is stable, the arms aid the elderly, and the seat accommodates even very large individuals. (*Photo courtesy: Source International, Shrewsbury, MA.*)

Figure 12-8. Guest chair can be used in exam or waiting room. (*Photo courtesy: David Edward Co., Baltimore, MD.*)

Figure 12-9. Clock. (*Photo courtesy: Peter Pepper Products, Inc., Compton, CA.*)

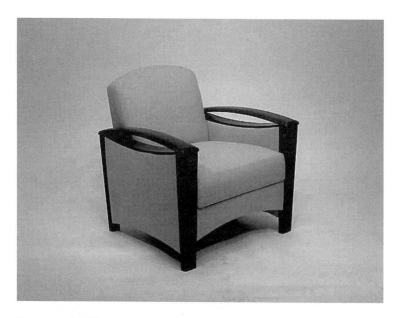

Figure 12-10. Uptown seating system includes individual chairs and modular seating in a variety of sizes and arm and back styles. (*Photo courtesy: Nemschoff, Sheboygan, WI.*)

not be too low or hard to get out of. The seating in Figures 12-10 and 12-11 is well suited to medical and dental waiting rooms, although there are many variations on this theme. Each of these is well balanced, so that it will not tip when someone pushes down on one arm only. Wooden arm caps protect the fabric where it is most vulnerable to soiling. Both of these manufacturers offer individual chairs as well as modular or ganged versions that accommodate more people in less space.

The Nemschoff Uptown® seating (Figure 12-10) is available in three different sizes, with five variations of arm cap styles and three different back details. A unique comfort feature is the spring seat construction. As tandem seating, two-, three-, and four-seat modules combine with individual chairs. Industrial hook-and-loop replaceable upholstery, mortise-and-tenon joinery, and totally replaceable components make this seating durable and somewhat of a lifetime purchase.

Figure 12-11. Modular waiting room seating. (*Photo courtesy: AGI Industries, Inc., High Point, NC.*)

Figure 12-12. Modular Georgia seating creates orderly appearance in waiting area of Whitfield County Health Department, Atlanta, Georgia. (*Photo courtesy: Brandrud Furniture Inc., Auburn, WA; Photographer: Warren Bond.*)

The modular seating in Figure 12-12 is both attractive and practical. It is easy to vacuum under the seating (no legs) and the separation between seat and back makes maintenance easy. Figure 12-13 demonstrates a creative approach to using modular seating that can be curved.

In selecting seating, one must be mindful of accommodating overweight individuals and sparing them the embarrassment of squeezing into a chair that is too nar-

row. Providing a few chairs without arms, or a loveseat, will serve the purpose.

Practices with a number of geriatric patients or patients with arthritic or orthopedic problems may wish to provide some high-backed seating such as that shown in Figures 12-14 and 12-15. The chair shown in Figure 12-15 has a rocking motion or flex that is quite soothing.

Figure 12-13. Waiting room of Fresno Cancer Center uses ADD Specialized Seating Technology (a division of KI) modular seating in an imaginative configuration. (*Interior design: Chambers Lorenz Design, Fresno, CA.*)

Figure 12-14. High-back Espree chair for geriatric patients or those with orthopedic problems. (*Photo courtesy: Thonet Industries, Statesville, NC.*)

Figure 12-15. High-back Rose chair with flexing seat and back. (*Photo courtesy: ADD Specialized Seating Technology [a division of KI], Los Angeles, CA; Design and engineering: Roger Leib, AIA.*)

Figure 12-16. Sand table with magnetized boats moved by levers under the table amuses young children. (*Photo courtesy: People Friendly Places, Inc., Northbrook, IL.*)

It is important for the parents' and staff's sanity to keep children well occupied—patients and siblings alike (Figures 12-16, 12-17, and 12-18). A small table or work counter will provide space for coloring or for playing games. Proper storage for toys may encourage the children to replace toys after use.

A great feature in a staff lounge is the specialized ADD Specialized Seating Technology De Stressor™ chair (Figure 12-19), which cushions the body and has a rocking motion. Lockers for personal belongings, a food prep area, dining table, and natural light—preferably with a view—will enable staff to refresh their energy.

Figure 12-17. Multistation interactive play unit requires little space in waiting room. (*Photo courtesy: People Friendly Places, Inc., Northbrook, IL.*)

Figure 12-18. Interactive play unit requires little space and keeps active toddlers entertained. (*Photo courtesy: People Friendly Places, Inc., Northbrook, IL.*)

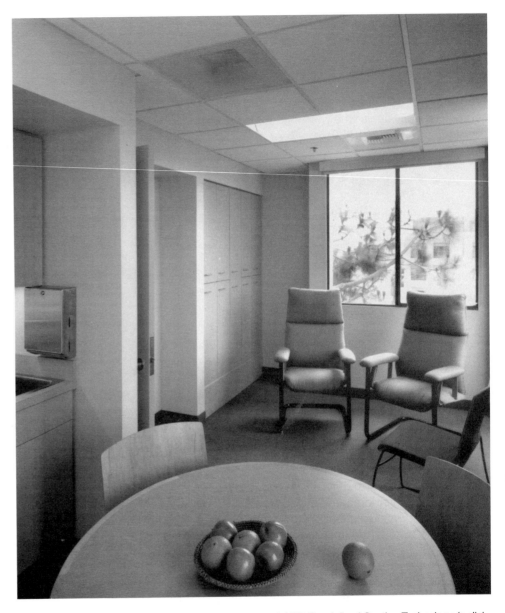

Figure 12-19. Clinic staff lounge features dining area and ADD Specialized Seating Technology (a division of KI) DeStressor™ chair with rocking motion. Room includes lockers for staff belongings. (*Design: Jain Malkin Inc.; Photographer: Steve McClelland.*)

Educational exhibits or artwork can be put to good use in a medical waiting room. The subject matter may provide useful information about the facility or its physicians or history, or explain birth defects, sports injuries, or other medical conditions.

Accommodating laptop computer users shows consideration for individuals who wish to make productive use of waiting time (Figure 12-20).

UPHOLSTERY FABRIC

There has been tremendous innovation in textile technology in recent years, resulting in fabrics that have the look and feel of silk, linen, chenille, bouclé, wools, and woven tapestries—all quite magnificent—that are, in reality, hardwearing synthetic fibers that are flame retardant, impervious to staining, and easy to clean, and that can withstand tremendous abrasion. Unlimited in range of patterns, colors, and type of weave, it has never been easier to brighten a waiting room with fabrics. The drab "workhorse" fabrics formerly associated with contract or institutional design are long gone.

Look for the following types of fabrics and fibers to assure top performance in medical and dental office settings.

Nylon is one of the most popular synthetic fibers. Although it is highly durable, 100 percent nylon upholstery fabrics sometimes pill and often lack the fine aesthetic character or "hand" that blended fabrics achieve. A nylon blended with other synthetic or natural fibers often provides the best solution. Nylon is resistant to many chemicals, water, and microorganisms, and has high resiliency.

Solution-dyed fabrics are 100 percent BASF Zeftron 200 Nylon. Some have a DuPont Teflon® fabric protector. Manufacturers offering these fabrics include DesignTex, Maharam, Arc Com, Architex International, Momentum, and Sina Pearson. These durable fabrics meet or exceed the 40-hour NAFM light fast (fading) requirement. They are recommended especially in areas where fabric or

Figure 12-20. Palette seating offers small tables and a place to plug in a laptop computer. (*Photo courtesy: Davis Furniture, High Point, NC.*)

seating is exposed to ultraviolet light. The BASF Zeftron fiber can even be cleaned with bleach.

Performance Plus fabrics are a blend of 66.5 percent Trevira FR and 33.5 percent polyester with a Scotchgard™ finish. DesignTex manufactures this product. It has very high abrasion performance, which makes it extremely durable.

Printed and woven Crypton is 100 percent polyester, an excellent solution where wet soiling is a problem. Crypton is finished with proprietary treatments consisting of a polymer latex and fluorochemical stain blocker that provides a total moisture barrier, yet it is "breathable." It is antibacterial, antifungal, and antimicrobial. It is soil and stain resistant, but cannot be cleaned with bleach. Manufacturers include Maharam, Fantagraph, DesignTex, Momentum, Arc Com, and C.F. Stinson.

Xorel fabrics by Carnegie are an option where extremely durable "industrial-strength" upholstery fabric is required. Woven from polyethylene, these textiles repel liquid stains and are washable, colorfast, antibacterial, and self-healing when punctured; hence, they are virtually indestructible. The fabric's high resistance to abrasion (often withstanding one million double rubs on the Wyzenbeek test) is another feature.

It is important to understand something about textile technology in selecting an appropriate fabric.

Durability

Measured by the Wyzenbeek abrasion test (ASTM D3597) under the standards set by ACT (Association of Contract Textile Companies), durability is critical to the selection of fabric in healthcare settings. In this test, a fabric is subjected to the revolving action of two abrasive wheels. The number of revolutions the fabric withstands before breaking a yarn is the fabric's rating. All fabrics carry this rating in their specifications. A rating of 30,000 double rubs with no wear qualifies a fabric for heavy-duty use; 15,000 double rubs classifies it for medium duty. This should be considered a minimum for any healthcare setting.

Light Fastness

A fadeometer exposes a portion of a fabric to a light source for a specific number of hours. The exposed section is compared to the unexposed section and then rated on a scale of 1 to 5 (no change) for fading. Typical for upholstery or wallcovering is a minimum standard of 40 hours with little or no change.

Soil and Staining

Various tests such as the oil repellency test evaluate a fabric's resistance to specific stains. Similar tests also evaluate the effectiveness of soil and stain repellents after having been applied to fabrics, comparing them to control samples.

Flammability

Although it is a concern in any healthcare facility, flammability is rarely an issue because most contract or institutional fabrics are Class A, the most stringent code classification. Nevertheless, one must always check this specification. The flammability and smoke generation characteristics of fabrics, as well as the composition of the filling in upholstered furniture, and the burn characteristics of the complete furniture assembly, are an issue in any "I" or institutional occupancy. California is one of a number of states that follows Technical Bulletin 133 for upholstered furniture, but it does not generally apply to medical and dental offices, just hospitals. When adhering to this code, it is the furniture manufacturer's responsibility to certify and label that the piece of furniture has complied.

The reader is referred to Chapter 15 for additional code information.

CHAPTER 13
Lighting

BIOLOGICAL EFFECTS OF LIGHT

Traditionally, lighting engineers and those in the design professions have been concerned with lighting in terms of vision or aesthetics. Until recently, the biological significance of light has been overlooked. The fabrication of incandescent and fluorescent lamps is based on the assumption that people will be exposed to sunlight as a normal part of each day and not be confined to a habitation of electrical illumination. These lamps emit a narrow spectrum of light that does not include ultraviolet.

Fluorescent light is light without heat, whereby ultraviolet radiation is converted into radiation of a longer wavelength. (Since the human eye is not sensitive to ultraviolet radiation, these wavelengths are lengthened by phosphors to which the eye is sensitive.) Different phosphors create different tints of fluorescent light. Thus, fluorescent lamps, in simplistic terms, are nothing more than glass tubes, the inner surface of which has been coated with phosphor powders, which, when excited by ultraviolet energy created within the arc stream, give off visible light. Most fluorescent lamp tints cost the same to manufacture, although, due to marketing demand, cool white always costs less than more appealing colors.

If people are to be confined for long periods away from sunlight, a balanced light that emits a fairly full spectrum of wavelengths is desirable. The illumination of our environment acts both to induce and to time glandular and metabolic functions affecting, among other things, milk produced, the quality and quantity of eggs laid, and stimulation or inhibition of sexual activity. Light dilates blood vessels, thereby increasing circulation. Sudden exposure to bright light stimulates the adrenal gland. Our biological time clocks—our circadian rhythms—are manipulated by light. Studies have shown that subjects who are forced to live in darkness for prolonged periods suffer sensory deprivation. The loss of environmental cues that tell the body what to do throws body systems out of kilter.

As populations increase and pollution keeps pace, those in urban centers spend increasingly more time in indoor environments. People confined to nursing homes or institutions who are not able to get outdoors similarly depend on their indoor environment to supply well-balanced light that includes some ultraviolet. Those who design such environments must be aware of not only the biological effects of light, but also the psychological effects, as well as the visual quality of the light.

Perhaps the optimal solution for lighting offices, homes, restaurants, hospitals, and hotels would be a system of changing light levels and tints. Since natural light changes throughout the day (warm and rosy at dawn and dusk, bright with a bluish cast at midday), should we not try to imitate these day-night cycles in our indoor environments?

TECHNICAL DATA

The sensations that we call color and light are our psychological interpretations of certain portions of the electromagnetic spectrum. How well we see colors depends on how closely the ingredients of artificial (electric) light sources match the ingredients of sunlight. Electric sources of light have varying degrees of each color—some have more warm wavelengths and some more cool. An incandescent bulb, for example, is high in orange and red and low in blue and violet; thus, it imparts a warm glow, but it is far from the color of daylight.

Fluorescent lamps are far more energy efficient than incandescent. Typically, fluorescents produce about 72 lumens (the amount of light generated at the light source) per watt, compared with 6 to 24 lumens per watt produced by an incandescent lamp. The fluorescent has an average life of 15,000 hours versus 750 to 2500 hours for the average incandescent. Furthermore, it takes 60 gallons of oil to burn one 100-watt bulb continuously for one year. With energy shortages having become a fact of life, fluorescents will usually be the major light source, complemented by halogens for special effects.

Fluorescent lamps have been improved in recent years, and more than 20 different colors are available. However, careful selection must be made after consulting manufacturers' lamp specification catalogs, because bulbs of the same wattage do not necessarily have equal lumen counts. There are often other quantitative and qualitative differences about a particular lamp from one manufacturer to another.

Fluorescent lamps are selected on the basis of lumen output, color temperature, and color rendition. The color temperature is expressed in kelvins. The higher the color temperature, the bluer the appearance and the closer to daylight; the lower the color temperature, the redder the appearance. The color rendering index (CRI) describes the ability of a lamp to render objects as they would be seen in outdoor sunlight, which has a CRI of 100. Thus, a lamp with a CRI of 80 renders the object 80 percent as accurately as outdoor sunlight. The closer the CRI to 100, the better the color rendition of the lamp. Below is a list of the most commonly used fluorescent lamps plus a few unique ones. The optimal color temperature for most areas of medical and dental facilities, with the exception of surgeries and dental operations, is 3500 kelvins with a CRI no lower than 80.

Cool White lamps are approximately 4100 kelvins with a CRI of 68. They intensify white, gray, blue, and green and do not blend well with incandescent.

Cool White Deluxe lamps are 4100 kelvins with a CRI of 89. Their color rendition is a big improvement over Cool White lamps, but the lumens per watt are reduced considerably, so more of them are needed to achieve the same level of illumination as with Cool White. They produce a white light with a slightly pink tint.

Warm White lamps are approximately 3000 kelvins with a CRI of 56. They slightly distort all colors and have a pink glow, but mix well with incandescent.

Warm White Deluxe lamps are 3000 kelvins with a CRI of 71. They greatly intensify warm colors, are not as pink as standard warm white, and blend well with incandescent.

Daylight lamps are 6500 kelvins and usually have a CRI of 75. This lamp produces a cold blue-white light, not enhancing to warm colors and incandescent light, but useful in a room where a large quantity of natural light is present.

Neutral White lamps are 3500 kelvins with a CRI of 64. These lamps fall between Cool White and Warm White, so they are good middle-of-the-road choice where budget does not permit a higher-quality lamp. The one with the highest CRI number is best. These lamps blend adequately with incandescent light.

Full-Spectrum lamps range from 5000 to 6500 kelvins with a CRI of 90 to 98. This is a high-quality lamp ideal for color-critical applications such as dental operatories. It produces a bright white light that simulates the full color and ultraviolet spectrum of sunlight. These are manufactured by several sources: Lumichrome by Lumiram is 6500 kelvins with a CRI of 98 and 5700 kelvins with a CRI of 95; Verilux by Verilux, Inc. is 6280 kelvins with a CRI of 94.5; Sylvania Octron 950 is 5000 kelvins with a CRI of 90. These lamps are ideal for dental operatories where exact color matching is critical. Specify high-frequency electronic ballasts to eliminate flicker. Another full-spectrum option is the TC-295 made by Western States Industries in Denver. It is 5550 kelvins with a CRI of 93.

The *Ultralume 3000* lamp is 3000 kelvins with a CRI of 85. Made by Phillips, this lamp enhances warm colors and has better color rendition than the warm white deluxe.

The *Pentron™ T5* lamp is available in various color temperatures with a CRI of 82. Made by Sylvania, the ⅝-inch diameter lamp gives 104 lumens per watt with 95 percent maintenance (constancy) over the life of the lamp.

The *SP35* lamp is 3500 kelvins with a CRI of 73. Made by General Electric (GE), this lamp renders skin tones very well, making it ideal for medical offices. It has the good color rendering properties of Cool White Deluxe and Warm White Deluxe, but has considerably more light output. Cool White Deluxe has 56 lumens per watt, while the SP35 offers 83 lumens per watt. The SP35 complements both cool and warm color palettes, producing a crisp light midpoint between cool white and warm white.

The *SPX35* is 3500 kelvins with a CRI of 82. Manufactured by GE, it is an enhanced version of the SP35 and is more expensive, but makes colors appear more vivid. It greatly enhances interiors.

Compact fluorescent lamps are available in standard color temperatures from 2700 kelvins (with a CRI of 81) to 4100 kelvins. If one does not specify a color temperature, usually 2700 kelvins will be supplied as it most closely resembles warm white or incandescent. Manufactured by many lamp companies, this type of fluorescent is a small twin or quad tube in a U shape, available in 7-, 9-, 13-, and 26-watt lamps. The color rendition is somewhat similar to incandescent, but tends to be a bit more pink, rather than yellow. The 7-watt lamp is equivalent to a 40-watt incandescent; the 9-watt lamp, to a 60-watt incandescent; and the 13-watt, to a 75-watt incandescent. These lamps are very popular because they combine the high efficiency and long life of fluorescent lamps with fairly good color rendition. Their size allows them to be used in downlights, wall sconces, and other types of fixtures that previously required incandescent bulbs. It is important to match the color temperature of compact fluorescents to the other sources of light being used.

Low-voltage lamps are of many types, the most common of which is the MR-16. These are 12-volt quartz halogen lamps that average 3000 kelvins and render colors vividly. The beam can be precisely focused to enhance textures or an art object or to add drama to a room. Low-voltage lamps accomplish a desired level of illumination with fewer watts than required by incandescent lamps, making them energy efficient. Additionally, the miniature size of the lamp allows it to be used in fixtures much smaller than those that accommodate incandescent bulbs. MR-16s give a clean, white light that enhances all colors. When specifying MR-16 lamps, it is necessary to note the desired width of the beam (spot or flood, narrow, medium, or wide beam). Look for long-life MR-16s rated for 4000 to 5000 hours.

The *ConstantColor Precise MR-16* lamp by GE delivers crisp white light with no color shift for the rated life of the lamp (5000 hours).

For comparison, an incandescent lamp is 2800 kelvins, and daylight (although it does vary with the time of day, the time of the year, and whether the sky is sunny or cloudy) is arbitrarily established at 6500 kelvins. The reader is encouraged to contact Osram-Sylvania in Danvers, Massachusetts, and Westinghouse in Bloomfield, New Jersey. Both manufacturers have excellent technical literature on their lamps. GE in Nela Park, Ohio, also publishes a number of interesting booklets. And design professionals should have a copy of the Illuminating Engineering Society of North America (IES) handbook on lighting healthcare facilities.

INNOVATION AND TRENDS

Lamp Technology

Great strides have been made in both lamp technology and fixture design in recent years. Fluorescent lamps with rare-earth phosphors have greatly improved color

Figure 13-2. Indirect pendant lighting provides soft illumination for corridors. (*Design: Jain Malkin Inc.; Photographer: Steve McClelland.*)

rendition; lamps like the slim T5 offer extremely high light output per watt, meaning fewer fixtures (less cost and reduced energy consumption); compact fluorescents in high wattages are now able to accommodate electronic ballasts and offer, in addition, excellent color rendition if one takes the time to choose and specify wisely. Overall, the trend is toward energy-efficient lamps with high light output, extremely long life, and excellent color rendition.

To replace the popular 300-watt halogen torchiere with a safer alternative (a number of imported poor-quality torchieres with unprotected bulbs have caused fires) that uses far less energy, GE has recently introduced a specialized compact fluorescent 55-watt 2D lamp that plugs into a fully dimmable electronic ballast. It uses 66 watts of power (ballast and lamp) and produces 4000 lumens of light, exceeding the output of the 300-watt halogen.

Heralded as one of the most dramatic lighting advances since 1965, the ceramic metal halide lamp will increasingly be used to achieve the ambience of incandescent and halogen sources. With color rendering of 80 to 85 CRI and a 3000 kelvins color temperature (which does, however, shift ±200 kelvins over the lamp's life), it produces 100 lumens per watt (very high performance) and has a life span of 20,000 to 30,000 hours.

Lighting Fixture Technology

A trend in commercial lighting is that there are many more options for indirect fixtures to replace the common 2-×4-foot lay-in luminaire that is the "building standard" fixture in all medical and dental offices. This type of fixture is cheap, creates glare in patients' eyes and on CRT monitors, and, unless electronic ballasts are used, produces flicker that can, in susceptible persons, create eyestrain and headaches. These negative features are compounded by the ubiquitous cool white lamps that are commonly used.

Demand Something Better!

Most physicians and dentists do not even think of inquiring about the color temperature of fluorescent lamps or even realize there are options. All fluorescent lamps (tubes) are coated with phosphors that represent a certain range of the visible color spectrum. Cool white is high in the blue-green range and thus produces a blue or "cold" reflection on all surfaces, including skin tone. Although lamps with more pleasant color attributes do not generally cost more to produce, they do cost more to purchase since the huge volume of cool white sales keeps the cost low. But don't let that deter you. The quality and character of lighting is, along with good space planning, the most important aspect of office design from a functional and aesthetic perspective. One can spend a considerable sum on interior design in terms of finishes and furniture, but if the lighting is "building standard," as described above, the overall effect will be compromised.

Humans are biologically sensitive to light. The quality and character of it affect us whether we realize it or not. Simply requesting a fluorescent lamp with better color characteristics (e.g., 3500 kelvins with a CRI of 80 to 85) will make a dramatic difference even with the building standard luminaire fixtures. The next step up would be to use a lay-in fluorescent luminaire such as the Lithonia Avante (Color Plate 5, Figure 3-99) or Focal Point's Luna, which fits in the standard grid system but is indirect (directs the light upward). An upgrade beyond this, in terms of indirect lighting, can be seen in Color Plate 40, Figure 13-1, and in Figures 3-18 and 13-2. Also consider wall sconces (Figures 13-3 and 13-4).

ENERGY CONSERVATION

Worse than not enough light is too much light. More is not better. The designer, if not qualified to do the lighting calculations, may wish to retain a lighting consultant or an electrical engineer. A high level of general illumination

Figure 13-3. Exam room ambience benefits from wall sconce and task light on desk. (*Design: Jain Malkin Inc.; Photographer: Glenn Cormier.*)

Figure 13-4. Wall sconces, pendant lights, and recessed downlights illuminate corridor and nurse station. (*Design: Jain Malkin Inc.; Photographer: Glenn Cormier.*)

washes out textures and colors. Much more interesting, not to mention energy efficient, is an interplay of high and low levels of illumination. In offices, we now light the task, not the entire room. Lighting, skillfully handled, can set up a rhythm of patterns, light, and shadow that can transform an otherwise commonplace interior into something quite spectacular.

Another practical way to prune watts is to install fixtures with dimmer controls and to use occupancy or motion sensors for rooms with frequent occupancy. Fluorescents must be ordered specifically with dimming ballasts. An attempt to save electricity by removing two of the four lamps in a four-lamp fixture without changing the ballast saves nothing. To achieve the highest transmission of light through the lens, one should specify only acrylic lenses, never polystyrene, which is less expensive but yellows with age. Specify high-frequency electronic ballasts to conserve energy and also to eliminate flicker.

The maintenance of light fixtures is extremely important to their performance. Technical equations permit one to calculate the *light loss factor,* which takes into account temperature and voltage variations, dirt on the lens, lamp depreciation, maintenance procedures, and atmospheric conditions. The ceiling height and the reflectance of walls and floor also affect the footcandle level (the measurement of light that reaches a given surface). Thus, when one speaks of a requirement of 100 *maintained* footcandles at a given task, one must start with a number of lamps somewhat in excess of that measurement to take into account the light loss factor and the interior finishes of the room.

MEDICAL OFFICE ELECTRICAL AND LIGHTING REQUIREMENTS

The electrical and lighting requirements for medical and dental offices differ greatly with the specialty and are discussed somewhat under each chapter. Chapter 10 discusses thoroughly the requirements of dental operatories, so that information will not be repeated here. Figure 13-5 shows the recommended electrical outlets for the

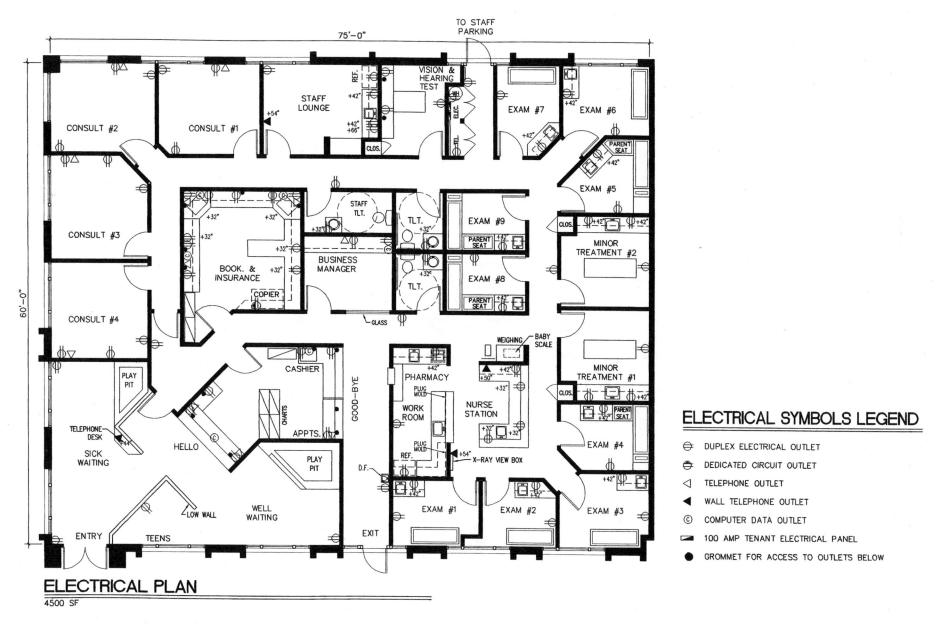

ELECTRICAL PLAN

4500 SF

ELECTRICAL SYMBOLS LEGEND

⊖ DUPLEX ELECTRICAL OUTLET

⊖ DEDICATED CIRCUIT OUTLET

◁ TELEPHONE OUTLET

◀ WALL TELEPHONE OUTLET

ⓒ COMPUTER DATA OUTLET

▭ 100 AMP TENANT ELECTRICAL PANEL

● GROMMET FOR ACCESS TO OUTLETS BELOW

Figure 13-5. Electrical plan for pediatrics suite in Figure 3-104. (*Design: Jain Malkin Inc.*)

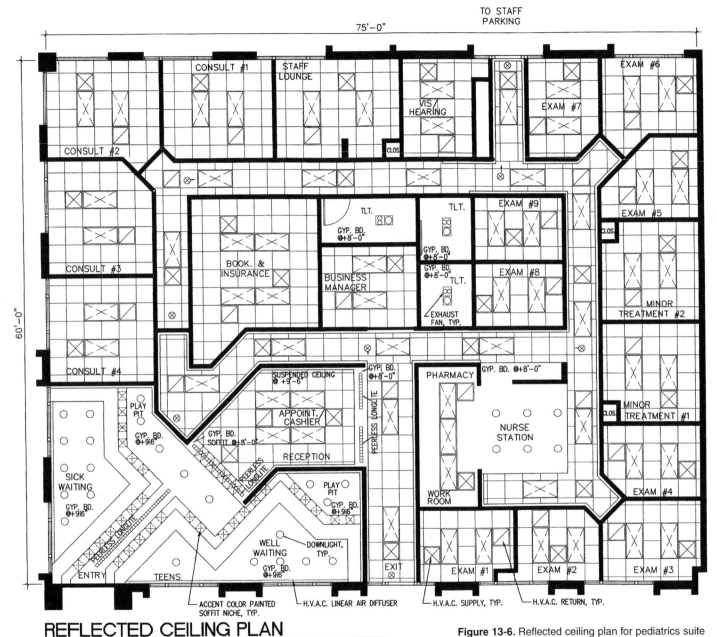

TO STAFF
PARKING

75'-0"

60'-0"

CONSULT #1   STAFF
              LOUNGE

CONSULT #2

VIS
HEARING   EXAM #6

CLOS.   EXAM #7

CONSULT #3   BOOK. &
                   INSURANCE

TLT.
GYP. BD.
@+8'-0"

TLT.

EXAM #9   EXAM #5

CLOS.

BUSINESS
MANAGER

GYP. BD.
@+8'-0"

GYP. BD.
@+8'-0"   TLT.

EXAM #8   MINOR
                  TREATMENT #2

CONSULT #4

EXHAUST
FAN, TYP.

SUSPENDED CEILING
@ +9'-6"

GYP. BD
@+8'-0"

GYP. BD. @+8'-0"

PLAY
PIT

GYP. BD.
@+9'6

APPOINT.
CASHIER

GYP. BD.
SOFFIT @+8'-0"

RECEPTION

PHARMACY

NURSE
STATION

MINOR
TREATMENT #1

CLOS.

SICK
WAITING

GYP. BD.
@+9'6

PLAY
PIT

GYP. BD.
@+9'6

WORK
ROOM

EXAM #4

ENTRY   TEENS

WELL
WAITING

GYP. BD.
@+9'6

DOWNLIGHT,
TYP.

EXIT

EXAM #1   EXAM #2   EXAM #3

ACCENT COLOR PAINTED
SOFFIT NICHE, TYP.

H.V.A.C. LINEAR AIR DIFFUSER

H.V.A.C. SUPPLY, TYP.

H.V.A.C. RETURN, TYP.

PEERLESS LONGLITE
PEERLESS LONGLITE
PEERLESS LONGLITE

REFLECTED CEILING PLAN

4500 SF

Figure 13-6. Reflected ceiling plan for pediatrics suite
in Figure 3-104. (*Design: Jain Malkin Inc.*)

pediatric suite first introduced in Figure 3-104. Figure 13-6 shows a typical reflected ceiling plan and switching diagram for the same pediatric suite.

Exam rooms need a maintained light level of 100 foot-candles. This can be achieved by two four-lamp (2-×4-foot) luminaires, either recessed (lay-in) or surface mounted. Physicians who require a high-intensity light for examinations will have a portable lamp or other light source for that purpose. Color Plate 5, Figure 3-99, shows an exam room with a Lithonia Avante indirect light source that conceals the lamps, especially important when patients are lying down looking up. A ceiling-mounted examination light adds high-intensity light where needed. The exam room in Figure 13-3 benefits from a combination of lighting types: compact fluorescent wall sconce, incandescent table lamp on desk, and indirect fluorescent overhead (out of view).

Nurse stations also require a maintained illumination of 100 footcandles. The nurse station in Figure 13-4 has halogen pendant lights, compact fluorescent downlights for ambient illumination, and wall sconces. The feeling is warm and nonclinical. A lower light level is appropriate for waiting rooms (30 to 50 footcandles), and the concentration of illumination should be where people are reading. The lighting may be indirect downlights or fluorescent luminaires or a combination of sources adding drama to the room rather than a wash of overall illumination as in Figure 13-7. The breast center waiting room in Color Plate 40, Figure 13-8, combines geometric forms, a sophisticated color palette, and a variety of light sources. Low voltage cable lighting is effective in corridors, especially when high ceilings are possible (Color Plates 9, 11, and 18, Figures 4-20, 4-24, 4-101, and 4-103).

The reader is referred to Color Plate 40, Figure 13-1, for an example of indirect fluorescent light in a pendant fixture. The ceiling reflects the light to illuminate the space without glare. Another type of pendant fixture that bounces light off of the ceiling by SPI is especially effec-

Figure 13-7. Variety in ceilings and lighting creates interest in a narrow, long waiting room. (*Design: Jain Malkin Inc.; Photographer: Glenn Cormier.*)

Figure 13-9. Fluorescent pendant lights in clinic administrator's office provide indirect light that bounces off ceiling and eliminates glare on CRT. (*Design: Jain Malkin Inc.; Photographer: Glenn Cormier.*)

tive where glare on computer monitors can be problematic (Figures 13-2 and 13-9).

Corridors need only about 20 footcandles of illumination, and the light certainly need not be confined to the ceiling. In fact, lighting mounted on the walls of a corridor often gives better color rendition to interior finishes than would those same lights mounted on the ceiling. Also, there is more glare when lights are mounted on the ceiling. Figure 13-10 shows the corridor of a dental suite. The vaulted ceiling and Italian pendant light fixtures create a residential ambience with a European flavor.

Decorative pendant lights are effective at reception desks (Color Plate 3, Figure 3-15). The lighting treatment in Color Plate 27, Figure 7-12, creates the effect of an outdoor sky and trellis in the waiting room of an ambulatory surgery center.

The consultation room requires approximately 50 footcandles of light concentrated over the desk. Additional lighting in a consultation room may be used to accent diplomas or artwork if the room is large enough to handle additional lighting.

Minor surgery rooms require from 100 to 150 maintained footcandles, depending on the types of procedures performed. Most minor surgery rooms will have a ceiling-mounted high-intensity surgical light in addition to two four-lamp fluorescents.

The lighting requirements of specialized rooms such as ophthalmology refraction rooms or radiology rooms are discussed under these specialties, as are any special considerations concerning the type or level of illumination for the individual suite as a whole.

Figure 13-10. Corridor, general dentistry office. (*Design: Carmel Repp, ASID, IIDA, San Diego, CA: Photographer: Kim Brun.*)

CHAPTER 14

Construction Methods and Building Systems

HEATING, VENTILATING, AND AIR CONDITIONING

The mechanical requirements of medical and dental offices are quite specialized in that the physical comfort of staff and patients is very important, and there are a great many variables in terms of room function, often within a small area. An *examination room,* for example, is typically 8×12 feet in size, and the patient (who spends more time in the room than the doctor) is usually undressed. The *waiting room,* by contrast, is designed to accommodate many people, and often they have sweaters or coats on their laps, which add to their body warmth. Not only does this room have a higher density (one person per 16 to 20 square feet compared with one person per 96 square feet in an exam room), but the occupants themselves generate heat.

A *nurse station* or *business office,* where fully clothed persons are busily moving about, has yet a different requirement. The *dental operatory,* typically 100 square feet, usually has three occupants and a high level of illumination. These rooms each have different comfort requirements in terms of temperature and varying load characteristics. The lighting load for a waiting room will be approximately 2 watts per square foot; for an examination room, 3.3 watts per square foot; for a dental operatory, 10 watts per square foot; for a nurse station or business office, 2.5 watts per square foot; and for corridors, 1 to 1.5 watts per square foot. In states where energy conservation legislation has been enacted, the allowable watts per square foot have been slashed to the point where it can be quite a challenge to light clinical rooms adequately. In California, for example, exam rooms are allowed 1.4 watts per square foot, a business office, 1.3 watts. This can be supplemented by task lighting, which falls outside these allowances. Refer to Chapter 13 to see how advances in technology have addressed the challenge of energy conservation.

The factors that must be considered in designing a functional heating, ventilating, and air-conditioning (HVAC) system are

1. Lighting load

2. Room occupancy

3. Equipment load

4. Comfort level based on room function

The capacity of the mechanical system should take into account requirements of such special tenants as a sports medicine facility, ambulatory surgical center, or clinical lab.

The type of HVAC system (equipment and method of distribution) may vary, but often it is a ducted air system that supplies heated, cooled, and fresh air. The system should be designed with maximum concern for sound control. Thus, each room may have its own supply and air return; undercutting doors and the use of transfer grilles for return air are to be avoided. Sound carried through the ducts of a ventilation system can be reduced in a number of ways.

A certain amount of sound will naturally be absorbed in the duct wall lining, and some will pass through the duct walls into the plenum. Additional insulation, duct linings, or package attenuation units can produce an even greater degree of sound control. However, a certain amount of white noise produced by the mechanical system is desirable for masking conversation from room to room.

Performance Spec

It is advisable to write a performance spec for the HVAC system to define goals about room zoning and after-hours operation (physicians often work late and on weekends) and to analyze equipment costs, projected energy use, and operating costs.

The need for after-hours HVAC operation must not be underestimated. Surgeons who live far from the hospital may sleep in their offices if called to the hospital late at night for an emergency. Others may open their offices on weekends to treat a sick patient. Extended evening and Saturday hours are fairly common for many dental and medical practices in order to accommodate people who work.

CONTROL OF ODORS

To prevent the spread of odors from radiography/fluoroscopy rooms, darkroom, toilets, cast room, laboratory, staff lounge, or other areas, the ventilation system should be designed so that negative air pressure, relative to adjoining corridors, is maintained. This can be accomplished by exhausting more air from these rooms than is supplied to them and by reversing this procedure in the corridors. Exhaust in these rooms should be at least 2 cubic feet per minute per square foot. *Air from fluoroscopic radiography rooms should not be recirculated when these rooms are in use, unless adequate odor removal equipment is incorporated in the ventilation system.*

PLUMBING

Plumbing in a medical or dental facility is not much different from that in other types of commercial buildings, but, by their very nature, medical office buildings have a high density of plumbing fixtures, and provisions must be made to locate them anywhere except along the perimeter of the building. No area should be too far from drainage to accommodate a slope of ¼ inch per foot within the given plenum depth. Plaster traps should be supplied in sinks for cast rooms, clinical laboratories, barium prep areas, dental laboratories, and sometimes in minor surgery rooms. Darkrooms and clinical laboratories should have acid-resistant waste piping. All medical and dental offices must be sprinklered.

MEDICAL GASES

Certain suites—dentists, oral surgeons, plastic surgeons—require medical gases. Building and fire codes are very strict regarding where and how medical gases are stored. Gases may be stored in mobile tanks that are wheeled from room to room as needed, or gases (nitrous oxide and oxygen) may be stored in tanks in a nearby room designed for that purpose and piped through degreased, sealed copper tubing (using only silver solder) to a flow meter in each room where gases are needed. If gases are located outside the suite, a pressure gauge must be located within the suite to monitor the supply. The reader is referred to Chapter 10 for a complete discussion of this topic. Building codes are very specific about the storage of medical gases with respect to the construction of the room and the required ventilation and fire protection.

Certain suites require compressed air and central suction. These tenants will usually have a vacuum pump and air compressor located in a small mechanical equipment room within the suite, but some medical buildings provide these utilities and pipe them to the suites. Vacuum piping is PVC Schedule 40. Suites requiring these utilities include dentists, oral surgeons, clinical laboratories, dental laboratories, endoscopy suites, ambulatory surgical centers, and plastic surgery suites.

Sound Control

Sound control is of utmost importance in a medical office, especially in examination rooms and consultation rooms. Unfortunately, all too many medical buildings are constructed with profit rather than function as the prime motivation, and partitions terminate at the finished ceiling and have no sound-attenuating properties. There are, however, several ways to reduce sound transmission without spending great sums of money:

1. All partitions should terminate 6 to 8 inches above the suspended ceiling. Thus, each room has its own ceiling, rather than dropping the suspended acoustic ceiling over the entire suite, with only the demising walls continuing above it.

2. Sound can be absorbed near its source through the use of carpet, wallcoverings, and acoustic ceiling tile.

3. Solid-core doors should be used.

4. Fiberglas batting should be added inside partitions between studs.

5. To control the passage of sound through walls, floors, and ceilings, acoustical "holes" should be avoided, such as those created by the use of pocket doors or when electrical outlets on opposite sides of a partition are positioned too close to each other, when doors are poorly fitted, when plumbing pipes or heating ducts are improperly fitted, or when partitions do not make proper contact with the ceiling.

6. A certain amount of white noise from the ventilation system will mask soft conversation from room to room.

7. A piped-in music system will also mask normal conversation. A CD player or cassette deck located in the business office with speakers in the waiting room and

corridors is preferable to innocuous prerecorded background music.

8. Certain rooms, such as psychiatrists' consultation rooms and audio rooms for hearing tests, need a high level of sound control. There are a number of ways to create a sound-attenuating partition. Creased Thermafiber insulation, application of sound board, isolation through the use of resilient channels, and staggered studs are four methods commonly used.

9. Return air grilles should not be located near each other. If the building has a plenum return, the grilles should have a minimum 4-foot sound boot (16-inch-diameter flexible ducting open at the other end). Open ends of sound boots should be turned away from each other.

MEDICAL/DENTAL OFFICE COMMUNICATION SYSTEMS

The reader is referred to Chapter 10 for a discussion of communication systems specifically for the dental office. Also refer to Chapter 3.

Many offices of more than 1500 square feet have some sort of interoffice communication system other than the telephone intercom. There are four conditions that may require signal notification:

1. To tell the doctor which room has the next patient

2. To call the doctor to the telephone

3. To call a nurse or aide when the doctor is in the examining room

4. To tell the staff where the doctor is

A small panel of signal lights mounted above exam room doors can indicate to the doctor when a patient has been prepared for examination. When the patient is ready, the nurse turns on the light code for a specific doctor. When the doctor enters the room, he or she turns off the light. This system requires additional modification for large busy practices, since several patients may be prepared and waiting for an individual doctor who will need some way of knowing the sequence.

The receptionist who handles the phone must know in which room each doctor can be found. A toggle switch for each physician must be located in each exam, treatment, or consultation room the doctor uses. When the doctor enters the room, he or she trips the switch, which lights a panel located at the reception desk.

Some offices do not use signal lights. A variety of "homemade" systems may be devised, one of which follows. Assume, for example, a group of three orthopedists: Each physician is assigned a color and a set of Plexiglas chips 4×5 inches in size. Each chip has a large number, 1 to 3 (since each physician has the use of three exam rooms). The chips are stored in a wall-mounted rack at the centrally located nurse station. When a nurse readies a patient, she puts that doctor's color chip in a slot on the door; thus, each doctor knows, by the color of the chip, if the patient in that room is his or hers, and, by the number, the order in which to examine the patients.

To call a nurse or aide when the doctor is in the exam room, a signal light can be used, but it may not be noticed—a distinct disadvantage. A preferred system is an annunciator panel, although it is limited by the number of sounds a person can reasonably discriminate. Each doctor would have a distinctive buzz or chime. When the nurse hears the signal, she consults a panel to determine what room the doctor is in, and proceeds to that room.

There are a variety of other interoffice communication systems available. Dealers who sell these products also install them. They can design a system to suit the needs of the individual office and can furnish the designer with the electrical specifications.

FIRE PROTECTION

Special consideration must be given to the type of fire-extinguishing system used in such suites as radiology or clinical labs, which contain a great deal of expensive computer-based equipment. Sprinklers would do considerable damage.

CHECKLIST

The following is a checklist of odds and ends to jog the designer's memory. It is not intended to be a complete inventory of requirements.

CODE REVIEW

- Occupancy type

- Occupancy load

- Number of required exits, separation of exits

- Radiation shielding

- Fire separations

- Handicapped bathrooms and other accessibility requirements

- Structural floor loading (chart file rooms)

PARTITIONS

- Sound control

- Continuation above suspended ceiling

- Fiberglas batting

- Verify construction of partitions with contractor when planning offices in a building not designed by the space planner (one may find that the contractor, in order to come in with a low bid, based his bid on 2½-inch studs, giving a finished wall that has to be "thickened" wherever plumbing and recessed plumbing accessories and/or X-ray view boxes occur)

- Verify or specify texture of finished wall

- Spec eggshell finish for walls for durability and cleanability
- Spec special ceiling heights, if required
- No texture on walls that will receive wallcovering
- Spec blocking in walls (or ceiling) to support X-ray view boxes, cassette pass boxes, dental operatory lights and X-ray heads, special light fixtures, casework, certain pieces of medical equipment, and for TV brackets

Doors

- Solid core
- Pocket doors
- Gate door with transaction shelf
- Door closers, smoke seals
- Hardware, keying of locks, function of locks
- Door finish: painted or stained, plastic laminate
- Door stops
- Type of door frame
- Spec width and height of doors
- Spec carpet height (plus pad, if any) for cutting doors
- Door assembly ratings (20 minute, 90 minute, etc.), if required

Plumbing

- Plaster traps
- Wrist- or foot-pedal control faucets
- Acid-resistant waste pipes
- Spec sizes of sinks; porcelain or stainless steel

- Vacuum breakers (darkrooms)
- Separate shutoffs for each fixture
- Floor drains in darkrooms, hot-water heater room
- ADA compliance for toilets

Communication Systems

- Telephones
- Intercom
- Signal lights
- Annunciator panel
- Music system: locate speakers
- Location of telephone terminal panel (requires electrical outlet and grounding)

Mechanical Systems

- Locate air compressor and vacuum
- Locate medical gases, natural gas
- Locate hot-water heater (if electric, requires outlet) and floor drain
- Exhaust fans (bathrooms, darkrooms, labs, cast rooms, staff lounges)

Casework

- Spec style of construction, types of drawer glides, hardware, hinges
- Detail handicapped accessibility at reception counter and sink locations
- Trash slots in exam cabinets, as required

LIGHTING/CEILING

- Do switching diagram
- Spec dimmers, as required (fluorescent fixtures require dimming ballasts)
- Spec color fluorescent lamps
- Spec lamp wattages
- Spec lenses of fixtures
- Spec color of grid (spline) suspended acoustic ceiling
- Illuminated exit signs

ELECTRICAL

- Note special outlets, 220-volt lines, floor receptacles
- Spec height of outlets
- Outlets over countertops should run horizontally
- Locate circuit breaker panel
- Locate intercom and phone, note wall phones

MISCELLANEOUS

- Locate scale spaces, as required, noting any that are to be recessed in the slab
- Fire extinguishing equipment

CHAPTER 15

Researching Codes and Reference Materials

Codes are designed to ensure life safety. As healthcare services have become more complex and sophisticated, the design and construction of these facilities have become more specialized. Paralleling the increasing complexity of diagnostic and treatment procedures is the development of numerous codes and standards designed to limit risk and make buildings relatively safe.

The problem is that codes occasionally contradict one another, and the language is frequently subject to interpretation. Often, the level of protection is a value judgment. The minimum standards per code may be inadequate for a facility serving the elderly, for example. Or the corollary may be true: The minimum standards may occasionally be excessive for a particular project. The cost of implementing them may make the project unfeasible. Thus, codes must be evaluated in terms of the following: (1) *What is an acceptable level of risk in terms of life safety?* (2) *Is the cost of that level of protection warranted or within the budget for the facility?* (3) *Are the codes or standards applicable to that facility redundant?*

Further complicating these issues is the fact that codes are written by one body and enforced by another. The local agent, who is responsible for interpretation and compliance, does not always understand the intent of the codes, and agents within the same office may disagree on interpretations. Nevertheless, codes are an important part of healthcare design, and designers need to be familiar with them. If anything, the next 10 years will bring more codes and regulations, not fewer. However, the recent introduction of the *International Building Code,* which will hopefully be adopted by all states, will do much to minimize the differences in codes among jurisdictions.

Codes cover the general areas outlined below.

FIRE PROTECTION

1. *Flammability of Materials:* especially carpet, wallcoverings, draperies, upholstery fillings and fabrics, and carpet and wallcovering adhesives

2. *Exiting Requirements:* number of exits, travel distances between doors of exit, corridor separations, sizes of doors and stairwells, construction of doors and walls and illumination of fire exits

3. *Storage:* how and where medical gases are to be used and stored; storage of combustible solid supplies

4. *Fire-Fighting Equipment:* locations of wet and dry standpipes; chemical fire extinguishers; and, in high-rise buildings, smoke evacuation shafts and central control station for fire department use

5. *Electrical Systems:* standards for wiring, equipment, and emergency power systems

6. Fire Detection Devices: locations of sprinklers, smoke detectors, and alarms

THE AMERICANS WITH DISABILITIES ACT OF 1990

Disabled persons are defined broadly to include the visually and hearing impaired; those with motor or neurological disorders; and individuals with arthritis, asthma, and cardiac insufficiency. The goal is to create spaces that are universally accessible to persons of different stature (height and weight), age, and abilities. The Americans with Disabilities Act (ADA) is civil rights legislation enacted to ensure equal access in public accommodations. Title III contains accessibility guidelines specifically related to building access. (Both federal and state codes provide for creating accessible places.)

The ADA is enforced through the U.S. Department of Justice (DOJ) through complaints of private citizens and other organizations. There is no "ADA police," but there are individual citezens or organized citizen groups and attorneys who file complaints with the DOJ.

The ADA affects the following facilities: restaurants and cafeterias; medical care facilities; businesses; retail shops, civic buildings, libraries; transient lodging; transportation; judiciary, legislative, and regulatory facilities; detention and correctional facilities; public housing; and public right-of-way areas.

1. Location of ramps, curb cuts, parking stalls; placement of exits and design configurations

2. Dimensions of elevators and restrooms, door widths and setbacks, and placement of restroom fixtures and accessories

3. Heights of countertops and work surfaces, public telephones, and drinking fountains

4. Audible and visible warnings at elevators and stairs

5. Elimination of protruding objects in corridors or lobbies

SANITATION

1. Cleanability of wallcovering, flooring, and other interior finishes

2. Asepsis (ability to support bacteria) of interior finish materials

3. Homogeneous character of materials to eliminate pores or cracks that may support bacterial growth

MINIMUM CONSTRUCTION REQUIREMENTS

1. Minimum sizes of rooms and minimum sizes of various departments (within a hospital, for example), location and number of windows, minimum ceiling heights, and relationship of various rooms to one another

2. Planning and programming decisions with regard to function (e.g., separation of clean and soiled functions in surgical facilities)

3. Accommodation of equipment: spaces for gurneys, drinking fountains, and public telephones. Minimum requirements for laundries, kitchens, laboratories, operating rooms, etc.

ENERGY CONSERVATION/ ENVIRONMENTAL IMPACT

State and local codes govern energy conservation and the ecological impact of a proposed building on its environment.

National Codes and Standards

The aforementioned code classifications may fall under the jurisdiction of city, county, state, or federal codes, in addition to the following nationally recognized standards:

Life Safety Code 101 and NFPA 99 (published by the National Fire Protection Association)

Uniform Fire Code

National Electrical Code (published by the National Fire Protection Association)

JCAHO (Joint Commission on Accreditation of Healthcare Organizations)

Building Officials and Code Administrators (BOCA)

Americans with Disabilities Act, Title III

Guidelines for Design and Construction of Hospital and Medical Facilities (published by the American Institute of Architects with assistance of the U.S. Department of Health and Human Services)

National Institute of Standards and Technology (U.S. Department of Commerce)

American Society for Testing and Materials (ASTM)

Underwriters' Laboratories

International Code Council

Recognized state building codes include the following:

International Building Code

Uniform Building Code (used by many western states)

Southern Standard Building Code

National Building Code

Some states have their own building code; others use a regional code that serves several neighboring states.

CERTIFICATE OF NEED

Prior to building a state-licensed healthcare facility or remodeling or expanding an existing one, the local health systems agency (HSA) must endorse the project and, in some states, a Certificate of Need (CON) must be obtained from the state. The CON is designed to prevent duplication of highly specialized facilities and equipment and to keep a lid on rising healthcare costs. States receiving federal funds under the National Health Planning and Resource Development Act of 1974 were required to introduce CON programs. Currently, 36 states have some type of CON regulations; however, a number of states have abandoned their CON programs.

ISSUES RELATING TO OUTPATIENT MEDICAL FACILITIES UNDER A HOSPITAL'S LICENSE

Hospitals often develop clinics or specialized outpatient facilities in MOBs on the hospital campus. Usually, these are barely distinguishable from non-hospital-based facilities of similar function or specialty, but—designer beware—these will be subject to levels of scrutiny and regulations that may, at times, seem excessive, or even capricious, for outpatient facilities. Some of these issues concern levels of infection control appropriate for hospitals but unusual when viewed within the context of an outpatient facility.

Most outpatient facilities operated under the hospital's license will be subject to JCAHO accreditation, which means they will be surveyed against the AIA *Guidelines for Design and Construction of Hospital and Healthcare Facilities* and will also be inspected by the local department of health services.

CODES RELATING TO MEDICAL OFFICE BUILDINGS

Code requirements for medical and dental offices are minimal compared to those for hospitals. The local building code will determine the type of construction for a particular medical building and site, the zoning requirements, and the fire zone.

Although state building codes vary, the following items are generally pertinent to planning individual medical and dental offices within a medical office building:

- Building type, number of floors, and square footage
- Minimum width of corridors
- Number of exits
- Accessible bathrooms
- Separation of exits
- Maximum length of dead-end corridors
- Minimum ceiling heights
- Construction of partitions
- Fire separations
- Radiation shielding
- Fire detection devices or sprinklers

Some of these items apply only to suites in excess of a specified square footage. Suites having an occupant load of 30 or more (generally 2900 square feet or larger), for example, in the *Uniform Building Code,* 1997 edition, must have at least two exits "separated by a distance equal to not less than one-half the length of the maximum overall diagonal dimension of the area served measured in a straight line between the center of such exits, or along the path of travel" and no more than a 20-foot dead-end corridor.

With an occupancy load of 100 or more, the suite would have to have corridors of one-hour fire-resistive construction. Codes applying to medical office buildings deal mainly with fire prevention and exiting in case of fire, as well as handicapped accessibility. The following principles are easy to understand in terms of space planning and construction.

ISOLATION OF RISK

If a facility is divided into sections by corridor separations, fire-resistive stairwell enclosures, and sealed vertical openings, the fire may be contained and prevented from spreading.

REQUIRED EXITS

The number of exits is based on the proposed occupancy load or the number of people using the space. Approved exits must lead directly out or to other means of egress, and doors may have to open in the direction of egress (depending on the occupant load). Exits may not be through kitchens, storage rooms, or spaces used for similar purpose. Thus, people will not be trapped in a building, and all exits will be clearly marked and accessible in case of fire.

SEPARATION OF EXITS

When more than one exit is required, each must be separated by a specified distance proportional to the size of the space to provide alternate access if one exit is blocked by fire.

STAIRS AND DOORS

Stairwells with fire-resistive enclosures and self-closing fire doors are intended to be smoke-free evacuation towers in case of fire. The stairs must be sufficiently wide to enable people on stretchers to be evacuated if necessary.

FIRE-WARNING OR FIRE-EXTINGUISHING DEVICES

Sprinkler systems are required in all facilities, particularly in laboratories, boiler rooms, large storage areas, or hazardous areas that are often unoccupied. Smoke or heat detectors and alarms are good warning devices where sprinklers are not feasible.

FLAMMABILITY TESTING

Building codes, regulations, and local ordinances are designed to restrict the use of flammable materials on walls, floors, and ceilings of buildings. The flammability characteristics of various interior finish materials influence the behavior of a fire. Although it is impossible to make a building and its furnishings absolutely "fireproof," it is desirable to limit the risk to a reasonable standard by ensuring that the major interior finishes will not support flame or generate smoke. The NFPA 101 Life Safety Code specifies the flame spread, smoke density, and fuel-contributed standards for floors and walls of hospitals.

CARPET

The flame retardance of a carpet is a significant factor in its selection for a healthcare facility. Carpet fibers have different melting points: Acrylics melt at 420 to 490 degrees Fahrenheit; nylons, 415 to 480 degrees; modacrylics, 275°F to 300°F. Polypropylene fuses at 285°F to 330°F; wool, which does not melt, scorches at approximately 400°F. Four factors affect the flammability of a carpet.

1. Type of face yarn

2. Type of construction and texture

3. Pile density

4. Underlayment or pad

There are two tests of carpet flammability.

The Pill Test (Deptartment of Commerce #DOCFF-1-70). A methenamine pill (a timed burning tablet) placed on the carpet is used to determine if a carpet will burn when ignited by a small incendiary source. Since April 1971, all carpet sold in the United States must pass the pill test.

Flooring Radiant Panel Test (ASTM 648). This is the most widely used test for carpet flammability. The radiant panel test evolved from extensive corridor fire test pro-

grams. The test measures the *critical radiant flux* (the minimum radiant energy necessary for a fire to continue to burn and spread) in watts per square centimeter (watts/cm^2). The lower the number, the greater the capacity for flame propagation.

0.45 watts per square centimeter is the minimum critical radiant flux recommended within corridors and exitways of hospitals and nursing homes. Class I = 0.45 watts per square centimeter or higher.

0.22 watts per square centimeter is the minimum critical radiant flux recommended within corridors and exitways of other occupancies except one-family and two-family dwellings. Class II = 0.22 to 0.44 watts per square centimeter.

These values provide a level of safety for a carpeted hospital corridor equal to or in excess of that now provided in the NFPA 101 Life Safety Code. Note that smoke density is as important as flame spread, since many people are killed by the smoke generated by a fire. The smoke density test is ASTM E-662.

WALLCOVERINGS

Interior finish materials (including wallcoverings) are grouped into three classes, according to their flame spread and smoke development characteristics. The Steiner Tunnel Test (ASTM E-84) is the standard test of flame spread for wallcoverings and ceiling materials. Codes qualify rooms by occupancy and specify which class of finish is applicable.

Class A Interior Finish. Flame spread 0–25, smoke developed 0–450

Class B Interior Finish. Flame spread 26–75, smoke developed 0–450

Class C Interior Finish. Flame spread 76–200, smoke developed 0–450

Where Class C is specified, Classes A and B are permitted; where Class B is specified, Class A is permitted. Where an approved and properly maintained sprinkler system is in place, the specified flame spread classification rating may be reduced by one classification, but in no case shall materials having a classification greater than Class III or Class C be used.

Wallcoverings are also classified according to weight and texture. Continuous smooth surfaces equal to enamel plaster—less apt to support bacterial growth or collect dirt—are required for operating rooms, recovery rooms, and sterilization areas. Textured wallcoverings may be used in waiting rooms, corridors, offices, and examination areas.

It is the designer's responsibility to verify the codes pertinent to a particular project. If local codes stipulate minimum flammability standards for finishes in a room, an exit corridor, or an area of a medical suite, then all interior finish materials must be evaluated with respect to vendor-provided laboratory test data supporting the flame spread classification claimed.

Wallcovering Specifications. Fabric-backed vinyl wallcoverings are classified into three general categories.

Type I. In accordance with federal specification CCC-W-408a, Type I must weigh a minimum of 7 ounces per square yard and may weigh up to 14 ounces per square yard. It usually has a lightweight scrim backing. Type I materials are acceptable for light commercial use such as offices and corridors with moderate traffic.

Type II. In accordance with federal specification CCC-W-408a, Type II must weigh a minimum of 13 ounces per square yard and may weigh up to 22 ounces per square yard. It usually has an Osnaburg or drill tear-resistant fabric backing. Type II materials are suitable for general commercial use in public corridors of hospitals, lobbies, waiting rooms, dining rooms, cafeterias, and other areas of high traffic and above-average abuse.

Type III. In accordance with federal specification CCC-W-408a, Type III must weigh in excess of 22 ounces per square yard. It usually has a broken twill fabric backing for maximum strength and tear resistance. Type III materials are suitable for areas receiving exceptionally hard wear and abrasion such as elevators, stores and shops, hospital corridors, and stairwells.

Wallcoverings in high-traffic areas can be ordered with a Tedlar® coating to give walls even greater protection. Tedlar is a tough preformed film of polyvinyl fluoride, which is laminated to the face of the vinyl wallcovering to make it resist stains such as lipstick, ballpoint pens, silver nitrate, and other indelible substances. Even harsh solvents and cleaning solutions will not mar the Tedlar coating, making it ideal for use in psychiatric hospitals, pediatric facilities, and other healthcare occupancies where walls are subject to graffiti and high abuse.

Page 568 blank

Appendixes

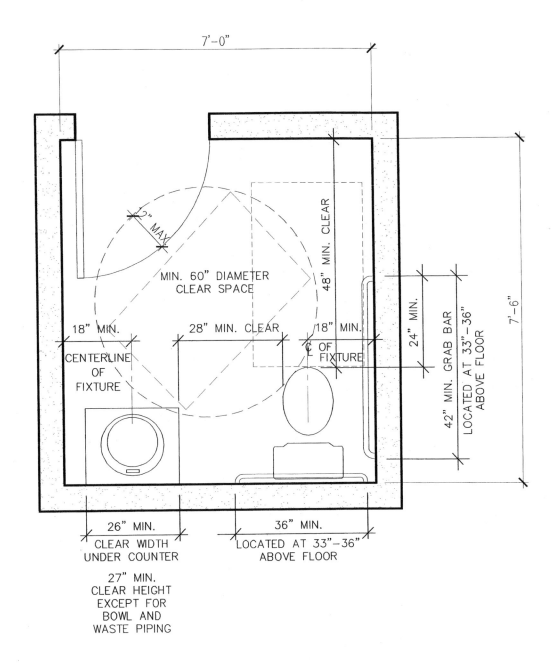

HANDICAPPED ACCESSIBLE TOILET

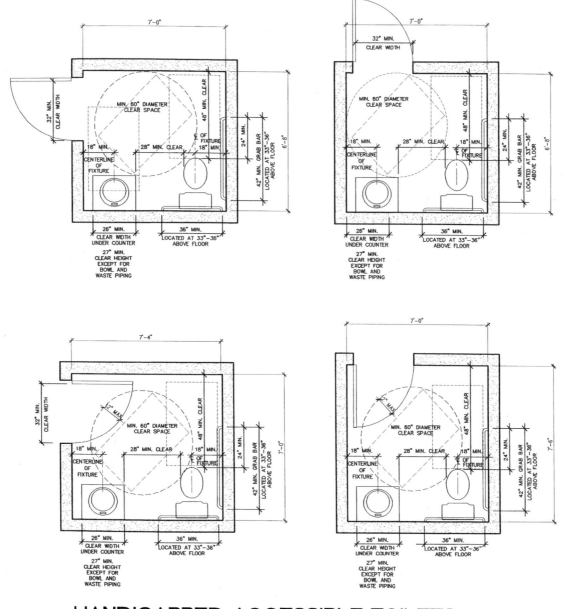

HANDICAPPED ACCESSIBLE TOILETS

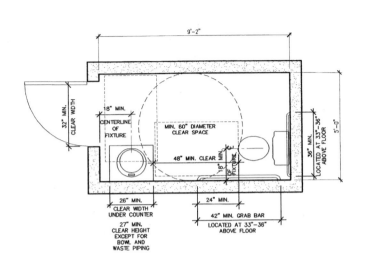

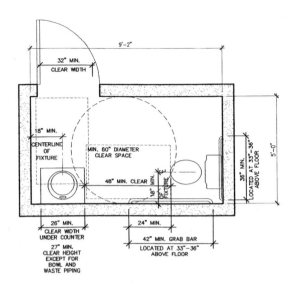

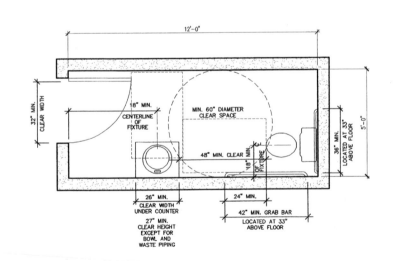

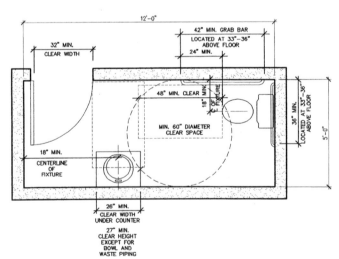

HANDICAPPED ACCESSIBLE TOILETS

Appendix 2

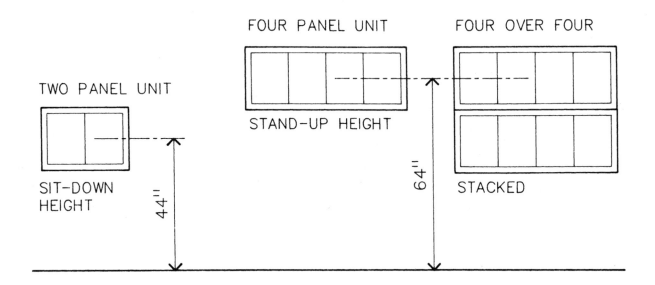

TWO PANEL UNIT

SIT-DOWN HEIGHT

FOUR PANEL UNIT

STAND-UP HEIGHT

FOUR OVER FOUR

STACKED

44"

64"

SUGGESTED MOUNTING HEIGHTS FOR VIEW BOX ILLUMINATORS

Appendix 3

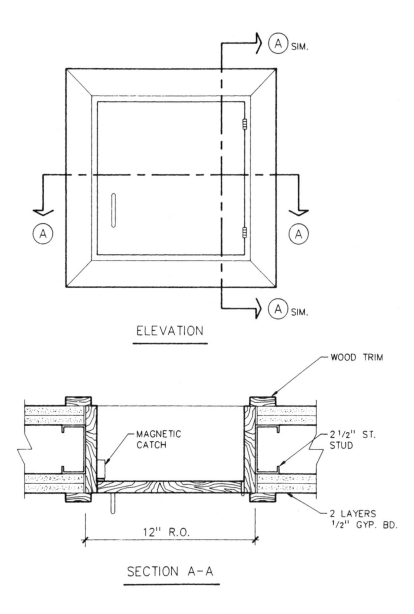

ELEVATION

WOOD TRIM

MAGNETIC
CATCH

2 1/2" ST.
STUD

2 LAYERS
1/2" GYP. BD.

12" R.O.

SECTION A-A

SPECIMEN PASS-THROUGH

Appendix 4

MEDICAL SPACE PLANNING QUESTIONNAIRE

Date: _____

Physician group name: _____

Telephone: _____ E-mail address: _____

Questionnaire filled out by: _____

Medical specialty: _____

Size of present office: _____ (SF)

Anticipated size of new office: _____ (SF)

Suite location requirements within building: _____

PROPOSED STAFF

Administration / Front Office:

Reception: _____   Separate Appts./Check-out: _____

Insurance: _____

Bookkeeping: _____

Office Manager: _____

Transcription: _____   Medical Records Clerk: _____

Other _____

_____

_____

Medical / Back Office:

Physicians: _____

Aides: _____ (medical assistants)

R.N.s: _____

L.V.N.s / L.P.N.: _____

Nurse Pract.: _____

1

Other: _____

_____

_____

BUSINESS OFFICE

Medical Records:

Do you use EMR (electronic medical records)? _____

If so, do you still require traditional medical chart storage for older "paper" charts? _____

_____

If EMR, describe the systems you use and how you access it in the exam room. _____

_____

_____

_____

_____

Are there other components of your paperless office we should be aware of? _____

_____

_____

No. chart file cabinets required: _____

Size chart file cabinets required: _____

If you do not use freestanding chart file cabinets, please describe what you do use and tell us how many lineal feet you require of this type chart filing.

_____

_____

We shall assume that the figures you give us include the projected growth you wish to plan for in the new office.

2

Details of Business Office Layout:
Describe the overall size of the business office and stipulate whether the bookkeeper, insurance staff, and office manager are included in one large space with modular workstations (prefabricated furniture and partitions) or if these individuals should have private offices.

_____

_____

_____

Insurance Bookkeeping:
In recent years, managed care has added complexity to billing and collections, often resulting in the need for additional staff. Please describe how you manage these functions, and how these staff relate to each other in an optimal situation which may or may not be what you currently have:

_____

_____

_____

_____

Filing needs (limited to bookkeeping and insurance): _____

_____

_____

Specialized Equipment:
Copy machine(s):   Floor model: _____   Countertop model: _____

Fax machine(s): _____

Postage-meter machine: _____

Other equipment (please describe): _____

_____

_____

Would you like to have a small workroom off the business office to accommodate this equipment?

_____

Computer Systems:
We shall assume each of your staff will require a CRT monitor at their workstations. Which of these individuals will **also** require a typewriter?

_____

_____

Printers (describe locations): _____

_____

Do you or your staff have an additional computer or printer networked with the hospital?

_____

Surgery Scheduling:
If relevant for your specialty, how do you handle surgery scheduling? Who, in your office, is responsible for this?

_____

_____

PATIENT PROFILE

Average number patients/day: _____ Office hours: _____ to _____

Composition of patients (describe age, gender, cultural mix): _____

_____

_____

DIAGNOSTIC INSTRUMENTATION

Do you use digital diagnostic instrumentation in your exam or procedure rooms that may require special accommodation in terms of room layout, utilities, or lighting?

_____

_____

_____

3

4

PROPOSED SUITE REQUIREMENTS (PROGRAM)

It would be helpful if you could provide approximate sizes and number of rooms needed. To guide you, we have listed in parentheses typical sizes of each room that accommodate most medical specialties.

Exam Rooms (8 x 12): _____

Minor Surgery/Special Procedures (12 x 12): _____

Consultation Room (Physician's office) (12 x 12): _____

Lab (8 x 10): _____

Nurse Stations (8 x 10): _____

    Combined with lab: _____ ? Separate: _____?

Storage: _____

Conference with Library (12 x 16): _____

Staff Lounge (small, 10 x 12): _____ (large, 12 x 16): _____

Patient Education Room (8 x 10): _____

Toilets (patients): _____ (staff): _____

Waiting Room (estimate 20 SF per person): _____

    Children's play area: _____?

SPECIALIZED ROOMS

ECG: _____ (with treadmill?): _____

Pulmonary Function Testing: _____ (with treadmill?): _____

Flex Sig. Procedure Room: _____ (with workroom?): _____

Ultrasound: _____

Endoscopy Suite: _____
(Includes prep and recovery area, clean and soiled utility rooms)

_____

_____

Mammography: _____

Cast Room: _____

Audio Room (specify if prefab booth used): _____

Allergy Test Rooms (provide detail on a separate page): _____

Chemo Infusion: _____

X-Ray: _____

    Existing or new equipment? _____

    Film or digital? _____

    Type of Films: _____

    Viewing Area/Tech Workstation _____

    Darkroom: _____

    Film Filing: _____ lineal feet: ___

    Automatic Processor: _____ Daylight? _____

Physical Therapy: _____

Office-based Surgery Suite (give details): _____

_____

_____

Ophthalmology:

    Field Room _____

    Mydriatic Room: _____

    No. Refraction Rooms: _____

    Data Collection Room: _____

    Office-based Surgery: _____

    Optical Dispensing: _____

Miscellaneous Rooms not listed above: _____

_____

_____

MISCELLANEOUS

1. Do you need medical gases (nitrous oxide, oxygen), vacuum, or compressed air?

_____

_____

2. If you are seeking accreditation by a professional association, Medicare certification, or state licensing for all or a portion of your suite, please provide details.

_____

_____

3. Will you be using conscious sedation in your special procedure room(s)?

_____

_____

_____
Signature

_____
Date

7

DENTAL SPACE PLANNING QUESTIONNAIRE

Date: _____

Dental group name: _____

Telephone: _____ E-mail address: _____

Questionnaire filled out by: _____

Dental specialty: _____

Dental equipment dealer: _____

Sales associate contact: _____ Phone: _____

Size present office: _____ (SF)   New office: _____ (SF)

Suite location requirements within building: _____

PATIENT PROFILE

Average number patients/day: _____ Office hours: _____ to _____

Composition of patients (age, socioeconomic level, cultural mix): _____

_____

PRACTICE METHODS

Digital Technology/Treatment Room

Patient monitor: _____ yes _____ no _____ shared with doctor

Location: _____ ceiling-mounted _____ post-mounted _____ other

Position: _____ patient's left _____ patient's right _____ radial arm

Type: _____ CRT/TV _____ flat screen _____ other

Use: _____ education _____ entertainment _____ size

Practice Mgmt. monitor: _____ yes _____ no   size: _____

Location: _____ rear _____ doctor's side _____ post-mounted

Type: _____ CRT/TV _____ flat screen _____ other

CPU location(s): _____ doctor's side _____ rear _____ USB hub

Will your computers be networked? _____

Total number monitors in treatment room: _____

Monitor input: _____ mouse _____ light pen _____ touch pad _____ wireless keyboard

Peripherals: _____ intraoral camera _____ printer _____ digital X-ray

_____ voice charting _____ computerized probes _____ blood pressure cuff

Other inputs (describe): _____

_____

Do you use lasers for anything but curing (e.g., cavity preparation, decay prevention, root canal treatment)?

_____

Type of laser: _____ CO_2 _____ Er:YAG _____ other

List equipment to be accommodated in treatment room: _____

_____

_____

Treatment Room—Other Features

Intraoral X-ray: _____ yes _____ no   Brand: _____

Location X-ray: _____ 12 o'clock _____ side _____ wall pass-through

Lighting: ____ clg.-mtd. _____ track-mtd. _____ post-mtd. _____ wall-mtd. _____ casework-mtd.

Centrally piped gases? _____

Casework: _____ custom _____ modular

Location: _____ sides _____ 12 o'clock column

If 12 o'clock, provide tray/cassette pass-through cabinet? _____

No. sinks/locations: _____

Communication system: _____

1

2

Room size: _____ No. openings/doors: _____

Operating microscope? _____ ceiling mount? _____

List equipment having space implications (air abrasion, CEREC, etc.): _____

_____

Type of Delivery System

Is doctor: _____ right-handed? _____ left-handed?

Do you practice: _____ two- _____ four- _____ six-handed dentistry?

Over the patient:

Dentist: _____ chair-mounted _____ post-mounted

Assistant: _____ chair-mounted _____ post-mounted

Side:

Dentist: _____ wall-mounted _____ cabinet-mounted _____ mobile cart

Assistant: _____ chair-mounted _____ post-mounted

Rear:

Dentist: _____ dual cart _____ fixed cabinet

Assistant: _____ mobile cart _____ fixed cabinet _____ flexible arm

PROPOSED STAFF

Front Office:

Reception: _____ Insurance: _____

Bookkeeping: _____ Office Manager: _____

Other: _____

Clinical:

Dentists: _____ Chairside Assistant: _____

Hygienists: _____ Lab Tech.: _____ Steri. Tech.: _____

3

BUSINESS OFFICE

Medical Records:

Do you do electronic patient charting? _____

If so, do you still require traditional chart storage for older "paper" charts?_____

No. chart file cabinets required: _____

Describe the system you use and how you access it in the treatment room: _____

_____

Are there other components of your paperless office we should be aware of? _____

_____

_____

Specialized Equipment:

Copy machine(s): _____ floor model _____ countertop model

Fax machine(s): _____

Postage meter: _____

Other equipment: _____

Would you like a small workroom off the business office to accommodate this equipment?

_____

Computer Systems:

We shall assume each of your staff will require a CRT monitor at his or her workstation.
Which of these individuals will also require a typewriter?

_____

Printers (describe locations): _____

Location of server: _____

4

Details of Business Office Layout:

Describe the overall size of the business office and stipulate whether the bookkeeper, insurance staff, and office manager are included in one large space or whether these individuals should have private offices.

_____

_____

PROPOSED SUITE REQUIREMENTS (approximate sizes of rooms)

Waiting room (estimate 20 SF per person): _____

No. of treatment rooms: _____ Size: _____

If Pedo or Ortho, do you use a treatment bay? _____ If so, how many chairs? _____

How many private treatment rooms or "quiet rooms" would you like? _____

Do you use chairside computers/monitors? _____

Exam/consultation rooms: _____ Size: _____

Hygiene Rooms: _____ Size: _____

Do you use a fully equipped standard operatory for hygiene or a dedicated room? _____

_____

X-ray: Equip each operatory with intraoral? _____ Film-based? _____

    Direct digital? _____ Phosphor storage plate? _____

    Central imaging room? _____

    Panoramic? _____ Film-based _____ Direct digital _____ Phosphor

    Pan/ceph? _____ Film-based _____ Direct digital _____ Phosphor

    Darkroom? _____ Type of processor: _____

    Processing alcove? _____

    Brand(s) of X-ray: _____

Lab:

    Specify type of lab work done in-house: _____

    _____ Size of lab: _____

5

Equipment: _____

_____

Sterilization: _____

List sterilization equipment: _____

_____

Do you use cassettes? _____

_____

Patient education room: _____ with sink _____?

Staff lounge: _____ Full-ht. ref. _____ Dishwasher _____ Garbage disposal _____?

Toilets: _____ (patient) _____ (staff)

Brushing area: _____ (for Peds or Ortho) _____ On-deck area

Vanity alcove (to repair make-up upon exiting suite): _____

Storage: _____ Housekeeping closet _____ Central media storage _____

Doctors' private office: _____ Shared? _____

    with toilet? _____ with shower? _____

Office manager: _____

Equipment room (for air compressor, vacuum): _____ inside suite _____ outside suite

Laundry/soiled holding: _____

Medical gas closet: _____

For Oral Surgeons:

No. exam/treatment rooms: _____ Size: _____

No. surgical operatories: _____ Size: _____

No. recovery beds: _____ with med gases? _____

Soiled holding room: _____

Clean linen/prep room: _____

6

Private exit for postsurgical patients? _____

Staff changing room/lockers? _____

For Periodontists:

No. exam/treatment rooms: _____ Size: _____

Implant surgery operatories and size: _____ Size: _____

_____

_____

UTILITIES

Central air abrasion? _____

Self-contained water system? _____ Type: _____

Nitrous Oxide and Oxygen: _____

_____ portable tanks _____ piped through wall

Vacuum: _____ treatment rooms _____ sterilization _____ lab

Location: _____ 12 o'clock column _____ side wall _____ dental unit

Compressed air: _____ treatment rooms _____ lab

Location: _____ 12 o'clock column _____ side wall _____ dental unit

Natural gas: _____

Add'l comments: _____

_____

_____

_____

_____

Signature

_____

Date

7

Index*